Maker Innovations Series

Jump start your path to discovery with the Apress Maker Innovations series! From the basics of electricity and components through to the most advanced options in robotics and Machine Learning, you'll forge a path to building ingenious hardware and controlling it with cutting-edge software. All while gaining new skills and experience with common toolsets you can take to new projects or even into a whole new career.

The Apress Maker Innovations series offers projects-based learning, while keeping theory and best processes front and center. So you get hands-on experience while also learning the terms of the trade and how entrepreneurs, inventors, and engineers think through creating and executing hardware projects. You can learn to design circuits, program AI, create IoT systems for your home or even city, and so much more!

Whether you're a beginning hobbyist or a seasoned entrepreneur working out of your basement or garage, you'll scale up your skillset to become a hardware design and engineering pro. And often using low-cost and open-source software such as the Raspberry Pi, Arduino, PIC microcontroller, and Robot Operating System (ROS). Programmers and software engineers have great opportunities to learn, too, as many projects and control environments are based in popular languages and operating systems, such as Python and Linux.

If you want to build a robot, set up a smart home, tackle assembling a weather-ready meteorology system, or create a brand-new circuit using breadboards and circuit design software, this series has all that and more! Written by creative and seasoned Makers, every book in the series tackles both tested and leading-edge approaches and technologies for bringing your visions and projects to life.

More information about this series at `https://link.springer.com/bookseries/17311`

ESP32 Formats and Communication

Application of Communication Protocols with ESP32 Microcontroller

Neil Cameron

Apress®

ESP32 Formats and Communication: Application of Communication Protocols with ESP32 Microcontroller

Neil Cameron
Edinburgh, UK

ISBN-13 (pbk): 978-1-4842-9378-2 ISBN-13 (electronic): 978-1-4842-9376-8
https://doi.org/10.1007/978-1-4842-9376-8

Managing Director, Apress Media LLC: Welmoed Spahr
Acquisitions Editor: Susan McDermott
Development Editor: James Markham
Coordinating Editor: Jessica Vakili

Distributed to the book trade worldwide by Springer Science+Business Media New York, 233 Spring Street, 6th Floor, New York, NY 10013. Phone 1-800-SPRINGER, fax (201) 348-4505, e-mail orders-ny@springer-sbm.com, or visit www.springeronline.com. Apress Media, LLC is a California LLC and the sole member (owner) is Springer Science + Business Media Finance Inc (SSBM Finance Inc). SSBM Finance Inc is a **Delaware** corporation.

For information on translations, please e-mail booktranslations@springernature.com; for reprint, paperback, or audio rights, please e-mail bookpermissions@springernature.com.

Apress titles may be purchased in bulk for academic, corporate, or promotional use. eBook versions and licenses are also available for most titles. For more information, reference our Print and eBook Bulk Sales web page at http://www.apress.com/bulk-sales.

Any source code or other supplementary material referenced by the author in this book is available to readers on the Github repository: https://github.com/Apress/ESP32-Formats-and-Communication. For more detailed information, please visit http://www.apress.com/source-code.

Printed on acid-free paper

Table of Contents

About the Author

Neil Cameron is an experienced analyst and programmer with a deep interest in understanding the application of electronics. Neil wrote the books *Arduino Applied: Comprehensive Projects for Everyday Electronics* and *Electronics Projects with the ESP8266 and ESP32: Building Web Pages, Applications, and WiFi Enabled Devices,* which are published by Apress. He has previously taught at the University of Edinburgh and at Cornell University.

About the Technical Reviewer

Mike McRoberts is the author of *Beginning Arduino* by Apress. He is the winner of Pi Wars 2018 and a member of Medway Makers. He is an Arduino and Raspberry Pi enthusiast. Mike McRoberts has expertise in a variety of languages and environments, including C/C++, Arduino, Python, Processing, JS, Node-RED, NodeJS, and Lua.

Preface

The ESP32 microcontroller is incorporated in several formats ranging from a development board to a camera-based module to an integrated watch with touch screen and GPS (Global Positioning System). The variety of different ESP32 formats illustrate the diversity of projects centered on the ESP32 microcontroller. *ESP32 Formats and Communication* develops projects with the ESP32 DEVKIT DOIT, TTGO T-Display V1.1, TTGO LoRa32 V2.1 1.6, ESP32-CAM, TTGO T-Watch V2 with GPS, and M5Stack Core2 modules.

Each ESP32 module format has different features, making some formats better suited for a particular project. The TTGO T-Display V1.1, TTGO LoRa32 V2.1 1.6, and M5Stack Core2 have built-in display screens. The TTGO LoRa32 V2.1 1.6 incorporates a LoRa (Long Range) module for transmitting and receiving messages. In Chapter 6, "LoRa and Microsatellites," satellites circling 550km above the Earth are tracked with the TTGO LoRa32 V2.1 1.6 module. The ESP32-CAM module is built around a 2M-pixel OV2640 camera. Chapter 11, "ESP-CAM Camera," describes streaming images with the WebSocket protocol to a remote ESP32 microcontroller connected to an LCD screen or with Wi-Fi communication to an app. Several projects are developed with the TTGO T-Watch V2 in Chapter 4, "TTGO T-Watch V2," with Bluetooth communication, GPS position detection and route tracking, infrared (IR) signaling, and accessing information over the Internet. The M5Stack Core2 module incorporates a touch LCD screen, Bluetooth and Wi-Fi communication, a microphone and speaker, as well as an accelerometer and gyroscope, making the M5Stack Core2 module extremely versatile. The M5Stack Core2 module features in several chapters.

The focus of the book is ESP32 microcontroller projects with different communication protocols. Wi-Fi communication to access information over the Internet or to control remote devices through an app is utilized in Chapter 12, "Control Apps"; Chapter 13, "Remote Control Motors"; and Chapter 14, "Remote Control ESP32-CAM Robot Car." The WebSocket protocol allows two-way real-time communication between an ESP32 microcontroller and a web page as illustrated in Chapter 8, "WebSocket, Remote Access, and OTA." Bluetooth Low Energy (BLE) communication is outlined in Chapter 5, "BLE Beacons," with the ESP32 microcontroller acting as a BLE beacon to transmit information to mobile phones, Android tablets, and other devices close to the beacon. Email communication with an ESP32 microcontroller and generation of QR (Quick Response) codes to instruct an ESP32 microcontroller to control a connected device are described in Chapter 7, "Email and QR Codes." Transmission and storage of image data and the fast display of images on an app are described in Chapter 10, "Managing Images." The MESH communication protocol, outlined in Chapter 3, "MESH Communication," enables communication between ESP32 microcontrollers without a Wi-Fi connection. The ESP-NOW protocol also enables communication between ESP32 devices without a Wi-Fi connection. In Chapter 9, "MQTT," a remote ESP32 microcontroller communicates with ESP-NOW to a second ESP32 microcontroller, which has a Wi-Fi connection to transmit smart meter data to a MQTT (Message Queueing Telemetry Transport) broker with the information displayed over the Internet and accessible from anywhere in the world. The ESP32 microcontroller–based Internet radio, MP3 player, and Bluetooth speaker projects in Chapter 2, "I2S Audio," all use the I2S (Inter-Integrated circuit Sound) communication protocol for transmission of encoded audio data. The ESP32 microcontroller transmits audio data to a Bluetooth speaker or receives audio data to output audio signals using an audio decoder.

Each chapter of the book focuses on a communication protocol and is stand-alone, so you can read any chapter without having to start from the beginning of the book. The order of chapters listed in the previous paragraph demonstrates the arbitrary nature of ordering communication protocols. The last three chapters develop the required apps and IoT techniques for remote control of an ESP32-CAM robot vehicle with an app displaying camera images, and the chapters benefit from being read sequentially.

Schematic diagrams were produced with *Fritzing* software (`www.fritzing.org`), with the emphasis on maximizing the clarity of the layout and minimizing overlapping connections between devices. All apps were built with *MIT App Inventor* (appinventor.mit.edu). Each app built is documented, and a level of experience with *MIT App Inventor* is assumed. My previous book *Electronics Projects with the ESP8266 and ESP32* includes several chapters on building apps, which incorporate remote-device control, GPS data, and *Google Maps*.

All sketches were built in the Arduino IDE (Integrated Development Environment). Some programming expertise with the Arduino IDE is assumed, but all sketches are completely described and comprehensively commented. Authors of libraries used in the book are acknowledged in each chapter with library details included in Chapter 15, "Libraries," which also demonstrates building a library.

All the Arduino IDE sketches and *MIT App Inventor* source code are available to download from *GitHub* (`github.com/Apress/ESP32-Formats-and-Communication`). The Arduino programming environment and libraries are constantly being updated, so information on the consequences of the updates is also available on the *GitHub* website.

CHAPTER 1

ESP32 Microcontroller

The ESP32 microcontroller has Wi-Fi and Bluetooth functionality, Bluetooth Low Energy (BLE) communication, independent timers, analog to digital and digital to analog converters (ADCs and DACs), capacitive touch sensors, and a Hall effect sensor. The ESP32 microcontroller includes two 240MHz cores, each with a Tensilica Xtensa 32-bit LX6 microprocessor. The ESP32 microcontroller is incorporated in several formats, ranging from a development board to an integrated watch with touch screen and GPS. The variety of different ESP32 formats illustrate the diversity of projects centered on the ESP32 microcontroller. The selected formats are the ESP32 DEVKIT DOIT, the TTGO T-Display V1.1, the TTGO LoRa32 V2.1 1.6, the ESP32-CAM, the TTGO T-Watch V2 with GPS, and the M5Stack Core2 module (see Figure 1-1). All formats incorporate the ESP32-D0WDQ6 chip, with either revision 1 (ESP32 DEVKIT DOIT and ESP32-CAM) or revision 3, except the TTGO LoRa32 V2.1 1.6, as the ESP32-PICO-D4 chip replaced the ESP32-D0WDQ6 chip of the TTGO LoRa32 V1.0. The selected range of ESP32 module formats is not exhaustive, but does represent a comprehensive range of modules available with the ESP32 microcontroller.

N. Cameron, *ESP32 Formats and Communication*,
https://doi.org/10.1007/978-1-4842-9376-8_1

Figure 1-1. *ESP32 microcontroller selection*

The ESP32 DEVKIT DOIT module has more broken-out GPIO (General-Purpose Input-Output) pins than the other ESP32 formats, but no display. Communication of the ESP32 DEVKIT DOIT with an OLED (Organic Light-Emitting Diode) or LCD (Liquid Crystal Display) screen is established with the I2C (Inter-Integrated Circuit) or SPI (Serial Peripheral Interface) communication protocol. The TTGO T-Display incorporates a multicolor TFT (Thin Film Transfer) LCD screen with two touch buttons and an external battery power option. The TTGO LoRa32 board has a built-in LoRa (Long Range) transceiver, a TF (TransFlash) or micro-SD (Secure Digital) card reader/writer, an OLED screen, and the facility for external battery power. The ESP32-CAM contains an OV2640 2M-pixel camera and a micro-SD card reader/writer. The TTGO T-Watch V2 and M5Stack Core2 both have a touch screen, a micro-SD card reader/writer, a three-axis accelerometer, a vibration motor, and a built-in battery. In addition, the TTGO T-Watch V2 includes a GPS receiver and an IR (infrared) transmitter, while the M5Stack Core2 has a three-axis gyroscope, a microphone, and a speaker. Details of each board are described in this chapter.

USB to UART Driver Installation

The USB (Universal Serial Bus) to UART (Universal Asynchronous Receiver-Transmitter) driver is ESP32 module specific as shown in Table 1-1, and within a module there are different drivers. The driver is viewed by connecting an ESP32 module to the USB port of a computer or laptop. Then in the computer *Control Panel,* select *Hardware and Sound* and select *Device Manager*. Click *Ports (COM & LPT)* to display the driver. The USB to UART driver files are located in the *C:\Windows\System32\drivers* folder.

Table 1-1. *USB to serial UART interface*

Commercial name	USB to UART	Driver file
ESP32 DEVKIT DOIT	Silicon Labs CP210x USB to UART	silabser.sys
TTGO T-Display V1.1	USB-Enhanced-SERIAL CH9102	CH343S64.SYS
TTGO LoRa32 V2.1 1.6 (year 2018)	Silicon Labs CP210x USB to UART	silabser.sys
TTGO LoRa32 V2.1 1.6 (year 2021)	USB-Enhanced-SERIAL CH9102	CH343S64.SYS
TTGO T-Watch V2	Silicon Labs CP210x USB to UART	silabser.sys
M5Stack Core2	USB-Enhanced-SERIAL CH9102	CH343S64.SYS
ESP32-CAM	USB-SERIAL CH340	CH341S64.SYS

The CP210x USB to UART Bridge driver is downloaded from `www.silabs.com/developers/usb-to-uart-bridge-vcp-drivers` with the *Downloads* menu. Save the *CP210x_Universal_Windows_Driver* zip file on the Desktop and right-click *Extract All.* In the extracted folder *CP210x_Universal_Windows_Driver*, right-click the *silabser.inf* file, select *Install,* and select *Open*. The computer or laptop may need to be restarted to complete the driver installation.

The CH9102F USB to UART chip replaced the Silicon Labs CP2104 chip. The CP2104 supports 12Mbps for USB with UART baud rates of 300bps–2Mbps, while the CH9102 chip supports UART baud rates of 50bps–4Mbps (`www.silabs.com/documents/public/data-sheets/cp2104.pdf`).

The M5Stack Core2 module USB to UART chip is either CH9102F or CP2104. A USB to UART driver is downloaded from `docs.m5stack.com/en/core/core2`. Save the *CH9102_VCP_SER_Windows* file on the Desktop, right-click the file, select *Run as administrator,* and select *Install anyway.* Similarly, save the *CP210x_VCP_Windows* zip file on the Desktop, right-click, and select *Extract All.* In the extracted folder, right-click the file *CP210xVCPInstaller_x64_v6.7.0.0,* select *Run as administrator,* and select *Install anyway.*

Arduino IDE

The Arduino IDE (Interactive Development Environment) software is downloaded from `www.arduino.cc/en/software`, with version 2.1.0 and the legacy 1.8.19 version currently available. The downloaded *.exe* file is double-clicked to start the installation. If both Arduino IDE versions 1.8.19 and 2.1.0 are installed on the same computer, then possible locations are

Version 1.8.19 – *C:\Program Files (x86)\Arduino*

Version 2.1.0 – *C:\Users\user\AppData\Local\Programs\Arduino IDE*

The default sketchbook location for storing sketches is *C:\Users\user\Documents\Arduino*.

In the Arduino IDE, either version 1.8.19 or version 2.1.0, select *File ➤ Preferences* and enter the URL (Uniform Resource Locator) `https://raw.githubusercontent.com/espressif/arduino-esp32/gh-pages/package_esp32_index.json` in the *Additional Boards Manager URLs* box. If there is already a URL in the box, then separate the URLs with a comma. The URL is defined on the Espressif website at `docs.espressif.com/projects/arduino-esp32/en/latest/installing.html`.

esp32 Boards Manager Version 2.0.N

ESP32 libraries are installed in the Arduino IDE by selecting *Tools ➤ Board ➤ Boards Manager*, entering *ESP32* in the *Filter* option to display *esp32* by *Espressif Systems*, and clicking *Install*.

In the Arduino IDE, an ESP32 module is identified by selecting *Tools ➤ Board* and then the required module within the category *ESP32 Arduino*. For example, selection of the ESP32 DEVKIT DOIT module is illustrated in Figure 1-2. Note that only the ESP32 module options relevant to this chapter are included in Figure 1-2, which shows the Arduino IDE version 1.8.19. The displayed information is identical with Arduino IDE version 2.1.0.

The ESP32 characteristics are defined in the Arduino IDE as *Tools ➤ Upload Speed, CPU Frequency, Flash Frequency, Flash Mode, Flash Size,* and *Partition Scheme*. For example, the ESP32 DEVKIT DOIT specification is defined by selecting *921600, 240MHz (WiFI/BT), 80MHz, DIO, 4MB (32Mb),* and *Default 4MB with spiffs*, respectively. The SPI Flash Mode setting of *QIO* (Quad Input/Output) is faster than the *DIO* (Dual Input/Output) setting, but not all settings are available to each device. If the *QIO* setting is unsupported, the message *rst:0x3 (SW_RESET),boot:0x13 (SPI_FAST_FLASH_BOOT)* is displayed after loading a sketch. Further details of SPI Flash Modes are available at `docs.espressif.com/projects/esptool/en/latest/esp32/advanced-topics`. Finally, in *Tools ➤ Port*, select the relevant COM port.

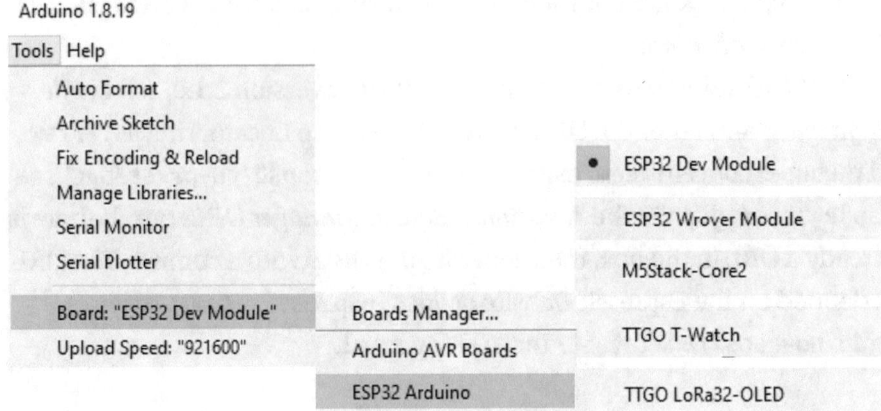

Figure 1-2. *Board selection in the Arduino IDE*

In the Arduino IDE, both the TTGO T-Display V1.1 and TTGO LoRa32 V2.1 1.6 modules are listed as *TTGO LoRa32-OLED* in the *ESP32 Arduino* list (see Figure 1-2). With *TTGO LoRa32-OLED* selected, the Arduino IDE *Tools ➤ Board Revision* option differentiates between the two modules, with the TTGO T-Display V1.1 module listed as *TTGO LoRa32 (No TFCard),* as shown in Figure 1-3. As noted for Figure 1-2, Figure 1-3 shows the Arduino version 1.8.19 screen, which includes the same information as Arduino IDE version 2.1.0.

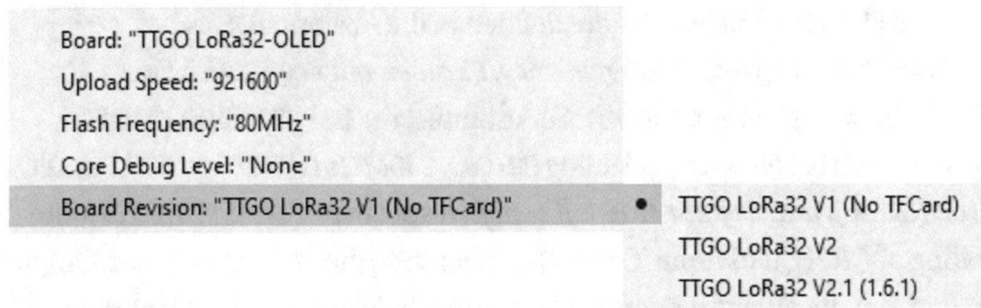

Figure 1-3. *Listing of TTGO LoRa32 modules*

In the Arduino IDE, the board or module name does not necessarily correspond to the commercial name, as shown in Table 1-2. Several board names are associated with the same microcontroller variant, such as the *ESP32 Dev Module* and the *ESP32 Wrover Module*, which are associated with the *esp32* variant. Details of the Arduino IDE board or module name and the corresponding variant are contained in the *boards* file in the *User\AppData\Local\Arduino15\packages\esp32\hardware\esp32\version* folder. The variant determines which *pins_arduino* file is referenced for defining features associated with the GPIO pins. The *pins_arduino* file is located in the *User\AppData\Local\Arduino15\packages\esp32\hardware\esp32\version\variants* folder.

Table 1-2. *ESP32 commercial names, board or module names and variants*

Commercial name	Board or module name	Board or module variant
ESP32 DEVKIT DOIT	ESP32 Dev Module	esp32
TTGO T-Display V1.1	TTGO LoRa32-OLED	ttgo-lora32-v1
TTGO LoRa32 V2.1 1.6	TTGO LoRa32-OLED	ttgo-lora32-v21new
TTGO T-Watch V2	TTGO T-Watch	twatch
M5Stack Core2	M5Stack-Core2	m5stack_core2
ESP32-CAM	ESP32 Wrover Module	esp32

The *pins_arduino* files for several boards and modules, based on the ESP32 microcontroller, generally define the TX (transmit) and RX (receive) pins for Serial communication as GPIO 1 and 3 and the SDA (Serial data) and SCL (Serial clock) pins for I2C communication as GPIO 21 and 22, with DAC1 and DAC2 on GPIO 25 and 26 (see Table 1-3). However, GPIO pin definitions for the SPI (Serial Peripheral Interface) communication protocol, as defined in the *pins_arduino* files, are variant dependent.

For example, MOSI is GPIO 23 for the *esp32* variant, but GPIO 27 for the *ttgo-lora32-v1* and *ttgo-lora32-v21new* variants. The SS (chip select) and SCK (Serial clock) pins are GPIO 5 and 18 for the *esp32* variant, but GPIO 18 and 5 for the *ttgo-lora32-v1* and *ttgo-lora32-v21new* variants. The SS pin for the *m5stack_core2* variant is GPIO 5 in the *pins_arduino* file, and the SS pin for the micro-SD card is GPIO 4, as shown on the back cover of the M5Stack Core2 module (see Figure 1-10a). In subsequent sections, which describe ESP32 boards or modules, GPIO pin definitions are based on the Espressif datasheet for the ESP32 microcontroller that is available in Section 2.2 of `www.espressif.com/sites/default/files/documentation/esp32_datasheet_en.pdf`. When GPIO values from the relevant *pins_arduino* file differ from those in the Espressif datasheet, the GPIO pin definitions are highlighted in the text.

Table 1-3. *GPIO associated with Serial, I2C, SPI communications and the DAC*

Variant	TX	RX	SDA	SCL	SS	MOSI	MISO	SCK	DAC1	DAC2
esp32	1	3	21	22	5	23	19	18	25	26
HSPI					15	13	12	14		
ttgo-lora32-v1	1	3	21	22	18	27	19	5	25	26
and OLED I2C			4	15						
ttgo-lora32-v21new	1	3	21	22	18	27	19	5	25	26
and SD card SPI					13	15	2	14		
twatch	33	34	21	22	13	15	2	14	25	26
m5stack_core2	1	3	32	33	5	23	38	18	25	26

The acronyms used in Table 1-3 refer to

Serial communication – TX, transmit; RX, receive

I2C communication – SDA, Serial data; SCK, Serial clock

SPI communication – SS, chip select; MOSI, main out secondary in; MISO, main in secondary out; SCK, Serial clock

ESP32 DEVKIT DOIT

The ESP32 DEVKIT DOIT module operates at 3.3V and is powered through a micro-USB connection at 5V or directly on the 3.3V VIN pin, but the former connection is recommended. The GPIO pins are not 5V tolerant, and the maximum current supply from a pin is 40mA.

In a sketch, pins are referenced by ESP32 microcontroller GPIO numbers. There are two 12-bit-resolution analog to digital converters with GPIO 32, 33, 34, 35, 36, and 39 for ADC1 and GPIO 2, 4, 12, 13, 14, 15, 25, 26, and 27 for ADC2. The ADC2 pins are not available as analog to digital conversion pins when Wi-Fi communication is in use. There are two digital to analog converter (DAC) pins (GPIO 25 and 26) with 8-bit resolution. Communication pins for I2C are GPIO 21 (SDA) and GPIO 22 (SCL) and for SPI (VSPI) are GPIO 19 (MISO), GPIO 23 (MOSI), GPIO 18 (CLK), and GPIO 5 (CS). A second SPI channel (HSPI) is available on GPIO 12, 13, 14, and 15 for MISO, MOSI, CLK, and CS, respectively. All GPIO pins, except the input-only pins (GPIO 34, 35, 36, and 39), support PWM (Pulse-Width Modulation), to generate a square wave with variable frequency and duty cycle, and all GPIO pins have interrupt functionality. The ESP32 microcontroller supports two I2S (Inter-Integrated circuit Sound) peripherals, *I2S0* and *I2S1*, with *I2S0* output routed directly to the internal DAC output channels on GPIO 25 and 26. Input-only pins SVP and

SVN (GPIO 36 and 39) are signal-positive and signal-negative inputs. There are nine capacitive touch pins (GPIO 2, 4, 12, 13, 14, 15, 27, 32, and 33). The built-in LED is on GPIO 2 and the LED is active *HIGH*. Several pins are available to the real-time clock (RTC) to trigger the ESP32 microcontroller from sleep mode. Internal pull-up resistors are connected to GPIO 0, 5, 14, and 15 with pull-down resistors on GPIO 2, 4, and 12. The ESP32 microcontroller contains a Hall effect sensor, which utilizes ADC1 channels 0 and 3.

The *BOOT* button is connected to GPIO 0, and pressing the *BOOT* button, when a sketch is running, pulls GPIO 0 to *LOW*. Pressing the *EN* (Enable) button, when a sketch is running, resets the ESP32 microcontroller.

Pin layout of the ESP32 DEVKIT DOIT with 30 pins is shown in Figure 1-4. GPIO pin functions are coded as *A#*, analog input; *T#*, capacitive touch; *input*, input only; *RTC*, real-time clock; *Rup*, built-in pull-up resistor; and *Rdn*, built-in pull-down resistor. In a sketch, ADC and touch pins are referenced either by the GPIO number or by A# or T#, respectively (see Figure 1-4). The *esp32\pins_arduino* file defines the SPI communication pins as the VSPI pins.

A PDF file of the schematic for the ESP32 DEVKIT module is available at `dl.espressif.com/dl/schematics/ESP32-Core-Board-V2_sch.pdf`.

Reference documentation for the ESP32 microcontroller is available at `docs.espressif.com/projects/esp-idf/en/latest/esp32/index.html`, particularly the "API Reference" section.

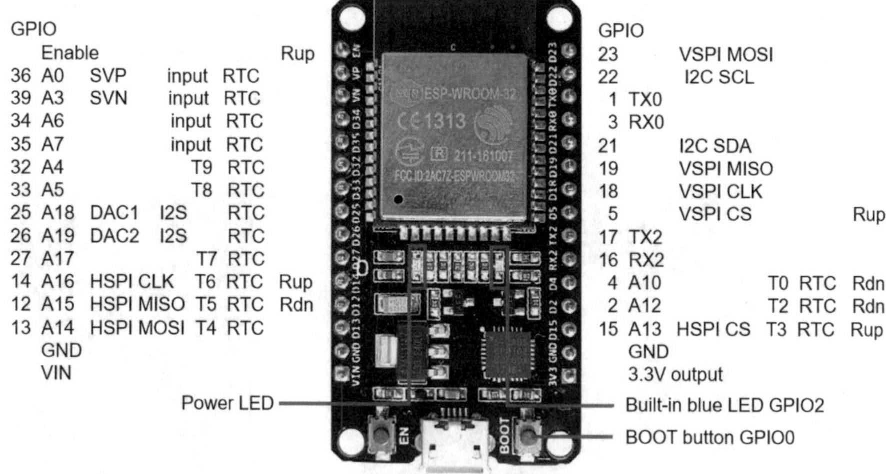

***Figure 1-4.** ESP32 DEVKIT DOIT pinout*

TTGO T-Display V1.1

The TTGO T-Display V1.1 module includes a TFT (Thin Film Transfer) ST7789 1.14" LCD screen with 135 × 240 pixels. The module includes two buttons and an ADC pin and is powered by either a USB-C connection or a battery with a two-pin JST connector. When powered by a USB-C connection, the battery is also charged.

Pin layout of the TTGO T-Display V1.1 is shown in Figure 1-5. GPIO pin functions are coded as *A#*, analog input; *T#*, capacitive touch; *input*, input only; and *Rup*, built-in pull-up resistor. All pins, except the input-only pins, support PWM to generate a square wave with variable frequency and duty cycle. The LCD backlight on GPIO 4 is controlled by PWM to vary the screen brightness. The two buttons on GPIO 0 and 35 both have built-in pull-up resistors with a button default state of *HIGH*. When interrupts are attached to the buttons, the buttons are active either when pressed (*HIGH* to *LOW*) or when released (*LOW* to *HIGH*) with the `attachInterrupt(digitalPinToInterrupt(GPIO), interrupt, option)` instruction and the *option* defined as `FALLING` or `RISING`, respectively.

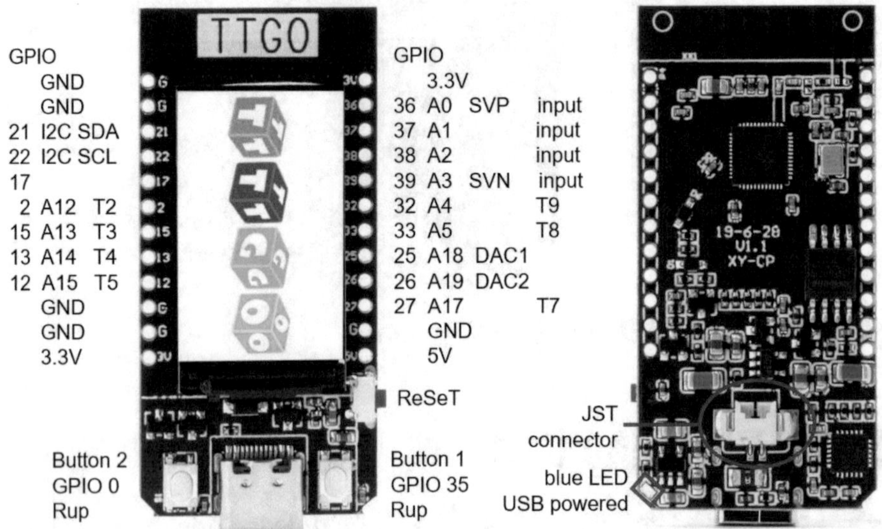

Figure 1-5. *TTGO T-Display V1.1 pinout*

The TTGO T-Display V1.1 factory test sketch is available at `github.com/Xinyuan-LilyGO/TTGO-T-Display/tree/master/TFT_eSPI/examples/FactoryTest`. After loading the *FactoryTest.ino* file into a blank sketch, load the three files *Button2.h*, *Button2.cpp*, and *bmp.h* into three tabs with the same names as the files. Figure 1-5 illustrates the initial screen of the factory test sketch. The current requirement of the TTGO T-Display V1.1 is displayed by the factory test sketch. With a 3.3V supply, the current requirements for deep sleep, to display the TTGO logo, or for Wi-Fi scanning are 15, 30, or 100mA, respectively, while with a 5V supply, the current requirements are increased to 25, 50, and 160mA.

A PDF file of the schematic for the TTGO T-Display V1.1 module is available at `github.com/Xinyuan-LilyGO/TTGO-T-Display/tree/master/schematic`.

Pulse-Width Modulation

The TFT screen backlight, *TFT_BL* on GPIO 4, is controlled by PWM with the *ledc* function instructions

```
int channel = 0, frequency = 1000, resolution = 8, duty = 32;
ledcAttachPin(TFT_BL, channel)
ledcSetup(channel, frequency, resolution)
ledcWrite(channel, duty)
```

where the parameters *channel, frequency, resolution,* and *duty* are the PWM output channel between 0 and 15; the square wave frequency (Hz); the 8-, 10-, 12-, or 15-bit PWM resolution; and the scaled duty cycle, respectively. For example, a resolution of 8 provides a range of values between 0 and $255 = 2^8 - 1$, with scaled duty cycles of 8, 16, 32, 64, 128, and 255 doubling the screen brightness. The TTGO T-Display V1.1 module quickly increases in temperature, and reducing the LCD brightness reduces the temperature, to an extent.

Analog to Digital Conversion

The two analog to digital converters, *ADC1* and *ADC2,* have six and seven available channels, respectively, consisting of GPIO 36, 37, 38, 39, 32, and 33 on *ADC1_CHANNEL_*0 to *ADC1_CHANNEL_*5 and GPIO 2, 15, 13, 12, 27, 25, and 26 on *ADC2_CHANNEL_*2 to *ADC2_CHANNEL_*5 and *ADC2_CHANNEL_*7 to *ADC2_CHANNEL_*9. Only the *ADC1* channel (pins A0 to A5) is available when Wi-Fi communication is in use.

The analog value and voltage on an ADC pin are measured with the `analogRead(pin)` and `analogReadMilliVolts(pin)` instructions, respectively. The default bit width or resolution is 12-bit, with a range of 9–12 bits equivalent to maximum analog values of 511, 1023, 2047, and $4095 = 2^{12} - 1$, respectively. The default voltage attenuation is 11dB, with options of 0, 2.5, 6, and 11dB. The ESP32 microcontroller ADC has a reference voltage of 1.1V, so ADC input voltages greater than 1.1V are reduced to $V_{IN}\sqrt{10^{(-dB/10)}} = V_{IN}10^{(-dB/20)}$. The attenuation options of 2.5, 6, and 11dB reduce the ADC input voltage by a factor of 1.33, 2.0, and 3.55, respectively. The bit width and voltage attenuation are defined with the `analogSetWidth(N)` and `analogSetAttenuation(N)` instructions, respectively. Details of the Arduino ADC instructions are available at `docs.espressif.com/projects/arduino-esp32/en/latest/api/adc.html`.

The ESP32 ADC library, *esp_adc_cal*, provides an alternative approach to characterizing the ADC functionality. The *esp_adc_cal* library is automatically incorporated in the Arduino IDE when the *esp32* Boards Manager is installed, with the library files located in file *User\AppData\Local\Arduino15\packages\esp32\hardware\esp32\version\cores\esp32*. Further details of the library are available at `docs.espressif.com/projects/esp-idf/en/v4.4.2/api-reference/peripherals/adc.html`. Definitions of the bit width and voltage attenuation are included in the `esp_adc_cal_characterize()` instruction, as shown in Listing 1-1. The bit width options are *ADC_WIDTH_BIT_9* to *ADC_WIDTH_BIT_12,* and the voltage attenuation options are *ADC_ATTEN_DB_0, ADC_ATTEN_DB_2.5, ADC_ATTEN_DB_6,* and *ADC_ATTEN_DB_11*. The ADC characterization instruction includes the analog to digital converter, *ADC_UNIT_1* or *ADC_UNIT_2,* and the ADC reference voltage of 1100mV as parameters. An ADC value is obtained with the `adcN_get_raw(ADC1_CHANNEL_C)` instruction, where *N* and *C* define the ADC and the channel number within the ADC, such as *ADC1* channel 1 equivalent to GPIO 37. The analog value is converted to millivolts with the `esp_adc_cal_raw_to_voltage` instruction.

For comparison, Listing 1-1 measures the voltage on GPIO 37 with the *esp_adc_cal* library instructions of `adc1_get_raw()` and `esp_adc_cal_raw_to_voltage()` and with the `analogRead()` and `analogReadMilliVolts()` instructions. There is little difference between the `esp_adc_cal_raw_to_voltage()` and `analogReadMilliVolts()` instructions for measuring a voltage on an ADC pin. The `adc1_get_raw()` and `analogRead()` instructions produce similar values.

Listing 1-1. ADC voltage measurement

```
#include <esp_adc_cal.h>                  // include ADC library
int ADCpin = 37;                          // ADC voltage pin
int count = 0, raw, analog, mVraw, mVanalog;

void setup()
{
  Serial.begin(115200);                   // Serial Monitor baud rate
}

void loop()
{                                         // characterization variable
  esp_adc_cal_characteristics_t adc_chars;
  esp_adc_cal_characterize(ADC_UNIT_1, ADC_ATTEN_DB_11,
                         ADC_WIDTH_BIT_12, 1100, &adc_chars);
  raw = adc1_get_raw(ADC1_CHANNEL_1);    // ADC reading on GPIO 37
                                          // convert reading to mV
  mVraw = esp_adc_cal_raw_to_voltage(raw, &adc_chars);
  analog = analogRead(ADCpin);            // read ADC pin
                                          // convert reading to voltage
  mVanalog = analogReadMilliVolts(ADCpin);
  count++;                                // display results
```

```
  Serial.printf("%d %d %d %d %d \n", count, raw, analog,
      mVraw, mVanalog);
  delay(100);
}
```

Input voltages of 500, 1000 ... 3000mV, plus 200 and 3100mV, provided a voltage range to test alternative methods of utilizing the ADC functionality. The average voltage measurements over the range of ADC input voltages, with a sample of 100 measurements per input voltage, are shown in Figure 1-6. The average measured voltages of 211, 507, 1018, 1527, 2030, 2545, 3011, and 3109mV indicated a linear relationship between the input and measured voltages with a positive bias of only 1.3% for an ADC input voltage of at least 500mV with the `analogReadMilliVolts()` instruction.

In contrast, with the `analogRead()` instruction, the average measured voltages of 96, 448, 1074, 1690, 2307, 2924, 3811, and 4038mV indicated a curvilinear relationship between the input and measured voltages with substantial positive bias for input voltages greater than 2V.

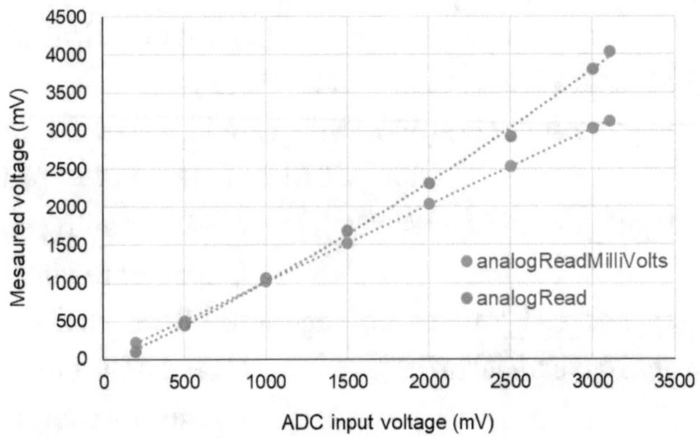

Figure 1-6. *ADC voltage measurement*

GPIO 34 is a 12-bit ADC pin connected to the battery JST connector. The battery voltage is measured with the `analogReadMilliVolts(34)*2` instruction, as a built-in voltage divider, consisting of two 100kΩ resistors (see Figure 1-7), halves the battery voltage on GPIO 34. The 10nF bypass capacitor shorts any noise on the voltage divider output to GND. When the TTGO T-Display V1.1 is solely USB powered, the ADC enable port, on GPIO 14, is automatically set *HIGH,* and the blue LED on the TTGO T-Display V1.1 module is turned on. When the TTGO T-Display V1.1 is battery powered, the ADC enable port must be set *HIGH* to activate the ADC on GPIO 34. The minimum battery voltage to power the TTGO T-Display V1.1 is 2.7V. When the TTGO T-Display V1.1 is USB powered, the battery is also charged through the built-in TP4054 battery management IC, and when charging is complete, the blue LED on the TTGO T-Display V1.1 module is turned off.

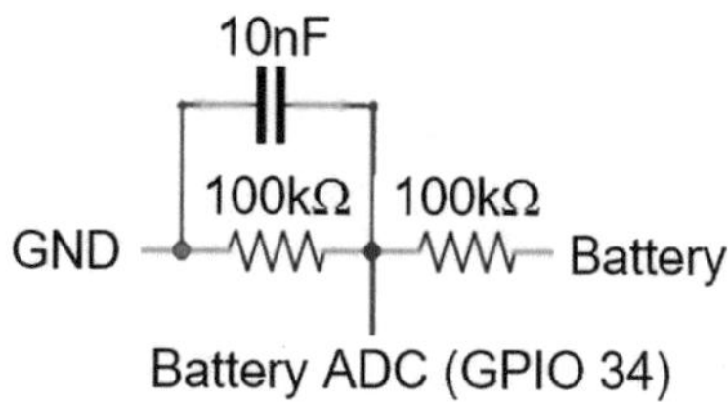

Figure 1-7. *Built-in voltage divider on GPIO 34*

The battery voltage is also calculated from the 12-bit ADC value, `analogRead()`, scaled by $4095 = 2^{12} - 1$, multiplied by 2, as the built-in voltage divider halves the voltage, multiplied by 3.3, which is the operating voltage of the ESP32 microcontroller, and multiplied by 1.1, which is the internal reference voltage of the ADC. The TTGO T-Display V1.1 battery voltage, measured by both methods, is displayed on the module LCD screen with the sketch in Listing 1-2. Details of the *TFT_eSPI* library used to display information on an LCD screen are given in Chapter 15, "Libraries."

Listing 1-2. Battery voltage

```
#include <TFT_eSPI.h>                     // include TFT_eSPI library
TFT_eSPI tft = TFT_eSPI();
int enPin = 14, battPin = 34;             // ADC enable and battery pins
int batt1;
unsigned long value, batt2;

void setup()
{
  pinMode(enPin, OUTPUT);                 // set ADC enable pin HIGH
  digitalWrite(enPin, HIGH);
  tft.init();
  tft.setTextColor(TFT_WHITE);
  tft.setTextSize(2);
  tft.setRotation(3);                     // landscape with USB on left
}

void loop()
{
  value = 0;
  batt2 = 0;
  for (int i=0; i<20; i++)                // take average of 20 readings
  {
    value = value + analogRead(battPin);// analog value
                                          // read millivolts
    batt2 = batt2 + analogReadMilliVolts(battPin);
  }
  value = value / 20;                     // average analog value
                                          // convert to millivolts
  batt1 = round((value * 2.0 * 3.3 * 1100.0)/4095.0);
  batt2 = round(2.0 * batt2 / 20.0);      // average millivolts value
  tft.fillScreen(TFT_BLUE);               // clear screen
```

```
  tft.setCursor(0,20);                          // display both battery voltages
  tft.printf(" analog %d mV \n\n readmV %d mV \n", batt1, batt2);
  delay(5000);
}
```

TTGO LoRa32 V2.1 1.6

The TTGO LoRa32 V2.1 1.6 module includes an SX1276 LoRa (Long Range) module with a frequency of 433, 868, or 915MHz, an SMA (SubMiniature version A) antenna, a micro-SD card reader/writer, and an SSD1306 0.96" OLED screen with 128 × 64 pixels. The module is powered by a micro-USB or a battery with a two-pin JST connector.

Pin layout of the TTGO LoRa32 V2.1 1.6 module is shown in Figure 1-8. GPIO pin functions are coded as *A#*, analog input; *T#*, capacitive touch; and *input*, input only. All pins, except the input-only pins, support PWM to generate a square wave with variable frequency and duty cycle. Only the ADC1 pins *A0, A3, A6,* and *A7* are available as analog to digital conversion pins when Wi-Fi communication is in use. All the left-side pins in Figure 1-8 (GPIO 36 to 25) support RTC, as well as GPIO 26.

GPIO 35 is a 12-bit ADC pin connected to the battery JST connector. An instruction for the battery voltage is `analogReadMilliVolts(35)*2`, as a voltage divider, consisting of two 100kΩ resistors, halves the battery voltage on the ADC pin. When battery powered, the power switch controls power to the module, but in older models (manufactured in 2018), the power switch controls power when the module is powered by USB or by battery. When USB powered, the battery is automatically charged. A red LED indicates USB power with the blue LED indicating that the battery is charging through the built-in TP4054 battery management IC. The green LED is controlled by GPIO 25 in the TTGO LoRa32 V2.1 1.6, but by GPIO 23 in V2.1 1.5.

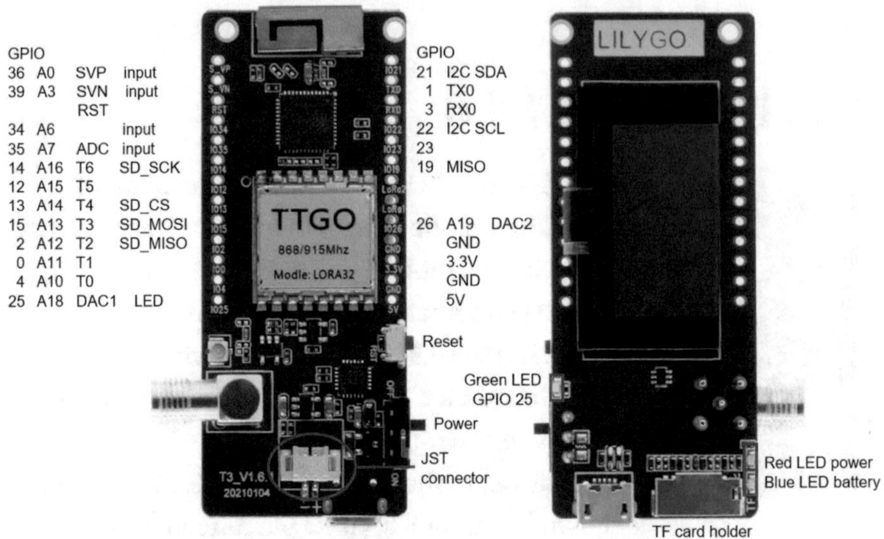

Figure 1-8. *TTGO LoRa32 V2.1 1.6 pinout*

The LoRa functionality of the TTGO LoRa32 V2.1 1.6 module is demonstrated in Chapter 6, "LoRa and Microsatellites." The SX1276 LoRa module communicates with the ESP32 microcontroller using the SPI protocol, and the *user\AppData\Local\Arduino15\packages\esp32\hardware\esp32\version\variants\ttgo-lora32-v21new\pins_arduino* file defines the SPI communication pins as GPIO 19, 27, 5, and 18 for MISO, MOSI, SCK, and SS, respectively, which differs from the corresponding VSPI pins of the ESP32 microcontroller, namely, 19, 23, 18, and 5.

The micro-SD card reader/writer accepts a FAT32-formatted 2MB card, but before compiling and loading a sketch, the micro-SD card must be removed, as the micro-SD card accesses GPIO 15, which is active during the boot process. The SPI communication pins for the micro-SD card are defined in the *ttgo-lora32-v21new\pins_arduino* file as GPIO 2, 15, 14, and 13 for *SD_MISO, SD_MOSI, SD_SCK,* and *SD_CS*, respectively. The SPI pins for the micro-SD card are similar to the ESP32 microcontroller HSPI pins of GPIO 12, 13, 14, and 15, but the SPI functions are different.

The ESP32 microcontroller hosts four SPI peripherals with SPI0 and SPI1 to access the flash memory, while SPI2 and SPI3 are general-purpose SPI controllers, referenced as HSPI and VSPI, respectively. Further details are available at `docs.espressif.com/projects/esp-idf/en/latest/esp32/api-reference/peripherals/spi_master.html`. Simultaneous SPI communication of the ESP32 microcontroller with the SX1276 LoRa module and the micro-SD card reader/writer utilizes the VSPI and HSPI peripherals. Two SPI objects are defined with the *SPI* library instructions `SPIClass hspi(HSPI)` and `SPIClass vspi(VSPI)` for the HSPI and VSPI peripherals. The SPI pins for communication with the micro-SD card and with the HSPI peripheral are defined with the instructions `hspi.begin(SD_SCK, SD_MISO, SD_MOSI, SD_CS)` and `SD.begin(SD_CS, hspi)`. Similar instructions, `vspi.begin(SCK, MISO, MOSI, SS)` and `LoRa.setSPI(vspi)`, for SPI communication with the LoRa module using the VSPI peripheral are not necessary as VSPI is the default SPI peripheral with pin definitions of *MISO, MOSI, SCK,* and *SS*. In the *ttgo-lora32-v21new\pins_arduino* file, the variables *MISO, MOSI, SCK,* and *SS* have the same values as the variables *LORA_MISO, LORA_MOSI, LORA_SCK,* and *LORA_CS*.

SPI communication with the LoRa module also requires definition of the reset and interrupt pins with the instruction `LoRa.setPins(LORA_CS, LORA_RST, LORA_IRQ)`, with *LORA_RST* and *LORA_IRQ* both defined in the *ttgo-lora32-v21new\pins_arduino* file.

A PDF file of the schematic for the TTGO LoRa32 V2.1 1.6 module is available at `github.com/LilyGO/TTGO-LORA32/blob/master/schematic1in6.pdf`.

TTGO T-Watch V2

The TTGO T-Watch V2 incorporates a 240 × 240-pixel ST7789V 1.54" LCD screen with a FT6336 capacitive touch screen controller, PCF8563 RTC, Quectel L76K GPS, BMA423 three-axis accelerometer, infrared signal transmitter, micro-SD card reader/writer, DRV2605L vibration motor driver, AXP202 power management unit, and 380mA lithium ion battery. The TTGO T-Watch V2 module includes 16MB of flash memory and 4MB of PSRAM (Pseudo-static RAM). The T-Watch V1 and V3 both include a MAX98357 class-D amplifier, with a PDM (Pulse-Density Modulation) microphone in the TTGO T-Watch V3, but not the GPS and micro-SD card reader/writer. The TTGO T-Watch V2 is turned on or off by pressing the power button on the side of the watch for 2s or 6s, respectively. Datasheets for components of the TTGO T-Watch V2 module are accessed from `github.com/Xinyuan-LilyGO/TTGO_TWatch_Library/blob/master/docs/watch_2020_v2.md` with a PDF file of the schematic available at `github.com/Xinyuan-LilyGO/TTGO_TWatch_Library/blob/master/Schematic/T_WATCH-2020V02.pdf`.

The *TTGO_TWatch_Library\src\board\twatch2020_v2.h* and the *user\AppData\Local\Arduino15\packages\esp32\hardware\esp32\version\variants\twatch\pins_arduino* files define the GPIO naming abbreviations, which are shown in Figure 1-9, with the layout corresponding to the ESP32 DEVKIT DOIT in Figure 1-4. The *TP#* function refers to the touch screen. Both the TFT LCD screen and the micro-SD card reader/writer communicate with the SPI protocol, using VSPI (GPIO 19, 0, 18, and 5 for MOSI, MISO, SCLK, and CS) and HSPI (GPIO 15, 4, 14, and 13), respectively. The I2C communication pins, SDA and SCL, are located on GPIO 21 and 22, with the touch screen I2C pins on GPIO 23 and 32. Interrupt pins for the RTC, the touch screen, the BMA423 three-axis accelerometer, and the AXP202 power management unit are located on

GPIO 37, 38, 39, and 35, respectively. The GPS transmit, receive, *1PPS*, and *WAKE* pins are located on GPIO 26, 36, 34, and 33. The GPS generates a precise one-pulse-per-second (*1PPS*) signal for the timing of GPS signal reception. There are three pairs of Serial communication pins (GPIO 1 and 3, 33 and 34, 17 and 16). The two DAC channels on GPIO 25 and 26 have 8-bit resolution. The infrared transmit pin (*TWATCH_2020_IR_PIN*) is located on GPIO 2.

The mapping of pairs of functions to a GPIO pin prevents simultaneous use of GPS and DAC2, GPS and Serial communication with TX1 and RX1, TFT screen backlight with DAC1, and SPI communication MISO with infrared signal transmission.

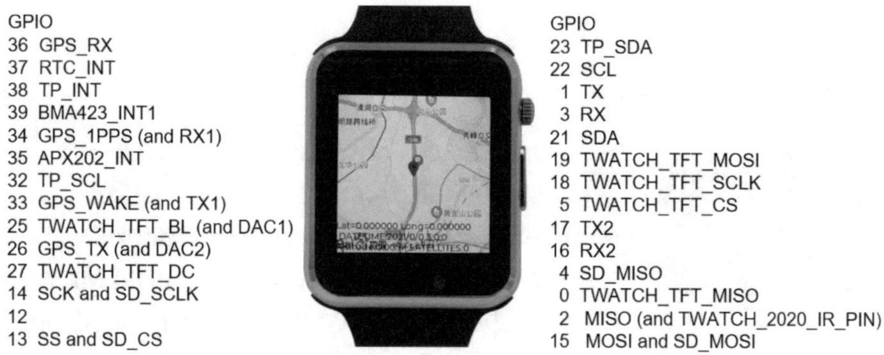

Figure 1-9. *TTGO T-Watch V2 pin layout*

TTGO T-Watch Installation

In the Arduino IDE, the TTGO T-Watch is identified by selecting *Tools* ➤ *Boards* ➤ *Boards Manager* ➤ *ESP32 Arduino* ➤ *TTGO T-Watch* with the TTGO T-Watch V2 specified by selecting *Tools* ➤ *Board Revision* ➤ *T-Watch-2020-V2*. The *TTGO_TWatch_Library.zip* file is downloaded from `github.com/Xinyuan-LilyGO/TTGO_TWatch_Library`. Example sketches for the TTGO T-Watch are opened in the Arduino IDE by selecting *File* ➤ *Examples* ➤ *TTGO TWatch Library* ➤ *BasicUnit*, with sketches specific to the GPS and DRV2605L motor of the TTGO T-Watch V2 module located in the folder *BasicUnit* ➤ *TwatcV2Special*.

The *TTGO_TWatch_Library* includes a version of the *TFT_eSPI* library. Therefore, it is not necessary to specify the TTGO T-Watch V2 module GPIO settings for the *TFT_eSPI* library by un-commenting the `#include <User_Setups/Setup45_TTGO_T_Watch.h>` instruction (see Chapter 15, "Libraries," section "TFT_eSPI Library"). Details of drawing graphics with the *TFT_eSPI* library are described in Chapter 15, "Libraries," and demonstrated in Chapter 4, "TTGO T-Watch V2."

M5Stack Core2

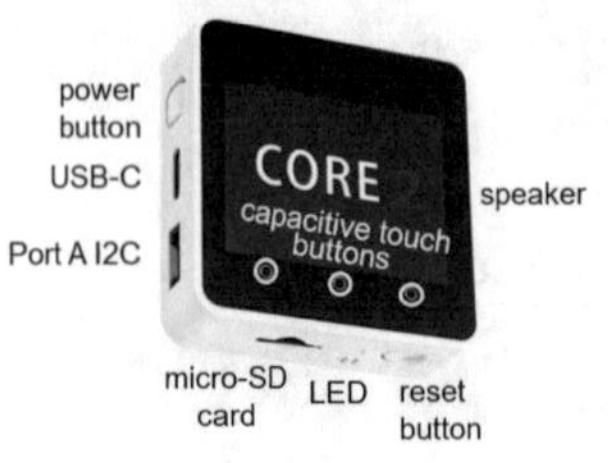

The M5Stack Core2 incorporates a 320 × 240-pixel ILI9342C 2" LCD screen with a FT6336 capacitive touch screen controller, 1W-09S speaker with a SPM1423 PDM MEMS microphone and NS4168 I2S power amplifier, BM8563 RTC, MPU6886 six-axis accelerometer and gyroscope, TF or micro-SD card reader/writer, vibration motor driver, AXP192 power management unit, and 390mA lithium ion battery. The M5Stack Core2 module includes 16MB of flash memory and 8MB of PSRAM (Pseudo-static RAM), which is double the TTGO T-Watch V2 PSRAM. The M5Stack Core2 is turned on or off by pressing the power button, on the side, briefly or for 6s, respectively. The reset button is located on the underside of the M5Stack Core2 module. The LCD screen contains three programmable capacitive touch buttons. There are two 12-bit-resolution ADCs with the eight-channel ADC1 on GPIO 32 to 39 and ten-channel ADC2 on GPIO 0, 2, 4, 12, 13, 14, 15, 25, 26, and 27.

The two DAC channels on GPIO 25 and 26 have 8-bit resolution. A four-pin Grove connector is located on the side of the M5Stack Core2 module for connecting M5Stack units with I2C communication on Port A. Details of M5Stack units are available at `docs.m5stack.com/en/unit/` with example sketches, for each unit, available in the Arduino IDE by selecting *File* ➤ *Examples* ➤ *M5Core2* ➤ *Unit.*

Under the rear cover of the M5Stack Core2 module, several GPIO pins are accessible (see Figure 1-10a). The microphone and the six-axis accelerometer and gyroscope are located on the cover, which must be completely closed to ensure connection between the modules and the microcontroller. The accessible GPIO pins include SPI (MOSI, MISO, and SCK), Port A, and internal I2C (SDA and SCL) and Serial communication, with the clock and data pins for the PDM microphone (*CLK* and *DAT*) and speaker (*LRCK* and *DOUT*) (see Figure 1-10b).

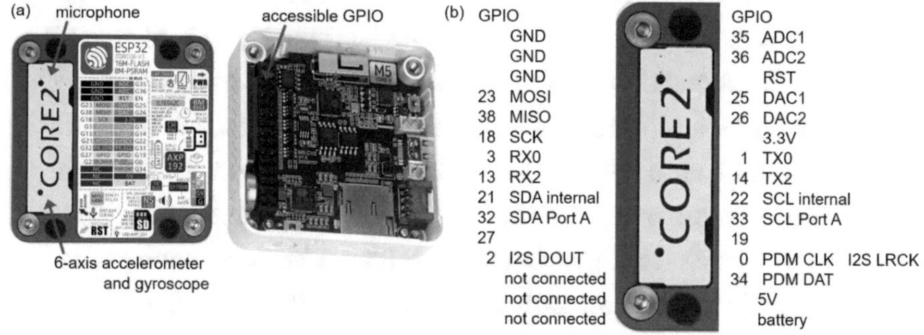

Figure 1-10. *M5Stack Core2 module (rear)*

The additional M5Stack Core2 GPIO pins and functions are illustrated in Figure 1-11.

GPIO	function
4	CS TF card
5	CS LCD
15	DC LCD
Variable	
AXP_DC3	LCD backlight
AXP_IO4	LCD RST
AXP_LDO2	LCD PWR

CORE 2

GPIO	function
12	BCLK speaker
AXP_IO2	SPK_EN
AXP_IO1	VCC LED
AXP_LD03	vibration motor
AXP_PWR	RTC INT
39	Touch INT
AXP_IO4	Touch RST

Figure 1-11. *M5Stack Core2 GPIO*

The M5Stack Core2 is powered through the USB-C port or internally by the 390mA lithium ion battery or externally through the 5V pin (see Figure 1-10b). For external power, the `M5.Axp.SetBusPowerMode(1)` instruction is required, as the default state is `SetBusPowerMode(0)` with the internal boost converter increasing the battery voltage to 5V. The LCD screen brightness is defined by the `M5.Axp.SetLcdVoltage(N)` instruction, with values between 2500 and 3300mV. The LCD backlight is turned off or on by the `M5.Axp.SetDCDC3(N)` instruction, with *N* equal to 0 or 1. Similarly, the green internal LED, located beside the micro-SD card slot, is turned on or off with the `M5.Axp.SetLed(N)` instruction. The built-in speaker is turned on or off with the `M5.Axp.SetSpkEnable(N)` instruction.

In general, M5Stack Core2 functions initialize sensors, such as the `M5.Imu.begin()` instruction, rather than defining the relevant GPIO, such as in the `audio.setPinout(BCLK, LRCK, DOUT)` instruction. In the Arduino IDE, example sketches are located in *File* ➤ *Examples* ➤ *M5Core2,* and additional sketches are available at `docs.m5stack.com/en/api/`. With the latter, select *CORE2 API* and then select a category, such as *AXP192* for power management sketches. Specification of the M5Stack Core2 and the GPIO descriptions are available at `docs.m5stack.com/en/core/core2`. Details of power management functions are available at `github.com/m5stack/M5Core2/blob/master/src/AXP192.cpp`.

M5Stack Core2 Installation

In the Arduino IDE, select *File* ➤ *Preferences* and enter the URL `https://m5stack.oss-cn-shenzhen.aliyuncs.com/resource/arduino/package_m5stack_index.json` in the *Additional Boards Manager URLs* box. If there is already a URL in the box, then separate the URLs with a comma.

The *M5Core2* library is installed in the Arduino IDE by selecting *Sketch* ➤ *Include Library* ➤ *Manage Libraries* and entering *M5Core2* in the *Filter* option to display *M5Core2* by *M5Stack* and clicking *Install*. There is no need to load the libraries listed as required, so select *Install 'M5Core2' only*.

In the *Tools* ➤ *Boards* ➤ *Boards Manager* drop-down list, select *M5Stack-Core2* as listed in the *ESP32 Arduino* section. In *Tools* ➤ *Upload Speed, CPU Frequency,* and *Partition Scheme*, select *921600, 240MHz (WiFI/BT),* and *Default (2× 6.5 MB app, 3.6 MB SPIFFS)*, respectively. In *Tools* ➤ *Port* select the relevant COM port.

A PDF file of the schematic for the M5Stack Core2 module is available from `docs.m5stack.com/en/core/core2`.

The M5Stack Core2 factory test sketch is installed by downloading the installer located at `m5stack.oss-cn-shenzhen.aliyuncs.com/EasyLoader/Windows/CORE/EasyLoader_M5Core2_FactoryTest.exe`. Copy the installer onto the computer Desktop, double-click the installer, click *More info,* and click *Run anyway*. In the *Core2_FactoryTest* installer panel, select the COM port and baud rate and click *Burn*. The M5Stack Core2 factory test sketch is available at `github.com/m5stack/M5Core2/tree/master/examples/FactoryTest`.

Images are displayed on the M5Stack Core2 LCD screen with instructions based on the *TFT_eSPI* library, which are outlined in Chapter 15, "Libraries." The *M5.Lcd* standard colors and instruction set are listed on `http://docs.m5stack.com/en/api/core2/lcd_api`, with example sketches.

The M5Stack Core2 and TTGO T-Watch V2 modules are multifunctional, with the features summarized in Table 1-4. Both modules have a TFT LCD touch screen, micro-SD card read and write function, real-time clock, three-axis accelerometer, and vibration motor and are powered by a lithium ion battery. In addition, the M5Stack Core2 module has a three-axis gyroscope, speaker, and microphone, while the TTGO T-Watch V2 module includes a GPS and an IR transmitter.

Table 1-4. *M5Stack Core2 and TTGO T-Watch V2 features*

Feature	M5Stack	T-Watch
LCD screen	ILI9342C	ST7789 TFT
Screen pixels	320 × 240	240 × 240
Touch sensor	FT6336U	FT6336
Motion sensor	MPU6886 Three-axis accelerometer Three-axis gyroscope	BMA423 Three-axis accelerometer
Real-time clock	BM8563	PCF8563
Power management	AXP192	AXP202
USB to UART	CH9102F	CP210x
Motor	Vibration motor	DRV2605
Audio	NS4168 speaker SPM1423 microphone	
GPS		L76K
Transmitter		Infrared
Button	3× capacitive touch	Button
Battery	390mAh	380mAh

M5Stack Core2 and Sound

The M5Stack Core2 speaker is available for audio (see Chapter 2, "I2S Audio"), but not for the *tone* function. The `tone(frequency, time)` instruction, which plays a sound at a given frequency for a set time, is available in the *Speaker* class of the *M5Unified* library. The *M5Unified* library is installed in the Arduino IDE by selecting *Include Library* from the *Sketch* menu and then *Manage Libraries*. In the *Filter* box, enter *M5Unified* and click *Install*.

Instructions to generate a sound are

```
#include <M5Unified.h>            // include M5Unified library
M5.Speaker.begin()                // initialize Speaker class
M5.Speaker.setVolume(80)          // volume from 0 to 255
M5.Speaker.tone(1000, 50)         // frequency (Hz) and time (ms)
```

For illustration, the *tone* function is combined with the three-axis accelerometer and capacitive touch buttons of the M5Stack Core2 module to produce a digital spirit level with a sound alarm (see Figure 1-12).

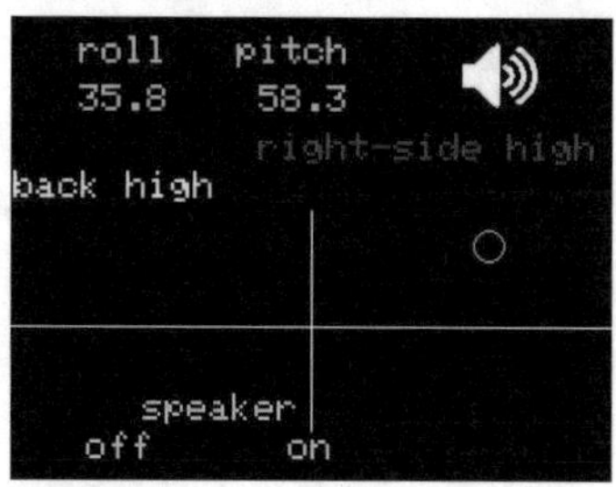

Figure 1-12. *Digital spirit level*

Several instructions in Listing 1-3 are specific to the M5Stack Core2 module and are preceded with *M5*. The *setup* function of the sketch initializes the accelerometer and the speaker, draws the axes of the digital spirit level, and displays the speaker image. In the *loop* function, the position of the spirit level "bubble" is derived from the accelerometer

X- and Y-axis readings. If the angle of the tilted M5Stack Core2 module deviates from limit values, then the speaker emits a beeping tone, and positional information is displayed on the LCD screen. Pressing the M5Stack Core2 touch screen button *BtnA* or *BtnB* turns off or on the speaker volume, respectively. Following the `if (M5.BtnX.wasPressed())` instruction, the `M5.update()` instruction updates the button pressed status. The `M5.BtnX.isPressed()` instruction requires the button to be pressed when the `M5.update()` instruction is next implemented.

Listing 1-3 includes the *M5Unified* library rather than the *M5Core2* library. The *M5Unified* library includes Bluetooth and web radio sketches, which demonstrate the FFT (Fast Fourier Transform) spectrum analysis display of the audio tracks. The Fast Fourier Transform is described in Chapter 2, "I2S Audio."

Listing 1-3. Digital spirit level

```
#include <M5Unified.h>          // include M5Unified library
#include "image.h"              // include bitmap image
float accX, accY, accZ, degX, degY;
int pitch = 15, roll = 30;      // different tilt thresholds
int x, y;                       // for X and Y axes

void setup()
{
  M5.begin();
  M5.Imu.begin();               // initialize accelerometer
  M5.Speaker.begin();           // and M5Unified speaker
  M5.Speaker.setVolume(80);     // volume range: 0 to 255
  M5.Lcd.setTextSize(2);
  M5.Lcd.setTextColor(GREEN, BLACK);
  M5.Lcd.fillScreen(BLACK);     // draw speaker image from image.h file
```

```
  M5.Lcd.drawBitmap(240, 10, speaker, 40, 40, WHITE);
                         // draw horizontal and vertical axes for "bubble"
  M5.Lcd.drawFastHLine (0, 160, 320, WHITE);
  M5.Lcd.drawFastVLine (160, 100, 120, WHITE);
}

void loop()
{
  M5.Imu.getAccel(&accX, &accY, &accZ); // 3-axis accelerometer data
  degY = atan(accY/accZ) * RAD_TO_DEG; // roll (tilt left or right)
  degX = asin(accX/sqrt(accX*accX+accY*accY+accZ*accZ));
  degX = degX * RAD_TO_DEG;             // pitch (take off and landing)
  M5.Lcd.setCursor(0, 10);
  M5.Lcd.print("   roll   pitch");   // switched when USB to left
  M5.Lcd.setCursor(0, 35);
  M5.Lcd.printf("%7.1f %7.1f", degX, degY);
  x = 160*(accX + 1);
  y = 60*(-accY + 1) + 100;
        // position of spirit level "bubble", co-ordinates of center, radius
  M5.Lcd.drawCircle(x, y, 8, GREEN);
  if(fabs(degY) > pitch || fabs(degX) > roll)
  {
    M5.Speaker.tone(1000, 50);          // sound freq Hz and time ms
                                        // over-write previous text
    M5.Lcd.fillRect (0, 60, 320, 40, BLACK);
    M5.Lcd.setCursor(0, 60);
    M5.Lcd.setTextColor(RED);           // display tilt message
    if(degX > roll) M5.Lcd.print("          right-side high");
    else if(degX < -roll ) M5.Lcd.print("left-side high");
    M5.Lcd.setCursor(0, 80);
    M5.Lcd.setTextColor(YELLOW);
```

```
    if(degY > pitch) M5.Lcd.print("back high");
    else if(degY < -pitch) M5.Lcd.print("front high");
  }                                     // over-write previous text
  else M5.Lcd.fillRect (0, 60, 320, 40, BLACK);
  if (M5.BtnA.wasPressed())
  {
    M5.Speaker.setVolume(0);            // turn off sound
    M5.Lcd.fillRect(240, 10, 40, 40, BLACK);
  }
  if (M5.BtnB.wasPressed())
  {                                     // turn on sound and
    M5.Speaker.setVolume(80);           // display speaker image
    M5.Lcd.drawBitmap(240, 10, speaker, 40, 40, WHITE);
  }
  M5.update();
  delay(200);                           // delay of 500ms is too jerky
  M5.Lcd.drawCircle(x, y, 8, BLACK); // over-write circle
                                        // redraw lines after black circle
  M5.Lcd.drawFastHLine (0, 160, 320, WHITE);
  M5.Lcd.drawFastVLine(160, 100, 120, WHITE);
  M5.Lcd.setTextColor(TFT_ORANGE, BLACK);
  M5.Lcd.drawString("speaker", 70, 195);
  M5.Lcd.drawString("off on", 40, 215); // display speaker labels
  M5.Lcd.setTextColor(GREEN, BLACK);
}
```

The first few lines of the bitmap image data for the speaker image are shown in Listing 1-4. Generation of the bitmap (BMP) image data is described in Chapter 10, "Managing Images."

Listing 1-4. Bitmap data for image

```
const unsigned char speaker [] PROGMEM = {
  0x00, 0x00, 0x00, 0x00, 0x00, 0x00, 0x00, 0x00,
  0x00, 0x00, 0x00, 0x00, 0x00, 0x00, 0x00, 0x00,
  0x00, 0x20, 0x00, 0x00, 0x00, 0x00, 0x70, 0x00,
  0x00, 0x00, 0x01, 0xf0, 0x07, 0x00, 0x00, 0x03, ... };
```

M5Stack Core2 M5GO Battery Base

The M5Stack Core2 M5GO battery base includes the SPM1423 PDM microphone and MPU6886 six-axis gyroscope and accelerometer, which are also located on the rear cover of the M5Stack Core2 module. In addition, ten SK6812 RGB LEDs and two expansion ports for ADC, DAC, or UART protocols are included in the M5Stack Core2 M5GO battery base. A 500mAh lithium ion battery replaces the 390mAh battery of the M5Stack Core2 module. The Port B and C expansion ports, located on the side of the battery base, connect to M5Stack units with four-pin Grove connectors for DAC2 (GPIO 26) and ADC2 (GPIO 36) and for RX2 (GPIO 13) and TX2 (GPIO 14), respectively.

The LEDs are controlled with GPIO 25 and the *FastLED* library, which is available in the Arduino IDE. Listing 1-5 illustrates flashing the LEDs.

Listing 1-5. Battery base LEDs

```
#include <FastLED.h>                    // include FastLED library
#define nLEDs 10                        // LEDs on battery base
CRGB leds[nLEDs];
#define LEDpin 25                       // int LEDpin = 25 doesn't
                                        // function with FastLED library
void setup()
{FastLED.addLeds<NEOPIXEL, LEDpin>(leds, nLEDs);}
```

```
void loop()
{
  fill_solid(leds, 10, CRGB::Red);       // turn on LEDs with red color
  FastLED.show();                        // update LED states
  delay(500);
  fill_solid(leds, 10, CRGB::Black);     // turn off LEDs
  FastLED.show();
  delay(500);
}
```

The PDM microphone in the M5GO battery base, as used in the book, was more sensitive than the microphone located on the rear cover of the M5Stack Core2 module.

Specification of the M5Stack Core2 M5GO battery base, a schematic, and the GPIO descriptions are available at `docs.m5stack.com/en/base/m5go_bottom2`.

ESP32-CAM

The ESP32-CAM module includes a 2M-pixel OV2640 image sensor with 1600 × 1200 pixels; a micro-SD card reader/writer; a COB (Chip on Board) LED, which flashes when taking a photo; and a red LED. The 5M-pixel OV5640 image sensor with 2592 × 1944 pixels is also available. JPEG (Joint Photographic Experts Group) files of images are stored on the micro-SD card or loaded on or streamed to a web page hosted by an Android tablet or mobile phone.

The pin layout of the ESP32-CAM module is shown in Figure 1-13 with *Rup* indicating the built-in pull-up resistor. There are three GND pins, a 3.3V pin, and a 5V input pin, and the VCC pin outputs 3.3V or outputs 5V when the corresponding jumper is closed. GPIO 0 determines the flashing mode state of the ESP32-CAM module, with the pin connected to GND when loading a sketch, as the pin has a built-in pull-up resistor. GPIO 2, 4, 12, 13, 14, and 15 are associated with the micro-SD card functionality. When the micro-SD card is not in use, the GPIO pins are available as output pins. The COB LED, which includes many LED chips bonded directly to a substrate to form a single module, and the red LED, which is active *LOW*, are accessed on GPIO 4 and 33, respectively.

A PDF file of the schematic for the ESP32-CAM module is available at `github.com/SeeedDocument/forum_doc/blob/master/reg/ESP32_CAM_V1.6.pdf`, with details of GPIO pins available at `github.com/raphaelbs/esp32-cam-ai-thinker/blob/master/docs/esp32cam-pin-notes.md`. GPIO 16 on the ESP32-CAM module is connected to the CS (chip select) pin of PSRAM. GPIO 0 and 16 are connected to an internal 10kΩ pull-up resistor. GPIO 1 and 3 are TX and RX Serial communication pins, respectively.

Figure 1-13. *ESP32-CAM pinout*

The ESP32-CAM module does not have a USB connector, and the module is connected to a laptop with a USB to serial UART (Universal Asynchronous Receiver-Transmitter) interface, such as an FT232RL FTDI USB to TTL Serial converter module. The Serial communication voltage of the USB to serial UART interface must be set at 3.3V, with the USB to serial UART interface RX and TX pins connected to the ESP32-CAM module TX and RX pins, respectively (see Figure 1-14 with connections in Table 1-5). The USB to serial UART interface 5V pin is connected to the ESP32-CAM module 5V pin. The camera unit is attached to the ESP32-CAM board by lifting the black tab on the ESP32-CAM board, sliding the camera unit into the connector, and closing the black tab. Prior to loading a sketch to the ESP32-CAM, GPIO 0 is connected to the GND pin, and then the *RESET* button is pressed. After the sketch is uploaded, GPIO 0 is disconnected from the GND pin, and the module *RESET* button is again pressed.

Figure 1-14. *USB to serial UART interface with the ESP32-CAM*

***Table 1-5.** USB to serial UART interface with the ESP32-CAM*

USB to serial UART	Connect to ESP32-CAM	
RXD	TX	
TXD	RX	
VCC	5V	
GND	GND	GPIO 0

In the Arduino IDE, from the *Tools* ➤ *Board* dropdown list, select *ESP32 Wrover Module.* In *Tools* ➤ *Partition Scheme,* select *Huge APP (3MB no OTA/1MB SPIFFS),* and in *Tools* ➤ *Port,* select the appropriate COM port.

Sketches to stream images to an LCD screen or to a web page are described in Chapter 11, "ESP32-CAM Camera." Development of an app to display streamed images is described in Chapter 12, "Control Apps."

ESP32-CAM-MB Module

The ESP32-CAM-MB module contains a CH340 USB to Serial communication chip, a micro-USB connector, a power indicator LED, and two buttons labeled *IO0* and *RST* (see Figure 1-15). When the button labeled *IO0* is pressed, ESP32-CAM GPIO 0 is connected to GND. The button labeled *RST* is not used. A sketch is loaded to the ESP32-CAM module by connecting the ESP32-CAM module to the ESP32-CAM-MB module, which is connected to the computer or laptop by the micro-USB connector. Prior to loading a sketch to the ESP32-CAM module, the ESP32-CAM-MB button labeled *IO0* is pressed, and then the ESP32-CAM *RESET* button, not the ESP32-CAM-MB button labeled *RST,* is pressed. The Serial Monitor displays the text *rst:0x1 (POWERON_RESET),boot:0x3*

(DOWNLOAD_BOOT(UART0/UART1/SDIO_REI_REO_V2))

waiting for download

After the sketch is uploaded, the ESP32-CAM *RESET* button is again pressed.

***Figure 1-15.** ESP32-CAM-MB and ESP32-CAM modules*

ESP32-CAM-CH340 Module

The ESP32-CAM-CH340 module combines the ESP32-CAM and ESP32-CAM-MB modules (see Figure 1-16). The COB LED and the red LED, which is active *LOW*, are accessed on GPIO 4 and 33, respectively. The blue LED flashes when a sketch is uploaded to the module. Prior to loading a sketch, the ESP32-CAM-CH340 GPIO 0 is connected to the GND pin, and then the module *RESET* button is pressed. The Serial Monitor displays the *POWERON_RESET* and *waiting for download* messages. After the sketch is uploaded, the module GPIO 0 is disconnected from the GND pin, and the module *RESET* button is again pressed.

Figure 1-16. *ESP32-CAM-CH340 module*

Image Resolution

The ESP32-CAM module supports a variety of image resolution options as shown in Table 1-6. The image resolution acronyms derive from the VGA (Video Graphics Array) acronym, with VGA images used in computer displays. The XGA, SXGA, and UXGA acronyms refer to eXtended, Super-extended, and Ultra-extended Graphics Array images with higher resolution than VGA. The letter H or Q in the acronyms for image resolution smaller than VGA refers to a half or a quarter of the VGA image resolution, such as HQVGA, which is an eighth of the VGA image resolution. Decreasing the image resolution from UXGA to QVGA increases the frame rate (Frames Per Second) from 3 FPS to 26 FPS (see Figure 1-17), with the image width, height, and pixel number, in multiples of 1024, shown in Table 1-6.

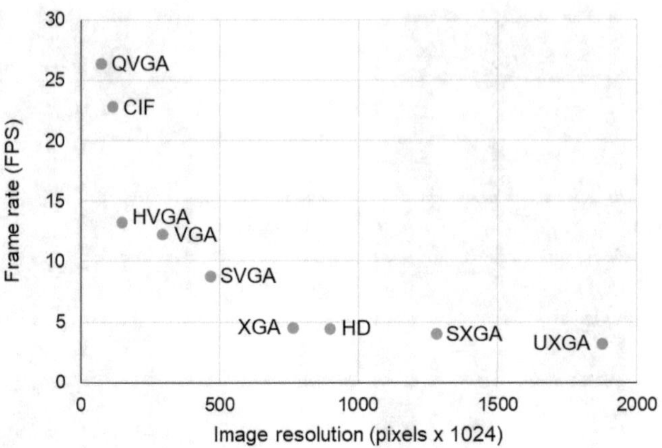

***Figure 1-17.** Image resolution and frame rate*

***Table 1-6.** ESP32-CAM VGA image resolution*

Image	UXGA	SXGA	XGA	SVGA	VGA	HVGA	QVGA	HQVGA	QQVGA
Width	1600	1280	1024	800	640	480	320	240	160
Height	1200	1024	768	600	480	320	240	176	120
Pixel (K)	1875	1280	768	468.75	300	150	75	41.25	18.75
FPS	3.1	4.0	4.4	8.7	12.2	13.2	26.3	26.3	26.3
Image code	13	12	10	9	8	7	5	3	1

The image resolution is defined by the image code (see Table 1-6) with the instructions

```
sensor_t * s = esp_camera_sensor_get()
s->set_framesize(s, (framesize_t)image_code)
```

or

```
sensor_t * s = esp_camera_sensor_get()
s->set_framesize(s, XXX)
```

with XXX equal to FRAMESIZE_ prefixing the image column heading in Table 1-6, such as FRAMESIZE_QVGA, as defined in the file *User\AppData\Local\Arduino15\packages\esp32\hardware\esp32\version\tools\sdk\esp32\include\esp32-camera\driver\include\sensor.h.*

Non-VGA image formats supported by the ESP32-CAM module are listed in Table 1-7. The HD (High Definition) and CIF (Common Intermediate Format) images are used in television and video teleconferencing, respectively.

Table 1-7. *ESP32-CAM non-VGA image resolution*

Image	HD	CIF	240 × 240	QCIF	96 × 96
Width	1280	400	240	176	96
Height	720	296	240	144	96
Pixel (K)	900	116	56.25	24.75	9
FPS	4.4	22.7	26.3	26.3	26.3
Image code	11	6	4	2	0

Microcontroller Developments

ESP32 microcontrollers based on the ESP32-D0WDQ6 chip are complemented with microcontrollers based on the ESP32-S3 and ESP32-C3 chips. The ESP32-S3 incorporates a dual-core 240MHz Tensilica Xtensa 32-bit LX7 microprocessor with a single-core 160MHz RISC-V 32-bit microprocessor included in the ESP32-C3 chip.

For example, the LilyGO T-Display ESP32-S3 module incorporates a TFT ST7789 1.9" LCD screen with 170 × 320 pixels, and the Seeed Studio Xiao ESP32C3 incorporates an ESP32-C3 chip (see Figure 1-18). Relative to the TTGO T-Display V1.1 module, the LilyGO T-Display ESP32-S3 module incorporates a larger LCD screen, while the Seeed Studio Xiao ESP32C3 is less than a third of the size of the ESP32 DEVKIT DOIT module.

***Figure 1-18.** ESP32, ESP32-S3, and ESP32-C3 modules (to size)*

The sketch in Listing 1-6 measures the time required to determine the first 10k prime numbers. The sketch may not be optimal, in terms of minimizing processing time, but is sufficient for establishing a benchmark.

Listing 1-6. Determine the first 10k prime numbers

```
int Nprimes = 9999;                      // required number of primes - 1
unsigned long number = 3;                // start from number 3
int count = 2;                           // prime number counter
unsigned int start;                      // store processing time
unsigned long ms;
int chk, limit, mod, divid;

void setup()
{
  Serial.begin(115200);
  Serial.print("\nCPU "); Serial.println(F_CPU/1000000);
  start = millis();                      // start of processing time
}
```

```
void loop()
{
  number = number + 2;         // exclude even numbers
  chk = is_prime(number);      // call function to check if prime number
  if (chk > 0) count++;        // increment counter when prime
  if (count > Nprimes)
  {
    ms = millis() - start;     // display results
    Serial.printf("Found %d primes in %d ms \n", count, ms);
    Serial.printf("Highest prime is %d \n", number);
    while(1) {};
  }
}

                               // function to check if prime number
int is_prime(unsigned long num)
{
  limit = sqrt(num);           // check divisors less than square root
  for (int divid = 3; divid <= limit; divid = divid + 2)
  {
    mod = num % divid;         // remainder after dividing
    if (mod == 0) return 0;    // not prime if zero remainder
  }
  return 1;                    // no divisor with zero remainder
}
```

The ESP32 DEVKIT DOIT and TTGO T-Display V1.1 modules are both ESP32 based, while the LilyGO T-Display ESP32-S3 and Seeed Studio Xiao ESP32C3 modules in Figure 1-18 are ESP32-S3 and ESP32-C3 based. With the V2.0.9 *esp32* Boards Manager installed and a 160MHz CPU frequency, the ESP32-S3-based module was faster than the ESP32-C3-based module, which was faster than the ESP32-based module (470 v 845 v 1079ms). For all the modules, the time to determine the first 10k prime numbers was dependent on the CPU frequency with time essentially doubling as CPU frequency halved (see Table 1-8). For the ESP32-based modules, the completion time with the V2.0.9 *esp32* Boards Manager installed was, surprisingly, double the time with the V1.0.5 *esp32* Boards Manager installed. All timings with the V2.0.9 *esp32* Boards Manager installed were made using the Arduino IDE 2.1.0 and were similar to timings using the Arduino IDE 1.8.19.

Table 1-8. *Time (ms) to determine 10k prime numbers for ESP32, ESP32-C3 and ESP32-S3 microcontrollers*

CPU Freq	ESP32 DEVKIT DOIT		XIAO ESP32-C3	T-Display ESP32-S3
(MHz)	V1.0.5	V2.0.9	V2.0.9	V2.0.9
240	357	715		313
160	537	1079	845	470
80	1087	2192	1678	951
40	2230	4534	3386	1943
20	4696	9747	6924	4062
10	10868	22702	14499	8915

Memory

Memory storage of the ESP32 microcontroller consists of RAM (Random Access Memory) and flash or program memory (PROGMEM). Flash memory is partitioned into several sections: application, OTA (Over the Air) updating, SPIFFS (Serial Peripheral Interface Flash File System), Wi-Fi, and configuration information. The allocation of flash memory to application, OTA, and SPIFFS is defined within the Arduino IDE by selecting *Tools ➤ Partition Scheme* to display a range of options.

For example, the 4MB flash memory is allocated by default as 1.2MB application, 1.3MB OTA, and 1.5MB SPIFFS or as 2MB application and 2MB SPIFFS with the *No OTA* option.

A sketch is stored in application memory with RAM storing variables created or manipulated in a sketch. RAM incorporates SRAM (Static RAM), which is divided into DRAM (Dynamic RAM) and IRAM (Instruction RAM) (see Figure 1-19). The ESP32 microcontroller has 520KB of SRAM, with the option to access 4MB or 16MB of external flash memory. SRAM is subdivided into SRAM0 (instruction bus), SRAM1 (instruction or data bus), and SRAM2 (data bus). Instructions are positioned in IRAM with the prefix `void IRAM_ATTR ISR()`, such as with an interrupt service routine (ISR). Further details are available at `docs.espressif.com/projects/esp-idf/en/latest/esp32/api-guides/memory-types.html`. Note that the abbreviations MB and KB refer to multiples of 1024^2 and 1024 bytes, respectively, while kB refers to 1000 bytes.

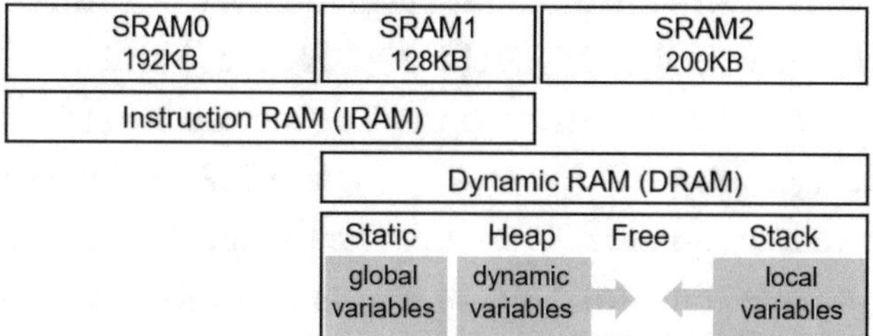

Figure 1-19. *Memory allocation*

Heap Memory

DRAM consists of static data, heap, and stack with the remainder termed *free memory*. Global and static variables are stored in static data, while the heap stores dynamic variables and data. The stack stores local variables and information from interrupts and functions, which increments while the sketch is running. After static data is defined at the start of a sketch, the heap, stack, and free memory sum to DRAM minus the static data. The increasing heap and stack memory requirements of DRAM are the main constraint of memory, and only 160KB of DRAM is available as heap.

The `ESP.getXX` instructions combine information from heap, 32-bit memory, and all internal memory rather than only from heap storage:

```
ESP.getHeapSize()                        // heap and 32-bit memory
ESP.getFreeHeap()                        // available internal memory
ESP.getHeapSize()-ESP.getFreeHeap()      // allocated heap
ESP.getMaxAllocHeap()                    // largest unallocated heap
```

The `ESP.getXX` instructions, listed at `github.com/espressif/arduino-esp32/blob/master/cores/esp32/Esp.h`, provide information on PSRAM, ESP32 chip, and sketch properties. For example, replace *Heap* with *Psram* in the heap instructions to obtain PSRAM properties. Sketch characteristics are provided with the `ESP.getSketchSize()` and `ESP.getFreeSketchSpace()` instructions. Flash memory size and frequency (Hz) are obtained with the `ESP.getFlashChipSize()` and `ESP.getFlashChipSpeed()` instructions. The instructions `ESP.getChipModel()`, `ESP.getChipRevision()`, and `ESP.getCpuFreqMHz()` provide information on the ESP32 chip. The `ESP.getEfuseMac()` instruction provides the MAC (Media Access Control) address with the six values in reverse order that is resolved with the instructions

```
int m[6]
for (int i=0; i<6; i++) m[i] = (ESP.getEfuseMac() >> 8*i) & 0xFF
Serial.printf("%02x:%02x:%02x:%02x:%02x:%02x \n",
  m[0],m[1],m[2],m[3],m[4],m[5])         // x is unsigned integer
```

Instructions for total heap, available heap, and largest unallocated block in heap are

```
heap_caps_get_total_size
  (MALLOC_CAP_DEFAULT)              // total heap size in bytes
heap_caps_get_free_size
  (MALLOC_CAP_DEFAULT)              // available heap
esp_get_free_heap_size()            // available heap
heap_caps_get_largest_free_block
  (MALLOC_CAP_DEFAULT)              // largest unallocated heap
```

Alternatively, a structure, *info*, containing heap information is constructed with the instructions

```
multi_heap_info_t info              // information structure
heap_caps_get_info
  (&info, MALLOC_CAP_DEFAULT)       // for heap information
info.total_free_bytes               // available heap
info.total_allocated_bytes          // allocated heap
info.largest_free_block             // largest unallocated heap
```

Listing 1-7 obtains memory characteristics for heap and demonstrates that several instructions provide the same information. In the first part of the *setup* function, the instructions `MALLOC_CAP_DEFAULT` and `MALLOC_CAP_INTERNAL` provide information on PSRAM and internal memory. The terms `MALLOC_CAP_DEFAULT` and `MALLOC_CAP_8BIT` are equivalent, but `MALLOC_CAP_INTERNAL` and `MALLOC_CAP_32BIT` arc only equal when there is no PSRAM.

Listing 1-7. Memory storage properties

```
void setup()
{
  Serial.begin(115200);                 // Serial Monitor baud rate
  Serial.println("\n total free alloc large");
  multi_heap_info_t info;               // information structure
                                        // heap memory
  heap_caps_get_info (&info, MALLOC_CAP_DEFAULT);
  Serial.printf("DEFAULT  %d %d %d %d \n",
                                        // total heap size
  heap_caps_get_total_size (MALLOC_CAP_DEFAULT),
  info.total_free_bytes,                // free heap
  info.total_allocated_bytes,           // allocated heap
  info.largest_free_block);             // largest unallocated block

                                        // internal memory
  heap_caps_get_info (&info, MALLOC_CAP_INTERNAL);
  Serial.printf("INTERNAL %d %d %d %d \n",
  heap_caps_get_total_size(MALLOC_CAP_INTERNAL),
  info.total_free_bytes,
  info.total_allocated_bytes,
  info.largest_free_block);

  Serial.printf("heap  %d %d %d %d \n", // "heap" characteristics
  ESP.getHeapSize(),ESP.getFreeHeap(),
  ESP.getHeapSize()-ESP.getFreeHeap(), ESP.getMaxAllocHeap());

                                        // equivalent instructions
  heap_caps_get_info (&info, MALLOC_CAP_DEFAULT);
  Serial.println("\nheap diff instructions same results");
  Serial.printf("free heap     %d %d %d \n",
  info.total_free_bytes,                // available heap
```

```
  heap_caps_get_free_size(MALLOC_CAP_DEFAULT),
  esp_get_free_heap_size());
  Serial.printf("largest block %d %d \n",
  info.largest_free_block,          // largest unallocated block
  heap_caps_get_largest_free_block(MALLOC_CAP_DEFAULT));
}

void loop()
{}
```

Further details are available at docs.espressif.com/projects/esp-idf/en/latest/esp32/api-reference/system/mem_alloc.html.

The constraint of limited SRAM capacity is reduced by defining variables as local rather than global or by storing constant data or text in PROGMEM. A variable defined in a function, only for use within the function, is termed a local variable, and when the function exits, the stack memory storing the local variable is released. In contrast, a global variable requires stack memory while the sketch is running. When printing a constant string *"abcd"*, the instruction `Serial.println(F("abcd"))` instructs the compiler to retain the string in PROGMEM, rather than copy the string, as a static variable, to SRAM.

Text or array variables are defined in PROGMEM with the instruction `const type variable_name[] PROGMEM = variable_value` or `const type array_name[] PROGMEM = {array_values}` for a variable or an array. Given that PROGMEM is non-volatile memory, variables stored in PROGMEM are constant as indicated by the *const* term in the instruction. For example, a string named *str* and an array named *data* with values {1, 2, 3} are stored in PROGMEM with the instructions

```
const char str[] PROGMEM = "some text"
const uint16_t data[] PROGMEM = {1, 2, 3}
```

The string is accessed from PROGMEM by copying the string to an SRAM buffer with the instructions

```
char buffer[12]
for (int i=0; i<12; i++)
     strcpy_P(buffer, (char *)pgm_read_byte(&(str[i])))
```

with the buffer size large enough to hold the string held in PROGMEM. The ith element of an array is accessed from PROGMEM with the `uint16_t value = pgm_read_word(data+i)` instruction. The `pgm_read_word` or `pgm_read_dword` instruction returns a 16-bit or a 32-bit value with the latter required for a pointer, as the ESP32 microcontroller pointers span 4 bytes or 32 bits.

Listing 1-8 illustrates storing an array and text in PROGMEM and then accessing the information from within the sketch. The *text* array combines the contents of the *text1*, *text2,* and *text3* arrays.

Listing 1-8. Memory storage

```
const int lookup[] PROGMEM = {2047,2402,2747,3071,3363};
const char text1[] PROGMEM = "ab12";
const char text2[] PROGMEM = "abc123";
const char text3[] PROGMEM = "abcd1234";
PGM_P const text[] PROGMEM = {text1,text2,text3};
int value;
char c;
char buffer[9];

void setup()
{
  Serial.begin(115200);
  for (int i=0; i<5; i++)          // contents of an array with integers
```

```
  {
    value = pgm_read_word(lookup+i);
    Serial.println(value);
  }
  for (int i=0; i<strlen_P(text2); i++)
  {                                // contents of an array with characters
    c = pgm_read_byte(text2+i);
    Serial.print(c);               // display one character at a time
  }
  Serial.println();
  for (int i=0; i<3; i++)          // combined contents of arrays
  {                                // copy array element to buffer
    strcpy_P(buffer,(PGM_P)pgm_read_dword(& text[i]));
    Serial.println(buffer);
  }
}

void loop()
{}
```

Non-volatile Memory

When power to the ESP32 microcontroller is turned off, data is retained in a portion of non-volatile memory (NVS). The *Preferences* library enables storing data in NVS, and the library is automatically installed in the Arduino IDE when the *esp32* Boards Manager is uploaded. The *Preferences* library replaces the *EEPROM* (Electrically Erasable Programmable Read-Only Memory) library. Data is stored in a *namespace* as key and value pairs, with several key and values pairs stored in a *namespace* and several *namespaces* stored in NVS. A *namespace* is defined with the `begin(namespace)` instruction, which enables read and write access to NVS, while the `begin(namespace, true)` instruction only enables read access, and the *namespace* title has a limit of 15 characters. The instruction format to save and retrieve a key and value pair is `putType("key", value)` and `getType("key", value)`, with the text *"key"* describing the stored value and *Type* defining the data type (see Table 1-9). For example, an integer variable, *state*, with a value of 3 is stored in or retrieved from NVS with the instruction `putInt("state", 3)` or `getInt("state", 0)`, respectively, with the variable *state* allocated a value of zero, if no value is stored in NVS. Details of the *Preferences* library are available at `espressif-docs.readthedocs-hosted.com/projects/arduino-esp32/en/latest/api/preferences.html`.

Table 1-9. *Preferences library data types*

Preferences type	Data type	Size (bytes)
Bool	bool	1
Char	int8_t	1
UChar	uint8_t	1
Short	int16_t	2
UShort	uint16_t	2
Int	int32_t	4
UInt	uint32_t	4
Long	int32_t	4
ULong	uint32_t	4
Long64	int64_t	8
ULong64	uint64_t	8
Float	float_t	8
Double	double_t	8
String	String	Variable
Bytes	uint8_t	Variable

The sketch in Listing 1-9 illustrates use of the *Preferences* library to store an LED state in NVS with a value, corresponding to the LED state, retained when the ESP32 microcontroller is powered off. The advantage of storing the variable in NVS is that the LED state when the ESP32 microcontroller is restarted is the same as prior to power off. The ESP32 DEVKIT DOIT module has a built-in blue LED on GPIO 2, and the *BOOT* button is connected to GPIO 0, when a sketch is running, with GPIO 0 set to *LOW* when the *BOOT* button is pressed.

In the sketch, the *Preferences* library is loaded, and a *namespace* called *"LED"* is initialized. When the *BOOT* button is pressed, the LED state is alternated, and the updated value of the *"state"* variable is stored in NVS with the `pref.putShort("state", LEDstate)` instruction. When the *EN* button is pressed, the ESP32 microcontroller is restarted, which has the same effect as the `ESP.restart()` instruction, and the value of the *"state"* key is obtained from NVS with the LED state updated to be the same as before the restart.

Listing 1-9. Stored data with Preferences

```
#include <Preferences.h>                    // include Preferences library
Preferences pref;                           // associate pref with library
int builtin = 2;                            // builtin LED on GPIO 2
int btn = 0;                                // BOOT button on GPIO 0
int LEDstate = 0;

void setup()
{
  Serial.begin(115200);                     // Serial Monitor baud rate
  pinMode(btn, INPUT);
  pinMode(builtin, OUTPUT);
  pref.begin("LED");                        // namespace called LED
  LEDstate = pref.getShort("state", 0);  // obtain state value from NVS
  digitalWrite(builtin, LEDstate);          // with default value of zero
  Serial.printf("LED state before reset %d \n", LEDstate);
}
```

```
void loop()
{
  if(digitalRead(btn) == LOW)          // BOOT button pressed
  {
    LEDstate = 1-LEDstate;             // update LED state
    digitalWrite(builtin, LEDstate);
    Serial.printf("LED state %d \n", LEDstate);
    pref.putShort("state", LEDstate); // update state value in NVS
    delay(500);                        // simple debounce
  }
}
```

Software Versions

Information on Espressif releases of the Arduino *esp32* Boards Manager with support for new boards, improvements, and bug fixes is available at `github.com/espressif/arduino-esp32/releases`. Details of software releases available when the book was written are listed in Table 1-10. Continuous software developments and web page revisions create a time limitation on the latest software release or information available on the Internet. Information on updates to Table 1-10 is available on the *GitHub* website for the book: `github.com/Apress/ESP32-Formats-and-Communication`. Details of installed libraries are included in Chapter 15, "Libraries."

Table 1-10. *Software releases*

Software	Version
CP210x Universal Windows Driver	v11.1.0 March 22, 2022
Arduino IDE	1.8.19 or 2.1.0
esp32 Boards Manager	V2.0.9

CHAPTER 2

I2S Audio

I2S (Inter-Integrated circuit Sound) is an audio standard for communicating PCM (Pulse-Code Modulation) or PDM (Pulse-Density Modulation) encoded digital audio data between devices. For example, audio input to a microphone is converted to a digital signal, which is subsequently converted to audio output. An ADC (analog to digital converter) device converts an analog signal to digital information, while a DAC (digital to analog converter) device converts a digital signal to an audio analog output. The ESP32 microcontroller supports two I2S (Inter-Integrated circuit Sound) peripherals, *I2S0* and *I2S1*, with *I2S0* output routed directly to the internal DAC output channels on GPIO 25 and 26.

An I2S signal includes audio data, an audio bit clock, and a frame or word select to indicate the left (*LOW*) or right (*HIGH*) channel. In contrast, asynchronous serial communication includes start and stop signals located before and after the transmitted data.

Analog to Digital

With PCM (Pulse-Code Modulation) encoding, the analog input signal is sampled at frequent, regular intervals, with sample values stored in binary format to form the digital signal. The resemblance between the analog input signal and the digital signal depends on both the PCM sampling rate and the PCM bit depth or resolution. Each signal sample is equated to the nearest set level, given the measurement resolution. For example,

N. Cameron, *ESP32 Formats and Communication*,
https://doi.org/10.1007/978-1-4842-9376-8_2

with 4-bit resolution and a signal range of –1 to 1, the $2^4 = 16$ set levels are ±0.0625, ±0.1875 ... ±0.9375. A signal sample of 0.30 is mapped to 0.3125, which is stored as $0.3125 \times 2^{(4-1)} + 2^{(4-1)} = 10$ or *B1010*. With positive and negative signal samples and R-bit resolution, there are $2^{(R-1)}$ set levels, in terms of magnitude, with an offset of $2^{(R-1)}$ to generate set levels with positive values. With 6-bit resolution, the signal sample is mapped to 0.296875, which is closer to the input signal, but requires two additional bits of data storage, and the signal sample is stored as $0.296875 \times 2^{(6-1)} + 2^{(6-1)} = 41$ or *B101001*. With R-bit resolution, the mapping of a sample, s, to a set level is $int[2^{(R-1)} \times (s + 1)]$. Conversion of a set level, L, to an analog value is $L/2^{(R-1)} - 1 + 1/2^R$.

The Nyquist-Shannon sampling theorem states that there is no signal distortion with PCM encoding if the sampling frequency is at least double the highest frequency of the analog signal. For example, the human voice frequency range is from 300Hz to 3400Hz, and telephone applications have an 8kHz sampling frequency. For CDs and DVDs, the sampling frequencies are 44.1kHz and 48kHz, respectively.

Figure 2-1 illustrates PCM encoding of a sine wave with a 200Hz sampling frequency. With 4-bit resolution, signal samples are mapped to one of the 16 set levels, which results in a stepped effect, while with 6-bit resolution and 64 set levels, the PCM voltage more closely represents the sine wave. Common PCM resolutions are 8-bit (telephone), 16-bit (CD audio), 20-bit, or 24-bit with 256, 65536, 1M, or 17M set levels. The PCM stored values are transformed to voltages by a digital to analog converter (DAC).

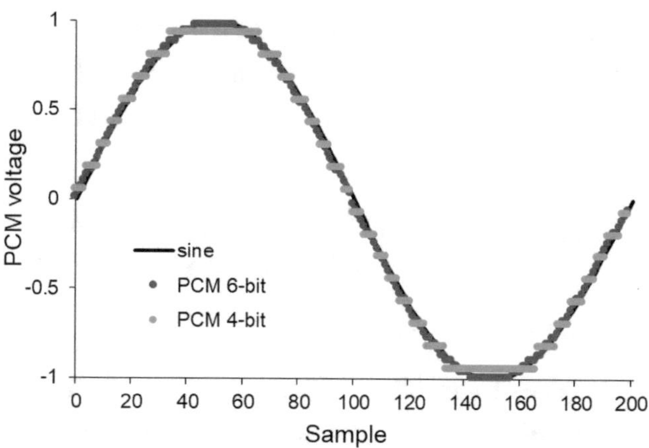

Figure 2-1. *Analog signal sampling with PCM*

With PDM (Pulse-Density Modulation) encoding, the analog input signal is also sampled at frequent, regular intervals, with each sample value mapped to either 0 or 1. Data storage with PDM encoding requires only 1 bit per sample, in contrast to PCM, which requires 8, 16, 20, or 24 bits per sample. The density of bits with value 1, in the digital signal, reflects the analog input signal. For example, given a sine wave as an analog input signal, the PDM digital signal consists, primarily, of bit values with 1 or 0 when the sine wave is at the peak or trough, respectively (see Figure 2-2a).

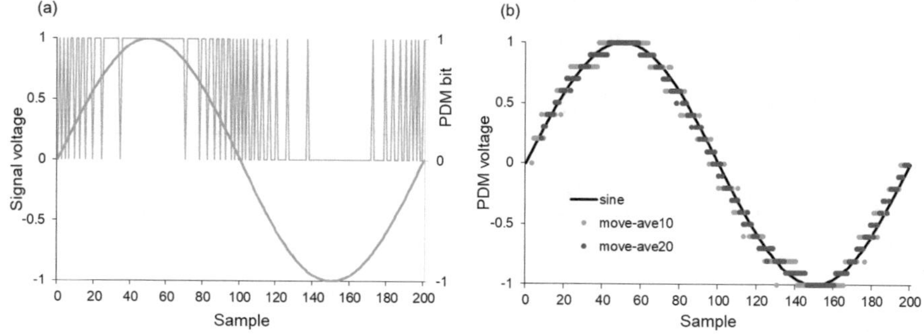

Figure 2-2. *Analog signal sampling with PDM*

The PDM digital signal is mapped to 1 or 0 if a function, *f*, which is based on the previous samples and the current sample of the analog input signal, is greater than or less than zero, respectively. The function, *f(i)*, is as follows:

If $x > 0$, then $f(i) = 1 - x$, where $x = s(i) - f(i - 1)$ and $s(i)$ is the ith sample.

If $x <= 0$, then $f(i) = -1 - x$.

For example, given a sampling frequency or rate of 200Hz and an analog input signal of a sine wave, the first six values of the PDM digital signal are shown in Table 2-1, with a sample equal to $sin(2 \times \pi \times (i - 1)/200)$. The first 32 values of the PDM signal are *B01010101 10110110 11101111 01111111*, and the increasing density of the high pulses is already apparent.

Table 2-1. *PDM encoding of analog signal samples*

i	Sample (s)	s(i) – f(i – 1)	Function (f)	PDM
1	0	–1 since f(0) = 1	0	0
2	0.0314	0.0314	0.9686	1
3	0.0628	–0.9058	–0.0942	0
4	0.0941	0.1883	0.8117	1
5	0.1253	–0.6864	–0.3136	0
6	0.1564	0.4701	0.5299	1

The PDM digital signal is converted to analog values by passing the digital signal through a low-pass filter, which essentially creates a moving average of the digital signal. For example, the first ten moving average values, each based on 20 values of the PDM digital signal, are *0.2, 0.3,*

0.3, 0.4, 0.4, 0.4, 0.5, 0.5, 0.5, and *0.5,* with the moving average equal to $2 \times \sum_{i=k}^{k+20} f(i)/20 - 1$. The PDM resolution, or number of effective levels, is the number of values in the moving average. Figure 2-2b illustrates the PDM values corresponding to moving averages based on 10 or 20 values. For comparison, PCM *N*-bit encoding is equivalent, in terms of resolution, to PDM encoding with a moving average based on 2^N sample values.

PDM encoding of audio signals with a sampling frequency of 2.8MHz is used by Sony and Sonic Studio as *Direct Stream Digital,* with substantially more complex methodology for converting a PDM digital signal to analog values than the illustrated moving average.

Direct Memory Access

PDM encoded audio data is transferred from an I2S device, such as a SPM1423 PDM microphone, to the CPU by the Direct Memory Access (DMA) controller. The DMA controller manages the data transfer, allowing the CPU to perform other tasks instead of waiting for the slow input or output transfer of data. The CPU initiates data transfer between SRAM (Static Random Access Memory) and the I2S device, with the transfer managed by the DMA controller. When data transfer is completed, the CPU receives an interrupt from the DMA controller to then either process the transferred data or to collate data for transmission. With at least two DMA buffers, the CPU processes data in one buffer, while the DMA transfers data to or from another buffer. Figure 2-3 illustrates the CPU receiving data from an I2S device and two DMA buffers.

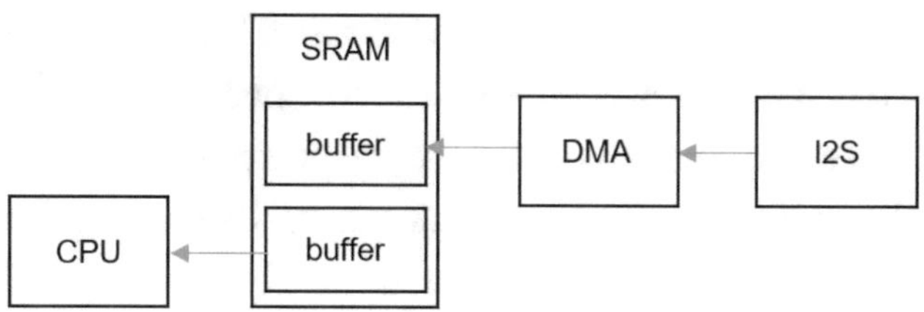

Figure 2-3. *Data from I2S device to CPU*

The DMA buffer size is 8–1024 samples, and DMA memory requirement is *buffers* × *buffer length* × *channels* × *bytes/sample*, which equates to 4KB for two buffers of 1024 samples, with recording in mono and 2 bytes or 16 bits per sample. The DMA buffers are stored in SRAM. A larger DMA buffer results in fewer interrupts from the DMA to the CPU, but generates a delay between the CPU instruction to transmit data and the start of data transfer, which is termed *latency*. The minimum number of DMA buffers is determined from the CPU data processing time, *T*; the sampling frequency, *F*; and the buffer size, *b*, as $(T \times F)/b$. For example, if the CPU processing time of data for transmission or analysis is 50ms for a data buffer of 1024 samples with a sampling frequency of 44.1kHz, then the minimum number of buffers is $(50 \times 10^{-3} \times 44100)/1024 = 2.15$, so three DMA buffers are required. Alternatively, the CPU is interrupted by the DMA controller at intervals of 23.2ms, equal to the buffer size divided by the sampling frequency, *b/F*, and the CPU data processing time of 50ms equates to 2.15 CPU interrupt intervals. At least three buffers are required.

I2S documentation is available at `docs.espressif.com/projects/esp-idf/en/latest/esp32/` by selecting *API Reference* ➤ *Peripherals API* ➤ *Inter-IC Sound (I2S)*. In the Espressif documentation, the required number of DMA buffers, DMA buffer size (samples), and CPU data processing time are termed *dma_desc_num*, *dma_frame_num*, and *polling_cycle*.

PDM Microphone

The M5Stack Core2 module incorporates a SPM1423 PDM MEMS microphone. A MEMS (Micro-electromechanical Systems) microphone is a combination of a sensor and an Application-Specific Integrated Circuit (ASIC) in a single package. An ASIC is an integrated circuit designed for a specific task, such as managing satellite transmissions or interfacing external memory with a microprocessor, rather than for general-purpose use. The sensor converts incoming sound pressure to capacitance values, which are transformed to analog or digital output by the ASIC. MEMS components are between 0.001 and 0.1mm in size, and MEMS devices range from 0.02 to 1.0mm in size.

In Listing 2-1, the digital signal from the M5Stack Core2 PDM microphone is displayed on the LCD screen of the module (see Figure 2-4a). The audio signal, consisting of a sine wave, was produced with the *Frequency Sound Generator* app by LuxDeLux that is available on *Google Play Store*. A large DMA buffer is recommended to capture complete sine waves, when displaying a sine wave input signal. The number of complete sine waves captured in a buffer, for a sine wave frequency of *W*Hz, is $(W \times b)/(4 \times F)$, where *F* is the sampling frequency and *b* is the DMA buffer size. For example, 5 or 12 complete sine waves are captured by the DMA buffer of 1024 samples, given a sine wave frequency of 861 or 2068Hz and a sampling frequency of 44.1kHz. In Figure 2-4a, the audio signal was generated as a sine wave of 861Hz, and the disjointed waveform is a consequence of the finite DMA buffer size.

The sine wave signal is sampled with F/W samples per cycle. Displaying sine wave values measured at intervals of $F/(2W) - 1$ samples results in interesting waveforms (see Figure 2-4b), with a signal frequency of 861Hz.

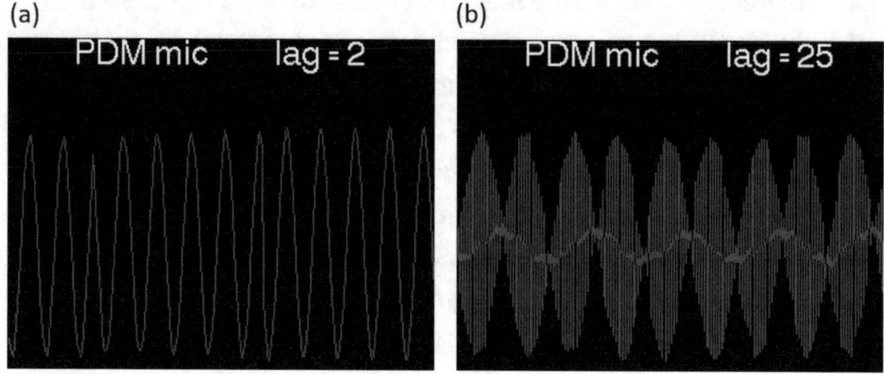

***Figure 2-4.** Sine wave signal sampling*

The first section of the sketch in Listing 2-1 loads the *driver/i2S* file, which is automatically included with the *esp32* Boards Manager. The file is located in *User\AppData\Local\Arduino15\packages\esp32\hardware\esp32\version\tools\sdk\esp32\include\driver\include*. The PDM microphone in the M5GO battery base, as used in this chapter, was more sensitive than the microphone located on the rear cover of the M5Stack Core2 module. The signal sample values were centered near zero for the microphone located on the rear cover of the M5Stack Core2 module, but around a value of 1100 for the microphone in the M5GO battery base. Minimum and maximum sample values, specific to the M5Stack Core2 module and the M5GO battery base, positioned the display waveform in the middle of the M5Stack Core2 LCD screen. In the sketch, values for the M5Stack Core2 module are commented out.

The *setup* function calls the *I2Sconfig* and *pinConfig* functions to configure the I2S protocol and define the PDM microphone pins. The ESP32 microcontroller receives signals from a PDM microphone, which requires the I2S mode settings of `I2S_MODE_RX` and `I2S_MODE_PDM`. The vertical line in the `.mode` instruction is a C++ bitwise *OR* operator. For example, with two bits the *OR* operator is equal to zero when both bits are zero, but otherwise is equal to one. The bit sampling resolution is defined as 16-bit with one channel. There are two DMA buffers of 1024 samples. The PDM microphones on the rear cover of the M5Stack Core2 module and in the M5GO battery base are both connected to GPIO 34 and 0.

The `.communication_format` instruction defines the format according to the ESP-IDF version used to compile the application, which is displayed with the `Serial.println(ESP_IDF_VERSION, HEX)` instruction. The ESP-IDF version consists of three components—major, minor, and patch—which are accessed with the format `ESP_IDF_VERSION_MAJOR`, as for the major component. For ESP-IDF versions earlier than or equal to 4.1.0, the communication format is `I2S_COMM_FORMAT_I2S`. The communication format options are defined in the *I2Sconfig* function by the instructions

```
#if ESP_IDF_VERSION > ESP_IDF_VERSION_VAL(4, 1, 0)
  .communication_format = I2S_COMM_FORMAT_STAND_I2S,
#else
  .communication_format = I2S_COMM_FORMAT_I2S,
#endif
```

The *loop* function calls the *wave* function to read the DMA buffer and display the waveform. The DMA buffer is read with the `i2s_read` instruction, which references the *I2S_NUM_0* channel, as do the `i2s_driver_install` and `i2s_set_pin` instructions, since *I2S_NUM_0* is the only I2S channel that supports PDM. The DMA buffer values, *buffer[i]*, are constrained to the defined minimum and maximum values and then mapped to values between 30 and 240, which is the number of available rows on the M5Stack Core2 LCD screen, as allocated by the sketch. The latest DMA buffer value is equated to the last element of the *yData* array, after all the array elements are shifted down one position. Lines between DMA buffer values, held in the *yData* array, are drawn in red, after overwriting the previous lines in black. Pressing the M5Stack Core2 button *BtnA*, *BtnB*, or *BtnC* increases, decreases, or sets the interval between displayed samples to one, respectively. A longer press is required for low values of the interval, as CPU processing time of the DMA buffer data is longer.

Listing 2-1. Display audio signal

```
#include <M5Core2.h>                 // include M5Core2 and
#include <driver/i2s.h>              // ESP32 I2S libraries
const int bufferLen = 1024;          // DMA buffer size (samples)
int N = 1, yData[320], yBase = 120;
int minY = 0, maxY = 2000;           // min and max values M5GO
// int minY = -600, maxY = 600;      // min and max values M5Stack
```

```
void setup()
{
  M5.begin();
  M5.Lcd.fillScreen(BLACK);                // initialize display
  M5.Lcd.setTextSize(1);
  M5.Lcd.setTextColor(WHITE, BLACK);
  M5.Lcd.drawString("PDM mic", 50, 0, 4);
  for (int i=0; i<320; i++) yData[i] = yBase;
  I2Sconfig();                             // configure I2S
  pinConfig();                             // and GPIO pins
}

void I2Sconfig()                           // function to configure I2S
{
  i2s_config_t i2s_config = {              // receive and PDM modes
    .mode = (i2s_mode_t)(I2S_MODE_MASTER | I2S_MODE_RX
                        | I2S_MODE_PDM),
    .sample_rate = 44100,                  // sample frequency
                                           // 16-bit sampling
    .bits_per_sample = I2S_BITS_PER_SAMPLE_16BIT,
                                           // mono channel sampling
    .channel_format = I2S_CHANNEL_FMT_ONLY_RIGHT,
    .communication_format = I2S_COMM_FORMAT_STAND_I2S,
    .intr_alloc_flags = ESP_INTR_FLAG_LEVEL1,
    .dma_buf_count = 2,                    // DMA buffers
    .dma_buf_len = bufferLen               // DMA buffer length
  };
  i2s_driver_install(I2S_NUM_0, &i2s_config, 0, NULL);
}
```

```
void pinConfig()                          // function to configure I2S pins
{
  i2s_pin_config_t pin_config = {
    .bck_io_num = I2S_PIN_NO_CHANGE,  // bit clock frequency
    .ws_io_num = 0,                   // word select (left /right) clock
    .data_out_num = I2S_PIN_NO_CHANGE, // data output
    .data_in_num = 34                 // data input
  };
  i2s_set_pin(I2S_NUM_0, &pin_config);
}

void loop()
{
  wave();                                 // call wave function
}

void wave()                               // function to read DMA
{                                         // buffer and display waveform
  size_t bits = 0;
  int16_t buffer[bufferLen] = {0};    // define and read I2S data buffer
  i2s_read(I2S_NUM_0, &buffer, sizeof(buffer), &bits,
           portMAX_DELAY);
  int bytes = bits / 8;                   // convert bits to bytes
  if(bytes > 0)
  {
    for (int i=0; i<bytes; i=i+N)
    {                                     // overwrite value
      M5.Lcd.drawLine(0, yData[0], 1, yData[1], BLACK);
```

```
                                          // shift one position
      for (int j=1; j<320; j++) yData[j-1] = yData[j];
                                          // constrain buffer values
      int temp = constrain(buffer[i], minY, maxY);
                                          // map to LCD height
      yData[319] = map(temp, minY, maxY, 30, 240);
      for (int j=1; j<319; j++)
      {                                   // overwrite and draw new line
        M5.Lcd.drawLine(j, yData[j-1], j+1, yData[j], BLACK);
        M5.Lcd.drawLine(j, yData[j], j+1, yData[j+1], RED);
      }
    }
  }
  if (M5.BtnA.isPressed())                // press button A to increase lag
  {
    N++;
    newValue();                           // call function to display lag
  }
  if (M5.BtnB.isPressed())                // press button B to decrease lag
  {
    N--;
    newValue();
  }
  if (M5.BtnC.isPressed())                // press button C to set lag to one
  {
    N = 1;
    newValue();
  }
  M5.update();
}
```

```
void newValue()                    // function to update displayed lag
{
  if(N > 60 || N < 1) N = 1;
  M5.Lcd.fillRect(200, 0, 120, 30, BLACK);
  String str = "lag = " + String(N);
  M5.Lcd.drawString(str, 200, 0, 4);
}
```

Fast Fourier Transform

A signal is decomposed into the component sine waves with the Fast Fourier Transform (FFT) methodology. For example, the waveform in Figure 2-5a consists of two sine waves with a lower-frequency sine wave providing the sinusoidal shape of the signal and a higher-frequency sine wave of smaller magnitude generating the signal "noise." The FFT decomposes the waveform and displays the frequencies and magnitudes of the signal and "noise" components (see Figure 2-5b), which are $\sin(2\pi \times t)$ and $\sin(2\pi \times 10t)/5$, where t is the time variable.

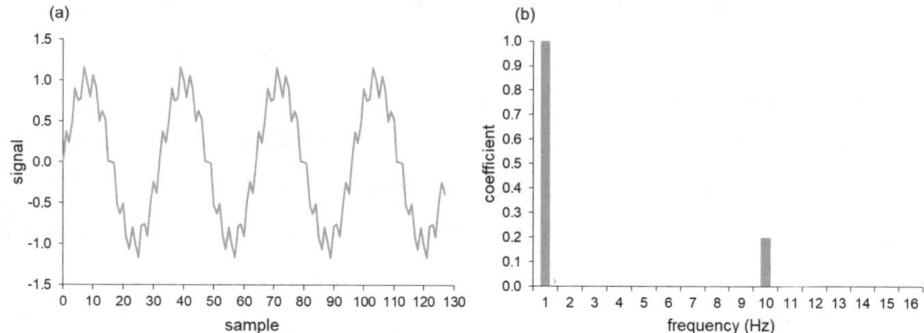

***Figure 2-5.** Fast Fourier Transform*

Audio processing uses FFT to filter noise from an audio signal, by subtracting the signal noise from the original signal to produce a clean signal. FFT parameterization of a signal requires substantially less data storage than the sample values stored with PCM (Pulse-Code Modulation) encoding.

Signal recognition is a second application of FFT with signals differentiated by either or both of the component frequencies and magnitudes. For example, a square wave is represented by the odd-numbered sine components, as $\frac{2}{\pi}\left[sin(2\pi ft)+\frac{1}{3}sin(3\times 2\pi ft)+\frac{1}{5}sin(5\times 2\pi ft)\ldots\right]$, while a sawtooth wave is represented by both the odd- and even-numbered sine components, as $\frac{1}{\pi}\sum_i \frac{1}{i} sin(i\times 2\pi ft)$, where f and t are the sine wave frequency and time variable. An FFT signal analysis, of square and sawtooth waves, detecting even-numbered sine components, identifies the signal as a sawtooth wave rather than a square wave.

Another application of FFT is JPEG compression of images, which uses FFT to identify high-frequency components of an image, to which the human eye is less sensitive. When only the lower-frequency information is retained, the data storage requirement of a compressed image typically reduces to 10% of the original requirement.

The *FFT* library, of Robin Scheibler, provides FFT analysis, with the library available to download within the Arduino IDE. An FFT analysis requires that the number of samples, N, is a power of two, such as 1024, with the waveform frequency, f, and sampling rate, R, determining the number of waveform cycles, $f\times N/R$, in the sample buffer. The FFT analysis generates, for each sample, a waveform component consisting of a real and an imaginary part. The magnitude of each FFT component is the square root of the sum of the real part squared and the complex part squared. For each sample, an FFT frequency is defined as the sample number, starting at zero, divided by the sampling rate. As an illustration, a signal with frequency of 2Hz is measured on 128 occasions with a sampling rate of 32, such that the samples cover 8 waveform cycles and the FFT frequency allocated to each sample is a multiple of 0.25 = 32/128. The FFT frequencies are plotted against the corresponding FFT magnitudes. FFT frequencies are limited to half the sampling rate, as aliased FFT components are generated when FFT frequencies are greater than half the sampling rate. The FFT methodology with Microsoft Excel is illustrated by Mike Holden (`www.youtube.com/watch?v=8nkKPR3-H1w`).

The FFT analysis of the noisy sine waveform in Figure 2-5a identified two sine wave components with frequencies of 1Hz and 10Hz and coefficients of 1 and 0.2 (see Figure 2-5b). The data consisted of 128 samples with a sampling rate of 32. FFT analyses of a square wave and of a sawtooth wave, both with values between 0 and 1, are shown in Figure 2-6a and b, respectively. The square waveform consists of odd-numbered (*C*) sine components with weights of *2/Cπ*, while the sawtooth waveform includes even- and odd-numbered sine components with weights of *1/Cπ*.

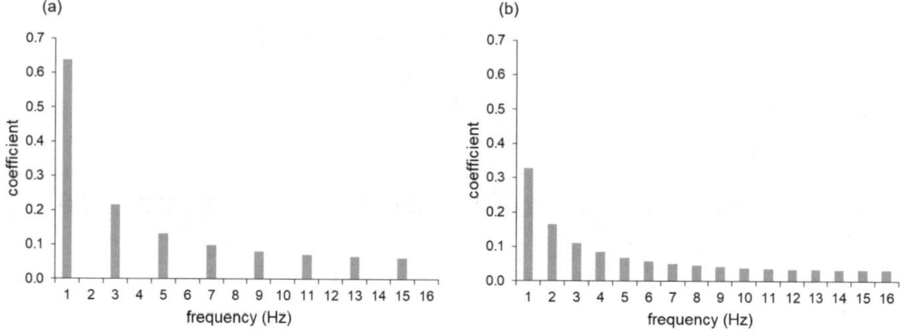

Figure 2-6. *Fast Fourier Transform of a square wave and a sawtooth wave*

The sketch in Listing 2-2 performs an FFT analysis of the audio data collected and displayed in Listing 2-1. The sketch is developed from the *File* ➤ *Examples* ➤ *M5Core2* ➤ *Unit* ➤ *PDM_SPM1423* sketch. The

FFTdisplay function is called in the *loop* function of Listing 2-1, by adding the `FFTdisplay()` instruction. The DMA buffer size is reduced from 1024 to 128, and the lag between displayed samples is increased from one to five, when displaying the audio waveform and the FFT frequency graph. The DMA buffer size for the FFT analysis, *FFTbufferLen,* is set to 1024; a variable to hold the number of elapsed milliseconds, *last,* is required; and a two-dimensional array, *x[2][24],* stores the FFT magnitudes and corresponding column number in the FFT frequency graph (see Figure 2-6). The changes to Listing 2-1 are listed in Table 2-2.

Table 2-2. *Changes to Listing 2-1 to include FFT display*

Instruction in Listing 2-1	New instruction
	#include <fft.h>
const int bufferLen = 1024	const int bufferLen = **128**
int N = 1	int N = **5**
	const int FFTbufferLen = 1024
	unsigned long last = 0
	int x[2][24]
In wave function	
yData[319] = map(temp, minY, maxY, 30, 240)	yData[319] = map(temp, minY, maxY, 30, **120**)
In loop function	
	FFTdisplay()

The displayed audio waveform in Figure 2-7 is constrained to the top half of the M5Stack Core2 LCD screen, as the FFT frequency graph is displayed in the lower half of the LCD screen. Each column in the FFT frequency graph corresponds to an increment of 250Hz. The audio waveform and FFT frequency graph for a generated 2055Hz sine wave signal are shown in Figure 2-7a, with a sampling interval of one. The estimated frequency of 2050Hz is similar to the frequency of the generated signal. The audio waveform and FFT analysis corresponding to a music track are shown in Figure 2-7b, with a sampling interval of five. FFT analysis of audio data from the music track demonstrates decomposition of the audio signal into a combination of sine waves.

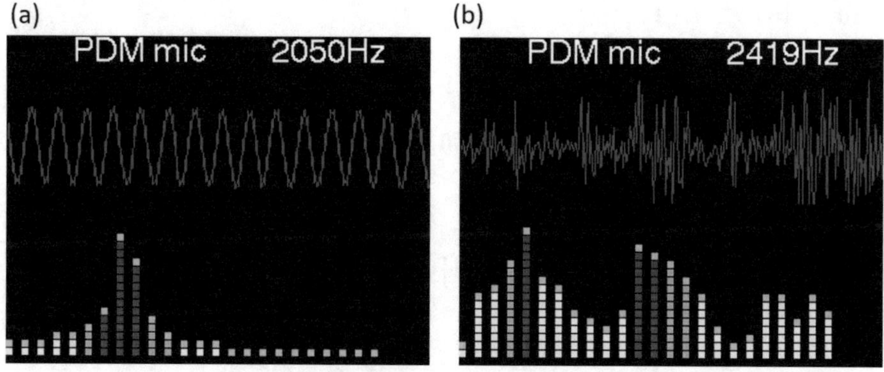

***Figure 2-7.** Fast Fourier Transform analysis of audio signals*

The format of the initial section of the *FFTdisplay* function (see Listing 2-2) is similar to the *wave* function (see Listing 2-1) as variables and matrices are defined, the DMA buffer is read, and the DMA buffer values are constrained. The FFT analysis is initiated with the `fft_execute(FFT)` instruction. The magnitude of each FFT component, the square root of the sum of the real part squared and the complex part squared, is calculated, constrained and mapped to between 0 and 255. After the FFT analysis, the `fft_destroy(FFT)` instruction frees up memory.

In the graph of FFT frequencies, the columns are color-coded with the highest three frequencies in red, the next three highest frequencies in orange, and the remaining frequencies in yellow. The top of each column is displayed in green. The FFT frequencies are sorted in descending order in the first row of the *x[rows][columns]* array while retaining the original column numbers in the second row, with the nested *sort* function (see Listing 2-3). Every second, the FFT frequency, corresponding to a weighted average of the three highest frequencies, is determined by the *calcFreq* function and displayed on the LCD screen.

Listing 2-2. Fast Fourier Transform

```
void FFTdisplay()
{
  int FFTn = FFTbufferLen;                      // FFTbufferLen defined
  int16_t FFTbuffer[FFTbufferLen] = {0};        // in main sketch
  size_t bits = 0;
  double data = 0;                              // FFT output values
  int FFTdata[128], plotData[24], temp;
  fft_config_t * FFT =
        fft_init(FFTn, FFT_REAL, FFT_FORWARD, NULL, NULL);
                                          // read I2S buffer every 100ms
  i2s_read(I2S_NUM_0, &FFTbuffer, sizeof(FFTbuffer), &bits,
    (100 / portTICK_RATE_MS));
                                                // constrain & map buffer
  for (int i=0; i<FFT->size; i++) FFT->input[i] =
    map(FFTbuffer[i], INT16_MIN, INT16_MAX, -2000, 2000);
  fft_execute(FFT);                             // FFT analysis
  for (int i=1; i<FFT->size/4; i++)
  {
    data = sqrt(pow(FFT->output[2*i],2)         // magnitude = real² +
          + pow(FFT->output[2*i+1],2));         // + imaginary²
    if(i - 1 < 128)
    {                                           // constrain and map
      data = constrain(data, 0, 2000);          // FFT magnitudes
```

```
    FFTdata[128-i] = map(data, 0, 2000, 0, 255);
  }
}
fft_destroy(FFT);                    // free-up memory space
for (int i=0; i<24; i++)
{
  temp = 0;
  for (int j=0; j<5; j++) temp = temp + FFTdata[i * 5 + j];
  temp = round(temp/5.0);            // average of 5 values
                                     // height of column = 16
  plotData[i] = map(temp, 0, 255, 0, 16);
}                                    // clear half LCD screen
M5.Lcd.fillRect(0,120,320,120, BLACK);
for (int i=0; i<24; i++)
{
  x[0][i] = plotData[i];             // FFT magnitude
  x[1][i] = i;                       // FFT column
}
sort();       // sort plotData in descending order, retain column values
for (int i=0; i<24; i++)             // FFT display with
{                                    // 24 columns, 16 blocks high
  int k = 23-i;                      // lowest frequency displayed first
  for (int j=0; j<16; j++)           // columns color coded
  {                                  // red, orange or yellow
    if((k == x[1][0] || k == x[1][1]
     || k == x[1][2]) && j < plotData[k])
    M5.Lcd.fillRect(i * 12, 234 - j * 6 - 5, 5, 5, RED);
    else if((k == x[1][3] || k == x[1][4] || k == x[1][5])
            && j < plotData[k])
      M5.Lcd.fillRect(i * 12, 234 - j * 6 - 5, 5, 5, ORANGE);
    else if(j < plotData[k])
```

```
        M5.Lcd.fillRect(i * 12, 234 - j * 6 - 5, 5, 5, YELLOW);
      else if(j == plotData[k])
        M5.Lcd.fillRect(i * 12, 234 - j * 6 - 5, 5, 5, GREEN);
    }                                    // column top in green
  }
  if(millis() - last > 1000)             // update main FFT frequency
  {
    last = millis();
    if(x[1][0] > 0)                      // if audio detected
    {
      float freq = freqCalc();           // function to calculate frequency
      String str = String(freq, 0) + "Hz";
      M5.Lcd.fillRect(200, 0, 120, 30, BLACK);
      M5.Lcd.drawString(str, 200, 0, 4);   // display frequency
    }
    else M5.Lcd.fillRect(200, 0, 120, 30, BLACK);
  }
}
```

The nested *sort* function (see Listing 2-3) sequentially compares pairs of values in the first row of the *x[rows][columns]* array. Values are interchanged if the value in the higher column is greater than the value in the lower column, but the original column numbers in the second row are retained.

The *freqCalc* function (see Listing 2-3) calculates an FFT frequency corresponding to a weighted average of the three highest frequencies.

Listing 2-3. Functions to sort data and derive main frequency

```
void sort()                     // sort first row of array into
{                               // descending order and retain column numbers
  int temp[2];
  for (int i=1; i<24; i++)      // nested sort for the ith column
  {
    for (int j=0; j<i; j++)     // then column 0 to column (i-1)
    {
      if(x[0][i] > x[0][j])     // if higher column value greater
      {                         // than lower column value
        for (int k=0; k<2; k++)
        {
          temp[k] = x[k][j];
          x[k][j] = x[k][i];    // then swap values
          x[k][i] = temp[k];
} } } } }

float freqCalc()                // function to calculate main frequency
{
  int sum1 = 0, sum2 = 0;
  for (int i=0; i<3; i++)       // for highest three values
  {                             // calculate weighted average
    sum1 = sum1 + (24 - x[1][i]) * x[0][i];
    sum2 = sum2 + x[0][i];      // and average column height
  }
  float freq = 250.0 * sum1/sum2;
  return freq;                  // return main frequency to sketch
}
```

Chris Greening designed an audio visualizer displaying the waveform, a graphic equalizer, and a spectrogram, using the FFT methodology, on an M5Stack Core2 module (`github.com/atomic14/m5stack-core2-audio-monitor`). Sarah Cartwright reconfigured the PlatformIO code to Arduino IDE code (`github.com/Sarah-C/m5stack-core2-audio-monitor`). It's an excellent visualization.

Digital to Analog

The PCM5102 and MAX98357 I2S decoder modules convert digital audio signals to analog output. The PCM5102 module is a stereo decoder, but cannot drive a speaker, while the MAX98357 module is a mono-decoder, and the built-in audio amplifier drives a 4Ω speaker. For amplified stereo output, a PCM5102 module with externally powered speakers or two MAX98357 modules with speakers are required. Both the PCM5102 and MAX98357 I2S decoder modules include a 16-bit DAC (digital to analog converter), which has higher signal resolution than the 8-bit DAC of the ESP32 microcontroller.

PCM5102 Decoder Module

The pinout of the PCM5102 decoder module is shown in Figure 2-8. Audio data input pins are located along the short side of the PCM5102 decoder module, with audio output pins positioned on the long side of the module. The PCM5102 decoder module audio data bit clock (*BCK*), audio data input (*DIN*), and audio data frame or word select clock (*LRCK*) are connected to the ESP32 module (see Table 2-4). For the audio output, default values for the latency filter (*FLT*), control of the sampling rate (*DEMP*), soft mute (*XSMT*), and format (*FMT*) are set with the soldered jumpers *H1L*, *H2L*, *H3L*, and *H4L*, respectively. Audio output is available through the audio jack to an externally powered speaker, such as used with a mobile phone. Stereo audio output to an externally powered right or left channel speaker is through the PCM5102 decoder module *ROUT* or *LROUT* pin with a GND pin (*AGND*) for each channel (see Figure 2-8).

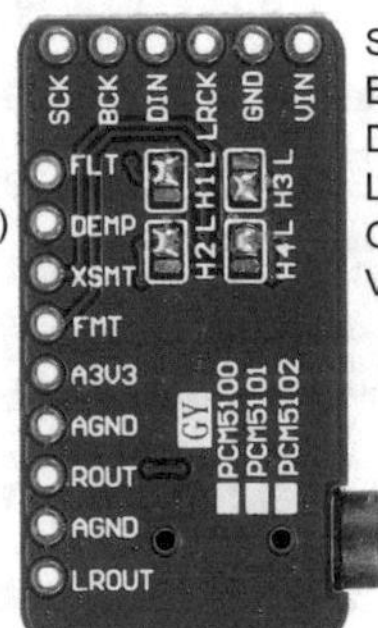

Figure 2-8. *PCM5102 decoder pinout*

MAX98357 Decoder Module

The MAX98357 decoder module outputs up to 3.2W to a 4Ω speaker with audio gains of 3, 6, 9, 12, and 15dB relative to 2.1dB. A speaker is connected to the MAX98357 decoder module plus ⊕ and minus ⊖ pins. The MAX98357 decoder module audio data bit clock (*BCLK*), audio data input (*DIN*), and audio data frame or word select clock (*LRC*) are connected to an ESP32 module (see Table 2-4 for an ESP32 DEVKIT DOIT module).

Audio output from the left or right channel is controlled by the voltage on the MAX98357 decoder SD (ShutDown) pin, with at least 1.4V for the left channel and between 0.77V and 1.4V for the right channel (see Table 2-3). When the voltage on the MAX98357 decoder SD pin is between 0.16V and 0.77V, the audio output is the average of the right and left channels. The MAX98357 decoder module includes a 1MΩ pull-up resistor between the SD and VIN pins with an internal 100kΩ pull-down resistor on the SD pin. When the SD pin is connected to GND, the audio output is shut down.

An additional pull-up resistor is required to obtain a specific output voltage, *VOUT*, on the SD pin. The additional resistor is in parallel with the MAX98357 decoder 1MΩ resistor, and both resistors are in series with the internal 100kΩ resistor (see Figure 2-9). The additional resistor is equal to $\frac{1000(VIN-VOUT)}{11\times VOUT-VIN}$ kΩ, where *VIN* is the voltage supply to the MAX98357 decoder module and *VOUT* is the required output voltage. The ESP32 module supplies 3.3V to the MAX98357 decoder module, and the additional resistor of 300kΩ results in 1.0V on the SD pin, which activates the right channel. The SD pin is connected directly to *VIN* or to an additional resistor of 100kΩ to set the left channel.

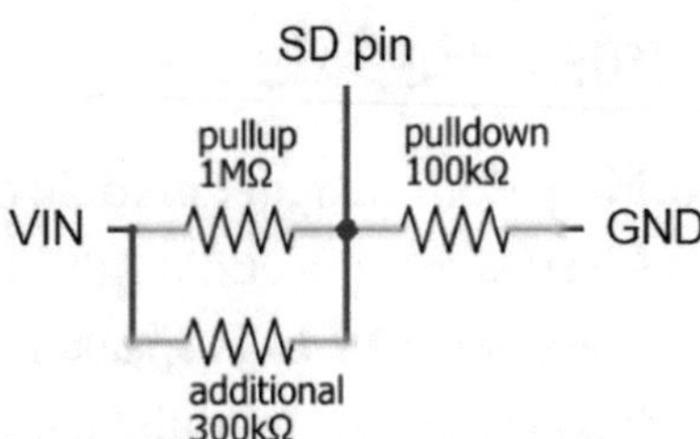

Figure 2-9. *Voltage divider for the MAX98357 module*

Figure 2-10 illustrates an ESP32 DEVKIT DOIT connected to two MAX98357 decoder modules for left and right channel output. The SD pin voltages on the MAX98357 modules for the left and right channels are 3.3 and 1.0V, respectively, with the latter due to addition of a 300kΩ resistor.

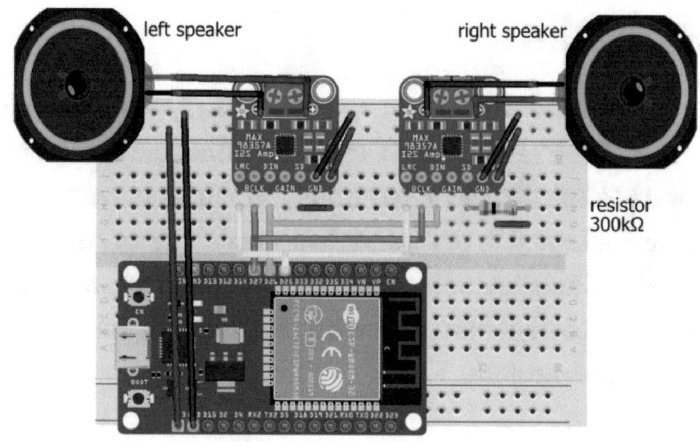

***Figure 2-10.** MAX98357 modules for left and right channels*

The MAX98357 module amplifier gain is determined by the resistance between the GAIN pin and the GND pin or the VIN pin (see Table 2-3). When GAIN is connected to GND or VIN, the amplifier gain is 12dB or 6dB, respectively. With a 100kΩ resistor between GAIN and GND or VIN, the amplifier gain is extended to 15dB or 3dB, respectively. The default gain is 9dB with the GAIN pin unconnected.

***Table 2-3.** MAX98357 GAIN and SD pin connections*

Connect GAIN pin	Gain	SD pin voltage	Additional resistor	Action
100kΩ and then GND	15dB	>1.4V	100kΩ	Left channel
GND	12dB	0.77–1.4V	300kΩ	Right channel
Unconnected	9dB	0.16–0.77V		Average of both channels
VIN	6dB	GND		Shut down
100kΩ and then VIN	3dB			

Internet Radio

Internet radio is developed with the ESP32 DEVKIT DOIT and M5Stack Core2 modules. The ESP32 DEVKIT DOIT is connected to either a PCM5102 or a MAX98357 decoder module, which is connected to an externally powered speaker or directly to a speaker, respectively. The M5Stack Core2 module includes a speaker, but the internal 8-bit DAC will have lower resolution than the 16-bit resolution of the PCM5102 or MAX98357 decoder module.

Internet Radio with an ESP32 Module

A PCM5102 or a MAX98357 decoder module is combined with an ESP32 DEVKIT DOIT to form an Internet radio (see Figure 2-11). Note that an externally powered speaker is required with a PCM5102 module. The MAX98357 module amplifier is adjusted by the voltage on a 10kΩ potentiometer. The mapping of voltage to digital value by the ESP32 microcontroller ADC (analog to digital converter) is linear between 0.5V and 2.5V, which corresponds to values between 620 and 3100 with a 12-bit ADC.

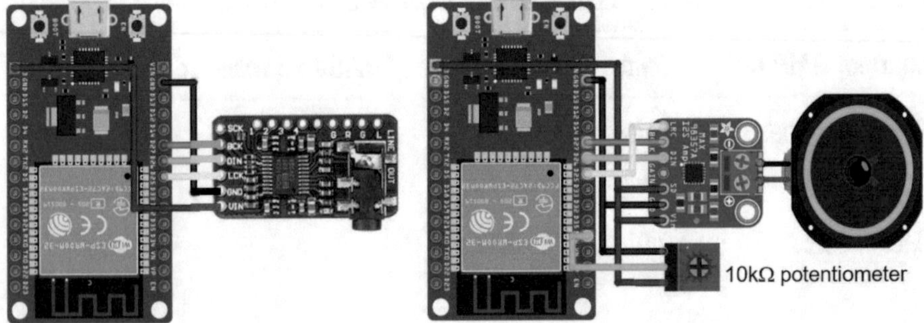

Figure 2-11. *Internet radio with PCM5102 and MAX98357 decoder modules*

Connections between the ESP32 DEVKIT DOIT and the PCM5102 or MAX98357 decoder module, for an Internet radio, are given in Table 2-4.

Table 2-4. *Internet radio with PCM5102 and MAX98357 decoder modules*

Component	Connect to ESP32
I2S module LRCK (audio data word clock)	GPIO 25
I2S module DIN (audio data input)	GPIO 26
I2S module BCK (audio data bit clock)	GPIO 27
I2S module SCK (system clock)	GND
I2S module VIN	3V3
I2S module GND	GND
Potentiometer signal	GPIO 34
Potentiometer VCC	3V3
Potentiometer GND	GND

The *Audio* library by Wolle, which is downloaded from `github.com/schreibfaul1/ESP32-audioI2S`, is recommended. A sketch for an Internet radio with one preset radio station is shown in Listing 2-4. The station name and title of each streamed track are displayed on the Serial Monitor. The first section of the sketch loads the libraries and defines the I2S pins, establishes a Wi-Fi connection, defines the radio station URL, and initiates the I2S decoder. The potentiometer value, used to change the volume of the MAX98357 module amplifier, is constrained to the linear region of the ADC and then mapped to a volume level between 0 (off) and 21 (high). The volume is updated at five-second intervals with the variable *lastTime* being the last time that the volume was updated. The *Audio* library *audio_showstation* and *audio_showstreamtitle* functions display the radio station name and the title of each streamed track.

Access to a Wi-Fi network and similarly to a MQTT broker requires a password, an SSID, or MQTT broker keys. Instead of storing the access information in the sketch with instructions like `char password[] = "Abcdef#99"`, the information is stored in a library that is referenced by the sketch. A text file with the extension *.h* is created to hold the access information, with the file placed in the Arduino IDE libraries folder. To determine the location of the Arduino IDE libraries folder, select *File* ➤ *Preferences* in the Arduino IDE; and the libraries folder is shown in the sketchbook location, such as *C:\Users\user\Documents\Arduino*. The access information file is referenced by the sketch with the instruction `#include <filename.h>`.

The sketch in Listing 2-4 represents a minimal Internet radio station with an ESP32 module. The facility to select from several preloaded stations and display station information on a ST7735 TFT LCD touch screen is given in Chapter 1 of *Electronics Projects with the ESP8266 and ESP32*.

Listing 2-4. Internet radio with an ESP32 module

```
#include <Audio.h>                    // include Audio
#include <WiFi.h>                     // and WiFi libraries
#include <ssid_password.h>            // file with Wi-Fi login details
Audio audio;                          // associate audio with library
int DIN = 26;                         // define decoder pins for
int BCK = 27;                         // data input, audio bit, clock
int LRCK = 25;                        // and the word select clock
int volPin = 34;                      // define potentiometer pin
int volume = 10, oldVol = 0;          // initial volume level
unsigned long lastTime = 0;
String str;
```

```
void setup()
{
  Serial.begin(115200);             // Serial Monitor baud rate
  WiFi.begin(ssid, password);       // initialize and connect to Wi-Fi
  while (WiFi.status() != WL_CONNECTED) delay(500);
  audio.setPinout(BCK, LRCK, DIN);  // initialize decoder
  audio.setVolume(volume);          // set volume level: 0 to 21
                                    // Classic FM
  audio.connecttohost("media-ice.musicradio.com/ClassicFM");
}

void loop()
{
  audio.loop();                     // update volume every 5s
  if(millis() - lastTime > 5000) getVolume();
}

void getVolume()                    // function to update volume
{
  volume = analogRead(volPin);      // read potentiometer value
                                    // constrain to linear region
  volume = constrain(volume, 620, 3100);
                                    // map analog values to volume
  volume = map(volume, 620, 3100, 0, 21);
  if(oldVol != volume)              // volume changed
  {
    audio.setVolume(volume);        // set volume
                                    // display new volume
    Serial.printf("volume %d \n", volume);
    oldVol = volume;
  }
```

```
  lastTime = millis();                // update volume reading time
}                                     // display radio station name
void audio_showstation(const char *info)
{
  Serial.printf("station %s \n",info);
}                                     // display title of streamed track
void audio_showstreamtitle(const char *info)
{
  Serial.printf("streamtitle %s \n", info);
}
```

Connecting to the radio station URL is not always successful as indicated by the message *"Request radio station URL failed!"*, in contrast to the message *"Connected to server in N ms"*, with the message displayed by the *Audio* library *audio_info* function using the instructions

```
void audio_info(const char *info)   // display URL connection status
{
  str = info;
  if(str.startsWith("Connected") || str.startsWith("Request"))
     Serial.printf("info %s \n", info);
}
```

If connection to the radio station URL fails, then connection is again attempted with the following instructions included in the *loop* function:

```
  if(str.startsWith("Request"))       // message "Request ..."
  {                                   // Classic FM
    audio.connecttohost("media-ice.musicradio.com/ClassicFM");
    str = "";                         // reset str
  }
```

A new radio station URL is entered on the Serial Monitor with the following instructions included in the *loop* function:

```
if(Serial.available())            // enter streamURL in Serial Monitor
{
  String newStation;
  audio.stopSong();                // stop existing playback
                                   // newStation defined as a String
  newStation = Serial.readString();
                                   // load new radio station URL
  audio.connecttohost(newStation.c_str());
}
```

Internet Radio with M5Stack Core2

Information on the selected radio station and the streamed track is displayed on the M5Stack Core2 screen with buttons to select radio stations and to control the volume provided by the touch screen facility. The I2S and speaker connections are illustrated on the rear panel of the M5Stack Core2 module (see Figure 2-12). The audio bit clock, word select clock, and data input pins are located on GPIO 12, 0, and 2, respectively.

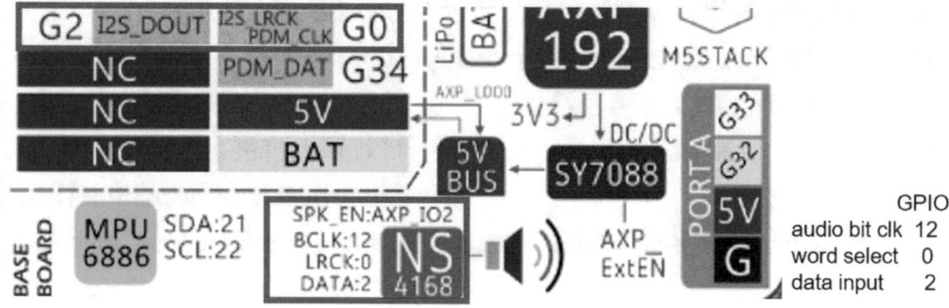

Figure 2-12. *I2S connections for M5Stack Core2*

The minimal Internet radio sketch in Listing 2-5, with one preset radio station and a volume setting between 0 and 21, requires only 31 lines of instructions.

The *setup* function enables the built-in speaker and the LCD screen, defines the I2S GPIO pins and volume, and connects to the Wi-Fi router and to the radio station URL. The *Audio* library *audio_showstreamtitle* function displays the streamed track title.

Listing 2-5. Internet radio minimal sketch

```
#include <M5Core2.h>                  // include M5Core2 library and
#include <ssid_password.h>            // file with Wi-Fi access details
#include <Audio.h>                    // include ESP32-audioI2S library
Audio audio;                          // associate audio with library

void setup()
{
  M5.begin();                         // initialize M5Stack module
  M5.Axp.SetSpkEnable(true);          // enable speaker
  M5.Lcd.setTextSize(2);              // define text size and color
  M5.Lcd.setTextColor(WHITE, BLACK);
  WiFi.mode(WIFI_STA);
  WiFi.begin(ssid, password);         // connect to Wi-Fi
  while (!WiFi.isConnected()) delay(500);
  audio.setPinout(12, 0, 2);          // I2S connection GPIO
  audio.setVolume(12);                // volume set at 12, range 0 to 21
  delay(500);                         // connect to radio station URL
  audio.connecttohost("media-ice.musicradio.com:80/ClassicFMMP3");
}

void loop()
{
  audio.loop();                       // manage audio streaming
}
```

```
void audio_showstreamtitle(const char *info)
{
  M5.Lcd.fillScreen(BLACK);
  M5.Lcd.setCursor (0, 50);
  M5.Lcd.print(String(info));          // display streamed track
}
```

The Internet radio sketch in Listing 2-6 displays radio station and streamed track information, and pressing the touch screen buttons changes the volume or the radio station. The streamed track title is parsed to ensure that words are not split. The Wi-Fi signal strength and battery level are displayed, with the battery level also presented as a color-coded bar graph. The LCD screen with the more comprehensive Internet radio is shown in Figure 2-13.

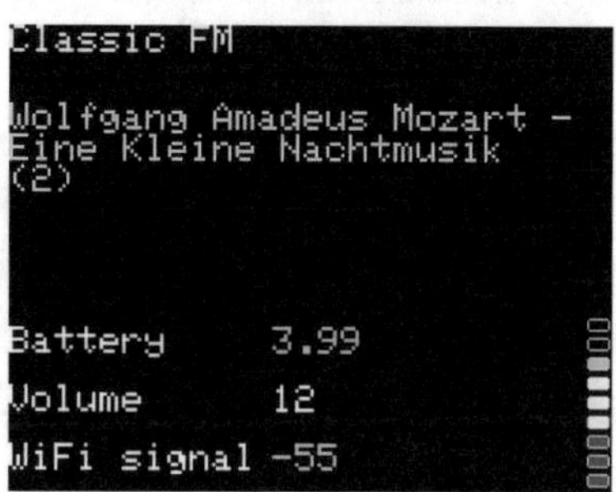

***Figure 2-13.** Internet radio with M5Stack Core2*

The structure of the first section and the *setup* function of the sketch are essentially the same as in Listing 2-5. The radio station URLs are stored in a character array defined with the C++ instruction `char const * name[N] = {...}`. Radio station URLs constantly change, but at the time of writing this chapter, the radio station URLs in Listing 2-6 were valid. The *GitHub* page for the book, `github.com/Apress/ESP32-Formats-and-Communication`, contains updates for sketches and URLs cited in the text.

When a new radio station URL is loaded, the *audio_showstation* function displays the radio station on the LCD screen. Some radio stations, such as Virgin Radio, do not provide the radio station name, and the two instructions

```
temp = String(URL[station])
if(temp.indexOf("virgin") != -1)
       M5.Lcd.drawString("Virgin Radio",0,0)
```

display a specific text when the radio station URL contains a particular substring, such as "*virgin*". Some radio stations do not provide a streamed track title, so when changing radio stations, the previous streamed title is blanked out. Similarly, some radio stations, such as BB Radio Berlin, substitute the streamed track title with the radio station name. In the *audio_showstreamtitle* function, the information is not displayed for those radio stations. A new radio station URL is entered on the Serial Monitor, rather than editing the sketch with the new URL.

Pressing the M5Stack Core2 touch screen button *BtnA, BtnB,* or *BtnC* selects the next or previous radio station or increments the volume, respectively. Following the `if (M5.BtnX.wasPressed())` instructions, the `M5.update()` instruction updates the button pressed status. The `M5.BtnX.isPressed` instruction requires the button to be pressed when the `M5.update()` instruction is next implemented.

The battery voltage bar graph consists of nine bars, which are 12 pixels wide and 7 pixels high with 3 pixels between bars. The `M5.Lcd.fillRoundRect(X,Y,W,H,R,(level > L) ? color : BLACK)` instruction draws a filled rectangle of width *W* and height *H* with rounded corners of radius *R,* starting at coordinates *(X,Y)*. If the condition *level* > *L* is true, then the rectangle is filled in *color* and otherwise in black. The `(A > B) C : D` part-instruction is equivalent to the `if(A > B) then C; else D;` instructions.

The *ESP32_audioI2S* library *audio_info* function provides additional information about the streamed data. The constraint that the *info* string contains the string *connect* restricts the displayed information to only relate to the connection status. For example, the displayed connection information is

> *Connect to new host:*
> *"http://media-ice.musicradio.com:80/ClassicFMMP3"*
>
> *Connection has been established in 55 ms,*
> *free Heap: 200636 bytes*

Listing 2-6. Internet radio with M5Stack Core2

```
#include <M5Core2.h>                 // include M5Core2 and
#include <ssid_password.h>           // file with Wi-Fi access details
#include <Audio.h>                   // include ESP32-audioI2S library
Audio audio;                         // associate audio with library
int BCLK = 12;                       // audio bit clock,
int LRC = 0;                         // word select clock and
int DOUT = 2;                        // data input pins
unsigned long last = 0;
uint16_t color;
int vol = 10;                        // volume between 0 and 21
int level;
float batt;
String title, newStation, temp;
const int maxStation = 6;            // number of radio station URLs
int station = 0;
char const * URL[maxStation] = {     // radio station URLs
"media-ice.musicradio.com:80/ClassicFMMP3", // Classic FM
"1940sradio1.co.uk:8100/stream/1/",         // 1940s radio
                                            // BB Radio Berlin
"irmedia.streamabc.net/irm-bbrberlinclub-mp3-128-4574783",
"radio.virginradio.co.uk/stream",           // Virgin radio
                                            // Radio Oslo
```

```
"stream.oneplay.no/oslo128",
                                          // Bayern3
"dispatcher.rndfnk.com/br/br3/live/aac/low?aggregator=radio-de"
};

void setup()
{
  M5.begin();                             // initialize M5Stack module
  M5.Axp.SetSpkEnable(true);              // enable speaker
  M5.Lcd.fillScreen(BLACK);
  M5.Lcd.setTextSize(2);                  // define text color and size
  M5.Lcd.setTextColor(WHITE, BLACK);
  M5.Lcd.setCursor(0,10);
  M5.Lcd.println("connecting");
  WiFi.mode(WIFI_STA);
  WiFi.begin(ssid, password);             // connect to Wi-Fi
  while (!WiFi.isConnected()) delay(500);
  M5.Lcd.println("WiFi connected");
  M5.Lcd.print(WiFi.localIP());           // display ESP32 IP address
  delay(2000);
  M5.Lcd.fillScreen(BLACK);               // initialize display screen
  M5.Lcd.drawString("Battery ", 0, 155);
  M5.Lcd.drawString("Volume ", 0, 185);
  M5.Lcd.drawString("WiFi signal ", 0, 215);
  displayBatt();
  audio.setPinout(BCLK, LRC, DOUT);       // I2S connection GPIO
  audio.setVolume(vol);                   // set initial volume
  delay(500);
  audio.connecttohost(URL[0]);            // connect to radio station URL
}
```

```
void loop()
{
  audio.loop();                       // manage audio streaming
  if (M5.BtnA.wasPressed())
  {
    vol++;
    if(vol > 21) vol = 0;
    audio.setVolume(vol);             // increase volume
    M5.Lcd.fillRect(140,185,30,20,BLACK);
    M5.Lcd.setTextColor(WHITE, BLACK);
                                      // updated displayed volume
    M5.Lcd.drawString(String(vol),140,185);
  }
  if (M5.BtnB.wasPressed())
  {
    station++;                        // increase radio station number
    if(station > maxStation-1) station = 0;
    audio.stopSong();                 // stop current streaming
                                      // update radio station URL
    audio.connecttohost(URL[station]);
    M5.Lcd.fillRect(0,0,319,20,BLACK);
    temp = String(URL[station]);      // display a station name
                                      // if none supplied
    M5.Lcd.setTextColor(YELLOW, BLACK);
    if(temp.indexOf("virgin") != -1)
         M5.Lcd.drawString("Virgin Radio",0,0);
  }
  if (M5.BtnC.wasPressed())
  {
    station--;                        // decrease radio station number
```

```
    if(station < 0) station = maxStation-1;
    audio.stopSong();
    audio.connecttohost(URL[station]);
    M5.Lcd.fillRect(0,0,319,20,BLACK);
    temp = String(URL[station]);
    M5.Lcd.setTextColor(YELLOW, BLACK);
    if(temp.indexOf("virgin") != -1)
         M5.Lcd.drawString("Virgin Radio",0,0);
  }
  M5.update();                          // update button "pressed" states
  if(Serial.available())                // radio station URL entered in
  {                                     // Serial Monitor for new URLs
    audio.stopSong();
    newStation = Serial.readString();
                                        // convert string to characters
    audio.connecttohost(newStation.c_str());
  }                                     // display battery voltage
  if(millis() - last > 60000) displayBatt();
}                                       // at minute intervals

void displayBatt()                      // function to display RSSI
                                        // and battery bar graph
{                                       // blank out previous RSSI
    M5.Lcd.fillRect(140,215,40,20,BLACK);
                                           // display low RSSI in red
    color = (WiFi.RSSI() < -70) ? RED : GREEN;
    M5.Lcd.setTextColor(color, BLACK);     // otherwise in green
    M5.Lcd.drawString(String(WiFi.RSSI()),140,215);
    batt = M5.Axp.GetBatVoltage();         // obtain battery voltage
    M5.Lcd.fillRect(140,155,50,20,BLACK);
    color = (batt < 3.5) ? RED : GREEN;  // display low voltage in red
```

```
    M5.Lcd.setTextColor(color, BLACK);  // otherwise in green
    M5.Lcd.drawString(String(batt),140,155);
                                        // number of bars for graph
    level = (M5.Axp.GetBatVoltage() - 3.2)/0.1;
    for (int i=0; i<9; i++)
    {
      color = GREEN;                    // green bars if 3.8-4.1V
      if(i<3) color = RED;              // red bars if 3.2-3.4V
      else if(i<6) color = YELLOW;      // yellow bars if 3.5-3.7V
      M5.Lcd.fillRoundRect(307,(230-(i*10)),12,7,2,(level>i)
                 ? color : BLACK);      // black above battery voltage
      M5.Lcd.drawRoundRect(307,(230-(i*10)),12,7,2,
             TFT_LIGHTGREY);
    }                                   // boundary around bars
    last = millis();                    // update time counter
}

void splitText(String text)             // see Listing 2-7

                                        // display radio station name
void audio_showstation(const char *info)
{
  Serial.print("station      ");Serial.println(info);
  M5.Lcd.fillRect(0,0,319,20,BLACK);    // overwrite previous name
  M5.Lcd.setTextColor(YELLOW, BLACK);
  title = String(info);
  M5.Lcd.drawString(title,0,0);
                                        // blank previous track as Virgin
  M5.Lcd.fillRect(0,40,319,80,BLACK);
}                                       // Radio provides no text
```

```
void audio_showstreamtitle(const char *info)
                                            // display title of streamed track
{
  Serial.print("streamtitle ");Serial.println(info);
                                            // overwrite previous title
  M5.Lcd.fillRect(0,40,319,80,BLACK);
  M5.Lcd.setTextColor(TFT_ORANGE, BLACK);
  title = String(info);
  M5.Lcd.setCursor(0, 40);                  // excluding third radio station
  if(station !=2) splitText(title);         // call function to split text
}

void audio_info(const char *info)           // for information purposes
{
  String chk = String(info);                // convert char array to string
  if(chk.startsWith("Connect")) Serial.println(info);
}
```

The *splitText* function to display text without splitting words is given in Listing 2-7. The `str.length()` instruction determines the length of the text, after adding a space at the end of the text, and determines positions of spaces in the text with the `str.indexOf(" ",` instruction. The instructions `str.indexOf("x")` and `str.indexOf("x", y)` locate the position of the substring *x* within the string, *str*, by searching from the first to the last character or from position *y* to the last character. Similarly, the instructions `str.lastIndexOf("x")` and `str.lastIndexOf("x", y)` locate the position of the substring *x* within the string by searching from the last to the first character or from position *y* to the first character.

A series of text substrings are displayed with each substring defined by the position of the last space plus one to the position of the next space with the `str.substring(firstC, lastC)` instruction. When the position of the penultimate space is reached, the remaining text is printed. The variable *line* is the number of characters that can be displayed on the M5Stack

Core2 LCD screen with a text size of two. When the position of a space is greater than the variable *line*, then the substring up to the position of the previous space is displayed.

Listing 2-7. Function to parse text

```
void splitText(String text)
{
  int line = 25, spaces[50], Nspaces = 0, firstC = 0, lastC = 1;
  String str = text + " ";          // add space at end of text
  int len = str.length();
  spaces[0] = -1;
  for (int i=0; i<50; i++)
  {
    if(spaces[i]+1 < len)          // not at end of text
    {                              // locate next space
      spaces[i+1] = str.indexOf(" ",spaces[i]+1);
      Nspaces++;                   // number of spaces
    }
    else i = 50;                   // found all spaces
  }
  for (int i=1; i<Nspaces+1; i++) // for each space
  {
    if(spaces[i]-lastC > line)     // current space past line length
    {
      lastC = spaces[i-1];         // finish position set to next space
                                   // display text between spaces
      M5.Lcd.println(str.substring(firstC, lastC));
      firstC = lastC+1;            // start position set to
    }                              // previous space+1
  }                                // display from last space
  M5.Lcd.println(str.substring(firstC, len-1));
}                                  // to end of text
```

MP3 Player

MP3 music files are played with an ESP32 module connected to an I2S decoder module and to a micro-SD card module, on which the MP3 files are stored. Alternatively, the M5Stack Core2 module combines a micro-SD card reader, an I2S decoder module, and a speaker for playing MP3 files, with an integrated LCD screen for displaying information about each MP3 file. Both options are described.

Play MP3 Files from the Micro-SD Card

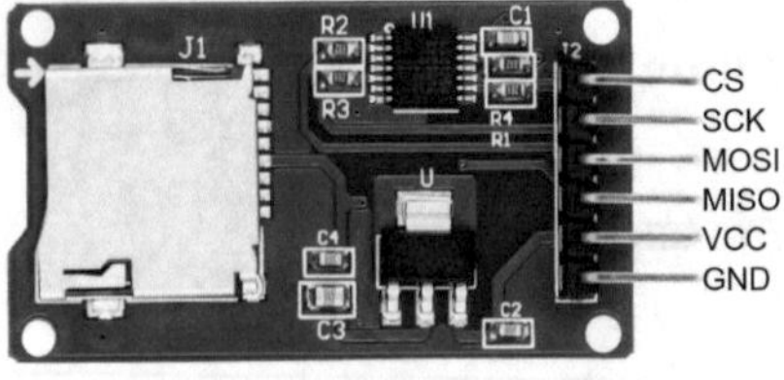

MP3 files stored on a micro-SD card are played by combining the ESP32 DEVKIT DOIT, an I2S decoder module, and a micro-SD card module (see Figure 2-14). Micro-SD card modules including a 3.3V AMS1117 voltage regulator are connected to 5V; otherwise, the micro-SD card module is connected to 3.3V. The ESP32 microcontroller communicates with the micro-SD card module using the SPI (Serial Peripheral Interface) protocol. The ESP32 microcontroller SPI bit rate of at least 8MHz exceeds the I2S audio bit clock rate of 1.41MHz, so SPI communication is not a limiting factor. A micro-SD card, formatted as FAT32, with 16GB storage was used in this chapter. The MP3 files were not contained in a specific folder on the micro-SD card, and file names consisted of alphanumeric text, which included spaces.

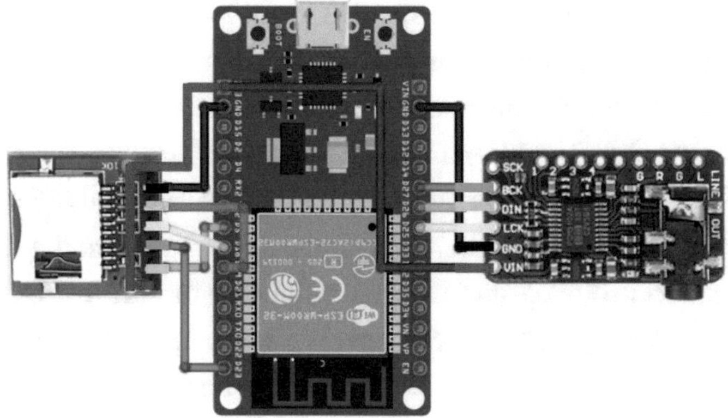

***Figure 2-14.** Micro-SD card and PCM5102 I2S decoder module*

Connections between a micro-SD card module and the ESP32 DEVKIT DOIT are given in Table 2-5, with connections for the I2S decoder module included in Table 2-4.

***Table 2-5.** Micro-SD card module connections to an ESP32 development board*

Component	Connect to ESP32
SD card module 3V3 or VCC	3V3 or VIN
SD card module CS (chip select)	GPIO 5
SD card module MOSI	GPIO 23
SD card module CLK or SCK	GPIO 18
SD card module MISO	GPIO 19
SD card module GND	GND

The sketch in Listing 2-8 illustrates sequentially playing files loaded on a micro-SD card with each file title displayed on the Serial Monitor. There is the option to preview files stored on the micro-SD card by playing only 10s of each track. In the first section of the sketch, the libraries and the SPI and I2S pins are defined. The SPI terms MOSI, MISO, SCK, and SS are reserved by the *SPI.cpp* file in the *SPI* library accessed by the ESP32 microcontroller, with the file located in *user\AppData\Local\Arduino15\packages\esp32\hardware\esp32\version\libraries\SPI\src*. Variable names defining the SPI pin numbers must differ from the reserved SPI terms, as in the instruction `int MOSIpin = 23`. In the *setup* function, the I2S and SPI communication protocols and the micro-SD card module are initialized, and the first track on the micro-SD card is played. In the *loop* function, the *playTime* variable determines when to play the next track on the micro-SD card if the option to preview files on the micro-SD card has been selected, which is implemented by un-commenting the instruction `if(millis() - playTime > 10000) playTrack()`.

The *playTrack* function is called when the currently playing track has finished or when the track preview time has elapsed. The next file on the micro-SD card is opened with the *openNextFile* function, and if the file is not a directory, as indicated by the *isDirectory* function, then the I2S decoder loads the file on the micro-SD card with the *connecttoSD* function. When the last file on the micro-SD card has been played, the micro-SD card directory is rewound, with the *rewindDirectory* function. The *play* variable indicates that a track is playing.

The *openNextFile, isDirectory,* and *rewindDirectory* functions are included in the *FS.cpp* file, accessed by the ESP32 microcontroller, with the *FS* library located in the same directory as the *SPI* library. The *SD* library references both the *SPI* and *FS* libraries, so the `#include <SPI.h>` and `#include <FS.h>` instructions are not required. The *Audio* library *audio_eof_mp3* function detects when a track has finished playing, and the function triggers the next track to play.

Listing 2-8. MP3 files on an SD card and I2C decoder

```
#include <Audio.h>                  // include Audio and
#include <SD.h>                     // SD libraries
Audio audio;                        // associate audio with library
File SDdir;                         // associate SDdir with SD library
int CS = 5;                         // SD Card pins
int MOSIpin = 23;                   // MOSI, MISO and SCK
int MISOpin = 19;                   // are reserved library terms
int SCKpin = 18;
int DIN = 26;                       // define decoder pins for
int BCK = 27;                       // data input, audio bit clock an
int LRCK = 25;                      // the word select clock
unsigned long playTime = 0;
int play = 0;                       // indicate track playing

void setup()
{
  Serial.begin(115200);             // Serial Monitor baud rate
  SPI.begin(SCKpin, MISOpin, MOSIpin); // initialize SPI
  SD.begin(CS);                     // and SD
  SDdir = SD.open("/");             // open SD directory
  audio.setPinout(BCK, LRCK, DIN);  // initialize decoder
  audio.setVolume(15);              // set volume level: 0 to 21
  playTrack();                      // play first track on SD card
}

void playTrack()                    // function to play tracks
{                                   // on SD card
  play = 0;
  while(play == 0)                  // while track not playing
```

```
  {
    File file = SDdir.openNextFile(); // open next file on SD card
    if (file == true)                 // found a file
    {
      if (!file.isDirectory())        // file is not a directory
      {
        Serial.print("playing ");Serial.println(file.name());
                                      // play track
        audio.connecttoSD(file.name());
        playTime = millis();          // time track started playing
        play = 1;                     // track playing
      }
    }
    else SDdir.rewindDirectory();     // rewind SD card directory
    file.close();
  }
}

void loop()
{
  audio.loop();
//  if(millis() - playTime > 10000) playTrack();
}                                     // play 10s of each track

void audio_eof_mp3(const char *info)  // action at end of file
{
  playTrack();                        // call playTrack function
}
```

Play MP3 Files with M5Stack Core2

The M5Stack Core2 module incorporates a micro-SD card reader/writer, an I2S decoder, an audio amplifier, and a speaker. The sketch for an M5Stack Core2 module, equivalent to Listing 2-8 for the combination of an ESP32 development board, micro-SD card reader module, PCM5102 I2S decoder module, and externally powered speaker, is given in Listing 2-9. The sketch is derived from the *File* ➤ *Examples* ➤ *SD* ➤ *SD_Test* and *File* ➤ *Examples* ➤ *ESP32-audioI2S* ➤ *M5Core2* sketches. The LCD screen displays information on the micro-SD card and the MP3 file content (see Figure 2-15a) and on the MP3 file being played (see Figure 2-15b).

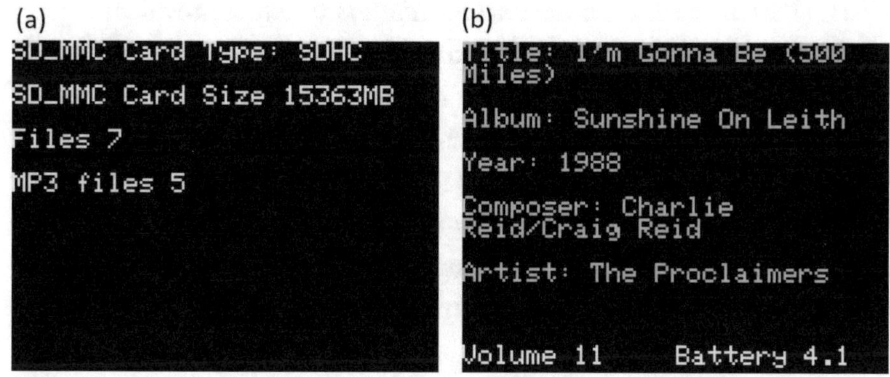

Figure 2-15. *MP3 player with M5Stack Core2*

Structures of the first section and of the *setup* function of the sketch are essentially the same as in Listing 2-8. The M5Stack Core2 buttons enable control of which MP3 file is played, while in Listing 2-8, the MP3 files are played sequentially. In Listing 2-9, the *getFiles* function displays information on the micro-SD card type and size and then calls the *listDir* function to identify and generate a list of the MP3 files. In the *loop* function, pressing an M5Stack Core2 touch screen button *BtnA*,

BtnB, or *BtnC* increases the volume or plays the next or previous MP3 file, respectively. When an MP3 file is finished playing, the next MP3 file is identified and played with the following instructions:

```
audio.stopSong()                          // stop playing current MP3 file
temp = file names[MP3play]                // identify next MP3 file name
audio.connecttoFS(SD, temp.c_str())  // play MP3 file on SD card
```

Sourcing MP3 files from the *file names* array enables moving between MP3 files, when there are non-MP3 formatted files on the SD card. When the volume is changed, the *battery* function is called to update the displayed volume, which is combined with the displayed battery voltage.

The *ESP32_audioI2S* library *audio_id3data* function provides information about an MP3 file, including the album, track title, year of publication, and composer and artist names, which is displayed on the M5Stack Core2 LCD screen. Additional MP3 file information is available with the *audio_id3data* function, but it is excluded from the display. For example, the *Content*, *Track*, and *Setting* variables contain the music type, such as Bluegrass, the album track number, and the encoding settings. The *Band* variable is generally the same as the *Artist* variable, but is often blank.

The *ESP32_audioI2S* library *audio_eof_mp3* function detects when playing an MP3 file has ended. The MP3 file number is incremented in the *audio_eof_mp3* function, and the *changeTrack* function is called to play the next MP3 file.

The *getFiles* function identifies the micro-SD card type, with the *SD* library categories of *CARD_MMC*, *CARD_SD*, and *CARD_SDHC* corresponding to Multi-Media Card, Secure Digital Standard Capacity (SDSC), and Secure Digital High Capacity (SDHC), respectively. SD card capacities are up to 2GB, 2–32GB, and 32GB–2TB for the *SDSC, SDHC,* and *SDXC* (Secure Digital eXtended Capacity) categories, respectively.

Listing 2-9. Play MP3 files with M5Stack Core2

```
#include <M5Core2.h>                    // include M5Stack and
#include <Audio.h>                      // ESP32-audioI2S library
Audio audio;
                                        // SPI and I2S GPIO pins
int SD_CS = 4, SD_SCK = 18, SD_MISO = 38, SD_MOSI = 23;
int I2S_BCLK = 12, I2S_LRC = 0, I2S_DOUT = 2;
uint8_t cardType;
uint64_t cardSize;
String temp, file names[20];            // array of MP3 files on SD card
int MP3play = 0, vol = 10, Nfiles = 0, Nmp3 = 0;
float batt;

void setup()
{
  M5.begin();                           // initialize M5Stack module
  M5.Axp.SetSpkEnable(true);            // enable speaker
  M5.Lcd.fillScreen(BLACK);
  M5.Lcd.setTextSize(2);                // define text color and size
  M5.Lcd.setCursor(0,0);
                                        // initialize SPI
  SPI.begin(SD_SCK, SD_MISO, SD_MOSI);
  SD.begin(SD_CS);
                                        // initialize I2S
  audio.setPinout(I2S_BCLK, I2S_LRC, I2S_DOUT);
  audio.setVolume(vol);                 // set volume level: 0 to 21
  getFiles();                           // call function to check SD card
//  Serial.println("list of MP3 files");
//  for (int i=0; i<Nmp3; i++) Serial.println(file names[i]);
  M5.Lcd.setCursor(0,0);
```

```
  M5.Lcd.fillScreen(BLACK);
  battery();                          // call function for battery voltage
  temp = file names[0];
                                      // play first MP3 file on SD card
  audio.connecttoFS(SD, temp.c_str());
//  Serial.printf("track %d %s \n", 0, temp.c_str());
}

void getFiles()                       // function to determine
{                                     // MP3 files on SD card
  M5.Lcd.setTextColor(YELLOW);
  if(!SD.begin())                     // check SD card is present
  {
    M5.Lcd.println("Card Mount Failed");
    return;
  }
  cardType = SD.cardType();           // determine and display
  if(cardType == CARD_NONE)           // SD card type
  {
    M5.Lcd.println("No SD_MMC card attached");
    return;
  }
  M5.Lcd.print("SD_MMC Card Type: ");
  if(cardType == CARD_MMC) M5.Lcd.println("MMC");
  else if(cardType == CARD_SD) M5.Lcd.println("SDSC");
  else if(cardType == CARD_SDHC) M5.Lcd.println("SDHC");
  else M5.Lcd.println("UNKNOWN");
                                      // display SD card size
  cardSize = SD.cardSize() / (1024 * 1024);
  M5.Lcd.printf("\nSD_MMC Card Size %lluMB\n", cardSize);
  listDir(SD, "/", 0);                // only access "top level" files
                                      // display total number of files
```

```
  M5.Lcd.printf("\nFiles %d \n", Nfiles);
                                      // and number of MP3 files
  M5.Lcd.printf("\nMP3 files %d \n", Nmp3);
  delay(3000);                        // time for user to read file data
}

void listDir(String dir, int level) // function to list files in
{                                     // an SD directory
  File SDdir = SD.open(dir);          // open SD directory
  File file = SDdir.openNextFile();  // open file on SD card
  while (file)                        // located a file
  {
    if (file.isDirectory())
    {
      Serial.printf("DIR %s \n", file.name());
                                      // move down a directory
      if(level) listDir(file.path(), level-1);
    }
    else                              // when file is not a directory
    {
      Serial.printf("   file %s \n", file.name());
      Nfiles++;                       // increment number of files
      temp = file.name();
      if(temp.indexOf(".mp3") > 2) // check if file name includes mp3
      {                               // add MP3 file path to array
        file names[Nmp3] = file.path();
        Nmp3++;                       // increment number of MP3 files
      }
    }
    file = SDdir.openNextFile();      // open next file
  }
}
```

```
void loop()
{
  audio.loop();                          // manage audio streaming
  if (M5.BtnA.wasPressed())
  {
    vol++;
    if(vol > 21) vol = 0;
    audio.setVolume(vol);                // increase volume
    battery();                           // call function to update
  }                                      // volume display
  if (M5.BtnB.wasPressed())
  {
    MP3play++;                           // increment MP3 file number
    if(MP3play > Nmp3-1) MP3play = 0;
    changeTrack();                       // play next MP3 file
  }
  if (M5.BtnC.wasPressed())
  {
    MP3play--;
    if(MP3play < 0) MP3play = Nmp3-1;
    changeTrack();                       // play previous MP3 file
  }
  M5.update();                           // update button “pressed” status
}

void battery()                           // function to display volume
{                                        // and battery voltage
  if(vol < 10) temp = "Volume  "+ String(vol);
  else temp = "Volume " + String(vol);
  M5.Lcd.setTextColor(YELLOW, BLACK);
  M5.Lcd.drawString(temp, 0, 220);   // display volume
```

```
  batt = M5.Axp.GetBatVoltage(); // get battery voltage
                                 // 1DP as batt is a real number
  temp = "Battery "+ String(batt,1);
                                 // display battery voltage
  M5.Lcd.drawString(temp, 160, 220);
  M5.Lcd.setTextColor(GREEN, BLACK);
}                                // function to display MP3 file data

void audio_id3data(const char *info)
{                                // convert char array to string
  String chk = String(info);     // exclude Content, Track ...data
  if(!(chk.startsWith("Content") || chk.startsWith("Track") ||
       chk.startsWith("Setting") || chk.startsWith("Publisher")
       ||chk.startsWith("Band"))) splitText(chk);
}                                // display information

                                 // end of file info contains file name
void audio_eof_mp3(const char *info)
{
  MP3play++;                     // increment MP3 file number
  if(MP3play > Nmp3-1) MP3play = 0;
  changeTrack();                 // at end of file, play next file
}

void splitText(String text)      // see Listing 2-7

void changeTrack()               // function to play next MP3 file
{
  audio.stopSong();              // stop playing current MP3 file
  temp = file names[MP3play];     // get MP3 file name from array
                                 // play MP3 file on SD card
  audio.connecttoFS(SD, temp.c_str());
```

```
//  Serial.printf("track %d %s \n", MP3play, temp.c_str());
  M5.Lcd.fillScreen(BLACK);
  M5.Lcd.setCursor(0,0);
  battery();                        // call function for volume & battery
}
```

The *listDir* function (see Listing 2-10) lists files at the top level of the SD card and within the first level of the directory with the `listDir("/", 0)` and `listDir("/", 1)` instructions, respectively. The `file.isDirectory()` instruction identifies if a file is a directory and then recursively displays all the files within each directory level.

Listing 2-10. File structure on a micro-SD card

```
void listDir(String dir, int level)
{
  File SDdir = SD.open(dir);        // start at top level of SD card
  File file = SDdir.openNextFile();
  while(file)
  {
    if(file.isDirectory())          // when file is a directory
    {                               // check files within a directory
      Serial.printf("DIR %s \n", file.name());
      if(level) listDir(file.path(), level-1);
    }           // when file is not a directory, display file name and size

    else Serial.printf("   %s size %dKB \n", file.name(),file.
    size()/1024);
    file = SDdir.openNextFile(); // next file
  }
}
```

Bluetooth Communication

Audio data is transmitted by an Android tablet or mobile phone to an ESP32 microcontroller using Bluetooth communication. Conversely, audio data is transmitted by the ESP32 microcontroller to a remote Bluetooth speaker with Bluetooth communication. Text is also transmitted by a Bluetooth communication app hosted by a mobile device to the ESP32 microcontroller. There are several Bluetooth communication apps to download from *Google Play Store*, and the *Bluetooth Terminal HC-05* app by MightyIT is recommended.

Transmission to ESP32

A Bluetooth device, such as an Android tablet or mobile phone, transmits audio data with Bluetooth communication to the ESP32 microcontroller. The Advanced Audio Distribution Profile (A2DP) defines streaming of audio data with Bluetooth communication between devices. The *BluetoothA2DPSink* library by Phil Schatzmann is recommended, with the library downloaded from `github.com/pschatzmann/ESP32-A2DP`.

The *bt_music_receiver_to_internal_dac* sketch in the *BluetoothA2DPSink* library by Phil Schatzmann interprets streamed audio data with Bluetooth communication using the ESP32 microcontroller 8-bit DAC. The audio jack signal and GND pins of an externally powered speaker are connected to GPIO 26 and GND, respectively.

Sound quality is increased with a higher-bit DAC compared with the ESP32 microcontroller 8-bit DAC. The PCM5102 I2S decoder module, connected to the ESP32 microcontroller, converts the received audio data to analog output (see Figure 2-16). Connections for the PCM5102 I2S decoder module to the ESP32 DEVKIT DOIT are given in Table 2-4.

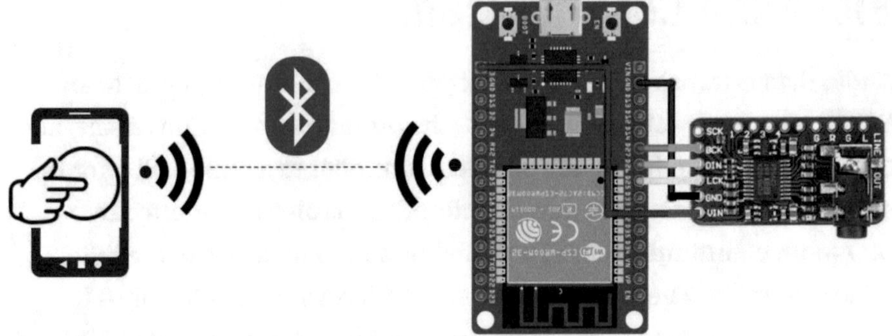

***Figure 2-16.** Bluetooth device, ESP32 development board, and PCM5102 decoder*

The *BluetoothA2DPSink* library default I2S pins for audio data input (*DIO*), audio bit clock (*BCK*), and word select clock (*LRCK*) are GPIO 22, 26, and 25. The I2S pins are user-defined in the sketch by the *pin_config* variable and implemented with the *set_pin_config* function (see Listing 2-11). The ESP32 microcontroller establishes a Bluetooth server called *BTmusic* with the `start("BTmusic")` instruction. Once an Android tablet or mobile phone is connected to the ESP32 microcontroller with Bluetooth communication, audio files played on the Android tablet or mobile phone are output on the speaker connected to the PCM5102 I2S decoder module.

Listing 2-11. Bluetooth signal to an ESP32 microcontroller

```
#include <BluetoothA2DPSink.h>          // include library
BluetoothA2DPSink BT;                   // associate BT with library

void setup()
{
  i2s_pin_config_t pin_config = {
  .bck_io_num = 27,                     // BCK (bit clock)
  .ws_io_num = 25,                      // LRCK (word select or frame)
  .data_out_num = 26,                   // DIO (data input)
  .data_in_num = I2S_PIN_NO_CHANGE};
```

```
  BT.set_pin_config(pin_config);        // update SPI pins
  BT.start("BTmusic");                  // establish Bluetooth server
}

void loop()                             // nothing in loop function
{}
```

The corresponding sketch for the M5Stack Core2 module is shown in Listing 2-12. The instructions differing from Listing 2-11 are commented.

Listing 2-12. Bluetooth signal to M5Stack Core2

```
#include <M5Core2.h>                    // include M5Core2 and
#include <Audio.h>                      // ESP32-audioI2S libraries
Audio audio;                            // associate audio with library
int BCLK = 12, LRC = 0, DOUT = 2;       // define I2S GPIO pins
#include <BluetoothA2DPSink.h>
BluetoothA2DPSink BT;

void setup()
{
  M5.begin();                           // initialize M5Stack module
  M5.Axp.SetSpkEnable(true);            // enable speaker
  i2s_pin_config_t pin_config = {
  .bck_io_num = BCLK,                   // BCK (bit clock)
  .ws_io_num = LRC,                     // LRCK (word select or frame)
  .data_out_num = DOUT,                 // DIO (data input)
  .data_in_num = I2S_PIN_NO_CHANGE
  };
  BT.set_pin_config(pin_config);
  BT.start("BTmusic");
  audio.setPinout(BCLK, LRC, DOUT);     // initialize audio
  delay(500);
}
```

```
void loop()
{
  audio.loop();                          // manage audio streaming
}
```

On the subject of Bluetooth, the *BluetoothSerial* library by Evandro Luis Copercini enables Bluetooth communication between a Bluetooth communication app, such as the *Bluetooth Terminal HC-05* app by MightyIT, hosted by an Android tablet or mobile phone and the M5Stack Core2 module. The *BluetoothSerial* library is installed when the *esp32* Boards Manager is installed. Listing 2-13 demonstrates sending text to the M5Stack Core2 module by a Bluetooth communication app with the M5Stack Core2 module also transmitting text to the Bluetooth communication app. In the simple example, when the transmitted text includes the letter *r* or g, the M5Stack Core2 screen color changes accordingly. The *M5.Lcd* integer representation of standard colors is listed on `docs.m5stack.com/en/api/core/lcd`.

Listing 2-13. Bluetooth and M5Stack Core2

```
#include <M5Core2.h>                     // include M5Stack and
#include <BluetoothSerial.h>             // Bluetooth Serial libraries
BluetoothSerial SerialBT;                // associate SerialBT with library
char c;
String str;
int color;

void setup()
{
  SerialBT.begin("M5Stack");             // initialize SerialBT
  M5.begin();                            // and M5Stack module
  M5.Lcd.setTextColor(WHITE);
  M5.Lcd.setTextSize(4);
}
```

```
void loop()
{
  while (SerialBT.available()>0)    // when text received by M5Stack
  {
    c = SerialBT.read();            // read character(s)
    str = str + c;
    if(c == 'g') color = 0x07E0;    // integer value for GREEN
    else if(c == 'r')
    {
      color = 0xF800;               // integer value for RED
                        // send response to connected Bluetooth app
      SerialBT.println("LCD screen now RED");
    }
  }
  if(str.length() > 0)
  {
    M5.Lcd.fillScreen(color);       // updated screen color
    M5.Lcd.setCursor(20,20);
    M5.Lcd.print(str);              // display message
    str = "";
    color = 0x0000;                 // integer value for BLACK
  }
  delay(100);
}
```

The *BluetoothSerial* library enables transmission between two Bluetooth devices. If one ESP32 module is connected to the Serial Monitor, then text entered on the Serial Monitor is sent, one character at a time, with either the `SerialBT.write(Serial.read())` or `SerialBT.write(c)` instruction for the character *c*. Chapter 4, "TTGO T-Watch V2," also uses the *BluetoothSerial* library for communication between two Bluetooth devices.

Transmission by ESP32

Transmission of audio data, with Bluetooth communication, by the ESP32 microcontroller to a remote Bluetooth speaker is the converse of the sketches in Listings 2-11 and 2-12. The *arduino-audio-tools* library by Phil Schatzmann is recommended, with the library available at `github.com/pschatzmann/arduino-audio-tools`. The additional libraries *arduino-libhelix* and *ESP32-A2DP* by Phil Schatzmann, available at `github.com/pschatzmann`, and the *SdFat* library by Bill Greiman, available at `github.com/greiman/SdFat`, are also required. The four libraries should be updated simultaneously, given developments to the libraries.

The sketch in Listing 2-14 is developed from the *examples-player/player-sdfat-a2dp* sketch in the *arduino-audio-tools* library. Audio data from MP3 files stored on a micro-SD card reader, connected to the ESP32 module, is transmitted with Bluetooth communication by the ESP32 microcontroller to the remote Bluetooth device. For this chapter, the remote Bluetooth device name was *Logitech BT Adapter*, but the name of your Bluetooth device must be included in Listing 2-14. A sketch to scan and identify remote Bluetooth device names is given in Listing 2-15. The MP3 files, located in the top directory of the micro-SD card with file name format of */abc.mp3*, are the Bluetooth signal source, as defined by the `AudioSourceSDFAT source("/", "mp3")` instruction. The MP3 audio files are decoded and streamed with the `MP3DecoderHelix decoder`, `A2DPStream out`, and `AudioPlayer player(source, out, decoder)` instructions.

When a new MP3 audio file is streamed, information from the MP3 file on the track title, album, and music genre is displayed on an OLED screen, connected to the ESP32 DEVKIT DOIT module. The *Adafruit SSD1306* library references the *Wire* and *Adafruit_GFX* libraries, which are loaded implicitly. An ESP32 DEVKIT DOIT module connected to a micro-SD card read/write module and a 128 × 64-pixel OLED screen is shown in Figure 2-17 with connections listed in Table 2-6.

The *AudioPlayer stop* and *next* functions, contained in the *arduino-audio-tools\src\AudioTools* folder, are illustrated in Listing 2-14. When the ESP32 DEVKIT DOIT module *BOOT* button, which is connected to GPIO 0, is pressed, the MP3 player is stopped, and the next MP3 audio file is played.

The *AudioLogger Info*, *Warning*, and *Error* options display the Bluetooth connection status and audio data transmission information. The *Info* option is recommended when developing a sketch, with the *Warning* option for a developed sketch.

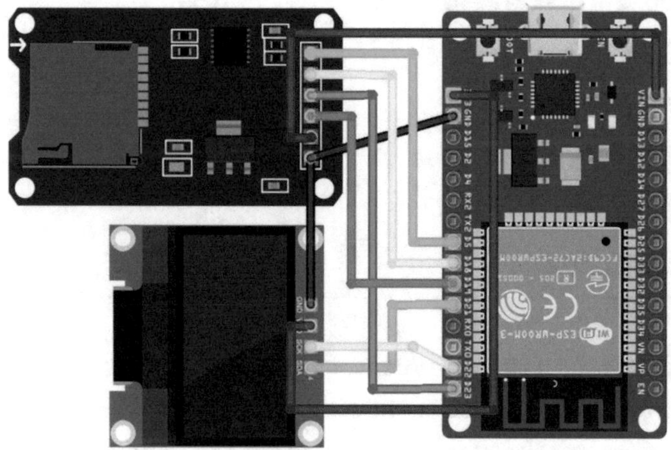

Figure 2-17. *Bluetooth transmission by an ESP32 microcontroller*

The micro-SD card module in Figure 2-17 includes a 3.3V AMS1117 voltage regulator, so is powered at 5V by the VIN pin of the ESP32 DEVKIT DOIT module. The OLED module is connected to the ESP32 DEVKIT DOIT module 3V3 pin.

Table 2-6. *OLED and micro-SD card module connections to an ESP32 development board*

Component	Connect to ESP32
SD card module 3V3 or VCC	3V3 or VIN
SD card module CS (chip select)	GPIO 5
SD card module MOSI	GPIO 23
SD card module CLK or SCK	GPIO 18
SD card module MISO	GPIO 19
SD card module GND	GND
OLED SDA	GPIO 21
OLED SCK	GPIO 22
OLED VCC	VIN
OLED GND	GND

Note that when a revised sketch is uploaded, the Bluetooth device connected to the ESP32 microcontroller must be reset. Similarly, when all MP3 audio files have been transmitted by the ESP32 microcontroller, the Bluetooth device must be reset before resetting the ESP32 microcontroller prior to replaying the MP3 audio files.

In Listing 2-14, libraries associated with Bluetooth transmission of audio data from MP3 files stored on a micro-SD card module are loaded, as well as the associated objects defined in the first section of the sketch. The *AudioLogger Warning* option and the Bluetooth device name are defined in the *setup* function. The *trackData* function displays the audio track title, album, and music genre on both the Serial Monitor and the OLED screen.

Listing 2-14. Bluetooth signal from an ESP32 microcontroller

```
#include <AudioTools.h>                // include libraries to decode
#include <AudioLibs/AudioA2DP.h>       // and stream MP3 files
#include <AudioLibs/AudioSourceSDFAT.h>
#include <AudioCodecs/CodecMP3Helix.h>
#include <Adafruit_SSD1306.h>          // Adafruit SSD1306 for OLED
int width = 128, height = 64;          // OLED dimensions
                                       // associate oled with library
Adafruit_SSD1306 oled(width, height, &Wire, -1);
String temp;
int bootBtn = 0;                       // ESP32 module BOOT button
const char *startFilePath="/";         // top-level folder on SD card
const char* ext="mp3";
                                       // source of audio data
AudioSourceSDFAT source(startFilePath, ext);
A2DPStream out;                        // streamed output
MP3DecoderHelix decoder;               // MP3 file decoder
AudioPlayer player(source, out, decoder);

void setup()
{
  Serial.begin(115200);                // Serial Monitor baud rate
  pinMode(bootBtn,INPUT_PULLUP);       // module BOOT button HIGH
                                       // OLED display I2C address
  oled.begin(SSD1306_SWITCHCAPVCC, 0x3C);
  oled.clearDisplay();
  oled.setTextColor(WHITE);            // set font color
  oled.setTextSize(1);                 // text size 6×8 pixels
  oled.display();
  AudioLogger::instance().begin(Serial, AudioLogger::Warning);
```

```
  auto cfg = out.defaultConfig(TX_MODE);
  cfg.name = "Logitech BT Adapter"; // Bluetooth device name
  out.begin(cfg);
  player.setVolume(1.0);            // set volume between 0 and 1
                                    // call function to display data
  player.setMetadataCallback(trackData);
  player.begin();
}

void trackData(MetaDataType type, const char* str, int len)
{
  temp = String(toStr(type));
                                    // display data on Serial Monitor
  Serial.printf("%s: %s \n", temp, str);
  if(temp == "Title")               // new audio track
  {
    oled.clearDisplay();
    oled.setCursor(0,0);
  }                                 // display track data on OLED
  oled.printf("%s: %s \n", temp, str);
  oled.display();
}

void loop()
{
  player.copy();                    // handle audio data
  if(digitalRead(bootBtn) == LOW)   // when BOOT button pressed
  {
    player.stop();                  // stop playing audio data
    delay(1000);
    player.next();                  // play next audio MP3 file
  }
}
```

The corresponding sketch for the M5Stack Core2 module is shown in Listing 2-15. The instructions differing from Listing 2-14 are commented. The two instructions:

```
SdSpiConfig sdcfg(SD_CS, DEDICATED_SPI, SD_SCK_MHZ(10));
AudioSourceSDFAT source(startFilePath, ext, sdcfg);
```

replace the `AudioSourceSDFAT source(startFilePath, ext)` instruction of Listing 2-14 to access to the micro-SD card.

Listing 2-15. Bluetooth signal from M5Stack Core2

```
#include <M5Core2.h>      // include M5Core2 library
#include <AudioTools.h>
#include <AudioLibs/AudioA2DP.h>
#include <AudioLibs/AudioSourceSDFAT.h>
#include <AudioCodecs/CodecMP3Helix.h>
const char *startFilePath = "/";
const char* ext = "mp3";
                          // define SPI pins and SD card as an SPI source
int SD_CS = 4, SD_SCK = 18, SD_MISO = 38, SD_MOSI = 23;
SdSpiConfig sdcfg(SD_CS, DEDICATED_SPI, SD_SCK_MHZ(10));
AudioSourceSDFAT source(startFilePath, ext, sdcfg);
A2DPStream out;
MP3DecoderHelix decoder;
AudioPlayer player(source, out, decoder);
float vol = 0.5;          // initial volume setting

void setup()
{
  M5.begin();             // initialise M5Stack module
  SPI.begin(SD_SCK, SD_MISO, SD_MOSI, SD_CS);    // initialise SPI
  SD.begin(SD_CS);                               // and SD card reader
  AudioLogger::instance().begin(Serial, AudioLogger::Warning);
```

```
  auto cfg = out.defaultConfig(TX_MODE);
  cfg.name = "Logitech BT Adapter";
  out.begin(cfg);
  player.setVolume(vol);
  player.setMetadataCallback(trackData);
  player.begin();
}

void trackData(MetaDataType type, const char* str, int len)
{
  Serial.printf("%s: %s \n", toStr(type), str);
}

void loop()
{
  player.copy();
  if(M5.BtnA.wasPressed())          // increase volume after
  {                                 // button A was pressed
    vol = vol + 0.1;
    if(vol > 1.0) vol = 0;
    player.setVolume(vol);
    Serial.printf("Volume %3.1f \n", vol);
  }
  if(M5.BtnB.wasPressed())          // after button B pressed
  {                                 // move to next track
    player.stop();
    delay(1000);
    player.next();
  }
  M5.update();                      // update button "pressed" states
}
```

Bluetooth Device Scanning

The Bluetooth device name is required when connecting the ESP32 microcontroller to a Bluetooth device. The *BluetoothSerial* library by Evandro Luis Copercini enables scanning for Bluetooth devices, and the library is installed when the *esp32* Boards Manager is loaded. Listing 2-16 scans for Bluetooth devices and displays the device names and corresponding RSSI (Received Signal Strength Indicator) values. Information on Bluetooth devices is held in the *BTScanResults* structure, *BTdevs*, with the device name and RSSI obtained with the *getName* and *getRSSI* functions within the *BTAdvertisedDevice* structure, *device*.

Listing 2-16. Bluetooth device scanning

```
#include <BluetoothSerial.h>         // include library and associate
BluetoothSerial SerialBT;            // SerialBT with library
int Ndev, lag = 5000;                // scan period of 5s

void setup()
{
  Serial.begin(115200);              // Serial Monitor baud rate
  SerialBT.begin();                  // initialize SerialBT
  Serial.printf("\nscanning for %ds \n", lag/1000);
                                     // scan for lag time
  BTScanResults * BTdevs = SerialBT.discover(lag);
  Ndev = BTdevs->getCount();         // number of Bluetooth devices
  if(Ndev > 0)
  {
    for (int i=0; i<Ndev; i++)
    {                                // display device name and RSSI
      BTAdvertisedDevice *device = BTdevs->getDevice(i);
      Serial.printf("%d. %s RSSI %d \n", i+1,
            device->getName().c_str(), device->getRSSI());
```

```
    }
  }
  else Serial.println("No BT device found");
}

void loop()
{}                                    // nothing in loop function
```

CHAPTER 3

MESH Communication

ESP-MESH

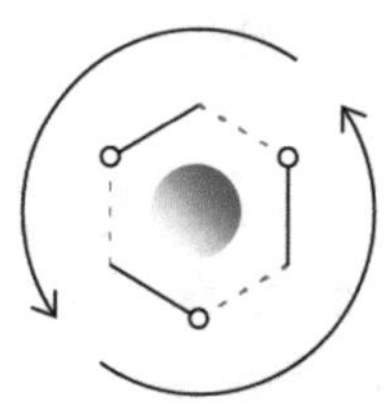

The ESP-MESH protocol enables communication between multiple ESP32 microcontrollers on a local area network. The ESP-MESH network provides single (one-to-one), broadcast (one-to-many), and mesh (many-to-many) communication between devices. ESP-MESH nodes do not require direct contact between all nodes, as the ESP-MESH protocol ensures that a message reaches the destination node by routing the message through the network (see Figure 3-1). The node topology is updated every three seconds, and the network self-organizes the connection of a new node to the network. Each node in the ESP-MESH network is automatically allocated an identity. Details of the ESP-MESH protocol are available at `docs.espressif.com/projects/esp-idf/en/latest/esp32/api-guides/esp-wifi-mesh.html`.

N. Cameron, *ESP32 Formats and Communication*,
https://doi.org/10.1007/978-1-4842-9376-8_3

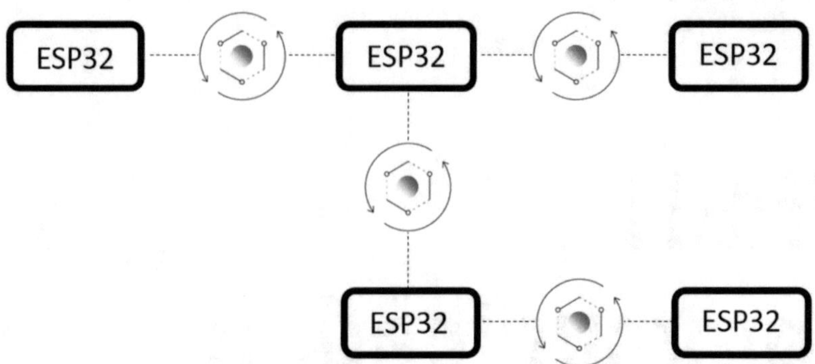

Figure 3-1. *ESP-MESH topology*

The *painlessMesh* library by Coopdis et al. is available in the Arduino IDE. The *painlessMesh* library references the *ArduinoJson, TaskScheduler,* and *AsyncTCP* libraries, so the corresponding `#include<library.h>` instructions are not required. The three libraries are available within the Arduino IDE.

Data is transmitted over the ESP-MESH network as a string, *sendMsg,* consisting of *name:value* pairs in JSON format. For example, an LED state, a value, and text are allocated to a JSON document, *doc,* defined as `DynamicJsonDocument doc(512)`, with the instructions

```
doc["LED"] = LEDstate
doc["value"] = 42
doc["text"] = "abcdef"
serializeJson(doc, sendMsg)
```

A message is broadcast by one node to all the nodes in the ESP-MESH network with the `mesh.sendBroadcast(sendMsg)` instruction where *mesh* is associated with the *painlessMesh* library by the `#include <painlessMesh.h>` and `painlessMesh mesh` instructions.

A received message is displayed with the sender node information using the instructions

```
mesh.onReceive(&recvMessage)  // call function when message received
                              // sender is node identity
void recvMessage(uint32_t sender, String &recvMsg)
{                             // recvMsg is message
                              // display message and sender node identity
  Serial.printf("%s from %d \n", recvMsg, sender)
}
```

A message is transmitted to a specific node identity by the `sendSingle` instruction. The identity of a node is obtained with the `getNodeId()` instruction. If the node identity is defined as a string, then the C++ *strtoul* instruction converts the string to a 32-bit integer with base 10. For example, a message is transmitted to node 2, which has identity *2127699893*, with the instructions

```
                              // node identity is converted to a number
String node2 = "2127699893"
uint32_t receiver = strtoul(node2.c_str(),NULL,10)
mesh.sendSingle(receiver, sendMsg)  // transmit message
```

An example ESP-MESH network consists of three ESP32 microcontrollers or nodes, with buttons connected to the node 1 module to control the states of a relay and an LED connected to the node 2 and node 3 modules, respectively (see Figure 3-2).

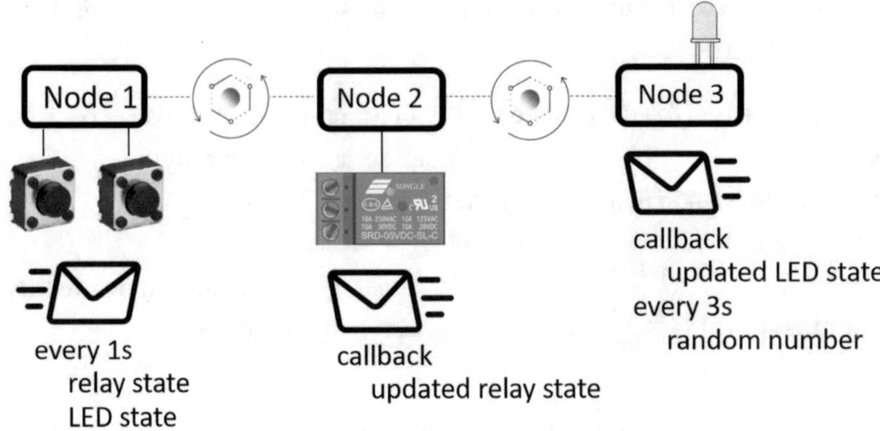

***Figure 3-2.** ESP-MESH layout and schedule*

Every second, node 1 broadcasts, to nodes 2 and 3, a JSON document containing the current relay and LED states. At 3s intervals, node 3 broadcasts a random number to simulate the transmission of sensor data. When a button connected to node 1, corresponding to the relay or the LED, is pressed, the relay or the LED state is updated by node 1. A change in the relay or the LED state is determined by node 2 or node 3, from the message transmitted by node 1. The relay or the LED, connected to node 2 or node 3, is turned on or off, and node 2 or node 3 transmits to node 1 a callback message containing the updated relay or LED state. Without the callback messages, node 1 would only receive the message broadcast by node 3. Node 1 interprets the received callback message and displays text describing the relay and LED states. The example demonstrates the bidirectional functionality of ESP-MESH.

Connections for the three ESP32 modules are shown in Figure 3-3. A TTGO T-Display V1.1 module, node 1, controls the switching of the relay and the LED connected to the ESP32 modules, which are nodes 2 and 3 in the ESP-MESH network. In the example, nodes 2 and 3 are a TTGO T-Display V1.1 module and an ESP32 DEVKIT DOIT module, respectively. The TTGO T-Display V1.1 module uses the *TFT_eSPI* library, and the library settings are defined in the *TFT_eSPI* ➤ *User_Setup_Select.h* file, by commenting out the line #include <User_setup.h> and un-commenting the line #include <User_setups/Setup25_TTGO_T_Display.h>. Details of the *TFT_eSPI* library are outlined in Chapter 15, "Libraries."

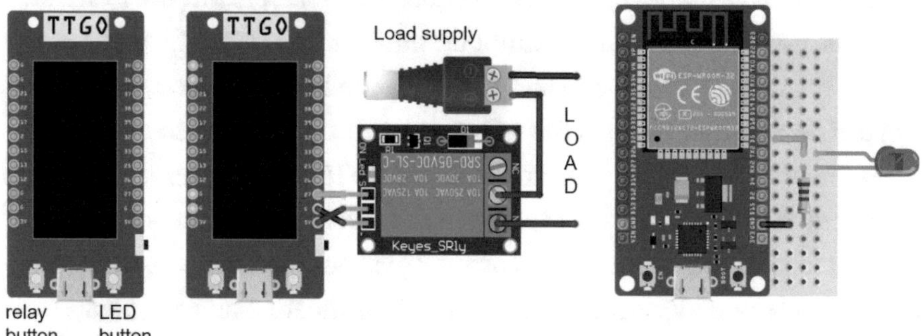

Figure 3-3. *ESP-MESH example*

When node 1 is initialized, the ESP-MESH is established, and the message *STARTUP: AP tcp server established on port 5555* is displayed on the Serial Monitor.

An example sequence of events is node 1 instructing a change in the LED state and then a change in the relay state. During the sequence, node 3 changes the variable *value*. The messages received by node 1 are

```
from node 3 {"relay":0,"LED":0,"value":83}
from node 3 {"relay":0,"LED":0,"value":74}  node 3 updated value
from node 3 {"relay":0,"LED":1,"value":74}  node 1 changed LED state
from node 2 {"relay":1,"LED":1,"value":78}  node 1 changed relay state
```

The sketch for node 1 in the example ESP-MESH network is given in Listing 3-1. The first section of the sketch includes the ESP-MESH name and password with the default port number of *5555*. The *taskSend* function defines message transmission timing. In the *setup* function, the ESP-MESH functions are declared. The `setDebugMsgTypes` instruction precedes the `init` instruction to display messages when the ESP-MESH network is established. The *sendMessage* function converts the JSON document, of *name:value* pairs, to the message, with the transmission interval defined by the `setInterval` instruction.

The *sendMessage* function is a *forward declaration* of the function, as the function is declared in the first section of the sketch, but the function contents are not defined. The compiler requires function information, such as data type for type checking, prior to the *setup* function, and the *forward declaration* enables the function definition later in the sketch.

On receipt of a message from the ESP-MESH network, node 1 converts the message to the *name:value* pairs, in the *recvMessage* function, and displays the named values. In the `printf` instruction displaying the node identity, the node identity is formatted as %u indicating an unsigned integer, rather than %d for a signed integer. For 16-bit integers, and similarly for 32-bit integers, an unsigned integer ranges from 0 to $2^{16} - 1 = 65535$, while the range of signed integers is -2^{15} to $2^{15} - 1$ equal to –32768 to 32767. Node identities are of the order of 2^{31}, such as 2127699893, which is within the 32-bit unsigned integer range of the ESP32 microcontroller.

Node connection changes to the ESP-MESH network are monitored with the *newConnectionCallback* function, which displays node identities of new connections. The *changedConnectionCallback* function generates a list of nodes with the `SimpleList<uint32_t> list = mesh.getNodeList()` instruction, with the number of nodes equal to `list.size()`. A node identity is obtained with the instruction `getNodeId()`.

For example, when a node is connected to the ESP-MESH network, the number of nodes is updated on the TTGO T-Display V1.1 LCD screen of node 1 with the following additional information displayed on the Serial Monitor:

```
New connection nodeID 3220294813   node identity
number of nodes 2                  nodes excluding node 1
Connection list
node1 2127700205                   node 1 identity
nodeID 2127699893                  existing node identity
nodeID 3220294813                  new node identity
```

Listing 3-1. MESH module with buttons and display (node 1)

```
#include <painlessMesh.h>           // include library
painlessMesh mesh;                  // associate mesh with library
Scheduler scheduler;                // associate scheduler with library
#include <TFT_eSPI.h>
TFT_eSPI tft = TFT_eSPI();          // associate tft with library
String ssid = "meshSSID";           // ESP-MESH name & password
String password = "meshPass";
int port = 5555;                             // ESP-MESH port
int relayButton = 0, LEDbutton = 35;         // LED and relay buttons
int LEDstate, relayState;
DynamicJsonDocument doc(512);                // JSON document

void sendMessage();
Task taskSend(TASK_SECOND * 1, TASK_FOREVER, &sendMessage);
                                             // task timing of 1s

void setup()
{
  Serial.begin(115200);
  pinMode(relayButton, INPUT_PULLUP);        // buttons active LOW
  pinMode(LEDbutton, INPUT_PULLUP);
  mesh.setDebugMsgTypes(ERROR | STARTUP); // before init  instruction
  mesh.init(ssid, password, &scheduler, port);
  mesh.onReceive(&recvMessage);              // set recvMessage function
                                             // ESP-MESH functions
  mesh.onNewConnection(&newConnectionCallback);
  mesh.onChangedConnections(&changedConnectionCallback);
  mesh.onNodeTimeAdjusted(&nodeTimeAdjustedCallback);
  scheduler.addTask(taskSend);               // schedule and enable
  taskSend.enable();                         // send message function
  tft.init();                                // initialize screen
```

```
  tft.setRotation(3);                     // landscape USB on left
  tft.setTextSize(2);
  tft.fillScreen(TFT_BLACK);              // clear screen
  tft.setTextColor(TFT_GREEN, TFT_BLACK);
  tft.setCursor(0,0);
  tft.print("Relay");                     // label buttons
  tft.setCursor(0,110);
  tft.print("LED");
  tft.setCursor(0,30);
  tft.print("nodes 0");
}

void sendMessage()                        // function to send message
{                                         // change relay state
  if (digitalRead(relayButton) == LOW)
      relayState = 1-relayState;
  doc["relay"] = relayState;              // update JSON document
  if (digitalRead(LEDbutton) == LOW) LEDstate = 1-LEDstate;
  doc["LED"] = LEDstate;
  String sendMsg;
  serializeJson(doc, sendMsg);            // serialize JSON doc
  mesh.sendBroadcast(sendMsg);            // broadcast message
  taskSend.setInterval((TASK_SECOND * 1)); // message timing of 1s
}                                         // function to receive message
void recvMessage(uint32_t sender, String &recvMsg)
{                          // display sender identity and message
  Serial.printf("from %u %s \n", sender, recvMsg .c_str());
  DeserializationError error = deserializeJson(doc, recvMsg);
  if (error)
  {
    Serial.print("deserializeJson() failed: ");
    Serial.println(error.c_str());
  }
```

```
  tft.setCursor(0,0);                 // relay state
  if(doc["relay"].as<long>() == 1) tft.print("Relay ON ");
  else tft.print("Relay OFF");
  tft.setCursor(0,60);                // generated data
  tft.printf("value %d   \n", doc["value"].as<long>());
  tft.setCursor(0,110);               // LED state
  if(doc["LED"].as<long>() == 1) tft.print("LED ON ");
  else tft.print("LED OFF");
}                                     // new node connected

void newConnectionCallback(uint32_t nodeID)
{                                     // display node identity
  Serial.printf("New connection nodeID %u \n", nodeID);
}                                     // function to list connected nodes

void changedConnectionCallback()
{                                     // number of nodes
  SimpleList<uint32_t> list = mesh.getNodeList();
  Serial.printf("number of nodes %d \n", list.size());
  tft.setCursor(0,30);
  tft.printf("nodes %d \n", list.size());
  Serial.println("Connection list");
                                      // node 1 identity
  Serial.printf("node1 %u \n", mesh.getNodeId());
  SimpleList<uint32_t>::iterator node = list.begin();
  while (node != list.end())          // list of nodes
  {                                   // *node is pointer
    Serial.printf("nodeID %u \n", *node);
    node++;                           // increment node
  }
}                                     // display synchronized timing
```

```
void nodeTimeAdjustedCallback(int32_t offset)
{
  Serial.printf("adjust %u offset = %d \n",
                mesh.getNodeTime(), offset);
}

void loop()
{
  mesh.update();                      // handle ESP-MESH
}
```

Listing 3-2 is for the node 3 ESP32 microcontroller. In the *setup* function, the *newConnectionCallback, changedConnectionCallback,* and *nodeTimeAdjustedCallback* functions are not required. The LED state, contained in the message transmitted by node 1, is updated in the *recvMessage* function. If the LED state has changed, an acknowledgment is transmitted only to node 1 by the *sendSingle* instruction. Instructions that differ from those in Listing 3-1 are annotated.

The sketch for the node 2 ESP32 microcontroller is based on Listing 3-2 with the relay on GPIO 27 replacing the LED on GPIO 5. In the *recvMessage* function, the relay state is defined by the `RelayState = doc["relay"]` instruction. A message is not transmitted on a regular basis by node 2, so the *sendMessage* function contains no instructions.

Listing 3-2. MESH module with LED and generated data (node 3)

```
#include <painlessMesh.h>
painlessMesh mesh;
Scheduler scheduler;
String ssid = "meshSSID";
String password = "meshPass";
int port = 5555;
```

```
int LEDpin = 5;                          // define LED pin
int LEDstate, oldLEDstate;               // new and old LED states
DynamicJsonDocument doc(512);

void sendMessage();
Task taskSend(TASK_SECOND * 1 , TASK_FOREVER, &sendMessage);

void setup()
{
  pinMode(LEDpin, OUTPUT);               // LED pin as OUTPUT
  mesh.init(ssid, password, &scheduler, port);
  mesh.onReceive(&recvMessage);
  scheduler.addTask(taskSend);
  taskSend.enable();
}

void sendMessage()                       // function to send message
{
  float value = random(0, 100);          // generate random number
  doc["value"] = value;                  // update name:value pair
  String sendMsg;
  serializeJson(doc, sendMsg);
  mesh.sendBroadcast(sendMsg);
                                         // message timing of 3s
  taskSend.setInterval((TASK_SECOND * 3));
}

void recvMessage(uint32_t sender, String &recvMsg)
{
  deserializeJson(doc, recvMsg);         // equate doc with message
  LEDstate = doc["LED"];                 // update LED state
  digitalWrite(LEDpin, LEDstate);        // turn on or off LED
```

```
  if(LEDstate != oldLEDstate)
  {                                      // if LED state changed
    oldLEDstate = LEDstate;              // update old LED state
    mesh.sendSingle(sender, recvMsg);    // send message to node 1
  }
}

void loop()
{
  mesh.update();
}
```

ESP-MESH and One Bluetooth Device

The ESP-MESH protocol enables communication between Bluetooth apps, hosted by Android tablets or mobile phones, over a greater range than only with Bluetooth communication. For example, a Bluetooth communication app, hosted by an Android tablet, communicates with an ESP32 microcontroller, and the message is transmitted over the ESP-MESH network (see Figure 3-4). There are several Bluetooth communication apps to download from *Google Play Store*, and the *Bluetooth Terminal HC-05* app by MightyIT is recommended.

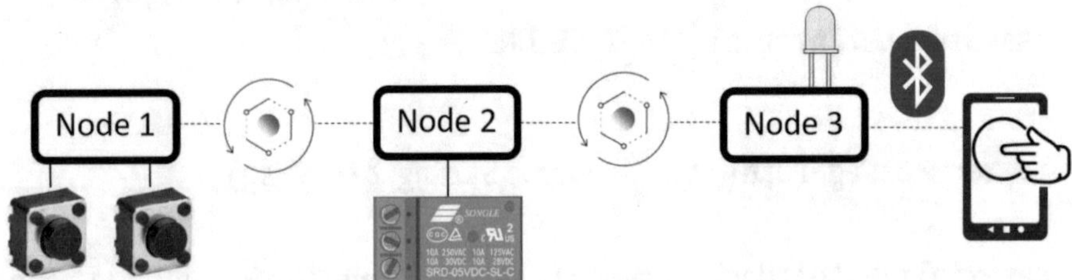

Figure 3-4. *ESP-MESH and Bluetooth communication (1)*

The *BluetoothSerial* library by Evandro Luis Copercini enables communication between a Bluetooth communication app, hosted by an Android tablet or mobile phone, and an ESP32 microcontroller. The *BluetoothSerial* library is installed when the *esp32* Boards Manager is installed. A Serial Bluetooth connection is established with the instructions

```
#include <BluetoothSerial.h>      // include Bluetooth library
BluetoothSerial SerialBT          // associate SerialBT with library
```

The Bluetooth communication app, with the name *ESP32 Bluetooth,* is defined in the *setup* function with the `SerialBT.begin("ESP32 Bluetooth")` instruction.

Text transmitted by a Bluetooth communication app, hosted by an Android tablet or mobile phone, and received by an ESP32 microcontroller is included in the JSON document, which is transmitted within the ESP-MESH network. Listing 3-2 for the node 3 ESP32 microcontroller in Figure 3-4 requires two further changes. Receipt of text is defined in the *loop* function by the `if(SerialBT.available()) BTtext = SerialBT.readString()` instruction with *BTtext* defined as a string. The instruction `doc["text"] = BTtext`, which is positioned immediately after the `doc["value"] = value` instruction in the *sendMessage* function, allocates the received text to the JSON document for transmission by node 3.

The JSON document now contains the four name:value pairs, such as *{"relay":0,"LED":1,"value":42,"text":"abcdef"}*. Listing 3-1 is updated to enable the node 1 ESP32 microcontroller to convert the received JSON formatted message to a character array, which is displayed with the *recvMessage* function, by adding the instructions

```
tft.fillRect(0, 85, 240, 40, TFT_BLACK)          // "delete" old text
tft.setCursor(0,85)              // position cursor and display new text
tft.printf("text %s \n", doc["text"].as<char*>())
```

prior to the `tft.setCursor(0,110)` instruction and display of the LED state.

ESP-MESH and Bluetooth Apps

Communication between several Bluetooth communication apps, hosted by Android tablets or mobile phones, independent of a WLAN (Wireless Local Area Network) or an ISP (Internet Service Provider), is achieved with an ESP-MESH network. A message is transmitted between a Bluetooth communication app, hosted by an Android tablet or mobile phone, and the corresponding ESP32 microcontroller, and the message is then transmitted between ESP32 microcontrollers over the ESP-MESH network.

For example, Figure 3-5 illustrates communication between two Bluetooth communication apps hosted by Android tablets over an ESP-MESH network. The left-side Bluetooth communication app, hosted by an Android tablet, transmits to the left-side ESP32 microcontroller, or node 1, text to be forwarded to the right-side Bluetooth communication app, hosted by an Android tablet, or command letters to control the relay or LED attached to other ESP32 modules in the ESP-MESH network. Text received by node 1 ESP32 microcontroller is transmitted to the left-side Bluetooth communication app, hosted by an Android tablet, by Bluetooth communication, and received data is also plotted on the Serial Monitor connected to node 1. The right-side ESP32 microcontroller, or node 3, communicates with the right-side Bluetooth communication app, hosted by an Android tablet, and transmits text and data across the ESP-MESH network to node 1. Node 2 responds to messages from node 1 by turning on or off the connected relay.

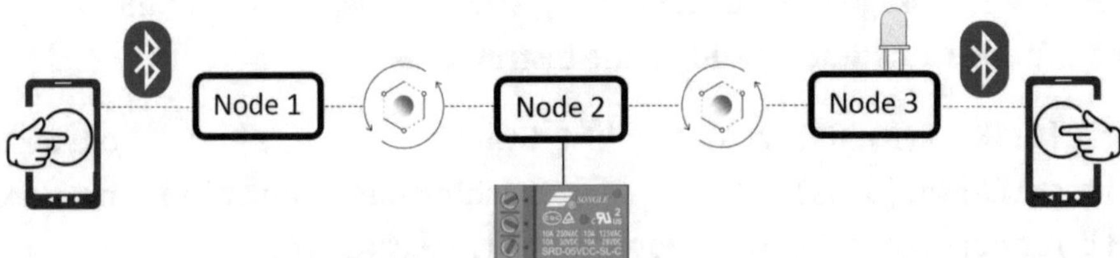

Figure 3-5. *ESP-MESH and Bluetooth communication (2)*

Listing 3-2 included the *painlessMesh* library, and Listing 3-1 also included the *TFT_eSPI* library and Serial communication to display information on the TTGO T-Display V1.1 LCD screen and the Serial Monitor. The two listings required 700617 bytes (0.67MB) and 754129 bytes (0.72MB) of program storage space, which was within the available 1310720 bytes or 1.25MB of ESP32 flash memory.

Inclusion of the *BluetoothSerial* library increases the program storage space to 1298757 bytes (1.24MB) for Listing 3-4 and to 1311061 bytes (1.25MB) for Listing 3-3. The sketch for node 3, Listing 3-4, was loaded to a TTGO T-Display V1.1 module, but only just. The standard *Partition Scheme* for the ESP32 DEVKIT DOIT is *Default 4MB with spiffs (1.2MB APP/1.5MB SPIFFS)*, but the program storage space is increased to 2MB by selecting the *No OTA (2MB APP/2MB SPIFFS)* option. *Partition Scheme* options are selected in the Arduino IDE *Tools* menu. The sketch for node 1, Listing 3-3, was loaded to an ESP32 DEVKIT DOIT module.

In both Listings 3-3 and 3-4, text transmitted by a Bluetooth communication app, hosted by an Android tablet, to the corresponding node is included in a JSON document and broadcast over the ESP-MESH network by the node with the *sendMessage* function. When a node receives a JSON document from the ESP-MESH network, the document is deserialized, in the *recvMessage* function, and the text is transmitted to the corresponding Bluetooth communication app, hosted by an Android tablet. If the text consists of more than three characters, then the text is displayed on the Bluetooth communication app.

In Listing 3-3 for node 1, if the first letter of text received from the corresponding Bluetooth communication app is the letter *L* or *R*, then node 1 changes the LED or relay state, and the updated state is displayed on the Bluetooth communication app. The received text and the updated LED or relay state are included in the JSON document broadcast over the ESP-MESH network. In Listing 3-4 for node 3 and adapted for node 2, a change in the relay or LED state is determined from the JSON document transmitted by node 1, and the relay or the LED, connected to node 2 or node 3, is turned on or off.

The deserialized JSON document, received from the ESP-MESH network by node 2 or 3, contains the *["LED"]* or *["relay"] name:value* pair, which determines if the LED or relay is turned on or off. Similarly, the deserialized JSON document received by node 1 includes the *["text"]* and *["value"] name:value* pairs to transmit the received text to the Bluetooth communication app, hosted by an Android tablet, and to plot the value on the Serial Monitor.

In the *Bluetooth Terminal HC-05* app by MightyIT, button settings are configured with a long press to enter the *Button Name* and the corresponding ASCII command letter. For example, *Button Names* of *LED* and *relay* are configured with the command letters of *L* and *R*. Pressing a *Bluetooth Terminal HC-05* app button broadcasts the command letter across the ESP-MESH network, and the LED or relay is turned on or off by the connected ESP32 microcontroller receiving the message.

Listing 3-3 is for the left-side ESP32 microcontroller or node 1 in Figure 3-5. Additional instructions to Listing 3-1 are annotated.

Listing 3-3. ESP-MESH and Bluetooth communication (node 1)

```
#include <painlessMesh.h>
painlessMesh mesh;
Scheduler scheduler;
String ssid = "meshSSID";
String password = "meshPass";
int port = 5555;
int LEDstate = 0, relayState = 0;   // LED and relay states
#include <BluetoothSerial.h>        // include Bluetooth library
BluetoothSerial SerialBT;           // associate SerialBT with library
String sendBT, oldBT = "";          // Bluetooth messages
char c;                             // character for command letter
DynamicJsonDocument doc(512);
```

```
void sendMessage();
Task taskSend(TASK_SECOND * 1, TASK_FOREVER, &sendMessage);

void setup()
{
  Serial.begin(115200);              // Serial Monitor baud rate
                                     // to plot transmitted values
  mesh.init(ssid, password, &scheduler, port);
  mesh.onReceive(&recvMessage);
  scheduler.addTask(taskSend);
  taskSend.enable();
  SerialBT.begin("ESP32 left");      // identify Bluetooth device
}

void sendMessage()
{
  doc["relay"] = relayState;
  doc["LED"] = LEDstate;
  doc["text"] = sendBT;              // text for Bluetooth app
  String sendMsg;
  serializeJson(doc, sendMsg);
  mesh.sendBroadcast(sendMsg);
  taskSend.setInterval((TASK_SECOND * 1));
  sendBT = "";                       // reset Bluetooth text message
}

void recvMessage(uint32_t sender, String &recvMsg)
{
  deserializeJson(doc, recvMsg);
  String recvBT = doc["text"];       // text from Bluetooth app
  Serial.printf("value %d \n", doc["value"].as<long>());
```

```
  if(recvBT != oldBT)
  {                                      // transmit to receiving Bluetooth app
    if(recvBT.length() > 3) SerialBT.print(recvBT);
    oldBT = recvBT;
  }
}

void loop()
{
  mesh.update();
  if(SerialBT.available())              // new Bluetooth message
  {
    sendBT = SerialBT.readString();  // read Serial buffer
    c = sendBT[0];                      // first letter of message
    switch (c)                          // switch...case on letter
    {
    case 'L':                           // letter = L (for LED)
      LEDstate = 1-LEDstate;            // alternate the LED state
                                       // transmit LED state to Bluetooth app
      if(LEDstate == 1) SerialBT.println("LED on");
      else SerialBT.println("LED off");
      break;
    case 'R':
      relayState = 1-relayState;    // similarly for the relay
      if(relayState == 1) SerialBT.println("relay on");
      else SerialBT.println("relay off");
      break;
    default: break;                     // no action, not L nor R
    }
  }
}
```

Listing 3-4 is for the right-side ESP32 microcontroller or node 3 in Figure 3-5. Additional instructions to Listing 3-2 are annotated.

Listing 3-4. ESP-MESH and Bluetooth communication (node 3)

```
#include <painlessMesh.h>
painlessMesh mesh;
Scheduler scheduler;
String ssid = "meshSSID";
String password = "meshPass";
int port = 5555;
int LEDpin = 5;
int LEDstate, oldLEDstate;
#include <BluetoothSerial.h>        // include Bluetooth library
BluetoothSerial SerialBT;           // associate SerialBT with library
String sendBT, oldBT = "";
DynamicJsonDocument doc(512);

void sendMessage();
Task taskSend(TASK_SECOND * 1 , TASK_FOREVER, &sendMessage);

void setup()
{
  pinMode(LEDpin, OUTPUT);          // LED pin as OUTPUT
  mesh.init(ssid, password, &scheduler, port);
  mesh.onReceive(&recvMessage);
  scheduler.addTask(taskSend);
  taskSend.enable();
  SerialBT.begin("ESP32 right");    // identify Bluetooth device
}

void sendMessage()
{
  float value = random(0, 100);
  doc["value"] = value;                 // update name:value pairs
```

```
  doc["text"] = sendBT;
  String sendMsg;
  serializeJson(doc, sendMsg);
  mesh.sendBroadcast(sendMsg);
  taskSend.setInterval((TASK_SECOND * 3));
  sendBT = "";
}

void recvMessage(uint32_t sender, String &recvMsg)
{
  deserializeJson(doc, recvMsg);
  String recvBT = doc["text"];          // received text
  if(recvBT != oldBT)
  {                                    // transmit to receiving Bluetooth app
    if(recvBT.length() > 3) SerialBT.print(recvBT);
    oldBT = recvBT;
  }
  LEDstate = doc["LED"];                // update LED state
  digitalWrite(LEDpin, LEDstate);       // turn on or off LED
  if(LEDstate != oldLEDstate)
  {
    oldLEDstate = LEDstate;
    mesh.sendSingle(sender, recvMsg); // transmit new LED state
  }                                     // to node 1
}

void loop()
{
  mesh.update();
  if(SerialBT.available())              // new Bluetooth message
    sendBT = SerialBT.readString();     // read Bluetooth Serial buffer
}
```

The sketch for node 2 is based on Listing 3-4 with the relay replacing the LED in the *recvMessage* function. No message is transmitted on a regular basis by node 2, so the *sendMessage* function contains no instructions. A Bluetooth device is not connected to node 2, so instructions related to Bluetooth messages and the *BluetoothSerial* library are not required.

CHAPTER 4

TTGO T-Watch V2

The TTGO T-Watch V2 incorporates a 240 × 240-pixel ST7789V 1.54" LCD screen with a FT6336 capacitive touch screen controller, PCF8563 RTC (real-time clock), Quectel L76K GPS (Global Positioning System), BMA423 three-axis accelerometer, infrared transmitter, TF (TransFlash) or micro-SD card reader/writer, DRV2605L vibration motor driver, AXP202 power management unit, and 380mA lithium ion battery.

The TTGO T-Watch V2 is turned on or off by pressing the power button on the side of the watch for 2s or 6s, respectively.

TTGO T-Watch Functionality

The TTGO T-Watch V2 functionality is illustrated with a range of applications including the following:

- Synchronize the watch time with the Network Time Protocol (NTP).
- A count-up and a count-down timer.
- Determine speed, altitude with the distance, and direction from the starting position.
- Obtain GPS position, altitude, and speed information.

N. Cameron, *ESP32 Formats and Communication*,
https://doi.org/10.1007/978-1-4842-9376-8_4

- Display a GPS satellite map with satellite tracking states.
- Measure the number of steps taken and distance traveled.
- Transmit and receive messages with a Bluetooth device.
- Transmit infrared signals to control a device.
- Source weather information with the *OpenWeatherMap* API (Application Programming Interface).
- Store data on a micro-SD card.
- Change the screen brightness with touch screen buttons.
- Monitor the battery voltage and ESP32 microcontroller temperature.
- Save battery power by turning off specific watch functions.

The sketch folder includes the main sketch (*TTGOWatch*), the *menu* sketch, a default display screen sketch (*displayTime*), functions for each application on separate tabs, a tab containing all the application bitmap images (*images.h*), and a tab (*image565.h*) for image(s) derived from .PNG files. The tabs containing instructions for each function have the same names as the application functions, such as *appBright*. A schematic of the sketch folder is shown in Figure 4-1. The structure of the *TTGOWatch* sketch was developed from the example sketch *File* ➤ *Examples* ➤ *TTGO TWatch Library* ➤ *ClientProject* ➤ *SimpleFramework*.

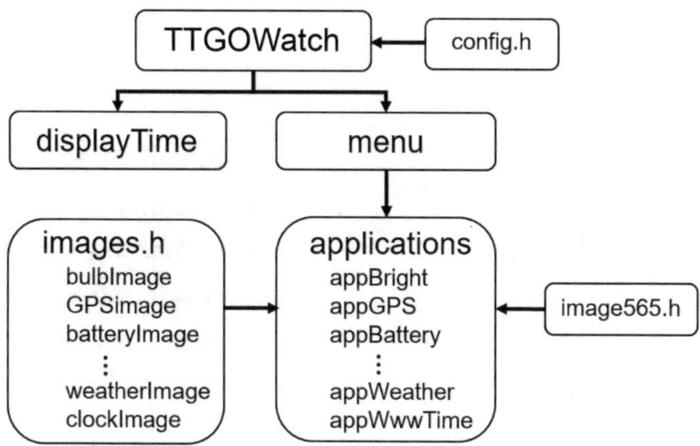

***Figure 4-1.** Schematic of the TTGOWatch sketch*

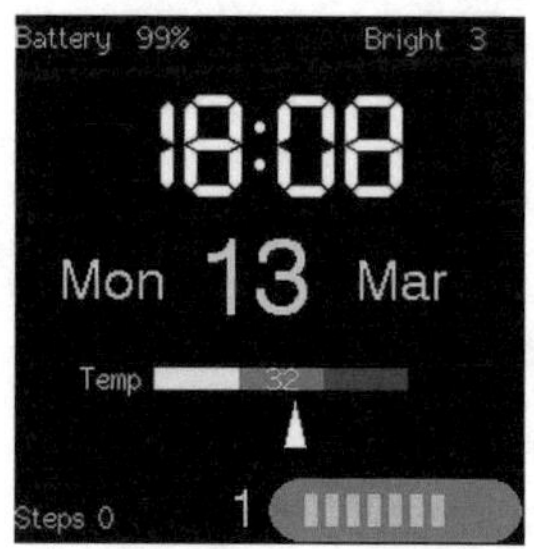

The default screen displays the current time, date, and day of week, month, battery charge percentage, screen brightness level, ESP32 microcontroller temperature, and animated seconds counter. The user selects an application by touching the highlighted application on a rolling menu, which is accessed by touching the default display screen, and the application output is displayed on the touch screen. Pressing the power button on the side of the watch puts the microcontroller into sleep mode to save battery power.

The instructions generally required to format the TTGO T-Watch V2 are shown in Listing 4-1.

Listing 4-1. Required instructions

```
#define LILYGO_WATCH_2020_V2      // define T-Watch model
#include <LilyGoWatch.h>          // include library
TTGOClass * ttgo;                 // associate objects with libraries
TFT_eSPI * tft;                   // graphics library
```

```
void setup()
{
  ttgo = TTGOClass::getWatch();
  ttgo->begin();                           // initialize ttgo object
  ttgo->openBL();                          // turn on backlight
  ttgo->bl->adjust(64);                    // reduce brightness from 255
  tft = ttgo->tft;                         // shorthand for object
  tft->fillScreen(TFT_BLACK);              // screen background color
                                           // text and background color
  tft->setTextColor(TFT_WHITE, TFT_BLACK);
  tft->setTextSize(1);                     // text size of 1 to 7
  tft->setCursor(0,0);                     // position cursor
}
```

Configuration File

The sketch in Listing 4-2 hosts the application sketches, which are functions located on separate tabs from the main sketch, for ease of access and readability. Details of libraries required for applications, a file containing the SSID and Wi-Fi network password, and the image files are listed on the *config.h* tab, as shown in Listing 4-2. The *TTGO_TWatch_Library* includes a version of the *TFT_eSPI* library, so the `#include <TFT_eSPI.h>` instruction is not required.

Listing 4-2. Configuration sketch

```
#define LILYGO_WATCH_2020_V2           // define T-Watch model as V2
#include <LilyGoWatch.h>               // include LilyGoWatch library
#include <HTTPClient.h>                // libraries for accessing
#include <WiFi.h>                      // Wi-Fi and URLs
#include <ssid_password.h>             // file with ssid and passwords
#include <ArduinoJson.h>               // library for JSON documents
#include <soc/rtc.h>                   // library for real-time clock
```

```
#include <BluetoothSerial.h>     // library for Bluetooth
#include <IRremoteESP8266.h>     // libraries for infrared signal
#include <IRsend.h>              // transmission
#include "images.h"              // icon image files
#include "image565.h"            // color image file
```

Main Sketch

The main sketch, shown in Listing 4-3, defines objects associated with each library. In the *setup* function, library objects for the touch screen backlight, RTC (real-time clock), GPS, and DRV2605 motor driver are initialized. Note that the `trunOnGPS()` instruction is not a typo. Shortcut terms are defined to make the sketch more readable, such as replacing the term `ttgo->tft` with `tft` to refer to the *TFT_eSPI* library object *tft*. The ADC (analog to digital converter) function, to monitor the battery voltage, and interrupts, activated by a short press on the power button or by the accelerometer, are enabled. The screen brightness is defined with the `ttgo->bl->adjust(N)` instruction, with the parameter *N* between 0 (off) and 255 (maximum). At the end of the *setup* function, the *displayTime* function is called to update the RTC time and the default display screen.

The *loop* function calls the *displayTime* function every second with the first parameter set to one when second (*ss*) is zero, to update the whole screen; otherwise, the first parameter is zero, to only update the seconds value. When a touch to the touch screen, which is displaying the menu, is released, the switch-case option calls the relevant function, based on the output of the *menu* function. The switch-case is not activated when the screen is touched, as that would repeatedly trigger the switch-case. When the called function is returned to the main sketch, the *displayTime* function updates the default display screen. If the power button is pressed, the *shutdown* function is called to disable several utilities and put the ESP32 microcontroller into sleep mode. The microcontroller wakes from sleep mode when the power button is pressed, which is the AXP202 power management unit interrupt pin *AXP202_INT* on GPIO 35.

Listing 4-3. Main sketch hosting application sketches

```
#include "config.h"                        // incorporate libraries
TTGOClass * ttgo;
TFT_eSPI * tft;
AXP20X_Class * power;                      // associate objects with libraries
BMA * bma;
Adafruit_DRV2605 * drv;
TinyGPSPlus * gps;
BluetoothSerial SerialBT;
IRsend irsend(TWATCH_2020_IR_PIN);  // references GPIO 2
unsigned long lastTime = 0;                // time display last updated
int IRQ = false;                           // power button interrupt
int irq = false;                           // step counter interrupt
uint8_t hh, mm, ss;                        // variables for displayTime app
int bright = 3;                            // and Bright app

void setup()
{
  ttgo = TTGOClass::getWatch();
  ttgo->begin();                           // initialize ttgo object
  ttgo->openBL();                          // turn on backlight
  ttgo->rtc->check();                      // compare RTC to compile time
  ttgo->rtc->syncToSystem();               // synchronize to system time
  ttgo->trunOnGPS();                       // trunOn is NOT a typo
  ttgo->gps_begin();                       // initialize GPS
  ttgo->enableDrv2650();                   // enable DRV2605 motor driver
  tft = ttgo->tft;
  bma = ttgo->bma;                         // shorthand for library objects
  drv = ttgo->drv;
  gps = ttgo->gps;
  power = ttgo->power;
```

```
                                    // initialize battery ADC
  power->adc1Enable(AXP202_VBUS_VOL_ADC1 |
           AXP202_VBUS_CUR_ADC1 | AXP202_BATT_CUR_ADC1 |
           AXP202_BATT_VOL_ADC1, 1);
                                    // enable button interrupt
  power->enableIRQ(AXP202_PEK_SHORTPRESS_IRQ, 1);
  power->clearIRQ();                // reset interrupt
  pinMode(AXP202_INT, INPUT_PULLUP); // power button interrupt
  attachInterrupt(AXP202_INT, [] {IRQ = 1;}, FALLING);
  pinMode(BMA423_INT1, INPUT);      // accelerometer interrupt
  attachInterrupt(BMA423_INT1, [] {irq = 1;}, RISING);
  ttgo->bl->adjust(64);             // reduce screen brightness
  displayTime(1, bright);           // display default screen
}

void loop()
{
  if(millis() - lastTime > 1000)    // call displayTime function
  {                                 // every second
    lastTime = millis();            // with full display updated
    displayTime(ss == 0, bright);   // every minute
  }
  int16_t x, y;
  if (ttgo->getTouch(x, y))         // screen touched
  {
    while (ttgo->getTouch(x, y)) {} // wait for touch release
    tft->fillScreen(TFT_BLACK);
    switch (menu())                 // switch-case based on
    {                               // menu function output
      case 0: break;                // exit switch-case
                                    // change screen brightness
      case 1: bright = appBright(); break;
```

```
      case 2: appGPS(); break;          // position data from GPS
      case 3: appBattery(); break;      // display battery status
      case 4: appBlue(); break;         // Bluetooth communication
      case 5: appSonyIR(); break;       // transmit infrared signal
      case 6: appStep(); break;         // step counter with GPS
      case 7: appTemp(); break;         // microcontroller temperature
      case 8: appTimer(); break;        // count-down and
                                        // count-up timer
      case 9: appWeather(); break;      // display OpenWeatherMap data
      case 10: appWwwTime(); break;     // synchronize with NTP time
      case 11: appGPSout(); break;      // data from GPS
      case 12: appSatellite(); break;  // GPS satellite positions
    }
    displayTime(1, bright);             // display default screen
  }
  if (IRQ) shutdown();                  // power button pressed
}                                       // to call shutdown function

void shutdown()                         // AXP202 interrupt triggered
{
  power->clearIRQ();                    // clear interrupt status
  ttgo->displaySleep();              // screen and touch in sleep mode
  power->setPowerOutPut(AXP202_LDO2, 0);    // disable backlight
                                     // disable touch screen function
  power->setPowerOutPut(AXP202_LDO3, 0);
  power->setPowerOutPut(AXP202_LDO4, 0);    // disable GPS
                                     // disable Touch Reset Enable
  power->setPowerOutPut(AXP202_EXTEN, 0);
                                     // wake up on power button
  power->setPowerOutPut(AXP202_DCDC2, 0);
```

```
  esp_sleep_enable_ext1_wakeup(GPIO_SEL_35,
    ESP_EXT1_WAKEUP_ALL_LOW);
  esp_deep_sleep_start();                    // initiate sleep mode
}
```

Default Display Screen

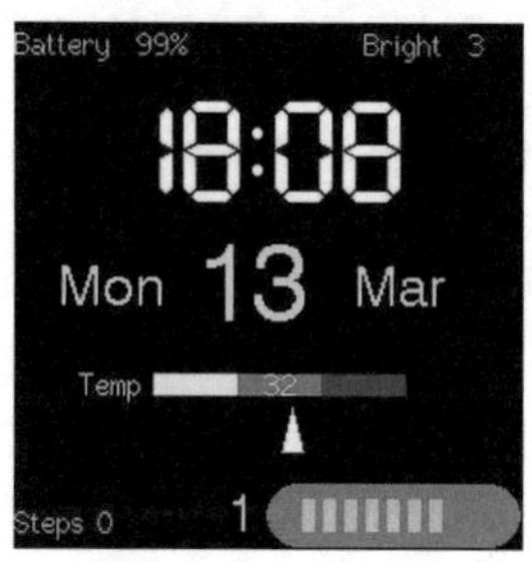

The sketch for the *displayTime* function, shown in Listing 4-4, includes parameters controlling screen updating and the brightness level. The instruction `RTC_Date tnow = ttgo->rtc->getDateTime()` obtains the current time parameters for second, minute, hour, day, month, and year. Note that there is no shorthand for the RTC, equivalent to `power = ttgo->power`. The current time is displayed with leading zeros for the hour and minute. The day of the week is obtained with the RTC function *getDayOfWeek*, with details in the library file *TTGO_TWatch_Library\src\drive\rtc\pcf8563.h*. In the arrays specifying strings for the month and day of week, the first element of the *months* array is blank with elements 1–12 equal to January–December, while for the *wkdays* array, the elements 0–6 equate to Sunday–Saturday.

A temperature bar, consisting of three rectangles (yellow, green, and red), indicates a low, medium, or high microcontroller temperature, which is displayed on the temperature bar. The position of the white triangle below the temperature bar indicates the temperature over the range of 10–50°C. The AXP202 power management unit `getTemp()` and `getBattPercentage()` instructions obtain the microcontroller temperature and battery percentage. A step count is displayed with the BMA423 three-axis accelerometer instruction `getCounter()`. The step counter application is described later in this chapter.

The animated seconds counter is updated every second. The number of tens of seconds is displayed, and the number of digits is represented with a series of bars overwritten on a rectangle with rounded corners.

Function-specific variables are defined in each function rather than being defined as global variables in the main sketch. The *TFT_eSPI* library functions are outlined in Chapter 15, "Libraries."

Listing 4-4. Default display screen

```
void displayTime(int update, int bright)    // default display screen
{
  RTC_Date tnow = ttgo->rtc->getDateTime(); // update RTC time
  hh = tnow.hour;
  mm = tnow.minute;
  ss = tnow.second;
  if (update)                               // update display screen
  {
    tft->fillScreen(TFT_BLACK);
    tft->setTextColor(TFT_WHITE);
    tft->setTextSize(1);                    // reduce text size to 1
    String hhmm = String(hh) +":";          // display time
    if(hh < 10) hhmm = "0" + hhmm;          // with leading zeros
    if(mm < 10) hhmm = hhmm + "0" + String(mm);
    else hhmm = hhmm + String(mm);
    tft->drawString(hhmm, 45, 35, 7);       // font 7 is 7-segment

    String months[] = {"","Jan","Feb","Mar","Apr","May","June",
                      "July","Aug","Sept","Oct","Nov","Dec"};
    String wkdays[] = {"Sun","Mon","Tues","Wed","Thur","Fri","Sat"};
    int wkday = ttgo->rtc->getDayOfWeek(
                      tnow.day, tnow.month, tnow.year);
    tft->setTextColor(TFT_GREENYELLOW);
```

```
    tft->drawString(wkdays[wkday], 20, 110, 4);
                                 // weekday, date & month
    tft->drawNumber(tnow.day, 85, 100, 6);
    tft->drawString(months[tnow.month], 160, 110, 4);

                                 // three color bars for microcontroller temp
    tft->fillRect( 65, 160, 40, 10, TFT_YELLOW);
    tft->fillRect(105, 160, 40, 10, TFT_DARKGREEN);
    tft->fillRect(145, 160, 40, 10, TFT_RED);
    tft->drawString("Temp", 30, 157, 2);
    float temp = power->getTemp();          // microcontroller temp
                                            // display temperature
    tft->drawNumber(round(temp), 118, 157, 2);
    int x = 35+3*round(temp);               // range 10 to 50°C
    tft->fillTriangle(x, 175, x-5, 195, x+5, 195, TFT_WHITE);

    tft->setTextColor(TFT_GREEN);           // display battery percent,
                                            // screen brightness level
    int batt_p = power->getBattPercentage();
    tft->drawString("Battery  "+ String(batt_p) + "%", 0, 2, 2);
    tft->drawString("Bright  " + String(bright), 165, 2, 2);
    tft->drawString("Steps " + String(bma->getCounter()),
                   0, 220, 2);
    tft->fillRoundRect(119, 210, 120, 29, 15, TFT_DARKCYAN);
  }
  int sval = ss/10;                         // seconds (tens)
  tft->setTextColor(TFT_ORANGE, TFT_BLACK);
  tft->drawNumber(sval, 100, 213, 4);
  sval = ss % 10;                           // seconds (units)
  if (sval > 0)
     tft->fillRect(126 + sval * 10, 217, 6, 15, TFT_ORANGE);
  else tft->fillRoundRect(119, 210, 120, 29, 15, TFT_DARKCYAN);
}                                           // seconds animation
```

Application Menu

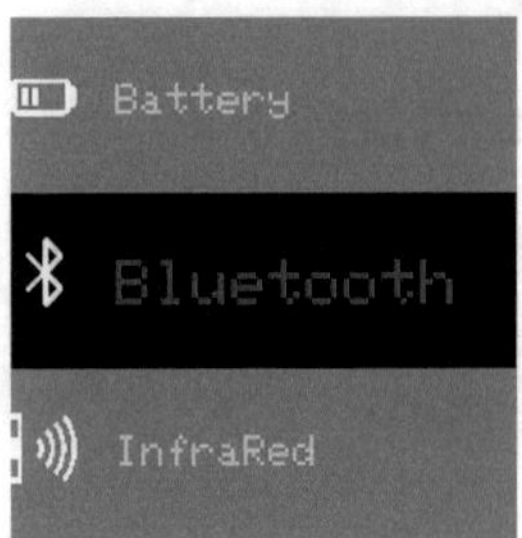

When the default display screen is touched, a rolling menu of three applications is displayed, with the menu moving up or down when a touch to the top or bottom third of the touch screen is released. When a touch to the middle of the touch screen is released, the function corresponding to the application title, displayed in the middle of the screen and highlighted in red, is called.

The *menu* function sketch, shown in Listing 4-5, holds the value of the *appN* variable, which increases or decreases depending on which third of the touch screen was touched. The *list* function displays three application titles, with the application title corresponding to the *appN* element of the *appTitle* array displayed in the middle of the touch screen. A 32 × 32-pixel icon for each application is displayed on the menu, with the *getIcon* function returning the matching bitmap image using the switch-case utility. Details on creating image bitmap files are described in Chapter 10, “Managing Images.”

If an application is added or deleted, then the *maxApp* variable in the *menu* function is set to the number of applications plus one, and the application title, to be displayed on the menu, is added or deleted in the *appTitle* array. The bitmap image corresponding to the application is included in the switch-case utility of the *getIcon* function, and the bitmap image file is located on the *image.h* tab. In the main sketch, Listing 4-3, the application function is added or deleted in the switch-case utility of the *loop* function.

Listing 4-5. Menu sketch

```
const int maxApp = 12;                  // number of apps plus one
String appTitle[maxApp] =               // application titles in menu
{"","Bright","GPS","Battery","Bluetooth","InfraRed","Step count",
    "Temp","Timer","Weather","www time","GPSout","Satellites"};
```

```
int menu()                           // function to update list
{                                    // when screen touched
  int appN = 0;                      // initial list starts with blank
  int exit = 0;                      // stay in menu until app selected
  list(appN);                        // call function to display app list
  int16_t x, y;
  while (!exit)                      // while app not selected
  {                                  // do nothing waiting for touch
    while (!ttgo->getTouch(x, y)) {}
                                     // then wait for touch release
    while (ttgo->getTouch(x, y)) {}
    {                                // middle app on list selected
      if (y > 80 && y < 160) exit = 1;
      appN = appN - int(y/80) + 1;   // move to next or previous app
      if (appN == maxApp) appN = 0;  // list starts with blank
                                     // list starts with last app
      else if (appN < 0) appN = maxApp - 1;
      list(appN);                    // call function to display app list
    }
  }
  tft->setTextSize(2);               // text size 2 as returning to an
                                     // app not to displayTime
  tft->setTextColor(TFT_GREEN);
  tft->fillScreen(TFT_BLACK);
  return appN;
}

void list(int N)                     // function to display app titles
{
  tft->fillScreen(TFT_DARKCYAN);
                                     // rectangle in center of screen
  tft->fillRect(0, 80, 240, 80, TFT_BLACK);
```

```
  tft->setTextSize(3);                   // large text for middle app
  tft->setTextColor(TFT_RED);
  tft->setCursor(50, 110);
  tft->println(appTitle[N]);             // display app title and draw icon
  if(N > 0) tft->drawBitmap(0, 100, getIcon(N), 32, 32, TFT_WHITE);
  tft->setTextSize(2);                   // small text for top & bottom app
  tft->setTextColor(TFT_ORANGE);
  int n = N-1;                           // previous app
  if (n < 0) n = maxApp - 1;
  tft->setCursor(50, 30);                // display app title at top of screen
  tft->print(appTitle[n]);               // with icon
  if(n>0) tft->drawBitmap(0, 20, getIcon(n), 32, 32, TFT_WHITE);
  n = N+1;                               // next app
  if (n > maxApp - 1) n = 0;
  tft->setCursor(50, 190);               // app title at bottom of screen
  tft->println(appTitle[n]);
  if(n>0) tft->drawBitmap(0, 180, getIcon(n), 32, 32, TFT_WHITE);
}

const unsigned char * getIcon(int N)     // switch-case for app icon
{
  switch (N)
  {
    case 1: return bulbImage; break;    // appBright, icon not
                                         // used in app
    case 2: return GPSimage; break;
    case 3: return batteryImage; break;
    case 4: return BTimage; break;       // appBlue
    case 5: return IRimage; break;       // appInfraRed, icon
                                         // not used
    case 6: return stepImage; break;
```

```
    case 7: return tempImage; break;        // icon not used in app
    case 8: return clockImage; break;       // appTimer, icon not
                                            // used in app
    case 9: return weatherImage; break;
    case 10: return clockImage; break;      // appWwwTime
    case 11: return GPSimage; break;        // appGPSout
    case 12: return GPSimage; break;        // appSatellite
    default: break;
  }
}
```

Screen Brightness

The lithium ion battery is rapidly drained with a high screen brightness (see the "Data Storage on a Micro-SD Card" section of this chapter), and reducing the screen brightness substantially reduces the temperature of the ESP32 microcontroller. The sketch to control screen brightness is shown in Listing 4-6. Screen brightness is set by the `ttgo->bl->adjust(N)` or `ttgo->setBrightness(N)` instruction, with the variable *N* between 0 (off) and 255 (maximum). Six round rectangles are numbered 1–6 for different brightness levels. While the touch screen is untouched or touched, nothing happens, due to the sequential `while(!ttgo->getTouch(x, y)) {}` and `while (ttgo->getTouch(x, y)) {}` instructions. When the touch screen is released, the touch position is converted to a brightness level, as buttons are 80 pixels wide and 50 pixels high. The string "*ABCD1234*" is displayed at the top of the screen to reflect the screen brightness to the user.

When the touch screen, corresponding to the *DONE* button at the bottom-right of the screen, is pressed, then the generated *key* parameter is greater than six, and the *appBright* function returns the brightness level to the main sketch.

Listing 4-6. Screen brightness

```
int appBright()                              // function to change screen
{                                            // brightness
  int row, col, key = 0;                     // brightness levels
  int level = 0, levels[] = {8, 16, 32, 64, 128, 192, 255};
  tft->fillScreen(TFT_BLACK);
  tft->setTextColor(TFT_WHITE);
  tft->drawString("ABCD1234", 60, 2, 2);
  tft->setTextColor(TFT_ORANGE);
  for (int r=0; r<2; r++)                    // draw buttons with numbers
  {                                          // 1 2 3
    for (int c=0; c<3; c++)                  // 4 5 6
    {
      tft->fillRoundRect(c*80, r*50+35, 75, 45, 6, TFT_DARKCYAN);
      tft->drawNumber(r*3+c+1, c*80+30, r*50+40, 2);
    }
  }
  tft->fillRoundRect(120, 200, 118, 35, 6, TFT_WHITE);
  tft->setTextColor(TFT_BLACK);
  tft->setCursor(155, 210);                 // draw button to exit function
  tft->print("DONE");
  int16_t x, y;
  while(key < 7)                            // key = 11 or 12 is "DONE"
  {                                         // do nothing waiting for touch
    while(!ttgo->getTouch(x, y)) {}
```

```
    while (ttgo->getTouch(x, y)) {}  // then wait for touch release
    col = int(x/80) + 1;             // button in column
                                     // number COL
    row = int((y-35)/50) + 1;        // button in row number ROW
    key = (row-1)*3+col;             // number on pressed button
    if(key < 7) level = key;
                                     // brightness levels 0 to 6
    ttgo->setBrightness(levels[level]);
  }
  return level;                      // return brightness level
}                                    // to main sketch
```

GPS Information

GPS information is displayed as a series of National Marine Electronics Association (NMEA) messages. Messages are prefixed with $GN followed by the message name, of RMC, GGA, GLL, and VTG, to provide information on time, latitude, and longitude. Speed over ground, altitude, and date are provided by the VTG, GGA, and RMC messages, respectively. The $GPGSV message provides positional information on each satellite or space vehicle (SV). Details on NMEA messages are available from several sources, such as `www.u-blox.com/en/product-resources`, and search for "*receiver description*" or Google "*u-blox NMEA-RMC.*"

The GGA and GLL messages contain time (*hhmmss*), latitude (*xx°xx'xx.x"N*), and longitude, with altitude included in the GGA message. The GSV message includes the number of satellites, satellite identity, elevation, azimuth, and signal strength. The RMC message includes time, latitude, longitude, direction, and date (*ddmmyy*), with direction and speed also included in the VTG message. Time data (*hhmmss*), day, month, and year are contained in the ZDA message.

An example of GPS NMEA messages is

```
$GNGGA,141155.000,5556.0,N,00311.0,W,1,07,2.7,61.2,M,52.9,M,,*63
$GNGLL,5556.0,N,00311.0,W,141155.000,A,A*5F
$GNGSA,A,3,10,12,23,24,25,32,,,,,,,4.7,2.7,3.8,1*3F
$GNGSA,A,3,76,,,,,,,,,,,,4.7,2.7,3.8,2*3E
$GPGSV,3,1,11,01,07,356,,10,23,266,32,12,60,209,10,15,14,167,,0*6C
$GPGSV,3,2,11,17,22,039,,19,38,075,,22,06,318,,23,10,235,23,0*60
$GPGSV,3,3,11,24,71,122,27,25,30,227,33,32,33,306,32,0*57
$GLGSV,1,1,03,70,,,41,86,,,32,76,41,261,24,0*40
$GNRMC,141155.000,A,5556.0,N,00311.0,W,0.08,323.43,271222,,,A,V*19
$GNVTG,323.43,T,,M,0.08,N,0.15,K,A*2A
$GNZDA,141155.000,27,12,2022,00,00*49
$GPTXT,01,01,01,ANTENNA OPEN*25
```

In the preceding example, the GPS NMEA messages were received at 14:11:55 on December 27, 2022, at position (55°56'N, 3°11'W) with an altitude of 61.2m, a speed of 0.15kmph, and a direction of travel of 323°. There were 11 satellites in view, and satellite identity 10 had an elevation of 23°, azimuth of 266°, and signal strength (carrier to noise ratio) of 32dB-Hz.

NMEA messages from the TTGO-T-Watch V2 GPS are displayed on the Serial Monitor with the sketch in Listing 4-7. The GPS Serial communication transmit (*TX*) and receive (*RX*) pins are GPIO 26 and 36, respectively, and the GPS baud rate is 9600Bd, as defined in the *TTGO_TWatch_Library* file *src\board\twatch2020_v2.h*. The *GPS_RX, GPS_TX,* and *GPS_BAUD_RATE* variables are defined in the sketch, even though they are defined in the *TTGO_TWatch_Library,* as the *TTGO_TWatch_Library* is not included in the sketch.

Listing 4-7. GPS NMEA messages

```
int GPS_RX = 36, GPS_TX = 26;
int GPS_BAUD_RATE = 9600;
String str;

void setup()
{
  Serial.begin(115200);
  Serial1.begin(GPS_BAUD_RATE, SERIAL_8N1, GPS_RX, GPS_TX);
}

void loop()
{
  while (Serial1.available()) Serial.write(Serial1.read());
}
```

If a restriction on the displayed NMEA messages is required, then the *loop* function in Listing 4-7 is replaced with the *loop* function in Listing 4-8 to display only the NMEA RMC messages.

Listing 4-8. Restriction on GPS NMEA messages

```
void loop()
{
  while (Serial1.available())
  {
    str = Serial1.readStringUntil('\n');
    if(str.startsWith("$GNRMC")) Serial.println(str);
  }
}
```

GPS Location

The NMEA messages are parsed to display the current time, altitude, speed, and number of tracked satellites with the latitude and longitude of the current position. After clearing the screen, the `while (!ttgo->getTouch(x, y))` instruction essentially provides a loop for GPS time and location information display, while the touch screen is not touched (see Listing 4-9). When the touch screen is touched and released, the *appGPSout* function returns to the main sketch.

When the GPS time is updated, the time components are displayed with the *%02d* format, which displays an integer with two digits and a leading zero. Similarly, when the altitude, speed, number of tracked satellites, or location is updated, the updated value is displayed. The *lag* variable is the number of seconds since the number of tracked satellites or the location was updated.

A GPS location requires four tracked satellites, each with a signal strength (carrier to noise ratio) of at least 15dB-Hz. A satellite map, such as in Figure 4-2, displaying more than four tracked satellites may not reflect a GPS location if the signal strength of several tracked satellites is low.

Listing 4-9. GPS location

```
void appGPSout()                       // function to display GPS location
{
  tft->fillScreen(TFT_BLACK);          //display GPS icon
  tft->drawBitmap(0, 0, GPSimage, 32, 32, TFT_WHITE);
  tft->setTextSize(2);                 // change text size to 2
  tft->setTextColor(TFT_YELLOW);
  tft->setCursor(80, 10);
  tft->print("GPS data");
  tft->setTextColor(TFT_GREEN, TFT_BLACK);
```

```
unsigned long last, lag;
int16_t x, y;
last = millis();
while (!ttgo->getTouch(x, y))    // wait for touch
{
  ttgo->gpsHandler();               // handle GPS signals
  if (gps->time.isUpdated())       // updated GPS time
  {
    tft->setCursor(0, 40);          // leading zeros for 2 digits
    tft->printf("tim %02d:%02d:%02d \n", gps->time.hour(),
                 gps->time.minute(),gps->time.second());
                                    // lag since last updated location
    lag = round((millis() - last)/1000.0);
    tft->setCursor(0, 220);
    if(lag > 0) tft->printf("lag %d   \n", lag);
  }
  if (gps->altitude.isUpdated()) // updated altitude
  {
    tft->setCursor(0, 70);
    tft->printf("alt %.1f m  \n", gps->altitude.meters());
  }
  if (gps->speed.isUpdated())      // updated speed
  {
    tft->setCursor(0, 100);         // display speed in mps
    tft->printf("spd %.1f mps  \n", gps->speed.mps());
  }
  if (gps->satellites.isUpdated()) // updated number of satellites
  {
    tft->setCursor(0, 130);
    tft->printf("sat %d  \n", gps->satellites.value());
  }
```

```
    if (gps->location.isUpdated())     // updated location
    {
      tft->setCursor(0, 160);
      tft->printf("lat %.5f \n", gps->location.lat());
      tft->setCursor(0, 190);
      tft->printf("lon %.5f \n", gps->location.lng());
      last = millis();                   // update last time when
    }                                    // new location received
  }
  while (ttgo->getTouch(x, y)) {}      // wait for touch release
}
```

Speed, Altitude, and Distance Covered

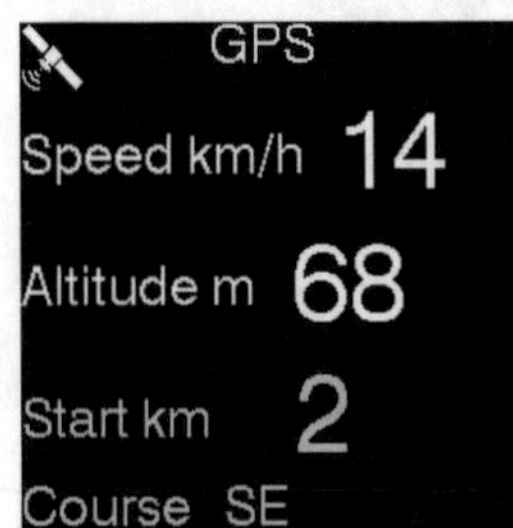

GPS functionality is demonstrated by the sketch in Listing 4-10 with speed and altitude updated continuously, while distance and course to a start position are updated every five seconds. The start position is defined by the latitude and longitude of the location when the GPS is first updated. The application is aimed at a cyclist, rather than a pedestrian, with the speed and altitude being the focus of the display. Measurement noise in the five-second updates of distance and course to the start position is likely to be small relative to the distance between the current and previous positions. The speed and altitude information is only displayed when a GPS location has been obtained.

Speed and altitude are obtained with the *gps* object instructions, but distance and course to the start position (*startLat, startLong*) from the current position (`location.lat(), location.lng()`) are obtained with *gps* object instructions preceded by `TinyGPSPlus::distanceBetween` and `TinyGPSPlus::courseTo`, respectively, with the course formatted as `TinyGPSPlus::cardinal`. Note that the start position latitude and longitude are formatted as *double* rather than *float*, as is the *course* variable.

The distance between two GPS positions is calculated by the Haversine formula as $2 \times R \times arcsin\left(\sqrt{B}\right)$ or by the spherical law of cosines as $R \times\ arccos\,(C)$, with R equal to the radius of the Earth of 6378km. The *TinyGS* library calculates the distance as $R \times asin\left(\sqrt{D}\right)$, with

$$B = sin^2\left(\Delta lat / 2\right) + cos\left(lat_1\right)cos\left(lat_2\right)sin^2\left(\Delta lon / 2\right)$$

$$C = sin\left(lat_1\right)sin\left(lat_2\right) + cos\left(lat_1\right)cos\left(lat_2\right)cos\left(\Delta lon\right)$$

$$and\ D = \left[\cos\left(lat_1\right)\sin\left(lat_2\right) - sin\left(lat_1\right)\cos\left(lat_2\right)cos\left(\Delta lon\right)\right]^2 + \left[cos\left(lat_2\right)\sin\left(\Delta lon\right)\right]^2$$

where (lat_i, lon_i) is GPS position coordinates and Δlon is the difference between longitude values.

Speed is expressed in units of mph, m/s, km/h, and knots with the `speed.mph()`, `speed.mps()`, `speed.kmph()`, and `speed.knots()` instructions, respectively. Altitude is expressed in meters, miles, kilometers, or feet with the `altitude.meters()`, `altitude.miles()`, `altitude.kilometers()`, or `altitude.feet()` instruction, respectively. Altitude is a weighted mean of several measurements. Given a sudden change in altitude, the displayed altitude is incrementally changed to the current altitude. The number of located satellites is obtained with the `satellites.value()` instruction. The C function `round` rounds a real number up or down to the nearest integer, as does the `int(x+0.5)` instruction.

Listing 4-10. GPS information

```
void appGPS()                              // function to display
{                                          // GPS information
  double startLat, startLon;               // start position
  double distance, course;
  unsigned long last = 0;
  int value, startFlag = 0;
  tft->fillScreen(TFT_BLACK);              // clear touch screen
                                           //display GPS icon
  tft->drawBitmap(0, 0, GPSimage, 32, 32, TFT_WHITE);
  tft->setTextSize(1);                     // reduce text size to one
  tft->setTextColor(TFT_YELLOW);
  tft->drawString("GPS", 90, 0, 4); // font size 4
  int16_t x, y;
  while (!ttgo->getTouch(x, y))            // wait for touch
  {
    ttgo->gpsHandler();                    // handle GPS signals
    if (gps->location.isUpdated())   // change in GPS location
    {
      if(startFlag == 1)        // start position already defined
      {                         // distance and course to start position
        distance = TinyGPSPlus::distanceBetween
                   (gps->location.lat(),
                   gps->location.lng(), startLat, startLon);
        course = TinyGPSPlus::courseTo(gps->location.lat(),
                 gps->location.lng(), startLat, startLon);
                                           // "delete" previous values
        tft->fillRect(120, 40, 100, 100, TFT_BLACK);
        tft->setTextColor(TFT_WHITE);
        tft->drawString("Speed km/h", 0, 50, 4);
                                           // display speed (km/h)
```

```
        value = round(gps->speed.kmph());
        tft->drawNumber(value, 150, 40, 6);
        tft->drawString("Altitude m", 0, 110, 4);
                                         // display altitude (m)
        value = round(gps->altitude.meters());
        tft->drawNumber(value, 130, 100, 6);
        if(millis() - last > 5000)       // at 5 sec intervals
        {
          last = millis();               // update last time
          tft->setTextColor(TFT_GREEN);
          tft->fillRect(50, 160, 180, 70, TFT_BLACK);
          tft->drawString("Start km", 0, 170, 4);
          value = round(distance/1000);  // convert distance to km
                                         // display distance
          tft->drawNumber(value, 130, 160, 6);
                                  // display course to start position
          tft->drawString("Course"+String(TinyGPSPlus::
                          cardinal(course)), 0, 210, 4);
        }
      }
      else if(startFlag == 0)            // GPS updated at
      {                                  // start position
        startFlag = 1;
        startLat = gps->location.lat();
        startLon = gps->location.lng();
      }
    }
  }
  while (ttgo->getTouch(x, y)) {}        // wait for touch release
}
```

GPS Satellite Map

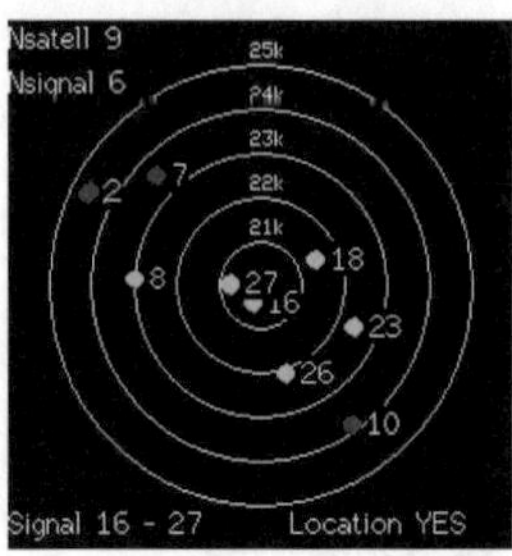

A circular map of GPS satellite positions showing the azimuth (degrees from North), the distance predicted from the satellite elevation angle, and from which satellites a signal is received by the Quectel L76K GPS module is illustrated in Figure 4-2, with the TTGO T-Watch V2 located in Edinburgh, Scotland. A green marker indicates a tracked-satellite signal. A website with GPS satellite position information is `in-the-sky.org/satmap_worldmap.php?gps=1`. Note that some satellites, such as *NAVSTAR77* and *GPS14,* are displayed on the satellite map with their *PRN* number, such as *PRN04* and *PRN22.* Satellite message data is encoded with a satellite-specific pseudo-random number (*PRN*) for receivers to differentiate between satellites, which are transmitting on the same frequency.

Figure 4-2. *Map of GPS satellite positions and the in-the-sky.org satellite map*

The NMEA *$GPGSV* message provides information on each tracked satellite. A *$GPGSV* message record contains information for a maximum of four satellites with several *$GPGSV* records received per message. An NMEA *$GPGSV* record contains the number of records, record number, number of satellites, and, for each satellite in the record, satellite identity, elevation (0–90°) angle, azimuth (0–359°) angle, and signal strength

(0–99dB-Hz). The signal strength of a non-tracked satellite is zero. The NMEA *$GPGSV* message consisting of three records for the nine satellites in the satellite map of Figure 4-2 is listed in Figure 4-3. Satellite identity 26 has an elevation, azimuth, and signal strength of 27°, 275°, and 23dB-Hz, respectively, and the signal strength for satellites 04 and 12 is zero.

```
        records
        satellites              identity,elevation,azimuth,signal
$GPGSV,3,1,09,02,31,054,23,04,09,338,0,12,19,092,0,22,26,237,22,0*69
$GPGSV,3,2,09,25,59,098,22,26,27,275,23,29,72,164,19,31,63,269,18,0*61
$GPGSV,3,3,09,32,13,222,16,0*5A
```

Figure 4-3. *NMEA $GPGSV message*

GPS satellites orbit the Earth with an altitude of 20200km and a period of 11hr and 58min, with satellites passing a location twice a day. At any one time, at least six satellites are in line of sight from anywhere on Earth. The distance (km) between a location and a satellite is a function of the satellite elevation (*Elev*) and altitude above the Earth (*Alt = 20200km*) and the Earth's radius (*Rad = 6378km*), with distance = $\sqrt{\alpha^2 + 2 \times Elev \times Alt + Alt^2} - \alpha^2$, where $\alpha = Rad \times \sin(Elev)$ (see `www.itu.int/rec/R-REC-S.1257`). Given the 0–90° range of satellite elevations, the satellite distances range from 25800 to 20200km (see Figure 4-2). The circular map position of a satellite has (*x, y*) coordinates of $(120 + D\sin(\theta), 120 - D\cos(\theta))$, for a satellite with distance *Dkm* and azimuth angle θ, which is relative to North (see Figure 4-4). The circular map is centered on the 240 × 240-pixel ST7789V 1.54" LCD screen of the TTGO T-Watch V2. The azimuth angle is transformed from degrees to radians by scaling with $\pi/180$ or by multiplying with the Arduino variable *DEG_TO_RAD*, which is defined in *C:\Program Files (x86)\Arduino\hardware\arduino\avr\cores\arduino\Arduino.*

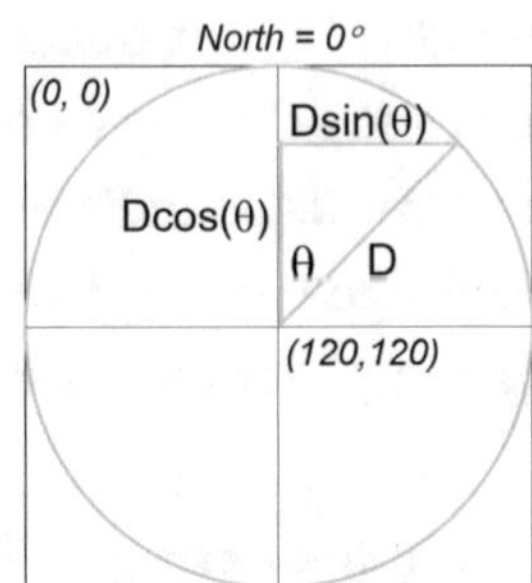

***Figure 4-4.** Calculate the satellite position on a map*

In Listing 4-11, the contour circles, with labels, are drawn, and the NMEA message is read and parsed to satellite elevations, azimuths, and signal strengths. Each satellite distance is calculated, with the satellite position plotted on the map with a green or red marker indicating a tracked- or non-tracked-satellite signal, respectively. The number of satellites, *Nsatell*; number of tracked satellites, *Nsignal*; and range of received signal strengths are displayed. The GPS location is displayed as *YES*, rather than *NO*, when the GPS latitude is greater than zero in the northern hemisphere. For the southern hemisphere, the GPS location is established when the GPS latitude is less than zero, with the `if(lat < 0) str = "YES"` instruction.

The NMEA message components are separated by commas, and the message is parsed with the C++ *strtok* function. In an NMEA message, a double comma indicates a missing record, which is replaced by **,***0,* with the `str.replace("\,\,","\,0\,")` instruction. The combination of a backslash and a comma is interpreted as a comma. The C++ *strtok* function parses a character array, rather than a string, and the NMEA message, *str*, is converted to a character array, *GPS*, with the `str.toCharArray(GPS,str.length())` instruction. Parsed message components are converted to integers or floats with the `atoi` or `atof` function.

Listing 4-11. Map of GPS satellite positions

```
void appSatellite()             // function to display satellite positions
{
  String str;
  char GPS[100];                // NMEA message
  char * pch;
  char * val[20];               // NMEA message values
              // identity, elevation, azimuth, signal and distance arrays
  int id[20], elev[20], azim[20], sgnl[20];
  float dist[20], alpha, lat, lon, spd;
  int Nrec, rec, Nsat, maxVal, strtVal, vals;
  int n, m, minSgnl, maxSgnl, Nsgnl;
  int16_t x, y;
                                // Serial output
  Serial1.begin(GPS_BAUD_RATE, SERIAL_8N1, GPS_RX, GPS_TX);
  tft->fillScreen(TFT_BLACK);
  for (int i=1; i<6; i++)
  {                             // map distance contours
    tft->drawCircle(120, 120, 20*i, TFT_YELLOW);
    tft->setTextSize(1);
    tft->setTextColor(TFT_WHITE, TFT_BLACK);
    tft->setCursor(115, (6-i)*20-10);  // distance labels 21k to 25k
    tft->printf("%dk", 20+i);
  }
  while (!ttgo->getTouch(x, y))        // wait for touch
  {
  while (Serial1.available())          // NMEA message available
  {
  str = Serial1.readStringUntil('\n');
```

```
    if(str.startsWith("$GNGLL"))          // NMEA location message
    {
      str.replace("\,\,","\,0\,");        // replace ,, with ,0,
      str.toCharArray(GPS,str.length());
      Serial.println(GPS);                // $GNGLL,5556.00000,
                                          // N,00311.00000,W
      pch = strtok(GPS, ",");             // parse to first comma
      pch = strtok(NULL, ",");            // parse to second comma
      lat = atof(pch);                    // convert to float
      Serial.printf("lat %9.4f \n", lat);
      str = "NO  ";
      if(lat > 0) str = "YES";            // GPS location established
      tft->drawString("Location " + str, 135, 220, 2);
    }
  if(str.startsWith("$GPGSV"))            // NMEA satellite message
  {
    str.replace("\,\,","\,0\,");          // replace ,, with ,0,
                                          // convert string to char array
    str.toCharArray(GPS,str.length());
    byte index = 0;                       // c++ strtok function
    pch = strtok(GPS, ",");               // parse GPS to first comma
    while (pch != NULL)                   // while parsed data available
    {                                     // equate data to next
      val[index] = pch;                   // array element
      index++;
      pch = strtok(NULL, ",");            // parse to next comma
    }
    Nrec = atoi(val[1]);                  // number of records
    rec = atoi(val[2]);                   // record number
    Nsat = atoi(val[3]);                  // total number of satellites
```

```
maxVal = min(rec*4, Nsat);          // cumulative satellite number
strtVal = (rec-1)*4;                // first satellite number in record
vals = maxVal-strtVal;              // number of satellites in record
for (int i=0; i<vals; i++)
{
  n = strtVal+i;
  id[n] =   atoi(val[4+4*i]);       // identity val[4, 8, 12, 16]
  elev[n] = atoi(val[5+4*i]);       // elevation val[5, 9, 13, 17]
  azim[n] = atoi(val[6+4*i]);       // azimuth val[6, 10, 14, 18]
  sgnl[n] = atoi(val[7+4*i]);       // signal val[7, 11, 15, 19]
                                    // distance in 1000km
  alpha = 6.378*sin(elev[n]*DEG_TO_RAD);
  dist[n] = sqrt(alpha*alpha+2*6.378*20.2+20.2*20.2)-alpha;
}
if(rec == Nrec)                     // finished processing messages
{
  minSgnl = 100;                    // determine minimum and
  maxSgnl = 0;                      // maximum signal strength
  Nsgnl = 0;                        // satellite signal received
  for (int i=0; i<Nsat; i++)
  {                                 // PI/180 = DEG_TO_RAD
    n = round(120.0 +
          (dist[i]-20.0)*20.0*sin(azim[i]*PI/180.0));
    m = round(120.0 -
          (dist[i]-20.0)*20.0*cos(azim[i]*DEG_TO_RAD));
                                    // color code satellites
    if(sgnl[i] > 0) tft->fillCircle(n, m, 4, TFT_GREEN);
    else tft->fillCircle(n, m, 4, TFT_RED);
                                    // satellite identity
    tft->drawString(String(id[i]), n+8, m-8 ,2);
                                    // satellite signals received
```

```
        if(sgnl[i] > 0) Nsgnl++;
                                        // maximum signal
        if(sgnl[i] > maxSgnl) maxSgnl = sgnl[i];
        if(sgnl[i] > 0 && sgnl[i] < minSgnl) minSgnl = sgnl[i];
      }                                 // display summary values
      tft->drawString("Nsatell "+String(Nsat)+" ", 0, 0, 2);
      tft->drawString("Nsignal "+String(Nsgnl)+" ", 0, 20, 2);
      str = String(minSgnl)+" - "+String(maxSgnl) + "  ";
                                        // resolve noise on maxSgnl
      if(str.length() > 9) str = "";
      tft->drawString("Signal " + str, 0, 220, 2);
    }
  }                                     // end of if(str.startsWith("$GPGSV"))
}                                       // end of while (Serial1.available())
}                                       // end of while (!ttgo->getTouch(x, y))
while (ttgo->getTouch(x, y)) {} // wait for touch release
}
```

Bluetooth Communication

The TTGO T-Watch V2 communicates with other Bluetooth devices to receive and transmit messages with Bluetooth communication. The TTGO T-Watch V2 is defined as a Serial Bluetooth device with the name *ESP32 Bluetooth* to which another Bluetooth device, such as an Android tablet or mobile phone, connects.

There are several Bluetooth communication applications to download from *Google Play Store*, and the *Bluetooth Terminal HC-05* app by MightyIT is recommended. Turn on the Bluetooth function of the Android tablet or mobile phone, open the *Bluetooth Terminal HC-05* app, scan for new devices, and pair the mobile device hosting the *Bluetooth Terminal HC-05* app with the ESP32 microcontroller. A message is transmitted by the *Bluetooth Terminal HC-05* app by entering alphanumeric characters in the *Enter ASCII Command* box and clicking *Send ASCII.*

A Bluetooth message received by the TTGO T-Watch V2 is displayed on the touch screen (see Figure 4-5b), with the touch screen cleared after several messages. The TTGO T-Watch V2 transmits a message to the connected Bluetooth device in response to a specified received message. For example, if the received message contains the text "*battery*", then the TTGO T-Watch V2 transmits the battery charge state (see Figure 4-5a).

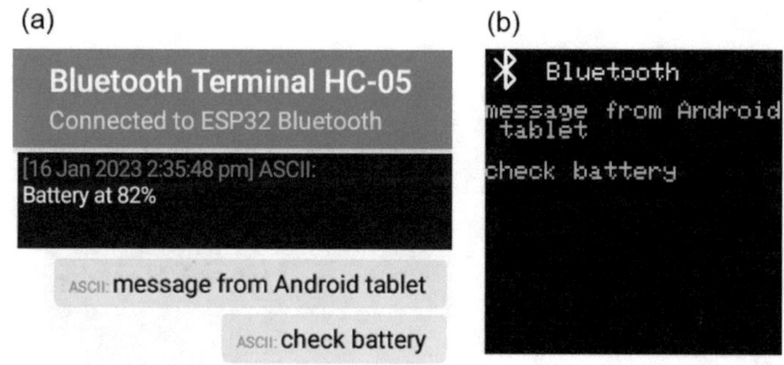

Figure 4-5. *Bluetooth communication*

In Listing 4-12, Serial Bluetooth communicates by transmitting one character at a time with the `write(c)` instruction for a character *c* or the `print(str)` instruction for a string *str*. When comparing the received message to a specific string, the carriage return, *\r*, and new line, *\n*, characters must be included in the comparison. The `while (!ttgo->getTouch(x, y))` instruction essentially provides a loop for handling Bluetooth communication, while the touch screen is not touched. When the touch screen is touched and released, the *appBlue* function returns to the main sketch. Note that the instruction `isChargeing()` is not a typo.

Listing 4-12. Bluetooth communication

```
void appBlue()                             // function to receive and
{                                          // transmit with Bluetooth
  SerialBT.begin("ESP32 Bluetooth");       // initialize Bluetooth
  clrScreen();                             // call clear screen function
  String str;
  int count = 0;
  int16_t x, y;
  while (!ttgo->getTouch(x, y))            // wait for touch
  {
    if(SerialBT.available())               // message received
    {
      str = SerialBT.readString();         // convert message to string
      count++;
      if(count > 5)                        // check if screen full
      {
        count = 0;                         // if so, clear screen
        clrScreen();
      }
      tft->println(str);                // display received message
    }                                   // check for substring in message
    if(str.indexOf("battery") != -1)
    {                                   // isChargeing is not a typo
      if (power->isChargeing()) str = "Battery charging";
      else str = "Battery at "+String(power->getBatt
      Percentage())+"%";
      SerialBT.println(str);            // transmit message
    }
  }
  while (ttgo->getTouch(x, y)) {}       // wait for touch release
}
```

```
void clrScreen()                        // function to clear screen
{
  tft->fillScreen(TFT_BLACK);           // display icon and text
  tft->drawBitmap(0, 0, BTimage, 32, 32, TFT_WHITE);
  tft->setCursor(50, 10);
  tft->setTextColor(TFT_YELLOW);
  tft->print("Bluetooth");
  tft->setTextColor(TFT_GREEN);
  tft->setCursor(0,40);
}
```

Infrared Signaling

Communication with infrared (IR) signals and details of infrared signal protocols or formats are available at `www.sbprojects.net/knowledge/ir/index.php`. In this chapter, communication with infrared signals is illustrated with the Sony protocol, which consists of three signal repeats separated by a pause of 25.2ms. An IR signal consists of a series of *LOW* pulses of multiples of 600μs, separated by *HIGH* pulses of 600μs. For example, the transmitted *START* signal, illustrated in Figure 4-6, begins with a 2400μs *LOW* pulse and ends with a 1200μs *LOW* pulse. A signal is characterized by an array of *LOW* pulses in multiples of 600μs, such as [4, 1,2,1,1, 2,2,1,2, 1,1,1,2], given the intervening *HIGH* pulses of a constant 600μs.

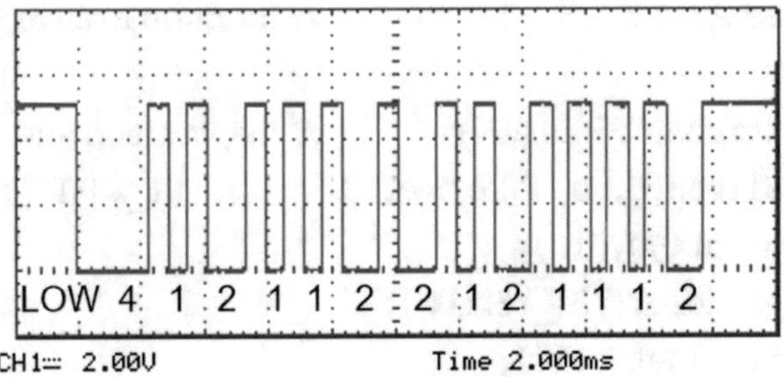

Figure 4-6. *Sony signal*

The signal, excluding the initial pulse, consists of 12 pulses and is represented by a three-character HEX code, each consisting of 4 bits. A binary representation of the transmitted *START* signal in Figure 4-6, excluding the initial pulse, is [0,1,0,0, 1,1,0,1, 0,0,0,1] or *0x4D1* in HEX code with the most significant bit (*MSByte*) first. However, Sony devices interpret IR signals as the least significant bit (*LSByte*) first. The *START* signal, excluding the initial pulse, is interpreted as *LOW* pulses with [2,1,1,1, 2,1,2,2, 1,1,2,1] multiples of 600μs, which has binary representation of [1,0,0,0, 1,0,1,1, 0,0,1,0] or *0x8B2* in HEX code.

Given that a signal from an IR transmitter, such as the TTGO T-Watch, is *MSByte* orientated and the Sony device interprets an IR signal with *LSByte* orientation, then a received IR signal must be converted from *LSByte* orientation to *MSByte* orientation for transmission. For example, a Sony device interprets the received *START* signal in Figure 4-6, excluding the initial pulse, as being represented by 12 bits, [1000 1011 0010], which is equivalent to *0x8B2* in HEX code. The three 4-bit sequences are converted, for transmission, by reversing the order of the three sequences and reversing the bit order of each 4-bit sequence. The converted *START* signal for transmission has binary representation [0100 1101 0001] or *0x4D1* in HEX code. The mapping of the 4-bit sequences of *0x0* to *0xF* is *0x0,0x8,0x 4,0xC,0x2,0xA,0x6,0xE,0x1,0x9, 0x5,0xD,0x3,0xB,0x7* and *0xF*, respectively. The received *START* signal, *0x8B2*, is easily converted to the transmitted signal of *0x4D1*, by mapping *0x2* to *0x4*, *0xB* to *0xD*, and *0x8* to *0x1*.

An IR signal is decoded with the VS1838B IR sensor, and the *IRremote* library by Ken Shirriff is recommended, with the library available in the Arduino IDE. The signal output pin of the VS1838B IR sensor is connected to GPIO 13 of the ESP32 DEVKIT DOIT module, with the VS1838B IR sensor powered by the 5V pin (see Figure 4-7).

Figure 4-7. *IR remote signal detection*

The sketch in Listing 4-13 converts an *LSByte*-orientated received signal to a signal with *MSByte* orientation for transmission. For example, the received *START* signal, *0x8B2,* by a Sony device is allocated to the *val* array as [*0x2, 0xB, 0x8*] by bit shifting the signal bits by 0, 4, or 8 positions and an *AND* operation with *0xF* = *B1111*. The *val* array is then mapped with the *mapv* array to the values of [*0x4, 0xD, 0x1*], which are displayed on the Serial Monitor. In the context of the TTGO T-Watch, the transmitted IR signal of *0x4D1* is received by the Sony device as *0x8B2,* as intended.

Listing 4-13. IR remote signal conversion

```
#include <IRremote.h>                    // include IRremote library
int IRpin = 13;                          // IR receiver pin
int recv, val[3];                        // mapped values
int mapv[] = {0,8,4,12,2,10,6,14,1,9,5,13,3,11,7,15};
```

```
void setup()
{
  Serial.begin(115200);                    // Serial Monitor baud rate
  IrReceiver.begin(IRpin);                 // initialize IR receiver
}

void loop()
{
  if(IrReceiver.decode())                  // IR signal received
  {                                        // IR signal components
    recv = IrReceiver.decodedIRData.decodedRawData;
    for (int i=0; i<3; i++) val[i+1] = (recv >> i*4) & 0xF;
                                           // display mapped values
    Serial.printf("data %X mapped %X%X%X \n",
            recv, mapv[val[1]], mapv[val[2]], mapv[val[3]]);
    delay(200);                            // delay before next IR signal
    IrReceiver.resume();
  }
}
```

The *IRremote* library `sendSony()` and `sendRaw()` instructions both transmit an IR signal to a Sony device, with the *sendRaw()* instruction being the generic method. Device name- or brand-specific instructions are listed in the *IRremote* library file *IRSend.hpp* with details in the corresponding *irBrand.hpp* file.

The `sendSony(code, N, Rep)` instruction transmits a signal with HEX *code* representation, consisting of *N LOW* pulses with the signal repeated *Rep* times. The instruction for the *START* signal package in Figure 4-6 is `sendSony(4D1, 12, 3)`.

The `sendRaw(raw, len, freq)` instruction transmits a signal consisting of a series of *HIGH* and *LOW* pulses, after an initial *LOW* pulse, with a total of *len* pulse lengths and a signal frequency of *freq* kHz, which is generally 38kHz. For example, the series of pulses for the *START* signal in Figure 4-6 is

[2400, 600, 600, 600,1200, 600, 600, 600, 600,

600,1200, 600,1200, 600, 600, 600,1200,

600, 600, 600, 600, 600, 600, 600,1200]μs.

The signal is defined by the *LOW* pulse multiples, such as the `signal[] = {4, 1,2,1,1, 2,2,1,2, 1,1,1,2}` instruction. The raw signal data is generated in Listing 4-14 with the instructions

```
                                        // LOW pulses and constant HIGH pulses
for (int i=0; i<13; i++) raw[2*i] = signal[i]*600;
for (int i=1; i<13; i++) raw[2*i-1] = 600;
```

and the signal is transmitted with the `sendRaw(raw, 25, 38)` instruction.

The sketch in Listing 4-14 transmits infrared signals to a Sony device, with the signals corresponding to buttons pressed on the touch screen. In the example, one row of three buttons is displayed with the signal *0x4D1* transmitted with the `sendSony` or `sendRaw` instruction and the signal *0x1D1* transmitted with the `sendSony` instruction. The two signals correspond to *START* and *STOP* for a particular Sony device. Note that the Sony device interprets the signals as *0x8B2* and *0x8B8*, respectively, as the Sony device interprets the signals as *LSByte* first.

The button layout and converting the touch position to the corresponding signal use the same method as described in the "Screen Brightness" section of this chapter. The `sendSony` instruction includes the number of repeat signal transmissions in a signal package, while the `sendRaw` instruction must be repeated three times with a defined interval between transmissions to generate the signal package.

Listing 4-14. Infrared signaling

```
void appSonyIR()                       // function to transmit infrared signals
{
  irsend.begin();                      // initialize library object
  int row, col, key = 0;
  String button[3] = {"Start", " ON", "Stop"};     // button text
  uint16_t raw[25];                    // array for signal data
                                       // LOW pulses for 0x4D1
  uint16_t signal[] = {4, 1,2,1,1, 2,2,1,2, 1,1,1,2};
  uint16_t pauseTime = 25200;          // interval (μs) between signals
  tft->fillScreen(TFT_BLACK);          // clear screen
  tft->setTextColor(TFT_ORANGE);
  int r = 0;                           // one row in the example
  for (int c=0; c<3; c++)              // draw buttons with text
  {                                    // from button[ ] array
    tft->fillRoundRect(c*80, r*50+35, 75, 45, 6, TFT_DARKCYAN);
    tft->drawString(button[c], c*80+5, r*50+40, 2);
  }
  tft->fillRoundRect(120, 200, 118, 35, 6, TFT_WHITE);
  tft->setTextColor(TFT_BLACK);
  tft->setCursor(155, 210);                 // button to exit function
  tft->print("DONE");
  int16_t x, y;
  while(key < 10)                           // key = 11/12 is "DONE"
  {
    while(!ttgo->getTouch(x, y)) {}         // do nothing waiting for touch
    while (ttgo->getTouch(x, y)) {}         // then wait for touch release
    col = int(x/80) + 1;                    // button in column number COL
    row = int((y-35)/50) + 1;               // button in row number ROW
    key = (row-1)*3+col;                    // button number
```

```
    if(key < 4)
    {                              // signal, bits, repeats
           if(key == 1) irsend.sendSony(0x4D1, 12, 3);
      else if(key == 3) irsend.sendSony(0x1D1, 12, 3);
      else if(key == 2)
      {                            // generate signal raw data LOW pulses
        for (int i=0; i<13; i++) raw[2*i] = signal[i]*600;
                                   // constant HIGH pulses
        for (int i=1; i<13; i++) raw[2*i-1] = 600;
        for (int j=0; j<3; j++)  // transmit 3 signal repeats
        {                          // data, signal length, kHz
          irsend.sendRaw(raw, 25, 38);
          delayMicroseconds(pauseTime);
        }                          // delay between signals
      }
      key = 0;                     // reset key to prevent repeat signals
    }
  }
}
```

Synchronization with the Network Time Protocol

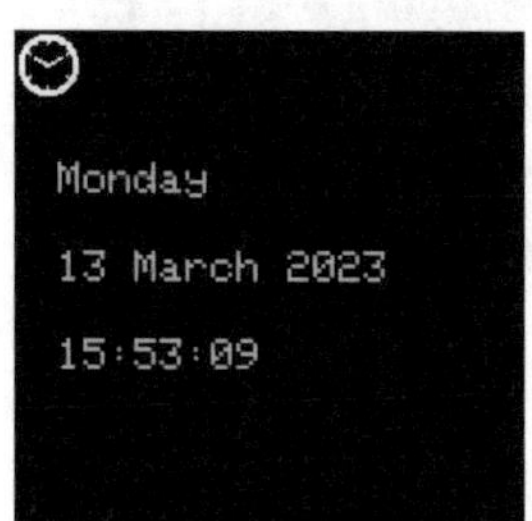

The TTGO T-Watch V2 time is synchronized with the Network Time Protocol (NTP) service using the local server pool as listed on `www.pool.ntp.org`, as the IP address of the local server pool is required in the sketch. For example, the German pool is `de.pool.ntp.org`. The built-in ESP32 microcontroller *configTime* function returns, in a structure, the time information accounting for the time zone and daylight saving time. The *configTime* function and the associated *getLocalTime* function are included in the *User\AppData\Local\Arduino15\packages\esp32\hardware\esp32\version\cores\esp32\esp32-hal-time* file. The NTP time structure format is defined at `www.cplusplus.com/reference/ctime/tm/` with the component labels defined at `www.cplusplus.com/reference/ctime/strftime/`. The time components are also accessed as `tnow.tm_parameter`, where *parameter* is equal to `year`, `mon`, `mday`, `hour`, `min`, or `sec`, as in Listing 4-15.

In Listing 4-15, a connection to the Wi-Fi network is established with the *WiFiconnect* function. If no connection is made during a five-second period, then control is returned to the main sketch. Once connected, the actual NTP time is displayed for five seconds, and then the TTGO T-Watch V2 is synchronized with the NTP time. The NTP time information is stored in a structure with labels `%A, %B %d %Y %H:%M:%S` for day of week, month, day, year, hour, minute, and second, respectively. The TTGO T-Watch V2 time is set by the *RTC* library `setDateTime` instruction, with the month number increased by one. Accessing the NTP time is described in Chapter 15, "Libraries."

Listing 4-15. Synchronization with the Network Time Protocol

```
void appWwwTime()                            // function to synchronize
{                                            // time with NTP
  int GMT = 0;                               // non-GMT adjustment (secs)
  int daylight = 3600;                       // daylight saving time (secs)
  tft->fillScreen(TFT_BLACK);                // clear screen
                                             // draw image
  tft->drawBitmap(0, 0, clockImage, 32, 32, TFT_WHITE);
  tft->setCursor(50, 10);
  tft->print("connecting");
  int wifiOK = WiFiconnect();                // connect to Wi-Fi network
  if(wifiOK == 0) return;                    // exit if no connection
                                             // built-in esp32 function
  configTime(GMT, daylight, "uk.pool.ntp.org");
  struct tm tnow;                            // NTP data as structure
```

```
  if (!getLocalTime(&tnow))
     tft->drawString("Error with time", 5, 30, 1);
  else
  {
    tft->fillRect(50, 10, 210, 110, TFT_BLACK);
    tft->setCursor(50, 10);
    tft->print("connected");
    for (int i=0; i<5; i++)           // display time for five seconds
    {
      tft->fillScreen(TFT_BLACK);
      tft->drawBitmap(0, 0, clockImage, 32, 32, TFT_WHITE);
      getLocalTime(&tnow);             // time from NTP
      tft->setCursor(20, 60);
      tft->print(&tnow, "%A \n");      // day of week
      tft->setCursor(20, 100);
      tft->print(&tnow, "%d %B %Y \n"); // date month year
      tft->setCursor(20, 140);
      tft->print(&tnow, "%H:%M:%S \n"); // hour : minute : second
      delay(1000);
    }                                  // set watch time to NTP time
    ttgo->rtc->setDateTime(tnow.tm_year, tnow.tm_mon + 1,
       tnow.tm_mday, tnow.tm_hour, tnow.tm_min, tnow.tm_sec);
  }
  WiFi.disconnect(true);         // disconnect Wi-Fi
  WiFi.mode(WIFI_OFF);
}

int WiFiconnect()                // function to connect to Wi-Fi network
{
  int wifiOK = 1;                // initial Wi-Fi connection indicator
  int count = 0;
```

```
  tft->setCursor(50, 120);
  WiFi.begin(ssid, password); // connect and initialize Wi-Fi
  while (WiFi.status() != WL_CONNECTED && wifiOK == 1)
  {
    delay(500);
    count++;                    // number of connection attempts
    tft->print(".");
    if(count > 9)               // attempted connection > 5 sec
    {
      tft->setCursor(50, 160);
      tft->print("no connection");
      delay(1000);              // time for user to read message
      WiFi.disconnect(true);    // disconnect Wi-Fi
      WiFi.mode(WIFI_OFF);
      wifiOK = 0;           // update Wi-Fi connection indicator
    }
  }
  return wifiOK;            // pass variable to appWwwTime function
}
```

If a Wi-Fi network connection is not available, the TTGO T-Watch V2 time would be set manually. The hours and minutes would be entered, using a button layout similar to the *appTimer* function in the "Timer" section of this chapter, and combined with the existing RTC values for year, month, and day. For example, if the variables *hh* and *mm* represent the user-entered hours and minutes, then the instructions to manually set the TTGO T-Watch V2 time are

```
RTC_Date mTime = ttgo->rtc->getDateTime()
ttgo->rtc->setDateTime(mTime.year, mTime.month, mTime.day, hh, mm, 0)
```

assuming that the day, month, and year currently used by the RTC are unchanged.

Source *OpenWeatherMap* API Data

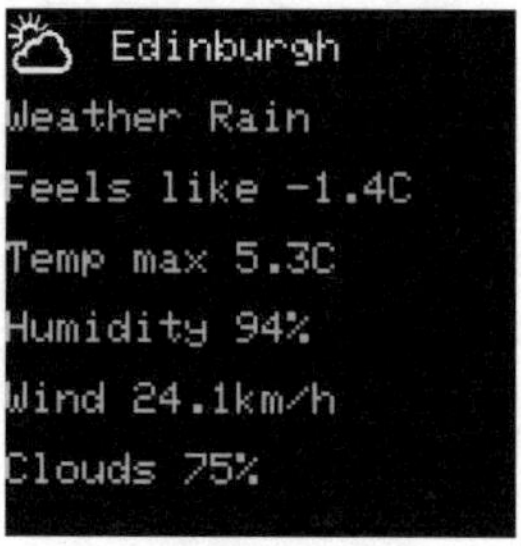

Weather information from the `OpenWeatherMap.org` is free to access within limits defined on the website. The *OpenWeatherMap* data requires a username, a password, an API (Application Programming Interface) key, and the city identity (ID) code. Details on opening an account and obtaining an API key for *OpenWeatherMap* are available at `openweathermap.org/appid`. The API key identifies the client to the web server. The city ID is obtained, from the `OpenWeatherMap.org` website, by entering the city name in the *Your city name* search box. Select the relevant city, and the city ID is the number at the end of the URL. For example, the Edinburgh URL is `openweathermap.org/city/2650225`. The URL to provide weather data in JSON format is `api.openweathermap.org/data/2.5/weather?id=cityID&units=metric&appid=APIkey`. When the web page is loaded, click the JSON header to display the JSON-formatted weather data.

The JSON-formatted data is allocated to a string containing the name:value pairs and is deserialized to a JSON document, with variables mapped to *values* associated with the *names* in the JSON document. For example, the JSON-formatted data *{"var1":"sunny", "var2":21.3, "var3":50}* contains three name and value pairs consisting of a string, a real number, and an integer. The JSON-formatted data is deserialized to a JSON document, and three variables are mapped to the *values* "sunny", 21.3, and 50. The corresponding instructions are

```
                                    // JSON formatted data
String data ={"var1":"sunny", "var2":21.3, "var3":50}
DynamicJsonDocument doc(1024)       // JSON document
deserializeJson(doc, data)          // deserialize JSON formatted data
```

```
String weather = doc["var1"]
float temp = doc["var2"]           // map variables to JSON document
int humidity = doc["var3"]
```

A filter is applied to the deserialization when a subset of the JSON-formatted data is required, which reduces the ESP32 microcontroller memory requirement. A second JSON document defines the filtered JSON-formatted data. For example, the instructions to filter the JSON data to only *var2* and *var3* are

```
StaticJsonDocument <200> filter   // JSON document with filter
filter ["var2"] = 1               // filter applied to var2 and var3
filter ["var3"] = 1
deserializeJson(doc, data, DeserializationOption::Filter(filter));
```

Note that the JSON documents containing the deserialized JSON-formatted data and the filter are defined as `DynamicJsonDocument` and `StaticJsonDocument` with the memory requirements formatted as `(N)` and `<N>`, respectively.

In Listing 4-16, a filter is applied to the JSON document to provide a subset of the *OpenWeatherMap* data, with values displayed on the TTGO T-Watch V2 touch screen.

The hierarchical format of the JSON data is required to both create the JSON data filter and deserialize the JSON data. For example, the "*feels like*" temperature is located at *["main"]["feels_like"]* and is included in the data filter with the `filter["main"]["feels_like"] = 1` instruction and is mapped to the variable *feels* with the `float feels = doc["main"]["feels_like"]` instruction.

A connection to the Wi-Fi network is established with the *WiFiconnect* function, which is described in the "Synchronization with the Network Time Protocol" section of this chapter. The *OpenWeatherMap* data is obtained by an HTTP request with the URL passed to the *http* function.

While the touch screen is untouched or touched, nothing happens, due to the sequential `while(!ttgo->getTouch(x, y)) {}` and `while (ttgo->getTouch(x, y)) {}` instructions. When the touch screen is released, the function returns to the main sketch.

Listing 4-16. Source OpenWeatherMap API data

```
void appWeather()          // function to display local weather information
{
  tft->fillScreen(TFT_BLACK);          // draw icon
  tft->drawBitmap(0, 0, weatherImage, 32, 32, TFT_WHITE);
  tft->setCursor(50, 10);
  tft->print("connecting");
  int wifiOK = WiFiconnect();          // defined on appWwwTime tab
  if(wifiOK == 0) return;              // no Wi-Fi connection
  String URL =
      "http://api.openweathermap.org/data/2.5/weather?";
                                       // URL with city code in bold
  URL = URL + "id=2650225&units=metric&appid=";
  URL = URL + APIkey;                  // include APIkey in URL
  String data = http(URL);             // source OpenWeatherMap data
  DynamicJsonDocument doc(1024);       // JSON document
  StaticJsonDocument<200> filter;      // filter for JSON data
  filter["weather"][0]["main"] = 1;
  filter["main"]["feels_like"] = 1;
  filter["main"]["temp_max"] = 1;      // define subset of JSON data
  filter["main"]["humidity"] = 1;
  filter["wind"]["speed"] = 1;
  filter["clouds"]["all"] = 1;
  filter["name"] = 1;                  // deserialize filtered JSON data
  deserializeJson
      (doc, data, DeserializationOption::Filter(filter));
```

```
  String main = doc["weather"][0]["main"];
  float feels = doc["main"]["feels_like"];
  float temp = doc["main"]["temp_max"];          // update variables
  float humidity = doc["main"]["humidity"];
  float wind = doc["wind"]["speed"];
  float clouds = doc["clouds"]["all"];
  String city = doc["name"];

  tft->fillScreen(TFT_BLACK);
  tft->drawBitmap(0, 0, weatherImage, 32, 32, TFT_WHITE);
  tft->setTextColor(TFT_YELLOW);
  tft->setCursor(50, 10);
  tft->printf("%s \n\n ", city);                  // display variables
  tft->setTextColor(TFT_GREEN);
  tft->printf("Weather %s \n\n ", main);
  tft->printf("Feels like %.1fC \n\n ", feels);
  tft->printf("Temp max %.1fC \n\n ", temp);
  tft->printf("Humidity %.0f%% \n\n ", humidity);
  float kmh = 3.6 * wind;                        // convert m/s to km/h
  tft->printf("Wind %.1fkm/h \n\n ", kmh);
  tft->printf("Clouds %.0f%% \n", clouds);

  WiFi.disconnect(true);
  WiFi.mode(WIFI_OFF);
  int16_t x, y;
  while(!ttgo->getTouch(x, y)) {}    // do nothing waiting for touch
  while (ttgo->getTouch(x, y)) {}    // then wait for touch release
}

String http(String URL)
{                       // function to source OpenWeatherMap data from URL
  HTTPClient http;                   // associate http with library
  http.begin(URL);                   // OpenWeatherMap URL
```

```
  http.GET();                        // HTTP request
  String data = http.getString();
  http.end();
  return data;                       // return data to function
}
```

Step Counter and Distance Measure

A step counter is based on the BMA423 three-axis accelerometer. The step count function is tested by raising the TTGO-T-Watch V2 to an angle of 15° and then to horizontal. The accelerometer section of Listing 4-17 is derived from the example sketch *File ➤ Examples ➤ TTGO TWatch Library ➤ BasicUnit ➤ BMA423_StepCount*. When the accelerometer interrupt is triggered, the *printStep* function is called to display the updated step count and distance walked.

The TTGO-T-Watch V2 GPS obtains the current location every second, but, in the sketch, the distance between the current and previous locations is measured at 15s intervals to reduce the measurement noise, rather than determining the distance every second. The start position is defined by the latitude and longitude when the GPS location is first updated. The application is aimed at a pedestrian, rather than a cyclist (see Listing 4-10), with the number of steps and distance being the focus of the display. A minimum distance of 8m during a 15s period is based on half the walking speed of 3.6km/h or 1m/s. The cumulative sum of the distances provides the total distance walked, which is displayed by the *printStep* function along with the number of tracked GPS satellites.

The total number of steps is stored in the accelerometer register, which is accessed with the `getCounter()` instruction. In contrast, the total distance walked and the previous location latitude and longitude variables are generated in the *appStep* function. When a function is called, variables defined in the function are set to default values, which are generally zero. The total distance walked and the previous location latitude and longitude variables are defined as *static*, to prevent resetting of the variables when the *appStep* function is called by the main sketch.

When the *RESET* button on the touch screen is pressed, the step counter and distance variables are reset to zero. The instruction to reset the step counter is, unsurprisingly, `resetStepCounter()`.

Listing 4-17. Step counter and distance measure

```
void appStep()                             // function for step counter
{                                          // and distance measure
  Acfg cfg;                                // accel parameter structure
  cfg.odr = BMA4_OUTPUT_DATA_RATE_100HZ;   // output data rate in Hz
  cfg.range = BMA4_ACCEL_RANGE_2G;         // gravity (g) range
                                           // bandwidth parameter
  cfg.bandwidth = BMA4_ACCEL_NORMAL_AVG4;
  cfg.perf_mode = BMA4_CONTINUOUS_MODE;    // performance mode
  bma->accelConfig(cfg);                   // configure accelerometer
  bma->enableAccel();                      // enable accelerometer
                                           // enable step count feature
  bma->enableFeature(BMA423_STEP_CNTR, true);
  bma->enableStepCountInterrupt();         // turn on step count interrupt
  int startFlag = 0;
  unsigned long lastGPS;
  static double lastLat, lastLon;          // retain last position
  static float distTotal;                  // retain total distance
  float dist;
  tft->fillScreen(TFT_BLACK);              // clear screen, draw icon
  tft->drawBitmap(0, 0, stepImage, 32, 32, TFT_WHITE);
  tft->setCursor(40, 20);
  tft->setTextColor(TFT_YELLOW);
```

```
tft->print("Step counter");
printStep(distTotal);           // display steps, distance & satellites
tft->fillRoundRect(120, 200, 118, 35, 6, TFT_WHITE);
tft->setTextColor(TFT_BLACK);
tft->setCursor(155, 210);
tft->print("RESET");

int16_t x, y;
while (!ttgo->getTouch(x, y))   // functions as a loop
{
  if (irq)                      // accelerometer interrupt triggered
  {
    irq = 0;                    // reset accelerometer interrupt
                                // wait for interrupt to reset
    while(bma->readInterrupt() != 1) {}
                                // if step counter set,
    if(bma->isStepCounter()) printStep(distTotal);
  }                             // update display
  ttgo->gpsHandler();           // handle GPS signals
  if(gps->location.isUpdated()) // updated location
  {
    if(startFlag == 1)          // start position already defined
    {                           // distance to previous position
      dist = TinyGPSPlus::distanceBetween(
                gps->location.lat(), gps->location.lng(),
                lastLat, lastLong);
      if((millis() - lastGPS > 15000) && dist > 8)
      {                         // minimum interval and distance
        lastGPS = millis();     // update timer
        distTotal = distTotal + dist;      // cumulative distance
        lastLat = gps->location.lat();     // update latitude
        lastLon = gps->location.lng();     // and longitude
```

```
        }
      }
      else if(startFlag == 0)          // GPS updated at
      {                                // start position
        startFlag = 1;
        lastLat = gps->location.lat();
        lastLon = gps->location.lng();
      }
    }
  }
  while (ttgo->getTouch(x, y)) {}      // wait for touch release
  if(x>155 && y>210)                   // reset button pressed
  {
    bma->resetStepCounter();           // reset steps and distance
    totalDist = 0;
    printStep(totalDist);              // display reset values
    delay(1000);                       // time for user to read update
  }
}

void printStep(float distVal)          // function to display steps,
{                                      // distance & satellites
  uint32_t step = bma->getCounter(); // get step data from register
  tft->setTextColor(TFT_GREEN);
  tft->fillRect(40, 70, 180, 100, TFT_BLACK);
  tft->setCursor(40, 70);
  tft->printf("Steps %d \n", step);  // display steps, distance
  tft->setCursor(40, 110);             // and satellite number
  tft->print("Distance ");tft->print(round(distVal), 0);
  tft->setCursor(40, 150);
  tft->printf("Satellites %d \n", gps->satellites.value());
}
```

Timer

A watch requires a count-up and count-down timer with the count-down timer utilizing the TTGO T-Watch V2 vibration motor driver to alert the user when the countdown is completed. The vibration motor driver accesses the *Adafruit_DRV2605* library, which is included in the *TTGO_TWatch_Library*, to play waveform patterns. Details of the 123 waveform patterns are available in the DRV2605 driver datasheet Table 11-2 at `ti.com/product/DRV2605`. A sequence of waveform patterns is generated by a series of `setWaveform(N, p)` instructions, loading waveform pattern *p* in position *N* of the series, starting at zero. The `setWaveform(N, 0)` instruction identifies the end of the series, and the `go()` instruction activates the vibration motor to play the series of waveforms. The example sketch *File* ➤ *Examples* ➤ *TTGO TWatch Library* ➤ *BasicUnit* ➤ *TwatcV2Special* ➤ *DRV2605_Basic* plays all 123 waveform patterns. Listing 4-18 plays waveform pattern 70, which is described in the datasheet as "*Transition ramp down long smooth 1 - 100 to 0%*".

The sketch in Listing 4-18 displays the time *00:00*, with one digit highlighted in yellow, and buttons labeled zero to nine. When a button is pressed on the touch screen, the highlighted digit changes to the button value, and the next digit is highlighted. After the *DONE* button is pressed, the timer counts down from the displayed time, and when the countdown is complete, the vibration motor is activated. Note that the variable *s*, for seconds, is defined as an integer, `int`, rather than an unsigned integer, `uint8_t`, as in the count-down timer, the variable sequence is *2, 1, 0, −1* before changing to *59, 58, 57….* When the *DONE* button is pressed and the displayed time is *00:00*, the count-up timer is started. The *TFT_eSPI* library `drawString(str, x, y, 7)` instruction displays the string *str* with digits formatted as a 7-segment display effect.

Listing 4-18. Timer sketch

```
void appTimer()
{                                             // minutes and seconds
  String ms, mmss[] = {"0", "0", ":", "0", "0"};
  unsigned long last = 0;
  int s, m, count;
  int row, col, key = 0, pos = 0;
  tft->fillScreen(TFT_BLACK);
  printTime(pos, mmss);                       // display timer time
  tft->setTextColor(TFT_ORANGE);
  for (int r=0; r<3; r++)                     // draw buttons with numbers
  {                                           // 1 2 3
    for (int c=0; c<3; c++)                   // 4 5 6
    {                                         // 7 8 9
      tft->fillRoundRect(c*80, r*50+35, 75, 45, 6,
                         TFT_DARKCYAN);
      tft->drawNumber(r*3+c+1, c*80+30, r*50+40, 2);
    }
  }
  tft->fillRoundRect(0, 185, 75, 45, 6, TFT_DARKCYAN);
  tft->drawNumber(0, 30, 192, 2);             // button with zero
  tft->fillRoundRect(120, 200, 118, 35, 6, TFT_WHITE);
  tft->setTextColor(TFT_BLACK);
  tft->setCursor(155, 210);                   // draw button to exit function
  tft->print("DONE");
  int16_t x, y;
  while(key < 11)                             // key = 11/12 is DONE
  {
    while(!ttgo->getTouch(x, y)) {}   // do nothing waiting for touch
    while (ttgo->getTouch(x, y)) {}   // then wait for touch release
```

```
    col = int(x/80) + 1;              // button in column number COL
    row = int((y-35)/50) + 1;         // button in row number ROW
    key = (row-1)*3+col;              // number on pressed button
    if(key == 10) key = 0;
    if(key < 11) mmss[pos] = key;     // position of digit in mm:ss
    pos++;                            // move to next position
    if(pos > 4) pos = 0;              // return to first position
    if(pos == 2) pos++;               // pos(2) is the colon on mm:ss
    printTime(pos, mmss);
  }                                   // minutes and seconds
  m = 10*mmss[0].toInt() + mmss[1].toInt();
  s = 10*mmss[3].toInt() + mmss[4].toInt();
  if(m+s == 0) count = 1;             // time set to zero so count up
  else count = -1;                    // otherwise count down
  tft->fillScreen(TFT_BLACK);         // clear screen
  tft->fillRoundRect(120, 200, 118, 35, 6, TFT_WHITE);
  tft->setTextColor(TFT_BLACK);
  tft->setCursor(145, 210);
  tft->print("FINISH");               // draw button to exit function
  tft->setTextColor(TFT_WHITE, TFT_BLACK);
  tft->setTextSize(1);                // need text size 1 for font 7
  while (!ttgo->getTouch(x, y))       // wait for touch
  {
    if(millis() - last > 1000)        // update timer every second
    {
      last = millis();
      ms = String(m) +":";            // display time mm:ss
      if(m < 10) ms = "0" + ms;       // include leading zeros
      if(s < 10) ms = ms + "0" + String(s);
```

```
      else ms = ms + String(s);
      tft->drawString(ms, 50, 50, 7); // font 7 for display of digits
      s = s+count;                    // update seconds
      if(s > 59)                      // minutes increased
      {
        s = 0;                        // seconds to zero
        m = m+1;                      // increment minutes
      }
      if(s < 0)                       // minutes decreased
      {
        s = 59;                       // seconds to 59
        m = m-1;                      // decrement minutes
      }
      if(m < 0)                       // timer reached 00:00
      {
        drv->selectLibrary(1);        // activate vibration motor
                                      // internal trigger mode
        drv->setMode(DRV2605_MODE_INTTRIG);
        drv->setWaveform(0, 70);      // vibrat. pattern 70 in
                                      // position 0
        drv->setWaveform(1, 0);       // end of waveforms
        drv->go();                    // activate vibration motor
        m = 0;
        s = 0;
                                  // stay in loop until screen pressed
      }
    }
  }
  while (ttgo->getTouch(x, y)) {}     // wait for touch release
}
```

```
                                      // function to display time (mm:ss)
void printTime(int pos, String timeMS[5])
{
  tft->setCursor(85, 2);
  tft->setTextSize(3);               // increase text size to 3
  for (int i=0; i<5; i++)            // display mm:ss
  {                                  // colors to overwrite previous values
    tft->setTextColor(TFT_WHITE, TFT_BLACK);
    if(i == pos) tft->setTextColor(TFT_YELLOW, TFT_BLACK);
    tft->print(timeMS[i]);
  }
  tft->setTextSize(2);               // reset to text size 2
}
```

Battery Voltage and Microcontroller Temperature

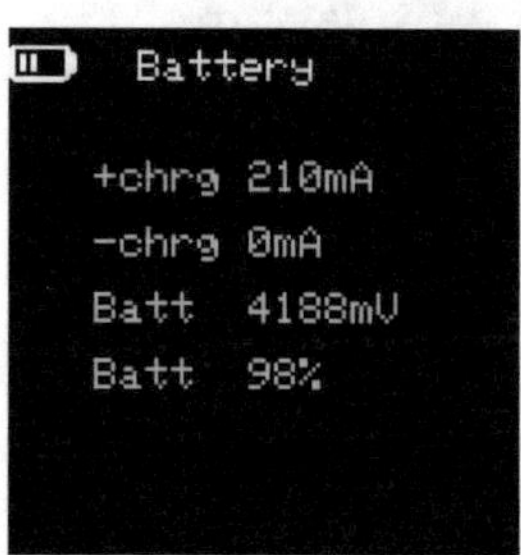

Battery voltage and the charging or discharging current are obtained with the AXP202 power management unit instructions power->getBattChargeCurrent(), getBattDischargeCurrent(), getBattVoltage(), and getBattPercentage(), as used in Listing 4-19. An AXP202 power management unit instruction, power->getTemp(), also provides the ESP32 microcontroller temperature (see Listing 4-20).

Listing 4-19. Battery charge sketch

```
void appBattery()                          // function to display battery
{                                          // voltage and current
  tft->fillScreen(TFT_BLACK);
  tft->drawBitmap(0, 0, batteryImage, 32, 32, TFT_WHITE);
  tft->setTextColor(TFT_YELLOW);
  tft->setCursor(60, 10);
  tft->print("Battery");
  tft->setTextColor(TFT_GREEN);
  unsigned long last = 0;
  int16_t x, y;
  while (!ttgo->getTouch(x, y))            // wait for touch
  {
    if(millis() - last > 5000)             // display every 5 seconds
    {
      last = millis();                     // update display time
                                           // charging current
      float chrg_p = power->getBattChargeCurrent();
                                           // discharging current
      float chrg_n = power->getBattDischargeCurrent();
                                           // battery voltage
      float batt_v = power->getBattVoltage();
      int   batt_p = power->getBattPercentage();       // battery %
      tft->fillRect(40, 60, 180, 120, TFT_BLACK);
      tft->setCursor(40, 60);
      tft->printf("+chrg %.0fmA \n", chrg_p);
      tft->setCursor(40, 90);
                                           // display battery state
      tft->printf("-chrg %.0fmA \n", chrg_n);
```

```
      tft->setCursor(40, 120);
      tft->printf("Batt  %0.fmV \n", batt_v);
      tft->setCursor(40, 150);
      tft->printf("Batt  %d%% \n", batt_p);
    }                                        // double %% displays %
  }                                          // wait for touch release
  while (ttgo->getTouch(x, y)) {}
}
```

In Listing 4-20, a color image is derived from a .PNG file, which requires the `setSwapBytes(true)` instruction, but the instruction is not required when drawing a bitmap image on the touch screen. Image formats, such as TIFF and PNG (Portable Network Graphics), store image data in most significant byte (*MSByte*) order, while the microcontroller stores and interprets data in least significant byte *(LSByte*) order. For example, the 32-bit or 4-byte integer *0x0A0B0C0D,* in HEX format, is stored as four 8-bit or 1-byte integers in four sequential memory byte locations as either *0x0A, 0x0B, 0x0C,* and *0x0D,* which is *MSByte* order, or as *0x0D, 0x0C, 0x0B,* and *0x0A,* which is *LSByte* order. Arithmetic operations of addition and multiplication are marginally simpler with *LSByte* order, as the operation starts with the least significant byte.

The terms *big-endian* and *little-endian,* suggested by Danny Cohen in the context of computer science, reflect the data ordering of *MSByte* and *LSByte.* In Jonathan Swift's book *Gulliver's Travels,* Lilliputians break a boiled-egg shell from the big end or from the little end and are called *Big-Endians* or *Little-Endians,* accordingly.

Listing 4-20. Microcontroller temperature sketch

```
void appTemp()                        // function to display
{                                     // IC temperature
    float temp = power->getTemp();    // get microcontroller temperature
    tft->fillScreen(TFT_BLACK);       // clear screen
    tft->setSwapBytes(true);          // required to retain image color
                                  // display color image as background
    tft->pushImage(30, 0, 183, 240, image565);
    tft->setTextColor(TFT_YELLOW, TFT_BLACK);
    tft->setCursor(60, 195);
                                      // display temperature
    tft->printf("Temp: %.1f \n", temp);

  int16_t x, y;
  while(!ttgo->getTouch(x, y)) {}     // do nothing waiting for touch
  while (ttgo->getTouch(x, y)) {}     // then wait for touch release
}
```

Data Storage on a Micro-SD Card

The TTGO-T-Watch V2 includes a TF (TransFlash) or micro-SD card reader/writer for accessing or storing data. Two examples of writing data to a micro-SD card are storage of the microcontroller temperature and battery discharge current over a range of screen brightness levels and storing GPS position and altitude data while walking or cycling a route.

The existence of a *filename* file on the micro-SD card is detected with the `if(SD.exists(filename)` instruction. If the *filename* file does not exist, the `SD.open(filename, FILE_WRITE)` instruction creates a new *filename* file. If the *filename* file already exists, the file is appended with the `SD.open(filename, FILE_APPEND)` instruction. The option to update an existing *filename* file or create a new file is obtained with the instructions

```
if(SD.exists(filename)) file = SD.open(filename, FILE_APPEND)
else file = SD.open(filename, FILE_WRITE)
```

An existing *filename* file is deleted with the `SD.remove(filename)` instruction.

Temperature, Current, and Screen Brightness

Figure 4-8 illustrates the increase in microcontroller temperature, due to the heat produced by the backlight, and battery discharge current with increasing touch screen brightness. Given the battery capacity of 380mA, a low screen brightness is recommended.

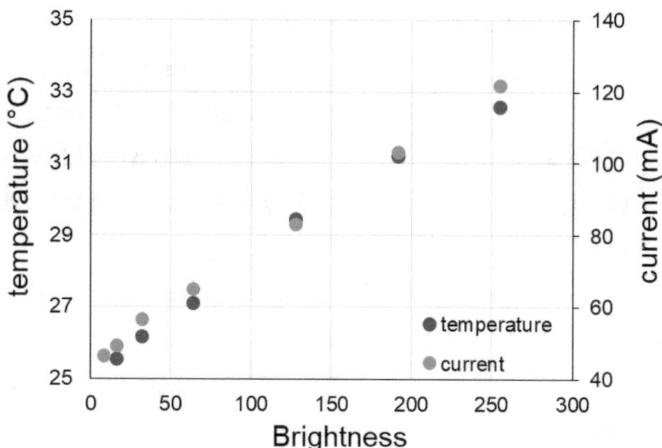

Figure 4-8. *Microcontroller temperature, battery discharge current, and screen brightness*

The instructions to detect and write data to a file on a micro-SD card are independent of the data, so the data recording section of Listing 4-21 is a separate function, *collectData*. In the first section of the sketch, the TTGO T-Watch V2 is formatted with the instructions from Listing 4-1. In the *setup* function, the micro-SD card is detected, SPI communication with the micro-SD card is initialized, and a new file is created. The file name and data header are defined in the first section of the sketch. In the *loop* function, the *collectData* function is repeatedly called, over a range of LCD screen brightness levels, and the returned string containing the collected data, *text*, is written to the file on the micro-SD card.

The *collectData* function returns a string, so the function is defined as a `String` rather than `void`. The *collectData* function collects the LCD screen brightness level, microcontroller temperature, battery discharge current, and data record number, which are displayed on the TTGO T-Watch V2 LCD screen and converted to a string.

Listing 4-21. Data storage on a micro-SD card sketch

```
#define LILYGO_WATCH_2020_V2
#include <LilyGoWatch.h>
#include <SD.h>                         // include SD library
File file;                              // associate file with SD library
SPIClass hspi(HSPI);                    // SD card uses HSPI
TTGOClass * ttgo;                       // associate objects with libraries
TFT_eSPI * tft;
AXP20X_Class * power;                   // required to access temperature
int count = 0, SDcard = 0;
                                        // file name on SD card
String text, filename= "/temp.txt";
                                        // data header
```

```
String header = "count, bright, temp, discharge";
                                        // brightness levels
int levels[] = {8, 16, 32, 64, 128, 192, 255};

void setup()
{
  ttgo = TTGOClass::getWatch();
  ttgo->begin();                        // initialize ttgo object
  ttgo->openBL();                       // turn on backlight
  tft = ttgo->tft;                      // shorthand for library objects
  power = ttgo->power;
                                        // ADC for battery current
  power->adc1Enable(AXP202_BATT_CUR_ADC1, true);
  tft->fillScreen(TFT_BLACK);
  tft->setTextColor(TFT_WHITE);
  tft->setCursor(0,0);
  tft->setTextSize(2);
                                        // connect micro-SD card
  hspi.begin(SD_SCLK, SD_MISO, SD_MOSI, SD_CS);
  if(!SD.begin(SD_CS, hspi)) tft->print("no SD card");
  else                                  // check for presence of SD card
  {
    SDcard = 1;                         // micro-SD card detected
    tft->print("SD card OK");
    file = SD.open(filename, FILE_WRITE);         // open new file
    file.print(header);                 // write column header to SD card
    file.println();                     // and new line character
    file.close();                       // close file after writing
  }
  delay(1000);                          // time for user to read message
}
```

```
void loop()
{
  for (int i=0; i<7; i++)            // different brightness levels
  {                                  // change brightness
    ttgo->setBrightness(levels[i]);
    for (int j=0; j<100; j++)        // 100 measurements per level
    {
      collectData(levels[i]);
      if(SDcard == 1)
      {
        file = SD.open(filename, FILE_APPEND);
        file.print(text);            // append string to file
        file.println();              // and new line character
        file.close();
      }
    }
    delay(10000);                    // 10s interval between levels
  }
  tft->fillScreen(TFT_BLACK);
  tft->setCursor(0, 40);
  tft->printf("data complete");
  while(1) {}                        // do nothing
}

String collectData(int level)
{
  float temp, chrg_n;
  temp = power->getTemp();           // microcontroller temperature
                                     // battery discharge current
  chrg_n = power->getBattDischargeCurrent();
  count++;
  tft->fillScreen(TFT_BLACK);
```

```
  tft->setCursor(40, 40);
  tft->printf("Bright %d \n", level);
  tft->setCursor(40, 70);
  tft->printf("Temp   %.1f \n", temp);      // display values
  tft->setCursor(40, 100);
  tft->printf("chrg-  %.0fmA \n", chrg_n);
  tft->setCursor(40, 130);
  tft->printf("count  %d \n", count);
  text = String(count)+","+String(level); // convert data to a string
  text = text +","+String(temp,1) +","+String(chrg_n,0);
  return text;
}
```

GPS Tracking Data

In the second example, GPS data is collected on the position (latitude and longitude) and altitude, during a walking or cycling route, and stored on the micro-SD card with a data record number. The GPS data is subsequently displayed using *GPS Visualizer*, developed by Adam Schneider. The GPS data file is uploaded from the micro-SD card to `www.gpsvisualizer.com`. Select *Choose an output format*, select *Google Maps*, and click *Map it*. At the top right of the map, there is a dropdown box for map types, and the *OSM (TF landscape)* option is shown in Figure 4-9. Route elevations are displayed by selecting *Look up elevations* from the menu at the top of the *GPS Visualizer* home page. Upload the GPS data file and select *Draw elevation profile*.

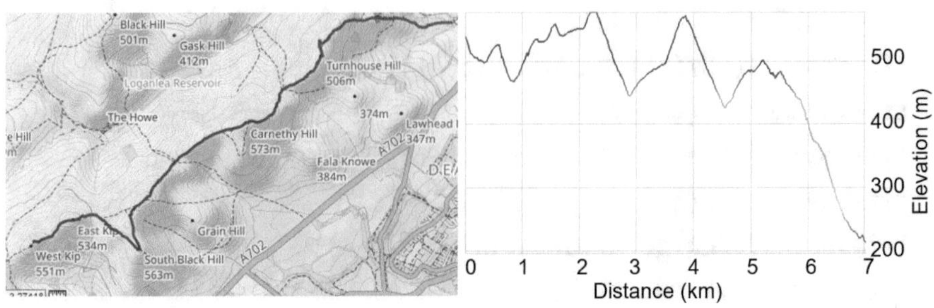

Figure 4-9. *Route map from GNSS data*

The sketch is a combination of Listing 4-21 to store data on a micro-SD card and Listing 4-9 to obtain GPS tracking data. The first section of the sketch is identical to that of Listing 4-21 with addition of the following instructions to load the *TinyGPS* library and define GPS position variables:

```
TinyGPSPlus *gps
unsigned long lastTime = 0, lastBatt = 0
double startLat, startLong, lastLat, lastLong, totalDist = 0
int startFlag = 0
```

In the *setup* function, the following instructions are included to define the screen brightness, measure battery voltage, and initialize the GPS:

```
ttgo->bl->adjust(48)          // set screen brightness
power->adc1Enable(AXP202_BATT_CUR_ADC1 | AXP202_BATT_VOL_ADC1, 1)
ttgo->trunOnGPS()             // trunOnGPS is not a typo
ttgo->gps_begin()             // initialize GPS
gps = ttgo->gps               // shorthand for library object
```

The *loop* and *collectData* functions are shown in Listing 4-22. The first detected GPS position is defined as the start position, and the updated GPS position and altitude data is written to the micro-SD card every 15 seconds. The battery voltage percentage is displayed every two minutes, and a fully charged battery powers the TTGO T-Watch V2 for 90 minutes.

In the *collectData* function, distances from the previous and start positions are displayed. The total distance is incremented, with the constraint that the distance covered is greater than 5m to reduce GPS noise. The `String(number, N)` instruction converts a real number to a string with *N* DP, which is used to retain the precision of GPS position data stored on the micro-SD card.

Listing 4-22. GPS position and altitude data and battery voltage

```
void loop()
{
  ttgo->gpsHandler();                 // handle GPS signals
  if (gps->location.isUpdated())  // change in GPS location
  {
    if(startFlag == 0)                // GPS updated at start position
    {
      startFlag = 1;
      startLat =  gps->location.lat();
      startLong = gps->location.lng();
      lastLat = startLat;
      lastLong = startLong;
    }
    if((millis() - lastTime > 15000) && startFlag == 1)
    {                                 // update GPS data every 15s
      lastTime = millis();
      collectData();                  // call function to collect GPS data
                                      // open an existing file
      file = SD.open(filename, FILE_APPEND);
      file.print(text);               // append string to file
      file.println();                 // and new line character
      file.close();
    }
  }
```

```
  if(millis() - lastBatt > 120000) // battery voltage updated 2min
  {
    tft->setTextSize(2);           // blank out previous value
    tft->fillRect(0,216, 240,240, TFT_BLACK);
    tft->setCursor(0,216);
    tft->printf("Battery %d  \n", power->getBattPercentage());
    lastBatt = millis();
  }
}

String collectData()               // function to collect GPS data
{
  double curLat, curLong, dist, startDist, alt;
  curLat = gps->location.lat();
  curLong = gps->location.lng();  // distance from previous position
  dist = TinyGPSPlus::distanceBetween
                  (curLat, curLong, lastLat, lastLong);
                                   // increment total distance
  if(dist > 5) totalDist = totalDist + dist;
                                   // distance from start position
  startDist = TinyGPSPlus::distanceBetween
             (curLat, curLong, startLat, startLong);
  lastLat = curLat;
  lastLong = curLong;
  alt = gps->altitude.meters();
  tft->setTextSize(3);
  tft->fillRect(0,0, 240,215, TFT_BLACK);
  tft->setCursor(0,0);             // display values: altitude (m)
  tft->printf("Alt   %.1f \n", alt);
```

```
  tft->printf("\nDist  %.1f \n", dist);      // distance covered
                                             // total distance
  tft->print("Total ");tft->println(round(totalDist), 0);
                                             // and from start
  tft->print("Start ");tft->println(round(startDist), 0);
                                             // speed (km/h)
  tft->printf("\nSpeed %.1f \n", gps->speed.kmph());
  tft->printf("Satellites %d \n", gps->satellites.value());
  count++;                                   // current GPS position
  text = String(count)+","+String(curLat,6)
         +","+String(curLong,6)+",";
                                             // altitude and distance
  text = text +String(alt)+","+String(totalDist)+",";
                                             // speed (km/h)
  text = text +String(gps->speed.kmph())+",";
                                             // number of satellites
  text = text +String(gps->satellites.value());
  return text;
}
```

Factory Firmware Installation

The factory firmware is installed by uploading the *twatch-2020-v2-220531.bin* file, which is located in the *TTGO_TWatch_Library\bin\2020-v2* folder. The firmware is uploaded with the Espressif Flash Download Tool, which is downloaded as a .zip file from `www.espressif.com/en/support/download/other-tools`. For this chapter, version *V3.9.4* of the Espressif Flash Download Tool dated 2023.02.21 was used. A PDF file containing details of the Espressif Flash Download Tool is included in the downloaded *flash_download_tool_3.9.4\ doc* folder.

In the unzipped *flash_download_tool* folder, double-click the application. In response to Microsoft Defender SmartScreen, click *More info* and click *Run anyway*. In the *Download Tool Mode* box, select *ESP32 ChipType*, select *Develop WorkMode*, and then click *OK*.

In the *ESP32 Flash Download Tool* box (see Figure 4-10), click the three dots in the first row to then locate the *twatch-2020-v2-220531.bin* file to be uploaded. Enter zero in the address box on the right side and click the left-side box to position a tick in the box. In the *SPI SPEED* and *SPI MODE* options, select *80MHz* and *QIO* (Quad Input/Output), respectively. Leave a tick in the *DoNotChgBIn* option. Select the COM port that the TTGO T-Watch V2 watch is connected to on the computer and click the *START* button of the *ESP32 Flash Download Tool*. After the upload is completed, which takes a few minutes, disconnect the TTGO T-Watch V2 watch from the computer. The factory firmware will automatically start. Details of the factory firmware by Dirk Broßwick are available at `github.com/sharandac/My-TTGO-Watch`.

***Figure 4-10.** Factory firmware installation*

CHAPTER 5

BLE Beacons

Bluetooth Low Energy (BLE) beacons transmit information to mobile phones, Android tablets, and other devices close to the beacon to initiate an action by the device. For example, a beacon triggers a mobile device to notify the user of a special offer from a nearby retailer. BLE beacons transmit information in pulses rather than on a continuous basis. A BLE beacon only transmits data, and an app on the mobile device interprets the beacon information. The BLE communication feature of the ESP32 microcontroller enables the ESP32 microcontroller to function either as a BLE beacon or as a recipient of messages from BLE beacons.

The iBeacon was developed by Apple to provide on-site offers and simplify payments. The iBeacon transmits a UUID (Universally Unique IDentifier) to identify the beacon, a major and a minor number to reference information from the app database, and a transmission power level. In a retail context, the UUID and major and minor numbers identify the retail area of a company, the specific store within the area, and the department within the store, respectively. When the user enters a specific department within the store, the mobile device receives a message from a nearby beacon and provides the user with details of a special offer relevant to that department within that store.

N. Cameron, *ESP32 Formats and Communication*,
https://doi.org/10.1007/978-1-4842-9376-8_5

This chapter describes the Eddystone-URL, Eddystone-TLM, and Eddystone-UID beacons and the iBeacon, with example sketches for the ESP32 microcontroller to transmit messages for each beacon type. Two-way communication with BLE between the ESP32 microcontroller, acting as an Eddystone beacon, and the *nRF Connect* app by Nordic Semiconductor is also described.

Eddystone Beacons

Google introduced Eddystone beacons to provide a URL (Eddystone-URL), beacon telemetry information (Eddystone-TLM), or a UUID (Eddystone-UID), which is similar to the iBeacon. The Eddystone-URL beacon transmits a URL, for a specific website, and the beacon transmission power level. The Eddystone unencrypted TLM beacon transmits telemetry information (beacon battery voltage, temperature, advertisement count, and time since power-up) for beacon management purposes. The Eddystone-UID beacon transmits a UUID, to allow an app to retrieve information from the app server. The Eddystone beacon was named after the Eddystone Lighthouse near the southwest coast of England.

Examples of Eddystone-URL and Eddystone-TLM beacons and the associated URL and telemetry information are shown in Figure 5-1. On viewing the Eddystone-URL beacon message with the *nRF Connect* app by Nordic Semiconductor, clicking *OPEN* (see Figure 5-1) opens the URL in the browser of the mobile phone or Android device hosting the *nRF Connect* app. Clicking *CLONE* stores the beacon information in the app *ADVERTISER* to enable access to the URL information when the mobile device is outside the beacon transmission range.

The general format of the Eddystone beacons and the iBeacon is shown in Table 5-1.

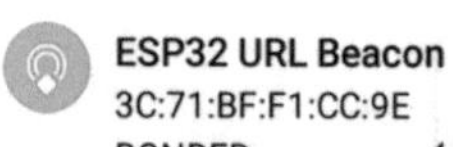

Figure 5-1. *Eddystone-URL and Eddystone-TLM beacons*

Eddystone beacon messages include the service UUID of *0xFEAA* and the frame type code of *0x00, 0x10,* or *0x20* corresponding to the Eddystone-UID, Eddystone-URL, or Eddystone-TLM beacon. The Eddystone-URL and Eddystone-UID beacon and the iBeacon messages include a TX power level at 0m and at 1m, respectively, in dBm, formatted as two's complement. The boxed text describes the two's complement format for interested readers.

> The N-bit numbers span either the positive numbers from 0 to $2^N - 1$ or the positive numbers from 0 to $2^{N-1} - 1$ and the negative numbers from -2^{N-1} to -1. For example, 8-bit numbers span either the positive numbers from 0 to 255 or the positive numbers from 0 to 127 and the negative numbers from –128 to –1. The 8-bit binary representation of the number 127 is *B01111111*, so an 8-bit binary-formatted number with the most significant bit equal to one represents a negative number. The two's complement system for N-bit numbers defines a negative number and the complement number to sum to 2^N. For example, the 8-bit complement of –90 is $166 = 2^8 + (-90)$. Alternatively, the complement is obtained by inverting the number's bits and adding one. For example, 90 = *B01011010* in binary representation, and the complement is *B10100101* + *B00000001* = *B10100110* = 166 with *B10100110* representing –90 in the two's complement format.

Table 5-1. *Beacon message composition*

Beacon	Service UUID	Frame type	Components				
Eddystone-URL	0xFEAA	0x10	TX power	URL scheme	URL		
Eddystone-TLM	0xFEAA	0x20	TLM version	Battery voltage	Temperature	Advertisement count	Time since power-up
Eddystone-UID	0xFEAA	0x00	TX power	UUID namespace	UUID instance		
iBeacon	0x4C00	0xFF	UUID	Major	Minor	RSSI	

The Eddystone-URL beacon includes the URL scheme code of *0x00, 0x01, 0x02,* or *0x03* corresponding to a URL prefix of http://www, https://www, http://, or https://. The URL is formatted as compressed encoding to reduce the beacon message length. One website to compress and encode a URL is `bitly.com`. For example, the URL `https://github.com/google/eddystone` is reduced to `https://bit.ly/3yOiW6V`, requiring only 14 bytes of storage with the URL scheme code of *0x03*.

The Eddystone-UID beacon includes a 16-byte or 128-bit UUID, formatted as 8-4-4-4-12 characters, a 10-byte namespace, and a 6-byte instance. One website to generate a UUID is `www.uuidgenerator.net`. An application of UID beacons is the GATT (Generic ATTribute) profile, described later in this chapter.

The Eddystone unencrypted TLM beacon includes the voltage as a 16-bit number, temperature in 8.8 fixed point notation, advertisement count, and time since power-up, expressed as a multiple of 0.1s, with the latter two variables stored as 32-bit numbers. The boxed text describes fixed point notation for interested readers.

Fixed point notation represents real numbers by N-bit numbers, such as a 16-bit number with the 8 most significant bits representing the integer part and the 8 least significant bits representing the fractional part. For example, the integer part and fractional part of the number 3.0625 are 3 and 0.0625, with the latter equal to 16/256. The real number is converted to 8.8 fixed point notation by bit shifting the integer part by eight positions, and the fractional part is multiplied by $256 = 2^8$. The 8.8 fixed point notation representation of 3.0625 is *B0000001100010000* consisting of the binary representation of 3 (*B0000011*) and 16 (*B00010000*).

Conversion of a 16-bit number to two 8-bit numbers requires right-shifting the 16-bit number by eight positions to identify the upper 8-bit number and operating an *AND* function with the number 255 (equal to $2^8 - 1$ or *0xFF* or *B11111111*) to obtain the lower 8-bit number. For example, right-shifting the number *B0000001100010000* by eight positions results in the number *B00000011* = 3, and the *AND* function with *0xFF* results in *B00010000* = 16. The real number is obtained by combining the upper 8-bit number, 3, with the lower 8-bit number, 16, which is divided by 256, to obtain 3 + 16/256 = 3.0625, as in the example.

An alternative is to use the C++ *highByte* and *lowByte* functions that extract the upper and lower bytes, respectively, from a 16-bit or 2-byte number. An example of the two functions is given in Listing 5-1 with the HEX value of *0xABCD* split into the high and low byte values of *0xAB* and *0xCD*. Note that *0xABCD* = $43981 = 171 \times 2^8 + 205$, equivalent to *0xAB* shifted eight positions + *0xCD*.

Listing 5-1. highByte and lowByte functions

```
int val = 0xABCD;                 // 16-bit variable
byte high, low;                   // 8-bit variables

void setup()
{
  Serial.begin(115200);           // Serial Monitor baud rate
  high = highByte(val);           // upper byte
  low = lowByte(val);             // lower byte
  Serial.printf("integers: %d %d \n", high, low);
  high = val >> 8;                // shift right 8 bits
  low = val & 0xFF;               // AND with B11111111
  Serial.printf("integers: %d %d \n", high, low);
}

void loop()                       // nothing in loop function
{}
```

A similar approach converts a 32-bit number to four 8-bit numbers, which is used in Listing 5-3. The four upper to lower 8-bit numbers are obtained by (1 = upper) right-shifting 24 positions, (2) right-shifting 16 positions and the *AND* function with *0xFF,* (3) right-shifting by 8 positions and the *AND* function with *0xFF,* and (4 = lower) the *AND* function with *0xFF,* respectively. The instructions are

```
number1 = val >> 24
number2 = val >> 16 & 0xFF
number3 = val >> 8  & 0xFF
number4 = val       & 0xFF
```

Eddystone-URL Beacon

An Eddystone-URL beacon containing the URL `bit.ly/3yOiW6V`, which maps to the URL `github.com/google/eddystone`, is generated in Listing 5-2, and then the ESP32 microcontroller sleeps. In sleep mode, the RTC (real-time clock) memory functions, while the ESP32 microcontroller CPU and memory are disabled, and the number of reboots and seconds since last reboot are stored in RTC memory.

The first section of the sketch defines the variables to be stored in RTC memory and the time variable, *timeData*, to store the number of seconds, `timeData.tv_sec`, since the microcontroller was reset. In the *setup* function, the time since reset is determined by the *gettimeofday* function, the BLE device is initialized, the *setBeacon* function is called to define the beacon message, and the beacon advertising is started. After advertising for the required period, the microcontroller goes into sleep mode to be woken with the RTC timer after *N* microseconds.

The *setBeacon* function generates the Eddystone-URL beacon message consisting of the service UUID of *0xFEAA*; the frame type for a URL beacon of *0x10*; the TX power set at –12dBm, which has a two's complement of 256 + (–12) = 244 = *0xF4*; the URL scheme value of *0x03* corresponding to https://; and the URL. The default beacon name is "*ESP32*", in the *BLEDevice* library, and a specific beacon name is advertised with the *setName* function. A text message, of up to 17 characters, is sent by the Eddystone-URL beacon, although the message is displayed in the format of a URL: http://message.

The *ESP32 BLE Arduino* library by Neil Kolban is automatically incorporated in the Arduino IDE when the *esp32* Boards Manager is installed. The *BLEDevice* component library references the component libraries of *BLEServer, BLEClient, BLEUtils, BLEScan,* and *BLEAddress,* so the corresponding `#include <library.h>` instructions are not required. The *BLEDevice* library is included in the Arduino IDE when the *ESP32 BLE Arduino* library is installed and is located in *user\AppData\Local\Arduino15\packages\esp32\hardware\esp32\version\libraries\BLE.*

Listing 5-2. Eddystone-URL beacon

```
#include <BLEDevice.h>          // include BLEDevice library
#include <sys/time.h>           // and the system time library
int sleepSec = 5;               // sleep 5 seconds, then wake up
unsigned long lag, uSec = 1000000;
RTC_DATA_ATTR int reboot = 0;   // number of reboots and last
RTC_DATA_ATTR time_t lastReboot; // reboot time in RTC memory
struct timeval timeData;        // time (s) since reset
BLEAdvertising *advertise;

void setup()
{
  Serial.begin(115200);          // Serial Monitor baud rate
  gettimeofday(&timeData, NULL); // time since reset
                                 // number and timing of reboots
  Serial.printf("%d reboots ", reboot++);
  Serial.printf("%ds since reboot \n",
                timeData.tv_sec - lastReboot);
  lastReboot = timeData.tv_sec;  // time(s) of last reboot
  BLEDevice::init("");
  advertise = BLEDevice::getAdvertising();
  setBeacon();                   // call beacon function
  lag = 0;                       // reset time lag
  advertise->start();            // start beacon advertising
  Serial.println("start advertising");
}

void setBeacon()                 // function to generate beacon message
{
  String URL = "bit.ly/3yOiW6V"; // URL to be broadcast
  char beaconData[17];           // beacon message array
  uint16_t UUID = 0xFEAA;        // Eddystone UUID
```

```
  BLEAdvertisementData advertData = BLEAdvertisementData();
  advertData.setCompleteServices(BLEUUID(UUID));
  beaconData[0] = 0x10;                // Eddystone frame type (URL)
  beaconData[1] = 0xF4;                // beacon TX power at 0m = -12
  beaconData[2] = 0x03;                // URL scheme for https://
  for (int i=0; i<URL.length(); i++) beaconData[i+3] = URL[i];
                                       // generate beacon message
  advertData.setServiceData(BLEUUID(UUID),
                std::string(beaconData, 17));
  advertise->setAdvertisementData(advertData);
  BLEAdvertisementData scanData = BLEAdvertisementData();
                                       // define beacon name
  scanData.setName("ESP32 URL Beacon");
  advertise->setScanResponseData(scanData);
}

void loop()
{
  if(millis() - lag > 5000)
  {
    advertise->stop();                 // stop beacon advertising
    Serial.println("stop advertising");
                                       // sleep for sleepSec seconds
    esp_deep_sleep(sleepSec * uSec);
  }
}
```

Eddystone-TLM Beacon

The Eddystone unencrypted TLM beacon contains the service UUID of *0xFEAA*, the frame type for a TLM beacon of *0x20*, the TLM version number of *0x00*, the beacon voltage as a 16-bit number, the beacon temperature in 8.8 fixed point notation, and the advertisement count and the time since power-up, expressed as a multiple of 0.1s, both as 32-bit numbers. In the sketch, battery voltage and temperature are generated from the ESP32 microcontroller reboot count to demonstrate inclusion of variables in a TLM beacon. The *setBeacon* function in Listing 5-3 replaces the *setBeacon* function in the sketch of Listing 5-2. Formatting the TLM beacon message accounts for the majority of *setBeacon* instructions.

Listing 5-3. Eddystone-TLM beacon

```
void setBeacon()                     // function to generate
{                                    // beacon message
  char beaconData[14];               // beacon message array
  uint16_t UUID = 0xFEAA;            // Eddystone UUID
  uint16_t voltage = reboot * 12;    // generated voltage
  float temp = (reboot * 1.1);       // and temperature
                                     // 8.8 fixed point notation
  uint16_t tempInt = (int)(temp * 256.0 + 1.0);
  BLEAdvertisementData advertData = BLEAdvertisementData();
  advertData.setCompleteServices(BLEUUID(UUID));
  beaconData[0] = 0x20;              // frame type (TLM)
  beaconData[1] = 0x00;              // TLM version
  beaconData[2] = (voltage >> 8);    // stored as 16-bit number
  beaconData[3] = (voltage & 0xFF);
  beaconData[4] = (tempInt >> 8);    // 8.8 fixed point notation
  beaconData[5] = (tempInt & 0xFF);
  beaconData[6] =  (reboot >> 24);   // stored as 32-bit number
  beaconData[7] = ((reboot >> 16) & 0xFF);
  beaconData[8] = ((reboot >> 8)  & 0xFF);
  beaconData[9] =  (reboot & 0xFF);
```

```
                                        // stored as 32-bit number
  beaconData[10] =  (timeData.tv_sec*10 >> 24);
                                        // with 0.1sec resolution
  beaconData[11] = ((timeData.tv_sec*10 >> 16) & 0xFF);
  beaconData[12] = ((timeData.tv_sec*10 >> 8) & 0xFF);
                                        // generate beacon message
  beaconData[13] =  (timeData.tv_sec*10 & 0xFF);
  advertData.setServiceData(BLEUUID(UUID),
                 std::string(beaconData, 14));
  advertise->setAdvertisementData(advertData);
  BLEAdvertisementData scanData = BLEAdvertisementData();
  scanData.setName("ESP32 TLM Beacon");
  advertise->setScanResponseData(scanData);
}
```

Eddystone-UID Beacon

The Eddystone-UID beacon contains the service UUID of *0xFEAA*; the frame type for a UID beacon of *0x00*; the TX power set at –12dBm, which has a two's complement of 256 + (–12) = 244 = *0xF4*; and the UUID 10-byte namespace and a 6-byte instance. Examples of Eddystone-UID and iBeacon URL are shown in Figure 5-2. Note that the iBeacon UUID is displayed in reverse pairwise order relative to the UUID provided in the sketch (see Listing 5-5). The UUID was generated on the `www.uuidgenerator.net` website.

Figure 5-2. *Eddystone-UID and iBeacon*

The *setBeacon* function in Listing 5-4 replaces the *setBeacon* function in the sketch of Listing 5-2. The UUID is mapped to the *beaconData* array with two characters for each element.

Listing 5-4. Eddystone-UID beacon

```
void setBeacon()              // function to generate beacon message
{
  char beaconData[20];        // beacon message array
  uint16_t UUID = 0xFEAA;     // Eddystone UUID
  BLEAdvertisementData advertData = BLEAdvertisementData();
  advertData.setCompleteServices(BLEUUID(UUID));
  beaconData[0] = 0x00;       // Eddystone frame type (UID)
  beaconData[1] = 0xF4;       // beacon TX power at 0m
  beaconData[2] = 0x05;       // UUID Namespace NID[0 to 9]
  beaconData[3] = 0x98;       // two characters
  beaconData[4] = 0x6D;       // for each array element
  beaconData[5] = 0x33;
  beaconData[6] = 0xF9;       // 05986d33-f920-4802-bbad-
  beaconData[7] = 0x20;
  beaconData[8] = 0x48;
  beaconData[9] = 0x02;
  beaconData[10] = 0xBB;
```

```
  beaconData[11] = 0xAD;
  beaconData[12] = 0x0C;        // UUID Instance BID[0 to 5]
  beaconData[13] = 0xFA;        // 0cfa43d07079
  beaconData[14] = 0x43;
  beaconData[15] = 0xD0;
  beaconData[16] = 0x70;
  beaconData[17] = 0x79;
  beaconData[18] = 0x00;        // reserved to 0x00
  beaconData[19] = 0x00;
                                // generate beacon message
  advertData.setServiceData(BLEUUID(UUID),
                  std::string(beaconData, 20));
  advertise->setAdvertisementData(advertData);
  BLEAdvertisementData scanData = BLEAdvertisementData();
  scanData.setName("ESP32 UID Beacon");
  advertise->setScanResponseData(scanData);
}
```

iBeacon

The iBeacon contains the iBeacon length of 26, the frame type of *0xFF,* the manufacturer identity for Apple of *0x4C00,* the UUID, the UUID major and minor components, and the RSSI at 1m, formatted as two's complement. The iBeacon message components are included using library instructions, for example, `setMajor()`. The UUID in Listing 5-5 is the same as in Listing 5-4 for the Eddystone-UID beacon. In the sketch, UUID major and minor components are generated from the ESP32 microcontroller reboot count to illustrate inclusion of variables in the iBeacon message. The *setBeacon* function in Listing 5-5 replaces the *setBeacon* function in the sketch of Listing 5-2. The *BLEBeacon* library is required to generate an iBeacon message with the `#include <BLEBeacon.h>` instruction added to the first section of the sketch.

Listing 5-5. iBeacon

```
void setBeacon()                              // function to generate
{                                             // beacon message
  char UUID[] = "05986d33-f920-4802-bbad-0cfa43d07079";
  BLEBeacon beacon = BLEBeacon();
  beacon.setManufacturerId(0x4C00);   // manufacturer ID for Apple
  beacon.setProximityUUID(BLEUUID(UUID));
  beacon.setMajor(3 * reboot);              // 16-bit integer
  beacon.setMinor(reboot);                  // 16-bit integer
  beacon.setSignalPower(0xBB);              // RSSI in two's complement
  BLEAdvertisementData advertData = BLEAdvertisementData();
  std::string serviceData = "";
  serviceData += (char)26;                  // length of beacon message
  serviceData += (char)0xFF;                // iBeacon frame type
  serviceData += beacon.getData();
  advertData.addData(serviceData);    // generate beacon message
  advertise->setAdvertisementData(advertData);
  BLEAdvertisementData scanData = BLEAdvertisementData();
  scanData.setName("ESP32 iBeacon");
  advertise->setScanResponseData(scanData);
}
```

Beacon Raw Data

Examples of Eddystone-URL and Eddystone-TLM beacon raw message data, corresponding to Figure 5-1, are shown in Tables 5-2 and 5-3, respectively. Raw data for the Eddystone-URL beacon message and the beacon name are shown in the second and third rows of Table 5-2, respectively. The beacon message with 20 (*0x14*) HEX character pairs consists of the Eddystone UUID in reversed HEX character pairs (*0xFEAA*), the frame type (*0x10*), the TX power in the two's complement format (*0xF4* equates to –12), the URL type for an https:// URL (*0x03*), and the URL of `bit.ly/3yOiW6V` (*0x62 69 74 … 57 36 56*). The beacon name contains 17 (*0x11*) HEX character pairs (*0x 45 53 50 … 63 6F 6E*).

Table 5-2. *Eddystone-URL beacon message data*

Length	Type	Content
03	0x03	0xAAFE
20	0x16	0xAAFE 10 F4 03 6269742E6C792F33793069573656
17	0x09	0x4553503332205524C20426561636F6E

Raw data for the Eddystone-TLM beacon message and the beacon name are shown in rows 2 and 3 of Table 5-3, respectively. The beacon message with 17 (*0x11*) HEX character pairs consists of the Eddystone UUID in reversed HEX character pairs (*0xFEAA*), the frame type (*0x20*), the beacon version (*0x00*), the beacon voltage of 72mV (*0x48*), the beacon temperature in 8.8 fixed point notation (*0x069A*), the advertisement count (*0x06*), and the time since power-up of 530 × 0.1s intervals (*0x0212*). The beacon temperature in HEX format (*0x069A*) represents the integer and fractional parts of 6 (*0x06*) and 154 (*0x9A*), respectively, for the real number of 6 + 154/256 = 6.6015625.

Table 5-3. *Eddystone-TLM beacon message data*

Length	Type	Content
03	0x03	0xAAFE
17	0x16	0xAAFE 20 00 0048 069A 000000 06 0000 0212
17	0x09	0x455350333220544C4D20426561636F6E

Raw data for an iBeacon message and the beacon name are included in Table 5-4. The beacon message with 26 (*0x1A*) HEX character pairs consists of the Apple manufacturer ID in reversed HEX character pairs (*0x004C*), the iBeacon type (*0x02*) and data length of 21 bytes (*0x15*), the URL (*05986d33-f920-4802-bbad-0cfa43d07079*) with character pairs in reverse order, the major (*0x09*) and minor (*0x03*) components, and the RSSI in the two's complement format (*0xBB* equates to -69). The beacon name contains 14 (*0x0E*) HEX character pairs (*0x 45 53 50 ... 63 6F 6E*).

***Table 5-4.** iBeacon message data*

Length	Type	Content
26	0xFF	0x4C00 02 15 7970D043FA0CADBB024820F9336D9805 0009 0003 BB
14	0x09	0x4553503332206942656163 6F6E

Conversion of alphanumeric characters to HEX-coded values, and vice versa, is demonstrated in a Microsoft Excel spreadsheet. A combination of the Microsoft Excel functions *CODE* and *DEC2HEX* converts alphanumeric characters to HEX-coded values, and conversely HEX-coded values are converted to alphanumeric characters with the *HEX2DEC* and *CHAR* functions. For example, the letter *H* is converted to *0x48* with *DEC2HEX(CODE("H"))* and *0x48* to the letter *H* with *CHAR(HEX2DEC(48))*.

BLE Communication

Bluetooth Low Energy (BLE) communicates on the same 2.4GHz frequency as Bluetooth communication, over a similar transmission range, but with reduced power consumption. BLE communication between a server and a client minimizes the server energy requirement, as the server notifies the connected client only when updated data is available. If the client periodically requested information from the server, which is termed polling, then the server would have to be continuously operational. The connected client requests notifications from the server, to avoid the server transmitting when the client does not require the notifications.

For example, the ESP32 DEVKIT DOIT module in Figure 5-3 is the server transmitting notifications to the client, which is the *nRF Connect* app or the TTGO T-Display V1.1 module. The server advertises its existence, and the client scans available BLE devices. When the client detects the required server, the client establishes a connection with the server. The data, such as a temperature in degrees Celsius or a battery level in percentage, to be transmitted with BLE communication is formatted as a service with component characteristics. The client formats the notification according to the service, such as *Battery Service*, and characteristic, such as *Battery Level*. The client turns on or off notifications from the server by transmitting a *Descriptor* attached to the corresponding characteristic.

The *nRF Connect* app by Nordic Semiconductor is recommended for BLE communication and is available on *Google Play Store*.

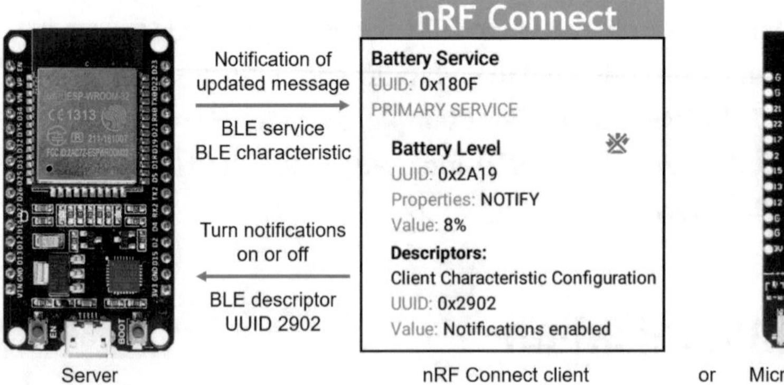

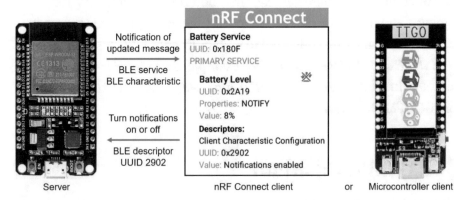

Figure 5-3. *BLE communication*

GATT Profile

The GATT (Generic ATTribute) profile defines the format of BLE-transmitted data. A BLE service, such as *Environmental Sensing,* includes characteristics, such as *Temperature* and *Humidity,* with the BLE service and characteristic each having a specific UUID. Details of the GATT services and characteristics are available at `www.bluetooth.com/specifications/assigned-numbers/`. The Assigned Numbers document details UUIDs of GATT services (section 3.4) and characteristics (section 3.8). For example, the UUIDs of the *Environmental Sensing* service and the *Temperature* characteristic are *0x181A* and *0x2A6E,* respectively. The Assigned Numbers document also lists the characteristics included in the *Environmental Sensing* (section 6.1) and *User Data* (section 6.2) services. Each characteristic format is defined in the GATT Specification Supplement document (section 3). A characteristic format is also obtained from `github.com/oesmith/gatt-xml`. For example, the *Temperature* characteristic has UUID *0x2A6E,* is stored as a 16-bit integer, is represented in degrees Celsius with 2DP, and has a valid range of –273.15° to 327.67°.

The client turns on or off notifications from the server with the *Client Characteristic Configuration,* which is a BLE descriptor attached to the corresponding BLE characteristic. The *Client Characteristic Configuration* descriptor is formatted as a 16-bit variable with a UUID of *0x2902,* and the first data bit indicates the notification status of *On* or *Off.*

BLE transmission of battery level and temperature by a server with the BLE notification viewed on the *nRF Connect* app is shown in Figure 5-4. The *Battery Level* and *Temperature* characteristics belong to the two services *Battery Service* and *Environmental Sensing,* and a separate *Client Characteristic Configuration* descriptor is required for each characteristic. In Figure 5-4, notification of the *Temperature* characteristic by the server is turned off, as indicated by the descriptor. The service and characteristic

UUIDs define the BLE notification formatting. In the *nRF Connect* app, the notifications are turned on or off by clicking the BLE arrows icon, as illustrated in Figure 5-4.

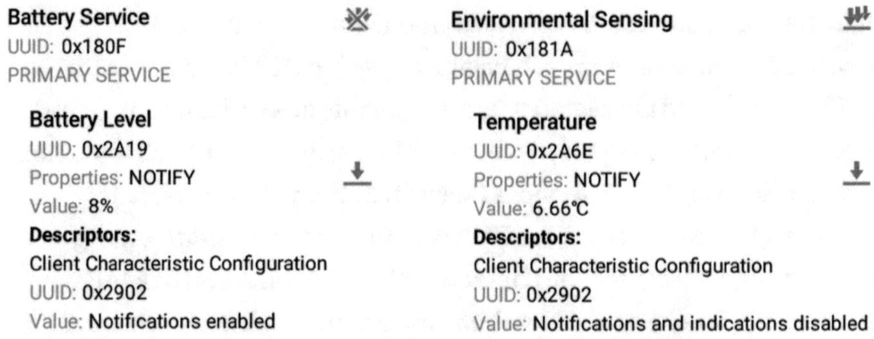

Battery Service
UUID: 0x180F
PRIMARY SERVICE

Battery Level
UUID: 0x2A19
Properties: NOTIFY
Value: 8%
Descriptors:
Client Characteristic Configuration
UUID: 0x2902
Value: Notifications enabled

Environmental Sensing
UUID: 0x181A
PRIMARY SERVICE

Temperature
UUID: 0x2A6E
Properties: NOTIFY
Value: 6.66°C
Descriptors:
Client Characteristic Configuration
UUID: 0x2902
Value: Notifications and indications disabled

Figure 5-4. *BLE communication with GATT characteristics*

In Listing 5-6, the BLE server is defined, and a BLE service, characteristic, and descriptor are defined separately for the *Battery Level* and *Temperature* characteristics, as the two characteristics belong to different services. In the *setup* function, the BLE descriptors are added to the corresponding characteristics, which are added to the corresponding services, which are added to the server. The *ServerCallback* function defines the server response to the client connecting to or disconnecting from the server. In the *loop* function, the server generates the battery level and temperature values, with the `setValue` instruction, which are transmitted to the client, with the `notify` instruction, provided the client both is connected to the server and has turned on notifications.

In the GATT Specification Supplement, the *Battery Level* and *Temperature* characteristics are formatted as an unsigned integer, *uint8*, between 0 and 100 and as a signed integer, *sint16*, between –273.15 and 327.67 with 2DP, respectively. In Listing 5-6, the temperature value is multiplied by 100 to retain 2DP and converted to a 16-bit integer, which is then split into the high and low bytes for transmission to the client with the `setValue(tempData, 2)` instruction, indicating that 2 bytes of data are to be transmitted.

When a client turns on or off notifications for a characteristic, the server updates the *BLE2902* library variable descriptor attached to the characteristic, as indicated by the `getNotifications()` instruction. In Listing 5-6, the temperature is a multiple of the battery level to illustrate formatting data for different characteristics. However, in Figure 5-4, notification of the temperature is disabled, resulting in the temperature reading of 6.66°C, while the battery level notification is independently enabled and a value of 8% is displayed. The *nRF Connect* app indicates that notifications for a characteristic are enabled or disabled with the *Client Characteristic Configuration* descriptor value and with the symbol adjacent to the displayed characteristic name.

Note that when a revised sketch is uploaded, the Bluetooth connection and the *nRF Connect* app may have to be disconnected and restarted.

Listing 5-6. BLE transmission with GATT characteristics

```
#include <BLEDevice.h>          // include BLE library
#include <BLE2902.h>            // and BLE2902 library
BLEServer * Server;             // define BLE server,
BLEService * battService;       // service and service UUID
                                // define characteristic UUID
BLEUUID battServUUID = BLEUUID((uint16_t)0x180F);
BLECharacteristic battChar(BLEUUID((uint16_t)0x2A19),
                  BLECharacteristic::PROPERTY_NOTIFY);
BLEDescriptor * battDesc;       // define BLE descriptor
BLE2902 * battNotfy;            // define notification status
BLEService * tempService;       // repeat for second service
BLEUUID tempServUUID = BLEUUID((uint16_t)0x181A);
BLECharacteristic tempChar(BLEUUID((uint16_t)0x2A6E),
                  BLECharacteristic::PROPERTY_NOTIFY);
BLEDescriptor * tempDesc;
```

```
BLE2902 * tempNotfy;
unsigned long lag;
int batt = 1, clientCon = 0;
float temp;
uint8_t tempData[2];
                                        // callback function
class ServerCallback : public BLEServerCallbacks
{
  void onConnect(BLEServer * Server)  // client connect to server
  {
    clientCon = 1;
    Serial.println("connected to client");
    delay(500);
  }                                   // client disconnect from server
  void onDisconnect(BLEServer * Server)
  {
    clientCon = 0;
    delay(500);
    Server->startAdvertising();       // server start advertising
    Serial.println("client disconnected\nstarted advertising");
  }
};

void setup()
{
  Serial.begin(115200);
  BLEDevice::init("ESP32");           // define BLE server name
  Server = BLEDevice::createServer();
  Server->setCallbacks(new ServerCallback());
                                      // add service to server
  battService = Server->createService(battServUUID);
```

```
                                    // add characteristic to service
  battService->addCharacteristic(&battChar);
  battDesc = new BLE2902();
                                    // add descriptor to characteristic
  battChar.addDescriptor(battDesc);
  battNotfy = (BLE2902*)battDesc;   // link notifier to descriptor
  battService->start();
                                    // repeat for second service
  tempService = Server->createService(tempServUUID);
  tempService->addCharacteristic(&tempChar);
  tempDesc = new BLE2902();
  tempChar.addDescriptor(tempDesc);
  tempNotfy = (BLE2902*)tempDesc;
  tempService->start();
  lag = 0;
                                    // start advertising services
  Server->getAdvertising()->start();
}

void loop()
{                                   // client connected to server
  if(clientCon == 1  && millis() - lag > 5000)
  {                                 // and advertising period expired
    batt++;
    if(batt > 99) batt = 1;
    battChar.setValue(batt);
    battChar.notify();              // notify battery service update
    temp = batt*1.11;
    tempData[0] = (uint16_t)(temp*100);          // upper and
    tempData[1] = (uint16_t)(temp*100) >> 8;     // lower bytes
```

```
    tempChar.setValue(tempData, 2);     // temperature format uint16_t
    tempChar.notify();
    Serial.printf("notify %d batt %d notify %d temp %.2f \n",
                  battNotfy->getNotifications(), batt,
                  tempNotfy->getNotifications(), temp);
    lag = millis();
  }
}
```

In Listing 5-6, the server transmits notifications to a client, which are viewed on the *nRF Connect* app by Nordic Semiconductor, with the notification format defined by a BLE service and characteristic. When the client is the ESP32 microcontroller, the notification is formatted by the UART (Universal Asynchronous Receiver-Transmitter) service for Serial communication. The Nordic Semiconductor UUIDs for UART services and receive/transmit characteristics are available at `infocenter.nordicsemi.com`, and search for *UART/Serial BLE*. The receive UUID *6E400003...* and transmit UUID *6E400002...* are relative to the client and are reversed when expressed relative to the server. Serial communication is not defined as a GATT service.

The sketch in Listing 5-7 for BLE with one-way Serial communication only differs from Listing 5-6 in the service and characteristic UUIDs and that the notification is formatted as a character array for display on the Serial Monitor.

Listing 5-7. BLE with one-way Serial communication

```
#include <BLEDevice.h>              // include BLE library
#include <BLE2902.h>                // and BLE2902 library
BLEServer * Server;                 // define BLE server,
BLEService * Service;               // service,
BLECharacteristic * Char;           // characteristic
BLEDescriptor * Desc;               // and descriptor
```

```
BLE2902 * Notfy;                      // UUIDs
char ServUUID[] = "6e400001-b5a3-f393-e0a9-e50e24dcca9e";
char CharUUID[] = "6e400003-b5a3-f393-e0a9-e50e24dcca9e";
int count = 0, clientCon = 0;
String str;
char msg[24];                         // char array to store message

                                      // same as Listing 5-6
class ServerCallback : public BLEServerCallbacks{};

void setup()
{
  Serial.begin(115200);
  BLEDevice::init("ESP32");           // define BLE device name,
  Server = BLEDevice::createServer();
  Server->setCallbacks(new ServerCallback());
                                      // add service to server
  Service = Server->createService(ServUUID);
                                      // add characteristic to server
  Char = Service->createCharacteristic(CharUUID,
                BLECharacteristic::PROPERTY_NOTIFY);
  Desc = new BLE2902();
  Char->addDescriptor(Desc);          // add descriptor to characteristic
  Notfy = (BLE2902*)Desc;             // link notifier to descriptor
  Service->start();
  Server->getAdvertising()->start();  // start advertising services
}

void loop()
{
  if(clientCon == 1)                  // client connected to server
  {
```

```
    count++;                                // create message
    str = "counts "+String(count)+","+String(0.5*count);
    str.toCharArray(msg, 24);               // convert to character array
    Char->setValue(msg);                    // set characteristic to message
    Char->notify();
    Serial.printf("notify %d msg %s \n",
                  Notfy->getNotifications(), msg);
    delay(5000);
  }
}
```

Two-Way Communication

The additional instructions to Listing 5-7 for two-way Serial communication between the server and the client, with server notifications viewed on the *nRF Connect* app, are given in Listing 5-8. After opening the *nRF Connect* app, scanning for the required device, and establishing a connection to the server, the Nordic UART service is displayed (see Figure 5-5a). The server notifications, for the *TX Characteristic*, are turned on or off by clicking the BLE arrows icon. When the single BLE arrow opposite *RX Characteristic* is pressed, a pop-up window for entering alphanumeric text appears, and the entered text is displayed as the *RX Characteristic* value (see Figure 5-5a). Entering the text *LED* results in the ESP32 microcontroller turning on or off the LED connected to the microcontroller GPIO 5 pin. The Serial Monitor, connected to the server, displays the sequence of the client turning on notifications and the client transmitting "*Bluetooth example*" and then "*LED*", which results in the LED being turned on (see Figure 5-5b).

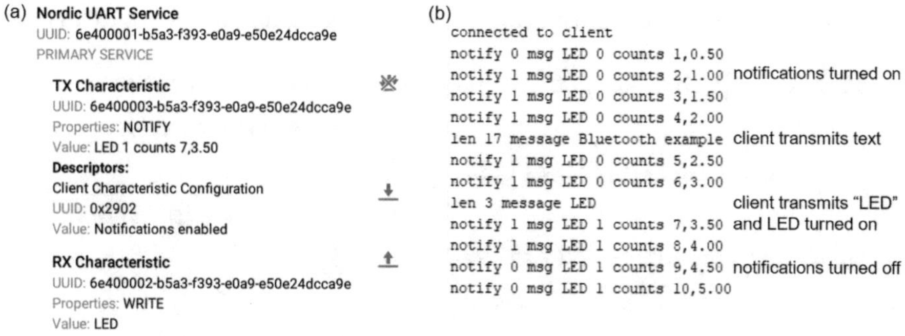

(a) Nordic UART Service
UUID: 6e400001-b5a3-f393-e0a9-e50e24dcca9e
PRIMARY SERVICE

TX Characteristic
UUID: 6e400003-b5a3-f393-e0a9-e50e24dcca9e
Properties: NOTIFY
Value: LED 1 counts 7,3.50
Descriptors:
Client Characteristic Configuration
UUID: 0x2902
Value: Notifications enabled

RX Characteristic
UUID: 6e400002-b5a3-f393-e0a9-e50e24dcca9e
Properties: WRITE
Value: LED

(b)
```
connected to client
notify 0 msg LED 0 counts 1,0.50
notify 1 msg LED 0 counts 2,1.00   notifications turned on
notify 1 msg LED 0 counts 3,1.50
notify 1 msg LED 0 counts 4,2.00
len 17 message Bluetooth example   client transmits text
notify 1 msg LED 0 counts 5,2.50
notify 1 msg LED 0 counts 6,3.00
len 3 message LED                  client transmits "LED"
notify 1 msg LED 1 counts 7,3.50   and LED turned on
notify 1 msg LED 1 counts 8,4.00
notify 0 msg LED 1 counts 9,4.50   notifications turned off
notify 0 msg LED 1 counts 10,5.00
```

Figure 5-5. *BLE with two-way Serial communication*

The instructions in Listing 5-8 define the *RX Characteristic* and UUID and establish the *RXCharCallback* function to convert the received notification from the client to a string for display on the TTGO T-Display V1.1 LCD screen. The function also turns on or off the LED if the received notification equals *"LED"*. In the *setup* function, the *RX Characteristic* is added to the server's service with the *PROPERTY_WRITE* property to indicate that the client transmits text, which is entered on the keypad of the *nRF Connect* app. In the *loop* function, the existing message display is updated to include the LED state. The *Refresh services* option may have to be selected on the Android tablet or mobile phone for display of the *RX Characteristic* data.

At the start of the sketch, the following instructions are inserted.

Listing 5-8. BLE with two-way Serial communication

```
BLECharacteristic * RXChar;     // define receive characteristic
                                // receive UUID
char RXUUID[] = "6e400002-b5a3-f393-e0a9-e50e24dcca9e";
int LED, LEDpin = 27;           // define LED pin
```

And before the *setup* function, the following instructions are inserted:

```
class RXCharCallback: public BLECharacteristicCallbacks
{                                          // receive callback function
  void onWrite(BLECharacteristic * RXChar)
  {                                        // received message from client
    std::string str = RXChar->getValue();
    Serial.printf("len %d message ", str.length());
    for (int i=0; i<str.length(); i++) Serial.print(str[i]);
    Serial.println();                      // turn on or off LED
    if(str == "LED") LED = !digitalRead(LEDpin);
    digitalWrite(LEDpin, LED);
  }
};
```

In the *setup* function, but before the `Service->start()` instruction, the following instructions are inserted:

```
  pinMode(LEDpin, OUTPUT);
                                           // add receive characteristic to server
  RXChar = Service->createCharacteristic(RXUUID,
           BLECharacteristic::PROPERTY_WRITE);
  RXChar->setCallbacks(new RXCharCallback());
```

In the *loop* function, the following instruction replaces the existing `str =` instruction:

```
str = "LED "+String(LED)+" "+"counts"
      +String(count)+","+String(0.5*count);
```

Notifications

The corresponding sketch to Listing 5-7 for one-way Serial communication with notifications viewed on a TTGO T-Display V1.1 LCD screen is given in Listing 5-9. The client is a TTGO T-Display V1.1 module, which includes an LCD screen to display notifications from the server, with the notifications turned on or off by clicking the right or left button on the TTGO T-Display V1.1 module. When the client connects to the required server, the server MAC address, the RSSI (Received Signal Strength Indicator) of the transmitted signal, and the distance between the server and client are displayed.

The RSSI is impacted by several factors, such as the distance or obstacles between transmitter and receiver. The log-distance path loss model predicts the RSSI as $RSSI_0 - 10N \times log_{10}(D/D_0)$, where $RSSI_0$ is the RSSI measured at D_0m distance from the transmitter; N is the path loss coefficient, equal to two through a vacuum; and D is the distance between the transmitter and receiver in meters. Given an RSSI, the predicted distance between a server and client is $D = 10^{((RSSI_0 - RSSI)/20)}$, with $RSSI_0$ = -69 at 1m distance, as illustrated in Figure 5-6.

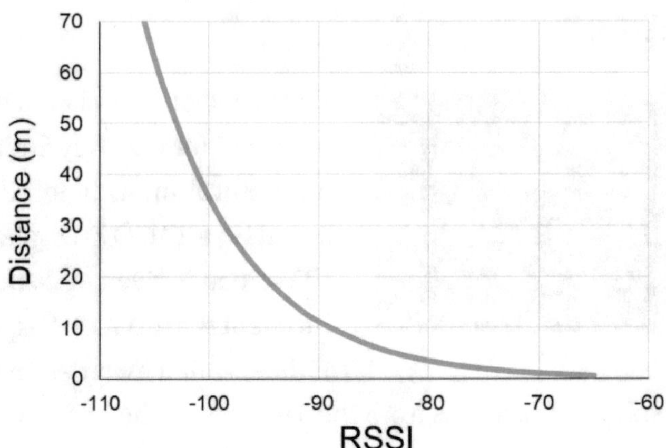

Figure 5-6. *RSSI and distance to BLE device*

In Listing 5-9, the BLE client, service, characteristic, and descriptor are defined, with the service and receive characteristic UUIDs. In the *setup* function, the BLE scanner is initialized with the *DeviceCallback* function to determine if a detected BLE device has the same name as the required server. In the *loop* function, the client scans for BLE devices, and when the required server is detected, the *serverConnect* function connects the client to the server; the BLE descriptor is added to the characteristic, which is added to the service; and the client turns on the server notifications. The *serverConnect* function also calls the *ClientCallback* function to define the client response when connecting to or disconnecting from the server.

When a server notification is received, the *callback* function converts the notification to a character array, which the client displays. The client turns on or off server notifications with the *notify* function, which sets the *Client Characteristic Configuration* descriptor value to *0x01* or *0x0*, respectively. The first 2 bits of the descriptor define the server notification and indication status, with the remaining 14 bits undefined. The `writeValue((uint8_t*)data, 2, true)` instruction defines the data array sent to the server, which consists of 2 bytes or 16 bits, with *true* indicating a response to the client.

A BLE message is formatted as a character array with variables converted to strings and the combined string, *str*, converted to the character array, *msg*, of length *N* characters with the `str.toCharArray(msg, N)` function. The *C++* `dtostrf(var, len, DP, array)` function converts a float value, *var*, to a character array, *array*, with length *len* characters and *DP* decimal points.

Listing 5-9. BLE with Serial communication for the client

```
#include <BLEDevice.h>                     // include BLE library
BLEAddress * ServerAddress;                // define server address,
BLEScan * BLEScan;                         // scanner,
BLEClient * Client;                        // client
BLERemoteService * Service;                // service
BLERemoteCharacteristic * Char;            // characteristic
BLERemoteDescriptor * Desc;                // descriptor
#include <TFT_eSPI.h>                      // include TFT_eSPI library
TFT_eSPI tft = TFT_eSPI();
char ServerName[] = "ESP32";               // name of required server
                                           // Service UUID
char ServUUID[] = "6e400001-b5a3-f393-e0a9-e50e24dcca9e";
                                           // transmit UUID
char CharUUID[] = "6e400003-b5a3-f393-e0a9-e50e24dcca9e";
char * msg;
float dist;
int RSSI, clientCon = 0, serverFnd = 0;
int leftButton = 0, rightButton = 35;   // module buttons

class DeviceCallback : public BLEAdvertisedDeviceCallbacks
{
  void onResult(BLEAdvertisedDevice advertisedDevice)
  {                                        // scanned servers
```

```
                                          // check server name
    if (advertisedDevice.getName() == ServerName)
    {                               // stop scanning when required server found
      advertisedDevice.getScan()->stop();
      RSSI = advertisedDevice.getRSSI();   // RSSI of received signal
      dist = pow(10, (-69.0-RSSI)/20.0);   // distance to server
      tft.fillScreen(TFT_BLUE);
      tft.setCursor(0,0);
      tft.printf("RSSI %d dist %.2f \n", RSSI, dist);
      ServerAddress =
          new BLEAddress(advertisedDevice.getAddress());
      serverFnd = 1;                       // found required server
    }
  }
};
                                          // callback function
class ClientCallback : public BLEClientCallbacks
{
  void onConnect(BLEClient* client)        // client connect to server
  {
    clientCon = 1;                         // display server name
    tft.printf("connected to %s \n", ServerName);
    delay(500);
  }
  void onDisconnect(BLEClient* client)
  {
    serverFnd = 0;
    clientCon = 0;
```

```
    tft.fillScreen(TFT_BLUE);          // clear screen
    tft.setCursor(0,20);
    tft.printf("%s disconnect \n", ServerName);
  }
};

void setup()
{
  pinMode(leftButton, INPUT_PULLUP);   // buttons active LOW
  pinMode(rightButton, INPUT_PULLUP);
  tft.init();
  tft.setRotation(3);                  // landscape USB to left
  tft.fillScreen(TFT_BLUE);            // blue screen for Bluetooth
  tft.setTextColor(TFT_WHITE, TFT_BLUE);
  tft.setTextSize(2);
  tft.setCursor(0,0);
  tft.println("BLE Client");
  BLEDevice::init("");                 // initialize client
  BLEScan = BLEDevice::getScan();      // and BLE scanner
                           // callback to notify BLE device detected
  BLEScan->setAdvertisedDeviceCallbacks(new DeviceCallback());
  BLEScan->setActiveScan(true);        // active obtains a scan response
}

void serverConnect(BLEAddress Address) // connect to BLE server
{                                      // server MAC address
  tft.printf("%s \n", Address.toString().c_str());
  Client = BLEDevice::createClient();  // initialize BLE client
                           // callback to manage connection to server
  Client->setClientCallbacks(new ClientCallback());
```

```
  Client->connect(Address);                 // connect to server
  Service = Client->getService(ServUUID); // initialize BLE service
                                            // add characteristic
  Char = Service->getCharacteristic(CharUUID);
                                            // add descriptor
  Desc = Char->getDescriptor(BLEUUID((uint16_t)0x2902));
  Char->registerForNotify(callback);       // request notifications
}                                    // callback to manage notification
void callback(BLERemoteCharacteristic * BLERemoteChar,
              uint8_t * data, size_t length, bool notfy)
{
  msg = (char*)data;                        // convert to character array
  tft.setCursor(0,80);
  tft.fillRect(0,80, 240, 50, TFT_BLUE);   // clear previous notification
                                     // update displayed notification
  tft.printf("message len %d \n", length);
  for (int i=0; i<length; i++) tft.print(msg[i]);
}

void notify(String state)                   // function to request
{                                           // notifications
  uint8_t data[] = {0x01, 0};               // define notification
  if(state == "off") data[0] = 0x0;         // status as on or off
                                            // transmit status to server
  Desc->writeValue((uint8_t*)data, 2, true);
  tft.setCursor(0, 50);
  tft.printf("notify %s \n", state);        // update displayed status
}
```

```
void loop()
{                                   // connect to server
  if(serverFnd == 1 && clientCon == 0)
            serverConnect(*ServerAddress);
                                    // otherwise scan 5s for server
  else if(serverFnd == 0) BLEScan->start(5, false);
                                    // buttons to turn on or off notifications
  if (digitalRead(leftButton) == LOW && clientCon == 1)
        notify("off");
  else if (digitalRead(rightButton) == LOW && clientCon == 1)
        notify("on ");
  delay(100);                       // crude debounce of buttons
}
```

BLE Scanning

In Listing 5-9, the BLE scanner is initialized with the *DeviceCallback* function to determine if a detected BLE device has the same name as the required server. Information on scanned BLE devices, including the device name, MAC address, RSSI, and distance from the scanning ESP32 microcontroller, is displayed with the sketch in Listing 5-10.

Listing 5-10. BLE scanner

```
#include <BLEDevice.h>        // include BLE library
BLEScan * BLEScan;            // define scanner and
int scan = 5;                 // scan time (secs)
int RSSI;
float dist;
```

```
class DeviceCallback : public BLEAdvertisedDeviceCallbacks
{
  void onResult(BLEAdvertisedDevice advertisedDevice)
  {                                          // BLE device name
    Serial.print("name ");
    Serial.print(advertisedDevice.getName().c_str());
    Serial.print(" address ");               // BLE device address
    Serial.print(advertisedDevice.getAddress().
                 toString().c_str());
    RSSI = advertisedDevice.getRSSI();       // RSSI of received signal
    dist = pow(10, (-69.0-RSSI)/20.0);       // distance to BLE device
    Serial.printf(" RSSI %d distance %.2f \n", RSSI, dist);
  }
};
void setup()
{
  Serial.begin(115200);
  BLEDevice::init("");                       // initialize BLE
  BLEScan = BLEDevice::getScan();            // and BLE scanner
  BLEScan->setAdvertisedDeviceCallbacks(new DeviceCallback());
  BLEScan->setActiveScan(true);              // obtain a scan response
}

void loop()
{                                          // number of scanned devices
  BLEScanResults res = BLEScan->start(scan, false);
  Serial.printf("%d Devices found\n", res.getCount());
  BLEScan->clearResults();
}
```

BLE Receive App

BLE messages transmitted by an ESP32 microcontroller, acting as an Eddystone beacon, are received by an app, built with *MIT App Inventor*, that scans for an advertising beacon and displays the BLE message. The *MIT App Inventor BluetoothLE* extension is required with details available at `iot.appinventor.mit.edu/#/bluetoothle/bluetoothleintro`. The *BluetoothLE* extension is downloaded as `edu.mit.appinventor.ble-20200828.aix` and is saved on the laptop or computer Desktop. The *BluetoothLE* extension is uploaded to *MIT App Inventor* by selecting the *Extension* palette on the left side of the Designer window of *MIT App Inventor*, selecting *Import extension*, and entering the location of the saved file. When an app including the *BluetoothLE* extension is installed on a mobile phone or Android table, the app permissions must include *Location*.

The BLE message content, in ASCII format, is converted to decimal format for transmission, and the app displays the beacon message in both formats (see Figure 5-7). The *Decimal.xoma.aix* extension by B. G. Kumaraswamy converts the decimal-formatted data to ASCII format. The *Decimal* extension is available at `community.appinventor.mit.edu/uploads/short-url/385f5ucPOOGnV2KF6etdeJEgPMe.aix`.

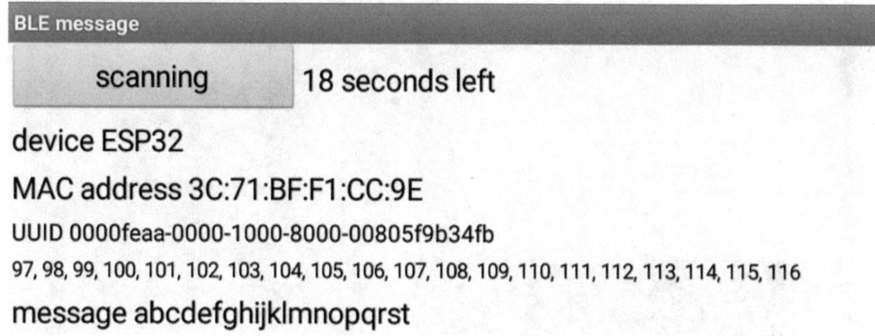

Figure 5-7. *BLE receive app*

The app layout includes a *HorizontalArrangement* containing a button to start scanning for BLE advertisements and a label for a counter variable (see Figure 5-8). Labels to display the BLE device name and MAC address, the advertised service UUID, and the beacon message in both decimal and ASCII formats are included. The *BluetoothLE* and *Decimal* extensions are incorporated in the app with the *Clock* component, which is located in the *Sensors* palette of the *MIT App Inventor* Designer window. The two extensions and the *Clock* component are displayed below the app layout as *Non-visible components*. The *ListView* component, located in the *User Interface* palette, contains the list of detected Bluetooth devices. In the *ListView* Properties, the default *BackgroundColor* and the *TextColor* are changed to white and black, respectively.

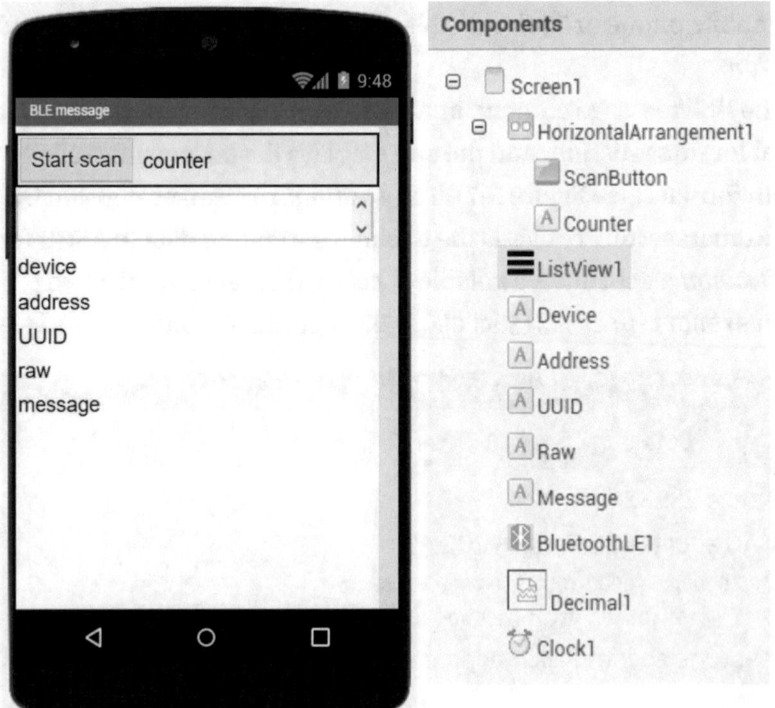

***Figure 5-8.** BLE receive app layout*

The app requires both the *StartScanning* and *ScanAdvertisments* blocks to detect advertising BLE devices, with scanning for an arbitrary period of 30s after the *Scan* button is clicked (see Figure 5-9). The long scanning period enables detection of changes in the BLE message. The *DeviceList* block provides a list of detected BLE devices, containing the MAC addresses, device names, and RSSI values, which does not include duplicates, unlike the *AdvertiserNames* block.

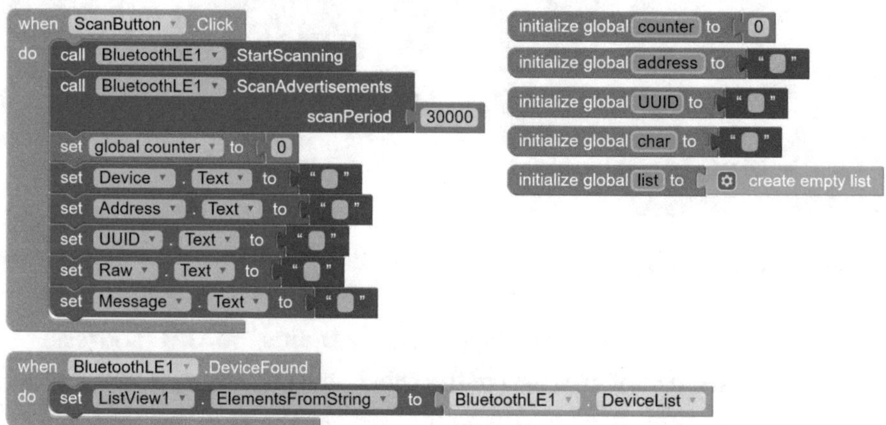

Figure 5-9. *BLE receive app scanning blocks*

The *Clock* component periodically checks if a BLE device name has been selected from the list of BLE advertiser devices, which is generated during scanning (see Figure 5-10). When a device is selected, the *getData* and *editData* procedures are called, and the remaining scanning time is displayed, based on the *Counter* variable, which increments with the *Clock* component. After the scanning period of 30s has elapsed, the *reset* procedure is called.

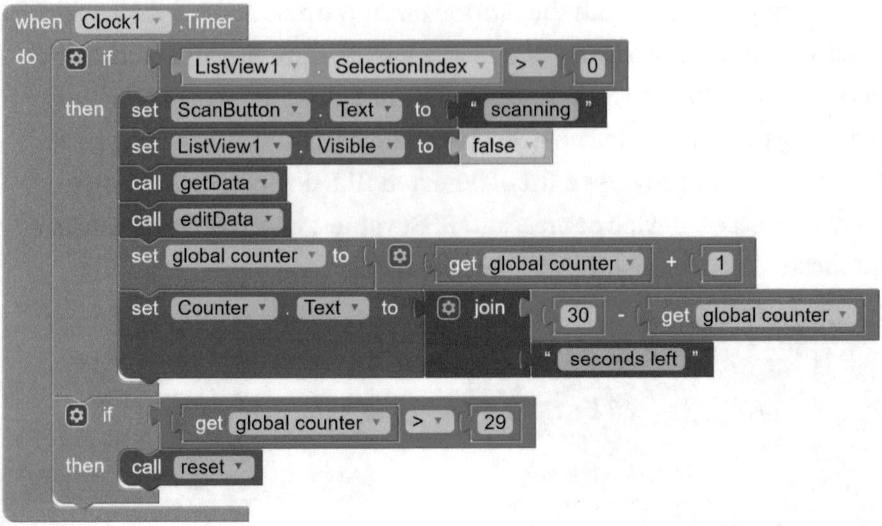

Figure 5-10. *BLE receive app timer blocks*

The *getData* procedure (see Figure 5-11) obtains the MAC address and the advertised service UUID of the selected BLE device, which are accessed by the *FoundDeviceAddress*, indexed by the *ListView* selected item, and *AdvertiserServiceUuids* blocks, respectively. The content of the BLE device message is accessed by the *AdvertisementData* block, which requires the BLE device MAC address and advertised service UUID.

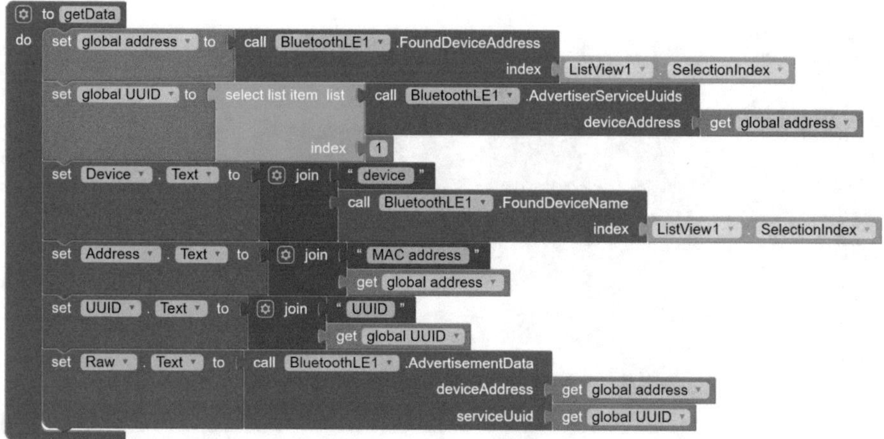

Figure 5-11. *BLE receive app data blocks*

The BLE device message is formatted as *[n,n,...,n]*, where *n* is a decimal number, and both square brackets are changed to a space character with the *replace all text* block. The BLE device message is converted from *csv* (comma-separated values) format to a list with the *list from csv row* block. With the *for each ... do* block, each item of the list is converted to ASCII format with the *DecimalToText* block of the *Decimal* extension (see Figure 5-12). Sequential characters of the BLE message are concatenated with the *join* block.

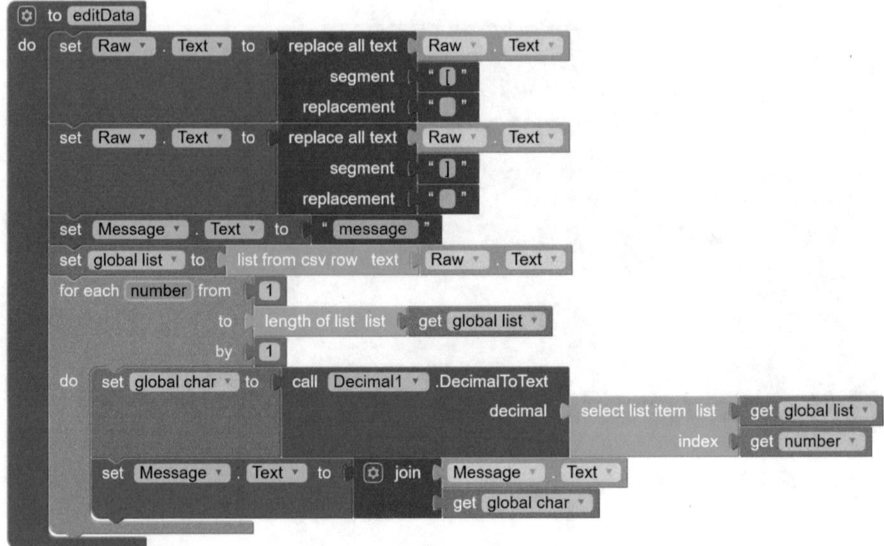

***Figure 5-12.** BLE receive app editing blocks*

At the end of the scanning period, scanning is stopped with the *StopScanning* block, the *Counter* and *ScanButton* variables are reset, and the *ListView* is reset to an empty list (see Figure 5-13).

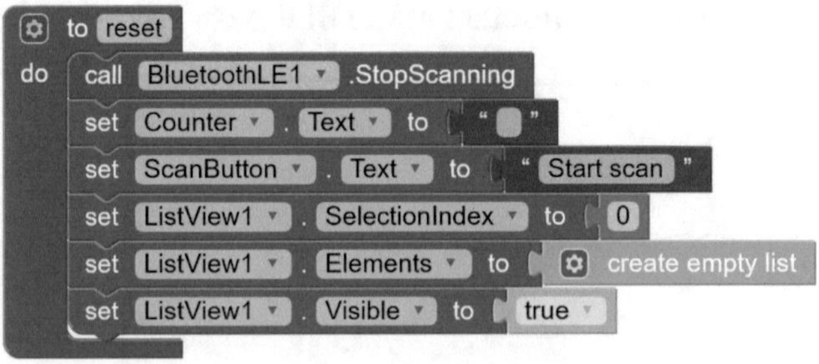

***Figure 5-13.** BLE receive app reset blocks*

The sketch for an ESP32 microcontroller to transmit BLE messages, while acting as an Eddystone beacon, is shown in Listing 5-11. The *setBeacon* function replaces the *setBeacon* function in the sketch of

Listing 5-2. The maximum length of the text message is 20 characters. The beacon name is not defined, as the default beacon name is "*ESP32*". The message is an alternating set of 20 characters, but a sensor description and reading or a device state are more pragmatic options for the message content.

Listing 5-11. Transmit text with an Eddystone beacon

```
void setBeacon()                  // function to generate beacon message
{
  String text;                    // message up to 20 char.
  if((reboot % 2) == 1) text = "abcdefghijklmnopqrst";
                   else text = "ghijklmnopqrstuvwxyz";
  char beaconData[20];            // beacon message array
  uint16_t UUID = 0xFEAA;         // Eddystone UUID
  BLEAdvertisementData advertData = BLEAdvertisementData();
  advertData.setCompleteServices(BLEUUID(UUID));
  for (int i=0; i<text.length(); i++) beaconData[i] = text[i];
  advertData.setServiceData(BLEUUID(UUID),
            std::string(beaconData, 20));
  advertise->setAdvertisementData(advertData);
}
```

nRF24L01 Module as a BLE Transceiver

The nRF24L01 radio transceiver module operates at 2.4GHz, the same frequency as Bluetooth Low Energy, and communicates with an Arduino Nano or Uno using Serial Peripheral Interface (SPI). The nRF24L01 module imitates a BLE beacon to transmit or receive BLE advertisements to or from an Android tablet or mobile phone hosting the *nRF Connect* app, which is available on *Google Play Store*. While the nRF24L01 module can transmit over 126 channels, only three channels, 2.402, 2.426, and 2.480GHz, are available as a BLE beacon. The nRF24L01 module transmits a message of up to 32 bytes, but when imitating a BLE device, 3 bytes are required for the CRC (Cyclic Redundancy Check) error checking code, 6 bytes for the MAC address, 5 bytes for device attributes, and 2 bytes for the packet header, which only leaves 16 bytes for a message. The nRF24L01 module is connected to an Arduino Nano or Uno identically when the module functions as a radio transceiver (see Figure 5-14 with connections in Table 5-5). The nRF24L01 module CE (transmit/receive) and CSN (standby/active mode) pins are connected to any Arduino GPIO pin, with GPIO 9 and 10 used in Listings 5-12 and 5-13.

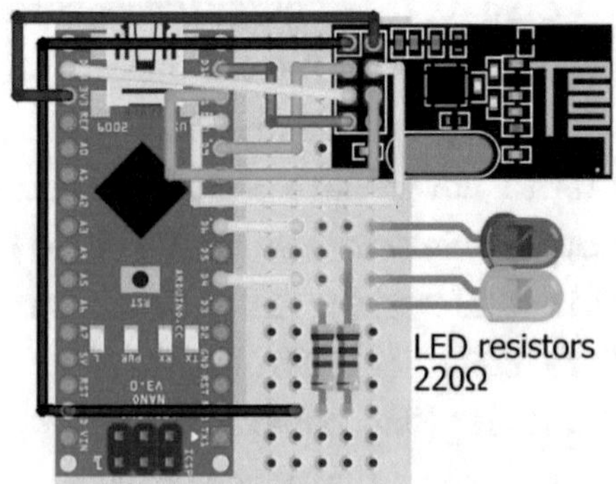

Figure 5-14. *nRF24L01 as a BLE transceiver*

Table 5-5. *Connections for nRF24L01 as a BLE transceiver*

Component	Connect to	and to
nRF24L01 GND	Arduino GND	
nRF24L01 CE	Arduino GPIO 9	
nRF24L01 SCK	Arduino GPIO 13	
nRF24L01 MISO	Arduino GPIO 12	
nRF24L01 VCC	Arduino 3.3V	
nRF24L01 CSN	Arduino GPIO 10	
nRF24L01 MOSI	Arduino GPIO 11	
Red LED long leg	Arduino GPIO 6	
Green LED long leg	Arduino GPIO 4	
LED short legs	220Ω resistor	Arduino GND

The *BTLE* library by Florian Echtler and the *RF24* library by J. Coliz are required for the nRF24L01 module to imitate a BLE beacon. Both libraries are available within the Arduino IDE. The built-in *SPI* library is also required. In Listing 5-12, the nRF24L01 module is named *nRFBLE* and transmits a value formatted as a BLE temperature characteristic, which has a temperature service UUID of *0x1809*.

Listing 5-12. nRF24L01 as a BLE transmitter

```
#include <BTLE.h>         // include BTLE, SPI
#include <SPI.h>          // and RF24 libraries
#include <RF24.h>
RF24 radio(9,10);         // associate radio with RF24
BTLE btle(&radio);        // and btle with BTLE library
float temp;
```

```
void setup()
{
  Serial.begin(115200);       // Serial Monitor baud rate
  btle.begin("nRFBLE");       // initialize BTLE device
}                             // with name nRFBLE

void loop()
{
  temp = random(1,100);
  nrf_service_data buf;       // define BLE service buffer
                              // and UUID
  buf.service_uuid = NRF_TEMPERATURE_SERVICE_UUID;
                              // convert variable to BLE format
  buf.value = BTLE::to_nRF_Float(temp);
                              // check message length
  if(!btle.advertise(0x16, &buf, sizeof(buf)))
       Serial.println("output error");
  else Serial.println(temp);
  btle.hopChannel();          // move to next BLE channel
  delay(5000);                // delay between transmissions
}
```

On the *nRF Connect* app, the *SCANNER* option is selected, the nRF24L01 BLE beacon is identified with the *SCAN* option, and the BLE message is available by clicking the nRF24L01 BLE beacon, named *nRFBLE* (see Figure 5-15).

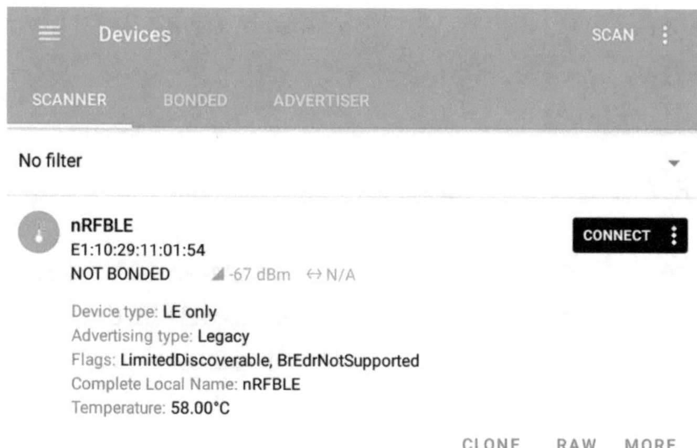

Figure 5-15. *BLE message transmitted by the nRF24L01 module*

A BLE advertisement is used to control a device attached to the Arduino Nano, which is connected to the nRF24L01 module, which imitates a BLE receiver. The BLE advertisement received by the nRF24L01 module contains the LED channel number and state, with the corresponding LED turned on or off by the Arduino microcontroller. A BLE advertisement is formatted as *xxxxN0Sxxx...xxx*, referencing the LED channel number (*N*) and state (*S*), respectively. Double-digit LED channel numbers are not available, as the Arduino Nano pins 10 to 13 are required for SPI communication. In Listing 5-13, the BLE advertisement consists of the LED channel number and state, which are extracted, and the corresponding LED is turned on or off, after the LED channel is defined as *OUTPUT*. Constraining a received message to contain exactly three characters functions as a filter for noise.

Listing 5-13. nRF24L01 as a BLE receiver

```
#include <BTLE.h>      // include BTLE, SPI
#include <SPI.h>       // and RF24 libraries
#include <RF24.h>
RF24 radio(9,10);      // associate radio with RF24
```

```
BTLE btle(&radio);                 // and btle with BTLE library
String str;
int channel, state;

void setup()
{
  Serial.begin(9600);              // Serial Monitor baud rate
  btle.begin("nRFBLE");            // initialize BTLE device
}                                  // with name nRFBLE

void loop()
{
  if(btle.listen())                // when BLE advertisement available
  {
    str = "";                      // increment string with BLE buffer
    for (int i=2; i<(btle.buffer.pl_size)-6; i++)
                    str = str + btle.buffer.payload[i];
    Serial.printf("payload %s \n", str);      // display payload
    if(str.length() == 3)
    {
      channel = str.toInt()/100;   // LED channel
      state = str.toInt() % 10;    // LED state
      pinMode(channel, OUTPUT);    // LED channel as OUTPUT
      digitalWrite(channel, state);           // turn on or off LED
    }
  }
  btle.hopChannel();               // move to next BLE channel
}
```

On the *nRF Connect* app, the *ADVERTISER* option is selected and the "+" symbol clicked to generate a new advertising packet. Enter the name of the advertisement, such as *Red LED On,* in the *Display name* section, click *ADD RECORD,* click *Manufacturer Data,* and in the *Company ID* value enter a four-digit channel number, such as *0006* or *0004,* to correspond with the Arduino GPIO pin connected to the red or green LED. In the *Data (HEX)* value, enter the two-digit LED state, such as *01* or *00,* to turn on or off the LED (see Figure 5-16). An advertisement is copied with the *CLONE* option, which is edited to generate a second advertisement, such as *Red LED Off* with data *<0x0006> 0x00* or *Green LED On* with data *<0x0004> 0x01*. The Serial Monitor should be closed and the Arduino reset after editing the *nRF Connect* app.

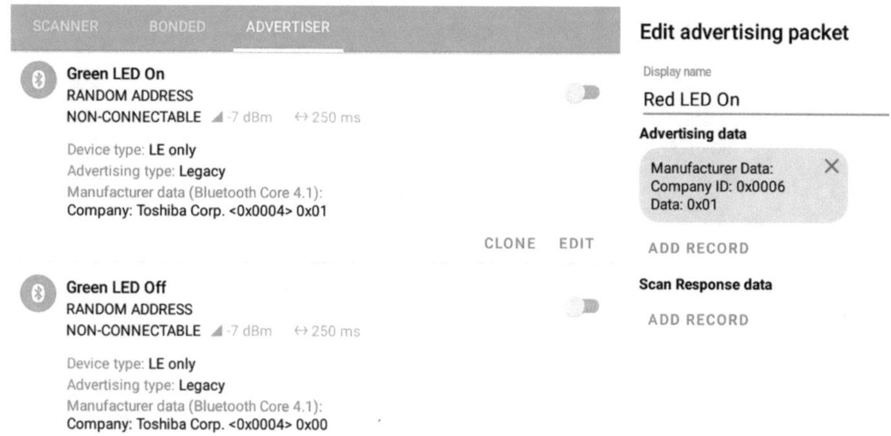

Figure 5-16. *nRF24L01 as a BLE receiver*

On the *nRF Connect* app, when an advertisement slide switch, opposite a *Display name,* is clicked (see Figure 5-16), the *Advertisement timeout* is displayed (see Figure 5-17). Edit the *Timeout* interval to 2000ms and click the box *Remember for this packet* to automatically switch off all advertisements after an interval of two seconds and then click *OK.* Alternatively, select *Until manually turned off,* and the BLE transmissions will repeat until manually turned off.

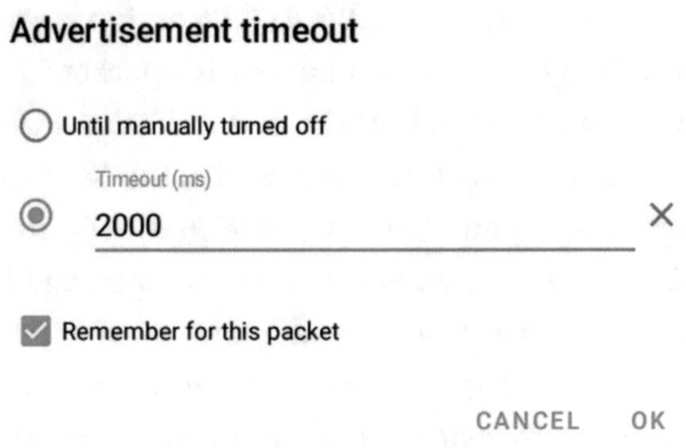

Advertisement timeout

Until manually turned off

Timeout (ms)

2000

Remember for this packet

CANCEL OK

Figure 5-17. *Timeout for BLE transmission*

CHAPTER 6

LoRa and Microsatellites

Different communication protocols operate at different frequencies, over different distances and with different data rates. RFID (Radio Frequency IDentification), Bluetooth, and Bluetooth Low Energy (BLE) technologies have lower data rates than Wi-Fi communication, which has a lower range than the mobile telecommunication technology standards of 2G–5G. LoRa (Long Range) is a low-power wide-area network (LPWAN) technology developed by Semtech. LoRa communication operates with a form of frequency modulation at lower frequencies than the 2.4GHz of Wi-Fi and Bluetooth communication. LoRaWAN (Long Range Wide Area Network) is the protocol for creating LoRa-based networks.

LoRa achieves a long transmission range by spreading a transmission across the available bandwidth, although the transmission bit rate is decreased. The LoRa signal spreading factor (SF) ranges from 7 to 12. For example, with a 125kHz bandwidth, increasing the SF from 7 to 10 increases the transmission range from 2km to 8km, but decreases the transmission bit rate from 5469bps to 977bps. Details of LoRa transmission

N. Cameron, *ESP32 Formats and Communication*,
https://doi.org/10.1007/978-1-4842-9376-8_6

range are available at lora-developers.semtech.com/documentation/tech-papers-and-guides/lora-and-lorawan. The transmission bit rate is defined as $SF \times BW \times \left(\frac{4}{4+CR}\right) / 2^{SF}$ for a bandwidth (BW) and coding rate (CR) (see the Semtech AN1200.22 and Semtech SX1276 documents).

The Semtech SX1276 and SX1278 LoRa modules are powered by 1.8–3.6V, but differ in frequency range, 137–1020MHz and 137–525MHz, respectively. LoRa frequencies, for signal transmission and reception, appropriate to each country are listed at www.thethingsnetwork.org/docs/lorawan/frequencies-by-country/. Both the SX1276 and SX1278 modules have LoRa spreading factors of 7–12 and a bandwidth of 8–500kHz, giving effective bit rates of up to 37.5kbps.

The TTGO LoRa32 V2.1 1.6 module includes a Semtech SX1276 LoRa module, with a frequency of 433, 868, or 915MHz, and an SMA (SubMiniature version A) antenna. This chapter uses a TTGO LoRa32 V2.1 1.6 module with a 433MHz frequency, and the module is described in Chapter 1, "ESP32 Microcontroller."

ESP32 as a LoRa Transmitter or Receiver

The *LoRa* library by Sandeep Mistry is recommended, with the library available in the Arduino IDE. The LoRa transmission frequency, in MHz, is defined by the LoRa.begin(NE6) instruction, with *N* equal to 433, 868, or 915. The C-plus notation NEM is equivalent to N × 10^M. The *LoRa* library supports SF of 7–12 and bandwidth of 7.8–250kHz with a default bandwidth of 125kHz. Available SF and bandwidth are listed on the *LoRa* library website. The maximum LoRa transmission length is 255 bytes with the *LoRa* library. Library functions are described at github.com/sandeepmistry/arduino-LoRa/blob/master/API.md.

Communication between the ESP32 microcontroller and a LoRa module uses SPI (Serial Peripheral Interface), which has two options: VSPI and HSPI. An interpretation of the VSPI and HSPI acronyms is Virtual, or software, and Hardware SPI. VSPI is the default SPI option, and the following instructions to initialize VSPI for LoRa communication are not required:

```
SPIClass vspi(VSPI)
vspi.begin(SCK, MISO, MOSI, SS)
LoRa.setSPI(vspi)
```

However, the instructions to define the LoRa module chip select (CS), reset (RST), and interrupt (IRQ) pins are required:

```
digitalPinToInterrupt(LORA_IRQ)
LoRa.setPins(LORA_CS, LORA_RST, LORA_IRQ)
```

Both VSPI and HSPI are utilized for communication between the ESP32 microcontroller of the TTGO LoRa32 V2.1 1.6 module and the LoRa module, for signal reception, and between the ESP32 microcontroller and the built-in micro-SD card reader/writer, to store LoRa signal data.

HSPI communication between the ESP32 microcontroller and the micro-SD card reader/writer is initialized with the instructions

```
SPIClass hspi(HSPI)
hspi.begin(SD_SCK, SD_MISO, SD_MOSI, SD_CS)
SD.begin(SD_CS, hspi))
```

In the *pins_arduino* file for the *ttgo-lora32-v21new* ESP32 board variant (see Chapter 1, "ESP32 Microcontroller"), the VSPI variables *SCK, MISO, MOSI, SS, LORA_RST,* and *LORA_IRQ* are defined as GPIO 5, 19, 27, 18, 23, and 36, with *SCK* equal to *LORA_CS*. The HSPI variables *SD_SCK, SD_MISO, SD_MOSI,* and *SD_CS* are defined as GPIO 14, 2, 15, and 13.

LoRa communication between two ESP32 microcontrollers acting as a transmitter or a receiver is demonstrated with two TTGO LoRa32 V2.1 1.6 modules. The transmitting device brackets a message with *#A* and *Z#* to form a packet and to differentiate received packets from noise. The receiving device writes the contents of a received packet to a micro-SD card inserted in the built-in SD card reader/writer of the TTGO LoRa32 V2.1 1.6 module.

For the situation, when a TTGO LoRa32 V2.1 1.6 module is battery powered, the battery voltage is displayed on the built-in OLED screen, along with the LoRa logo and the transmitted or received message. The built-in LED is flashed when a message is transmitted or received.

The sketch for the transmitting device is given in Listing 6-1. The *SPI* library is referenced by the *LoRa, SD,* and *Adafruit_SSD1306* libraries, with the latter referencing the *Wire* and *Adafruit GFX* libraries, so the `#include <SPI.h>`, `#include <Wire.h>`, and `#include <Adafruit_GFX.h>` instructions are not required. The SX1276 LoRa module frequency, spreading factor, and bandwidth and the interrupt pin are defined in the *setup* function. In the *loop* function, a generated packet is transmitted every five seconds. The built-in LED is flashed at each transmission by being turned on for the time taken to transmit the LoRa packet and update the OLED screen, and the LED is then turned off. The TTGO LoRa32 V2.1 1.6 module battery voltage is displayed by the *battVolt* function, prior to transmitting a package, with the voltage on the module ADC (analog to digital converter) pin, GPIO 35, doubled as a built-in voltage divider halves the ADC input voltage (see Chapter 1, "ESP32 Microcontroller").

Generating a bitmap of an image, such as the LoRa logo, is described in Chapter 10, "Managing Images." The image data is stored in flash or programmable memory, *PROGMEM*, which has more capacity than RAM, where variables are created and manipulated in a sketch. The LoRa logo data is included on a separate tab, *logo.h,* with the instructions

```
int logoWidth = 50;
int logoHeight = 30;
const uint8_t PROGMEM logo[] = {
0x0, 0x0, 0x0, 0x0, 0x0, 0x0, 0x0, 0x0, 0x1F,0xFF,0x0, 0x0, 0x0, 0x0,
0x0, 0x78,0x3, 0xC0,0x0, 0x0, 0x0, 0x0, 0x0, 0x0, 0x0, 0x0, 0x0, 0x0,
0x0, 0x7, 0xFC,0x0, 0x0, 0x0, 0x0, 0x0, 0x1C,0x7, 0x0, 0x0, 0x0, 0x0,
```

and intermediate lines

```
0x0, 0x1F,0xFF,0x0, 0x0, 0x0, 0x0, 0x0, 0x0, 0x0, 0x0, 0x0, 0x0, 0x0
};
```

Each image row contains 50 pixels, requiring 7 bytes with the last byte right-filled with zeros. The *logo* array contains 210 values for 30 image rows with 7 values, representing up to 56 pixels, per row.

Listing 6-1. LoRa transmit

```
#include "logo.h"                    // tab with LoRa logo data
#include <LoRa.h>                    // include LoRa library and
#include <Adafruit_SSD1306.h>        // Adafruit SSD1306 for OLED
int width = 128;                     // OLED dimensions
int height = 64;                     // associate oled with library
Adafruit_SSD1306 oled(width, height, &Wire, -1);
int LEDpin = 25;                     // built-in LED
int battPin = 35;                    // ADC for battery voltage
float battery;
unsigned long lastTime;
String txt, packet, recv;
int counter = 0, packetSize;
```

```
void setup()
{
  pinMode(LEDpin, OUTPUT);              // define input and output GPIO
  pinMode(battPin, INPUT);
  digitalPinToInterrupt(LORA_IRQ);      // set pin as interrupt
                                        // define LoRa module pins
  LoRa.setPins(LORA_CS, LORA_RST, LORA_IRQ);
  LoRa.setSpreadingFactor(9);           // define spreading factor
  LoRa.setSignalBandwidth(62.5E3);      // set bandwidth to 62.5kHz
                                        // 433MHz transmission
  while (!LoRa.begin(433E6)) delay(500);
                                        // OLED display I2C address
  oled.begin(SSD1306_SWITCHCAPVCC, 0x3C);
  oled.setTextColor(WHITE);             // set font color
  oled.setTextSize(1);                  // text size 6×8 pixels
  oled.display();
}
void loop()
{
  if(millis() - lastTime > 5000)        // 5s transmission interval
  {
    lastTime = millis();                // update transmission time
    digitalWrite(LEDpin, HIGH);
    battVolt();                         // call battery voltage function
    screen();                           // and OLED display function
    if(counter % 2 == 0) txt = "ABC";
    else txt = "FGH";
    packet = "#A"+txt+String(counter)+"Z#";          // create packet
    counter++;
    LoRa.beginPacket();                 // start LoRa transmission
    LoRa.print(packet);                 // transmit packet
```

```
    LoRa.endPacket();                   // close LoRa transmission
  }
  digitalWrite(LEDpin, LOW);
  packetSize = LoRa.parsePacket();  // detect received packet
  if (packetSize > 0)
  {
    recv = "";                          // read packet
    while(LoRa.available()) recv = LoRa.readString();
    screen();
  }
}

void screen()                           // function for OLED display
{
  oled.clearDisplay();                  // display LoRa logo
  oled.drawBitmap(30, 0, logo, logoWidth, logoHeight, WHITE);
  oled.setCursor(0,35);
  oled.printf("sent %s \n", packet);  // display transmitted value and
  oled.setCursor(0,45);
  oled.print(recv);                     // received confirmation message
  oled.setCursor(0,55);
                                        // display battery voltage
  oled.printf("battery %4.0fmV \n", battery);
  oled.display();
}

void battVolt()                         // function to measure
{                                       // battery voltage
  battery = 0;                          // average of 20 readings
  for (int i=0; i<20; i++)
      battery = battery + analogReadMilliVolts(battPin);
  battery = battery*2.0/20.0;
}
```

The receiving TTGO LoRa32 V2.1 1.6 module displays, on the built-in OLED screen, the interval between received packets, the RSSI (Received Signal Strength Indicator), the signal to noise ratio (SNR), and the packet length. The packet bracketing terms, *#A* and *Z#*, are removed to display the received message. For confirmation, the receiving device transmits the received packet to the transmitting device, which is also displayed by the transmitting device.

The RSSI, measured in decibels (dBm), quantifies the received signal power as $10^{(dBm/10)}$mW. The RSSI ranges from 0dBm to –120dBm, with a value greater than -50dBm indicating a strong signal, while a weak signal has an RSSI of less than -90dBm. The RSSI is impacted by several factors, such as the distance or obstacles between transmitter and receiver. Given an RSSI, the predicted distance between transmitting and receiving devices is $D = 10^{((RSSI_0 - RSSI)/20)}$, with $RSSI_0 = -69$ at 1m distance, where $RSSI_0$ is the RSSI measured at a fixed distance from the transmitter (see Chapter 5, “BLE Beacons”).

The SNR is the difference between the signal power and the background noise, with a positive SNR indicating that the received signal operates above the noise baseline. LoRa can operate below the noise baseline, which is the limit of signal sensitivity for non-LoRa devices.

The sketch for the receiving device is given in Listing 6-2. The *setup* function is similar to Listing 6-1, except for the micro-SD card management instructions to detect the presence of the micro-SD card, to determine the micro-SD card type and capacity, and to either erase an existing *filename* file or create a new file. In the *loop* function, the bracketing terms of a received packet are checked to differentiate the packet from noise and are removed with the `packet.substring(2, packet.length()-2)` instruction to then display the received message.

The received packet is read either with the instruction

```
while(LoRa.available()) packet = LoRa.readString()
```

which reads characters from the Serial buffer into a string, or the instruction

```
while(LoRa.available()) packet = packet + (char)LoRa.read()
```

which reads the Serial buffer 1 byte at a time, with the byte converted to a character and added to a string.

Signal information is written to the micro-SD card with the instructions

```
file = SD.open(filename, FILE_APPEND)   // open and append to file
file.print(data)                        // write data to file
file.println()                          // new line character
file.close()                            // close file
```

As in Listing 6-1, the time taken to receive the LoRa packet, write to the micro-SD card, and update the OLED screen is sufficient to flash the built-in LED.

Listing 6-2. LoRa receive

```
#include "logo.h"                       // tab with LoRa logo
#include <LoRa.h>                       // include LoRa library
#include <SD.h>                         // and SD library
File file;                              // associate file with SD library
SPIClass hspi(HSPI);                    // SD card uses HSPI
#include <Adafruit_SSD1306.h>           // Adafruit SSD1306 for OLED
int width = 128;                        // OLED dimensions
int height = 64;
                                        // associate oled with library
Adafruit_SSD1306 oled(width, height, &Wire, -1);
int LEDpin = 25;                        // module LED
int battPin = 35;                       // ADC GPIO for battery
int count = 0, SDcard = 0, SDsize;
uint8_t SDtype;
```

```
String packet, filename = "/LoRadata.txt";   // filename for data
                                             // file header
String text, header = "lag,RSSI,SNR,msg,bytes,battery";
int RSSI, dist, packetSize, interval;
float SNR, battery;
unsigned long lastTime = 0, chkTime = 0;

void setup()
{
  pinMode(LEDpin, OUTPUT);                       // define output and
  pinMode(battPin, INPUT);                       // input GPIO
  digitalPinToInterrupt(LORA_IRQ);               // set pin as interrupt
  LoRa.setPins(LORA_CS, LORA_RST, LORA_IRQ);     // define LoRa pins
  while (!LoRa.begin(433E6)) delay(500);         // 433MHz transmission
  oled.begin(SSD1306_SWITCHCAPVCC, 0x3C);        // I2C address
  oled.setTextColor(WHITE);                      // set font color
  oled.setTextSize(1);                           // text size 6×8 pixels
  oled.clearDisplay();
  oled.drawBitmap(30, 0, logo, logoWidth, logoHeight, WHITE);
  oled.setCursor(0, 35);
                                       // initialize SPI for SD card
  hspi.begin(SD_SCK, SD_MISO, SD_MOSI, SD_CS);
  delay(50);                           // time to initialize HSPI
  if(!SD.begin(SD_CS, hspi))           // check for presence of SD card
  {
    oled.print("SD card error");       // do nothing, if no SD card
    oled.display();
  }
  else                                 // when SD card present
  {
    SDcard = 1;
    SDsize = SD.cardSize()/(1024*1024);      // SD card size in MB
```

```
    SDtype = SD.cardType();             // get SD card type
    if(SDtype == CARD_MMC) oled.print("SD type MMC");
    else if(SDtype == CARD_SD) oled.print("SD type SDSC");
    else if(SDtype == CARD_SDHC) oled.print("SD type SDHC");
    else oled.print("SD type UNKNOWN");
    oled.setCursor(0, 45);
                                        // display card type and size
    oled.printf("SD size %d MB \n", SDsize);
    oled.display();
                                        // delete existing file
    if(SD.exists(filename)) SD.remove(filename);
    file = SD.open(filename, FILE_WRITE);        // create new file
    file.print(header);                 // write header to file
    file.println();
    file.close();
  }
  delay(2000);                          // time for user to read SD card
}                                       // information

void loop()
{
  packetSize = LoRa.parsePacket();      // detect received packet
  if(packetSize > 0)
  {
    packet = "";                        // read packet and build message
    while(LoRa.available()) packet = packet + (char)LoRa.read();
    if (packet.startsWith("#A") && packet.endsWith("Z#"))
    {                                   // packet = #A value Z# not noise
      digitalWrite(LEDpin, HIGH);
      battVolt();                       // call battery voltage function
                                        // interval between packets
      interval = round((millis() - lastTime)/1000);
```

```
      lastTime = millis();           // update transmission time
      RSSI = LoRa.packetRssi();      // signal RSSI
      SNR = LoRa.packetSnr();        // signal to noise ratio
                                     // distance to transmitter
      dist = round(pow(10, (-69.0-RSSI)/20.0));
      LoRa.beginPacket();            // start LoRa transmission
      LoRa.print("recv " + packet);  // transmit packet
      LoRa.endPacket();              // close LoRa transmission
      if(SDcard > 0)
      {                              // write data to SD card
        text = String(interval)+","+String(RSSI)+","
               +String(SNR)+",";
        text = text + String(packet)+","
               +String(packetSize)+",";
        text = text + String(battery, 0);       // 0 decimal places
        file = SD.open(filename, FILE_APPEND);
        file.print(text);
        file.println();
        file.close();
      }
      screen();                      // OLED display function
      digitalWrite(LEDpin, LOW);     // no need for delay
    }
  }
}

void screen()                        // function for OLED display
{
    oled.clearDisplay();             // display LoRa logo
    oled.drawBitmap(75, 0, logo, logoWidth, logoHeight, WHITE);
    oled.setCursor(0,0);
    oled.printf("lag %d \n", interval);        // display interval,
    oled.setCursor(0,10);
```

```
    oled.printf("RSSI %d \n", RSSI);              // RSSI and SNR
    oled.setCursor(0,20);
    oled.printf("SNR   %4.2f \n", SNR);
    oled.setCursor(0,30);
                                            // display distance to transmitter
    oled.printf("dist  %d m \n", dist);
                                            // display received bytes
//  oled.printf("bytes %d \n", packetSize);
    oled.setCursor(0,40);
    oled.print("msg   ");                   // display edited message
    oled.print(packet.substring(2, packet.length()-2));
    oled.setCursor(0,50);                   // display battery voltage
    oled.printf("battery %4.0fmV \n", battery);
    oled.display();
}

void battVolt()                             // as in Listing 6-1
```

ESP32 and LoRa Satellites

TinyGS is an open network of Ground Stations, consisting of ESP32 microcontrollers with Semtech SX126x or SX127x LoRa modules, to receive signals from LoRa satellites. There are currently several satellites—Norby, FEES, Gossamer, SATLLA-2A and SATLLA-2B, MDQubeSAT-1, and FossaSat-2E1 to FossaSat-2E13—with more satellites planned. The satellite frequencies include 402, 433, 868, and 918MHz. Details of the TinyGS satellites are available at `tinygs.com/satellites`. The satellites have an altitude of 540–570km and a period of 96 minutes, enabling frequent and predictable signal reception from the satellites by a LoRa receiving module.

Several ESP32 LoRa modules are supported as ground stations for TinyGS, with details given at `github.com/G4lile0/tinyGS`. The TTGO LoRa32 V2.1 1.6 module, which incorporates an OLED screen, was used in this chapter. A potential ground station built with an ESP32 DEVKIT DOIT module, a 433MHz Semtech SX1278 LoRa module, and an OLED screen received test signals using the test satellite, but was unable to receive signals from the LoRa satellites.

Installation and Configuration

TinyGS uses the *Telegram* app as the communication channel, which requires joining the *tinyGS Community* with the *Telegram* app, which is available on *Google Play Store*. The *Telegram* app requires a username and a mobile phone number. Open the website `tinygs.com`, and at the bottom on the web page, click *TELEGRAM*, which opens the *Telegram* app. Select *JOIN GROUP* in the *Telegram* app and select *Get credentials* and click *START*. The message */mqtt* generates the required MQTT account. The TinyGS configuration parameters of *MQTT Username* and *MQTT Password*, as listed in Table 6-1, refer to the *tinyGS Community* MQTT User and Pass, respectively.

To install the TinyGS source code on an ESP32 LoRa module, such as the TTGO LoRa32 V2.1 1.6 module, the *TinyGS_Uploader_WINDOWS.exe* file is downloaded from `github.com/G4lile0/tinyGS/releases`, saved to the computer Desktop, and double-clicked to load the *TinyGS uploader* (see Figure 6-1). Version 2105260 was used for this chapter. The ESP32 LoRa module is connected to the computer hosting the Arduino IDE, the *TinyGS uploader Refresh* button is clicked to identify the ESP32 LoRa module port, and the *Upload tinyGS firmware* button is clicked.

Figure 6-1. *TinyGS uploader*

The ESP32 LoRa module generates a software access point, *My TinyGS*. Connect to the local network of *My TinyGS*; select the URL *192.168.4.1*, as indicated on the OLED screen of the TTGO LoRa32 V2.1 1.6 module, to display the TinyGS menu (see Figure 6-2a); and select *Configure parameters* to display the System configuration form (see Figure 6-2b).

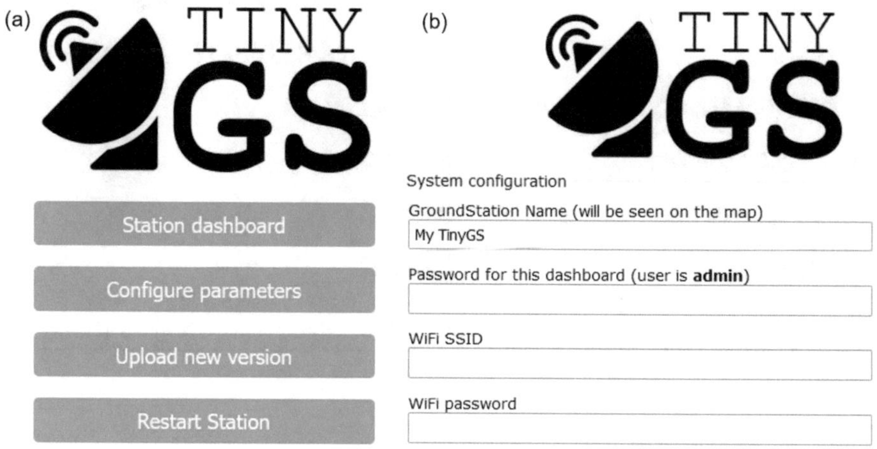

Figure 6-2. *TinyGS menu and configuration*

The parameters required for ground station configuration are shown in Table 6-1.

Table 6-1. *TinyGS configuration parameters*

Configuration parameter	Notes
GroundStation Name	Name shown on the TinyGS website
Password for this dashboard	Your choice of password
Wi-Fi SSID	Your WLAN network SSID
Wi-Fi password	Your WLAN network password
Latitude (3 decimals)	Map position of ground station, which
Longitude (3 decimals)	will be shown on the TinyGS website
Time Zone	For example, Europe/London
Server address	Preset as mqtt.tinygs.com
Server Port	Preset as 8883
MQTT Username	*tinyGS Community* MQTT User
MQTT Password	*tinyGS Community* MQTT Pass
Board type	For example, 433MHz TTGO LoRa32 V2
Enable TX (HAM licence / no preamp)	Deselect
Allow automatic tuning	Select
Allow sending telemetry to third party	Deselect
Test mode	Deselect
Automatic firmware update	Select

The configuration option *Allow automatic tuning* is selected for TinyGS to automatically optimize the LoRa parameters for maximizing reception of satellite packages, given positions of the ground station and satellites. After clicking *Apply*, the ground station is initialized, and the software access point, *My TinyGS*, is disconnected. Reconnect to your WLAN network and enter the URL shown on the OLED screen of the TTGO LoRa32 V2.1 1.6 module, such as *Connected 192.168.1.12*, to display the TinyGS menu (see Figure 6-2a). The ground station is now configured.

The *Station dashboard* option is selected in the TinyGS menu to display the ground station dashboard with the MQTT and Wi-Fi connection status, the name and frequency of the satellite currently being listened to, and the spreading factor, coding rate (*CR + 4*), and bandwidth of the LoRa module (see Figure 6-3). If a username and password are requested by the TinyGS menu, the username is *admin* with the password as entered when configuring the Tiny LoRa module.

Groundstation Status	
Name	LoRa receiver
Version	2105260
MQTT Server	CONNECTED
WiFi	CONNECTED
Radio	READY
Test Mode	DISABLED

Modem Configuration	
Listening to	FossaSat-2E3
Modulation	LoRa
Frequency	401.70
Spreading Factor	11
Coding Rate	8
Bandwidth	125.00

Figure 6-3. *Ground station dashboard*

Test Station Configuration and Test Message

A ground station configuration is confirmed by transmitting a test message from the ground station to a test ground station, which is a second ESP32 LoRa module. The test ground station is configured in the same manner as the ground station, but with a different name.

Both the ground station and the test ground station must be tuned to transmit or receive from the test satellite named *ISM_433*. Tuning the ground station or the test ground station is accessed through the *Telegram* app. In the *Telegram* app, select the *TinyGS Personal Bot* option and send the message */weblogin* to obtain a login link URL. In a web browser, open the login link URL to display the TinyGS *User Console* listing both the ground station and test ground station. Click the ground station and select *OPERATE* to display the ground station tuning options screen (see Figure 6-4). In *Automatic Tuning*, select *Disabled* (see Figure 6-4a), and in *Manual Tuning Satellite Name*, select *ISM_433* (see Figure 6-4b), which is the test satellite. Click *SAVE CONFIG* and then close the display ground station tuning options screen. Repeat the settings for the test ground station.

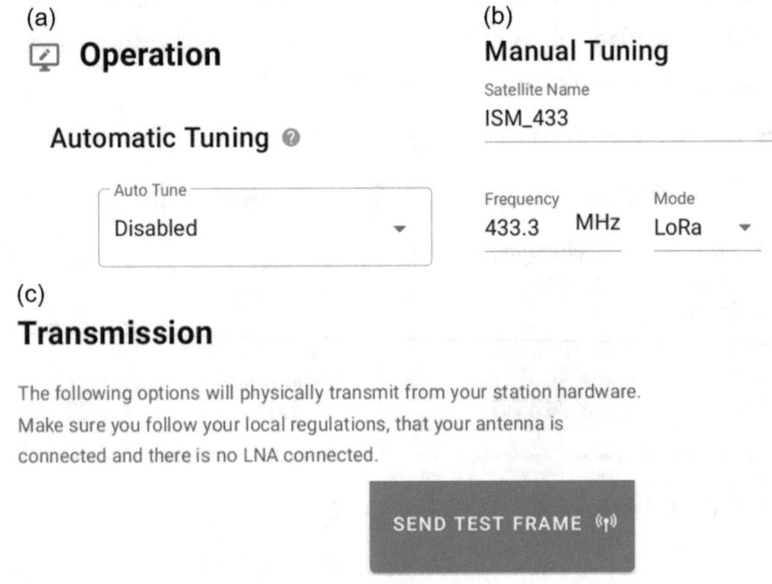

Figure 6-4. *Ground station tuning options*

For the ground station, return to the TinyGS menu (see Figure 6-2a). Select *Configure parameters* and select both *Enable TX (HAM licence / no preamp)* and *Test mode* and then click *Apply*. When *Station dashboard* is selected in the TinyGS menu, the ground station is now shown as being in *Test mode* and listening to *ISM_433* (see Figure 6-5). Repeat the configuration for the test ground station, but only select *Test mode*.

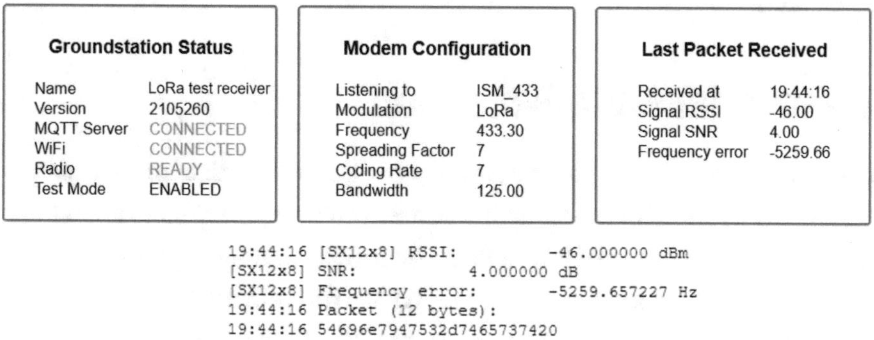

Groundstation Status

Name	LoRa test receiver
Version	2105260
MQTT Server	CONNECTED
WiFi	CONNECTED
Radio	READY
Test Mode	ENABLED

Modem Configuration

Listening to	ISM_433
Modulation	LoRa
Frequency	433.30
Spreading Factor	7
Coding Rate	7
Bandwidth	125.00

Last Packet Received

Received at	19:44:16
Signal RSSI	-46.00
Signal SNR	4.00
Frequency error	-5259.66

```
19:44:16 [SX12x8] RSSI:          -46.000000 dBm
[SX12x8] SNR:              4.000000 dB
[SX12x8] Frequency error:       -5259.657227 Hz
19:44:16 Packet (12 bytes):
19:44:16 54696e7947532d7465737420
```

Figure 6-5. *Transmission to test the ground station*

The ground station transmits a test message by entering *p* in the *Enter command* bar, which is located below *Station dashboard* (see Figure 6-3) of the TinyGS menu. A confirmation message *Sending test packet to nearby stations!* is displayed. The test ground station *Station dashboard* now displays the test message, in HEX format, as *54696e7947532d7465737420* (see Figure 6-5). The test message equates to *TinyGS-test*, by converting HEX to ASCII alphanumeric characters with `www.rapidtables.com/convert/number/hex-to-ascii.html` or by two characters at a time in Microsoft Excel with *CHAR(HEX2DEC(two-characters))*. A test message is also transmitted by the ground station by clicking *SEND TEST FRAME* in the *Transmission* section of the ground station tuning options screen (see Figure 6-4c).

After transmission and reception of the test message by the ground station and the test ground station, respectively, both stations are reset by selecting either *Enabled 433* or *Enabled 868-915*, as appropriate, in the *Automatic Tuning* option (see Figure 6-4a) of the ground station tuning options screen and clicking *SAVE CONFIG*. For the ground station, in the

TinyGS menu (see Figure 6-2a), select *Configure parameters* and deselect both *Enable TX (HAM licence / no preamp)* and *Test mode* and then click *Apply*. For the test ground station, only the *Test mode* option needs to be deselected.

Antenna for LoRa Reception

A quarter-wave ground-plane antenna consists of a vertical monopole of length 0.95 × λ/4, with the transmission wavelength, λ, equal to *c/f*, where *c* is the speed of light (299,792,458m/s or approximately 300Mm/s), *f* is the LoRa transmission frequency, and 0.95 is the velocity factor for the relative transmission speed through metal. The four radials have length 0.95 × 0.28 × λ, rather than 0.95 × 0.25 × λ (see `m0ukd.com/calculators`). With a transmission frequency of 433MHz, the 16.4cm vertical monopole is connected to 18.4cm radials with an SO-239 connector. A schematic of the quarter-wave ground-plane antenna is shown in Figure 6-6a with the male and female SO-239 connectors (Figure 6-6b). The signal and GND plane of the quarter-wave ground-plane antenna are connected to the TTGO LoRa32 V2.1 1.6 module by soldering wires to the SMA antenna pins (Figure 6-6c). The distance between the TTGO LoRa32 V2.1 1.6 module and the quarter-wave ground-plane antenna should be minimized.

Figure 6-6. *Quarter-wave ground-plane antenna*

Microsatellite Tracking

The TinyGS dashboard displays information about the current satellite being listened to and signal information. Selection of *Allow automatic tuning*, in the ground station configuration, maximizes reception of signals from several satellites with the dashboard displaying when a change in the tracked satellite occurs. For example, during a 30-minute period, a range of satellites was listened to as the coverage area of each satellite included the ground station location (see Figure 6-7a). Note that with the configuration option *Automatic firmware update* selected, the ground station periodically checks for firmware updates, which are installed automatically with the OTA (Over the Air) protocol. When a satellite packet is received by the ground station, the TinyGS dashboard displays the signal RSSI and SNR, packet length, and content (see Figure 6-7b). For example, a section of the Norbi packet contained the HEX-coded string *42524B204D57203A3035615F3031*, which equated to *BRK MW :05a_01*.

```
(a) 12:04:05 [SX12x8] Starting to listen to FossaSat-2E4
    12:06:05 [SX12x8] Starting to listen to Norbi
    12:09:05 [SX12x8] Starting to listen to FossaSat-2E1
    12:12:05 [SX12x8] Starting to listen to FossaSat-2E6
    12:14:05 [SX12x8] Starting to listen to FossaSat-2E5
    12:19:05 [SX12x8] Starting to listen to MDQubeSAT-1
    12:27:05 [SX12x8] Starting to listen to FossaSat-2E2
    12:27:23 Checking for firmware Updates...
    12:31:05 [SX12x8] Starting to listen to SATLLA-2A
    12:32:05 [SX12x8] Starting to listen to SATLLA-2B
    12:33:05 [SX12x8] Starting to listen to FossaSat-2E3

(b) 12:08:38 [SX12x8] RSSI:          -128.000000 dBm
    [SX12x8] SNR:           -12.000000 dB
    [SX12x8] Frequency error:       5295.308594 Hz
    12:08:38 Packet (143 bytes):
    12:08:38 8effffffff0 ... 42524b204d57205645523a3035615f3031
```

Figure 6-7. *Microsatellite monitoring and signal reception*

The TinyGS website, `tinygs.com`, provides more signal information than the TinyGS dashboard, as illustrated by Figure 6-8 for the same signal as shown in Figure 6-7. The map highlights the ground stations in the satellite coverage area, with ground stations in green receiving a CRC (Cyclic Redundancy Check) error-free signal from the satellite. The signal information includes the distance to and elevation of the satellite, in addition to the signal RSSI and SNR displayed by the TinyGS dashboard. Details on the TTGO LoRa32 V2.1 1.6 module include the frequency, spreading factor (SF), coding rate (CR), and bandwidth (BW). The satellite information includes

Diameter of the satellite coverage area (5197km in Figure 6-8)

Transmission power, temperature (2000mW and 19°C in Figure 6-8)

Voltage, total power, temperature

Solar panel power, battery capacity, charge power

Median, maximum and minimum solar panel temperatures

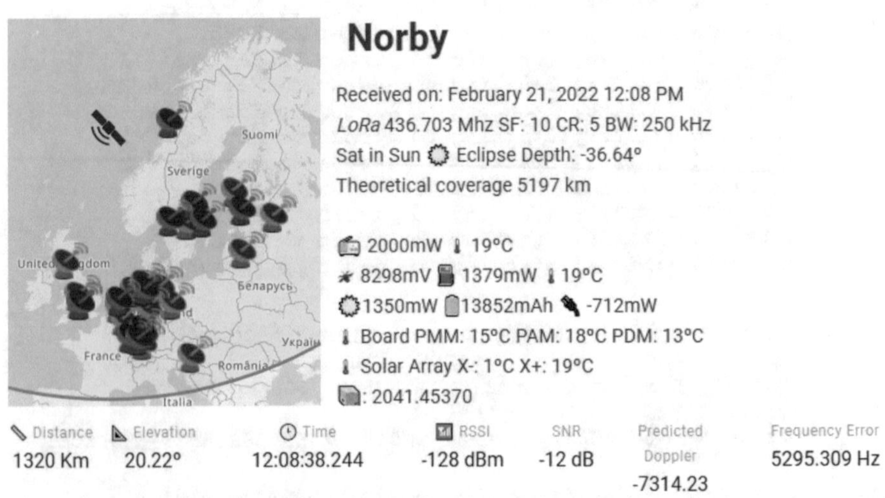

Figure 6-8. *Satellite signal detail*

The distance (km) between the ground station and a satellite is a function of the satellite elevation (*Elev*) and altitude above the Earth ($Alt = 570km$) and the Earth's radius ($Rad = 6378km$), with distance = $\sqrt{\alpha^2 + 2 \times Elev \times Alt + Alt^2} - \alpha^2$, where $\alpha = Rad \times \sin(Elev)$ (see www.itu.int/rec/R-REC-S.1257). A series of satellite signals was recorded over time to provide context to the signal information. The greater the satellite distance from the ground station, the lower the elevation angle as seen from the ground station (see Figure 6-9). An overhead satellite has an elevation of 90°, while a satellite on the horizon has a low elevation.

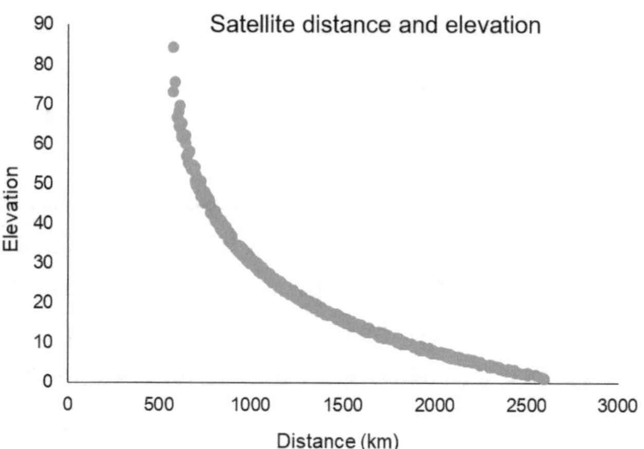

Figure 6-9. *Satellite distance and elevation from the ground station*

A high RSSI was associated with a high SNR, and satellite signals with no CRC errors had higher RSSI and higher SNR than signals with CRC errors (see Figure 6-10a). The SNR of –15dB for signals with no CRC errors may be a threshold, as the majority of signals with a CRC error had an SNR of less than –15dB. A low SNR is indicative of a CRC error, but it is not necessarily the cause of a CRC error. There was no difference in signal SNR with satellite elevation for signals with or without CRC errors (see Figure 6-10b).

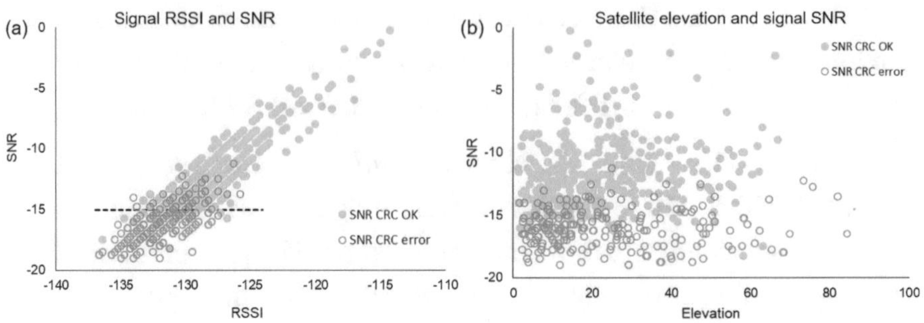

***Figure 6-10.** Satellite elevation and distance, signal SNR and RSSI*

The satellite predicted Doppler and frequency error indicate the direction of travel of the satellite relative to a ground station. The predicted Doppler is positive as the satellite moves toward the ground station, with the opposite for the frequency error.

The TinyGS website, `tinygs.com`, also provides information on a satellite's current latitude and longitude, altitude and velocity, and predicted pass times with elevation and azimuth over a ground station. In the ground station view, select the required ground station and click the satellite marked on the globe to display the satellite pass information (see Figure 6-11).

Name	Latitude	Longitude	Altitude	Velocity
SATLLA-2B	66.34°	-3.71°	500.97 km	7.62 km/s

Passes

Countdown	Start	End	El	Az
ONGOING	04.01 21:02:59	21:14:14	50°	69.03°
00:01:26:15	04.01 22:37:22	22:47:47	19°	268.80°
00:12:46:40	05.01 09:57:47	10:08:32	23°	92.27°

***Figure 6-11.** Predicted satellite passes over a ground station*

Satellite information is also available from `www.n2yo.com` including ten-day satellite pass times over a ground station. A satellite name, for example, *Norbi,* is entered in the web page *Search* box. LoRa satellites are included in the *Amateur Radio* category.

CHAPTER 7

Email and QR Codes

Email and QR (Quick Response) codes are both ubiquitous, and projects with the ESP32 microcontroller incorporate both technologies. Transmitting information or images by email with the ESP32 microcontroller and generating a QR code instructing an ESP32 microcontroller to control a device are described in this chapter.

Email

The ESP32 microcontroller sends an email (electronic mail) with text and image attachments by either Gmail, Outlook, or Hotmail. The *ESP_Mail_Client* library by Mobizt (K. Suwatchai) is recommended, with the library available in the Arduino IDE. An email is sent through an SMTP (Simple Mail Transfer Protocol) server. The sender email account should not be a personal email account, as a coding problem may result in the account being temporarily suspended. In this chapter, email examples are illustrated with Gmail.

The sender's Gmail account must have *2-Step Verification* turned on and an *app password*, which is a 16-character password providing the ESP32 microcontroller with permission to access the Gmail account.

N. Cameron, *ESP32 Formats and Communication*,
https://doi.org/10.1007/978-1-4842-9376-8_7

In the Gmail account, select the *Google Account* logo at the top right, select *Manage your Google Account*, select *Security*, and under *Signing in to Google*, select *2-Step Verification* and select *Get started*. After entering the Gmail account password, a Google verification code is texted to the mobile phone number registered to the Gmail account, and then select *Turn on 2-Step Verification*. Return to the options under *Signing in to Google* and click the forward arrow to the right of *App passwords*. In the *Select app* field, select *Mail*, and in the *Select device* field, select *Other (Custom name)* and give the device a name, such as *ESP32*. Finally, click *Generate*. The 16-character password, generated by Google, is used as the Gmail account password in a sketch for sending an email. Further information is available at `support.google.com/accounts/answer/185833`.

An email containing a formatted message, a counter variable, and two images as attachments is shown in Figure 7-1. Names and email addresses of the sender and the recipient are defined in the sketch, along with the email subject and the message identity. The email message identity, set to *nnn.nnn@gmail.com*, uniquely defines the email message and is arbitrarily based on the number of seconds, *nnn.nnn*, that the sketch has been running.

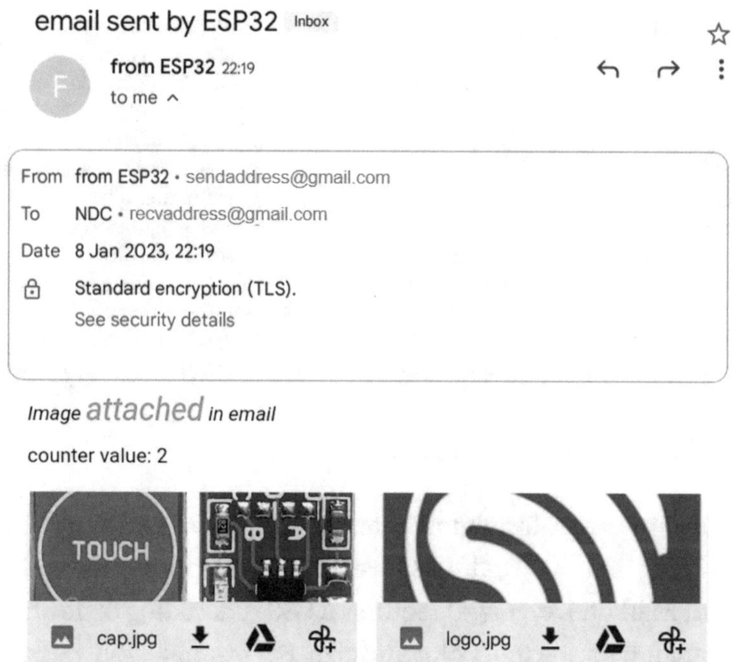

***Figure 7-1.** Email and attachments sent by ESP32*

A section of the original email message content is shown in Figure 7-2 with details of the email transmission time, priority, descriptive names and email addresses of the sender and receiver, email subject, and message identity. The content types of the message text and images, with the transfer encoding, are defined in the sketch (see Listing 7-1). The original email message content also lists the attached files and the file sizes.

```
Delivered-To: <recvaddress@gmail.com>                     recipient email address
X-MSMail-Priority: Normal                                 email priority setting
From: from ESP32 <sendaddress@gmail.com>                  sender name and email address
To: NDC <recvaddress@gmail.com>                           recipient name and email address
Subject: email sent by ESP32                              message subject
Message-ID: <129.43@gmail.com>                            unique email message identity
Date: Sun, 8 Jan 2023 22:19:09 +0000                      transmission time
Content-Type: text/html; charset="utf-8"                  message text format
Content-transfer-encoding: 7bit                           transfer encoding
Content-Type: image/jpg; Name="cap.jpg"                   name, size of image file in SPIFFS
Content-Disposition: attachment; filename="cap.jpg"; size=190541
Content-transfer-encoding: base64                         image transfer encoding
Content-Type: image/jpg; Name="logo.jpg"                  name of HEX coded image
Content-Disposition: attachment; filename="logo.jpg"; size=13485
```

Figure 7-2. *Original email message*

An email message, formatted as text, is simply defined as a string, such as `String str = "Test message"`. A message formatted with HTML (HyperText Markup Language) requires a CSS (Cascading Style Sheets) style instruction for the font color and size. For example, the message *"Image attached in email"* is defined by

```
String str ="<p><i>Image <span style=\"color:#009900;
      font-size:20px;\"> attached</span> in email</i></p>"
```

The term `<i>` defines the italics format of the complete text, while the CSS `style` definition defines the text color and font for only the text bracketed by the `<span>` terms. The adjacent backslash, \, and quote, ", characters are interpreted as a " character.

An email message can only contain a text or an HTML-formatted message, but not both.

An image file attached to an email is either stored in SPIFFS (Serial Peripheral Interface Flash File System), or the image data, formatted as an array of HEX values, is stored in PROGMEM. Chapter 10, "Managing Images," describes uploading files to SPIFFS and converting an image to an array of HEX values for storage in PROGMEM. When including an image in an email, there is no difference between uploading a file to SPIFFS and converting the JPEG or PNG file to HEX values. Both options are utilized in Listing 7-1.

An image file is uploaded to SPIFFS with the *ESP32 Sketch Data Upload* option in the Arduino IDE *Tools* menu. Note that, at the time of writing this chapter, the *ESP32 Sketch Data Upload* option was not available with Arduino IDE version 2.1. The image file, in either JPEG or PNG format, is stored in the *data* folder, which must be created, within the sketch folder and is referenced by the sketch as */image.jpg*, for example. Prior to compiling and uploading the sketch in the Arduino IDE, ensure that both a *Board* and a *Port* are selected and that the Serial Monitor is closed. Click the *ESP32 Sketch Data Upload* option and select the *LittleFS* option, as the *ESP_Mail_Client* library requires the *LittleFS* library. The *SPIFFS* option is for use with the *SPIFFS* library. Once the message *LittleFS Image Uploaded* is displayed, compile and upload the sketch.

The image file *image.jpg* is attached to an email by defining the location of the file in SPIFFS and specifying the flash storage type, as SPIFFS is one of the partitions of flash memory. Instructions for an email to include an image stored in SPIFFS are

```
file.path = "/image.jpg"            // file location in SPIFFS
file.storage_type = esp_mail_file_storage_type_flash
addAttachment()                     // include image in email
```

Alternatively, an image is converted to an array of HEX values, *imagaData*, and stored in PROGMEM, with the array loaded to a separate tab in the sketch. Chapter 10, “Managing Images,” describes converting a JPEG or PNG image to an array of HEX values, storing the array in PROGMEM, and incorporating the array in a sketch. Instructions for an email to include image data, which is stored in PROGMEM, are

```
static const uint8_t imageData[] PROGMEM = {0xFF ... 0xE0}
blob.data = imageData                     // image data array
blob.size = sizeof(imageData)             // size of data array
addAttachment()                           // include image in email
```

In Listing 7-1, the email includes an HTML-formatted message, with an updated counter value, and two images. The capacitive touch module image is stored in SPIFFS, and the logo image is converted to HEX values for storage in PROGMEM. Pressing a switch, which is active *LOW*, triggers sending the email and updating the counter, which is incorporated in the email message. An LED is turned on for the duration of generating and sending the email. The email could also be triggered by a sensor reading exceeding a threshold or after a defined time period has elapsed, instead of pressing a switch. In an energy-saving scenario, the ESP32 microcontroller obtains a sensor reading, emails the time and sensor information, and then returns to sleep mode for a set time period.

An email is sent with either of the TTGO T-Display V1.1, TTGO LoRa32 V2.1 1.6, or ESP32 DEVKIT DOIT module. The TTGO T-Display V1.1 module has switches on GPIO 0 and on GPIO 35, while the TTGO LoRa32 V2.1 1.6 module includes an LED on GPIO 25. Listing 7-1 defines an LED on GPIO 25 and a switch on GPIO 0, so an additional LED or switch must be connected to the TTGO T-Display V1.1 or TTGO LoRa32 V2.1 1.6 module, respectively. Alternatively, the ESP32 DEVKIT DOIT module includes a built-in LED on GPIO 2, and the *BOOT* button is connected to GPIO 0, which is pulled *LOW* when the *BOOT* button is pressed. Listing 7-1 is adapted for the ESP32 DEVKIT DOIT module by changing the *LEDpin* to GPIO 2.

The initial section of Listing 7-1 defines the email host and port and the text or HTML-formatted content of the email message with details of the email sender and recipient. The email host is *smtp.gmail.com, smtp.office365.com*, or *stmp.live.com* for the Gmail, Outlook, or Hotmail sender email addresses, respectively, with the corresponding ports of *465*, *587*, and *465*.

In the *setup* function, a Wi-Fi connection is established, and the email session and message details are defined. A descriptive name and file media type or mime are defined for each attached image, with `file` or `blob` instructions to attach an image stored in SPIFFS or PROGMEM, respectively. Each image definition is completed with an `addAttachment` instruction, and the `resetAttachItem` instruction resets the image attachment definitions.

In the *loop* function, the message HTML code is updated with the incremented counter value, with the string holding the HTML code converted to a C-style, null-terminated string by the `c_str()` function. Similarly, the email message identity is generated from the number of elapsed seconds, with the instruction `String(millis()/1000.0,3)` to retain three digits after the decimal point. The email is sent with the `MailClient.sendMail` instruction.

The *sendCallback* function is called repeatedly to describe the emailing process of *Sending message header, message body, attachments, Closing the session*, and *Message sent successfully*.

An email is sent to several recipients, with each recipient's email address defined in a separate `addRecipient()` instruction, with the instruction `clearRecipients()` prior to redefining recipients. The `empty()` instruction clears data from the email object to free memory.

The character set for a text or an HTML-formatted message is defined by the `text.charSet = "us-ascii"` or `html.charSet = "utf-8"` instruction, respectively, and the `transfer_encoding = Content_Transfer_Encoding::enc_7bit` instruction, with both text and HTML format having the same transfer encoding. In Listing 7-1, the text option is commented out as an email message can only contain a text or an HTML-formatted message, but not both. The encoding format options are *enc_7bit* (not encoded), *enc_8bit* (not encoded), *enc_qp* (quoted-printable encoded), *enc_base64* (encoded), and *enc_binary* (not encoded). In the sketch, the *enc_7bit* (not encoded) option is selected.

Listing 7-1. Send an email with a message and images

```
#include <ESP_Mail_Client.h>          // include library
#include <ssid_password.h>            // file with logon details
#include "logo.h"                     // include image data tab
SMTPSession smtp;                     // associate smtp with SMTP
                                      // connection
ESP_Mail_Session session;             // session with email access,
SMTP_Message message;                 // message with email content
SMTP_Attachment att;                  // and att with attachments

char emailSender[] = "xxxx";          // change xxxx to sender email
char emailPassword[] = "xxxx";        // and xxxx to sender password
char emailName[] = "from ESP32";      // sender name (text)
char emailSubject[] = "email sent by ESP32";
char emailRecipient[] = "xxxx";       // change xxxx to recipient
char emailRcptName[] = "xxxx";        // and to recipient name (text)
char emailHost[] = "smtp.gmail.com";
uint16_t emailPort = 465;
String baseStr = "sample text for message ";
String str, baseHTML, header, newStr, newHTML;
int switchPin = 0, LEDpin = 25;       // switch and LED pins
int counter = 0;

void setup()
{
  Serial.begin(115200);
  pinMode(switchPin, INPUT_PULLUP);
```

```
  pinMode(LEDpin, OUTPUT);              // SPIFFS library loaded
  if(SPIFFS.begin()) Serial.println("SPIFFS OK");
  WiFi.begin(ssid, password);           // initialize and connect Wi-Fi
  while (WiFi.status() != WL_CONNECTED) delay(500);
  Serial.print("IP address ");Serial.println(WiFi.localIP());
  str = "<p><i>Image <span style=\"color:#009900;";
  baseHTML = str +
    "font-size:20px;\">attached</span> in email</i></p>";
  smtp.callback(sendCallback);          // callback funct on
                                        // session close
  session.server.host_name = emailHost;
  session.server.port = emailPort;
  session.login.email = emailSender;
  session.login.password = emailPassword;
  message.sender.name = emailName;
  message.sender.email = emailSender; // repeat sender email
  message.subject = emailSubject;
  message.addRecipient(emailRcptName,
  emailRecipient);                      // recipient email
  message.priority =
        esp_mail_smtp_priority::esp_mail_smtp_priority_normal;
                                        // instructions for text message
//  message.text.charSet = "us-ascii";
//  message.text.transfer_encoding =
//                 Content_Transfer_Encoding::enc_7bit;
                                // instructions for HTML code message
  message.html.charSet = "utf-8";
  message.html.transfer_encoding =
                 Content_Transfer_Encoding::enc_7bit;
```

```
  att.descr.filename = "/cap.jpg";        // name of image
  att.descr.mime = "image/jpg";           // JPEG formatted image
  att.file.path = "/cap.jpg";             // file location in SPIFFS
  att.file.storage_type = esp_mail_file_storage_type_flash;
  att.descr.transfer_encoding =
              Content_Transfer_Encoding::enc_base64;
                                     // attach image (SPIFFS) to email
  message.addAttachment(att);

  message.resetAttachItem(att);           // clear attached item data
  att.descr.filename = "logo.jpg";
  att.descr.mime = "image/jpg";
  att.blob.data = imageData;              // image data array
                                          // in PROGMEM
  att.blob.size = sizeof(imageData);      // size of image data array
  att.descr.transfer_encoding =
               Content_Transfer_Encoding::enc_base64;
  message.addAttachment(att);             // attach image (data
                                          // array) to email

  if (!smtp.connect(&session)) return;    // connect email session
}

void loop()
{
  if(digitalRead(switchPin) == LOW)       // when switch pressed
  {
    digitalWrite(LEDpin, HIGH);           // turn on LED
    counter++;                            // increment counter
                                       // text message commented out
//  newStr = baseStr + String(counter);
//  message.text.content = newStr.c_str();
```

```
    newHTML = baseHTML +
          "<p>counter value: " + String(counter) + "</p>";
    message.html.content = newHTML.c_str(); // HTML code message
    message.clearHeader();                  // reset email header
    header = "Message-ID:<"
            + String(millis()/1000.0) + "@gmail.com>";
    message.addHeader(header);
                                            // false: keep session open
    if (!MailClient.sendMail(&smtp, &message, true))
        Serial.println("Error sending email, " +
                       smtp.errorReason());
    digitalWrite(LEDpin, LOW);
  }
}

void sendCallback(SMTP_Status status)       // function for
{                                           // email send status
  Serial.println(status.info());            // print current status
                                            // email sent success
  if (status.success()) Serial.println("email OK");
}
```

QR Codes

The QR (Quick Response) code is a two-dimensional barcode (see Figure 7-3) invented by Masahiro Hara of Denso Wave, a Japanese automotive company. Information held on a QR code includes text, an email address and message, a phone number, or a web page URL. Scanning a QR code displays information on the user's device (by scanning Figure 7-3a), sends an email (by scanning Figure 7-3b), or makes a phone call from the user's device or opens a web page on the user's device (by scanning Figure 7-3c). Several QR code generators are available, and the *QRCode Monkey* (`www.qrcode-monkey.com`) is recommended for generating a QR code from a comprehensive range of functions.

***Figure 7-3.** QR code functions of text, email, and web page*

Responses to scanning the QR codes in Figure 7-3a and b are shown in Figure 7-4a and b. Text is displayed on scanning the QR code in Figure 7-3a. When the *NEW EMAIL* option is clicked, after scanning the QR code in Figure 7-3b, an email is generated to the email address with "QR codes" as the title and "Send an email by scanning a QR code" as the text. Scanning the QR code in Figure 7-3c opens a browser at the website incorporated in the QR code.

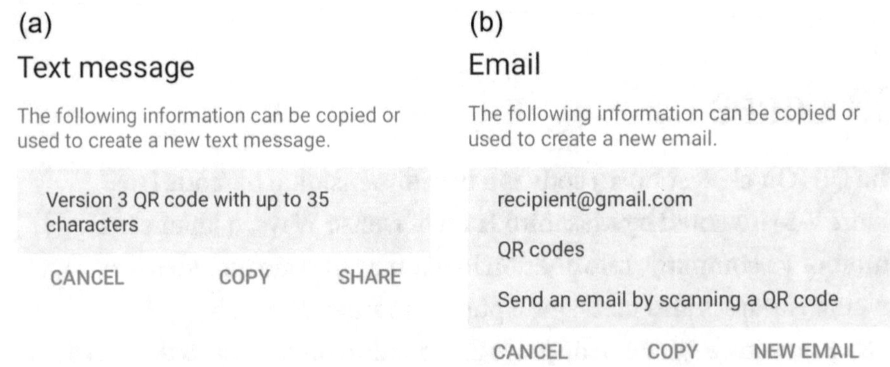

***Figure 7-4.** Responses to scanning QR codes for text and email*

An image is included in the QR code to identify, to the user, the function of the QR code. For example, with the *QRCode Monkey* web page, click *ADD LOGO IMAGE* and upload the image (see Figure 7-3b and c). On the right of the *QRCode Monkey* web page, click *Create QR Code* and then click *Download PNG* to save the QR code. The default size of the QR code is 1000 × 1000 pixels, with a low- to high-quality range of 200 × 200 to 2000 × 2000 pixels. A high pixel number is recommended if a complex picture image is included in the QR code.

The QR code version number defines the amount of information held by a QR code. For example, QR code version 3 (see Figure 7-5a) or version 10 stores a maximum of 35 or 174 characters, respectively, with the QR code consisting of 29 × 29 or 57 × 57 pixels, as the QR code dimension equals (4 × version number + 17) pixels. Further details on QR code versions are available at `www.qrcode.com/en/about/version.html`. A QR code contains finder, alignment, and timing patterns with version and format information for reading the QR code (see Figure 7-5a). The timing patterns connect the finder patterns and consist of alternate black and white pixels. The dark module is a single pixel always positioned at the top-right corner of the bottom-left finder pattern. The information content is positioned in the QR code in a zigzag series of two columns starting from the bottom-right corner (see Figure 7-5b).

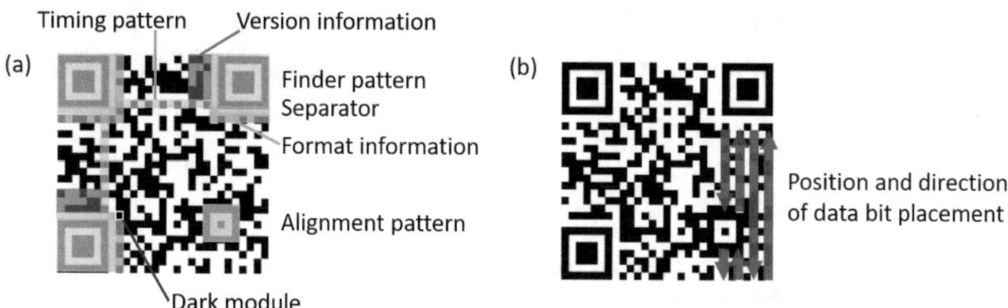

Figure 7-5. *QR code structure*

QR codes are generated by and displayed on an M5Stack Core2 module (see Listing 7-2). The `qrcode("http://URL", x, y, W, N)` instruction creates a version *N* QR code of width *W* pixels for a URL with the QR code displayed at position (*x, y*) of the LCD screen. In the sketch, a new URL is entered on the Serial Monitor, and the M5Stack Core2 module displays the corresponding QR code.

Listing 7-2. QR code generation

```
#include <M5Core2.h>
String url;

void setup()
{
  M5.begin();                          // display M5Stack QR code
  M5.Lcd.qrcode("http://www.m5stack.com", 0, 0, 200, 3);
}

void loop()
{
  if(Serial.available())               // URL entered on Serial Monitor
  {
    url = Serial.readString();
    url = "http://" + url;             // include http:// prefix
    M5.Lcd.qrcode(url, 0, 0, 200, 3);  // display QR code version 3
  }
}
```

HTTP and XML HTTP Requests

The QR code in Figure 7-3c contains the URL of a web page to display information. Rather than the QR code having a passive role, the QR code has an active role through controlling a device. If a web page is used to control a device, connected to an ESP32 module, then scanning a QR code, which contains the web page URL, would also control the device. Prior to describing control of a device by scanning a QR code, the control of a device through a web page is outlined.

As an example, a web page consists of a control button and text displaying the state of an LED connected to an ESP32 module. The web page URL (Uniform Resource Locator) is the IP address of the ESP32 microcontroller, which is the server. When the web page button is clicked, the client, which is the browser hosting the web page, makes an HTTP request to the server for information associated with the URL (see Figure 7-6a). The server calls a function mapped to the URL, updates the LED state, turns on or off the LED, and responds to the client with the updated HTML code for the whole web page (see Figure 7-6b).

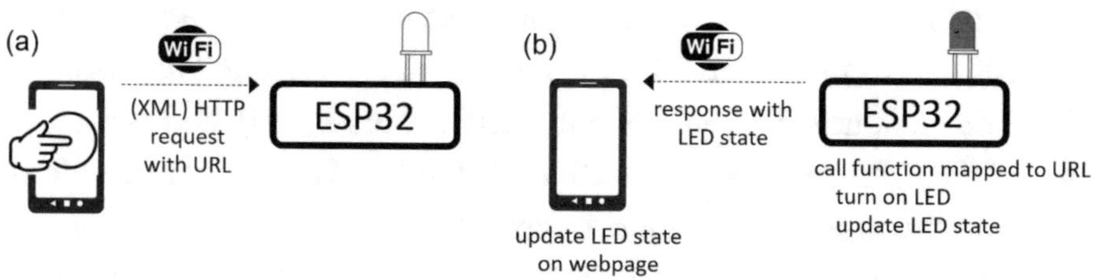

Figure 7-6. *Control an LED through a web page*

The web page with the two LED states is shown in Figure 7-7a and b. The IP address of the ESP32 microcontroller used in this chapter is 192.168.1.2. The web page and button are not formatted, as this section of the chapter focuses on the HTTP request instructions. However, a formatted web page and buttons are illustrated in Figure 7-9 and Listings 7-6 and 7-7. The content of the serverIP/LEDurl changes from *OFF* to *ON* or from *ON* to *OFF*, as shown in Figure 7-7c and d.

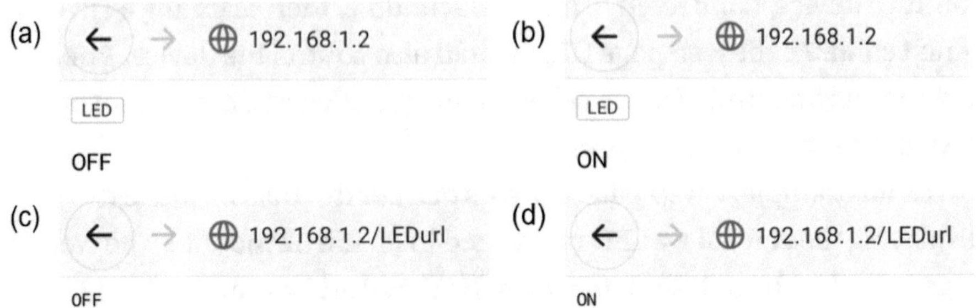

Figure 7-7. *Updated web page with XML HTTP requests*

In Listing 7-3, the first section of the sketch loads the *WebServer* library by Ivan Grokhotkov, which is installed with the *esp32* Boards Manager, and the file containing the SSID and password of the Wi-Fi router. The default HTTP COM port, on which the server listens for HTTP requests, is *80*, as indicated in the `WebServer server (80)` instruction. In the *setup* function, the Wi-Fi connection is established, and the *editHTML* function is called, to load the default web page, when the URL of the server IP address is entered on a browser. The `server.on("/LEDurl", LEDfunct)` instruction maps the URL in the HTTP request, serverIP/LEDurl, to the *LEDfunct* function, which updates the LED state and calls the *editHTML* function, which contains the HTML code to update the web page. The `server.handleClient()` instruction in the *loop* function manages HTTP requests from the client.

The *editHTML* function equates a string, *page*, to the web page HTML code, updates the *LEDlabel* variable with a value of *ON* or *OFF*, and then uploads the whole web page with the `server.send(200, "text/html", page)` instruction. The string *page* is a *string literal*, which contains no variables, and is bracketed by the `R"(` and `)"` characters, which are extended to `R"str(` and `)str"`, where *str* is a string, such as === or +++, which is not included in the *string literal*.

From the client perspective, when the web page button is clicked, a client HTTP request with URL of serverIP/LEDurl is triggered by the `onclick='location.href="/LEDurl"` instruction, where *location.href* (Hyperlink REFerence) is the combination of the server IP address and the */LEDurl* term. The client loads the whole web page with the updated HTML code included in the server response to the client HTTP request.

A 2ms delay in the *loop* function of Listing 7-3 prevented an ESP32 DEVKIT DOIT module from intermittently resetting, while a TTGO T-Display V1.1 module did not reset when the delay was omitted. The 2ms delay is included in example sketches of the *WebServer* library. The LED is connected with a 220Ω resistor to GPIO 12 of an ESP32 module.

The HTML code for the web page is updated by replacing the *LEDlabel* term with the text *ON* or *OFF*, depending on the value of the *LEDstate* variable being equal to one or zero.

Listing 7-3. HTTP request

```
#include <WebServer.h>               // include webserver library
WebServer server (80);               // associate server with library
#include <ssid_password.h>           // Wi-Fi SSID and password file
int LEDstate = 0, LEDpin = 12;       // LED state and GPIO pin

void setup()
{
  Serial.begin(115200);              // Serial Monitor baud rate
  pinMode(LEDpin, OUTPUT);           // define LED pin as output
  WiFi.begin(ssid, password);        // connect and initialize Wi-Fi
  while (WiFi.status() != WL_CONNECTED) delay(500);
  Serial.println(WiFi.localIP());    // display ESP32 IP address
  server.begin();                    // initialize server
  server.on("/", editHTML);          // load default web page
  server.on("/LEDurl", LEDfunct);    // map URL to function
}
```

```
void LEDfunct()                          // function mapped to URL
{
  LEDstate = 1 - LEDstate;
  digitalWrite(LEDpin, LEDstate);        // update LED state
  editHTML();                            // call function to update HTML
}

void editHTML()
{
  String page = R"(
  <!DOCTYPE html><html><head>
  <meta name='viewport'
        content='width=device-width, initial-scale=1.0'>
  <meta charset='UTF-8'>
  </head>
  <body>
  <button onclick='location.href="/LEDurl";'>LED</button>
  <p>LEDlabel</p>
  </body></html>
  )";                                    // LEDstate on web page
  page.replace("LEDlabel", LEDstate ? " ON" : "OFF");
  server.send(200, "text/html", page);  // load updated web page
}
void loop()
{
  server.handleClient();                 // manage HTTP requests
  delay(2);                              // prevent ESP32 resetting
}
```

An XML (eXtensible Markup Language) HTTP (HyperText Transfer Protocol) request results in updating specific web page variable(s), rather than updating the whole web page following an HTTP request. For web pages containing substantial information, it is advantageous, certainly in terms of time, to only update specific variables rather than the whole web page. The combination of an XML HTTP request with JavaScript commands to manage the XML HTTP request is AJAX (Asynchronous JavaScript And XML). Listing 7-4 incorporates the server response to the client XML HTTP request, with differences from Listing 7-3 annotated.

Listing 7-4. XML HTTP request

```
#include <WebServer.h>
WebServer server (80);
#include <ssid_password.h>
#include "buildpage.h"          // HTML code for web page
int LEDstate = 0, LEDpin = 12;
String str;

void setup()
{
  Serial.begin(115200);
  pinMode(LEDpin, OUTPUT);
  WiFi.begin(ssid, password);
  while (WiFi.status() != WL_CONNECTED) delay(500);
  Serial.println(WiFi.localIP());
  server.begin();
  server.on("/", base);         // load default  web page
  server.on("/LEDurl", LEDfunct);
}

void base()                     // function to transmit HTML code
{                               // for default web page to client
  server.send(200, "text/html", page);
}
```

```
void LEDfunct()
{
  LEDstate = 1 - LEDstate;
  digitalWrite(LEDpin, LEDstate);
  str = (LEDstate == HIGH ? "ON" : "OFF"); // map LEDstate to
                                           // ON or OFF
  server.send(200, "text/plain", str);     // server response to
}                                          // client XML HTTP request

void loop()
{
  server.handleClient();
}
```

The HTML code for the web page with the XML HTTP request is included as a string literal, the character array *page[]*, which is stored in PROGMEM, on a separate tab, *buildpage.h*, as shown in Listing 7-5. Clicking the web page button calls the *update* function with the `button onclick = 'update()'` instruction, which opens an XML HTTP request referencing the serverIP/LEDurl with the `xhr.open('GET', 'LEDurl', true)` instruction. The server response is mapped to the *LEDstate* identity with the `document.getElementById('LEDstate').innerHTML = this.responseText` instruction, which is displayed on the web page with the `<span id='LEDstate'>val</span>` instruction, with *val* being the default value. The client XML HTTP request only updates the *LEDstate* identity on the web page, rather than updating the whole web page.

Listing 7-5. HTML code for a web page with an XML HTTP request

```
char page[] PROGMEM = R"(
<!DOCTYPE html><html><head>
<meta name='viewport'
      content='width=device-width, initial-scale=1.0'>
<meta charset='UTF-8'>
```

```
</head>
<body>
<button onclick = 'update()'>LED</button>
<p><span id='LEDstate'>OFF</span></p>
<script>
function update()                        // function called when
{                                        // button clicked
  var xhr = new XMLHttpRequest();        // XML HTTP request
  xhr.onreadystatechange = function()   // status of XML HTTP request
  {
    if (this.readyState == 4 && this.status == 200)
    document.getElementById('LEDstate').innerHTML =
              this.responseText;
  };                                     // identifier LEDstate updated
  xhr.open('GET', 'LEDurl', true);       // URL accessed
  xhr.send();                            // transmit XML HTTP request
}
</script>
</body></html>
)";
```

When the web page button labeled *LED* is clicked, the web page is updated as shown in Figure 7-7a and b, with the server response to the client XML HTTP request illustrated in Figure 7-7c and d. In the sketch (see Listing 7-4), the URL serverIP/LEDurl is mapped to the *LEDfunct* function to turn on or off the LED, to update the string consisting of the LED state, and to transmit the server response to the client XML HTTP request.

The process of updating a web page element with a client XML HTTP request and the server response is listed and annotated in Table 7-1.

Table 7-1. XML HTTP request

Source	Instruction	Note
Web page	<button onclick = 'update()'>	Client button clicked, call *update* function.
Web page	xhr.open('GET', 'LEDurl', true)	Function calls HTTP request with URL.
Sketch	server.on("/LEDurl", LEDfunct)	Server maps URL to *LEDfunct* function.
Sketch	digitalWrite(LEDpin, LED)	Server turns on or off LED.
Sketch	str = (LED == HIGH ? "ON" : "OFF")	Server maps string to ON or OFF.
Sketch	server.send(200, "text/plain", str)	Server transmits string.
Web page	document.getElementById('LEDstate'). innerHTML = this.responseText	Client updates identifier *LEDstate* with response from server.

QR Codes and XML HTTP Requests

Scanning a QR code containing the serverIP URL controls an LED, connected to an ESP32 module, rather than clicking a control button on a web page. The QR code is generated with *QRCode Monkey* (`www.qrcode-monkey.com`) by entering the serverIP URL in the *Your URL* box. A QR code containing the *http://192.168.1.2* URL is shown in Figure 7-8a.

Figure 7-8. *QR codes for one LED URL and for green and red LED URLs*

When the QR code storing the server IP address (see Figure 7-8a) is scanned by an app on an Android tablet or mobile phone, the app opens the web page with the LED control button, as shown in Figure 7-7a. Scanning the QR code has only replaced entering the server IP address into the browser, to display the default web page.

To demonstrate control of devices by scanning QR codes, a web page contains buttons to individually control two LEDs (see Figure 7-9), with the LEDs connected with 220Ω resistors to an ESP32 module on GPIO 12 and GPIO 13.

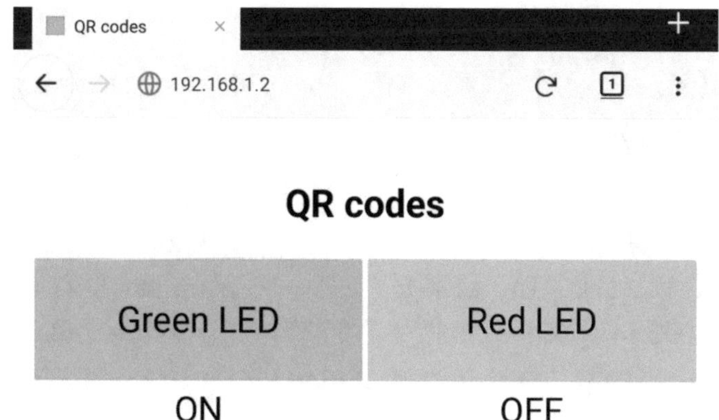

Figure 7-9. *Green and red LED control web page*

With two control buttons on the web page, the process of clicking a web page button to turn on or off an LED and update a web page element in response to a client XML HTTP request is identical to a web page with one control button. Listing 7-6, to control two LEDs, is similar to Listing 7-4, to control one LED, with replacement of the *LEDstate* variable, the *LEDpin* GPIO pin, and the *LEDfunct* function by the *LEDG* and *LEDR* variables, the *LEDGpin* and *LEDRpin* GPIO pins, and the *LEDGfunct* and *LEDRfunct* functions.

Listing 7-6. Control two LEDs through a web page

```
                                          // define LED pins
int LEDG = 0, LEDR, LEDGpin = 13, LEDRpin = 12;

void setup()                              // additional instructions
{                                         // to Listing 7-4
  pinMode(LEDGpin, OUTPUT);               // define LED pins as output
  pinMode(LEDRpin, OUTPUT);
  server.on("/LEDGurl", LEDGfunct);       // map URLs to functions
  server.on("/LEDRurl", LEDRfunct);
}

void base()                               // same as Listing 7-4

void LEDGfunct()                          // function to turn on
{                                         // or off green LED
  LEDG = 1 - LEDG;                        // alternate LED state
  digitalWrite(LEDGpin, LEDG);            // update LED state
  str = (LEDG == HIGH ? "ON" : "OFF");    // set str to LED state
  server.send(200, "text/plain", str);    // transmit LED state
}                                         // to client
```

```
void LEDRfunct()                    // similar function for red LED
{
  LEDR = !digitalRead(LEDRpin);     // different method to
  digitalWrite(LEDRpin, LEDR);      // alternate LED state
  str = (LEDR ? "ON" : "OFF");
  server.send(200, "text/plain", str);
}

void loop()                         // same as Listing 7-4
```

Listing 7-7 contains the AJAX code for the client to maintain the web page with control buttons for two LEDs. Apart from the addition of the HTML styling code and displaying the LED control buttons and LED states in a table, the structure of Listings 7-5 and 7-7 is similar. The *update* function in Listing 7-7 includes a parameter to indicate which LED control button was clicked. The *update* function sets the *URL* and *state* variables to the corresponding URL and identifier associated with the green or red control button, such as server IP/LEDGurl and *LEDGstate.*

For example, when the web page button for the red LED is clicked, the *id* identifier is mapped to *LEDR,* with the *URL* and *state* variables equated to /LEDRurl and *LEDRstate,* respectively. The server response to the client XML HTTP request updates the *state* variable, which is now equal to *LEDRstate,* and the web page is updated.

Listing 7-7. XML HTTP requests with two LEDs

```
char page[] PROGMEM = R"(
<!DOCTYPE html><html><head>
<meta name='viewport'
      content='width=device-width, initial-scale=1.0'>
<meta charset='UTF-8'>
<title>QR codes</title>
```

```
<style>
body {margin-top:50px; font-family:Arial; text-align:center}
.btn {display:block; width:280px; margin:auto; padding:30px;
      font-size:30px; color:black; text-decoration:none}
.gn {background-color:DarkSeaGreen}
.rd {background-color:Thistle}
td {font-size:30px; text-align:center}
</style></head>
<body>
<h1>QR codes</h1>
<center>
<table style='width:50%'>
<tr><td><button class = 'btn gn' id='LEDG'
         onclick = 'update(id)'>Green LED</button></td>
    <td><button class = 'btn rd' id='LEDR'
         onclick = 'update(id)'>Red LED</button></td></tr>
<tr><td><span id='LEDGstate'>OFF</span></td>
    <td><span id='LEDRstate'>OFF</span></td></tr>
</table>
</center>
<script>
function update(butn)          // function called when button clicked
{
  var URL, state;
  if(butn == 'LEDG')           // green LED button clicked
  {
    URL = 'LEDGurl';           // XML HTTP request location
    state = 'LEDGstate';       // green LED identifier
  }
  else if(butn == 'LEDR')      // red LED button clicked
  {
    URL = 'LEDRurl';
```

```
    state = 'LEDRstate';
  }
  var xhr = new XMLHttpRequest();       // XML HTTP request
  xhr.onreadystatechange = function()  // status of XML HTTP
  {                                     // server response
    if (this.readyState == 4 && this.status == 200)
    document.getElementById(state).innerHTML =
                         this.responseText;
  };                                    // identifier state updated
  xhr.open('GET', URL, true);           // URL accessed
  xhr.send();                           // transmit XML HTTP request
}
</script>
</body></html>
)";
```

QR Codes and WebSocket

When a control button is clicked on the web page controlling one or more devices, the client transmits an XML HTTP request to the server, containing the URL associated with the control button. The server maps the URL to a function, which turns on or off the corresponding device, and the updated device state is included in the server response, with which the client updates the device state on the web page.

In contrast, if the URL associated with a control button, such as server IP/LEDGurl, is refreshed, the server triggers the corresponding function, such as *LEDGfunct*, to change the LED state and transmit the updated LED state to the client. However, the web page is not updated, as the *update* function in the AJAX code (see Listing 7-7) is not called by the client. Scanning a QR code containing the URL associated with a control button, as in Figure 7-8b, has the same effect as refreshing the URL associated with the control button.

Furthermore, if one user controls a device through the web page and a second user scans the QR code for the same device, then the first user will not know the current device state, as the web page is not updated when the QR code is scanned. Similarly, if two remote users each control the same device through a web page by clicking the web page button, then the web pages of the two remote users are updated independently. Each remote user will only know the current state of the device after the control button is clicked on the user's browser.

The WebSocket protocol resolves the updating of a web page with control buttons when a QR code is scanned. The independent web page updating for two remote users is also resolved by the WebSocket protocol, as both web pages are updated simultaneously. The WebSocket protocol enables two-way communication between the server and client rather than the server only responding to a client request. The *WebSocketsServer* library, listed under *WebSockets,* by Marcus Sattler is available in the Arduino IDE.

The XML HTTP request in Listing 7-7 is replaced by the WebSocket client transmitting, to the WebSocket server, the identity, *LEDG* or *LEDR,* of the control button clicked on the web page. On receiving a message from the client, the server calls the *wsEvent* function to turn on or off the appropriate LED, and the *readLED* function broadcasts the JSON-formatted state of both LEDs to all clients (see Figure 7-10). The server broadcast ensures that web pages of all clients are updated simultaneously. When each client receives a broadcast from the server, the message content, which is JSON formatted as *rx.data,* is parsed to update both LED states on the web page, rather than only the LED associated with the clicked control button. Updating both LED states on each client web page ensures that the effect of clicking a control button by one user is reflected on the web page of another client as well as on the user web page.

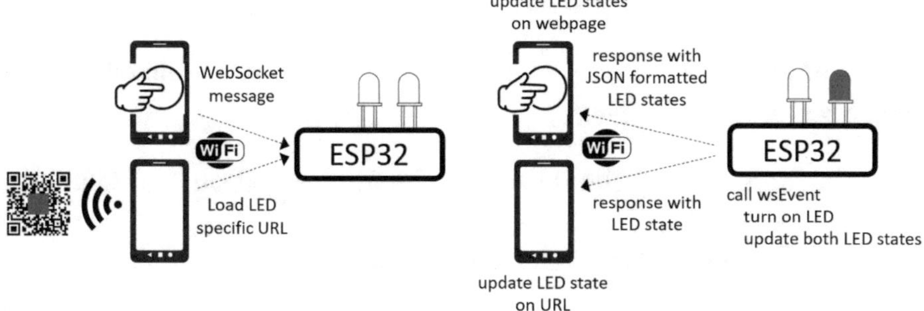

Figure 7-10. *WebSocket protocol*

When a QR code is scanned, for example, to control the red LED, the server calls the *LEDRfunct* function to turn on or off the red LED in response to the client XML HTTP request with the serverIP/LEDRurl, and the *readLED* function broadcasts the JSON-formatted state of both LEDs to all clients with the WebSocket protocol. In addition, a server response is generated with the `server.send(200, "text/plain", strR)` instruction, and the string *strR*, which has the value *ON* or *OFF*, displays the updated LED state to the user scanning the QR code (see Figure 7-10).

The WebSocket instructions are readily incorporated into Listings 7-6 for the server and 7-7 for the AJAX code. The *wsEvent* (see Listing 7-8) and *readLED* (see Listing 7-9) functions are defined to handle the WebSocket message from a client and to broadcast the updated LED states, in JSON format, to all clients.

In Listing 7-6, the additional instructions to include the *WebSockets* library are

```
#include <WebSocketsServer.h>            // include Websocket library
                                         // set WebSocket port 81
WebSocketsServer websocket = WebSocketsServer(81)
String strR, strG, json
int LEDpin
```

In the *setup* function, two instructions initialize the WebSocket:

```
websocket.begin()                          // initialize WebSocket
websocket.onEvent(wsEvent)
```

In the *loop* function, the `websocket.loop()` instruction is added.

Listing 7-8. WebSocket wsEvent function

```
void wsEvent(uint8_t n, WStype_t type, uint8_t * message,
  size_t length)
{
  if(type == WStype_TEXT)
  {
    str = "";                              // convert message to string
    for (int i=0; i<length; i++) str = str + char(message[i]);
                                           // determine required LED
    LEDpin = (str == "LEDG" ? LEDGpin : LEDRpin);
                                           // turn on or off LED
    digitalWrite(LEDpin, !digitalRead(LEDpin));
    readLED();                             // call readLED function
  }
}
```

Listing 7-9. Addition of the readLED function

```
void readLED()                             // function to broadcast
                                           // LED states to clients
{
  strG = String(digitalRead(LEDGpin)); // determine LED states
  strR = String(digitalRead(LEDRpin));
  strG = (strG == "1" ? "ON" : "OFF"); // convert LED states
  strR = (strR == "1" ? "ON" : "OFF"); // to "ON" or "OFF"
```

```
  json =  "{\"var1\": \"" + strG + "\",";      // partition with comma
  json += " \"var2\": \"" + strR + "\"}"; // end with close bracket
                                              // broadcast to clients
  websocket.broadcastTXT(json.c_str(), json.length());
}
```

The *LEDGfunct* function instructions are updated to

```
void LEDGfunct()                              // function to turn on or
{                                             // off green LED
  LEDG = !digitalRead(LEDGpin);
  digitalWrite(LEDGpin, LEDG);                // update LED state
  readLED();                    // call function to broadcast to all clients
  server.send(200, "text/plain", strG);       // server response to
}                                             // AJAX request
```

with the *LEDRfunct* function updated in a similar manner.

In Listing 7-7, the HTML instruction `<body>` is replaced with `<body id='initialize'>`, and the AJAX code bracketed by `<script>` and `</script>` is replaced by Listing 7-10. When a web page is loaded, the *init* function opens the WebSocket connection at *ws://server IP address:81/*. When the client receives a message from the server, the message, held in the variable *rx.data,* is parsed to the two objects, *var1* and *var2,* as constructed by the server *readLED* function, and mapped to the two LED states.

Listing 7-10. AJAX code with WebSocket

```
<script>
var wskt;
document.getElementById('initialize').onload = function()
{init()};
```

```
function init()
{
  wskt = new WebSocket('ws://' +
              window.location.hostname + ':81/');
  wskt.onmessage = function(rx)
  {
    var obj = JSON.parse(rx.data);
    document.getElementById('LEDGstate').innerHTML = obj.var1;
    document.getElementById('LEDRstate').innerHTML = obj.var2;
  };
}

function update(butn)
{
  wskt.send(butn);
}
</script>
```

CHAPTER 8

WebSocket, Remote Access, and OTA

This chapter describes establishing a software-enabled access point (*softAP*) with the ESP32 microcontroller to communicate with another ESP32 microcontroller or to host a remote web-based Serial Monitor or to host a remote web-based dashboard for graphical display of data. The WebSocket protocol allows two-way real-time communication between two ESP32 microcontrollers acting as server and client. *WebSerial* provides a ready-built web page–based Serial Monitor to display information transmitted by a remote ESP32 microcontroller when developing or running a remote project. Similarly, a ready-built web page–based dashboard, *ESP-Dash*, displays sensor data and device states monitored by a remote ESP32 microcontroller. Both *WebSerial* and *ESP-Dash* are based on the WebSocket protocol.

WebSocket

In Chapter 7, "Email and QR Codes," the server is the ESP32 microcontroller, and the client is the browser hosting a web page, when both the server and client are connected to the same WLAN (Wireless Local Area Network). In this chapter, both the server and client are ESP32 microcontrollers. The WebSocket protocol allows two-way real-time

N. Cameron, *ESP32 Formats and Communication*,
https://doi.org/10.1007/978-1-4842-9376-8_8

communication between the server and client, with the client sending a request to the server to switch from an HTTP protocol to a WebSocket protocol using the same port as HTTP (HyperText Transfer Protocol). Communication between ESP32 microcontrollers with the WebSocket protocol is an alternative communication protocol to ESP-NOW (see Chapter 9, "MQTT").

In this chapter, WebSocket communication between server and client(s) only requires the IP address of the ESP32 microcontroller acting as the server. A WLAN is established, without Internet access, with the server defined as a *softAP*, and the server IP address is obtained with the `WiFi.softAPIP()` instruction. The `WiFi.localIP()` instruction provides the IP address of the ESP32 microcontroller with an Internet connection. Access to the WLAN requires a password, which must contain at least eight alphanumeric characters.

In the sketches listed in Table 8-1, the client transmits a message, "*WebSocket message NN abc*", to the server every two seconds, with the WebSocket protocol. The client uses a WebSocket callback function, *wsEvent*, to manage an acknowledgment message, *"msg rcvd NN"*, from the server. In the sketches shown in Table 8-2, the server displays the received message on the Serial Monitor and sends an acknowledgment to the client.

The *WebSockets* and *ArduinoWebSockets* libraries, by Markus Sattler and Gil Maimon, respectively, enable communication between ESP32 microcontrollers with the WebSocket protocol. Both libraries are available in the Arduino IDE. The *WebSockets* library enables several clients to connect to a server, while the *ArduinoWebSockets* library connects one client to a server. Table 8-1 includes sketches for the two libraries with the ESP32 microcontroller transmitting to the receiving ESP32 microcontroller. Similarly, sketches, using the two libraries, for the receiving ESP32 microcontroller are listed in Table 8-2.

The WebSocket communication channel definitions for the server and client are library specific. For the *WebSockets* library, the server and client instructions defining the channel are `WebSocketsServer(channel)` and begin(serverIP address, channel, "/"). For the *ArduinoWebSockets* library, the instructions are server.listen(channel) and client.connect(serverIP address, channel, "/"), respectively. A received message, *RXmsg*, is displayed on the Serial Monitor with the Serial.printf("%s \n", RXmsg) or Serial.println(RXmsg.data()) instruction for the *WebSockets* or *ArduinoWebSockets* library, respectively.

The *ArduinoWebSockets* library requires several instructions to manage the WebSocket connection. The server instruction if(server.poll()) client = server.accept() maintains the WebSocket connection. When the server transmits a message to the client with the client.send(message) instruction, the client sketch must include the if(client.available()) client.poll()instruction to check for new messages.

With the *WebSockets* library, several clients are able to connect to a server, and when clients transmit messages to the server, the client number, *n*, is accessible in the *wsEvent* function void wsEvent(uint8_t n, WStype_t type, uint8_t * RXmsg, size_t length). A message is transmitted by the server to client number *n* with the websocket.sendTXT(n, "message") instruction. The server transmits a message to all clients with the websocket.broadcastTXT("message") instruction. If the client response depends on the content of the received message, then the received message is compared to a string, for example, *"abcd"*, with the if(strcmp((char *)RXmsg, "abcd") == 0) instruction.

The websocket.sendTXT(n, "msg rcvd " + str) instruction constructs a message by combining two existing strings, but a generated string, for example, String(value), is not a valid parameter. The instruction Serial.printf("%s \n", RXmsg) avoids having to cast the message *RXmsg* as a character array in the Serial.print((const char *) RXmsg) instruction.

The print-formatted instruction, `printf`, includes the parameter `%s` or `%c` for printing a string or a character, respectively, plus the new line character `\n`, as in the examples:

```
printf ("characters: %c %c \n", 'a', 'b')      // characters: a b
printf ("string: %s \n", "abc")                // string: abc
printf ("float: %4.2f \n", 3.141)              // float: 3.14 (2DP)
printf ("integer: %d \n", 123)                 // integer: 123
```

Table 8-1 includes sketches for the transmitting device using the *WebSockets* and *ArduinoWebSockets* libraries, with Table 8-2 containing the corresponding sketches for the receiving ESP32 microcontroller. In Tables 8-1 and 8-2, the receiving ESP32 microcontroller is defined as the server and the transmitting ESP32 microcontroller as the client, but the opposite is also valid. The transmit-receive or client-server orientation enables several clients to transmit messages to the server, with the server able to reply to specific clients using the *WebSockets* library.

Table 8-1. *Transmit a message to a receiving ESP32*

WebSockets transmit (client)	ArduinoWebSockets transmit (client)
#include <WebSocketsClient.h>	#include <ArduinoWebsockets.h>
	using namespace websockets;
WebSocketsClient websocket;	WebsocketsClient client;
char ssid[ ] = "ESP32_WebSocket";	char ssid[ ] = "ESP32_WebSocket";
char password[ ] = "pass1234";	char password[ ] = "pass1234";
String TXmsg = "WebSocket message ";	String TXmsg = "WebSocket message ";
unsigned long lag;	unsigned long lag;

(*continued*)

Table 8-1. *(continued)*

WebSockets transmit (client)	ArduinoWebSockets transmit (client)
int count = 0;	int count = 0;
void setup()	void setup()
{	{
Serial.begin(115200);	Serial.begin(115200);
WiFi.begin(ssid, password);	WiFi.begin(ssid, password);
while(WiFi.status() != WL_CONNECTED)	while(WiFi.status() != WL_CONNECTED)
delay(500);	delay(500);
Serial.print("softAP Address ");	Serial.print("softAP address ");
Serial.println(WiFi.softAPIP());	Serial.println(WiFi.softAPIP());
websocket.begin("192.168.4.1", 81, "/");	client.connect("192.168.4.1", 81, "/");
websocket.onEvent(wsEvent);	client.onMessage(wsEvent);
}	}
void wsEvent(WStype_t type, uint8_t * RXmsg, size_t length)	void wsEvent (WebsocketsMessage RXmsg)
{	{
if(type == WStype_TEXT) Serial.printf("callback \"%s\" \n", RXmsg);	Serial.printf("callback %s \n", RXmsg.data());
}	}

(continued)

Table 8-1. *(continued)*

WebSockets transmit (client)	ArduinoWebSockets transmit (client)
void loop()	void loop()
{	{
websocket.loop();	if(client.available()) client.poll();
if(millis() - lag > 2000)	if(millis() - lag > 2000)
{	{
count++;	count++;
websocket.sendTXT(TXmsg +String(count) + " abc");	client.send(TXmsg + String(count) + " abc");
lag = millis();	lag = millis();
}	}
}	}

In the sketches in Table 8-2, the server displays the received message from a client and sends an acknowledgment to the client. With the *WebSockets* library, the *wsEvent* function is triggered when a message is received by either the server or the client. In contrast, with the *ArduinoWebSockets* library, the server *loop* function manages the WebSocket connection, message reception, and sending an acknowledgment. With the *ArduinoWebSockets* library, the displayed received message does not incorporate the client number, as the server connects to one client only.

Table 8-2. *Receive a message from a transmitting ESP32*

WebSockets receive (server)	ArduinoWebSockets receive (server)
#include <WebSocketsServer.h>	#include <ArduinoWebsockets.h>
	using namespace websockets;
WebSocketsServer websocket = WebSocketsServer(81);	WebsocketsServer server;
	WebsocketsClient client;
char ssid[ ] = “ESP32_WebSocket”;	char ssid[ ] = “ESP32_WebSocket”;
char password[ ] = “pass1234”;	char password[ ] = “pass1234”;
String str;	String str;
void setup()	void setup()
{	{
Serial.begin(115200);	Serial.begin(115200);
WiFi.softAP(ssid,password);	WiFi.softAP(ssid, password);
Serial.print(“softAP address ”);	Serial.print(“softAP address ”);
Serial.println(WiFi.softAPIP());	Serial.println(WiFi.softAPIP());
	server.listen(81);
websocket.begin();	
websocket.onEvent(wsEvent);	
}	}

(*continued*)

Table 8-2. *(continued)*

WebSockets receive (server)	ArduinoWebSockets receive (server)
void wsEvent(uint8_t n, WStype_t type, uint8_t * RXmsg, size_t length)	void loop()
{	{
	if(server.poll()) client = server.accept();
if(type == WStype_TEXT)	if(client.available())
{	{
	WebsocketsMessage RXmsg = client.readBlocking();
Serial.printf("RXmsg \"%s\" from device %d \n", RXmsg, n);	Serial.printf("RXmsg \"%s\" \n", RXmsg.c_str());
str = "";	
for (int i=0; i<length; i++)	
if (isDigit(RXmsg[i])) str = str + char(RXmsg[i]);	str = "len " + String(RXmsg.length());
websocket.sendTXT(n, "msg rcvd " +str);	client.send(str);
}	}
}	}
void loop()	
{ websocket.loop(); }	

A message with the *WebSockets* library is formatted as a character array, rather than a string, which aids text manipulation, such as identifying digits in an alphanumeric message with the `isDigit(RXmsg[i])` instruction.

Data included in a transmitted text message is combined as JSON-formatted name:value pairs, which are parsed by the receiving microcontroller into the data components. For example, the *JsonConvert* function to combine four variables into a JSON-formatted string (see Listing 8-1) is called with the `JsonConvert(height, width, length, weight)` instruction, and the message containing the string, *json*, is transmitted with the `websocket.sendTXT(json)` or `webSocket.broadcastTXT(json)` instruction for the *WebSockets* library or the `client.send(json)` instruction for the *ArduinoWebSockets* library.

Listing 8-1. JSON formatting data

```
String JsonConvert(int val1, int val2, int val3, int val4)
{
  json  = "{\"val1\": \"" + String(val1) + "\",";
  json += " \"val2\": \"" + String(val2) + "\",";
  json += " \"val3\": \"" + String(val3) + "\",";
  json += " \"val4\": \"" + String(val4) + "\"}";
  return json;
}
```

Instructions to parse a received message into components are given in Listing 8-2 for the *WebSockets* and *ArduinoWebSockets* libraries, with the latter commented out. The *ArduinoJson* library is included in a sketch with the `#include <ArduinoJson.h>` instruction, and the variable *jsonDoc* is defined by the `DynamicJsonDocument jsonDoc(1024)` instruction. The *ArduinoJson* library, by Benoît Blanchon, is available in the Arduino IDE.

Listing 8-2. Parsing a JSON-formatted string

```
  DeserializationError error = deserializeJson(jsonDoc, RXmsg);
// DeserializationError error =
//          deserializeJson(jsonDoc, RXmsg.data());
  height = jsonDoc["val1"];
  width  = jsonDoc["val2"];
  length = jsonDoc["val3"];
  weight = jsonDoc["val4"];
```

Strings and Character Arrays

The "WebSocket" section of the chapter included the `if(strcmp((char *) RXmsg, "abcd") == 0)` instruction to compare a received message with the text "*abcd*". The *strcmp* function and the `(char *)` term relate to a `String` variable and to the pointer to a character array, respectively. Uses of strings and character arrays are described.

String management has an impact on the heap memory requirement within DRAM (see Chapter 1, "ESP32 Microcontroller"). For example, combining the two strings "*abcd*" and "*wxyz*" with the instructions

```
String str1 = "abcd", str2 = "wxyz", str
str = str1 + "&" + str2
```

requires four strings, "*abcd*", "*wxyz*", "*abcd&*", and "*abcd&wxyz*", to be stored in heap. The number of strings held in heap is reduced to only one with the two string concatenation instructions of `str1.concat("&")` and `str1.concat("wxyz")`.

Passing strings to a function duplicates the required number of strings held in heap. For example, when the `printOled(str1, str2)` function is called, two new strings are created by the *printOled* function, when defined as `void printOled(String txt1, String txt2)`, irrespective of the names of the string variables in the function. The number of strings held in heap is not increased when referencing strings with pointers, using the "&" symbol, in the *printOled* function as in `void printOled(String &txt1, String &txt2)`. Pointers are used to reference images as Sprites in the *TFT_eSPI* library with the `TFT_eSprite img = TFT_eSprite(&tft)` instruction (see Chapter 10, "Managing Images").

Strings are compared with the `strcmp(str1, str2)` instruction, which compares the two strings character by character and returns the index of the first character that differs, with a zero return indicating that strings are identical. For example, the `strcmp(variable, "servo")` instruction has value zero when the *variable* string is equal to "*servo*".

A character array is stored in static memory within DRAM, rather than heap memory. A character array differs from a string as the array elements are individually accessible. A character array is defined with the `char array[] = "some letters"` instruction, and the length of the array, `strlen(array)`, is the number of characters plus one, as the last element of the array is the *NULL* character to indicate the end of the text. An array is overwritten with the `strcpy(array, "new text")` instruction, and character arrays are concatenated with the `strcat(array1, array2)` instruction.

A character array is referenced by a pointer to the array with the `const char * array = "some letters"` instruction and must not be subsequently changed, as the array is effectively read-only. The array definition instruction is preceded by `const` to indicate a constant. The pointer referencing the array is passed to a function with the `void printOled(char *arr1, char *arr2)` instruction. Note that the pointer to a string or to a character array is indicated with the & or * term, respectively.

The `if(strcmp((char *)RXmsg, "abcd") == 0)` instruction cited at the start of the section compares the character array *RXmsg*, which is referenced by a pointer, with the string "*abcd*". If the content of a character array matches a string, then the value zero is returned, and otherwise a non-zero value is returned. However, the `if(strcmp((char *)RXmsg, str) == 0)` instruction will fail, when the variable *str* is defined as a string, which would require comparing a character array to a string. The `text.c_str()` instruction returns a pointer to an array containing the characters in the string text, to enable comparison between a character array and a string. Listing 8-3 provides comparisons between a string, a character array, and a character array referenced by a pointer. A string is converted to a character array and vice versa for comparing alphanumeric text.

Listing 8-3. String and character array comparisons

```
String a = "abcd";                    // string
char b[] = "hijk";                    // character array
const char * c = "rstu";              // pointer to character array
const char * d = "wxyz";

void setup()
{
  Serial.begin(115200);
  Serial.printf("pointer and string %d \n", strcmp(c, "abcd"));
  Serial.printf("pointer and c_str %d \n",
           strcmp(c, a.c_str()));
  Serial.printf("pointer and char %d \n", strcmp(c, b));
  Serial.printf("two pointers %d \n", strcmp(c, d));
  char charA[100];
  a.toCharArray(charA, a.length());   // convert string to character array
  Serial.printf("two char %d \n", strcmp(charA, b));
  String strB = String(b);            // convert character array to string
  Serial.printf("two c_str %d \n",
           strcmp(a.c_str(), strB.c_str()));
  Serial.printf("two strings %d \n", strcmp("abcd", "1234"));
}

void loop()
{}
```

WebSerial

A web page to mirror the Serial Monitor (see Figure 8-1) is generated by the *WebSerial* library of Ayush Sharma, with the library available within the Arduino IDE. When developing a project with a remote ESP32 microcontroller, such as with OTA (Over the Air) updating, the *WebSerial* web page displays information from the ESP32 microcontroller. The `print` and `println` instructions display information on the *WebSerial* web page, as for a Serial Monitor, without the need to build HTML instructions for a web page. The ESP32 libraries *WiFi* and *ESPAsyncWebServer* are referenced by the *WebSerial* library, so do not have to be explicitly referenced by the sketch. The *ESPAsyncWebServer* library by Hristo Gochkov is downloaded from `github.com/me-no-dev/ESPAsyncWebServer`.

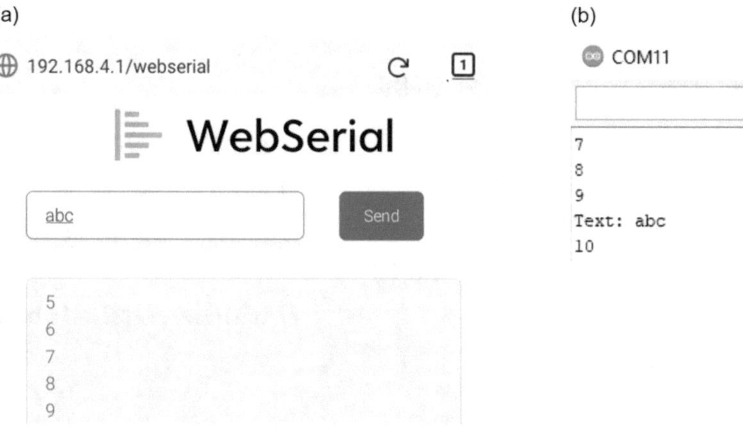

Figure 8-1. *Output to a WebSerial web page and to a Serial Monitor*

The *WebSerial* web page is accessed with the ESP32 microcontroller IP address as *IP/webserial*. The ESP32 microcontroller either is connected to an existing Wi-Fi network in station mode or acts as a server, as a software-enabled access point (*softAP*). The default WLAN status is joint access point and station mode, which is also set with the `WiFi.mode(WIFI_AP_STA)` instruction. The ESP32 microcontroller is specifically defined as in station mode or as an access point with the `WiFi.mode(WIFI_STA)` or `WiFi.mode(WIFI_AP)` instruction, respectively. The `WiFi.begin(ssid, password)` or `WiFi.softAP(ssidAP, passwordAP)` instruction connects the ESP32 microcontroller to an existing WLAN or establishes the ESP32 microcontroller as a *softAP*. The `print(WiFi.localIP())` or `print(WiFi.softAPIP())` instruction displays the IP address of the ESP32 microcontroller connected to a Wi-Fi network or acting as a *softAP*.

When the ESP32 microcontroller is a *softAP*, the Android tablet, mobile phone, or computer hosting the browser must be connected to the software-enabled access point, *ssidAP*, for example, *ESP32_WebSerial* as in Listing 8-4.

The sketch to display a count on the web page generated by the *WebSerial* library, as shown in Figure 8-1a, with the ESP32 microcontroller acting as a *softAP*, is given in Listing 8-4.

Listing 8-4. WebSerial web page

```
#include <WebSerial.h>                  // include WebSerial library and
AsyncWebServer server(80);              // associate server with library
char ssidAP[] = "ESP32_WebSerial";      // microcontroller as access point
char passwordAP[] = "pass1234";
int count = 0;                          // with the required channel

void setup()
{
  Serial.begin(115200);                 // Serial Monitor baud rate
  WiFi.softAP(ssidAP, passwordAP);      // connect to softAP device
  Serial.println(WiFi.softAPIP());      // display softAP address
  WebSerial.begin(&server);             // initialize WebSerial
  server.begin();                       // and AsyncWebServer
}
```

```
void loop()
{
  Serial.println(count);         // display to Serial Monitor
  WebSerial.println(count);      // and to WebSerial web page
  count++;
  delay(1000);
}
```

Alphanumeric text entered in the *Type here* box on the *WebSerial* web page is displayed on the Serial Monitor (see Figure 8-1b) by including the *TypeHere* function in Listing 8-4

```
void TypeHere(uint8_t *text, size_t length)
{
  Serial.print("Text: ");
  for(int i=0; i<length; i++) Serial.print((char)text[i]);
  Serial.println();
}
```

with the *TypeHere* function defined in the *setup* function by the `WebSerial.msgCallback(TypeHere)` instruction.

Web Dashboard

A web page dashboard to display information from sensors connected to an ESP32 module is generated by the *ESP-Dash* library of Ayush Sharma. The library is listed as *ESP-DASH* in the Arduino IDE. The dashboard is built with cards, each with a different format. The generic card displays text or a number, the temperature and humidity cards are self-explanatory, the status card displays one of four state categories, and the progress card displays a number as a horizontal bar. The slider or button card consists of an interactive slider or an interactive button to control a device connected to the ESP32 module. The dashboard also includes a bar chart function. The *ESP-Dash* dashboard is useful when developing a project without needing to write HTML code for a temporary web page.

The dashboard in Figure 8-2 includes two generic cards, a temperature card, a status card, a progress card, a slider card, and a button card.

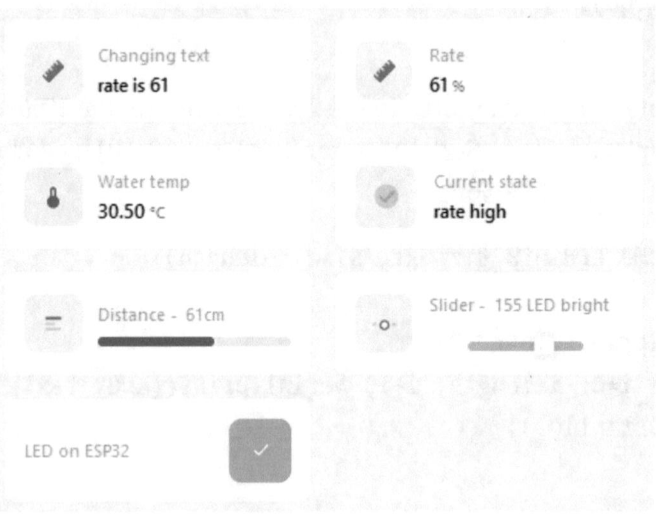

Figure 8-2. *Dashboard*

The status and button card definitions include the card name, the card type, and descriptive text. The generic, temperature, and humidity card definitions additionally include a symbol, such as *°C* or *%*. The progress and slider card definitions include the minimum and maximum values of the horizontal bar. Listing 8-5 defines the card definitions, such as `Card progCard(&dashboard, PROGRESS_CARD, "Distance", "cm", 1, 100)` for the progress card name *progCard*, describing a *Distance* with values ranging from 1 to 100cm. Card values and the dashboard are updated with the instructions `cardname.update(variable)` and `dashboard.sendUpdates()`, respectively.

The status card has four categories of *idle, warning, success,* and *danger* associated with gray, yellow, green, and red images (see Figure 8-2 for the *success* symbol) and four messages. In Listing 8-5, a state category, held in the string array *state,* is converted to a character array, *chr,* with the instruction `state[value].toCharArray(chr, 8)`. The size of the character array, *chr,* is the state category with most letters, which is *warning,* plus one. The status card is updated with both a message and the image corresponding to *chr.*

The button and slider cards require a *callback* function with variables representing the button state or the slider value, which are updated within the *callback* function by the `cardname.update(variable)` and the `dashboard.sendUpdates()` instructions. The button and slider callback functions are defined in the *setup* function. The slider value is updated when the slider is *released* on the web page.

The *ESP-Dash* library references the *WiFi* and *ESPAsyncWebServer* libraries, so the instructions `#include <WiFi.h>` and `#include <ESPAsyncWebServer.h>` are not required. The ESP32 microcontroller is either connected to an existing Wi-Fi network in station mode or is a server acting as a *softAP* device, which does not require a Wi-Fi connection to a router. When using the *softAP* functionality, the browser is connected to the *softAP* device named *"ESP32_Dashboard",* for example, as in Listing 8-5, rather than the WLAN router. The dashboard URL is the default *softAP* address of *192.168.4.1.*

Listing 8-5 demonstrates the dashboard with generic cards displaying text or an integer, the temperature card, the status card, and the progress card. A random value populates the cards with a state category derived from the value divided by 25 and a maximum value of 100. The button and slider cards turn on or off the built-in LED on GPIO 2 of an ESP32 DEVKIT DOIT module and control the LED brightness.

Listing 8-5. Dashboard

```
#include <ESPDash.h>                    // include ESPDash library
AsyncWebServer server(80);              // associate server with
                                        // ESPAsyncWebServer
ESPDash dashboard(&server);             // and dashboard with ESPDash
char ssidAP[] = "ESP32_Dashboard";      // microcontroller as access point
char passwordAP[] = "pass1234";
                                        // text
Card textCard(&dashboard, GENERIC_CARD, "Changing text");
                                        // rate%
Card rateCard(&dashboard, GENERIC_CARD, "Rate", "%");
                                        // temp°C
Card tempCard(&dashboard, TEMPERATURE_CARD, "Water temp", "°C");
                                        // state
Card stateCard(&dashboard, STATUS_CARD, "Current state");
Card progCard(&dashboard, PROGRESS_CARD, "Distance", "cm", 1, 100);
Card slider(&dashboard, SLIDER_CARD, "Slider", "LED bright", 0, 255);
                                        // LED
Card button (&dashboard, BUTTON_CARD, "LED on ESP32");
                                        // bar chart
Chart graph(&dashboard, BAR_CHART, "Random values");
int LEDon, LEDpin = 2;                  // ESP32 built-in LED
String state[] = {"idle","warning","success","danger"};
String message[] = {"rate low","rate medium","rate high",
                    "rate extreme"};
String Xaxis[] = {"N-5","N-4","N-3","N-2","N-1","NOW"};
int Yaxis[] = {0,0,0,0,0,0};
char chr[8];                   // 7 letters + 1 as "warning" is the longest string
unsigned long lag = 0;
```

```
                                        // LED PWM parameters
int channel = 0, freq = 5000, resolution = 8;
int value, LEDpwm, graphN = 0;
float temp;
String str;

void setup()
{
  Serial.begin(115200);                 // Serial Monitor baud rate
  pinMode(LEDpin, OUTPUT);
  ledcAttachPin(LEDpin, channel);       // PWM parameters for LED
  ledcSetup(channel, freq, resolution);
  WiFi.softAP(ssidAP, passwordAP);      // connection to
                                        // softAP device
  Serial.println(WiFi.softAPIP());      // display SoftAP address
  server.begin();                       // initialize server
  button.attachCallback([&](bool LEDval)    // attach button callback
  {
    button.update(LEDval);              // update button card
    Serial.println("button "+String((LEDval) ? "on" : "off"));
    LEDon = LEDval;
  });
  slider.attachCallback([&](int slideVal)   // attach slider callback
  {
    slider.update(slideVal);            // update slider
    Serial.println("Slider "+String(slideVal));
    LEDpwm = slideVal;
  });
  graph.updateX(Xaxis, 6);              // define X-axis with 6 values
}
```

```
void loop()
{
  if(millis() > lag + 2000)             // interval between updates
  {
    lag = millis();                     // turn LED off if button is off
    if(LEDon == 0) ledcWrite(channel, 0);
    else ledcWrite(channel, LEDpwm);    // update LED brightness
    value = random(1, 100);             // generate random number
    graphN++;
    if(graphN > 4)                      // update graph every 5 cycles
    {                                   // shift data one position
      for (int i=0; i<5; i++) Yaxis[i] = Yaxis[i+1];
      Yaxis[5] = value;                 // incorporate new data point
      graph.updateY(Yaxis, 6);          // Y-axis data with 6 values
      graphN = 0;                       // reset counter
    }
    str = "rate is " + String(value);   // append value to string
    textCard.update(str);               // update generic card
                                        // with string
    rateCard.update(value);             // generic card with integer,
    temp = value * 0.5;
    tempCard.update(temp);              // temperature card with float,
    progCard.update(value);             // progress card with integer
    value = value/25;                   // convert value to one of
                                        // four categories
    state[value].toCharArray(chr, 8);   // convert string to char array
                              // update state card message and image
    stateCard.update(message[value], chr);
    dashboard.sendUpdates();            // update dashboard
  }
}
```

The bar chart function is illustrated in Figure 8-3. A bar chart is defined with the `Chart graph(&dashboard, BAR_CHART, "title")` instruction, which has the same format as a `Card` instruction. The chart X-axis is defined, in the *setup* function when the X-axis values are fixed, with the `graph.updateX(Xaxis, N)` instruction, where *Xaxis* is a string array containing the *N* values on the X-axis (see Listing 8-5). Similarly, specific Y-axis values are defined as `Yaxis[i] = y`, with the integer array defined as `int Yaxis[] = {0,0...0}`, to contain default values, and the chart Y-axis values are updated with the `graph.updateY(Yaxis, N)` instruction. In Listing 8-5, the bar chart is updated every five cycles, with the latest value displayed on the right side of the bar chart.

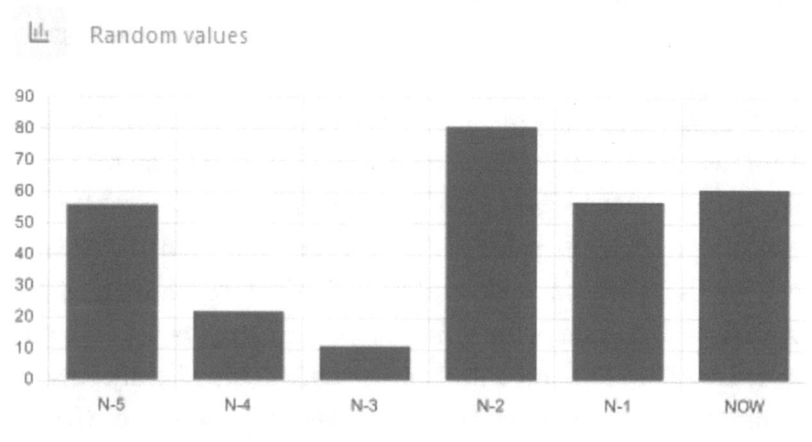

Figure 8-3. *Dashboard bar chart*

Over the Air (OTA)

When the ESP32 microcontroller is remotely located, an updated sketch is loaded onto the ESP32 microcontroller with the OTA protocol. The initial version of the sketch is uploaded, with a Serial connection, by selecting the *Upload* option in the *Sketch* menu of the Arduino IDE. The ESP32 microcontroller is then moved to a remote location, and subsequent updates of the sketch are uploaded, over a Wi-Fi connection, to the remote ESP32 microcontroller. In the Arduino IDE, after saving the updated sketch, select the *Export Compiled Binary* option in the *Sketch* menu. The generated binary file, which is now located in the *sketch* folder as *sketch.ino.esp32.bin,* is uploaded to the ESP32 microcontroller using the *ElegantOTA* library by Ayush Sharma. The library is available in the Arduino IDE, and Ayush Sharma also wrote the *ESP-DASH* and *WebSerial* libraries.

The *ElegantOTA* library provides a web page, with the URL based on the IP address of the ESP32 microcontroller (IP address/update), to upload the binary file (see Figure 8-4). Note that the ESP32 microcontroller and the computer hosting the Arduino IDE must be connected to the same WLAN. With the *Firmware* option selected, the *Browse* button is clicked to then identify the location of the binary file, which is uploaded with the OTA protocol to the ESP32 microcontroller. The ESP32 chip identity provides a unique identity for the *ElegantOTA* library. The chip identity of *31c4f5fc,* in Figure 8-4, is derived from four components of the ESP32 MAC address of *fc:f5:c4:31:9d:98,* obtained with the `ESP.getEfuseMac()` instruction (see the "Memory" section of Chapter 1, "ESP32 Microcontroller").

192.168.1.149/update

ElegantOTA

Firmware Filesystem

Browse... No file selected.

31c4f5fc - ESP32

Figure 8-4. *Over the Air*

Listing 8-6 illustrates the OTA protocol. The *ElegantOTA* library references the *WiFi*, *WiFiClient*, and *WebServer* libraries, so the corresponding `#include <library.h>` instructions are not required. In the *setup* function, the Wi-Fi connection is established, and the ESP32 microcontroller IP address is displayed, as the user requires the IP address for the *ElegantOTA* web page URL. For illustration, a sketch, which displays the LED lag time on the default web page, is updated by changing the LED lag time, and the updated sketch is uploaded with OTA. The *ElegantOTA* is started with the `ElegantOTA.begin(&server)` instruction. An OTA name and password are included in the `ElegantOTA.begin(&server, OTAhost, OTApass)` instruction to provide some security for requests to the OTA web page or firmware uploads to the ESP32 microcontroller.

For example, Listing 8-6 is compiled and initially uploaded over the Serial connection. The LED lag time is reduced from 1000ms to 200ms, the sketch is saved, and the *Export Compiled Binary* option is selected, instead of the *Upload* option, in the *Sketch* menu of the Arduino IDE. The *ElegantOTA* web page is loaded with the serverIP/update URL, and the binary file is uploaded over a Wi-Fi connection to the ESP32 microcontroller.

Listing 8-6. Over the Air

```
#include <ElegantOTA.h>                  // include ElegantOTA library
WebServer server(80);                    // initialize server
#include <ssid_password.h>
char OTAhost[] = "ESP32board";           // OTA name and password
char OTApass[] = "admin1";
int LEDpin = 2;
int lag = 1000;                          // LED lag time (ms)
String str;

void setup()
{
  Serial.begin(115200);                  // Serial Monitor baud rate
  pinMode(LEDpin, OUTPUT);
  WiFi.mode(WIFI_STA);                   // Wi-Fi station mode
  WiFi.begin(ssid, password);            // initialize and connect Wi-Fi
  while (WiFi.status() != WL_CONNECTED) delay(500);
  Serial.print("IP address: ");          // display ESP32 IP address
  Serial.println(WiFi.localIP());
  ElegantOTA.begin(&server);             // start ElegantOTA
  server.begin();                        // start server
  server.on("/", base);                  // load default web page
}

void loop()
{
  server.handleClient();                 // manage HTTP requests
                                         // turn on or off LED
  digitalWrite(LEDpin, !digitalRead(LEDpin));
  delay(lag);
}
```

```
void base()                                  // function called when
{                                            // web page loaded
  str = "Time lag " + String(lag);
  server.send(200, "text/plain", str);      // send response to client
}
```

CHAPTER 9

MQTT

MQTT

Message Queueing Telemetry Transport (MQTT) is a publish-subscribe network protocol that includes communication between ESP32 microcontrollers on different Wi-Fi networks. MQTT was developed in 1999 by Andy Stanford-Clark and Arlen Nipper for connecting oil pipeline telemetry systems. The MQTT broker enables data transfer between devices on different Wi-Fi networks without breaching firewall safeguards. When a device on one Wi-Fi network requests information from a second device on another network, the information is allowed through the network firewall, as the request came from the Wi-Fi network. Provision of information by a MQTT client to a MQTT broker is termed *publish*, and *subscrib*e is the term to access information through the MQTT broker. There are several MQTT brokers, and the Cayenne MQTT broker (`developers.mydevices.com`) is used in this chapter. The ESP32 microcontroller is a MQTT client communicating with a MQTT broker. A MQTT dashboard is accessible from anywhere in the world to provide remote access to information from sensors or for remote control of devices connected to an ESP32 module. MQTT is illustrated with the ESP32 microcontroller transmitting air quality measures or energy usage readings, provided by a smart meter, to a MQTT broker for display on the MQTT broker dashboard.

N. Cameron, *ESP32 Formats and Communication*,
https://doi.org/10.1007/978-1-4842-9376-8_9

CO2 and TVOC

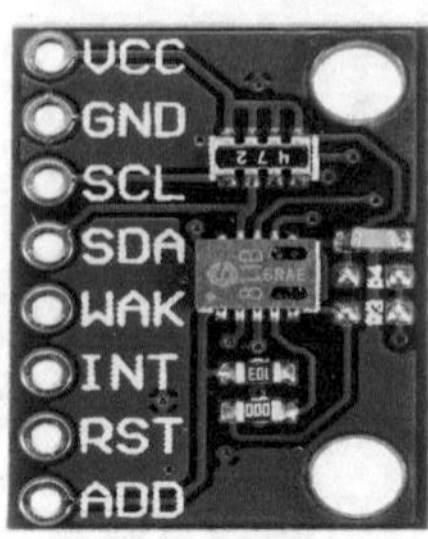

Carbon dioxide (CO2) and total volatile organic compounds (TVOC) are indicators of air quality. Equivalent carbon dioxide (eCO2) and equivalent total volatile organic compounds (eTVOC) are measured by the CCS811 module. The measurable eCO2 and eTVOC ranges are 400–33000ppm and 0–29000ppb, respectively. Suggested normal values for eCO2 and eTVOC levels are <500ppm and <50ppb, respectively, with >1500ppm and >1000ppb for poor air ventilation. The Adafruit CCS811 module (not shown) measures eCO2 and eTVOC from 400 to 8192ppm and from 0 to 1187ppb, respectively. The *Adafruit CCS811* library is for the Adafruit CCS811 module. The CCS811 HDC1080 module measures eCO2, eTVOC, temperature, and relative humidity, as the module includes an HDC1080 sensor in addition to the CCS811 sensor. The *CCS811* library by Maarten Pennings is recommended and is downloaded from `github.com/maarten-pennings/CCS811`.

The CCS811 module requires a voltage of 1.8–3.6V and communicates with I2C (Inter-Integrated Circuit). The default I2C address of *0x5A* is changed to *0x5B* by setting the *ADD* pin to *HIGH*. The CCS811 module is reset by setting the *RST* pin to *LOW*. Connections between a CCS811 module and an ESP32 DEVKIT DOIT module are given in Table 9-1.

The CCS811 module operates in constant-power mode with sampling every second or in low-power mode with sampling at 10s or 60s intervals. Constant-power mode is initiated with the `start(CCS811_MODE_1SEC)` instruction, and the *WAK* pin is connected to GND. The instruction `start(CCS811_MODE_10SEC)` or `start(CCS811_MODE_60SEC)` initiates low-power mode, and the *WAK* pin is connected to a GPIO pin, such as GPIO 19 (see Figure 9-1). The `CCS811 ccs811(19)` instruction identifies GPIO 19 as attached to the module *WAK* pin. If the *WAK* pin is connected to GND, then the instruction is `CCS811 ccs811(-1)`. The interval between start-up and the first reading is 4, 33, or 200s for a sampling interval of 1, 10, or 60s, respectively.

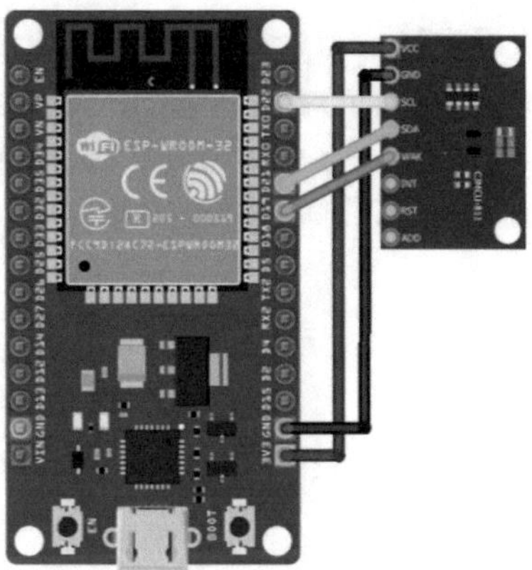

Figure 9-1. *TVOC and CO_2 measurement*

Table 9-1. *TVOC and CO_2 measurement*

CCS811 module	ESP32
VCC	3V3
GND	GND
SCL	GPIO 22
SDA	GPIO 21
WAK	GPIO 19

Equivalent carbon dioxide (eCO2) and total volatile organic compounds (eTVOC) are measured at 10s intervals in Listing 9-1. Given a valid data reading, *eCO2* and *eTVOC* values and the interval between readings are displayed on the Serial Monitor, and the state of an activity indicator LED, which is the built-in LED on GPIO 2, is alternated. Each second between readings, the no data error status triggers the display, on the Serial Monitor, of a dot as a state indicator. With the *CCS811* library, if an error is detected, an error message consisting of a letter series indicates the error source. Details of the *errstat* letter series are included in the *ccs811.cpp* file of the *CCS811* library. The *CCS811* library references the *Wire* library, so the `#include <Wire.h>` instruction is not required.

Listing 9-1. TVOC and CO2 measurement

```
#include <ccs811.h>                    // include CCS811 and
#include <Wire.h>                      // Wire libraries
CCS811 ccs811(19);                     // nWAKE connected to GPIO 19
uint16_t CO2, TVOC, errstat, rawdata;
unsigned long last, diff;
int LEDpin = 2, LED = 0;               // LED as activity indicator

void setup()
{
  Serial.begin(115200);                // Serial Monitor baud rate
  pinMode(LEDpin, OUTPUT);
  digitalWrite(LEDpin, LED);           // turn off LED
  Wire.begin();                        // initialize I2C
  ccs811.begin();                      // initialize CCS811
  ccs811.start(CCS811_MODE_10SEC);     // set reading interval at 10s
}

void loop()
{                                      // read CCS811 sensor data
  ccs811.read(&CO2, &TVOC, &errstat, &rawdata);
  if(errstat == CCS811_ERRSTAT_OK)     // given valid readings
  {
    diff = millis() - last;
```

```
    last = millis();                    // interval since last reading
    LED = 1-LED;                        // turn on or off indicator LED
    digitalWrite(LEDpin, LED);          // display readings
    Serial.printf("\n int %d CO2 %dppm TVOC %dppb \n",
                 diff, CO2, TVOC);
  }                                     // print dot between readings
  else if(errstat == CCS811_ERRSTAT_OK_NODATA)
          Serial.print(".");
  else if(errstat & CCS811_ERRSTAT_I2CFAIL)
          Serial.println("I2C error");
  else
  {                                     // display error message
    Serial.print("errstat = "); Serial.print(errstat,HEX);
    Serial.print(" = ");
    Serial.println(ccs811.errstat_str(errstat));
  }
  delay(1000);                          // arbitrary delay of 1s to display
}                                       // dot between readings
```

MQTT, CO2, and TVOC

Equivalent carbon dioxide (eCO2) and total volatile organic compounds (eTVOC) readings are forwarded by the ESP32 microcontroller to a MQTT broker for display on the MQTT broker dashboard (see Figure 9-2). The eCO2 and eTVOC readings, which are taken every 60s, and a count-down indicator, which is updated every 5s, are displayed on the MQTT broker dashboard. An LED, connected to the ESP32 module, is controlled through the MQTT broker dashboard.

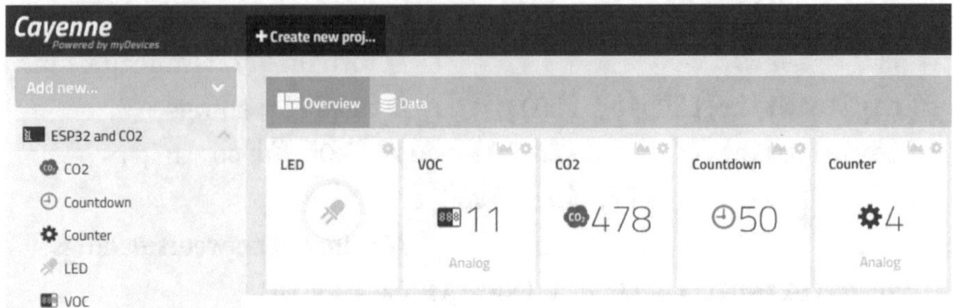

Figure 9-2. *TVOC and CO2 measurement and MQTT broker*

Cayenne provides a dashboard to display information from devices connected to an ESP32 microcontroller. The Cayenne dashboard is visible on `developers.mydevices.com` after logging in with the *SIGN IN* option. Information from devices is displayed numerically or as a dial or graphically, with binary variables displayed as *ON/OFF*. A device is turned on or off from the Cayenne dashboard, which provides both local and remote access to a device.

Details on the Cayenne MQTT broker are available at `developers.mydevices.com/cayenne/docs/intro`, and the *CayenneMQTT* library is available in the Arduino IDE. Communication between the ESP32 microcontroller and Cayenne MQTT broker is through virtual channels, which are numbered *V0, V1, V2,* etc. Data is sent to the Cayenne MQTT broker for display on the Cayenne dashboard with the instruction

```
Cayenne.virtualWrite(virtual channel, variable, type code, unit code)
```

where the *type* and *unit* codes define attributes of the variable. For example, the `Cayenne.virtualWrite(V3, light, "lum", "lux")` instruction transmits the *light* variable, a measure of luminosity in lux, on virtual channel *V3*. Including *type* and *unit* codes in the `Cayenne.virtualWrite()` instruction automatically configures the Cayenne dashboard with the variable description, a relevant icon, and a unit of measurement. A list of variable *type* and *unit* codes is given in the library file *CayenneMQTT\ src\ CayenneUtils\ CayenneTypes.h*. The generic *type* code of `prox` is used in Listing 9-2. Note that `Cayenne.virtualWrite()` instructions are limited to 60 per minute.

The ESP32 microcontroller is added as a Cayenne dashboard device by selecting *Add new* on the top left-hand side of the dashboard, selecting *Device/Widget*, and selecting *Bring Your Own Thing*. The corresponding MQTT username and password, Client ID, and MQTT server and port details are generated by the Cayenne MQTT broker. Copy the MQTT username and password and the Client ID to the sketch, and then compile and upload the sketch. Alternatively, the MQTT username, password, and Client ID along with the Wi-Fi SSID and password are included in the access information file, such as *ssid_password.h* (see Listing 9-2).

Cayenne dashboard widgets are defined by selecting *Add new* on the top left-hand side of the dashboard, selecting *Device/Widget*, and selecting *Custom Widgets*. An analog device is defined by selecting *Value (Display widget)* and entering the chosen widget name, such as *VOC*, and the device name corresponding to the ESP32 microcontroller, such as *ESP32 and CO2*. Select *Data*, enter the required category such as *Analog Sensor*, select the virtual channel number to correspond with the sketch, choose an icon, and select *Add Widget*. For a controlling widget, the selections are *Button (Controller widget)*, *Digital Actuator* in the *Data* option, and *Digital (0/1)* in the *Unit* option.

Figure 9-3 shows examples of defining an analog device, *VOC*, and a controller widget, *LED*, linked to virtual channels 4 and 0, on the Cayenne dashboard.

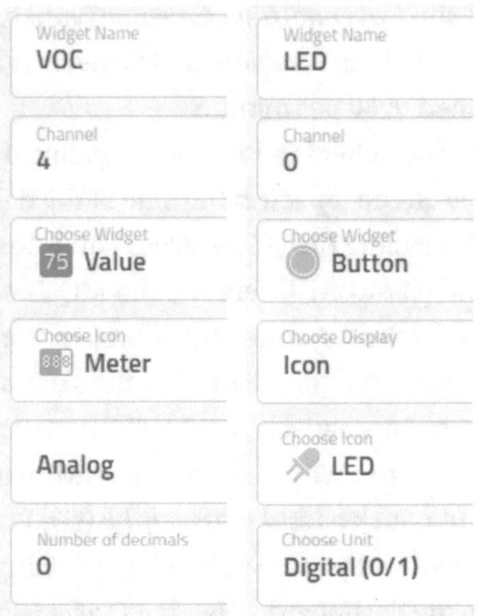

***Figure 9-3.** Analog and controlling widget definitions*

The sketch in Listing 9-2 is based on Listing 9-1. A `delay` instruction is not included in the *loop* function, as a delay would block the ESP32 microcontroller from receiving input by the MQTT broker. When the LED state is changed by the MQTT broker, the ESP32 microcontroller receives the updated state, on Cayenne virtual channel 0, with the `CAYENNE_IN(0)` and `getValue.asInt()` instructions. The ESP32 microcontroller receives a real number and a string with the functions `getValue.asDouble()` and `getValue.asString()`, respectively. Rather than taking one observation every 60 seconds, determined by the `start(CCS811_MODE_60SEC)` instruction, an alternative option would transmit, to the MQTT broker, the average of six measurements taken every 10 seconds.

Listing 9-2. TVOC and CO2 measurement and MQTT broker

```
#include <Wire.h>                  // include Wire and
#include <ccs811.h>;               // CCS811 libraries
#include <CayenneMQTTESP32.h>  // Cayenne MQTT library
#include <ssid_password.h>     // file with logon details
//char ssid[] = "xxxx";            // change xxxx to your Wi-Fi SSID
//char password[] = "xxxx";        // change xxxx to your Wi-Fi password
//char username[] = "xxxx";        // change xxxx to Cayenne username
//char mqttpass[] = "xxxx";        // change xxxx to Cayenne password
//char clientID[] = "xxxx";        // change xxxx to Cayenne client identity
CCS811 ccs811(19);                 // CCS811 nWAKE on GPIO 19
uint16_t CO2, TVOC, errstat, rawdata;
int LEDpin = 2;                    // LED as activity indicator
int LEDMQTTpin = 4;                // LED controlled with MQTT
int count = 0, countDown = 200;
unsigned long LEDtime = 0, countTime;

void setup()
{                                  // initiate Cayenne MQTT
  Cayenne.begin(username, mqttpass, clientID, ssid, password);
  pinMode(LEDpin, OUTPUT);         // define LED pins as output
  digitalWrite(LEDpin, LOW);       // turn off LEDs
  pinMode(LEDMQTTpin, OUTPUT);
  digitalWrite(LEDMQTTpin, LOW);
  Wire.begin();                    // initialize I2C
  ccs811.begin();                  // initialize CCS811
  ccs811.start(CCS811_MODE_60SEC);        // set reading interval at 60s
}
```

```
void loop()
{
  Cayenne.loop();                     // Cayenne loop function
                                      // read CCS811 sensor data
  ccs811.read(&CO2, &TVOC, &errstat, &rawdata);
  if(errstat == CCS811_ERRSTAT_OK)    // given valid readings
  {
    count++;                          //increment reading counter
    countDown = 60;
    countTime = millis();             // set countdown time
                                      // send data to MQTT
    Cayenne.virtualWrite(V3, CO2, "prox", "");
    Cayenne.virtualWrite(V4, TVOC, "prox", "");
    Cayenne.virtualWrite(V6, count, "prox","");
    Cayenne.virtualWrite(V7, countDown, "prox","");
    LEDtime = millis();
    digitalWrite(LEDpin, HIGH);       // turn on indicator LED
  }                                   // turn off LED after 100ms
  if(millis() - LEDtime > 100) digitalWrite(LEDpin, LOW);
  if(millis() - countTime > 5000)     // countdown interval 5s
  {
    countTime = millis();             // update countdown time
    countDown = countDown - 5;        // update countdown
                                      // send to MQTT
    Cayenne.virtualWrite(V7, countDown, "prox","");
  }
}

CAYENNE_IN(0)                         // Cayenne virtual channel 0
{                                     // turn on or off LED
  digitalWrite(LEDMQTTpin, getValue.asInt());
}
```

MQTT and Smart Meter

An ESP32 module is connected to a smart meter and provides energy usage readings to a MQTT broker for display on the MQTT broker dashboard. The ESP32 module is battery powered, and the battery voltage is also transmitted to the MQTT broker to alert the user when to replace or charge the battery. Power consumption is measured at one-minute intervals, with the ESP32 microcontroller in deep sleep mode between readings, to save battery power. The deep sleep function enables the ESP32 microcontroller to wake up, measure, and transmit energy usage, power consumption, and battery voltage to the MQTT broker and then return to deep sleep.

Figure 9-4 illustrates the power consumption measured every minute over a 60-minute period. A 2kW kettle was switched on at 7:30 a.m. and again at 8:15 a.m. with an 8kW shower used briefly at 8:00 a.m. The baseline power usage was 300W.

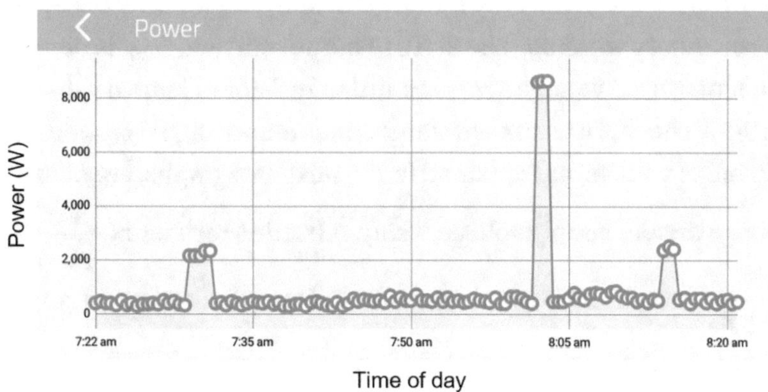

Figure 9-4. *MQTT dashboard of power consumption*

Energy Usage Measurement

Current usage is measured with the SCT013 current transformer, which is a current clamp meter. When a conductor (cable) supplying a load is clamped, the conductor is effectively the primary winding of a current transformer. The wire coil around the SCT013 current transformer core is the secondary winding. The alternating current in the conductor produces an alternating magnetic field in the SCT013 core, which induces an alternating current in the secondary winding, which is converted to a voltage and quantified by the ESP32 microcontroller analog to digital converter (ADC).

The SCT013 current transformer outputs a maximum current of 50mA given a load maximum current usage of 100A, as the SCT013 current transformer includes 2000 coil turns. The current in the secondary winding is the current in the primary winding divided by the number of coil turns on the secondary winding. The SCT013 output current, I_{OUT}, is determined from the measured voltage across a burden resistor of known value (see Figure 9-5). The SCT013 current transformer output signal is combined with an offset voltage, as explained in the next paragraphs, equal to half of the voltage divider supply voltage, *Vsply*. A burden resistor of $\frac{Vsply/2}{\sqrt{2} \times IOUT}\Omega$ $= \frac{1.65}{\sqrt{2} \times 0.05}\Omega$ or 23.3Ω is required, and a 22Ω burden resistor is sufficient. The scalar of $\sqrt{2}$ converts the RMS (Root Mean Square) SCT013 current transformer output, I_{OUT}, to the peak current of an AC (alternating current) signal. Further details on measuring current and apparent power with the SCT013 current transformer are available at `learn.openenergymonitor.org/electricity-monitoring/ct-sensors/introduction`.

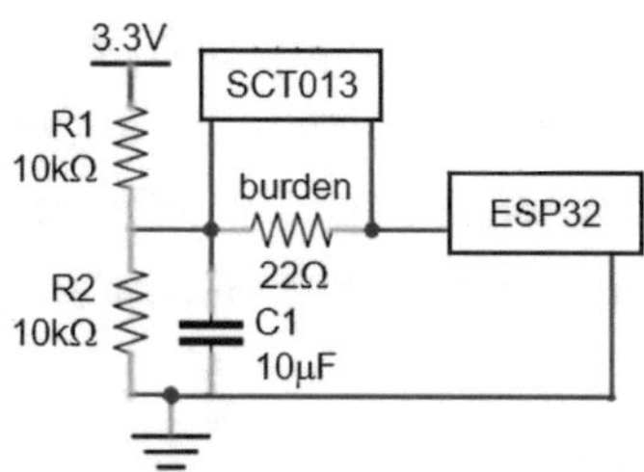

***Figure 9-5.** SCT013 current transformer connections*

The SCT013 output current, I_{OUT}, is alternating current (AC), and the measured voltage across the burden resistor follows a sinusoidal wave or sine curve (see Figure 9-6). The SCT013 output current corresponding to a load current of L amps is $L \times \sqrt{2} \times 0.05/100$ A, given the SCT013 maximum current of 50mA with a load maximum current of 100A. When measured with an oscilloscope, the peak-to-peak voltage across the burden resistor, R, is $2 \times I_{OUT} \times$ R volts, with the factor of two reflecting the positive and negative AC signal of the SCT013 current transformer. For example, a load current of 20A RMS corresponds to an SCT013 output current of 14.1mA $= 20 \times \sqrt{2} \times 0.05/100$ A, and a peak-to-peak voltage, measured with an oscilloscope, across the 22Ω burden resistor of 622mV = 2 × 14.1mA × 22Ω.

The peak-to-peak voltage is measured with the analog to digital converter (ADC) of the ESP32 microcontroller. The ADC only measures positive voltages, and a direct current (DC) offset voltage is combined with the SCT013 AC output, which is centered on zero. The offset voltage is provided by a voltage divider, formed by resistors *R1* and *R2* (see Figure 9-5). The combined AC and DC signal has minimum and maximum voltages of $Vsply/2 \pm I_{OUT} \times$ R volts. For example, a load current of 20A RMS corresponds to minimum and maximum voltages of 1339 and 1961mV = 3.3V/2 ± 311mV and a peak-to-peak voltage of 622mV. Without the offset voltage, the maximum and minimum voltages of the sinusoidal signal, as measured by the ESP32 microcontroller ADC, are 311 and 0, respectively (see Figure 9-6). If an offset DC voltage is not added to the sinusoidal AC voltage and the ADC-measured voltage is just doubled, then clipping of the AC signal will result in an underestimate of the peak-to-peak voltage.

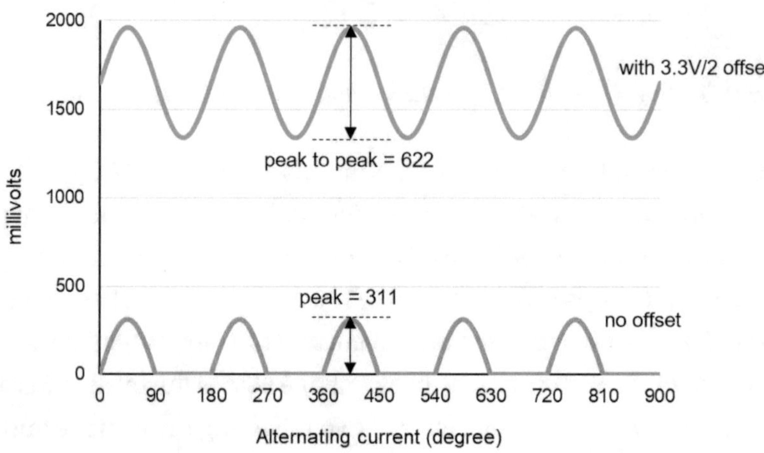

Figure 9-6. *SCT013 current transformer sensor readings*

The load usage current simplifies to $P2P/\sqrt{2}R$ RMS amps, given the peak-to-peak voltage, *P2P* volts, of the combined AC and DC signal across the burden resistor, *R*. From the earlier example, a peak-to-peak voltage of 622mV and a 22Ω burden resistor correspond to a load usage of 20A RMS.

For this chapter, the current usage of a hairdryer at the high setting was estimated with the SCT013 current transformer. The peak-to-peak voltage, measured with the ESP32 microcontroller ADC, of 280mV equated to a current of 9.0A RMS, which was consistent with the current of 8.52A RMS, when measured with a multimeter. At low current loads, the voltage measured, on an oscilloscope, across the SCT013 burden resistor formed a clipped sinusoidal wave, which negatively biased the estimated current usage.

Wi-Fi, MQTT, and Smart Meter

Monitoring energy usage with the data forwarded to a MQTT broker, to display on the MQTT broker dashboard, requires an ESP32 microcontroller with a low current requirement, when the ESP32 microcontroller is battery powered. An ESP32 DEVKIT DOIT module requires 51mA when active, between 58 and 130mA when accessing a Wi-Fi network, and 12mA in deep sleep mode. The corresponding current requirements of a TTGO T-Display V1.1 module are 38mA, 45–113mA, and 325μA. A battery will power a TTGO T-Display V1.1 module longer than an ESP32 DEVKIT DOIT module, primarily due to the lower deep sleep current requirement of the TTGO T-Display V1.1 module.

Connections between a TTGO T-Display V1.1 module, an SCT013 current transformer, a burden resistor, and a voltage divider are shown in Figure 9-7 and listed in Table 9-2.

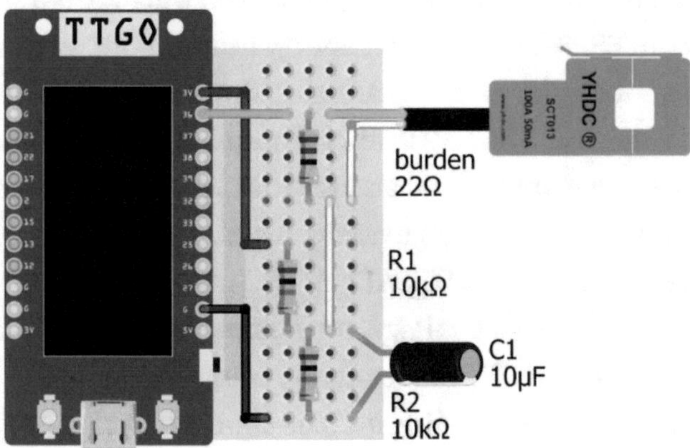

***Figure 9-7.** ESP32 with an SCT013 current transformer sensor*

Table 9-2. SCT013 connections

Component	Connect to	SCT013 wire color
SCT013 signal	ESP32 GPIO 36	Red, but green in Figure 9-6
SCT013 signal	22Ω burden resistor	
SCT013	22Ω burden resistor	White
SCT013	Voltage divider midpoint	
Voltage divider 10kΩ resistors	ESP32 3V3 and GND	
10µF capacitor positive	Voltage divider midpoint	
10µF capacitor negative	GND	

The sketch for an SCT013 current transformer, acting as a smart meter, connected to an ESP32 module with energy usage information sent to a MQTT broker, for display of information on the MQTT broker dashboard, is shown in Listing 9-3. The ESP32 microcontroller RTC (real-time clock) is active in deep sleep mode, and an incrementing counter is stored in the RTC memory at each energy reading. A counter to be stored in RTC memory is defined with the `RTC_DATA_ATTR int counter` instruction. The SCT013 current transformer voltage, the battery voltage, and the counter are transmitted to the MQTT broker at one-minute intervals.

In the *setup* function of Listing 9-3, the connection to the MQTT broker is established, and the *taskFunction* is called to obtain the SCT013 current transformer voltage across the burden resistor and the battery voltage. When the TTGO T-Display V1.1 is battery powered, the ADC enable port on GPIO 14 must be set *HIGH* to activate the ADC on GPIO 34. In the *getCurrent* function, the initial readings from the SCT013 current transformer, which may be noisy, are discarded. A total of 500 voltage readings took 51.6ms to complete, ensuring that the minimum and maximum voltages were detected as readings were taken over 2.5 cycles, given the 50Hz frequency of the AC signal and cycle length of 20ms. After a delay to allow time for transmission to the MQTT broker, the microcontroller goes into deep sleep mode. Without the time delay, the MQTT broker dashboard is not updated.

Listing 9-3. Smart meter and MQTT

```
#include <WiFi.h>
#include <CayenneMQTTESP32.h>          // Cayenne MQTT library
#include <ssid_password.h>             // file with logon details
int battPin = 34, enabPin = 14, SCTpin = 37;
float mA, current, RMS, battery;
int volt, minVolt, maxVolt, mV, power;
RTC_DATA_ATTR int count = 0;           // store count in RTC memory
int Nread = 500;                       // number of current readings
                                       // shorthand 60×10⁶ for 60secs
unsigned long cnectTime = 0, micro = 60E6;

void setup()
{
  pinMode(enabPin, OUTPUT);
  digitalWrite(enabPin, HIGH);
                                       // restart after fixed time
  esp_sleep_enable_timer_wakeup(micro);
  cnectTime = millis();
  Cayenne.begin(username, mqttpass, clientID, ssid, password);
  cnectTime = millis() - cnectTime;    // 3.5 - 4s to re-connect
  taskFunction();                      // call task function
  delay(500);                          // time to complete transmission
  esp_deep_sleep_start();              // ESP32 in deep sleep mode
}
```

```
void taskFunction()
{                                   // battery voltage
  battery = analogReadMilliVolts(battPin)*2.0/1000.0;
  count++;
  getCurrent();                     // call function to measure current
                                    // send data to MQTT
  Cayenne.virtualWrite(V3, RMS, "prox", "");
  Cayenne.virtualWrite(V4, mV, "prox", "");
  Cayenne.virtualWrite(V5, power, "prox", "");
  Cayenne.virtualWrite(V6, battery, "prox", "");
  Cayenne.virtualWrite(V7, count, "prox", "");
  Cayenne.virtualWrite(V8, cnectTime, "prox", "");
}

void getCurrent()                   // function to calculate current usage
{
  maxVolt = 0;
  minVolt = 5000;
                                    // ignore initial readings
  for (int i=0; i<100; i++) analogRead(SCTpin);
  for (int i=0; i<Nread; i++)
  {                                 // SCT013 output voltage
    volt = analogReadMilliVolts(SCTpin);
                                // update maximum and minimum voltages
    if(volt > maxVolt) maxVolt = volt;
    if(volt < minVolt) minVolt = volt;
  }
  mV = maxVolt - minVolt;           // peak to peak mV
  mA = 0.5*mV/22.0;                 // mV with burden resistor to mA
```

```
  current = mA*100.0/50.0;      // mA to current usage in amps
  RMS = current/sqrt(2.0);      // RMS current usage
  power = 230.0 * RMS;          // convert current to power
}

void loop()                     // nothing in loop function
{}
```

A TTGO T-Display V1.1 module was powered by an 18650 Li-ion battery mounted in an 18650 battery V3 micro-USB charging shield. After 5199 wake-measure-transmit-deep sleep cycles, each lasting 68s, the battery voltage dropped to 2.4V, and the battery stopped powering the microcontroller. There was a gradual decrease in battery voltage over 90 hours, followed by a rapid decline (see Figure 9-8).

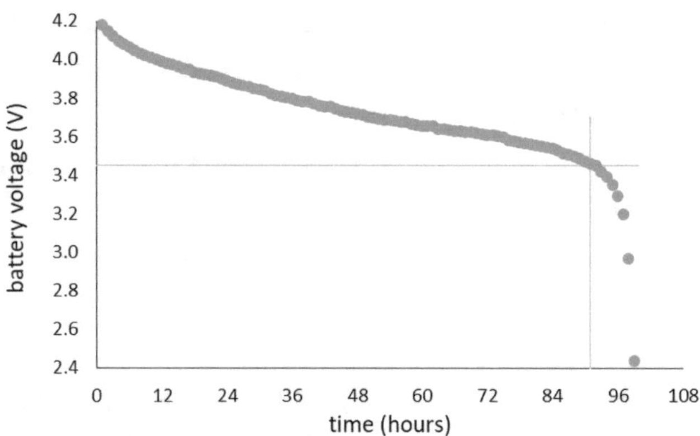

Figure 9-8. *18650 battery discharge curve*

A practical smart meter must be powered on a single battery for longer than four days. Extending the one-minute interval between SCT013 current transformer readings will increase the time powered by the battery, but will decrease the resolution of daily cumulative energy usage. Combining several high-capacity 18650 batteries in an 18650 battery V3 micro-USB charging shield or in an 18650 battery case is one solution.

Wi-Fi Connection to a Router

Occasionally, the ESP32 microcontroller does not connect to a MQTT broker through a router Wi-Fi connection. The sequence of instructions

```
#include <CayenneMQTTESP32.h>   // Cayenne MQTT library
#include <ssid_password.h>      // file with logon details
void setup()
{
  Cayenne.begin(username, mqttpass, clientID, ssid, password)
```

combines Wi-Fi connection to the router and connection to the Cayenne MQTT broker. The connection problem is resolved by separating the connection process into the two components with the instructions

```
#include <WiFi.h>                    // include Wi-Fi library and
WiFiClient client;                   // associate client with library
#include <CayenneArduinoMQTTClient.h>
                                     // associate Cayenne with library
CayenneArduinoMQTTClient Cayenne;
#include <ssid_password.h>           // file with logon details
void setup()
{
  WiFi.begin(ssid, password);   // initialize and connect Wi-Fi
  while (WiFi.status() != WL_CONNECTED) delay(500);
                                     // pass Wi-Fi client to MQTT broker
  Cayenne.begin(client, username, mqttpass, clientID);
```

The number of Wi-Fi connection attempts to the router is monitored by combining the instruction `while (WiFi.status() != WL_CONNECTED) delay(500)` with an instruction to increment a counter.

Espressif notes that the *esp_deep_sleep* function does not thoroughly shut down connections with the Wi-Fi and Bluetooth communication protocols (see `docs.espressif.com/projects/esp-idf/en/latest/esp32/api-reference/system/sleep_modes.html`). Wi-Fi or Bluetooth connections are closed with the `WiFi.disconnect()` and `WiFi.mode(WIFI_OFF)` instructions or the `btStop()` instruction before implementing the `esp_deep_sleep_start()` instruction.

ESP-NOW, MQTT, and Smart Meter

In Listing 9-3, a battery-powered ESP32 microcontroller transmitted SCT013 current transformer data to a MQTT broker with Wi-Fi communication (see Figure 9-9a). Connection to a MQTT broker and data transmission required 2210ms and 5ms, respectively (see Table 9-3). In an alternative arrangement, a battery-powered ESP32 microcontroller transmits data, with the ESP-NOW protocol, to a second ESP32 microcontroller, which is not battery powered and has a permanent connection to a MQTT broker (see Figure 9-9b). The second ESP32 microcontroller forwards the data to a MQTT broker. ESP-NOW requires only 364μs to establish communication with the recipient ESP32 microcontroller and just 227μs to transmit data (see Table 9-3), which is faster than transmitting data directly to a MQTT broker. The advantage of two ESP32 microcontrollers and the combination of ESP-NOW and Wi-Fi communication is the lower connection and data transmission times with the ESP-NOW protocol, which should enable the battery-powered ESP32 microcontroller to operate for a longer period. The ESP-NOW communication protocol is also described in Chapter 14 of *Electronics Projects with the ESP8266 and ESP32.*

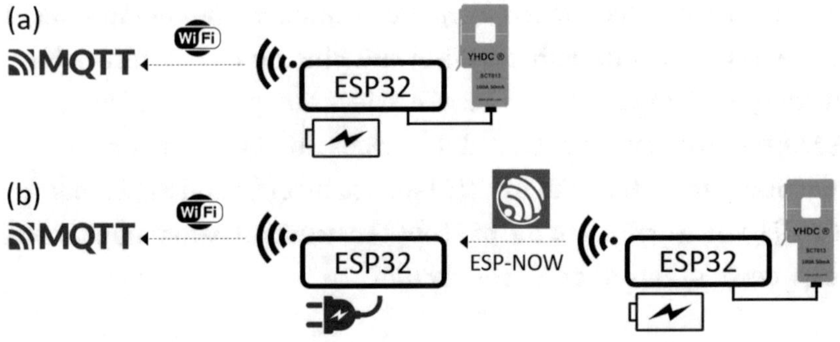

Figure 9-9. *ESP-NOW, smart meter, and MQTT*

For ESP-NOW communication between two ESP32 microcontrollers, when one microcontroller is connected to a router for Wi-Fi communication, the ESP-NOW communication channel must be the same as the Wi-Fi communication channel. Wi-Fi routers automatically switch to the least congested channel, and the available networks must be scanned to identify the communication channel of the specified router. Figure 9-10 illustrates a router switching between communication channels over a 30-hour time period.

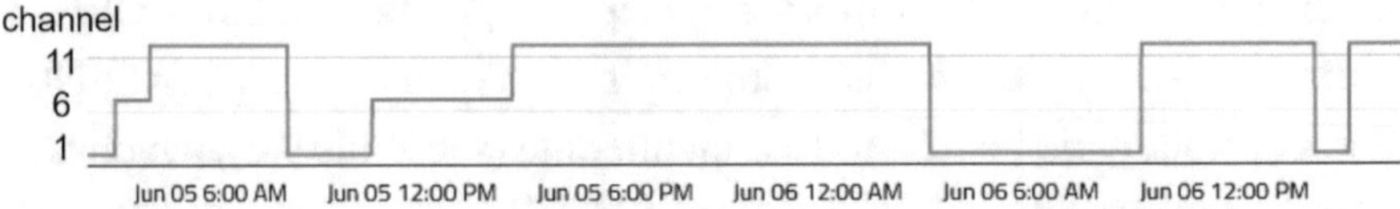

Figure 9-10. *Router switching communication channels*

The sketch for a battery-powered ESP32 microcontroller, transmitting data with the ESP-NOW protocol to a second ESP32 microcontroller, is based on Listing 9-3. The *WiFi* and *esp-wifi* libraries are required to scan available networks and to both define the communication channel and manage deep sleep mode of the ESP32 microcontroller. The sketch scans available networks to determine the router communication channel, as used by the second ESP32 microcontroller, which is defined as the

ESP-NOW receiver, with MAC (Media Access Control) address defined in the *receiveMAC* array. The MAC address of a microcontroller is obtained with the *WiFi* library `WiFi.macAddress()` instruction and is also displayed by the Arduino IDE when a sketch is compiled and loaded. The ESP32 microcontroller MAC address in Listing 9-4 must be replaced by the MAC address of your ESP32 microcontroller. The `esp_now_peer_info_t receiver = {}` instruction is required to prevent the *"E (66) ESPNOW: Peer interface is invalid"* error message.

The router SSID is compared to available network SSIDs with the C++ *strcmp* function. The function compares two strings character by character and returns the index of the first character that differs, with a zero return indicating that strings are identical. Alternatively, the router SSID and a network SSID are compared with the `if(SSIDstr == WiFi.SSID(i).c_str())` instruction, with the router SSID, *SSIDstr*, defined as a string rather than a character array.

In Listing 9-4, the instructions for ESP-NOW communication replace the instructions in Listing 9-3 to connect with and transmit data to a MQTT broker. The *taskFunction* is called to obtain the SCT013 current transformer data, battery voltage, and router communication channel, which are contained in a structure, *payload*, for transmission. Following data transmission, there is a 500ms delay for receipt of the transmission callback, before the ESP32 microcontroller is moved to deep sleep mode with the instructions `esp_sleep_enable_timer_wakeup(micro)` and `esp_deep_sleep_start()`.

Listing 9-4. ESP-NOW transmitting ESP32

```
#include <WiFi.h>             // include ESP-NOW and Wi-Fi
#include <esp_wifi.h>         // libraries
#include <esp_now.h>          // receiving ESP32 MAC address
uint8_t receiveMAC[] = {0x94, 0xB9, 0x7E, 0xD2, 0x20, 0xEC};
char ssid[] = "XXXX";         // replace with your router SSID
typedef struct                // structure for data
```

```
{
  int mV;                              // SCT013 voltage
  float battery;                       // battery voltage
  int channelPL;                       // router Wi-Fi channel
  int countPL;                         // data counter
  int rep;                             // repeated transmissions
} dataStruct;
dataStruct payload;
int battPin = 36, SCTpin = 37;         // battery pin when USB powered
int chk, scan, channel = 0;
                                       // number of current readings
int Nread = 500, volt, minVolt, maxVolt;
RTC_DATA_ATTR int count = 0;           // store count in RTC memory
unsigned long micro = 60E6;            // shorthand 60×106 for 60secs

void setup()
{
  WiFi.mode(WIFI_STA);                 // ESP32 in station mode
  scan = WiFi.scanNetworks();          // number of found Wi-Fi devices
  for (int i=0; i<scan; i++)
  {                                    // compare to router SSID
    if(!strcmp(ssid, WiFi.SSID(i).c_str()))
    {
      channel = WiFi.channel(i);       // router Wi-Fi channel
      i = scan;                        // exit the "for" loop
    }
  }
  esp_wifi_set_channel(channel, WIFI_SECOND_CHAN_NONE);
  esp_now_init();                      // initialize ESP-NOW
```

```
                                 // establish ESP-NOW receiver
  esp_now_peer_info_t receiver = {};
  memcpy(receiver.peer_addr, receiveMAC, 6);
  receiver.channel = channel;    // ESP-NOW receiver channel
  receiver.encrypt = false;
  esp_now_add_peer(&receiver);   // add ESP-NOW receiver
                                 // sending data callback function
  esp_now_register_send_cb(sendData);
                                 // restart after fixed time
  esp_sleep_enable_timer_wakeup(micro);
  taskFunction();                // call task function
  esp_now_send(receiveMAC,
        (uint8_t *) &payload, sizeof(payload));
                              // interval for callback before deep sleep
  delay(500);
  esp_deep_sleep_start();        // ESP32 in deep sleep mode
}

void taskFunction()              // manage data collection
{
  getCurrent();                  // call function to measure current
  payload.battery = analogReadMilliVolts(battPin)*2.0/1000.0;
  payload.channelPL = channel;   // router Wi-Fi channel
  payload.countPL = count++;     // incremented counter
  payload.rep = 0;               // transmission repeats
}

void getCurrent()                // function to calculate current usage
{
  maxVolt = 0;                   // minimum and maximum values
  minVolt = 5000;                // ignore initial readings
  for (int i=0; i<100; i++) analogReadMilliVolts(SCTpin);
  for (int i=0; i<Nread; i++)
```

```
  {                                      // SCT013 output voltage
    volt = analogReadMilliVolts(SCTpin);
                               // update maximum and minimum voltages
    if(volt > maxVolt) maxVolt = volt;
    if(volt < minVolt) minVolt = volt;
  }
  payload.mV = maxVolt - minVolt;   // peak to peak mV
}

void sendData(const uint8_t * mac, esp_now_send_status_t chkS)
{                                        // function to count transmissions
  if(chkS != 0)                          // transmission not received
  {
    payload.rep++;                       // increment transmission number
    esp_now_send(receiveMAC,
            (uint8_t *) & payload, sizeof(payload));
  }                                      // re-transmit data
}

void loop()                              // nothing in loop function
{}
```

A TTGO T-Display V1.1 module is powered through the USB connector of an 18650 battery V3 micro-USB charging shield (see Figure 9-11). The 18650 Li-ion battery is directly connected to GPIO 36 and to GND for measurement of the battery voltage.

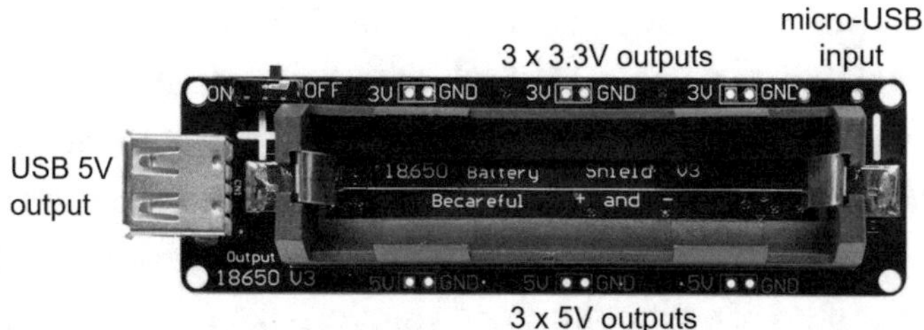

Figure 9-11. *18650 battery V3 micro-USB charging shield*

The sketch for the ESP32 microcontroller that receives data transmitted with the ESP-NOW protocol and then transmits, with Wi-Fi communication, data to a MQTT broker is given in Listing 9-5. Data is received in a structure, defined in Listing 9-4 for the transmitting ESP32 microcontroller, with the processed data then transmitted to a MQTT broker in the *receiveData* function.

Information is displayed on a TTGO T-Display V1.1 module LCD screen by the *display* function, with text colors defined in the *TFT_eSPI.h* file of the *TFT_eSPI* library (see Chapter 15, "Libraries"). For consistency of letter and digit sizes, numbers are converted to strings and displayed with the *drawString* instruction rather than with the *drawNumber* instruction. Labels are displayed once on a TTGO T-Display V1.1 module LCD screen by the *layout* function, rather than redisplaying the labels when data values are updated.

In Wi-Fi station mode, defined by the `WiFi.mode(WIFI_AP_STA)` or `WiFi.mode(WIFI_STA)` instruction, the ESP32 microcontroller periodically enters power-saving mode and sets Wi-Fi communication to standby. Consequently, data transmissions are not received by the ESP32 microcontroller, when the microcontroller is in power-saving mode. Power saving is prevented with the `WiFi.setSleep(WIFI_PS_NONE)` instruction, which increases the ESP32 microcontroller power requirement, but Wi-Fi communication by the ESP32 microcontroller is not interrupted.

The *time* library is required to determine daily power usage, based on the time of data reception. Methods to obtain the current time are described in Chapter 15, "Libraries." Daily power usage, determined from the SCT013 current transformer data, is constantly incremented until the time, *hhmm*, of data receipt is less than the previous time, *hhmmOld*, indicating the start of a new day. For example, if data is received every five minutes, then reception times of *23:58* and *00:03*, which equate to *hhmmOld* and *hhmm* values of 1438 and 3, respectively, identify the start of a new day.

Listing 9-5. ESP-NOW receiving ESP32

```
#include <TFT_eSPI.h>              // include TFT_eSPI library
TFT_eSPI tft = TFT_eSPI();         // associate tft with library
#include <WiFi.h>                  // include Wi-Fi and ESP-NOW
#include <esp_now.h>               // libraries
#include <CayenneMQTTESP32.h>      // Cayenne MQTT library
#include <ssid_password.h>         // file with logon details
typedef struct                     // structure for data
{
  int mV;                          // SCT013 voltage
  float battery;                   // battery voltage
  int channelPL;                   // router Wi-Fi channel
  int countPL;                     // data counter
  int rep;                         // repeated transmissions
} dataStruct;
dataStruct payload;
int power;
float mA, current, RMS, kWh = 0, lag;
unsigned long last = 0;
#include <time.h>                  // include time library
int GMT = 0, daylight = 3600;      // GMT and daylight saving offset
```

```
int hh, mm, ss, hhmm, hhmmOld;       // in seconds
struct tm timeData;

void setup()
{
  WiFi.setSleep(WIFI_PS_NONE);       // prevent Wi-Fi sleep mode
  WiFi.mode(WIFI_AP_STA);            // access point and station mode
  esp_now_init();                    // initialize ESP-NOW
                                     // receiving data callback function
  esp_now_register_recv_cb(receiveData);
  Cayenne.begin(username, mqttpass, clientID, ssid, password);
  configTime(GMT, daylight, "uk.pool.ntp.org");       // NTP pool
                                     // wait for connection to NTP
  while (!getLocalTime(&timeData)) delay(500);
                                     // set current hhmm value
  hhmmOld = 60*timeData.tm_hour + timeData.tm_min;
  layout();                          // function for LCD display labels
}
                                     // function to receive data
void receiveData(const uint8_t * mac, const uint8_t * data,
                 int len)
{                                    // copy data to payload structure
  memcpy(&payload, data, sizeof(payload));
  mA = 0.5*payload.mV/22.0;          // convert SCT013 voltage
  current = mA*100.0/50.0;           // to current
  RMS = current/sqrt(2.0);           // convert to RMS current
  power = 230.0 * RMS;               // convert to power (Watt)
  lag = (millis() - last)/1000.0;    // interval between receiving
  last = millis();                   // ESP-NOW transmissions
  getLocalTime(&timeData);           // update current time
```

```
  hh = timeData.tm_hour;
  mm = timeData.tm_min;
  ss = timeData.tm_sec;
  hhmm = 60*hh + mm;                        // update hhmm value
                                            // reset power for new day
  if(hhmm < hhmmOld) kWh = power/(3600.0*1000);
                                            // increment power
  else kWh = kWh + power*lag/(3600.0*1000);
  hhmmOld = hhmm;
                                            // send data to MQTT broker
  Cayenne.virtualWrite(V3, lag, "prox", "");
  Cayenne.virtualWrite(V4, payload.channelPL, "prox", "");
  Cayenne.virtualWrite(V5, power, "prox", "");
  Cayenne.virtualWrite(V6, payload.battery, "prox", "");
  Cayenne.virtualWrite(V7, payload.countPL, "prox", "");
  Cayenne.virtualWrite(V8, kWh, "prox", "");
  display();                     // function to display data on LCD screen
}

void layout()                               // function for LCD display labels
{
  tft.init();                               // initialize LCD screen
  tft.setRotation(3);                       // landscape with USB on left
  tft.setTextSize(1);
  tft.fillScreen(TFT_BLACK);                // colors from TFT_eSPI.h
  tft.setTextColor(TFT_GREEN,TFT_BLACK);
  tft.drawString("power", 0, 0, 4);  // labels for power and kWh
  tft.drawString("kWh", 0, 35, 4);
  tft.setTextColor(TFT_YELLOW,TFT_BLACK);
```

```
                                        // labels for battery and count
  tft.drawString("battery", 0, 70, 4);
  tft.drawString("count", 0, 105, 4);
}

void display()                          // function to display data on
{                                       // LCD screen
  tft.fillRect(100, 0, 140, 135, TFT_BLACK);
  tft.setTextColor(TFT_GREEN,TFT_BLACK);
  String txt = String(power);           // convert variable to string
  tft.drawString(txt, 100, 0, 4);       // display current and
  txt = String(kWh);                    // cumulative power
  tft.drawString(txt, 100, 35, 4);
  tft.setTextColor(TFT_YELLOW,TFT_BLACK);
  txt = String(payload.battery);        // display battery voltage
  tft.drawString(txt, 100, 70, 4);
  txt = String(payload.countPL);        // display data counter
  tft.drawString(txt, 100, 105, 4);
  tft.setTextColor(TFT_RED,TFT_BLACK);
  tft.drawString("time", 190, 0, 4); // display data reception time
  if(hh > 9) txt = String(hh); else txt = "0"+String(hh);
  tft.drawString(txt, 200, 35, 4);
  if(mm > 9) txt = String(mm); else txt = "0"+String(mm);
  tft.drawString(txt, 200, 70, 4);
  if(ss > 9) txt = String(ss); else txt = "0"+String(ss);
  tft.drawString(txt, 200, 105, 4);
}
```

```
void loop()                               // nothing in loop function
{
  Cayenne.loop();
}
```

Wi-Fi or Wi-Fi and ESP-NOW

The cycle times of the two scenarios to transmit energy usage data to a MQTT broker are shown in Table 9-3. The first scenario consists of a battery-powered ESP32 microcontroller transmitting data, by Wi-Fi communication through a router, to a MQTT broker. The second scenario consists of a battery-powered ESP32 microcontroller transmitting data, with the ESP-NOW protocol, to a non-battery-powered ESP32 microcontroller, which forwards the data, by Wi-Fi communication through a router, to a MQTT broker (see Figure 9-9). The main difference in transmission cycle times of the two scenarios was the longer time required to scan available networks and to determine the router communication channel of the receiving ESP32 microcontroller than to connect to a MQTT broker with Wi-Fi communication. While the data transmission time with ESP-NOW communication was shorter than with Wi-Fi communication, the difference was small relative to the time to connect to a MQTT broker or to scan available networks.

Table 9-3. *Transmission cycle times*

Task	One ESP32 Wi-Fi only	Two ESP32s ESP-NOW and Wi-Fi
Restart from deep sleep mode.	300ms	300ms
Scan available networks.		2462ms
Connect to MQTT broker over Wi-Fi.	2210ms	
Connect to receiving ESP32 with ESP-NOW.		0.36ms
Collect data.	51.6ms	51.6ms
Transmit data.	5.0ms	0.23ms
Time to complete transmission or receive callback.	500ms	500ms
Total time	3067ms	3314ms

The current requirements during the transmission cycle, for a battery-powered transmitting ESP32 microcontroller, in the two scenarios are shown in Figure 9-12. The ESP32 microcontroller communicating directly with the MQTT broker is shown in Figure 9-12a, with the scenario of two ESP32 microcontrollers transmitting data with ESP-NOW and Wi-Fi communication shown in Figure 9-12b. An initial 300ms is required for restarting the ESP32 microcontroller after deep sleep mode, followed by either connecting to the Wi-Fi router or scanning available networks to determine the router communication channel, prior to communication with the ESP-NOW protocol. The 500ms delay period after data transmission is not apparent in the current requirement graph for the first scenario, but is visible for the second scenario. The area under the current graph, measured in milliamp-seconds (mAs), is inversely related to the length of time that a battery, of capacity *N* mAh, can supply power to a transmitting ESP32 microcontroller. The ESP32 microcontroller, which transmitted data directly to a MQTT broker, required 65% of the charge (226 vs. 348mAs) of the ESP32 microcontroller that scanned available networks to determine the router communication channel before transmitting data with the ESP-NOW protocol to a second ESP32 microcontroller.

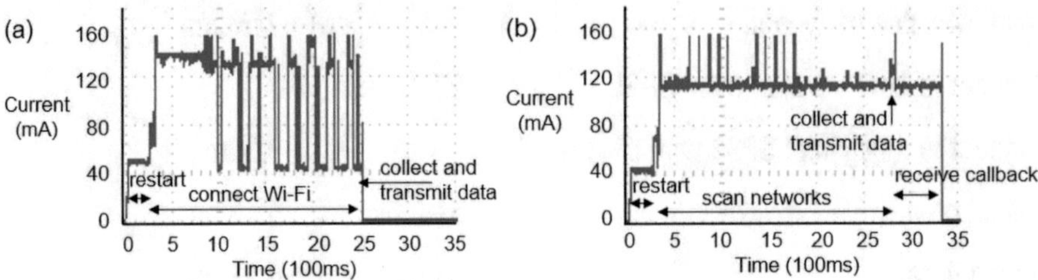

***Figure 9-12.** Current requirements with Wi-Fi or with ESP-NOW and Wi-Fi*

CHAPTER 10

Managing Images

An image is displayed on a web page by referencing the JPEG, GIF (Graphics Interchange Format), or PNG file directly. In contrast, to display an image on an OLED screen or an LCD screen, the image JPEG, GIF, or PNG file is converted to a file containing the image data, with the file format dependent on the display device. For a black-and-white OLED (Organic Light-Emitting Diode) screen, each image pixel is represented by a zero or a one. For a color image displayed on an LCD (Liquid Crystal Display) screen, information on the red, green, and blue components of each pixel is required. This chapter describes formatting images for display on an OLED screen and on an LCD screen. Displaying an image on a web page, with the image held directly in SPIFFS (Serial Peripheral Interface Flash File System) or the image data stored in the sketch, is also described.

The JPEG (Joint Photographic Experts Group) format is applicable to complex images, such as digital photographs and images with tonal changes in color. The GIF (Graphics Interchange Format) and PNG (Portable Network Graphics) formats are suitable for less complex images, such as line drawings or graphics with solid areas of color.

N. Cameron, *ESP32 Formats and Communication*,
https://doi.org/10.1007/978-1-4842-9376-8_10

Image Bitmap

A black-and-white image is characterized by a bitmap or a map of the bits representing the image. For example, the 6 × 7 (width × height)-pixel image of a tick symbol in Figure 10-1 is characterized by the bitmap *0x01, 0x03 ... 0x00,* with a value of zero or one for each pixel. A bitmap is a series of numbers in binary format, which is converted to HEX format, which requires fewer digits than decimal format. For example, the decimal number 12345 is equal to *0x3039* in HEX format, with the *0x* prefix indicating a HEX-formatted number. An 8-bit binary or two-digit HEX number represents up to eight pixels, as illustrated in Figure 10-1.

32	16	8	4	2	1	binary	decimal	HEX
						000001	1	0x01
						000011	3	0x03
						000110	6	0x06
						101100	44	0x2C
						111000	56	0x38
						010000	16	0x10
						000000	0	0x00

Figure 10-1. *Bitmap*

For illustration only, Listing 10-1 displays the tick symbol on the LCD screen of the TTGO T-Display V1.1 module. Note that the 6 × 7-pixel size of the tick symbol is very small. The image bitmap is stored in flash or programmable memory, PROGMEM, where the sketch is also stored, rather than in SRAM, where variables are created and manipulated in a sketch. The `drawBitmap(x, y, width, height, image, color)` instruction displays the image starting at the (*x, y*) coordinates, referencing the *image* data array, with the image width and height in pixels.

Listing 10-1. Display an image with a bitmap

```
const unsigned char tick [] PROGMEM = {  // store image bitmap
0x01, 0x03, 0x06, 0x2C, 0x38, 0x10, 0x00  // in PROGMEM
};
#include <TFT_eSPI.h>                     // include TFT_eSPI library
TFT_eSPI tft = TFT_eSPI();                // associate tft with library
int imageW = 6, imageH = 7;               // image width and height

void setup()
{
  tft.init();                             // initialize screen
  tft.fillScreen(TFT_BLACK);              // screen background color
                                          // draw image
 tft.drawBitmap(20, 20, tick, imageW, imageH, TFT_WHITE);
}

void loop()                               // nothing in loop function
{}
```

Each pixel of an 8-bit color image consists of red, green, and blue components, with a component having a value between 0 and 255 or $2^8 - 1$. Android tablets and mobile phones display colors with a pixel color represented by 3 × 8 bits, *RGB888* format, or 24-bit color depth. An alternative is the *RGB565* format, in which the last 3, 2, and 3 bits of the red, green, and blue components are dropped, with an additional green bit as the human eye is more sensitive to graduations of green than to red or blue. The *RGB565* format, with 16-bit color depth, requires 2 bytes to store a pixel color, rather than 3 bytes with the *RGB888* format. The *RGB565* format represents $2^{16} = 65536$ colors, rather than 2^{24} or about 17 million colors with the *RGB888* format.

For example, the olive green color in Figure 10-2 has red, green, and blue components of *95, 153, 66* in *RGB888* format. The red component in binary format of *B0101111* is reduced to *B01011* by dropping the last 3 bits.

The last 2 and 3 bits of the green and blue components are also dropped resulting in values of *B100110* and *B01000*, respectively. The reduced red, green, and blue components are combined, *B01011|100110|01000*, to the *RGB565* value, which is formatted as high and low bytes of *B01011100* and *B11001000* that equate to *0x5C* and *0xC8*, respectively. The *RGB565* value of *0x5CC8* has red, green, and blue components of 88, 152, 64, after bit shifting the red, green, and blue components by three, two, and three positions, respectively. For example, bit shifting the red component of *B01011* = 11 by three positions, which is the equivalent of multiplying by $8 = 2^3$, equates the red component of the *RGB565* value to *B01011000* = 88. The red, green, and blue components of an RGB565-formatted color are equal to the highest multiple of 8, 4, and 8, respectively, lower than the original color value.

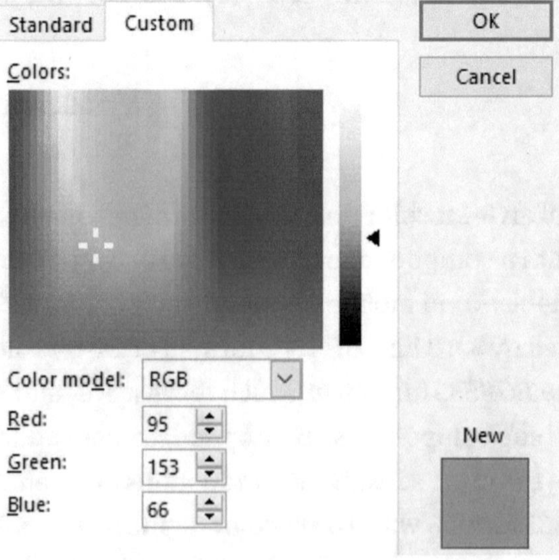

Figure 10-2. *Color palette*

A color image is displayed on an LCD screen in a comparable manner to Listing 10-1, with an element of the image data array representing the red, green, and blue components of one pixel. In contrast, when displaying a black-and-white image, one element of the image data array represents the states of up to eight pixels. A 135 × 240-pixel black-and-white image requires 4050 bytes of memory storage, while the corresponding color image with *RGB565* format requires 64800 bytes or 63kB of program storage space.

Display a Black-and-White Image

An application of displaying black-and-white images is to indicate options in a rolling menu with the user selecting an option on the touch screen (see Chapter 4, “TTGO T-Watch V2”).

Prior to displaying an image in black and white, the website `javl.github.io/image2cpp` by Jasper van Loenen converts a JPEG- or PNG-formatted image to an image data array. After the image file is loaded, in the *Image Settings* section, select the *Canvas size*, which is the dimension of the image to be displayed, such as 64 × 128 or 135 × 240 pixels for an OLED or LCD screen (see Figure 10-3). The image file is either imported with the required width and height or is scaled within the website. In the *Scaling* section, the options are *original size, scale to fit,* and *stretch to fill canvas*. There are options to center, rotate, or flip the image. The scaled image is displayed in the *Preview* section.

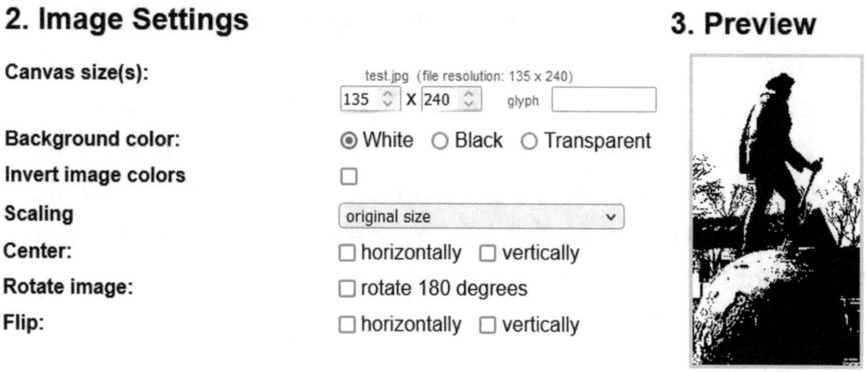

2. Image Settings

Canvas size(s): test.jpg (file resolution: 135 x 240) 135 X 240 glyph

Background color: White Black Transparent

Invert image colors

Scaling original size

Center: horizontally vertically

Rotate image: rotate 180 degrees

Flip: horizontally vertically

3. Preview

Figure 10-3. *Define an image to convert to HEX values*

In the *Output* section (see Figure 10-4), select *Arduino code* in the *Code output format* field and click *Generate code*. In the example, the image data file consists of 4080 HEX values, in 255 rows of 16 columns. The 4080 HEX values represent up to 32640 pixels, as a HEX value defines the states of up to eight pixels, consistent with the 135 × 240 = 32400 pixels of the image. The output file includes the `const unsigned char imageData[] PROGMEM {...}` instruction to store the image data file in PROGMEM (see Figure 10-4). In a sketch, the image data from the output file is stored on a separate tab to make the sketch more easily interpretable.

4. Output

Code output format Arduino code

Identifier/Prefix:

Draw mode: Horizontal - 1 bit per pixel

Generate code Copy Output

```
// 'test', 135x240px
const unsigned char test [] PROGMEM = {
	0xff, 0xff, 0xff, 0xff, 0xff, 0xff, 0xff, 0xff, 0xff, 0xff, 0xff, 0xff,
	0xfe, 0xff, 0xff, 0xff, 0xff, 0xff, 0xff, 0xff, 0xff, 0xff, 0xff, 0xff,
	0xff, 0xfe, 0xff, 0xff, 0xff, 0xff, 0xff, 0xff, 0xff, 0xff, 0xff, 0xff,
```

Figure 10-4. *Convert an image to HEX values*

A sketch to display an image is identical to Listing 10-1 apart from the image data array dimensions and that array values are held on a separate tab.

A black-and-white image is displayed on an OLED screen with the *Adafruit SSD1306* library, which references the *Wire* and *Adafruit_GFX* libraries, which are loaded implicitly. An ESP32 DEVKIT DOIT module connected to a 64 × 128-pixel OLED screen is shown in Figure 10-5 with connections listed in Table 10-1.

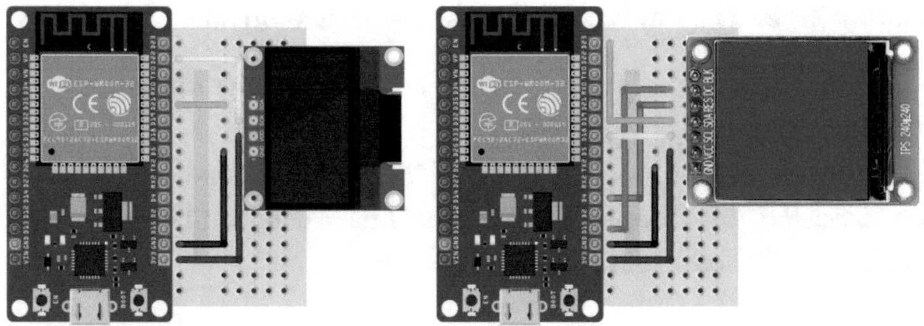

Figure 10-5. *ESP32 with an OLED screen and LCD screen*

Table 10-1. *ESP32 and an OLED screen and LCD screen*

1.3" 240 × 240 TFT LCD	TFT_eSPI	To ESP32	OLED screen	To ESP32
SDA (SPI data)	TFT_MOSI	GPIO 23	SDA	GPIO 21
	TFT_MISO	Unconnected		
	TFT_CS	Unconnected		
SCK (SPI clock)	TFT_SCLK	GPIO 18	SCL	GPIO 22
BLK (backlight)		Unconnected		
DC (data or command)	TFT_DC	Default GPIO 2 GPIO 15		
RES (reset)	TFT_RST	GPIO 4		
VCC		3.3V	VCC	3.3V
GND		GND	GND	GND

Listing 10-2 illustrates displaying a 64 × 128-pixel image on an OLED screen, with the image data array, *test,* held on the tab *image.h*. The sketch illustrates displaying an image in the four orientations, with the `setRotation(N)` instruction to rotate the displayed image by $N \times 90°$, with N equal to 0 equivalent to landscape mode. The default I2C (Inter-Integrated Circuit) address of the OLED screen is *0x3C*.

Listing 10-2. Display a black-and-white image on an OLED screen

```
#include "image.h"                       // tab with image data array
#include <Adafruit_SSD1306.h>            // include libraries
int oledW = 128, oledH = 64;             // OLED width and height
int imageW = 64, imageH = 128;           // image width and height
Adafruit_SSD1306 oled(oledW, oledH, &Wire, -1);

void setup()
{                                        // initialize OLED
  oled.begin(SSD1306_SWITCHCAPVCC, 0x3C);
}

void loop()
{
  for (int i=0; i<4; i++)                // for four rotation settings
  {
    oled.clearDisplay();                 // clear OLED display
    oled.setRotation(i);                 // 0 & 2 landscape 1 & 3 portrait
                                         // draw image
    oled.drawBitmap(0, 0, test, imageW, imageH, WHITE);
    oled.display();
    delay(3000);                         // delay between image rotations
  }
}

// 'test', 64x128px                      // image width × height
const unsigned char test [] PROGMEM = {
0xff, 0xff, 0xff, 0xff, 0xff, 0xff, 0xff, 0xff, 0xff, 0xff, ...
0xff, 0xff, 0xff, 0xff, 0xff, 0xff, 0xff, 0xff, 0xff, 0xff, ...
```

The I2C address of the OLED screen is required to identify the screen in the sketch. Listing 10-3 scans for I2C devices connected to the ESP32 module, with device I2C addresses displayed on the Serial Monitor. On transmitting to an I2C device, the device returns a zero, indicating a successful transmission. The I2C addresses 0–7, *0x00* to *0x07*, and 120–127, *0x78* to *0x7F*, are reserved and are not scanned. I2C addresses of sensors and modules are available at `learn.adafruit.com/i2c-addresses/the-list`.

Listing 10-3. I2C device scanner

```
#include <Wire.h>                          // include Wire library
int device, row;

void setup()
{
  Wire.begin();                            // initialize I2C bus
  Serial.begin(115200);                    // Serial Monitor baud rate
}

void loop()
{
  device = 0;                              // reset I2C device counter
  row = 1;
  Serial.println("\nI2C Scanner");         // display header
  Serial.print("    0  1  2  3  4  5  6  7  8  9");
  Serial.println("    A  B  C  D  E  F");
  Serial.print  ("00                ");
  for (int i=8; i<120; i++)                // scan through channels 8 to 119
  {
    Wire.beginTransmission(i);             // transmit to device at address i
    if(Wire.endTransmission() == 0)        // device response to transmission
    {
      Serial.print(" ");
```

```
      if (i < 16) Serial.print("0");
      Serial.print(i, HEX);          // display I2C address in HEX
      device++;
    }
    else Serial.print(" --");        // no device with I2C address
    if ((i + 1) % 16 == 0)           // next row in displayed results
    {
      Serial.printf("\n%d0", row);   // display row header
      row++;
    }
  }                                  // display scan results
  Serial.printf("\nFound %d device(s) \n", device);
  delay(5000);
}
```

The image displayed on an OLED screen in Listing 10-2 is also displayed on a 1.3" 240 × 240-pixel TFT ST7789 LCD screen, connected to an ESP32 DEVKIT DOIT module, with Listing 10-4. Connections are shown in Figure 10-5 and listed in Table 10-1. The *TFT_eSPI* library is used to display images on an LCD screen, as described in Chapter 15, "Libraries." In the *TFT_eSPI* library, comment out `#include <User_setup.h>` in the *User_Setup_Select.h* file and un-comment `#include <User_Setups/Setup24_ST7789.h>`. In the *TFT_eSPI* ➤ *User_Setups* ➤ *Setup24_ST7789* file, the default *TFT_eSPI DC* pin is mapped to GPIO 2, which is connected to the ESP32 DEVKIT DOIT built-in blue LED. The *DC* pin is mapped to GPIO 15 by changing the instruction `#define TFT_DC 2` to `#define TFT_DC 15`.

Listing 10-4. Display a black-and-white image on an LCD screen

```
#include "image.h"                   // tab with image data array
#include <TFT_eSPI.h>                // include TFT_eSPI library
TFT_eSPI tft = TFT_eSPI();           // associate tft with library
int imageW = 64, imageH = 128;       // image width and height
```

```
void setup()
{
  tft.init();                          // initialize screen
}

void loop()
{
  for (int i=0; i<4; i++)              // for four rotation settings
  {
    tft.fillScreen(TFT_BLACK);         // clear OLED display
    tft.setRotation(i);                // 0 & 2 landscape 1 & 3 portrait
                                       // draw image
    tft.drawBitmap(0, 0, test, imageW, imageH, TFT_WHITE);
    delay(3000);                       // delay between image rotations
  }
}
```

Display a Color Image

A JPEG-, PNG-, or GIF-formatted image is converted to an *RGB565* image data array with the website `www.rinkydinkelectronics.com/t_imageconverter565.php` by Henning Karlsen. After an image is loaded, select *Convert to .c file* and click *Make File*. A preview of the image is displayed (see Figure 10-6), and a text file containing the image data array is downloaded. The image data array is copied and pasted into the *image.h* tab of the sketch in Listing 10-5, with the first few rows shown.

For information, the András Jelky statue in Figures 10-3, 10-6, and 10-10 is located in Baja, Hungary, and commemorates the life of an eighteenth-century adventurer, who traveled the world.

ImageConverter (UTFT)
The picture 'test.jpg' is being processed...
Click here to download your file

Figure 10-6. *Convert a color image to HEX values*

The Henning Karlsen image converter does not resize a JPEG-, PNG-, or GIF-formatted image, and the maximum file size is 300kB. A program, such as Microsoft Windows *Paint,* is required to resize an original image to the dimensions of the displayed image.

Listing 10-5 is virtually identical to Listing 10-4 apart from replacing the instruction

```
tft.drawBitmap(0, 0, test, imageW, imageH, TFT_WHITE)
```

with the instructions

```
tft.setSwapBytes(true)
tft.pushImage(0, 0, imageW, imageH, test)
```

The instructions drawBitmap and pushImage display an image starting at the (*x, y*) coordinates, equal to (0,0), and reference the *test* array, with the image width and height in pixels. The setSwapBytes instruction converts image byte order. Image data is stored in most significant byte (*MSByte*) order, while the microcontroller interprets data in least significant byte *(LSByte*) order. For example, the 32-bit or 4-byte integer *0x0A0B0C0D,* in HEX format, is stored as four 8-bit or 1-byte integers in four sequential memory byte locations as either *0x0A, 0x0B, 0x0C,* and *0x0D,* which is *MSByte* order, or *0x0D, 0x0C, 0x0B,* and *0x0A,* which is *LSByte* order. The setSwapBytes(true) instruction reverses the byte order, to store the image data in *LSBbyte* order.

Displaying an original color image in black and white requires less memory than displaying the color image. For example, a sketch to display the 135 × 240-pixel image in Figure 10-6 in black and white or in color required 243kB or 303kB of PROGMEM, a difference of 60kB. A color image requires 2 bytes per pixel, while a black-and-white image only requires 1 byte for eight pixels. When displayed in black and white or in color, a 135 × 240-pixel image with 32400 pixels requires 4kB or 63kB, a difference of 59kB. The difference in sketch memory requirements of 60kB is essentially due to the difference in the required image storage of 59kB.

Listing 10-5. Display a color image on an LCD screen

```
#include "image.h"                  // tab with image data array
#include <TFT_eSPI.h>               // include TFT_eSPI library
TFT_eSPI tft = TFT_eSPI();          // associate tft with library
int imageW = 135, imageH = 240;     // image width and height

void setup()
{
  tft.init();                       // initialize screen
  tft.fillScreen(TFT_BLACK);
  tft.setSwapBytes(true);           // required to retain image color
```

```
                                          // draw image
  tft.pushImage(0, 0, imageW, imageH, test);
}

void loop()                               // nothing in loop function
{}

const unsigned short test[32400] PROGMEM={
0xBEBE, 0xBEBE, 0xBEBE, 0xBE9E, 0xBE9E, 0xBE9E, 0xBE9E, 0xBE9E, ...
0xBE9E, 0xBE9E, 0xBE9E, 0xBE9E, 0xBE9E, 0xBE9E, 0xBE9E, 0xBE9E, ...
0xB69E, 0xB69E, 0xB67E, 0xB67E, 0xAE9E, 0xAE7E, 0xAE7E, 0xAE7E, ...
```

Bitmap and X Bitmap

Existing black-and-white images and color images are converted to image data arrays for inclusion in a sketch to display the image, while new black-and-white images are created in a graphics package, such as Microsoft Windows *Paint*. For example, several hundred snowflake images are displayed on an LCD screen in Listing 10-13, which requires a snowflake image to be created, as an existing snowflake image is not available.

In Microsoft Windows *Paint*, a new image is resized to the required dimensions, $W \times H$ pixels, with the *Gridlines* option selected and the pencil *Tool* clicked on the relevant squares of the grid to generate the required image. For example, a snowflake image generated with dimensions 13 × 13 pixels is shown in Figure 10-7. The image file is saved in PNG format.

Figure 10-7. *Generated snowflake image*

The corresponding bitmap data file for the image is generated with Jasper van Loenen's converter available at `javl.github.io/image2cpp`, as described in the "Display a Black-and-White Image" section of the chapter. After loading the saved PNG file, a canvas size of 13 × 13 pixels is selected (see Figure 10-8), with a transparent background color and inverted image colors. A preview image is displayed in section 3 of the website.

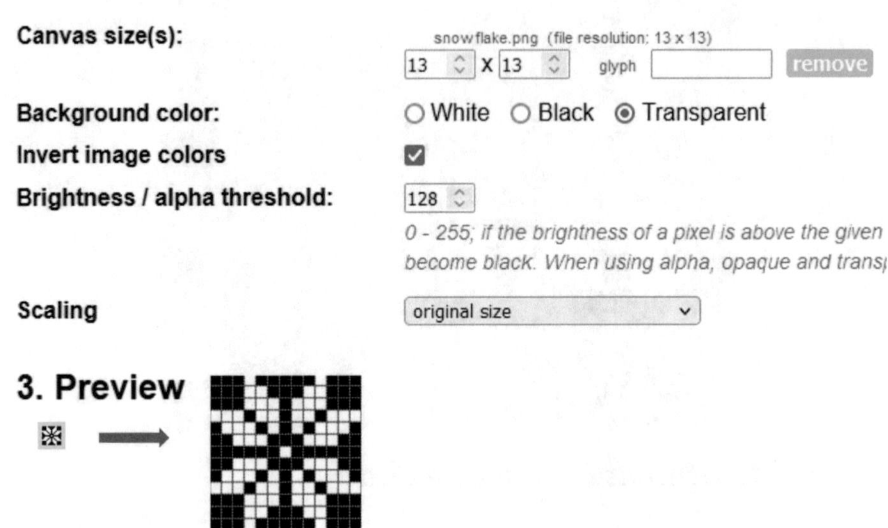

Figure 10-8. *Inverted image saved to bitmap format*

The image bitmap data file is obtained by clicking the *Generate code* option in section 4 of the website. For example, the bitmap data file corresponding to the snowflake image in Figure 10-7 is shown in Listing 10-6.

Listing 10-6. Image bitmap data file

```
// 'snowflake', 13x13px
const unsigned char snowflake [] PROGMEM = {
  0x10, 0x40, 0x18, 0xc0, 0x1d, 0xc0, 0xed, 0xb8, 0x75, 0x70,
  0x38, 0xe0, 0x02, 0x00, 0x38, 0xe0, 0x75, 0x70, 0xed, 0xb8,
  0x1d, 0xc0, 0x18, 0xc0, 0x10, 0x40
};
```

The bitmap data file for a 13 × 13-pixel image consists of 13 pairs of HEX values, with one pair for each row of the image. Two 8-bit numbers are concatenated to represent a 13-bit number plus three redundant bits.

For example, the third row of the snowflake image in Figure 10-7 has a binary representation of *B00011101|11000,* with *1* representing a white square and *0* a transparent square. The binary representation is split into 8-bit and 5-bit numbers, *B00011101* and *B11000,* with the 5-bit number right-filled with *B000,* to produce the HEX values of *0x1D* and *0xC0,* as shown in Listing 10-6.

An alternative to the bitmap (BMP) format is the X bitmap (XBM) format, which combines the second 8-bit number with the first 8-bit number rather than the reverse, as with the BMP format. For example, the binary representation of *B00011|10111000* for the third row of the snowflake image in Figure 10-7 is split into the second (8-bit) and first (5-bit) numbers *B10111000* and *B00011* with the first number left-filled with *B000,* to produce the HEX values of *0xB8* and *0x03,* respectively. The XBM data file is given in Listing 10-7.

Listing 10-7. Image X bitmap data file

```
int flakeW = 13, flakeH = 13;
const unsigned char snowflake[] PROGMEM = {
  0x08, 0x02, 0x18, 0x03, 0xB8, 0x03, 0xB7, 0x1D, 0xAE, 0x0E,
  0x1C, 0x07, 0x40, 0x00, 0x1C, 0x07, 0xAE, 0x0E, 0xB7, 0x1D,
  0xB8, 0x03, 0x18, 0x03, 0x08, 0x02
};
```

An image saved in BMP format is converted to XBM format with Mladen Adamovic's converter available at `www.online-utility.org/image/convert/to/XBM`. The converted image file is saved as *filename.XBM,* which is opened by a word processor package, such as *WordPad,* to display the file contents, as shown in Listing 10-7.

A bitmap (BMP)-formatted file contains a file header (bitmap identifier, file size, width, height, color options, and bitmap data starting point) and the bitmap pixels, each with a different color. An X bitmap (XBM)-formatted file stores information on a black-and-white image, with the

XBM file containing the pixel information as plain text, as shown in Listing 10-7. The *TFT_eSPI* library of Bodmer supports both BMP- and XBM-formatted image files, with an image displayed using the instructions `drawBitmap` and `drawXBitmap`, respectively.

Send an Image in Email

Sending an email containing an image attachment with the ESP32 microcontroller is described in Chapter 7, "Email and QR Codes." A JPEG-, PNG-, or GIF-formatted image to be included in an email is converted to an image data array of HEX values with the website `tomeko.net/online_tools/file_to_hex.php?lang=en` by Tomasz Ostrowski. There is no file size constraint with Tomasz Ostrowski's image converter, but the converter does not resize a JPEG-, PNG-, or GIF-formatted image. For example, the first few rows of HEX values from converting the image in Figure 10-6 are shown in Figure 10-9. The options to *"Use 0x and comma as separator"* and to *"Insert newlines after each 16B"* are required and recommended, respectively, with the latter making the image data array more manageable.

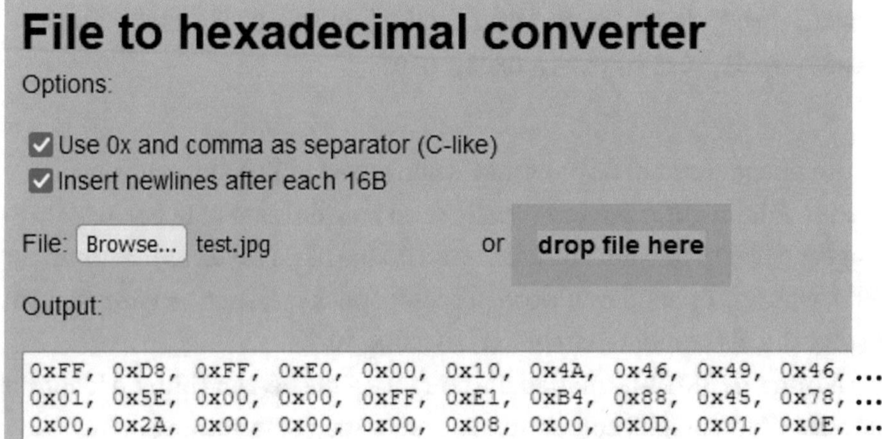

Figure 10-9. *Convert an image to HEX format*

The image data array is copied and pasted into the *image.h* tab of the sketch with the first few rows shown:

```
const uint8_t imageData[] PROGMEM = {
0xFF, 0xD8, 0xFF, 0xE0, 0x00, 0x10, 0x4A, 0x46, 0x49, 0x46, ...
0x01, 0x5E, 0x00, 0x00, 0xFF, 0xE1, 0xB4, 0x88, 0x45, 0x78, ...
0x00, 0x2A, 0x00, 0x00, 0x00, 0x08, 0x00, 0x0D, 0x01, 0x0E, ...
...
};
```

To check that the HEX values correspond to the original image, the website `codepen.io/abdhass/full/jdRNdj` by Abdul Hassan converts the image data array of HEX values to an image. Note that the *0x* preceding a HEX value and the separating commas are excluded, either by editing the image data array output from the image to HEX conversion or by deselecting the *"Use 0x and comma as separator"* option in the *File to hexadecimal converter* when converting the image. For example, Figure 10-10 shows the first few rows of HEX values from the converted JPEG image and the resulting image.

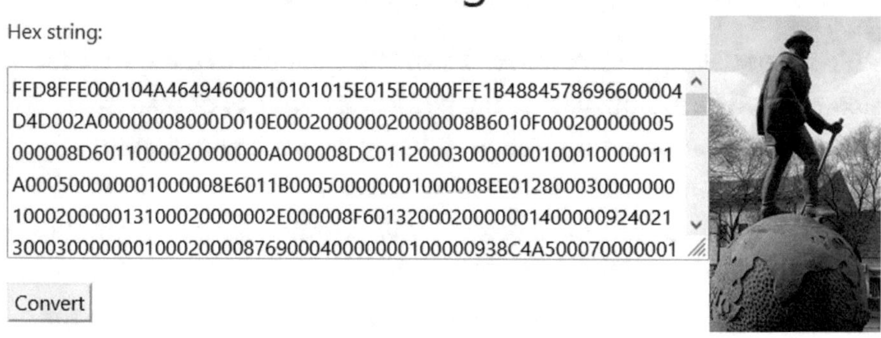

Figure 10-10. *Convert HEX-formatted data to an image*

Several websites associated with image data converters have been described. Table 10-2 lists the various converter functions and associated websites.

Table 10-2. *Image converters*

Image conversion	Website
JPEG, PNG, or GIF image to RGB565 data array	www.rinkydinkelectronics.com/t_imageconverter565.php
JPEG or PNG image to HEX data array for black-and-white image	javl.github.io/image2cpp
JPEG, PNG, or GIF image to HEX data array for color image	tomeko.net/online_tools/file_to_hex.php?lang=en
HEX data array to black-and-white image or to color image	codepen.io/abdhass/full/jdRNdj
BMP-formatted image to XBM format	www.online-utility.org/image/convert/to/XBM

Store the Image File in SPIFFS

SPIFFS (Serial Peripheral Interface Flash File System) is a file system for microcontrollers to store data or image files and write to or read from files stored in flash memory. The partition of flash memory for SPIFFS is adjusted within the Arduino IDE depending on the requirements of a sketch. For example, the default SPIFFS partition for the ESP32 microcontroller is 1472kB. SPIFFS has a flat structure as directories are not supported. A file with path *temp/filename.txt* creates a file called *temp/filename.txt* and not a file called *filename.txt* in the *temp* directory.

Chapter 7, "Email and QR Codes," describes attaching an image in an email sent by the ESP32 microcontroller, with the JPEG-formatted image stored directly in SPIFFS. The advantage of SPIFFS, in the context of email, is that the image file does not have to be converted into an image data array and then stored in PROGMEM.

The ESP32 microcontroller uses the *LittleFS* and *SPIFFS* libraries, which are automatically incorporated in the Arduino IDE when the *esp32* Boards Manager is installed in the Arduino IDE. The *LittleFS* library is recommended as the read and write functions are faster than with the *SPIFFS* library, and the *LittleFS* library includes directories. Although SPIFFS has a flat structure, files are allocated to *directories* by prefixing the file name with a *directory* name, such as */dir/filename.txt*. The *8-3* file naming convention for a file name (eight characters) and extension (three characters) is recommended.

The *LittleFS* and *SPIFFS* libraries both use the instruction parameters `FILE_READ`, `FILE_WRITE`, and `FILE_APPEND` to read a file from the start, to create and then write to a file, and to append to a file, respectively. The *LittleFS* library instruction `createDir(dir)` creates a directory *dir*. The *LittleFS* library provides a list of files in SPIFFS with the directory structure, which is not provided by the *SPIFFS* library.

The sketch in Listing 10-8 demonstrates opening, writing to, reading from, renaming, and deleting a file stored in SPIFFS. The *LittleFS* library generates a SPIFFS hierarchical structure, which is demonstrated with the *hierarchy* function.

Listing 10-8. Write, read, and append a file in SPIFFS

```
#include <LittleFS.h>                    // include LittleFS library
String dirAname = "/dirA";
String dirBname = "/dirB";
String file1 = "/dirA/tstfile1.txt";     // structure /dir/ file
String file2 = "/dirA/tstfile2.txt";     // level      0    1
```

```
String file3 = "/dirB/tstfile3.txt";
unsigned long lag;

void setup()
{
  Serial.begin(115200);       // define Serial Monitor baud rate
  if(LittleFS.begin()) Serial.println("LittleFS OK");
  createDir(dirAname);        // create directory
  createDir(dirBname);
                              // open file to write
  File file = LittleFS.open(file1, FILE_WRITE);
  file.println("ABC");        // add record with ABC
  file.println("123");        // instead of print("xxx\n")
  file.close();
  fileContent(file1);         // function to display file content
  dirContent(dirAname);       // and directory content
  file = LittleFS.open(file1, FILE_APPEND);    // append to a file
  file.println("XYZ");
  file.close();
  LittleFS.rename(file1, file2);               // change file name
  fileContent(file2);
                              // delete a file
//  if(LittleFS.exists(file2)) LittleFS.remove(file2);
  file = LittleFS.open(file1, FILE_WRITE);     // create a new file
  file.close();
  file = LittleFS.open(file3, FILE_WRITE);
  file.close();
  dirContent("/");            // list of directories
  dirContent(dirAname);       // files in directory
```

```
  Serial.println("\nSPIFFS hierarchy");
  hierarchy("/", 1);             // function for SPIFFS hierarchy
  lag = millis();
  LittleFS.format();             // delete all files in SPIFFS
  lag = millis() - lag;
  Serial.printf("\ntime to delete: %u \n", lag);
  dirContent("/");
}

void dirContent(String dname)   // function to display directory content
{                                // open directory
  File dir = LittleFS.open(dname);
  Serial.printf("\n%s content\n", dir.name());
  File file = dir.openNextFile();            // open file in directory
  while(file)
  {                              // display file details
    Serial.printf("file %s size %d \n", file.name(),file.size());
    file = dir.openNextFile();
  }
}

void fileContent(String fname)  // function to display file content
{                                // open file and display content
  File file = LittleFS.open(fname, FILE_READ);
  Serial.printf("\nFile content of %s \n", file.name());
  while(file.available()) Serial.write(file.read());
  file.close();
}
```

```
void createDir(String dirname)              // create a directory
{
  if(LittleFS.mkdir(dirname))
          printf("directory %s OK \n", dirname);
}

void hierarchy(String dirname, int level)  // function to display
{                                           // sorted list of file names
  File root = LittleFS.open(dirname);       // in each directory
  File file = root.openNextFile();
  while (file)
  {
    if(file.isDirectory())                  // when file is a directory
    {                                    // check files within directory
      Serial.printf("DIR content of %s \n", file.name());
      if(level) hierarchy(file.path(), level-1);
    }                                    // display file name and size
    else Serial.printf(" File %s size %d \n",
                     file.name(),file.size());
    file = root.openNextFile();
  }
}

void loop()                                 // nothing in loop function
{}
```

When uploading files to SPIFFS, the Arduino IDE requires a separate plugin for the ESP32 microcontroller. Note that, at the time of writing this chapter, the plugin to upload files to SPIFFS was not available with Arduino IDE version 2.1. Instructions for installing and running the plugin are available at `github.com/me-no-dev/arduino-esp32fs-plugin`. The file *ESP32FS-1.1.zip* is downloaded, and the unzipped *esp32fs.jar* (Java Archive) file containing the plugin must be located in the *Sketchbook location\tools\ESP32FS\tool* folder, with the *Sketchbook location* folder defined in the Arduino IDE by selecting *File ➤ Preferences*. If the Arduino IDE is open, then the Arduino IDE must be closed and restarted after the *esp32fs.jar* file is moved to the *tool* folder. The Arduino IDE *Tools* menu will then include the *ESP32 Sketch Data Upload* option (see Figure 10-11).

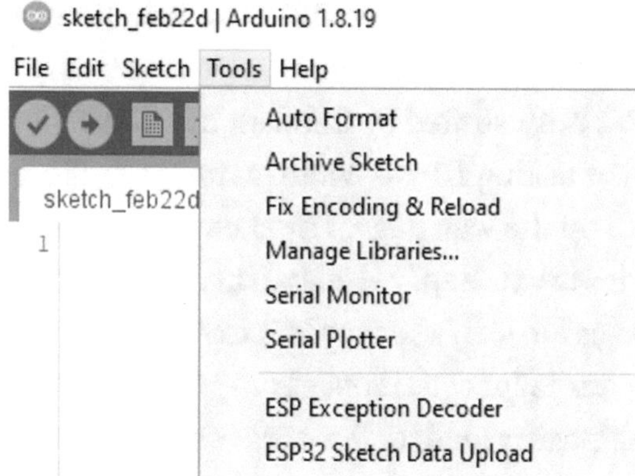

***Figure 10-11.** Plugin details for uploading files to SPIFFS*

The *mklittlefs* folder containing the *mklittlefs* application is required, with the folder located in *User\AppData\Local\Arduino15\packages\esp32tools*, in which the *esptool_py* folder is located. The *mklittlefs* folder is downloaded through `github.com/lorol/LITTLEFS`.

A text file or image file is stored in SPIFFS by locating the file in the *data* folder within the sketch folder. In the Arduino IDE, select the *Sketch* menu, click *Show Sketch Folder*, create a folder named *data*, and then move the file into the *data* folder. A file *filename.txt* or *image.jpg* is referenced in the sketch as */filename.txt* or */image.jpg*. Prior to compiling and uploading the sketch in the Arduino IDE, ensure that both a *Board* and a *Port* are selected and that the Serial Monitor is closed. In the Arduino IDE, select the *Tools* menu, click the *ESP32 Sketch Data Upload* option, and select the *LittleFS* option. The *SPIFFS* option is for use with the *SPIFFS* library. Once the message *LittleFS Image Uploaded* is displayed, compile and upload the sketch.

Image URL in the Sketch

A JPEG-, PNG-, or GIF-formatted image, to be included on a web page, is either specified by the image source URL (Uniform Resource Locator) or by the image data array. Displaying images on a web page, with the image specified by a URL, is illustrated by the sketch in Listing 10-9 with the web page HTML code in Listing 10-10. When an image is clicked, an alternative image is displayed on the web page. The sketch is adapted from `www.w3schools.com/js/tryit.asp?filename=tryjs_lightbulb`. The URLs of the lightbulb images are `www.w3schools.com/js/pic_bulboff.gif` and `www.w3schools.com/js/pic_bulbon.gif`.

When the web page is loaded, the `<img src='https://www...` instruction loads the image corresponding to the URL. When a web page image is clicked, the *switchImage* function is called to display the image corresponding to the URL, which is determined by whether or not the current URL contains the *bulbon* substring. The `src.match('string')` instruction searches for the specified *string* in the image URL. For example, if the *bulb on* image is currently displayed and the web page image is clicked, then the image URL is updated to `www.w3schools.com/js/pic_bulboff.gif`, as the current image URL contains the substring *bulbon*, and the *bulb off* image is displayed.

Listing 10-9. Display images on web page

```
#include <WebServer.h>              // WebServer library for ESP32
WebServer server(80);
#include <ssid_password.h>
#include "buildpage.h"              // HTML and JavaScript code

void setup()
{
  Serial.begin(115200);             // Serial Monitor baud rate
  WiFi.begin(ssid, password);       // initialize and connect Wi-Fi
  while (WiFi.status() != WL_CONNECTED) delay(500);
  Serial.print("IP Address ");
  Serial.println(WiFi.localIP());   // display ESP32 IP address
  server.begin();
  server.on("/", base);             // function for default web page
}
void base()                         // function to return HTML code
{
  server.send(200, "text/html", page);
}
void loop()
{
  server.handleClient();            // manage HTTP requests
}
```

Listing 10-10. HTML code for the web page

```
char page[] PROGMEM = R"(
<!DOCTYPE html>
<html>
<body>
<img id='bulb' onclick='switchImage()'
```

```
  src='https://www.w3schools.com/js/pic_bulboff.gif'
  width='100' height='180'>
<p>Click the bulb to turn on or off</p>
<script>
function switchImage()
{
  var image = document.getElementById('bulb');
  if (image.src.match('bulbon'))
  {image.src = 'https://www.w3schools.com/js/pic_bulboff.gif';}
  else
  {image.src = 'https://www.w3schools.com/js/pic_bulbon.gif';}
}
</script>
</body>
</html>
)";
```

The sketches in Listings 10-9 and 10-10 require an Internet connection to source the images. If an Internet connection is not available when the sketch is used, then the server response to a client HTTP request includes the corresponding image data array loaded with the sketch. Note that the ESP32 microcontroller is acting as a software-enabled access point with the default IP address of *192.168.4.1*. An image defined by a URL, such as `www.w3schools.com/js/pic_bulbon.gif`, is saved by right-clicking the displayed image, selecting *Save Image As...*, and then saving the file to the required location on a laptop or computer. An image is converted to an image data array with Tomasz Ostrowski's image converter (`tomeko.net/online_tools/file_to_hex.php?lang=en`), as described in the "Send an Image in Email" section of the chapter.

Listings 10-11 and 10-12 are the equivalent of Listings 10-9 and 10-10 when no Internet connection is available and the ESP32 microcontroller acts as a software-enabled access point. Only the instructions differing from those in Listing 10-9 are commented. The *WebServer* library instruction `send_P` indicates that the information is stored in PROGMEM, and the size of the data is included in the instruction. The `send_P` instruction is recommended for large files.

When a web page image is clicked, the *switchImage* function, in Listing 10-12, defines the image URL, and the corresponding image data array is displayed. For example, when the web page *bulb off* image is clicked, the *switchImage* function sends an HTTP request with the URL *serverIP address/on*, and the server calls the corresponding *bulbon* function to send an HTTP response with the image data in the *onHEX* array. The client displays the image with the `<img id='iden'` and `image = document.getElementById('iden')` instructions, where *iden* is the identifier linking the image with the response to the HTTP request.

Listing 10-11. Display images on a web page with no Internet connection

```
#include <WebServer.h>
WebServer server(80);
char ssidAP[] = "ESP32_image";        // access point ssid and password
char passwordAP[] = "pass1234";
#include "buildpage.h"
#include "images.h"                   // image data arrays

void setup()
{
  Serial.begin(115200);
  WiFi.softAP(ssidAP,passwordAP);   // initialize access point
  Serial.print("softAP address ");
  Serial.println(WiFi.softAPIP()); // display access point IP
```

```
  server.begin();
  server.on("/", base);
  server.on("/on", bulbon);        // map functions to URLs
  server.on("/off", bulboff);
}
void bulbon()                      // function to send response with
{                                  // bulb on image data
  server.send_P(200, "image/gif", onHEX, sizeof(onHEX));
}
void bulboff()                     // function to send response with
{                                  // bulb off image data
  server.send_P(200, "image/gif", offHEX, sizeof(offHEX));
}
void base()
{
  server.send(200, "text/html", page);
}
void loop()
{
  server.handleClient();
}
```

Listing 10-12. HTML code for a web page with no Internet

```
char page[] PROGMEM = R"(
<!DOCTYPE html>
<html>
<body>
<img id='bulb' onclick='switchImage()' src='off'
      width='100' height='180'>
<p>Click the bulb to turn on or off</p>
<script>
```

```
function switchImage()
{
  var image = document.getElementById('bulb');
  if (image.src.match('on')) {image.src = 'off';}
  else {image.src = 'on';}
}
</script>
</body>
</html>
)";
```

The first few rows of the *onHex* array for the *bulb on* image are

```
const char onHEX [] PROGMEM = {
0x47, 0x49, 0x46, 0x38, 0x39, 0x61, 0x64, 0x00, 0xB4, 0x00, ...
0xFF, 0xFF, 0xCC, 0xFF, 0xFF, 0x99, 0xFF, 0xFF, 0x66, 0xFF, ...
0xCC, 0xFF, 0xFF, 0xCC, 0xCC, 0xFF, 0xCC, 0x99, 0xFF, 0xCC, ...
```

Display Images as a Sprite

A Sprite enables flicker-free graphic updates on an LCD screen, such as redrawing foreground images over a static background image. Images are drawn on a Sprite, which is notionally an invisible graphics screen held in RAM, and after the Sprite is completed, the Sprite is displayed, at a specified position, on the LCD screen.

LCD Screen

The advantage of displaying images as a Spite is demonstrated by replacing the *img* instructions in Listing 10-13 with *tft* instructions. The Sprite image movements are smooth and continuous, unlike those of the *tft* images. The display and movement of Sprite images are demonstrated on a 1.3" 240 × 240-pixel TFT ST7789 LCD screen. Connections between the LCD screen and an ESP32 DEVKIT DOIT module are shown in Figure 10-5 and listed in Table 10-1.

A Sprite consisting of a background image and many foreground images is illustrated in Listing 10-13, which displays several hundred snowflakes falling in front of a static background image. The sketch was developed from the sketch by Hans-Günther Nusseck (`www.hackster.io/hague`). The background image is converted to an *RGB565* image data array, as described in the "Display a Color Image" section of the chapter. The foreground image of a snowflake is converted to an X bitmap image, as described in the "Bitmap and X Bitmap" section of the chapter. The image data arrays for the background and foreground images, `bckgnd` and `snowflake`, are located on separate tabs, *background.h* and *snowflake.h,* and are stored in PROGMEM with the `const unsigned char bckgnd[] PROGMEM {...}` instruction for the `bckgnd` array.

In the first section of the sketch, the Sprite *img* is defined with a pointer to the *tft* object, as required to display the Sprite. An array structure is defined to hold the position and speed of each foreground image. The LCD screen parameters *TFT_WIDTH* and *TFT_HEIGHT* are defined in the *TFT_eSPI* library *User_Setups\Setup24_ST7789* file.

In the *setup* function, the LCD screen is initialized, and the Sprite color depth and full-screen dimensions are defined. The background image is derived from a JPEG image, and 16-bit color depth is required for the range of image colors, while an 8-bit color depth is sufficient for a foreground graphics image. The initial position and speed of each foreground image are generated, with the images uniformly distributed across the width of the LCD screen. The foreground images are uniformly distributed above the screen, as random(height/2)-height/2-flakeH, to extend the time before each foreground image appears at the top of the LCD screen. The variables *height* and *flakeH* are the heights of the LCD screen and snowflake image, respectively.

In the *loop* function, the background image is loaded to the Sprite, which is held in RAM, with the img.pushImage(x, y, width, height, image) instruction. The top-left corner of the image, of *width* and *height* pixels, is located at position (*x, y*) of the LCD screen. The updated position of each foreground image includes a random component, random(-5,5) × speed[i], to give the foreground images an appearance of floating, with a positive-biased random element in the vertical direction. The foreground images are added to the Sprite with the drawXBitmap(x, y, image, width, height, color) instruction. The pushImage and drawXBitmap instructions have the same format, apart from *color* in the latter instruction. At the end of the *loop* function, the Sprite is displayed on the LCD screen with the pushSprite(x, y) instruction, with the coordinates of the top-left corner of the Sprite equal to (*x, y*). The pushSprite instruction moves the sprite from RAM to Character Generator RAM (CGRAM), which is a memory location provided by the display for character generation.

Listing 10-13. Display images as a sprite

```
#include <TFT_eSPI.h>                    // include TFT_eSPI library
TFT_eSPI tft = TFT_eSPI();               // associate tft with library
TFT_eSprite img = TFT_eSprite(&tft);     // Sprite image pointer to tft
#include "background.h"                  // background in RGB565 format
#include "snowflake.h"                   // foreground in XBM format
                                         // LCD screen dimensions
int width = TFT_WIDTH, height = TFT_HEIGHT;
int colorDepth = 8;                      // 1, 4, 8 or 16-bit colors
```

```
const int Nflake = 500;                   // const to define array size
int x[Nflake], y[Nflake];
float speed[Nflake];
float dx, dy;

void setup()
{
  tft.init();                             // initialize LCD screen
  img.setSwapBytes(true);                 // required to retain image color
  img.setColorDepth(colorDepth);          // Sprite color depth
  img.createSprite(width, height);        // full screen Sprite
  for (int i=0; i<Nflake; i++)            // create foreground images
  {
    x[i] = random(width);                 // horizontally distributed
                                          // foreground image above screen
    y[i] = random(height/2)-height/2-flakeH;
    speed[i] = random(10,30)/200.0;       // foreground image speed
  }
}

void loop()
{                                         // add background image to Sprite
  img.pushImage(0, 0, width, height, bckgnd);
  for (int i=0; i<Nflake; i++)            // move foreground images
  {
    dx = random(-5,5);                    // random makes image "float"
    dy = 10 + random(-5,5);               // add 10 to make image fall
    x[i] = x[i] + round(dx*speed[i]);
    y[i] = y[i] + round(dy*speed[i]);
    constrain(x[i], 0, width-flakeW);            // keep images on screen
```

```
                                        // add foreground image to Sprite
    img.drawXBitmap(x[i], y[i], snowflake, flakeW, flakeH,
                    TFT_WHITE);
  }
  img.pushSprite(0, 0);                 // display Sprite on LCD screen
  delay(5);
}
```

The image data array for the foreground image of a snowflake is given in Listing 10-7. The image size of 13 × 13 pixels requires (16 × 13)/8 = 26 bytes as the X bitmap format left-fills the binary bitmap of a row to a multiple of eight. The left-filled zero values are not included when the image is displayed on an LCD screen.

M5Stack Core2 and Accelerometer

The integrated TFT LCD screen, accelerometer, and PSRAM of the M5Stack Core2 module enable extending Listing 10-13 to include multiple background scenes, triggering the snowstorm by vertically or horizontally shaking the M5Stack Core2 module and with virtually no constraint on the number of snowflakes. The format of Listing 10-14 is the same as Listing 10-13, with the addition of a second background data array, `bckgnd2`, located on the *background2.h* tab and the two instructions

```
M5.IMU.getAccelData(&accX,&accY,&accZ)   // read accelerometer
if(fabs(accY) > 2 || fabs(accX) > 2)     // vertical or horizontal shake
```

to read the accelerometer values. The orientation of the accelerometer dimensions, *x*, *y*, and *z* is left-right, up-down, and forward-backward, respectively, relative to the M5Stack Core2 module buttons at the bottom of the module. The `abs(x)` and `fabs(y)` instructions return the absolute value of an integer and of a real number (float), respectively. The `dx = -accX*10.0 + accY*random(-5,5)` instruction updates the position of each foreground image based on the shaking action in the X-axis, primarily, with a random component weighting to the Y-axis, to give the foreground images an appearance of floating.

When the M5Stack Core2 button *BtnA* is pressed, the background image of the Sprite is alternated. Pressing M5Stack Core2 button *BtnB* displays a battery level indicator consisting of nine bars, colored green, yellow, or red to reflect a high (3.8–4.1V), medium (3.5–3.7V), or low (3.2–3.4V) battery voltage. The `Axp.GetBatVoltage()` and `Axp.GetBatCurrent()` instructions provide the battery voltage and current, respectively. When the M5Stack Core2 button *BtnC* is pressed, the M5Stack Core2 TFT LCD screen brightness, *N*, is incremented with the instruction `Axp.SetLcdVoltage(N)`.

The built-in LED is turned off or on with the `Axp.SetLed(0 or 1)` instruction. Similarly, the vibration motor is turned on and off with the `Axp.SetLDOEnable(3, state)` instruction, with *state* equal to one or zero, respectively. The power and time that the motor vibrates are determined by the `Axp.SetLDOVoltage(3, power)` instruction and the *delay()* function, respectively.

Listing 10-14. Display images as a sprite (2)

```
#include <M5Core2.h>                // include M5Core2 library
                                    // Sprite image pointer to img
TFT_eSprite img = TFT_eSprite(&M5.Lcd);
#include "background.h"
#include "background2.h"            // backgrounds in RGB565 and
#include "snowflake.h"              // foreground in XBM formats
int width = 320, height = 240;      // LCD dimensions
int colorDepth = 16;                // 1, 4, 8 or 16-bit colors
const int Nflake = 250;             // const to define array size
int x[Nflake], y[Nflake];
float speed[Nflake];
float dx, dy;
```

```
float accX, accY, accZ;                    // accelerometer values
int background = 0, level, volt = 2500;
uint16_t color;
String text;

void setup()
{
  M5.begin();                              // initialize M5Stack module
  M5.Axp.SetLed(0);                        // turn off in-built LED
  M5.Axp.SetSpkEnable(0);                  // turn off speaker
  M5.IMU.Init();                           // initialize accelerometer
  img.setColorDepth(colorDepth);           // Sprite color depth
  img.createSprite(width, height);         // full screen Sprite
  img.pushImage(0, 0, 320, 240, bckgnd);   // create background image
}

void loop()
{
  if (M5.BtnA.wasPressed()) background = 1-background;
  if(background == 0) img.pushImage(0, 0, 320, 240, bckgnd);
                                           // change backgrounds
  else img.pushImage(0, 0, 320, 240, bckgnd2);

                                       // accelerometer val > threshold
  M5.IMU.getAccelData(&accX,&accY,&accZ);
  if(fabs(accY) > 2 || fabs(accX) > 2)     // absolute value for float
  {
    for(int i=0; i < Nflake; i++)
    {
      x[i] = random(width);                // snowflakes horizontally
      y[i] = random(height/2)-             // distributed and
             height/2-flakeH;              // above screen
```

```
      speed[i] = random(10,30)/200.0; // speed for each snowflake
    }
  }
  else
  {
    for (int i=0; i<Nflake; i++)        // move snowflakes
    {                               // -accX to correspond to M5 movement
      dx = -accX*10.0 + accY*random(-5,5);
                                        // random(-5, 5) on accY
      dy =  accY*10.0 + accY*random(-5,5);
      x[i] = x[i] + round(dx*speed[i]);
                                        // update snowflake position
      y[i] = y[i] + round(dy*speed[i]);
      constrain(x[i], 0, width-flakeW); // keep images on screen
      img.drawXBitmap(x[i], y[i], snowflake, flakeW, flakeH,
                      TFT_WHITE);
    }
  }
  img.pushSprite(0, 0);                 // display Sprite on LCD screen

  if (M5.BtnB.isPressed())
  {
    battLevel();                        // call function to display battery
    motor();                            // call function to vibrate motor
  }
                                        // increment screen brightness
  if (M5.BtnC.wasPressed()) volt = volt+100;
  if(volt > 3300) volt = 2500;
  M5.Axp.SetLcdVoltage(volt);           // update LCD brightness
  M5.update();                          // update button “pressed” status

}
```

```
void battLevel()                          // function to display battery voltage
{                                         // battery level 3.2 - 4.1V
  level = (M5.Axp.GetBatVoltage() - 3.2)/0.1;
                                          // white rectangle behind graph
  M5.Lcd.fillRect(160, 100, 160, 140, WHITE);
  for (int i=0; i<level; i++)       // only display colored bars
  {
    color = GREEN;                        // battery voltage 3.8-4.1V
    if(i<3) color = RED;                  // 3.2-3.4V
    else if(i<6) color = YELLOW;          // 3.5-3.7V
    M5.Lcd.fillRoundRect(307, (230-(i*10)), 12, 7, 2,
      (level>i) ? color : BLACK); // black above battery voltage bar
    M5.Lcd.drawRoundRect(307,(230-(i*10)),12,7,2,TFT_LIGHTGREY);
  }
  M5.Lcd.setTextColor(BLACK);
  text = "LCD " + String(volt);     // display LCD brightness
  M5.Lcd.drawString(text, 180, 110, 4);
  text = "Level "+String(level);    // drawString cannot build string
  M5.Lcd.drawString(text, 180, 140, 4);
                                          // display battery voltage
  text = String(M5.Axp.GetBatVoltage())+"V";
  M5.Lcd.drawString(text, 180, 170, 4);
                                          // display current usage with 0DP
  text = String(M5.Axp.GetBatCurrent(),0)+"mA";
  M5.Lcd.drawString(text, 180, 200, 4);
}
```

```
void motor()                              // function for vibration motor
{
  M5.Axp.SetLDOVoltage(3, volt);          // vibration motor voltage
  for (int i=0; i<5; i++)
  {
    M5.Axp.SetLed(1);                     // turn on built-in LED
    M5.Axp.SetLDOEnable(3, 1);            // turn on vibration motor
    delay(500);
    M5.Axp.SetLed(0);                     // turn off built-in LED
    M5.Axp.SetLDOEnable(3, 0);            // turn off vibration motor
    delay(500);
  }
}
```

Transparent Sprite

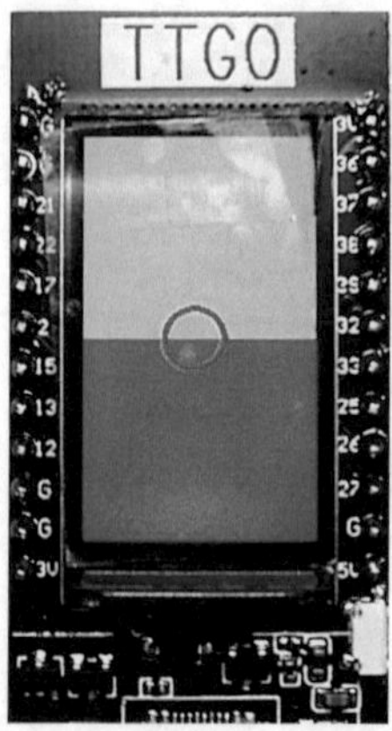

A transparent Sprite consists of a solid and a transparent component. When a transparent Sprite is positioned or moved over another image or background, the image or background is visible through the transparent component of the Sprite. The illustrative sketch in Listing 10-15 displays a ring, as a transparent Sprite, with the two colors of the screen background visible through the transparent center of the ring on the LCD screen of a TTGO T-Display V1.1 module.

The `pushSprite(x, y, color)` instruction positions a Sprite at the (x, y) coordinates, relative to the LCD screen, and the color defines the transparent color. The Sprite, shaped as a ring, is defined with the two instructions `fillCircle(20, 20, 20, TFT_RED)` and `fillCircle(20, 20, 15, TFT_BLACK)`. The smaller circle, which has the same color as the `pushSprite` instruction, is transparent.

Listing 10-15. Transparent Sprite

```
#include <TFT_eSPI.h>                    // include TFT_eSPI library
TFT_eSPI tft = TFT_eSPI();               // associate tft with library
TFT_eSprite img = TFT_eSprite(&tft);     // Sprite image pointer to tft

void setup()
{
  tft.init();                            // initialize LCD screen
  tft.setRotation(1);                    //rotation 1 = USB-C on RHS
                                         // rectangle over half the screen
  tft.fillRect(0, 0, 120, 135, TFT_GREEN);
  tft.fillRect(120, 0, 120, 135, TFT_BLUE);
  img.createSprite(40, 40);
                          // centre (x, y), relative to Sprite, radius, color
  img.fillCircle(20, 20, 20, TFT_RED);
                                         // smaller circle
  img.fillCircle(20, 20, 15, TFT_BLACK);
  img.pushSprite(100, 50, TFT_BLACK);    // position relative to screen
}

void loop()                              // nothing in loop function
{}
```

A more comprehensive sketch illustrating transparent Sprites is given in Listing 10-16. The user moves a paddle at the bottom of the screen, with the left and right buttons on the TTGO T-Display V1.1 module, to intercept a ring, which is bouncing around the LCD screen. When the paddle position coincides with the ring position, the score is incremented and displayed on the LCD screen. The LCD screen consists of a constant background image with the ring, the paddle, and the text, to display the score, defined as transparent Sprites.

The Sprites are defined in the first section of the sketch and the Sprite sizes in the *setup* function. The background Sprite, *back*, is the size of the 240 × 135-pixel LCD screen of the TTGO T-Display V1.1 module. The ring Sprite, *img*, consists of two circles of radii 14 and 9 pixels, with the smaller circle being transparent, centered at coordinates (14, 14) relative to the Sprite of 28 × 28 pixels. The size of the ring Sprite was chosen not to be a multiple of the TTGO T-Display V1.1 module LCD screen size, to ensure that the ring bounces around the screen. The paddle Sprite, *pad*, is a filled rectangle, and the text Sprite, *txt*, is defined as white text on black. The black color, *TFT_BLACK*, is the transparent color, which is the color of the inner circle of the ring Sprite and the background color of the text Sprite.

When the right or left button, on the TTGO T-Display V1.1 module, is pressed, the paddle Sprite is moved ten pixels to the right or to the left, relative to the user holding the TTGO T-Display V1.1 module with the USB-C port at the bottom. The right button is associated with a rising interrupt, which is active when the button is released, as the button is connected to a built-in pull-up resistor. The left button is associated with a falling interrupt, which is active when the button is pressed. The two interrupts also differ in the method to update the paddle position, *padY*. One interrupt increases the paddle position, which moves the paddle to the left of the LCD screen, while the other interrupt sets a flag, *padFlag,* to unity with the flag indicating that, in the *loop()* function, the paddle position is to be decreased, which moves the paddle to the right of the LCD screen. The rising and falling interrupts and different methods of updating the paddle position are only for illustration.

The Sprite X-direction is alternated when the ring Sprite *x*-coordinate, the "vertical" position, is zero or 212, similarly for the ring Sprite Y-direction when the "horizontal" position is zero or 107. The "vertical" and "horizontal" limits of 212 and 107 correspond to the TTGO T-Display V1.1 module LCD screen size of 240 × 135 pixels minus the ring Sprite width of 28 pixels.

The score is incremented when the *y*-coordinate or "horizontal" position of the ring Sprite and the paddle position coincide. The difference between the centers of the ring Sprite and the paddle is $(x + 14) - (padY + 20) = (x - padY - 6)$, given the 28-pixel diameter of the ring Sprite and the 40-pixel paddle length. When the score is a multiple of three, the "speed" of the ring Sprite is incremented by increasing the "vertical" distance, *dx,* between sequential positions of the ring Sprite. The *x*-coordinate or "vertical" position of the ring Sprite is $x + xDir * dx$, where *x* is the previous position and *xDir* is the direction of travel.

The background image is displayed with the `setSwapBytes(true)` instruction as the image was derived from a .JPEG file, for which data is stored in most significant byte (*MSByte*) order, while the ESP32 microcontroller interprets data in least significant byte (*LSBbyte*) order. The ring and text Sprites are combined with the background image by the `pushToSprite(&image, x, y, color)` instruction. The *setSwapBytes* state of the background image must be set to false before combining the Sprite images; otherwise, red pixels appear blue, blue pixels appear green, and green pixels appear red.

The default orientation of the text Sprite is vertical relative to the USB-C port at the bottom of the TTGO T-Display V1.1 module, while the required orientation of the text Sprite is horizontal. The text Sprite is rotated 270° with the `pushRotated(&image, 270, color)` instruction, where *image* is the background image on which the text Sprite is displayed. The points of rotation for the background image and for the text Sprite are defined with the `back.setPivot(0,120)` and `txt.setPivot(0, 0)` instructions in the *setup()* function. The point of rotation for the background image moves the text Sprite to the "top left" of the TTGO T-Display V1.1 module LCD screen, with the rotation point of the text Sprite equal to top-left corner.

Listing 10-16. Transparent Sprites in a paddle game

```
#include <TFT_eSPI.h>                    // include TFT_eSPI library
TFT_eSPI tft = TFT_eSPI();               // associate tft with library
TFT_eSprite back = TFT_eSprite(&tft);    // Sprite for background
TFT_eSprite img = TFT_eSprite(&tft);     // image Sprite is a ring
TFT_eSprite txt = TFT_eSprite(&tft);     // Sprites to display text
TFT_eSprite pad = TFT_eSprite(&tft);     // and the paddle
#include "background.h"                  // background in 565 format
int btnRpin = 35, btnLpin = 0;           // right and left buttons
int xDir = 1, x = 0, y = 30;             // direction and position of ring
int dx = 1, dy = 1;                      // increments to move ring
int lag = 10;                            // speed in x direction
volatile int padFlag = 0, padY = 50;     // paddle position
int score = 0, total = 0, scoreFlag = 0; // game scores
String scores;
```

```
void setup()
{
  tft.init();                                  // initialize display
  tft.setRotation(1);                          // rotation 1 = USB on RHS
  back.createSprite(240, 135);                 // background Sprite size
  back.setPivot(0,120);                        // rotation point
  img.createSprite(28, 28);                    // Sprite to display ring
  img.fillCircle(14, 14, 14, TFT_RED);         // red larger circle
  img.fillCircle(14, 14, 9, TFT_BLACK);        // and black inner circle
  pad.createSprite(10, 40);                    // Sprite to display paddle
  pad.fillRect(0, 0, 10, 40, TFT_GREEN);       // as a green rectangle
  txt.createSprite(100, 30);                   // Sprite to display text
  txt.setTextSize(2);
  txt.setTextColor(TFT_RED, TFT_BLACK);        // red on black
  txt.setPivot(0, 0);                          // rotation point
  pinMode(btnRpin,INPUT);
  pinMode(btnLpin,INPUT);              // right button active when released
  attachInterrupt(digitalPinToInterrupt(btnRpin), Yup, RISING);
  attachInterrupt(digitalPinToInterrupt(btnLpin), Ydown, FALLING);
}                                      // left button active when pressed

IRAM_ATTR void Yup()                   // flag that right button was pressed
{ padFlag = 1; }
IRAM_ATTR void Ydown()                 // move paddle down screen
{ padY = padY + 10; }                  // (towards bottom)
```

```
void loop()
{
  x = x + xDir * dx;                      // increment x position, change
  if(x < 0 || x > 212) xDir = -xDir; // direction at end of screen
  y = y + dy;                             // change y direction at
  if(y < 0 || y > 107) dy = -dy;          // top or bottom of screen
  if(x > 212)                             // when ring at bottom of screen
  {
    total++;                              // increment total number
    if(abs(y - padY - 6) < 15) score++; // increment score
    if(score % 3 == 0) dx++;              // increment ring Sprite change
  }                                       // in the x-co-ordinate
  if(padFlag > 0)                         // right button pressed
  {
    padFlag = 0;                          // reset paddle flag
    padY = padY - 10;                     // move paddle towards top
  }                                       // of screen
                                          // text to display scores
  scores = String(score) + "/" + String(total);
  back.setSwapBytes(true);                // required to retain image color
                                          // create background image
  back.pushImage(0, 0, 240, 135, backgnd);
  back.setSwapBytes(false);               // reset setSwapBytes state
  txt.drawString(scores, 0, 0, 2);        // position within Sprite area
                                          // rotate text Sprite 270°
  txt.pushRotated(&back, 270, TFT_BLACK);
  pad.pushToSprite(&back, 230, padY);  // paddle Sprite position
```

```
                                // ring Sprite position (x, y)
  img.pushToSprite(&back, x, y, TFT_BLACK);
  back.pushSprite(0,0);         // TFT_BLACK is transparent color
  delay(lag);                   // time lag (ms) between displays
}
```

Memory Requirements

The ESP32 microcontroller includes 520KB of RAM (Random Access Memory). For ESP32 modules without PSRAM, the maximum available 160KB of DRAM (Dynamic RAM), within RAM, constrains the Sprite size. Some ESP32 modules, such as the ESP32-CAM module, have an additional RAM chip, known as PSRAM (Pseudo-static RAM) or external SPI RAM, as the ESP32 microcontroller and RAM communicate with SPI. PSRAM extends the possible size of a Sprite.

The *TFT_eSPI GitHub* site, `github.com/Bodmer/TFT_eSPI`, notes that 16-bit or 8-bit Sprites are limited to about 200 × 200 or 320 × 240 pixels, respectively, with the ESP32 microcontroller. A Sprite of width, *W*, and height, *H*, pixels with *N*-bit color depth requires $N \times (W \times H)/8$ bytes with 16-bit (65536 colors), 8-bit (256 colors), 4-bit (16 colors), or 1-bit (black and white) color depth available. For example, a 16-bit or 8-bit 240 × 240-pixel Sprite requires 115.2kB (112.5KB) or 57.6kB (56.25KB) of memory, respectively. If the maximum available RAM for a Sprite is 90KB, due to reduced heap memory availability from the increased stack memory requirements, then the 16-bit 240 × 240-pixel Sprite is not allocated sufficient RAM. Reducing the Sprite color depth of 8- or 16-bit (default) reduces the RAM requirement. ESP32 memory capacity and components are described in Chapter 1, "ESP32 Microcontroller."

The sketch in Listing 10-17 illustrates the impact on heap by sequentially including the *TFT_eSPI* library, a 500-integer array as a global variable, and an 8-bit or a 16-bit color depth Sprite with 240 × 240 pixels, with the results shown in Table 10-3. An integer array of size *N* requires

4*N* bytes, as the ESP32 microcontroller stores integers with 32 bits or 4 bytes. The example integer array and 8-bit or 16-bit Sprite require 2000 and 57600 or 115200 bytes of memory, respectively. Heap availability is reduced by including the integer array and the Sprite in the sketch, but for different reasons. The integer array is a global variable, which is stored in static data, as is the *TFT_eSPI* library. A consequence of increasing static data is a reduction in available heap. In contrast, the Sprite is stored in heap, rather than in static data, which also reduces the available heap.

Increasing the color depth of the Sprite from 8-bit to 16-bit doubles the memory requirement of the Sprite from 57600 to 115200 bytes, and the allocated heap is increased accordingly (see Table 10-3). However, the largest block of unallocated heap is reduced from 116724 bytes to 110580 bytes, which is less than the required memory for the 16-bit Sprite, and the Sprite is not loaded to memory. The solution is to reduce the Sprite color depth to 8-bit.

Table 10-3. *Changes in static data and heap size (bytes)*

Variables incrementally included in a sketch	**Static data**	**Allocated heap**	**Available heap**	**Largest block of unallocated heap**
None	16376	25232	271312	118772
Change in static data and heap				
TFT_eSPI library	364	192	–624	0
Integer array [500]	**2000**	0	–2000	–2048
Sprite 8-bit color, 240 × 240 pixels	384	**57604**	**–58004**	–6144
Or Sprite 16-bit color, 240 × 240 pixels	384	**115204**	**–115604**	–6144

Listing 10-17. Heap size with a large array

```
#include <TFT_eSPI.h>                     // include TFT_eSPI library
TFT_eSPI tft = TFT_eSPI();                // associate tft with library
TFT_eSprite img = TFT_eSprite(&tft);      // Sprite image pointer to img
int A[500];                               // integer array

void setup()
{
  Serial.begin(115200);                   // Serial Monitor baud rate
  Serial.println();
  A[0] = 1;                               // array size in bytes
  Serial.printf("Size of A %d bytes \n", sizeof(A));
  img.setColorDepth(8);                   // Sprite color depth
  img.createSprite(240, 240);             // Sprite dimensions
  multi_heap_info_t info;                 // information structure
  heap_caps_get_info(&info, MALLOC_CAP_DEFAULT);
  Serial.printf("total %d alloc %d free %d large %d \n",
                                          // total heap size in bytes
  heap_caps_get_total_size(MALLOC_CAP_DEFAULT),
  info.total_allocated_bytes,             // allocated heap
  info.total_free_bytes,                  // available heap
  info.largest_free_block);               // largest unallocated heap
}

void loop()                               // nothing in loop function
{}
```

Display Time with Sprites

The smooth and continuous Sprite image movement is combined with the Network Time Protocol (NTP) to generate an analog clock displayed on a 1.3" 240 × 240-pixel TFT ST7789 LCD screen, which is connected to an ESP32 module. Connections between the ESP32 DEVKIT DOIT module and the LCD screen are shown in Figure 10-15 and listed in Table 10-1. The rotation of one Sprite, such as a clock hand, on another Sprite, such as the clock dial, is developed from the *Rotated_Sprite_2* example in the *TFT_eSPI* library. Obtaining the current time and date from the Network Time Protocol is described in Chapter 15, "Libraries." In the *TFT_eSPI* library file *Setup24_ST7789.h*, the ESP32 *TFT_DC* pin is mapped to GPIO 2, which is connected to the ESP32 DEVKIT DOIT built-in blue LED. The *TFT_DC* pin is mapped to GPIO 15 by changing the instruction `#define TFT_DC 2` to `#define TFT_DC 15`.

The analog clock is generated in Listing 10-18. Sprite objects are created for each component of the clock, consisting of the clock face or dial and the hour, minute, and second hands, with corresponding functions to create each Sprite. The *drawDial* function creates the *dial* Sprite (`createSprite`) with the width and height of the LCD screen, defines the background color (`fillScreen`), provides a border (`drawRoundRect`), draws a circular border around the dial by overlaying a white-filled circle over a larger blue-filled circle (`fillCircle`), and calls the *lines* function to draw the one- and five-minute markers within the clock face and the digits around the clock face. The width, and similarly the height, of an LCD screen is defined with either the *tft.width* function or the variable *TFT_WIDTH*, which are generated by the *TFT_eSPI* library.

The one- and five-minute markers are positioned at 6° and 30° intervals, respectively. The marker start and end positions are located on circles with radii of *dialR* and (*dialR* – *len*), respectively, as shown in

Figure 10-12, where *dialR* is the radius of the clock face and *len* is the length of the one- or five-minute markers. For example, the start coordinates for a minute marker are [$centX + dialR \times \cos(\theta)$, $centY + dialR \times \sin(\theta)$]. The coordinates of the center of the clock face are (*centX*, *centY*), where *centX* and *centY* are half the width and height of the LCD screen, respectively. The angle, θ, has a value of zero at the right side of the clock face, when the LCD screen connections are at the top of the LCD screen module. The digits around the clock face are calculated as $(\theta + 90)/30$, for θ between 0° and 360°, which represents rotating the digits anti-clockwise by 90°. The digits are positioned around a circle with radius $dialR + 15$.

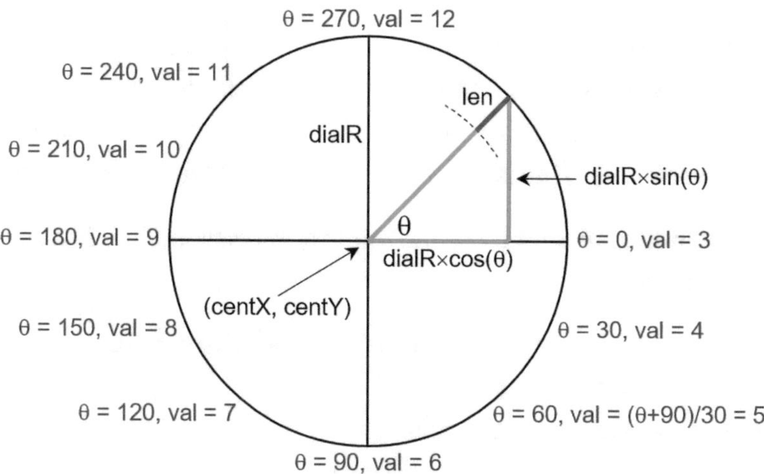

Figure 10-12. *Derivation of the clock face*

A Sprite is created for each clock hand with the *drawHour*, *drawMinute*, and *drawSecond* functions. The hour and minute hands consist of a rectangle with a line drawn through the length of the rectangle. A second hand consists of a rectangle of width 3 pixels. Each hand is pivoted at coordinates (*wid2*, 10), where *wid2* is half the width of the hand. A more elaborate hour hand is generated by a long triangle, of width *wid* and length *len*, overlaying a circle, of radius *wid2*, with the instructions

```
hourh.setPivot(wid2, wid2)                    // pivot point of hand
hourh.fillCircle(wid2, wid2, wid2, color)     // circle center and radius
                                              // triangle overlaying circle
hourh.fillTriangle(0, wid2, wid, wid2, wid2, len, color)
```

A Sprite is rotated relative to another Sprite with the `pushRotated` instruction for 1-, 8-, and 16-bit-per-pixel Sprites, which requires the corresponding `setColorDepth` instruction when creating a Sprite. The hour, minute, and second hand Sprites are aligned to the central pivot point of the clock face Sprite and rotate about the pivot point, for the angles *hh, mm,* and *ss*, with the instructions

```
dial.setPivot(centX, centY)           // clock face pivot point
hourh.pushRotated(&dial, hh)          // position hour, minute and
minuteh.pushRotated(&dial, mm)        // second hands on clock face
secondh.pushRotated(&dial, ss)        // at angles hh, mm and ss
```

The rotation angles for the hour, minute, and second hands are calculated from

```
hh = 30 * timeData.tm_hour + timeData.tm_min/2 + 180
mm = 6 * timeData.tm_min + 180
ss = 6 * timeData.tm_sec + 180
```

as one hour represents a rotation of 30° on a 12-hour clock face. With the LCD screen connections at the top of the LCD screen module, 180° is added to the hour, minute, or second angle for the appropriate orientation of the clock hands. Instructions for obtaining the current time and data information from the Network Time Protocol are described in Chapter 15, "Libraries."

The clock face Sprite with the rotating hour, minute, and second hand Sprites, pushed to the clock face Sprite, is displayed by the `pushSprite(x, y)` instruction, with the Sprite positioned at coordinates (*x, y*), relative to the top-left corner of the LCD screen. The day of the week and month are displayed on the clock face with the display position opposite to the minute hand position, so that the minute hand does not obstruct the information. A delay between LCD screen updates of longer than 100ms results in a jerky transition between updates. The `deleteSprite` instruction releases heap memory.

Listing 10-18. Analog watch face

```
#include <TFT_eSPI.h>              // include TFT_eSPI library
TFT_eSPI tft = TFT_eSPI();
TFT_eSprite dial = TFT_eSprite(&tft);       // Sprite objects for dial
TFT_eSprite hourh = TFT_eSprite(&tft);      // and for clock hands
TFT_eSprite minuteh = TFT_eSprite(&tft);
TFT_eSprite secondh = TFT_eSprite(&tft);

#include <WiFi.h>                  // include Wi-Fi library
#include <ssid_password.h>         // file with logon details
#include <time.h>                  // include time library
int GMT = 0, daylight = 3600;      // GMT and daylight saving offset (sec)
int hh, mm, ss, wd, dd, mn;
int posx, posy;
struct tm timeData;                // time structure
String day[] = {"Sun","Mon","Tues","Wed","Thur","Fri","Sat"};
String mon[] = {"Jan","Feb","Mar","Apr","May","Jun",
    "Jul","Aug","Sep","Oct","Nov","Dec"};
                                   // define screen dimensions
int width = tft.width(), height = TFT_HEIGHT;
                                   // center of screen position
int centX = width/2, centY = height/2;
int dialR = 95;                    // clock face radius for white area
int Llong = 20, Lshort = 10;       // lengths of minute markers
```

```
void setup()
{
  WiFi.begin(ssid, password);        // initialize and connect to Wi-Fi
  while (WiFi.status() != WL_CONNECTED) delay(500);
  configTime(GMT, daylight, "uk.pool.ntp.org");
  while (!getLocalTime(&timeData)) delay(500);
  WiFi.disconnect(true);             // disconnect Wi-Fi
  WiFi.mode(WIFI_OFF);

  tft.init();                        // initial LCD screen
  drawDial();                        // function to display clock face
  drawHour(11, 70, TFT_LIGHTGREY); // function to create clock hands
  drawMinute(11, 90, TFT_LIGHTGREY); // width, length and color
  drawSecond(3, 90, TFT_BLACK);      // of clock hand
}

void loop()
{
  getLocalTime(&timeData);           // obtain current time and date
  hh = 30 * timeData.tm_hour + timeData.tm_min/2 + 180;
  mm = 6 * timeData.tm_min + 180;    // zero degrees at bottom of circle
  ss = 6 * timeData.tm_sec + 180;    // with screen connections at top
  wd = timeData.tm_wday;             // day of week
  dd = timeData.tm_mday;             // date
  mn = timeData.tm_mon;              // month
  drawDial();
  hourh.pushRotated(&dial, hh);      // position hour, minute and
  minuteh.pushRotated(&dial, mm);    // second hands on clock face
  secondh.pushRotated(&dial, ss);
  dial.pushSprite(0,0);              // push clock Sprite
  delay(100);                        // interval between screen updates
```

```
  dial.deleteSprite();                 // delete Sprite
}

void drawDial()                        // function to display clock face
{
  dial.createSprite(width, height);    // pivot point of clock face
  dial.setPivot(centX, centY);         // on which clock hands rotate
  dial.setColorDepth(8);
  dial.fillScreen(TFT_DARKGREY);
                                       // screen border
  dial.drawRoundRect(0, 0, width, height, 10, TFT_WHITE);
                                    // blue outline circle around clock
  dial.fillCircle(centX, centY, dialR + 5, TFT_NAVY);
  dial.fillCircle(centX, centY, dialR, TFT_WHITE);
  lines (6, Lshort, TFT_BLACK);        // degrees between markers
  lines (30, Llong, TFT_BLUE);         // for one and five minutes
  dial.setTextColor(TFT_NAVY);
  dial.setTextSize(1);                 // position day and month
  if(timeData.tm_min > 20 && timeData.tm_min < 40)
         {posx = 100; posy = 55;}
  else if(timeData.tm_min <= 20) {posx = 60; posy = 85;}
  else {posx = 140; posy = 85;}
                                       // display day of week
  dial.drawString(day[wd], posx, posy, 4);
                                       // and month
  dial.drawString(mon[mn], posx, posy+30, 4);
                                       // date in fixed position
  if(dd > 9) dial.drawNumber(dd, 90, 140, 7);
  else dial.drawNumber(dd, 110, 140, 7);

}
```

```
                                          // function to draw minute markers
void lines (int increm, int len, int color)
{
  int x0, y0, x1, y1, val, dev;
  float sx, sy;
                                          // increments of 6 or 30 degrees
  for (int j=0; j<360; j=j+increm)
  {
    sx = cos(j * DEG_TO_RAD);             // co-ordinates of marker
    sy = sin(j * DEG_TO_RAD);
    x0 = round(centX + dialR * sx);       // position on dial perimeter
    y0 = round(centY + dialR * sy);
    x1 = round(centX + (dialR - len) * sx); // position inside dial
    y1 = round(centY + (dialR - len) * sy);
    dial.drawLine(x0, y0, x1, y1, color);   // draw minute marker
    if(increm == 30)                      // for five minute markers
    {             // 0° = right-side of dial, rotate values 90° anti-clockwise
      if(j > 270) val = (j-270)/30;
      else val = (j+90)/30;
      dev = 6;                            // adjust for digits > 9
      if(val > 9) dev = 18;
                                    // positioned at top-left corner of number
      x1 = round(centX + (dialR + 15) * sx - dev);
      y1 = round(centY + (dialR + 15) * sy - 10);
      dial.setTextColor(TFT_WHITE);
      dial.drawNumber(val, x1, y1, 4); // numbers around dial
    }
  }
}
```

```
                                    // function to draw hour hand
void drawHour(int wid, int len, int color)
{
  int wid2 = wid/2;
  hourh.setColorDepth(8);
  hourh.createSprite(wid, len);     // Sprite width and length
  hourh.fillSprite(TFT_WHITE);
  hourh.setPivot(wid2, 10);         // pivot point of hour hand
  hourh.fillRect(0, 0, wid, len, color);
                                    // line through middle of rectangle
  hourh.drawLine(wid2, 0, wid2, len, TFT_BLACK);
}

                                    // function to draw minute hand
void drawMinute(int wid, int len, int color)
{
  int wid2 = wid/2;
  minuteh.setColorDepth(8);
  minuteh.createSprite(wid, len);
  minuteh.fillSprite(TFT_WHITE);
  minuteh.setPivot(wid2, 10);
  minuteh.fillRect(0, 0, wid, len, color);
  minuteh.drawLine(wid2, 0, wid2, len, TFT_BLACK);
}

                                    // function to draw second hand
void drawSecond(int wid, int len, int color)
{
  secondh.setColorDepth(8);
  secondh.createSprite(wid, len);
  secondh.fillSprite(TFT_WHITE);
  secondh.setPivot(1, 10);
  secondh.fillRect(0, 0, wid, len, color);
}
```

Extension to M5Stack Core2

The sketch in Listing 10-18 to display an analog clock on a 1.3" 240 × 240-pixel TFT ST7789 LCD screen is extended to display on the M5Stack Core2 module, which includes a 2" 320 × 240-pixel TFT ILI9342C LCD screen. Changes to the sketch refer to the M5Stack library instructions and to the difference in LCD screen size.

In the first section of the sketch, add the #include <M5Core2.h> instruction and replace the two instructions #include <TFT_eSPI.h> and TFT_eSPI tft = TFT_eSPI() with the TFT_eSprite dial = TFT_eSprite(&M5.Lcd) instruction. In the TFT_eSprite hourh = TFT_eSprite(&tft) instruction, replace &tft with &dial, similarly for the corresponding *minuteh* and *secondh* definitions. Set the *width* and *height* variables to 320 and 240, respectively.

In the *setup* function, replace the tft.init() instruction with the M5.begin() instruction.

In the *drawDial* function, add 40 to the *x*-coordinate when displaying day, month, and date, as in

```
dial.drawString(day[wd], 40+posx, posy, 4)
dial.drawString(mon[mn], 40+posx, posy+30, 4)
if(dd > 9) dial.drawNumber(dd, 40+90, 140, 7)
else dial.drawNumber(dd, 40+110, 140, 7)
```

Throughout the sketch, delete the TFT_ prefix for all colors.

Compress HTML Code

Several example sketches include a tab containing HEX-formatted data, which often contains HTML code for a web page. The sketch Arduino IDE *File* ➤ *Examples* ➤ *ESP32* ➤ *Camera* ➤ *CameraWebServer* is an example with the *camera_index.h* file containing the array *index_ov2640_html_gz*. The term *gz* in the file name indicates a *Gzipped* HEX file format.

To convert the HEX-formatted file to readable HTML code, open the website `gchq.github.io/CyberChef/` and paste the contents of the HEX-formatted file to the *Input* screen:

- In the *Operations* box on the left side, enter *Find* and then drag the *Find/Replace* option (in the *Utils* dropdown list) to the *Recipe* screen. In the *Find* box, enter a comma. Deselect options to only leave the *Global match* option.
- In the *Operations* box on the left side, enter *Remove* and then drag the *Remove whitespace* option (in the *Utils* dropdown list) to the *Recipe* screen. Deselect options to only leave the *Spaces* and *Linefeeds* options.
- In the *Operations* box on the left side, enter *From* and then drag the *From Hex* option (in the *Data format* dropdown list) to the *Recipe* screen. Click *Delimiter* and select the *0x* option.
- In the *Operations* box on the left side, enter *Gunzip* and then drag the *Gunzip* option (in the *Compression* dropdown list) to the *Recipe* screen.
- Click *BAKE!*, and the HTML code is displayed in the *Output* screen.

Conversely, HTML code is converted to a *Gzipped* HEX format by essentially reversing the previous process:

- Paste the HTML code in the *Input* screen. Then in the *Operations* box on the left side, enter *Gzip* and then drag the *Gzip* option (in the *Compression* dropdown list) to the *Recipe* screen. Click *Compression type* and select the *Dynamic Huffman Coding* option.
- In the *Operations* box on the left side, enter *To Hex* and then drag the *To Hex* option (in the *Data format* dropdown list) to the *Recipe* screen. Click *Delimiter* and select the *0x with comma* option. Click *Bytes per line* and select the *16* option. Note the length of the output file that is displayed at the top of the *Output* screen.
- Click *BAKE!*, and the *Gzipped* HEX data is displayed in the *Output* screen.

Listing 10-19 loads the web page HTML code given the *Gzipped* HEX-formatted data in Listing 10-20. The length of the data is either included as `sizeof(htmlcode_gz)` or the value, obtained when converting the HEX-formatted file to readable HTML code, is included explicitly in the sketch. The *WebServer* library instruction `send_P` indicates that the information is stored in PROGMEM, and the size of the data is included in the instruction. The `send_P` instruction is recommended for large files.

Listing 10-19. Load a web page with HTML code in Gzipped HEX format

```
#include <WebServer.h>      // include WebServer library
WebServer server(80);       // associate server with library
#include <ssid_password.h>
#include "buildpage.h"      // HTML code
```

```
void setup()
{
  Serial.begin(115200);             // Serial Monitor baud rate
  WiFi.begin(ssid, password);       // initialize and connect Wi-Fi
  while (WiFi.status() !=WL_CONNECTED) delay(500);
  Serial.println(WiFi.localIP());
  server.begin();
  server.on("/", base);             // function for default web page
}

void base()
{                                   // file in GZIP format
  server.sendHeader("content-encoding", "gzip");
                                    // send file
  server.send_P(200, "text/html", htmlHEX, sizeof(htmlHEX));
//  server.send_P(200, "text/html", htmlHEX, fileLength);
}

void loop()
{
  server.handleClient();            // manage HTTP requests
}
```

The *buildpage.h* tab includes the corresponding *Gzipped* HEX data, given in Listing 10-20. If the HTML code in Listing 10-21 is directly included in the *buildpage.h* tab, then the *base* function only includes the `server.send(200, "text/html", page)` instruction, and the HTML code is bracketed with `char page[] PROGMEM = R"(` and `)";`.

Listing 10-20. HTML code in Gzipped HEX format

```
int fileLength = 551;
const char htmlHEX[] PROGMEM = {
0x1f,0x8b,0x08,0x00,0x09,0x5e,0x39,0x60,0x00,0xff,0x2d,0x8c,
0xbd,0x0d,0xc4,0x20,0x0c,0x46,0x7b,0xa6,0x70,0x26,0x60,0x01,
0x8b,0x3a,0x45,0xae,0x63,0x01,0x02,0xbe,0x1c,0x12,0x81,0x08,
0x5c,0x1c,0xdb,0xf3,0x97,0xea,0x49,0x9f,0xdf,0x33,0x6e,0x2e,
0x59,0xae,0x0f,0xc1,0xae,0x3f,0x87,0x12,0xf8,0xe3,0x3b,0x0c,
0x90,0x71,0x1d,0xec,0x39,0x90,0x62,0x2a,0x3c,0xef,0x28,0xd7,
0x20,0x50,0xbe,0xc2,0x99,0x5c,0x55,0x42,0xd3,0x9f,0xe1,0x9b,
0x32,0x14,0x9b,0x89,0x22,0xcc,0xc0,0x5c,0xc6,0xc7,0x6e,0x2e,
0xa5,0x17,0xe3,0x73,0x03,0xba,0x51,0x8a,0xd2,0x70,0x00,0x00,
0x00
};
```

Listing 10-21. HTML code

```
<!doctype HTML>
<html>
<head>
<title>test HTML</title>
</head>
<body>
Text for screen test again
</body>
</html>
```

CHAPTER 11

ESP32-CAM Camera

The ESP32-CAM camera module incorporates the ESP32 microcontroller, a 2M-pixel OV2640 camera, and a TF (TransFlash) or micro-SD (Secure Digital) card reader/writer. Camera images are either stored on the micro-SD card or displayed on an LCD screen or streamed to a web page. This chapter outlines streaming images to an LCD screen connected to the ESP32-CAM module or to an LCD screen connected to a remote ESP32 module or to a web page.

Decoding JPEG images to display on an LCD screen requires the *TJpg_Decoder* library, by Bodmer, which references the *LittleFS* library. The *LittleFS* library is used for accessing SPIFFS (Serial Peripheral Interface Flash File System) and is automatically included in the Arduino IDE when *esp32 version 2.0.N* Boards Manager is installed. With an *esp32 version 1.0.N* Boards Manager installation, sketches including the *TJpg_Decoder* library will not compile, as the *LittleFS* library is not automatically installed.

N. Cameron, *ESP32 Formats and Communication*,
https://doi.org/10.1007/978-1-4842-9376-8_11

Stream Images Directly to an LCD Screen

The ESP32-CAM module streams images directly to a 2.4” 320 × 240-pixel ILI9341 SPI TFT LCD screen (see Figure 11-1), which is equivalent to the QVGA (Quarter Video Graphics Array) image resolution. Further details of image resolution for the ESP32-CAM camera are given in Chapter 1, “ESP32 Microcontroller.”

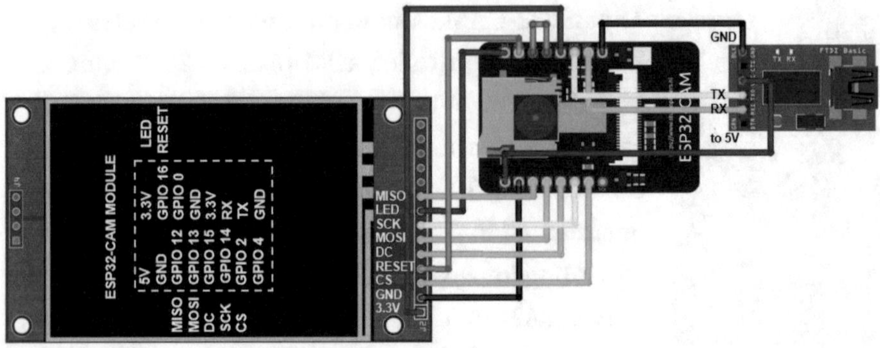

Figure 11-1. *ESP32-CAM and ILI9341 TFT LCD screen*

Images are streamed using SPI (Serial Peripheral Interface) communication. The MOSI (main out secondary in), MISO (main in secondary out), and DC (data command) connections are not predefined for the ESP32-CAM module, although the Serial clock corresponds to GPIO 14. The GPIO pin allocation in Table 11-1 minimizes overlapping connections and excludes GPIO 4, which is connected to the ESP32-CAM COB LED. The DC pin identifies bit streams containing data or commands with the DC pin state *HIGH* for a data bit stream or *LOW* for a command. The MISO pin is not required.

Table 11-1. *ILI9341 LCD to ESP32-CAM connections*

ILI9341 LCD	To ESP32-CAM
VCC	3V3
GND	GND
CS (chip select) or SS (secondary select)	GPIO 2
RESET	GPIO 16
DC (data command)	GPIO 15
MOSI or SDI (secondary data in)	GPIO 13
SCK or SCL (Serial clock)	GPIO 14
LED (LCD screen)	3V3
MISO or SDO (secondary data out)	GPIO 12

The *TFT_eSPI* and *TJpg_Decoder* libraries, by Bodmer, enable streaming of ESP32-CAM images to an ILI9341 LCD screen and are available within the Arduino IDE. The *TFT_eSPI* library references the *User_Setup_Select.h* file to define the screen drivers and settings for several screen types. To specify settings for the ILI9341 LCD screen, in the *User_Setup_Select.h* file, comment out the line `#include <User_setup.h>` and un-comment the line `#include <User_Setups/ Setup42_ILI9341_ESP32.h >`. The GPIO pin definitions in the *Setup42_ILI9341_ESP32.h* file are suitable for an ESP32 DEVKIT DOIT module, but not for the ESP32-CAM module as GPIO 18 and 23 are not available. Comment out the GPIO pin definitions for *TFT_MISO* to *TFT_RST* and insert the pin definition instructions of Listing 11-1.

Listing 11-1. TFT_eSPI library User_Setup settings

```
#define TFT_MISO 12      // MISO (main in secondary out)
#define TFT_MOSI 13      // MOSI (main out secondary in)
#define TFT_SCLK 14      // Serial clock
#define TFT_CS    2      // Chip select
#define TFT_DC   15      // Data command
#define TFT_RST  16      // Reset
```

A sketch to stream ESP32-CAM images to an ILI9341 LCD screen is given in Listing 11-2. The first section of the sketch loads the libraries for the ESP32-CAM module and calls the *configCamera* function to configure the ESP32-CAM module, with GPIO pin connections on the *config_pins.h* tab (see Listing 11-3). The screen orientation is set as portrait or landscape with the instruction `setRotation(N)` with a value of 0 or 1, respectively, or a value of 2 or 3 to rotate the screen image by 180°.

The *TJpg_Decoder* library decompresses a JPEG-formatted image for display on the ILI9341 LCD screen. Listing 11-2 is developed from the sketch in Arduino IDE *File* ➤ *Examples* ➤ *TJpg_Decoder* ➤ *Flash_array* ➤ *Flash_Jpg*. The library enables image scaling by a factor of 1, 2, 4, or 8, with no scaling, equivalent to a factor of 1, which is used in the sketch. The *tftOutput* function displays the decompressed image on the ILI9341 LCD screen. If image pixel coordinates are outside the frame size of the ILI9341 LCD screen, then image processing is stopped with the instruction `if(y >= tft.height()) return 0`.

The `setSwapBytes` instruction converts image byte order. Image data is stored in most significant byte (*MSByte*) order, while the microcontroller interprets data in least significant byte *(LSByte)* order. For example, the 32-bit or 4-byte integer *0x0A0B0C0D,* in HEX format, is stored as four 8-bit or 1-byte integers in four sequential memory byte locations as either *0x0A, 0x0B, 0x0C,* and *0x0D*, which is *MSByte* order, or *0x0D, 0x0C, 0x0B,* and *0x0A*, which is *LSByte* order.

The *loop* function includes only three instructions, with the instruction `TJpgDec.drawJpg(0,0,(const uint8_t*) frame->buf, frame->len)` drawing the image held in the *frame* buffer with length *len*, starting at the LCD screen coordinates of *(0, 0)*.

Prior to loading a sketch to the ESP32-CAM, GPIO 0 is connected to the GND pin, and then the *RESET* button is pressed. After the compiled sketch is uploaded, GPIO 0 is disconnected from the GND pin, and the module *RESET* button is again pressed. Power to the ESP32-CAM module may have to be disconnected and reconnected for the camera images to appear on the ILI9341 LCD screen.

Frame rates of 7.1, 10.0, and 16.7 FPS (Frames Per Second) were achieved with image resolution of QVGA (320 × 240 pixels), HQVGA (240 × 160 pixels), and QQVGA (160 × 120 pixels), respectively. Image resolution is changed by updating the parameter in the `config.frame_size` instruction in Listing 11-3 to `FRAMESIZE_HQVGA` or `FRAMESIZE_QQVGA`.

Listing 11-2. ESP32-CAM and ILI9341 TFT LCD screen

```
#include <esp_camera.h>               // include camera library and
#include "config_pins.h"              // camera configure pins tab
#include <TJpg_Decoder.h>             // include JPEG decoder library
#include <TFT_eSPI.h>                 // include TFT_eSPI library,
TFT_eSPI tft = TFT_eSPI();            //    associate tft with library

void setup()
{
  configCamera();                     // function to configure camera
  tft.begin();                        // initialize TFT LCD screen
  tft.setRotation(3);                 // landscape orientation
  tft.fillScreen(TFT_BLACK);
  TJpgDec.setJpgScale(1);             // jpeg image scale factor
  TJpgDec.setSwapBytes(true);         // convert image byte order
  TJpgDec.setCallback(tftOutput);     // call tftOutput function
}
```

```
bool tftOutput                          // function to decode JPEG image
(int16_t x, int16_t y, uint16_t w, uint16_t h, uint16_t* bitmap)
{                                       // constrain displayed image
  if(y >= tft.height()) return 0;
                                        // clip image to screen boundaries
  tft.pushImage(x, y, w, h, bitmap);
  return 1;                             // return 1 to decode next block
}

void loop()
{                                       // get image from camera
  camera_fb_t * frame = esp_camera_fb_get();
  TJpgDec.drawJpg(0,0,(const uint8_t*) frame->buf, frame->len);
  esp_camera_fb_return(frame);   // return frame buffer to driver
}
```

The ESP32-CAM camera configuration instructions (see Listing 11-3) are included on the *config_pins.h* tab rather than in the main sketch, for easier interpretation of the latter.

Listing 11-3. ESP32-CAM module configuration

```
camera_config_t config;                 // camera configuration parameters
void configCamera()
{
  config.ledc_channel = LEDC_CHANNEL_0;
  config.ledc_timer = LEDC_TIMER_0;
  config.pin_d0 = 5;
  config.pin_d1 = 18;
  config.pin_d2 = 19;
  config.pin_d3 = 21;
```

```
  config.pin_xclk = 0;                          // external clock
  config.pin_pwdn = 32;                         // power down
  config.pin_d4 = 36;
  config.pin_d5 = 39;
  config.pin_d6 = 34;
  config.pin_d7 = 35;
  config.pin_pclk = 22;                         // pixel clock
  config.pin_vsync = 25;                        // vertical synchronization
  config.pin_href = 23;                         // horizontal reference
  config.pin_sscb_sda = 26;                     // I2C data
  config.pin_sscb_scl = 27;                     // I2C clock
  config.pin_reset = -1;
  config.xclk_freq_hz = 20000000;               // clock speed of 20MHz
  config.pixel_format = PIXFORMAT_JPEG;         // JPEG file format
  config.frame_size = FRAMESIZE_QVGA;           // 320×240 pixels
  config.jpeg_quality = 10;                     // image quality index
  config.fb_count = 1;                          // frame buffer count
  esp_err_t err = esp_camera_init(&config);     // initialize camera
  if (err != ESP_OK)
  {
    Serial.print("Camera initialize failed with error");
    Serial.println(err);
    return;
  }
}
```

For this chapter, the ESP32-CAM module is configured with GPIO pin numbers in Listing 11-3, which correspond to the *AI Thinker ESP32-CAM* module, even though the *ESP32 Wrover Module* is selected in the Arduino IDE *Tools* ➤ *Board* ➤ *ESP32 Arduino* menu. For your ESP32-CAM module, the *AI Thinker ESP32-CAM* option may have to be selected in the *Tools* ➤ *Board* ➤ *ESP32 Arduino* menu. Several *ESP32 Wrover Module* GPIO pin numbers differ from those of the *AI Thinker ESP32-CAM* module, as shown in Table 11-2.

Table 11-2. *ESP32-CAM module-specific GPIO*

Module pin	ESP32 Wrover	AI Thinker ESP32-CAM
config.pin_d0	GPIO 4	GPIO 5
config.pin_d1	GPIO 5	GPIO 18
config.pin_d2	GPIO 18	GPIO 19
config.pin_d3	GPIO 19	GPIO 21
config.pin_xclk	GPIO 21	GPIO 0
config.pin_pwdn	-1	GPIO 32

Stream Images to a Remote LCD Screen

ESP32-CAM images are streamed to a remote 2.4" 320 × 240-pixel ILI9341 SPI TFT LCD screen using the WebSocket communication protocol (see Figure 11-2). The ESP32-CAM microcontroller acts as the client with the receiving ESP32 module, connected to the ILI9341 LCD screen, acting as the server.

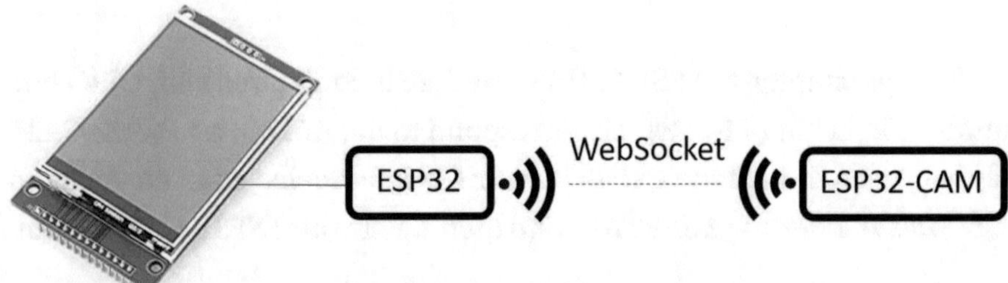

Figure 11-2. *Stream images to a remote LCD screen*

A WLAN is established, which does not have Internet access, with a software-enabled access point, *softAP*, allocated to the receiving ESP32 microcontroller with the default *softAP* IP address of *192.168.4.1*. The ESP32-CAM microcontroller, or client, has a default IP address of *192.168.4.2*. The WLAN password should contain at least eight alphanumeric characters. The WebSocket client connects to the WebSocket server with the server *softAP* IP address. When 320 × 240-pixel or QVGA images are transmitted between ESP32 devices, a frame rate of at least 7 FPS is obtained with the *WebSockets* library by Markus Sattler. The *WebSockets* library is available in the Arduino IDE. Connections between the ILI9341 LCD screen and the receiving ESP32 DEVKIT DOIT module are shown in Figure 11-3 and Table 11-3.

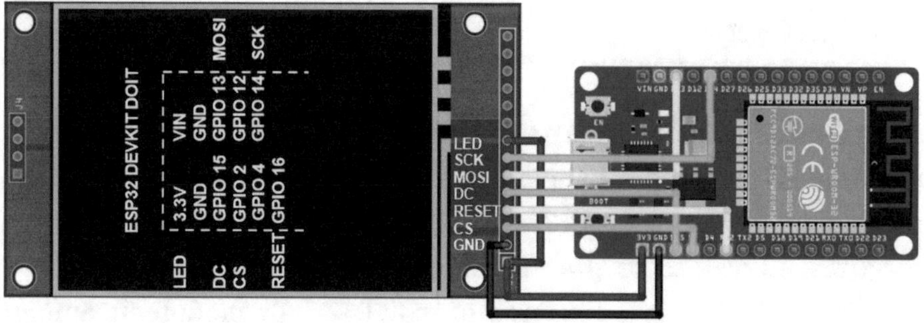

Figure 11-3. *ILI9341 LCD screen and ESP32 development board*

Table 11-3. *ILI9341 LCD screen to ESP32 development board connections*

ILI9341 LCD screen	To ESP32
VCC	3V3
GND	GND
CS (chip select) or SS (secondary select)	GPIO 2
RESET	GPIO 16 (RX2)
DC (data command)	GPIO 15
MOSI or SDI (secondary data in)	GPIO 13
SCK or SCL (Serial clock)	GPIO 14
LED (LCD screen)	3V3

In the sketch for the ESP32-CAM module acting as the client, the image data is transmitted in binary format to the server with the `sendBIN` instruction (see Listing 11-4). The ESP32-CAM camera configuration image resolution is set to *FRAMESIZE_QVGA* on the *config_pins.h* tab (see Listing 11-3), as in the example of an ESP32-CAM module streaming images directly to an ILI9341 LCD screen (see Listing 11-2).

Listing 11-4. ESP32-CAM—client

```
#include <esp_camera.h>              // include camera library and
#include "config_pins.h"             // camera configure pins tab
#include <WebSocketsClient.h>        // WebSocket client library
WebSocketsClient websocket;          // associate websocket with lib
char ssidAP[] = "ESP32CAM";          // softAP ssid and password
char passwordAP[] = "pass1234";
```

```
void setup()
{
  Serial.begin(115200);            // initialize and connect to Wi-Fi
  WiFi.begin(ssidAP, passwordAP);
  while(WiFi.status() != WL_CONNECTED) delay(500);
                                   // client softAP IP address
  Serial.print("client softAP address ");
  Serial.println(WiFi.localIP());
                                   // server softAP IP address
  websocket.begin("192.168.4.1", 81, "/");
  configCamera();                  // function to configure camera
}

void loop()
{
  websocket.loop();                // handle WebSocket data
                                   // get image from camera
  camera_fb_t * frame = esp_camera_fb_get();
  websocket.sendBIN((uint8_t *)frame->buf, (size_t)frame->len);
  esp_camera_fb_return(frame);   // return frame buffer to driver
}
```

The sketch for the ESP32 module, connected to the ILI9341 LCD screen, acting as the server (see Listing 11-5) is based on Listing 11-2, which is for an ESP32-CAM module connected directly to an ILI9341 LCD screen. The server establishes the *softAP* WLAN, and the server default *softAP* IP address is displayed. The average FPS (Frames Per Second) rate is calculated as a moving average based on 50 observations with a circular buffer. Comments in Listing 11-5 are for the additional instructions to Listing 11-2, to emphasize the WebSocket and circular buffer instructions.

The image dimensions are obtained in the *wsEvent* function with the instructions

```
uint16_t wdth, hght
TJpgDec.getJpgSize(&wdth, &hght, RXmsg, length)
Serial.printf("image %d %d \n", wdth, hght)
```

Listing 11-5. Remote ILI9341 TFT LCD screen—server

```
#include <TJpg_Decoder.h>
#include <TFT_eSPI.h>
TFT_eSPI tft = TFT_eSPI();
#include <WebSocketsServer.h>          // WebSocket server library
                                       // WebSocket on port 81
WebSocketsServer websocket = WebSocketsServer(81);
char ssidAP[] = "ESP32CAM";
char passwordAP[] = "pass1234";
unsigned long last;
int FPS, FPSs[50], sum = 0, N = 0;     // circular buffer array
float mean;

void setup()
{
  Serial.begin(115200);
  WiFi.softAP(ssidAP, passwordAP);     // initialize softAP WLAN
  Serial.print("server softAP address ");
  Serial.println(WiFi.softAPIP());     // server IP address
  websocket.begin();                   // initialize WebSocket
  websocket.onEvent(wsEvent);          // call wsEvent function
  tft.begin();                         //    on WebSocket event
  tft.setRotation(3);
  tft.fillScreen(TFT_BLACK);
```

```
  TJpgDec.setJpgScale(1);
  TJpgDec.setSwapBytes(true);
  TJpgDec.setCallback(tftOutput);
  tft.setTextColor(TFT_RED);        // font color display FPS
  tft.setTextSize(2);
                                    // initialize circular buffer
  for (int i=0; i<50; i++) FPSs[i] = 0;
}

bool tftOutput
(int16_t x, int16_t y, uint16_t w, uint16_t h, uint16_t* bitmap)
{
  if(y >= tft.height()) return 0;
  tft.pushImage(x, y, w, h, bitmap);  // move bitmap data to LCD
  return 1;
}
                                    // function called on WebSocket event
void wsEvent(uint8_t num, WStype_t type, uint8_t * RXmsg,
             size_t length)
{
  last = millis();                  // update last image time
                                    // decompress JPEG image
  TJpgDec.drawJpg(0,0, RXmsg, length);
  FPS = millis() - last;            // interval between images
  circular();                       // update circular buffer
  tft.setCursor(220,220);           // position cursor bottom right
  tft.print("FPS ");tft.print(mean, 1);   // display FPS
}
```

```
void circular()                    // function for circular buffer
{
  sum = sum - FPSs[N];             // subtract oldest value from sum
  sum = sum + FPS;                 // add current value to sum
  FPSs[N] = FPS;                   // update circular buffer
  N++;                             // increment buffer position
  if(N > 50-1) N = 0;              // back to "start" of circular buffer
  mean = 1000.0/(sum/50.0);        // moving average FPS
}

void loop()
{
  websocket.loop();                // handle WebSocket data
}
```

After the compiled sketches are uploaded to the ESP32-CAM module and the remote ESP32 module is connected to the ILI9341 LCD screen, both ESP32 microcontrollers should be reset, by pressing the respective *RST* or *EN* module button. The ESP32 module connected to the ILI9341 LCD screen, that is, the server, is reset before the ESP32-CAM module, which is the client.

The sketch in Listing 11-5 for the receiving ESP32 microcontroller or server uses the *WebSockets* library to communicate with the ESP-CAM microcontroller or client. An alternative to the *WebSockets* library is the *ArduinoWebSockets* library by Gil Maimon. The *WebSockets* and *ArduinoWebSockets* libraries are both used in Chapter 8, "WebSocket, Remote Access, and OTA." A sketch with the *ArduinoWebSockets* library for the ESP32-CAM module, acting as the client, is similar to the sketch (see Listing 11-4) with the *WebSockets* library, but the instructions defining the WebSocket connection

```
#include <WebSocketsClient.h>   // WebSocket client library
WebSocketsClient websocket      // associate websocket with lib
```

are replaced with the instructions

```
#include <ArduinoWebsockets.h>       // ArduinoWebSockets library
using namespace websockets
WebsocketsClient client              // associate client with library
```

The `websocket.begin("192.168.4.1, "/")` instruction to initialize the WebSocket connection is replaced with the `client.connect("192.168.4.1", 81, "/")` instruction. Lastly, the `websocket.sendBIN((uint8_t *)frame->buf, (size_t)frame->len)` instruction to transmit the image data is replaced with

```
client.sendBinary((const char *)frame->buf, frame->len)
```

Likewise, the sketch for the receiving ESP32 microcontroller, acting as the server, with the *ArduinoWebSockets* library is similar to the sketch (see Listing 11-5) with the *WebSockets* library. The instructions defining the WebSocket server connection

```
#include <WebSocketsServer.h>        // WebSocket server library
                                     // websocket on port 81
WebSocketsServer websocket = WebSocketsServer(81)
```

are replaced with the instructions

```
#include <ArduinoWebsockets.h>       // include library
using namespace websockets
WebsocketsServer server              // associate server and
WebsocketsClient client              // client with library
```

The `websocket.begin()` instruction defining the server *softAP* WebSocket connection is replaced with the server connection instruction `server.listen(81)`. Instructions in the WebSocket event *wsEvent* function are moved to the *loop* function as shown in Listing 11-6.

Listing 11-6. ArduinoWebSockets library—server

```
void loop()
{
  if(server.poll()) client = server.accept();
  if(client.available())
  {
    WebsocketsMessage RXmsg = client.readBlocking();
    last = millis();
    TJpgDec.drawJpg(0, 0, (const uint8_t*) RXmsg.c_str(),
                    RXmsg.length());
    FPS = millis() - last;
    circular();
    tft.setCursor(220,220);
    tft.print("FPS ");tft.print(mean, 1);
  }
}
```

The average frame rate of images displayed on the ILI9341 LCD screen with the *WebSockets* library is generally one frame per second higher than with the *ArduinoWebSockets* library.

Stream Images to TTGO T-Watch

Streaming images from an ESP32-CAM module to the 240 × 240-pixel ST7789V 1.54" LCD of a TTGO T-Watch requires a few changes to Listing 11-5. Streamed images with frame rates of at least 10 FPS (Frames Per Second) are displayed on a TTGO T-Watch screen.

At the start of the sketch, the `#include <TFT_eSPI.h>` and `TFT_eSPI tft = TFT_eSPI()` instructions are replaced by the instructions

```
#define LILYGO_WATCH_2020_V2          // define T-Watch model
#include <LilyGoWatch.h>              // include library
TTGOClass * ttgo                      // associate objects with libraries
TFT_eSPI * tft
```

In the *setup* function, the `tft.begin()` instruction is replaced by the following instructions:

```
ttgo = TTGOClass::getWatch()
ttgo->begin()                         // initialize ttgo object
ttgo->openBL()                        // turn on backlight
ttgo->bl->adjust(64)                  // reduce brightness from 255
tft = ttgo->tft
```

The `tft->setRotation(2)` instruction replaces the `tft.setRotation(3)` instruction.

In the *tftOutput* function, the `if (y >= tft.height()) return 0` instruction is replaced by the `if (y >= 240) return 0` instruction, as `tft.height()` is not defined in the TTGO T-Watch subset of the *TFT_eSPI* library.

In the *wsEvent* function, the `tft->setCursor(120,220)` instruction replaces the `tft.setCursor(220,220)` instruction, to reposition the displayed FPS value.

Throughout the sketch, the `tft.` instruction prefix is replaced by the `tft->` prefix.

Stream Images to M5Stack Core2

Streaming ESP32-CAM images to the 320 × 240-pixel ILI9342C 2” LCD of an M5Stack Core2 module requires fewer changes to Listing 11-5 than streaming to a TTGO T-Watch.

The `#include <M5Core2.h>` instruction replaces the `#include <TFT_eSPI.h>` and `TFT_eSPI tft = TFT_eSPI()` instructions at the start of the sketch.

In the *setup* function, the `M5.begin()` instruction replaces the `tft.begin()` instruction.

Throughout the sketch, the `M5.Lcd.` instruction prefix replaces the `tft.` prefix.

Stream Images Over Wi-Fi

The ESP32-CAM module streams images to a web page with frame rates ranging from 3 FPS with UXGA (1600 × 1200 pixels) format to 26 FPS with QQVGA (160 × 120 pixels) format. The *CameraWebServer* sketch, accessed in the Arduino IDE by *File* ➤ *Examples* ➤ *ESP32* ➤ *Camera*, includes face recognition and face detection functions, with options to change numerous image characteristics. The ESP32-CAM module supports a variety of image resolution options, which are described in Chapter 1, "ESP32 Microcontroller."

A sketch to stream ESP32-CAM images to a web page is given in Listings 11-7 to 11-11 with the GPIO pin configuration file in Listing 11-3 and a schematic of the sketch in Figure 11-4. The main sketch calls the *configCamera* function to define the ESP32-CAM microcontroller GPIO pins and the initial image resolution. The *startServer* function defines the server and image streaming ports and also maps the web page and image streaming to the *page_handler* and *stream_handler* functions, respectively. The *page_handler* function loads the HTML and AJAX code for the web page, which is stored in the *page* array. The *stream_handler* function manages the ESP32-CAM image streaming. In a subsequent section of the chapter, the web page supports both streaming ESP32-CAM images and controlling external devices, connected to the ESP32-CAM module, with the latter controlled by the *device_handler* function.

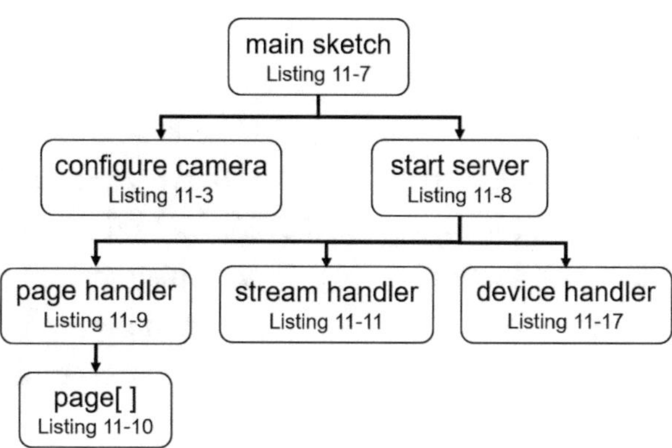

Figure 11-4. *Sketch schematic for streaming camera images*

The main sketch and each function are included on separate tabs to make the sketch more interpretable. The *buildpage.h* tab includes the HTML and AJAX code for the web page, and the *stream_handler.h* tab contains the *stream_handler* function. The remaining tabs are *configCamera, startServer,* and *page_handler*. The image resolution is defined on the *config_pins.h* tab (see Listing 11-3), with the `config.frame_size = FRAMESIZE_QVGA` instruction for an image of 320 × 240 pixels.

The main sketch (see Listing 11-7) includes libraries, connects to the Wi-Fi network, and calls the *configCamera* and *startServer* functions. Note that the *configCamera* function (see Listing 11-3) is identical to that used to stream images to an LCD screen either directly connected to the ESP-CAM module or connected to a remote ESP32 module.

Listing 11-7. Main sketch for streaming camera images

```
#include <WiFi.h>                  // include libraries
#include <esp_camera.h>
#include <esp_http_server.h>
#include <ssid_password.h>         // file with SSID and password
#include "buildpage.h"             // webpage HTML & AJAX code
#include "stream_handler.h"        // stream handler function
```

```
void setup()
{
  Serial.begin(115200);                  // Serial Monitor baud rate
  WiFi.begin(ssid, password);            // initialize and connect Wi-Fi
  while (WiFi.status() != WL_CONNECTED) delay(500);
  Serial.println(WiFi.localIP());        // display server IP address
  configCamera();                        // functions to configure camera
  startServer();                         // and start server
}

void loop()                              // nothing in loop function
{}
```

The *startServer*, *page_handler*, and *stream_handler* functions are derived from sections of the *CameraWebServer* sketch.

The *startServer* function (see Listing 11-8) links the default web page URL to the *page_handler* function (see Listing 11-9), which responds to the HTTP GET request with the HTML and AJAX code contained in the *page[ ]* array, which is a *string literal*. The *startServer* function also links the */stream* URL to the *stream_handler* function, which manages image streaming, also in response to HTTP GET requests.

Listing 11-8. Start server sketch

```
void startServer()
{
  httpd_handle_t esp32_httpd = NULL;    // define esp32_httpd and
  httpd_handle_t stream_httpd = NULL;   // stream_httpd handlers
  httpd_config_t config = HTTPD_DEFAULT_CONFIG();
  httpd_uri_t page_uri =                // link / URL to page_handler
{.uri="/", .method = HTTP_GET, .handler = page_handler,
          .user_ctx = NULL};
  httpd_uri_t stream_uri =              // link /stream to stream_handler
```

```
{.uri="/stream", .method=HTTP_GET, .handler=stream_handler,
                 .user_ctx=NULL};
  if (httpd_start(&esp32_httpd, &config) == ESP_OK)
      httpd_register_uri_handler(esp32_httpd, &page_uri);
  config.server_port = 81;
  config.ctrl_port = config.ctrl_port + 1;   // required for streaming
  if (httpd_start(&stream_httpd, &config) == ESP_OK)
    httpd_register_uri_handler(stream_httpd, &stream_uri);
}
```

Listing 11-9. page_handler

```
static esp_err_t page_handler(httpd_req_t *req)
{
  httpd_resp_set_type(req, "text/html");
  return httpd_resp_send(req, (const char *)page,
                         strlen(page));
}
```

The HTML and AJAX code for the web page (see Listing 11-10) is a string literal, bracketed by the "+++(and)+++" characters. A title for the web page is defined and an image loaded on port *81* with the */stream* URL, as declared in the *startServer* function. The URL to display streamed images is `http://serverIP:81/stream`, which is constructed with the `var site = 'http://' + window.location.hostname + ':81/stream'` instruction. The parameter *window.location.hostname* returns the host of the URL, which is the server IP address, such as *192.168.1.4*. In Chapter 7, "Email and QR Codes," a similar instruction `window.location.href` returned the URL of a web page.

Listing 11-10. HTML and AJAX code for a web page

```
const char page[] PROGMEM = R"+++(
<!doctype html><html><head>
<meta name='viewport'
      content='width=device-width,initial-scale=1.0'>
<meta charset='UTF-8'>
<title>ESP32</title>
<style>
body {font-family:Arial; text-align:center; margin-top:5px;}
</style>
</head>
<body>
<h1>ESP32 image streaming</h1>
<img id='stream' src=''>
<script>
var site = 'http://' + window.location.hostname + ':81/stream';
window.onload = document.getElementById('stream').src = site;
</script>
</body>
</html>
)+++";
```

In the *stream_handler* function (see Listing 11-11), the instruction `httpd_resp_send_chunk()` returns the JPEG buffer as 64-bit sections in response to the client HTTP GET request, with the instruction `snprintf((char *)part_buf, 64,...)` generating the 64-bit sections of the JPEG buffer. The *static* keyword creates a variable specific to a function, and the value of the variable is maintained between repeated calls to the function.

Listing 11-11. stream_handler

```
#define Boundary "123456789000000000000987654321"
static const char* ContentType =
     "multipart/x-mixed-replace;boundary=" Boundary;
static const char* StreamBound = "\r\n--" Boundary  "\r\n";
static const char* StreamContent =
     "Content-Type: image/jpeg\r\nContent-Length: %u\r\n\r\n";

static esp_err_t stream_handler(httpd_req_t *req)
{
  camera_fb_t * frame = NULL;      // associate frame with esp_camera
  uint8_t * jpgBuffer = NULL;      // JPEG buffer
  size_t jpgLength = 0;            // length of JPEG buffer
  char * part_buf[64];
  esp_err_t res = ESP_OK;          // error status
  res = httpd_resp_set_type(req, ContentType);
  if (res != ESP_OK) return res;
  while (true)
  {
   frame = esp_camera_fb_get();   // get camera image
   if (!frame)
      {Serial.println("Camera capture failed");
      res = ESP_FAIL; }            // set JPEG buffer length
   else {jpgLength = frame->len; jpgBuffer = frame->buf;}
   if (res == ESP_OK)             // no error, stream image
   {
    size_t hlen = snprintf((char *) part_buf, 64,
                  StreamContent, jpgLength);
    res = httpd_resp_send_chunk(
          req, (const char *) part_buf, hlen);
   }
```

```
    if (res == ESP_OK)
      res = httpd_resp_send_chunk(
            req, (const char *) jpgBuffer, jpgLength);
    if (res == ESP_OK)
      res = httpd_resp_send_chunk(
            req, StreamBound, strlen(StreamBound));
    if (frame)      // return frame buffer for reuse
      {esp_camera_fb_return(frame);
      frame = NULL; jpgBuffer = NULL;}
    else if (jpgBuffer) {free(jpgBuffer); jpgBuffer = NULL;}
    if (res != ESP_OK) break;
  }
  return res;
}
```

Web Page with Control Functions

The baseline sketch to stream images to a web page (see the previous section) is developed to include control functions to change the image resolution, to control devices connected to the remote ESP32 module with either web page buttons or sliders, and to display device information on the web page. The device controlling functionality is described before inclusion of image streaming.

The web page consists of a button to control a binary-state device, such as an LED; a slider to control a device with multiple settings, such as a servo motor; and buttons to transmit text to the server, which is an ESP32 microcontroller, when clicked (see Figure 11-5). One scenario is to control a remote vehicle in the forward, backward, left, or right direction with an ESP32-CAM module mounted on a panning or tilting servo motor and the built-in COB LED of the ESP-CAM module controlled to brighten areas for camera imaging. The web page is developed both with the WebSocket communication protocol and with the *esp_http_server* library, which is used in the sketch to stream ESP32-CAM images to a web page. The WebSocket approach is easier to interpret and assists in understanding the *esp_http_server* library functions. Note that the servo motor must be externally powered with the external power source GND connected to the ESP32-CAM module GND.

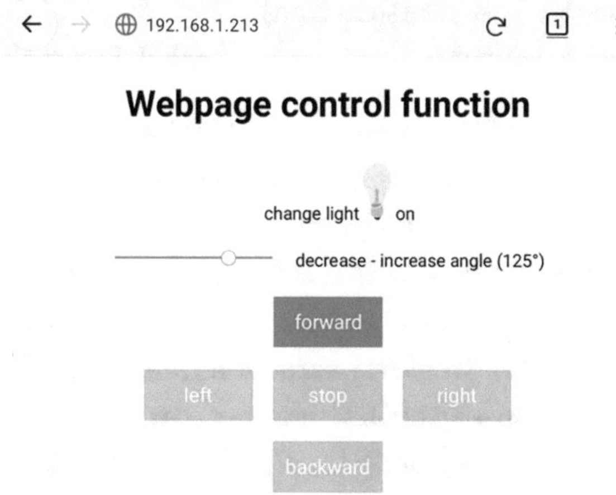

Figure 11-5. *Web page control functions with WebSocket*

WebSocket

The sketch for the control function web page consists of three parts: the main sketch (see Listing 11-12), the HTML and AJAX code for the web page (see Listing 11-13), and the WebSocket event sketch (see Listing 11-14). Listings 11-13 and 11-4 are included on the *buildpage.h* and *wsEvent* tabs.

The main sketch loads the *WebServer* and *WebSocketsServer* libraries, loads the *buildpage.h* file containing the HTML and AJAX code for the web page, initiates and connects to the Wi-Fi network, and defines the square wave frequency for controlling the servo motor.

All ESP32 microcontroller GPIO pins, except the input-only pins (GPIO 34, 35, 36, and 39), are PWM (Pulse-Width Modulation) pins to generate a square wave with variable duty cycle. Three *ledc* function instructions are required for PWM

```
ledcAttachPin(wavePin, channel)       // define PWM channel
                                      // frequency (Hz) and resolution
ledcSetup(channel, freq, resolution)
ledcWrite(channel, duty)              // scaled duty cycle (0 to 255)
```

with the parameters PWM output channel (*channel*) between 0 and 15, GPIO pin to output the square wave (*wavePin*), square wave frequency (*freq*), PWM resolution (*resolution*), and duty cycle (*duty*). The ESP32-CAM microcontroller accesses *ledc_channel_0* on *ledc_timer_0,* as indicated in Listing 11-3, so other *ledc* channels are utilized for controlling a servo motor. The *ledc* instructions are available at `github.com\espressif\arduino-esp32\blob\master\cores\esp32\esp32-hal-ledc.c` or in the file *User\AppData\Local\Arduino15\packages\esp32\hardware\esp32\version\cores\esp32\esp32-hal-ledc.cpp*. The ESP32 microcontroller uses 8-, 10-, 12-, or 15-bit resolution for PWM, providing ranges from 0 to 255, 1023, 4095, or 32767, respectively.

A Tower Pro SG90 servo motor moves to an angle between 0° and 180° with a square wave signal of frequency 50Hz and pulse length between 500μs and 2500μs. The pulse length corresponds to a duty cycle between 2.5% and 12.5%, as the square wave has a 20ms pulse length. The required servo motor angle is converted to a duty cycle of $2.5 + 10 \times angle/180$, which is then scaled according to the PWM resolution. For example, moving a servo motor to an angle of 45° requires a 50Hz square wave signal with a duty cycle of 5%. Given an 8-bit PWM resolution with a maximum value of $255 = 2^8 - 1$, the scaled duty cycle is $0.05 \times 255 = 12.75$, and the instructions to generate the required square wave are

```
ledcSetup(channel, 50, 8)              // 50Hz & 8-bit resolution
                                       // scaled duty cycle
duty = round((2.5+10*angle/180)*(pow(2,8)-1)/100.0)
ledcWrite(channel, duty)               // generate square wave
```

Listing 11-12. Main sketch with WebSocket

```
#include <WebServer.h>                 // include Webserver library
WebServer server;                      // associate server with library
#include <WebSocketsServer.h>          // include Websocket library
                                       // set WebSocket port 81
WebSocketsServer websocket = WebSocketsServer(81);
#include <ssid_password.h>             // file with SSID and password
#include "buildpage.h"                 // webpage HTML & AJAX code
int lightPin = 13;
int servoPin = 14;
int channel = 10, freq = 50, resol = 8;
String str, text[3], direct = "null", Ndirect;
int comma1, comma2, light = 0, Nlight, servo = 20,
Nservo, duty;

void setup()
{
  Serial.begin(115200);                // Serial Monitor baud rate
  pinMode(lightPin, OUTPUT);
  ledcAttachPin(servoPin, channel);    // attach servoPin to channel
  ledcSetup(channel, freq, resol);     // define square wave frequency
  WiFi.begin(ssid, password);          // connect and initialize Wi-Fi
  while (WiFi.status() != WL_CONNECTED) delay(500);
  Serial.println(WiFi.localIP());      // display web server IP address
  server.begin();
```

```
  server.on("/", base);                // load default webpage
  websocket.begin();                   // initialize WebSocket
  websocket.onEvent(wsEvent);          // wsEvent on WebSocket event
}

void base()                            // function to return HTML code
{
  server.send(200, "text/html", page);
}

void loop()
{
  server.handleClient();               // manage HTTP requests
  websocket.loop();                    // handle WebSocket data
}
```

The HTML and AJAX code for the web page is contained in the *page* array as a string literal, bracketed by the `R"+++(` and `)+++"` characters. When the web page is loaded, the *init* function is called to open the WebSocket connection at `ws://serverIP:81/`. The content of the web page is formatted as a table, with the first row, spanning two columns, containing a button, an image, and text describing the button state as *On* or *Off*. When the button is clicked, the *changeLight* function is called to update the *lightVal* variable, which is the LED state of zero or one, to update the light state of *on* or *off* on the web page code and to alternate the bulb image, which is downloaded from the `www.w3schools.com` website. If the current image URL contains the string *bulboff*, then the image URL is changed to the URL for the *bulb on* image and vice versa. The location of an image, to download from a website, is obtained by right-clicking the image and selecting *View Image Info* or *Copy Image Location* and including the image location in the AJAX code.

The second table row contains a slider to select the servo angle. The slider is defined with the option *input autocomplete='on' value='20'*, which sets the slider initial position to *value*, as the default is the middle position. When the slider is moved, the *sendSlider* function is called to update the displayed slider position and the *sliderVal* variable. The three rows of direction buttons span three columns of a second table, and when a button is clicked, the *direction* function is called to update the *directVal* variable, reset all the button states, and set the clicked button state to *on*.

When the light button or direction buttons are clicked or the slider position is changed, the *lightVal, sliderVal,* and *directVal* variables are transmitted, with the WebSocket protocol, by the client to the server with the `wskt.send()` instruction.

Listing 11-13. Control function web page

```
const char page[] PROGMEM = R"+++(
<!doctype html><html><head>
<meta name='viewport'
      content='width=device-width,initial-scale=1.0'>
<meta charset='UTF-8'>
<title>ESP32</title>
<style>
body {font-family:Arial; text-align:center; margin-top:5px;}
table {margin: auto}
td {padding: 8px;}
.btn {display:block; width:100px; margin:auto; padding:10px;
      font-size:18px; color:white; text-decoration:none;}
.on {background-color: SteelBlue;}
.off {background-color: LightSteelBlue;}
</style>
</head>
```

```
<body id='initialize'>
<h1>Webpage control function</h1>
<table align='center'><tr>
<td colspan = '2'><input type='radio' id='r1'
     onclick='changeLight()'>change light
<img id='bulb' width='25' height='50'
     src='https://www.w3schools.com/jsref/pic_bulboff.gif'>
<span id='lightId'>off</span></td>
</tr><tr>
<td><input autocomplete='on' type='range' min='20' max='160'
     value='20' class='slider' id='Slider'
     oninput='sendSlider()'></td>
<td><label id='sliderId'>decrease - increase angle (20&deg)
</label></td>
</tr><tr>
<td colspan = '3' align='center'>
<button class='btn onclick='direction("forward",id);'>forward
</button></td>
</tr></table>
<table><tr>
<td align='center'><button class='btn off' id='L'
     onclick='direction("left",id);'>left</button></td>
<td align='center'><button class='btn on'  id='S'
     onclick='direction("stop",id);'>stop</button></td>
<td align='center'><button class='btn off' id='R'
     onclick='direction("right",id);'>right</button></td>
</tr><tr>
<td colspan = '3' align='center'><button class='btn off' id='B'
     onclick='direction("backward",id);'>backward</button></td>
</tr></table>
<script>
```

```
var sliderVal = 20;
var lightVal = 0;
var directVal = "null";
document.getElementById('initialize').onload = function()
{init()};
function init()
{
  wskt = new WebSocket('ws://' +
                   window.location.hostname +':81/');
}
function sendSlider()
{
  sliderVal = document.getElementById('Slider').value;
  document.getElementById('sliderId').innerHTML =
     'decrease - increase angle ('+
      sliderVal.toString() + '&deg)';
  wskt.send(sliderVal +','+ lightVal +','+ directVal);
}
function changeLight()
{
  lightVal = 1 - lightVal;
  if(lightVal == 1) {lightTag = 'on';}
  else {lightTag = 'off';}
  document.getElementById('lightId').innerHTML = lightTag;
  document.getElementById('r1').checked=false;
  var image = document.getElementById('bulb');
  if (image.src.match('bulboff'))
       {image.src =
           'https://www.w3schools.com/js/pic_bulbon.gif';}
```

```
  else {image.src =
     'https://www.w3schools.com/js/pic_bulboff.gif';}
  wskt.send(sliderVal +','+ lightVal +','+ directVal);
}
function direction(direct,butn)
{
  document.getElementById('F').className = 'btn off'
  document.getElementById('B').className = 'btn off'
  document.getElementById('L').className = 'btn off'
  document.getElementById('R').className = 'btn off'
  document.getElementById('S').className = 'btn off'
  document.getElementById(butn).className = 'btn on'
  directVal = direct;
  wskt.send(sliderVal +','+ lightVal +','+ directVal);
}
</script>
</body></html>
)+++";
```

When the server receives a message from the client, the *wsEvent* function is called, which loads the received message into a string, which is parsed into the servo angle, the light state, and the button direction by locating the positions of commas separating the values. The LED state is updated, the servo angle is mapped to the duty cycle for a square wave signal to move the servo motor to the required position, and the button direction is updated. For a message containing many substrings, separated by commas, the string could be parsed with the C++ *strtok* instruction, as in Chapter 4, "TTGO T-Watch V2," Listing 4-11, rather than with the `str.substring()` instruction. The *wsEvent* function is included on the *wsEvent* tab.

Listing 11-14. WebSocket event

```
void wsEvent(uint8_t n, WStype_t type, uint8_t * message,
             size_t length)
{
  if(type == WStype_TEXT)
  {
    str = "";                          // build string from characters
    for (int i=0; i<length; i++) str = str + char(message[i]);
    comma1 = str.indexOf(",");         // comma positions
    comma2 = str.lastIndexOf(",");
                                       // substrings between commas
    text[0] = str.substring(0, comma1);
    text[1] = str.substring(comma1+1, comma2);
    Nservo = text[0].toInt();          // convert string to integer
    Nlight = text[1].toInt();
    Ndirect = str.substring(comma2+1);
    if(Nlight != light)
    {
      light = Nlight;
      digitalWrite(lightPin, light);   // update LED state
      Serial.printf("light %d \n", light);
    }
    if(Nservo != servo)
    {
      servo = Nservo;
      duty = round((2.5+servo/18.0)*(pow(2,resol)-1)/100.0);
      ledcWrite(channel, duty);        // update servo position
      Serial.printf("servo %d pulse %d \n", servo, duty);
    }
```

```
    if(Ndirect != direct)
    {
      direct = Ndirect;        // update direction text
      Serial.printf("direction %s \n", direct);
    }
  }
}
```

esp_http_server

A sketch to generate the control function web page in Figure 11-5 is developed with the *esp_http_server* library rather than using the *WebSocket* library. The five component parts of the sketch are the main sketch (see Listing 11-15); the *startServer* function (see Listing 11-16), which calls the *page_handler* (see Listing 11-9) and *device_handler* functions (see Listing 11-17); and the HTML and AJAX code for the web page (see Listing 11-13).

The main sketch in Listing 11-15 includes the *WiFi* and *esp_http_server* libraries, which replace the *WebServer* and *WebSocketsServer* libraries in Listing 11-12.

Listing 11-15. Main sketch with esp_http_server

```
#include <WiFi.h>                    // include WiFi and
#include <esp_http_server.h>         // esp_http_server libraries
#include <ssid_password.h>           // file with SSID and password
#include "buildpage.h"               // webpage HTML & AJAX code
int lightPin = 13;
int servoPin = 14;
int channel = 10, freq = 50, resol = 8;
int pulse;
```

```
void setup()
{
  Serial.begin(115200);          // Serial Monitor baud rate
  pinMode(lightPin, OUTPUT);
                                 // attach servoPin to channel
  ledcAttachPin(servoPin, channel);
                                 // define square wave frequency
  ledcSetup(channel, freq, resol);
  WiFi.begin(ssid, password);    // initialize and connect Wi-Fi
  while (WiFi.status() != WL_CONNECTED) delay(500);
                                 // display web server IP address
  Serial.println(WiFi.localIP());
  startServer();
}

void loop()                      // nothing in loop function
{}
```

The *startServer* function, in Listing 11-16, is equivalent to Listing 11-8, with references to *stream_handler* replaced by *device_handle*r and instructions for the streaming port deleted.

Listing 11-16. startServer with esp_http_server

```
void startServer()
{                                // define esp32_httpd handler
  httpd_handle_t esp32_httpd = NULL;
  httpd_config_t config = HTTPD_DEFAULT_CONFIG();
  httpd_uri_t page_uri =         // link URL to page_handler
{.uri="/", .method = HTTP_GET, .handler = page_handler,
          .user_ctx = NULL};
  httpd_uri_t device_uri =       // link /update to device_handler
```

```
{.uri="/update",.method=HTTP_GET, .handler=device_handler,
      .user_ctx=NULL};
  if (httpd_start(&esp32_httpd, &config) == ESP_OK)
  {
    httpd_register_uri_handler(esp32_httpd, &page_uri);
    httpd_register_uri_handler(esp32_httpd, &device_uri);
  }
  config.server_port = 81;
}
```

The *page_handler* function in Listing 11-9 is unchanged. In Listing 11-13, the HTML and AJAX code for the web page is unchanged, except for replacement of the repeated `wskt.send(sliderVal +','+ lightVal +','+ directVal)` instruction by the HTTP GET request instructions:

In the *sendSlider* function:

```
var xhr = new XMLHttpRequest()
xhr.open('GET', '/update?device=servo&level='+ sliderVal, true)
xhr.send()
```

In the *changeLight* function:

```
var xhr = new XMLHttpRequest()
xhr.open('GET', '/update?device=light&level='+ lightVal, true)
xhr.send()
```

And in the *direction* function:

```
var xhr = new XMLHttpRequest()
xhr.open('GET', '/update?device=button&level='+ direct, true)
xhr.send()
```

Note that the complete sketches with the *esp_http_server* library are included on *GitHub* (`github.com/Apress/ESP32-Formats-and-Communication`).

The *device_handler* function in Listing 11-17 is equivalent to the WebSocket *wsEvent* function (see Listing 11-14). The first half of the *device_handler* function performs error checking, and in the second half, the devices connected to the ESP32 module are controlled depending on the *device* and *level* parameters included in the client HTTP GET requests of the *startServer* function in Listing 11-16.

The *device* and *level* parameters of the client HTTP GET request are mapped to the *variable* and *value* parameters in the `httpd_query_key_value` instructions in Listing 11-17. The mapping of *device* and *level* to *variable* and *value* is included in the instructions

```
if(httpd_query_key_value(buf, "device", variable,
      sizeof(variable)) == ESP_OK
&& httpd_query_key_value(buf, "level", value,
      sizeof(value)) == ESP_OK) {}
```

The *variable* parameter is compared to the *light, servo,* or *button* string to determine which device to control using the *value* parameter.

Listing 11-17. Device handler with esp_http_server

```
static esp_err_t device_handler(httpd_req_t *req)
{
  char*  buf;
  size_t buf_len;
  char variable[32] = {0,};
  char value[32] = {0,};
  buf_len = httpd_req_get_url_query_len(req) + 1;
  if(buf_len > 1)
  {
    buf = (char*)malloc(buf_len);
    if(!buf) {httpd_resp_send_500(req); return ESP_FAIL;}
    if(httpd_req_get_url_query_str(req, buf, buf_len) == ESP_OK)
    {
```

```
    if(httpd_query_key_value(buf, "device", variable,
          sizeof(variable)) == ESP_OK
    && httpd_query_key_value(buf, "level", value,
          sizeof(value)) == ESP_OK) {}
    else {free(buf); httpd_resp_send_404(req); return ESP_FAIL;}
    }
    else {free(buf); httpd_resp_send_404(req); return ESP_FAIL;}
    free(buf);
  }
  else {httpd_resp_send_404(req); return ESP_FAIL;}

  int x = atoi(value);               // convert value char to integer
  if(!strcmp(variable, "light"))     // HTTP request with "light"
  {
    digitalWrite(lightPin, x);       // x = 0 or 1
    Serial.printf("light %d \n", x);
  }                                  // HTTP request with "servo"
  else if(!strcmp(variable, "servo"))
  {                                  // x = 20 to 160
    pulse = round(pow(2,resol)*(2.5 + x/18.0)/100.0);
    ledcWrite(channel, pulse);
    Serial.printf("servo %d pulse %d \n", x, pulse);
  }                                  // HTTP request with "button"
  else if(!strcmp(variable, "button"))
  {
    String str = value;              // convert value char to string
    Serial.printf("button %s \n", str);
  }
  return httpd_resp_send(req, NULL, 0);
}
```

Web Page with Image Streaming and Control Functions

A flexible web page to stream ESP32-CAM images and to remotely control devices attached to the ESP32 module is obtained by combining the sketches for image streaming (Listings 11-7 to 11-11) with the sketches for web page control (Listings 11-15 to 11-17).

The main sketch for web page control (Listing 11-15) is extended by loading the *esp_camera* library and the *stream_handler* function at the start of the sketch and calling the *configCamera* function (see Listing 11-3) in the *setup* function, with the instructions

```
#include <esp_camera.h>
#include "stream_handler.h"
configCamera()
```

The *configCamera* function instructions are included on the *configCamera* tab. The *startServer* function for web page control (Listing 11-16) is extended by including the *stream_handler* instructions of

```
  httpd_handle_t stream_httpd = NULL;
  httpd_uri_t stream_uri =
{.uri="/stream", .method=HTTP_GET,
      .handler=stream_handler, .user_ctx=NULL};
  config.ctrl_port = config.ctrl_port + 1;
  if (httpd_start(&stream_httpd, &config) == ESP_OK)
    httpd_register_uri_handler(stream_httpd, &stream_uri);
```

The *page_handler* (Listing 11-9), *stream_handler* (Listing 11-11), and *device_handler* (Listing 11-17) functions are unchanged. The *stream_handler* function instructions are included on the *stream_handler.h* tab.

The HTML and AJAX code for the web page (Listing 11-10) is replaced with Listing 11-13 with the addition of the two instructions in the *script* section

```
<img id='stream' src=''>
window.onload = document.getElementById('stream').src =
    'http://' + window.location.hostname + ':81/stream'
```

and replacement of the `wskt.send(sliderVal +','+ lightVal +','+ directVal)` instruction by the HTTP GET request instructions:

In the *sendSlider* function:

```
var xhr = new XMLHttpRequest()
xhr.open('GET', '/update?device=servo&level='+ sliderVal, true)
xhr.send()
```

In the *changeLight* function:

```
var xhr = new XMLHttpRequest()
xhr.open('GET', '/update?device=light&level='+ lightVal, true)
xhr.send()
```

And in the *direction* function:

```
var xhr = new XMLHttpRequest()
xhr.open('GET', '/update?device=button&level='+ direct, true)
xhr.send()
```

ESP32-CAM Image Resolution

The ESP32-CAM image resolution is changed within the web page by a second slider mapped to the *changeFrame* function in the HTML and AJAX code for the web page. The instructions for the image resolution slider

```
<input autocomplete='on' type='range' min='0' max='13'
value='5' class='slider' id='frame' oninput='changeFrame()'>
<label id='frameId'>framesize QVGA 320x240</label>
```

are similar to the slider for the servo motor angle in Listing 11-13. The 14 image resolution options are given in Listing 11-18, with the slider having minimum and maximum values of 0 and 13. When the slider is moved, the image resolution slider calls the *changeFrame* function, which displays the selected image resolution on the web page. Instructions for the *changeFrame* function are given in Listing 11-18.

Note that image resolution refers to the dimensions, measured in pixels, of an image, while frame size refers to the dimensions, measured in cm, of a displayed image. Several of the *esp-camera.h* library instructions, such as `frame_size = FRAMESIZE_QVGA`, use *frame* as a synonym for *image*. For consistency with the instructions, the term *frame* is used in a sketch, such as *changeFrame* as in Listing 11-18, while *changeImage* would be more appropriate.

Listing 11-18. Change image resolution function

```
function changeFrame()
{
  const frames = ["96x96",
  "QQVGA 160x120","QCIF 176x144","HQVGA 240x176","240x240",
  "QVGA 320x240", "CIF 400x296", "HVGA 480x320", "VGA 640x480",
  "SVGA 800x600", "XGA 1024x768","HD 1280x720",
  "SXGA 1280x1024", "UXGA 1600x1200"];
  frameVal = document.getElementById('frame').value;
  document.getElementById('frameId').innerHTML =
     'framesize ' + frames[frameVal]; // frameVal.toString();
  var xhr = new XMLHttpRequest();
```

```
  xhr.open('GET', '/update?device=frame&level=' +
          frameVal, true);
  xhr.send();
}
```

The instructions for the server response to the client HTTP GET request to control the image resolution, which are included in the *device_handler* function of Listing 11-17, are

```
else if(!strcmp(variable, "frame"))      // HTTP request with "frame"
{
  sensor_t * s = esp_camera_sensor_get();
                                          // update image resolution
  s->set_framesize(s, (framesize_t)x);   // x = 0 to 13
  Serial.printf("image resolution %d \n", x);
}
```

CHAPTER 12

Control Apps

MIT App Inventor enables building applications or apps, which provides the opportunity to design an app, rather than using an app downloaded from *Google Play Store*. After completing the app design and build stages, the app is immediately available to download to an Android tablet or mobile phone. The *MIT App Inventor* app design website, `ai2.appinventor.mit.edu`, is accessed by clicking *Create Apps!* on `appinventor.mit.edu`. When building an app, the option to simultaneously display the developing app on an Android tablet or mobile phone is provided by the *MIT App Inventor Companion* app (*MIT AI2 Companion*), which is downloaded from *Google Play Store*. For example, the effect of changing the screen position of an image on *MIT App Inventor* is instantly realized on the *Companion* app. Both the computer, on which the app is developed, and the Android tablet or mobile phone hosting the *MIT App Inventor Companion* app must be on the same WLAN (Wireless Local Area Network). Building an app with *MIT App Inventor* is comprehensively described with examples in Chapters 10–13 of *Electronics Projects with the ESP8266 and ESP32*. Details on the *MIT App Inventor Companion* app are available at `appinventor.mit.edu/explore/ai2/setup-device-wifi.html`.

One objective of this chapter is to design and build the components of an app to display streamed images from an ESP32-CAM module and transmit control parameters for devices connected to the ESP32-CAM

N. Cameron, *ESP32 Formats and Communication*,
https://doi.org/10.1007/978-1-4842-9376-8_12

module. This chapter also describes the control of WS2812 5050 RGB LEDs, connected to an ESP32 module, with Bluetooth or with Wi-Fi communication between the app and the ESP32 microcontroller.

App to Display a Web Page

An app to display a web page is easily built on *MIT App Inventor* (see Figure 12-1). The app is hosted by a device, such as an Android tablet or mobile phone, which has a Wi-Fi connection to a WLAN. A default URL for the *WebViewer* component is defined as the *HomeURL* located in the *WebViewer Properties* palette.

Figure 12-1. *Web page display app*

The app layout (see Figure 12-2) consists of the *WebViewer* component, which is located in the *User Interface* palette, the *URLtext* textbox for the user to enter the web page URL, and the *URLbutton* button. The web page URL is entered in the *URLtext* textbox, and the web page is loaded when the *URLbutton* button, which is labeled *Load URL*, is clicked. A default URL for the *WebViewer* component is defined as the *HomeURL* located in the *WebViewer Properties* palette.

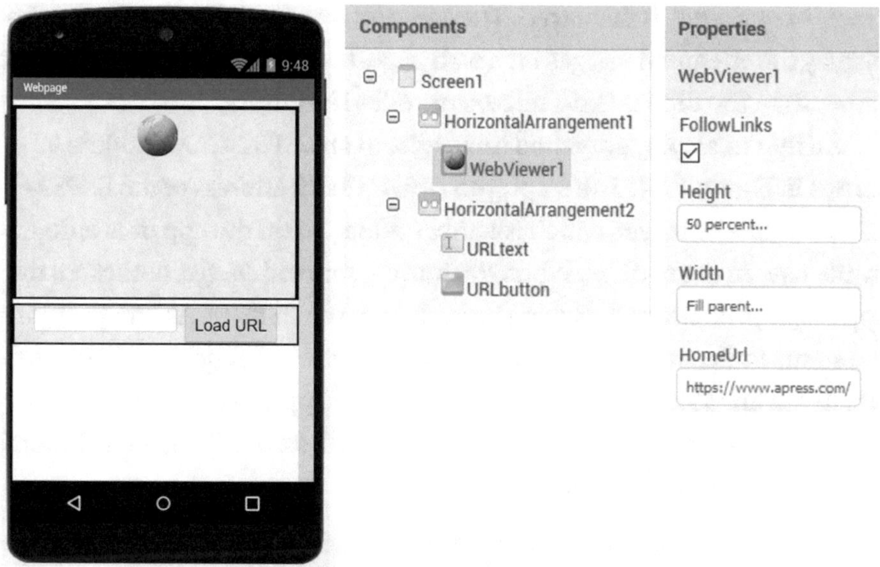

Figure 12-2. *Web page display app layout*

The *MIT APP Inventor* instruction blocks for the app are shown in Figure 12-3, with the entered URL automatically preceded by *http://*.

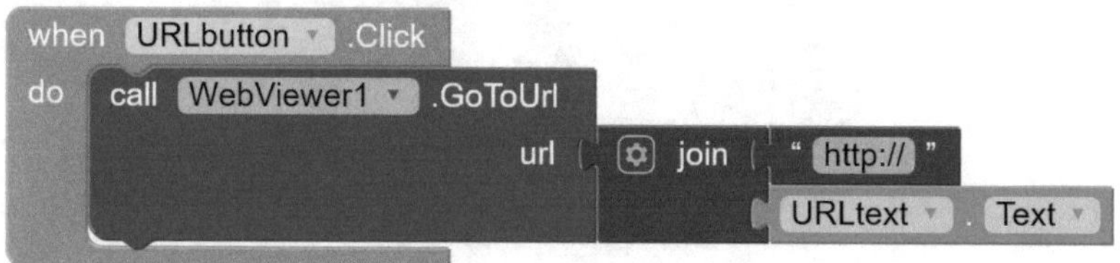

Figure 12-3. *Blocks to display a web page*

App to Display Streamed Images

The *WebViewer* component displays a web page on an app by including the web page URL as a parameter. If the IP address of an ESP32-CAM module, which is streaming images, is loaded to the *WebViewer* component, then the error message *"Header fields are too long for the server to interpret"* is displayed. The solution is to load the HTML code, to display the streamed images on a web page, to the *WebViewer* component, rather than the ESP32-CAM microcontroller IP address.

An app to display streamed images from an ESP32-CAM module is shown in Figure 12-4. The displayed URL is the IP address of the ESP32-CAM module or server, which is either preloaded on the app or is entered by the user in the textbox. When the button, marked *Image*, is clicked, the app displays or stops displaying images from the ESP32-CAM module, and the status indicator displays the color-coded text: *on* or *off*. The frame, in which the image is displayed, is resized on the app screen, by entering a percentage value between 0 and 100 in the textbox. The image resolution is not changed, only the frame size.

Figure 12-4. *Display streamed ESP32-CAM images app*

The app layout is shown in Figure 12-5, which is similar to the app layout to display a web page (see Figure 12-2), with the addition of a button to turn on or off the display of streamed images and a textbox to enter the required frame size.

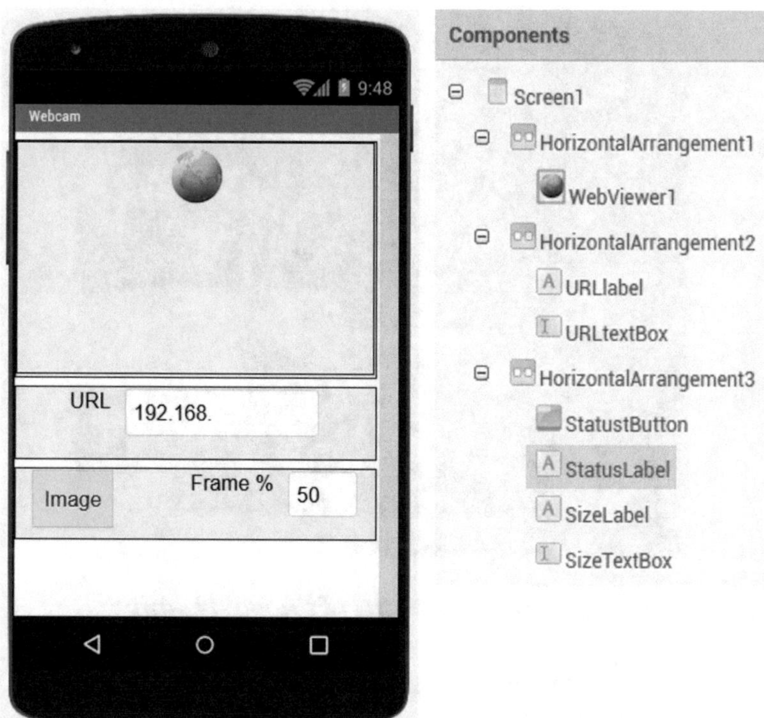

***Figure 12-5.** Display streamed ESP32-CAM images app layout*

Blocks to update the status label and control the display of streamed images from the ESP32-CAM module are shown in Figures 12-6 and 12-7. When the status button is clicked, the status variable and status label are updated, with either the *procedure* called to load the web page HTML code or the display of streamed images stopped.

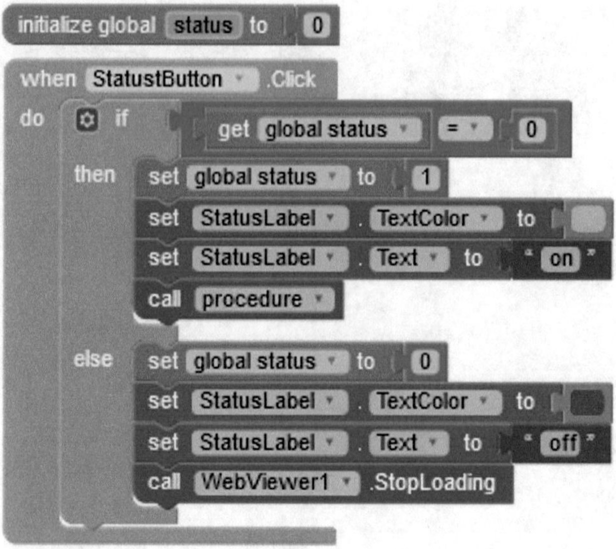

Figure 12-6. *Blocks to display status of image streaming*

The web page HTML code is loaded as a URL to the *WebViewer* component (see Figure 12-7), with the frame size and the IP address of the ESP32-CAM microcontroller incorporated from the values entered in the *SizeTextBox* and the *URLtextBox* textboxes, respectively. The HTML code is preceded by `data:text/html`, so the client interprets the subsequent data as HTML code rather than a URL. Turning on or off the image display and changing the frame size are both functions of the app, and no information is passed from the app to the ESP32-CAM microcontroller, which is continuously streaming images.

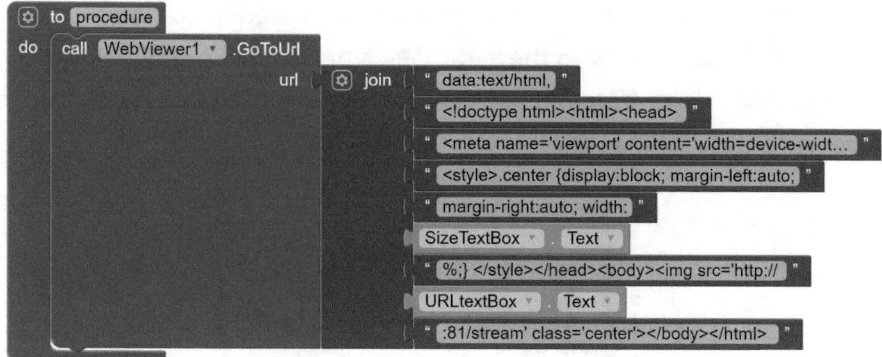

Figure 12-7. *Blocks to display streamed ESP32-CAM images*

The web page HTML code loaded as a URL (see Listing 12-1) is similar to the HTML and AJAX code for streaming images to a web page over a Wi-Fi connection in Listing 11-10.

Listing 12-1. HTML code for a web page

```
<!doctype html>
<html>
<head>
<meta name='viewport'
      content='width=device-width,initial-scale=1.0'>
<style>
.center {display: block; margin-left: auto; margin-right: auto;
         width: N%;}
</style>                                    // N: value in SizeTextbox
</head>
<body>
                                            // URL: value in URLtextBox
<img src='http://URL:81/stream' class='center'>
</body>
</html>
```

A schematic of the sketch for the ESP32-CAM module to stream images is shown in Figure 12-8 with the main sketch and each function included on the separate tabs of *configCamera*, *startServer*, and *stream_handler.h*, to make the sketch more interpretable.

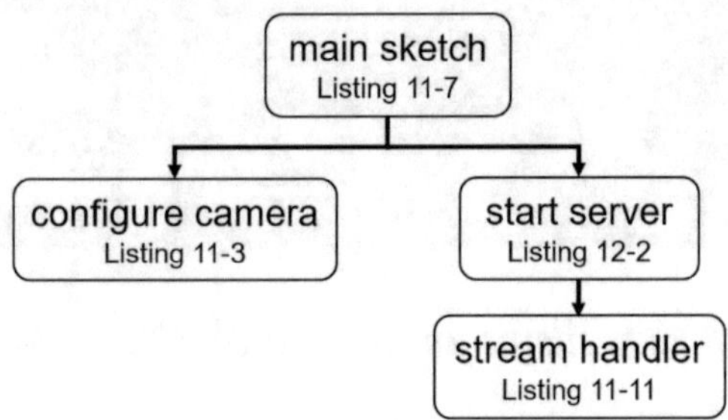

Figure 12-8. *Display streamed ESP32-CAM images on an app*

The sketch to stream images from the ESP32-CAM module to an app is similar to the sketch to stream images to a web page, as described in Chapter 11, "ESP32-CAM Camera." The main sketch is identical to Listing 11-7, except that the `#include "buildpage.h"` instruction is not required, as the streamed camera images are not displayed on a web page. Likewise, the *page_handler* function (see Listing 11-9) is not needed. In the *startServer* function (see Listing 11-8), only the *stream_handler* function instructions are required, as shown in Listing 12-2. The *configCamera* (see Listing 11-3) and *stream_handler* functions (see Listing 11-11) are both unchanged.

Listing 12-2. startServer with an image streaming app

```
void startServer()
{
  httpd_handle_t stream_httpd = NULL;   // stream_httpd handler
  httpd_config_t config = HTTPD_DEFAULT_CONFIG();
  httpd_uri_t stream_uri =              // link /stream to stream_handler
```

```
{.uri="/stream", .method=HTTP_GET,
      .handler=stream_handler,.user_ctx=NULL};
  config.server_port = 81;
  config.ctrl_port = config.ctrl_port + 1;  // required for streaming
  if (httpd_start(&stream_httpd, &config) == ESP_OK)
    httpd_register_uri_handler(stream_httpd, &stream_uri);
}
```

App to Transmit and Receive Data

In Chapter 11, "ESP32-CAM Camera," a web page with control functions enabled remote control of devices connected to an ESP32 module. In this chapter, the equivalent scenario is developed with an app transmitting and receiving data to and from the ESP32 microcontroller to control or provide information on devices connected to the ESP32 module. In the demonstration app (see Figure 12-9), the app transmits, to the ESP32 microcontroller, a random number generated by the app and button-specific text when one of the two arrow buttons on the app is clicked. In response, the ESP32 microcontroller transmits text, related to the received text, and a function of the received number to the app, which are displayed on the app. Both the ESP32 microcontroller and app are connected to the same WLAN (Wireless Local Area Network) for Wi-Fi communication between the ESP32 microcontroller and the app. Alternatively, a software-enabled access point, *softAP*, is provided by the ESP32 microcontroller for communication with the app.

The app layout and components are shown in Figure 12-9. A button image is uploaded in the *Media* palette and then mapped to the button in the button *Properties* palette (see Figure 12-9). The *Web* component, located in the *Connectivity* palette and displayed below the app layout as a *Non-visible component*, transmits the *HTTP GET* request to the server, which is the ESP32 microcontroller.

***Figure 12-9.** App layout to transmit and receive data*

When a button is clicked, the *procedure* is called with text, specific to each button, as a parameter. The *procedure* generates a random number and the *HTTP GET* request URL. The URL consists of the server IP address and the *direction* and *value* parameters, which correspond to the button-specific text and the random number, respectively (see Figure 12-10). The server IP address is prepopulated with `http://192.168`, so only the last two numbers of the server IP address are entered in the SSID textbox.

In an *HTTP GET* request, parameters are formatted as *name=value* pairs, such as *direct=R*, and are separated by the ampersand, &, symbol. For example, the URL when the right button is clicked and the random number 42 is generated is `http://192.168.1.219/button?direct=R&value=42`, for a server IP address of *192.168.1.219*. The *Web* component transmits, to the server, the *HTTP GET* request of *GET /button?direct=R&value=42 HTTP/1.1*.

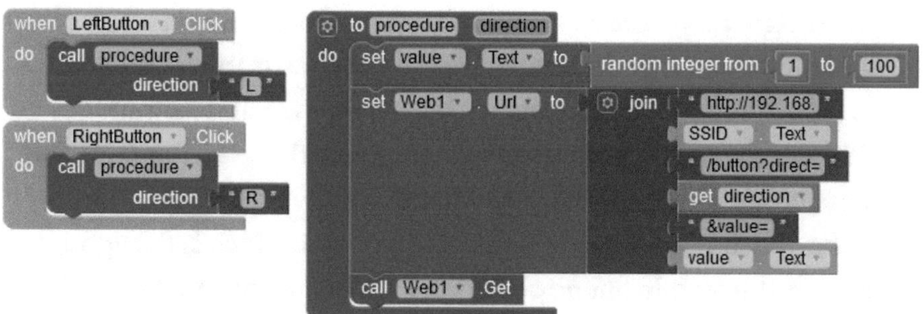

Figure 12-10. *Blocks for an app to transmit data*

The server response, to the client *HTTP GET* request, contains text with the direction, dependent on which app button was pressed, and a number, equal to double the value generated by the app, with the two components separated by a comma. On receipt of the server response to the *HTTP GET* request, the *Web* component initiates the *GotText* component (see Figure 12-11). In the *GotText* component, the server response is split according to the comma separator, with the two components displayed on the app in the *ResponseText* and *ResponseValue* textboxes.

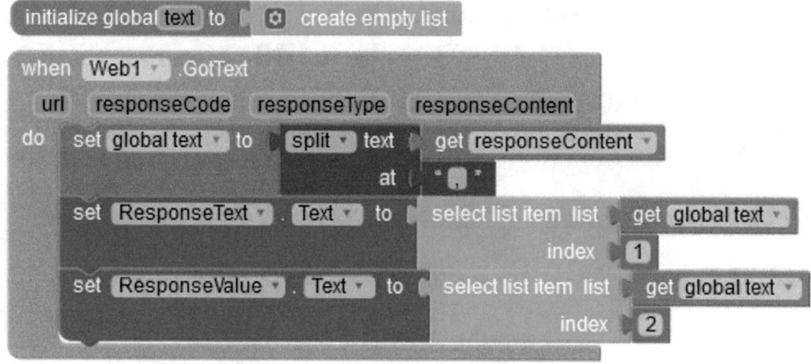

Figure 12-11. *Blocks for an app to receive data*

The sketch for the ESP32 microcontroller, acting as the server, is given in Listing 12-3. The *WiFiClient* and *WiFiServer* libraries are referenced by the *WiFi* library, so the `#include <WiFiClient.h>` and `#include <WiFiServer.h>` instructions are not required. In the *setup* function, the Wi-Fi connection and server are initialized.

In the *loop* function, a connection to the client, which is the app (technically the mobile phone or Android tablet hosting the app), is established, and when a client *HTTP GET* request is received, a string, *str*, is mapped to the received message up to the carriage return character, *\r*. The ESP32 *WiFi* library does not have the equivalent *server.arg("value")* instruction of the *ESP8266WiFi* library, so the string is split into components using the *indexOf* function. The *HTTP GET* request is formatted as *GET /button?direct=letter&value=number HTTP/1.1* and contains the *name=value* pairs of *direct=letter* and *value=number*. The *number* parameter is located between the *"value"* and *"HTTP"* substrings, with the substring starting positions obtained with the *indexOf* function. The *direct* parameter is obtained by simply determining if the *HTTP GET* request contains the letter *R*.

For example, the server response to the *HTTP GET* request, of *GET / button?direct=R&value=42 HTTP/1.1*, after the right button on the app is clicked and the number 42 is generated by the app is

HTTP/1.1 200 OK	HTTP header with response code of 200
Content-type:text/html	inform client of server response type
<blank line>	indicate start of HTTP response
right,84	content of HTTP response
<blank line>	indicate end of HTTP response

as, in the sketch, the number received by the server is doubled and transmitted to the client.

Listing 12-3. App to transmit and receive data

```
#include <WiFi.h>                     // include WiFi library
WiFiClient client;                    // associate client and server with
WiFiServer server(80);                //  WiFiClient and WiFiServer lib
#include <ssid_password.h>            // file with SSID and password
String str, reply, value;
int indexS, indexF, valueN;

void setup()
{
  Serial.begin(115200);               // Serial Monitor baud rate
  WiFi.begin(ssid, password);         // initialize and connect Wi-Fi
  while (WiFi.status() != WL_CONNECTED) delay(500);
  Serial.println(WiFi.localIP());     // display server IP address
  server.begin();                     // initiate server
}

void loop()
{
  client = server.available();
  if (client)                         // initialize client connection
  {                                   // no client request, do nothing
    while (!client.available()) {};
                                      // map str to HTTP GET request
    str = client.readStringUntil('\r');
    Serial.println(str);              // display HTTP GET request
    indexS = str.indexOf("value");    // position of "value" in string
    indexF = str.indexOf("HTTP");
                                      // value=NNN HTTP
    value = str.substring(indexS+6, indexF-1);
    valueN = 2*(value.toInt());       // transform received value
```

```
    reply = "left";
                                              // str contains "R"
    if(str.indexOf("R") != -1) reply = "right";
    reply = reply +","+ String(valueN);
                                              // HTTP header & response code
    client.println("HTTP/1.1 200 OK");
                                              // \n to generate blank line
    client.println("Content-type:text/html\n");
    client.println(reply);                    // transmit HTTP response
    client.stop();                            // close connection
  }
}
```

App with Image Streaming and Control Functions

An app to stream ESP32-CAM images and control devices connected to an ESP32 module combines the image streaming app with the app to transmit and receive data. One scenario is to control a remote robot car in the forward, backward, left, or right direction with the ESP32-CAM module mounted on the robot car. This chapter focuses on developing the app, while Chapter 14, "Remote Control an ESP32-CAM Robot Car," describes building the sketch to control the robot car given the directions transmitted by the app. The app displays the streamed ESP32-CAM images and includes control buttons for forward, backward, left, and right directions and for stop (see Figure 12-12). A slider controls the image resolution with 14 categories ranging from 96 × 96 pixels to UXGA (1600 × 1200 pixels). Changing the image resolution of images displayed on a web page is described in Chapter 11, "ESP32-CAM Camera," and the same methodology is applied to control image resolution with the app. Changing the size of the frame, in which the image is displayed, is described in this chapter in the "App to Display Streamed Images" section. The displayed URL is the IP address of the ESP32-CAM microcontroller, which is either preloaded on the app or entered by the user in the textbox.

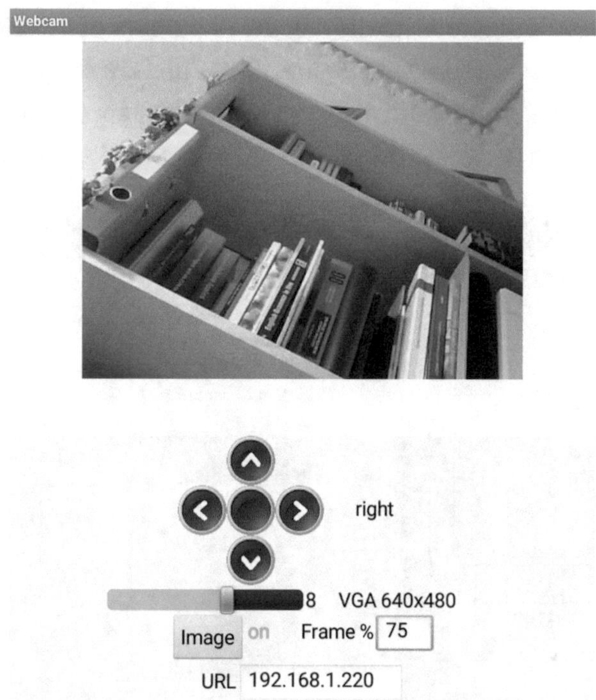

Figure 12-12. *App with image streaming and control functions*

The app layout (see Figure 12-13) includes the *WebViewer* component, which is contained in a *HorizontalArrangement,* with the height reduced from 400 to 75 for the purpose of showing all the app components in the figure. A *TableArrangement,* located in the *Layout* palette, holds the buttons and a label, with the number of table columns and rows defined in the *TableArrangement Properties* palette (see Figure 12-14). The horizontal *Slider* component, located in the *User Interface* palette, determines the image resolution category. The colors of the left and right portions of the slider, the slider width, and minimum and maximum slider values are defined in the slider *Properties* palette (see Figure 12-14). The *FrameValue* and *FrameSize* textboxes display the slider value and the image resolution description. The *StatusButton* button, to turn on or off the display of streamed images; the *SizeTextBox* textbox, to enter the required frame size; and the *URLtextBox* textbox, to display the IP address of the ESP32-CAM module, are identical to those in Figure 12-4. The *Web* component, located in the *Connectivity* palette and displayed below the app layout as a *Non-visible component*, performs the *HTTP GET* request with the server.

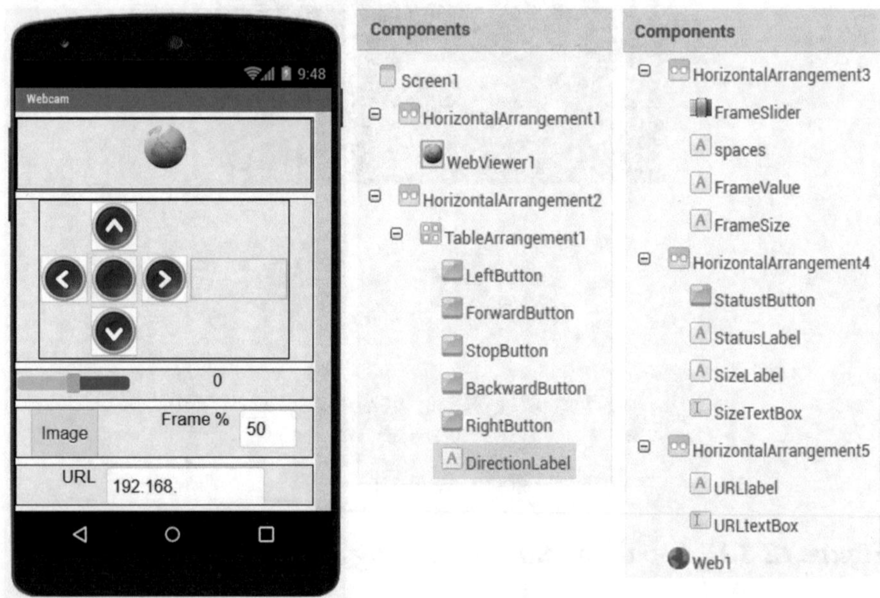

***Figure 12-13.** App layout with image streaming and control functions*

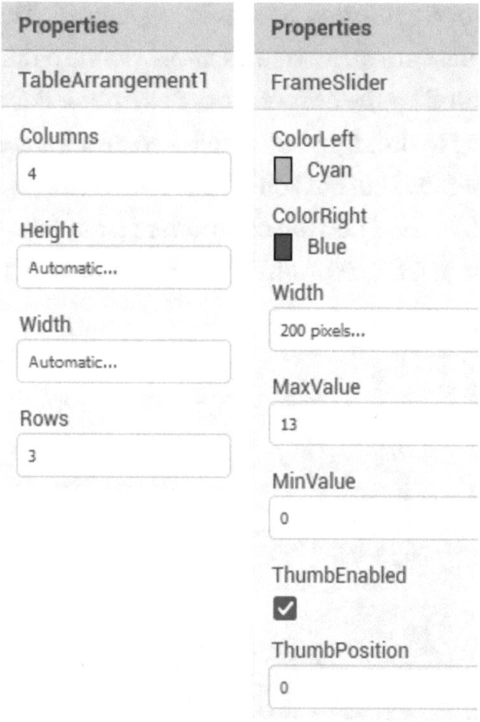

Properties

TableArrangement1

Columns

4

Height

Automatic...

Width

Automatic...

Rows

3

Properties

FrameSlider

ColorLeft

Cyan

ColorRight

Blue

Width

200 pixels...

MaxValue

13

MinValue

0

ThumbEnabled

ThumbPosition

0

Figure 12-14. *Table arrangement and slider properties*

The app blocks to display streamed images from the ESP32-CAM module, change the frame size, and update the status label are identical to the blocks in Figures 12-6 and 12-7. Blocks for transmitting the *HTTP GET* request to the server, which is the ESP32-CAM microcontroller, and receiving data in the server response to the *HTTP GET* request are similar to the blocks in Figures 12-10 and 12-11.

When a direction button is clicked, the *procedure2* procedure is called (see Figure 12-15) to generate the *HTTP GET* request URL containing the *direct* and *frame* parameters, corresponding to the direction button-specific text and the slider value, which is the slider *thumbPosition.* Note that there are five button blocks with *direct* set to *R, L, F, B,* or *S* corresponding to the *RightButton, LeftButton, ForwardButton,*

BackwardButton, or *StopButton* button being clicked. The parameters of an *HTTP GET* request are formatted as *name=value* pairs, such as *direct=R* or *frame=8*, separated by the ampersand, &, symbol. For example, the URL corresponding to the right button clicked and a slider position of 8 is `http://192.168.1.220/button?direct=R&frame=8`, for a server IP address of *192.168.1.220*. The *Web* component transmits, to the server, the *HTTP GET* request of *GET /button?direct=R&frame=8 HTTP/1.1*.

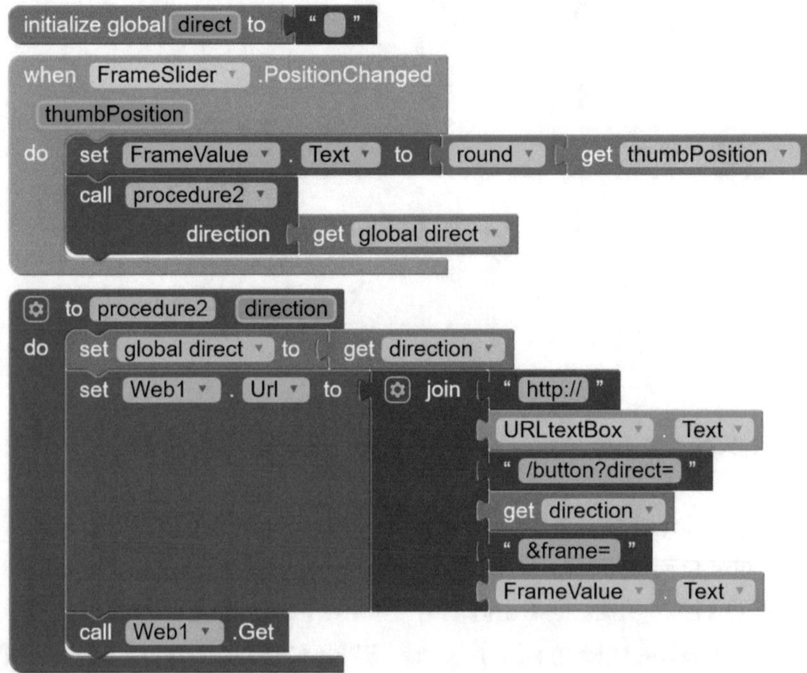

Figure 12-15. *Blocks for HTTP GET request procedure and slider*

The server response to the client *HTTP GET* request contains the text describing the direction, such as *forward*, and the image resolution, such as *HVGA 480×320*. The *Web GotText* component splits the server response, with the comma separator, and displays the component strings on the app in the *DirectionLabel* and *FrameSize* textboxes (see Figure 12-16).

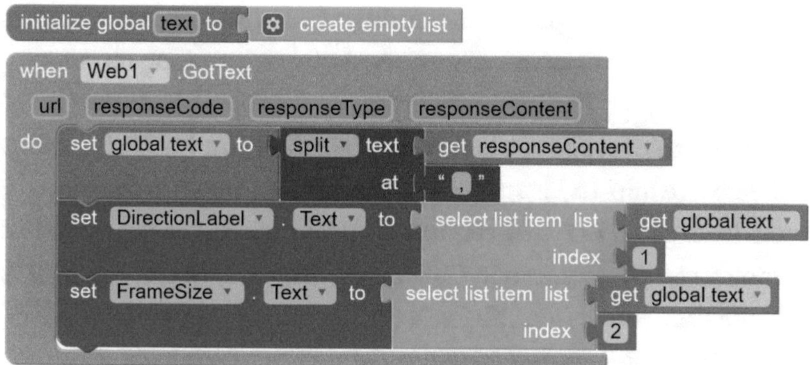

Figure 12-16. *Blocks for response to HTTP GET request*

The sketch to display streamed ESP32-CAM images and manage the client *HTTP GET* requests (see Listing 12-4) is a combination of Listings 12-3 and 11-7, excluding the *buildpage.h* tab containing the HTML and AJAX code for a web page (Listing 11-10) and the *page_handler* function (see Listing 11-9), as the streamed camera images are displayed on an app and not on a web page. In the *setup* function, a WLAN connection is established, and the ESP32-CAM microcontroller IP address is displayed, as the information is required by the client, which is the app, to connect to the server, which is the ESP32 microcontroller. Alternatively, a software-enabled access point, *softAP*, is provided by the ESP32 microcontroller for communication with the app. The *frames* array contains the descriptions of the image resolution options.

The *loop* function extracts the image resolution and the direction from the *HTTP GET* request, in the same manner as in Listing 12-3. The *indexOf* function is used to identify the position of the image resolution value, *N*, as the *HTTP GET* request contains the sequence *frame=N HTTP*. The ESP32-CAM image resolution is updated, and the server response to the client *HTTP GET* request contains a description of the direction of travel and the image resolution.

The focus of this chapter is on building apps with a control function. Chapter 13, "Remote Control Motors," describes controlling motors with an app. Chapter 14, "Remote Control an ESP32-CAM Robot Car," combines app design and the control of DC motors for building a robot car controlled by an app. In Listing 12-4, the server response to the direction extracted from the *HTTP GET* request is only to return the direction text. In the motor control scenario in Chapter 14, "Remote Control an ESP32-CAM Robot Car," the `if(str.indexOf("R") != -1)` instruction calls the corresponding motor control function, rather than defining a string, as in Listing 12-4.

Listing 12-4. App with image streaming and control functions

```
#include <WiFi.h>                    // include libraries
#include <esp_camera.h>
#include <esp_http_server.h>
WiFiClient client;                   // associate client and server with
WiFiServer server(80);               // WiFiClient and WiFiServer lib
#include <ssid_password.h>           // file with SSID and password
// char ssidAP[] = "ESP32CAM";       // softAP SSID and password
// char passwordAP[] = "pass1234";
#include "stream_handler.h"          // stream handler function
String str, reply, direct;
String frames[] = {"96x96","QQVGA 160x120","QCIF 176x144",
                   "HQVGA 240x176", "240x240","QVGA 320x240",
                   "CIF 400x296", "HVGA 480x320","VGA 640x480",
                   "SVGA 800x600", "XGA 1024x768","HD 1280x720",
                   "SXGA 1280x1024","UXGA 1600x1200"};
int indexS, indexF, frm, oldfrm = 0;
```

```
void setup()
{
  Serial.begin(115200);                  // Serial Monitor baud rate
// WiFi.softAP(ssidAP, passwordAP); // option for softAP
// Serial.println(WiFi.softAPIP());
  WiFi.begin(ssid, password);            // initialize and connect Wi-Fi
  while (WiFi.status() != WL_CONNECTED) delay(500);
  Serial.println(WiFi.localIP());        // display server IP address
  configCamera();                        // functions to configure camera
  startServer();                         //   and start server
  server.begin();                        // initiate server
}

void loop()
{
  client = server.available();
  if (client)                            // initialize client connection
  {                                      // no client response, do nothing
    while (!client.available()) {};
    str = client.readStringUntil('\r');     // map str to message
    indexS = str.indexOf("frame");       // position of "frame" in string
    indexF = str.indexOf("HTTP");
                                         // convert to integer
    frm = (str.substring(indexS+6, indexF-1)).toInt();
    if(frm != oldfrm)                    // image resolution changed
    {
      oldfrm = frm;
      sensor_t * s = esp_camera_sensor_get();
                                         // update image resolution
      s->set_framesize(s, (framesize_t)frm);
```

```
      Serial.printf("image resolution %d \n", frm);
    }
    direct = "left";
                                            // str contains "R"
    if(str.indexOf("R") != -1) direct = "right";
    else if(str.indexOf("F") != -1) direct = "forward";
    else if(str.indexOf("B") != -1) direct = "backward";
    else if(str.indexOf("S") != -1) direct = "stop";
    reply = direct +","+ frames[frm];
    client.println("HTTP/1.1 200 OK");  // HTTP header & response
                                        // \n to generate blank line
    client.println("Content-type:text/html\n");
    client.println(reply);              // transmit HTTP response
    client.stop();                      // close connection
  }
}
```

App Sliders

The *MIT App Inventor* slider position is mapped to a range of values for controlling a device, such as the speed of a DC motor, the time interval between events, or the volume of a speaker. For example, a slider range, defined as 0–100, is mapped to an 8-bit PWM (Pulse-Width Modulation) value between 0 and 255 to generate a square wave, with the corresponding duty cycle, to control the speed of a DC motor. Servo motor control is described in Chapter 13, "Remote Control Motors." The *MIT App Inventor* slider component is a horizontal component, which is sufficient for controlling motor speed or the left-right direction of a servo motor, but a circular slider or a vertical slider may have a more relevant visual appearance than a horizontal slider. Applications of a circular slider and a vertical slider are described.

Circular Slider

Controlling the direction of a robot car powered by two DC motors requires either two linear sliders or a circular slider. The circular slider horizontal and vertical positions correspond to the left-right and forward-backward positions of two linear sliders. Speeds of two DC motors are defined by the horizontal and vertical positions of the circular slider, equal to $Rcos(\theta)$ and $Rsin(\theta)$, respectively, for an angle θ° and radius *R* of the circular slider (see Figure 12-17). Relative to a clock face, the slider positions of 3 o'clock and 12 o'clock are equal to angles of 0° and 90°, with the angle increasing in an anti-clockwise direction.

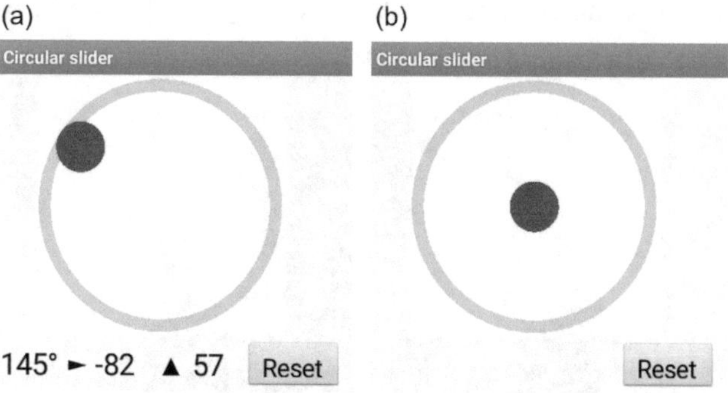

Figure 12-17. *Circular slider*

For example, left-only or forward-only directions correspond to circular slider positions of 180° or 90° with horizontal and vertical positions of (*–R, 0*) and (*0, R*), respectively. Figure 12-17a illustrates a circular slider position for moving the robot car in a left-forward direction at a 145° angle. With a circular slider radius of 100, the horizontal and vertical position values are –82 and 57, respectively. When the *Reset* button is clicked, the circular slider position is moved to the neutral position at the center (see Figure 12-17b).

On *MIT App Inventor*, the circular slider is formed with large (gray), white, and small (red) *Ball* components, which are located in the *Drawing and Animation* palette, of radius 100, 90, and 20, respectively (see Figure 12-17). The white *Ball* overlays the large *Ball* to create the circular slider ring with the small *Ball* indicating the circular slider position. The app includes labels for the circular slider position angle, the horizontal and vertical positions, and a reset button. The horizontal and vertical positions of the small *Ball* centered on the circular slider are $R + (R - r)\cos(\theta)$ and $R - (R - r)\sin(\theta)$, respectively, for an angle of θ° with R and r equal to the radii of the large *Ball* and small *Ball*, respectively (see Figure 12-18). On *MIT App Inventor*, the origin is at the top-left corner of the canvas, and when the ball moves down the screen, with angles of 90°–270°, the vertical position increases from zero to $2R$. With the origin at the *conventional* bottom-left corner, the vertical position of $R + (R - r)\sin(\theta)$ decreases from $2R$ to zero with angles of 90°–270°.

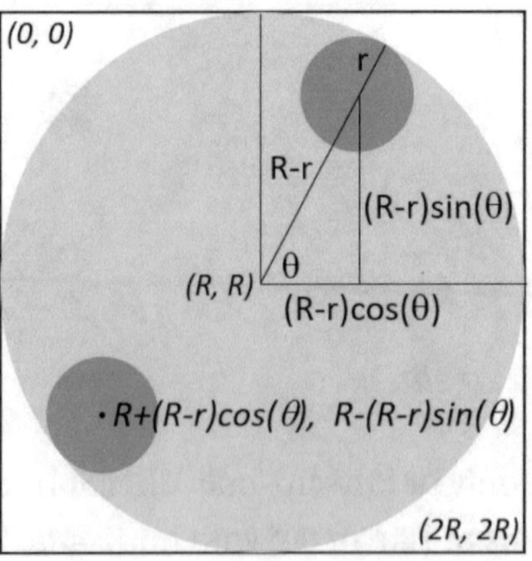

Figure 12-18. *Circular slider derivation*

The layout of the circular slider is shown in Figure 12-19, with the *OriginAtCenter* option selected for each *Ball* component and *Ball* center position equal to (*R, R*), where *R* is the radius of the large (gray) *Ball* component. A *Canvas* component, also located in the *Drawing and*

Animation palette, is a two-dimensional touch-sensitive panel with the touched location equal to (*x, y*) coordinates relative to the (*0, 0*) coordinates of the top-left corner of the *Canvas* component. The *Canvas* line width is 2 pixels, so a *Canvas* width of 204 pixels is required for a large *Ball* of radius 100 pixels.

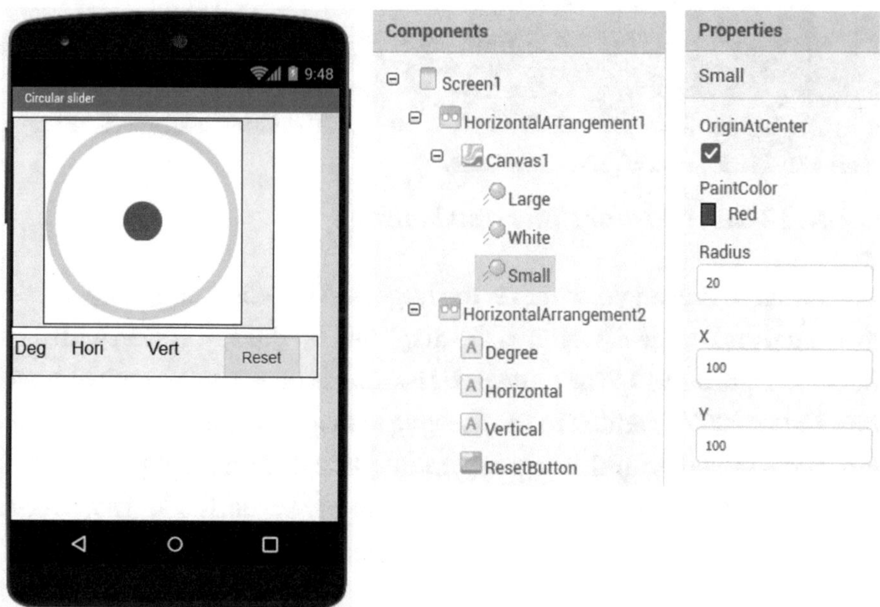

Figure 12-19. *Circular slider app layout*

When the small (red) *Ball* component is dragged over the *Canvas* component to an (*x, y*) coordinate position, the direction of movement, relative to the large *Ball* center, is the large *Ball Heading* with headings of 0° and 90° toward the right and to the top of the screen, respectively (see Figure 12-20).

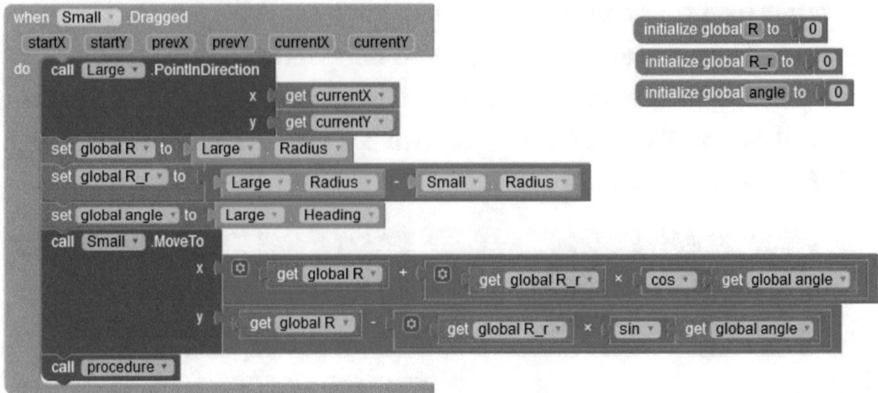

***Figure 12-20.** Circular slider app blocks (1)*

The small *Ball* angle, which is the large *Ball Heading*, and the horizontal and vertical positions are displayed on the app screen with blocks in Figure 12-21. The large *Ball Heading* is negative for angles greater than 180°, so 360° is added to the *heading* to display the *degree* value on the app. The *ALT* codes for the degree symbol (*Alt 248*) and the right (*Alt 16*) and up (*Alt 30*) arrows are obtained from the website `unicode-table.com/en/alt-codes` and are entered in the relevant textboxes.

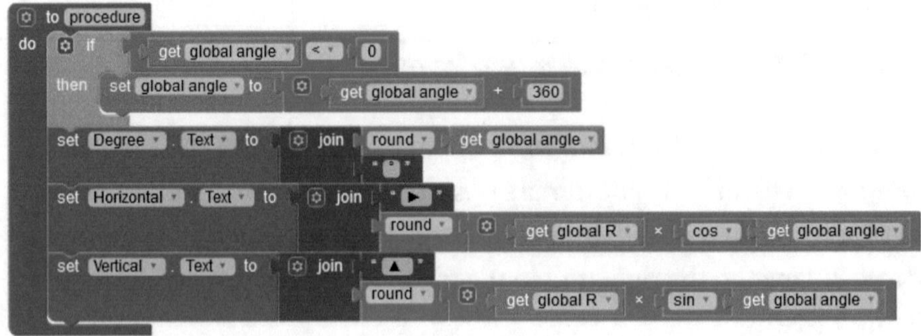

***Figure 12-21.** Circular slider app blocks (2)*

When the *Reset* button is clicked, the small *Ball* center is moved to the center of the large *Ball* at position (*R, R*), and the displayed angle and horizontal and vertical positions are reset (see Figure 12-22).

Figure 12-22. *Circular slider reset*

Vertical Slider

MIT App Inventor slider components are horizontal, which is sufficient for controlling DC motor speed or the left-right direction of a servo motor. A vertical slider is more appropriate for controlling the tilt position of a servo motor in a pan-tilt bracket (see Figure 12-23).

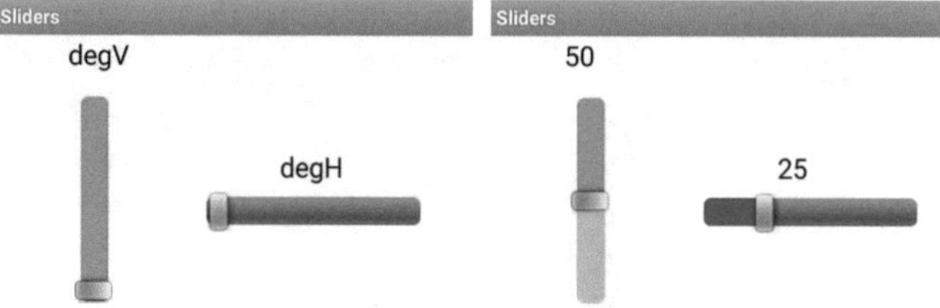

Figure 12-23. *Vertical and horizontal sliders*

Juan Antonio Villalpando provides an extension to rotate a label, a textbox, an image, a button, or a slider on *MIT App Inventor*. On the website `kio4.com/appinventor/294_extension_crear_componente.htm`, select and save the file *com.KIO4_CreateView.aix*, which is the fourth version. On *MIT App Inventor*, select the *Extension* palette on the left side of the Designer window, select *Import extension*, select *From my computer*, click *Browse* to locate the saved file, and select *Import*. The extension component *KIO4_CreateView* is displayed in the *Extension* palette. The extension is dragged onto the app screen and is displayed below the app layout as a *Non-visible component*.

A vertical slider is defined with blocks, in contrast to a horizontal slider, which is defined by the *Slider* component properties. For example, Figure 12-24 illustrates the app layout for a vertical (left side) and a horizontal slider, *Slider1* (right side). The impact of changing the vertical slider properties is viewed through the *MIT App Inventor Companion* app (*MIT AI2 Companion*), as the app layout only displays a horizontal *Slider* component, with the *KIO4_CreateView* extension displayed as a *Non-visible component*.

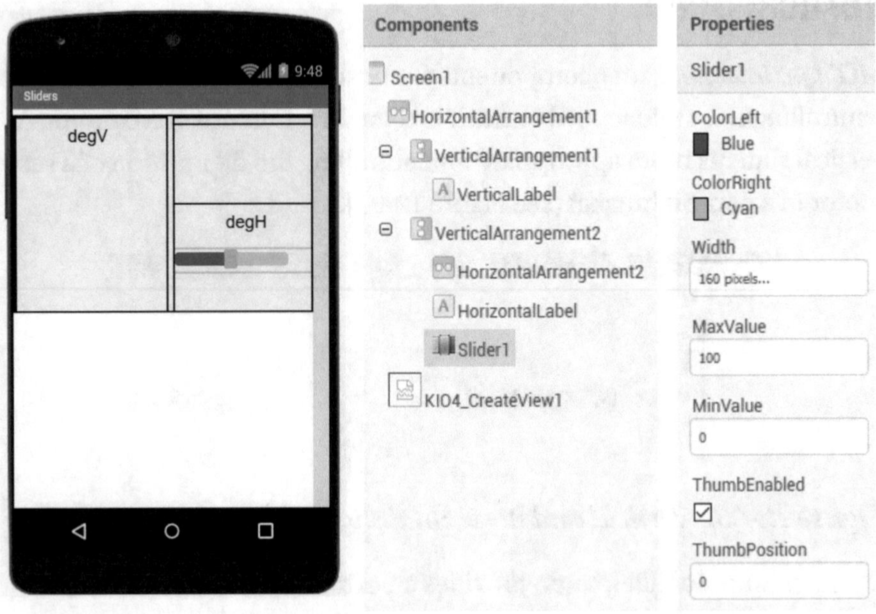

***Figure 12-24.** Vertical and horizontal slider app layout*

A *VerticalArrangement* contains the vertical slider, and the vertical slider properties defined in the block (see Figure 12-25) are relative to a horizontal slider. For a vertical slider, the *rotate* property is set at 90. The *width* property is the height of the vertical slider and conversely for the *height* property. A vertical slider width of 40 pixels, set with the *height* property, is recommended. There must be sufficient space above the vertical slider within the *VerticalArrangement*, which is set with the *topMargin* property; otherwise, the top of the vertical slider is not shown. For example, vertical sliders of height 100, 150, or 200 pixels require a *topMargin* property of at least 30, 60, or 80 pixels, respectively. The *minValue* and *maxValue* property values are equal to the maximum (top) and minimum (bottom) values of the vertical slider.

The *initialPosition* property is the vertical slider position when the app screen is initialized. The slider color changes from the *ProgressColor* to the *backgroundColor* property, as the slider position moves to the top of the vertical slider.

Figure 12-25. *Vertical slider initialize*

When the vertical slider is no longer touched, the vertical slider is effectively redrawn with the *KIO4_CreateView.Slider* block repeated, but with the initial position updated to the vertical slider position or the *thumbPosition* (see Figure 12-26). The two block structures, *Screen1. Initialize* and *KIO4_CreateView.StopTrackingTouch*, are identical apart from inclusion of the *KIO4_CreateView.RemoveViewAt* block and replacement of the *initialPosition* property from zero to *get thumbPosition* in the *KIO4_CreateView.slider* block.

Figure 12-26 only displays the *initialPosition* component of the *KIO4_CreateView.Slider* block, rather than repeat all the blocks shown in Figure 12-25.

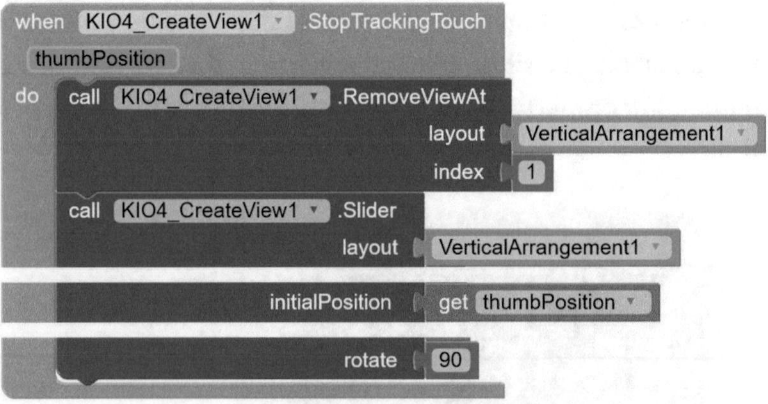

***Figure 12-26.** Vertical slider update*

The vertical slider or horizontal slider positions are accessed with the *PositionChanged* block (see Figure 12-27).

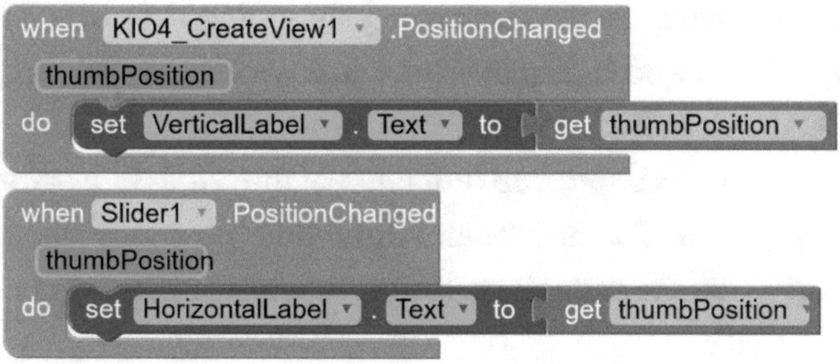

when KIO4_CreateView1 .PositionChanged
thumbPosition
do set VerticalLabel . Text to get thumbPosition

when Slider1 .PositionChanged
thumbPosition
do set HorizontalLabel . Text to get thumbPosition

Figure 12-27. *Vertical and horizontal slider positions*

The main difference between a vertical slider and a horizontal slider is that the vertical slider properties are defined in blocks, while the horizontal slider properties are defined in the app layout. A vertical slider also requires the *MIT App Inventor Companion* app (*MIT AI2 Companion*) to evaluate changes made to the slider properties.

Horizontal Slider Touchdown and Touchup

The vertical slider blocks include the *PositionChanged* and *StopTrackingTouch* blocks, which provide the slider position during and after slider movement. For example, the *PositionChanged* block is used to control the brightness of an LED, while the *StopTrackingTouch* block would be preferable to control a servo motor rather than continuously updating the servo motor position as the slider is moved.

An extension for the *touchdown* and *touchup* slider positions on *MIT App Inventor* is provided by Bryan. On the website `github.com/WatermelonOof/SliderTools-AI2-Kodular-Extension`, select and save the file *com.watermelonice.SliderTools.aix*, which is version 1.2. On *MIT App Inventor*, select the *Extension* palette on the left side of the Designer window, select *Import extension*, select *From my computer*, click *Browse* to locate the saved file, and select *Import*. The extension component

SliderTools is displayed in the *Extension* palette. The extension is dragged onto the app layout and is displayed as a *Non-visible component* (see Figure 12-29).

The *touchdown* and *touchup* functions of the *SliderTools* extension are illustrated by an app. The current and final slider positions when the slider is moved and when the slider is no longer moved are displayed on the app (see Figure 12-28).

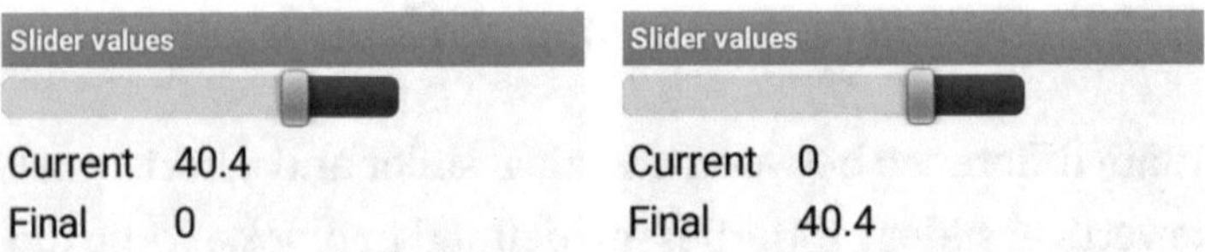

Figure 12-28. *Horizontal slider positions*

The app layout and components are shown in Figure 12-29, which include the *SliderTools* extension.

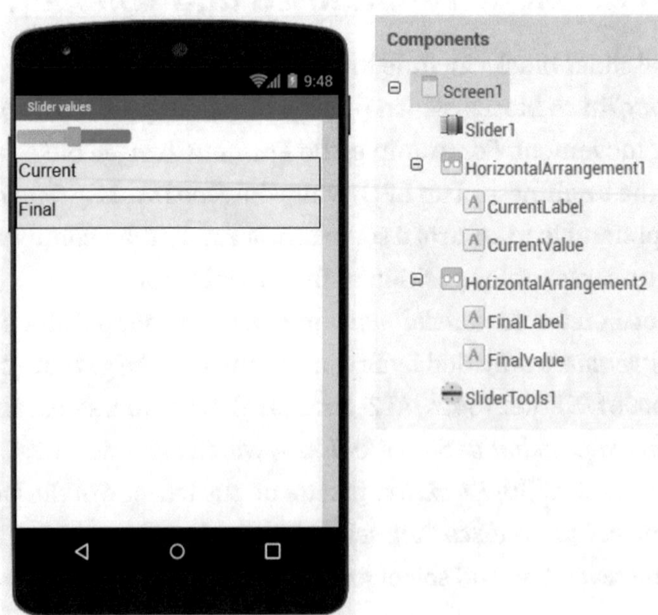

Figure 12-29. *Horizontal slider app layout*

With the *SliderTools* extension, the slider, for which the current and final positions are to be displayed, is registered with the extension when the app is loaded (see Figure 12-30). The *Changed* block provides the current slider position, *progress*, which is displayed in the *CurrentValue* label, and the *TouchDown* block sets the *FinalValue* label to zero. When the slider is no longer moved, the *TouchUp* block sets the *FinalValue* label to the last slider position, held by the *CurrentValue* label, and the *CurrentValue* label is then set to zero.

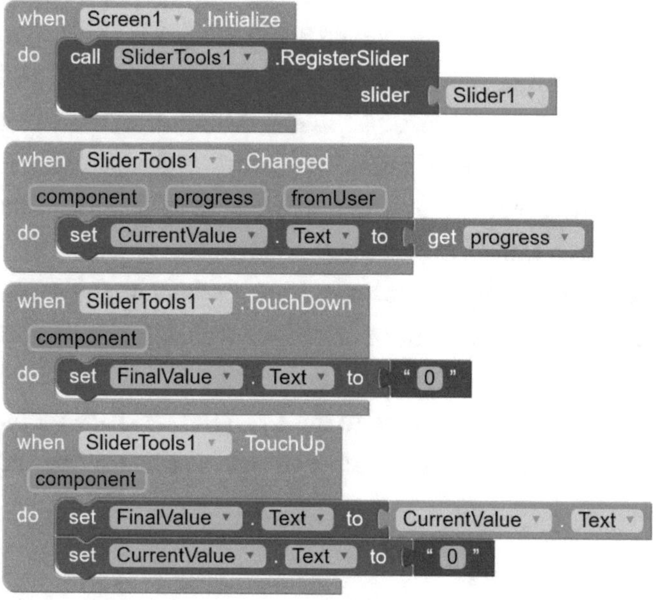

Figure 12-30. *Blocks for horizontal slider positions*

App to Control WS2812 RGB LEDs

An app to transmit and receive data, which was described earlier in the chapter, used Wi-Fi communication with the ESP32 microcontroller through a WLAN connection or through a software-enabled access point provided by the ESP32 microcontroller. The ESP32 microcontroller also supports Bluetooth communication, and the app, to control WS2812 5050 RGB LEDs, interacts with the ESP32 microcontroller by Bluetooth communication. The app is easily converted from Bluetooth to Wi-Fi communication, and both options are described.

Bluetooth Communication

A color is selected on a color wheel in an app, with a Bluetooth connection to the ESP32 microcontroller, which controls the color of a WS2812 5050 RGB LED ring or strip. A WS2812 5050 RGB LED refers to a WS2812 controller chip incorporated in an RGB (Red Green Blue) LED, which has dimensions of 5.0 × 5.0mm. *Neopixel* is the Adafruit brand name for individually addressable RGB LEDs. The *Adafruit_Neopixel* library, which is available within the Arduino IDE, is applicable to WS2812 5050 RGB LED strips and rings, as well as to *Neopixel* products.

The color selection app consists of a color wheel image loaded onto an *MIT App Inventor Canvas* component with a *Ball* component indicating the selected color on the color wheel (see Figure 12-31). The *Canvas* and *Ball* components are both located in the *Drawing and Animation* palette. A color wheel image is obtained from a Google search on "*rgb color wheel 320*".

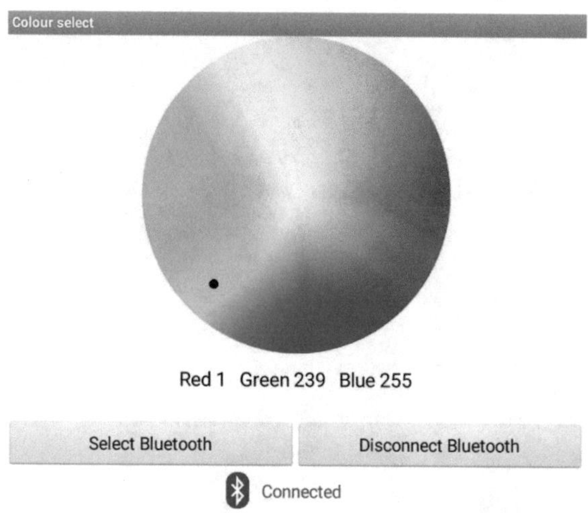

Figure 12-31. *Color selection on a color wheel app with Bluetooth*

The app layout consists of a *Canvas* and a *Ball* component with a *Label* component to display the RGB color components (see Figure 12-32). The color wheel image is uploaded as the *BackgroundImage* property of the *Canvas* component with *Height* and *Width* properties of 320 pixels. The *Ball* component initial (*x*, *y*) coordinates of (160, 160) place the *Ball* component at the center of the color wheel. A *Listpicker* component, to display available Bluetooth devices; a *Button* component, to connect or disconnect the Bluetooth connection; and a *Label* component, to display the Bluetooth connection status, are included in the app layout. The *BluetoothClient* component, located in the *Connectivity* palette on the left side of the Designer window, is displayed below the app layout as a *Non-visible component.*

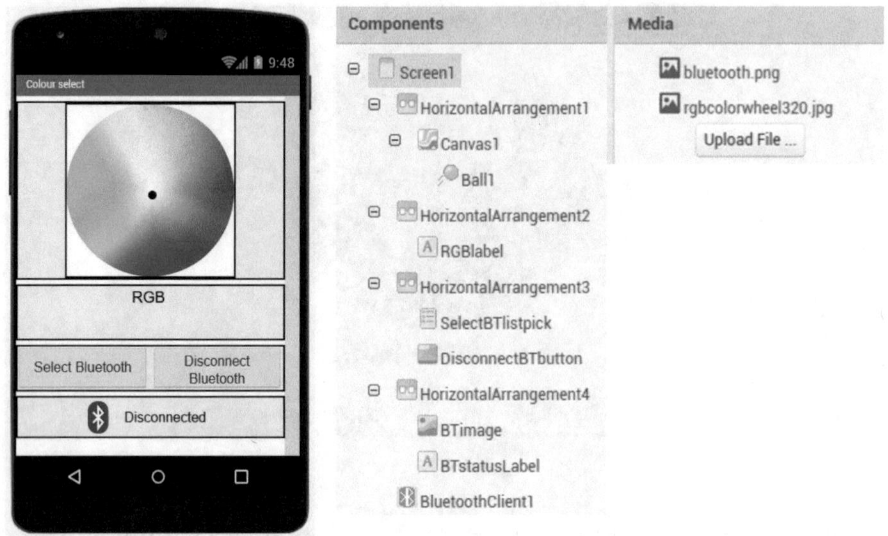

***Figure 12-32.** Color selection app layout with Bluetooth*

The *split color* block derives the RGB color components of the pixel identified by the position of the *Ball* component (see Figure 12-33). Each pixel has four parameters held in a *split color* list, consisting of the three RGB color components and a color saturation value. The *labels* procedure is called to obtain the RGB color components from the list indexed one to three (see Figure 12-34), which are combined with "*Red*", " *Green*", and "*Blue*" text to form the *RGBlabel* text.

Figure 12-33. *Color components*

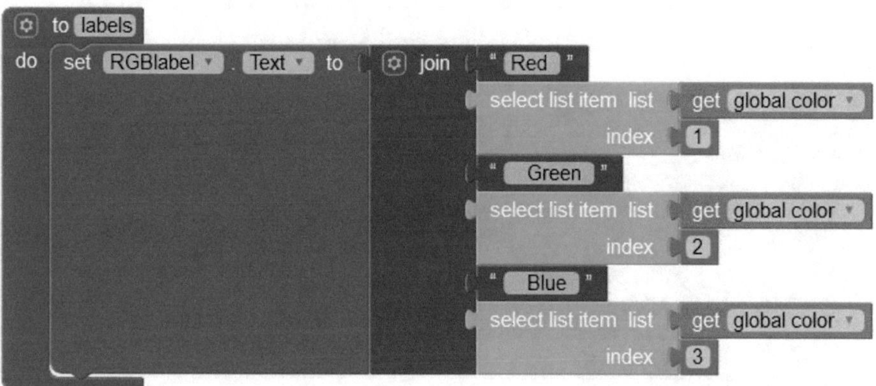

Figure 12-34. *Color components with Bluetooth*

After the *Ball* component is dragged across the *Canvas* component and the screen is no longer touched, the *RGBlabel* text is transmitted to the ESP32 microcontroller by Bluetooth communication from the Android tablet or mobile phone hosting the app (see Figure 12-35).

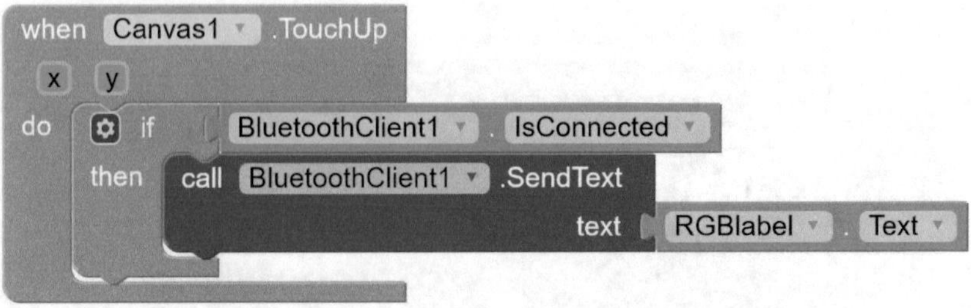

when Canvas1 .TouchUp
x y
do if BluetoothClient1 . IsConnected
then call BluetoothClient1 .SendText
text RGBlabel . Text

***Figure 12-35.** Bluetooth communication*

When the *SelectBTlistpick Listpicker* button is clicked, a Bluetooth connection to the selected device is made, and the text *Connected* is displayed as black text (see Figures 12-31 and 12-36). The *DisconnectBTbutton* button enables disconnection of the Bluetooth connection, and *Disconnected* is displayed as red text.

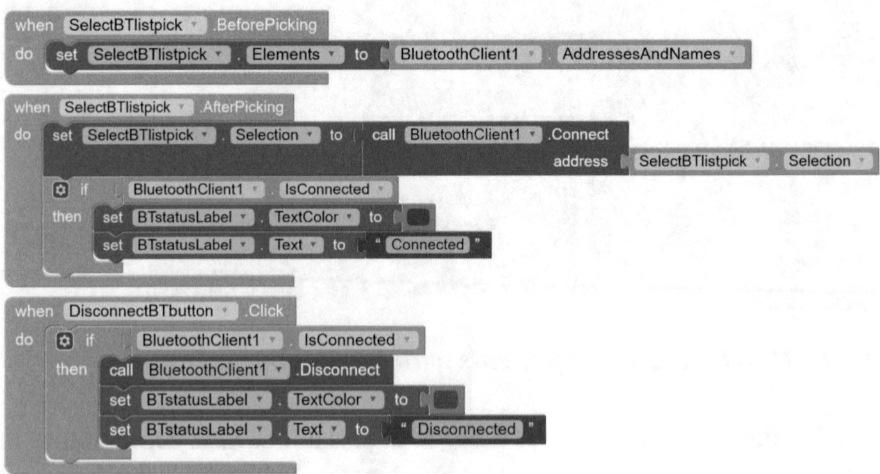

***Figure 12-36.** Bluetooth connection*

The color selection app is demonstrated with an ESP32 DEVKIT DOIT module connected to a WS2812 5050 RGB LED ring consisting of 12 LEDs (see Figure 12-37).

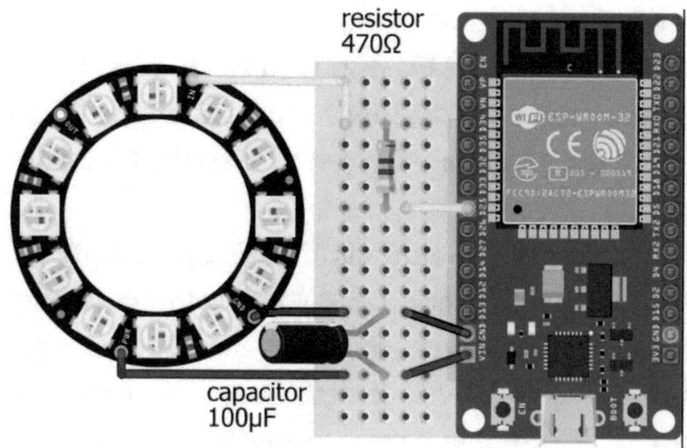

***Figure 12-37.** WS2812 RGB LED ring and ESP32 development board*

A 100μF capacitor is connected across the power supply to the WS2812 5050 RGB LED ring to protect the LEDs from a current surge when the power supply is turned on. A 470Ω resistor is fitted between the *data in* pin of the WS2812 5050 RGB LED ring and the ESP32 module *data* pin to prevent voltage spikes on the data line, which could damage the first RGB LED of the ring (see Figure 12-37 with connections in Table 12-1).

***Table 12-1.** WS2812 RGB LED strip and microphone with ESP8266 development board*

Component	Connect to	and to
LED ring VCC	ESP32 5V	100μF capacitor positive
LED ring GND	ESP32 GND	100μF capacitor negative
LED ring DI (data in)	470Ω resistor	ESP32 GPIO 25

An RGB LED uses up to 60mA with all three LEDs at full brightness. When an ESP32 module is powered by USB, the 5V pin supplies 400mA, so an absolute maximum of six RGB LEDs at full brightness are powered by the ESP32 module 5V pin. If the RGB LEDs are turned on at brightness level of 1, 40, or 100, with a scale of 1–255, then the current usage of a WS2812 5050 RGB LED ring, with 12 LEDs, is 15, 75, or 160mA, respectively. Therefore, a WS2812 5050 RGB LED ring, with 12 LEDs, with maximum brightness of 100 is safely powered by the ESP32 development board 5V pin.

The sketch in Listing 12-5 controls a WS2812 5050 RGB LED ring from the RGB values supplied, with Bluetooth communication, by the Android tablet or mobile phone hosting the app. The message received by the ESP32 microcontroller has format "*Red.N...Green.N...Blue.N*", with *N* representing a number between 0 and 255 and a dot indicating a space. The message is parsed into the three RGB color components with substrings from the fourth character to the character prior to the letter *G*, from the sixth character after the letter *G* to the character prior to the letter *B*, and from the fifth character after the letter *B* to the end of the string. The RGB color components are converted to a 32-bit integer, as required by the *Adafruit_NeoPixel* library. The instructions `fill(color)` and `show()` set the RGB LED color and update the RGB LED display.

Listing 12-5. WS2812 color selection with Bluetooth

```
#include <BluetoothSerial.h>     // include BluetoothSerial library
BluetoothSerial SerialBT;
#include <Adafruit_NeoPixel.h>  // include Neopixel library
int LEDpin = 25;                // define data pin
int LEDnumber = 12;             // number of LEDs on ring
int32_t color;                  // color is 32-bit or signed long
                                // associate ring with Neopixel library
Adafruit_NeoPixel ring(LEDnumber, LEDpin,
                                NEO_GRB + NEO_KHZ800);
String str, substr;
char c;
int R,G,B, indexS, indexF;
```

```
void setup()
{
  Serial.begin(115200);                     // Serial Monitor baud rate
                                            // initialize Bluetooth
  SerialBT.begin("ESP32 Bluetooth");
  ring.begin();
  ring.setBrightness(1);                    // LED ring brightness
  ring.show();
}

void loop()
{
  if(SerialBT.available())                  // character in Bluetooth buffer
  {
    str = "";                               // reset string
    while(SerialBT.available()>0)
    {
      c = SerialBT.read();                  // accumulate buffer to a string
      str = str + String(c);
    }
    Serial.println(str);                    // display string on Serial Monitor
    indexS = 4;                             // parse red color component
    indexF = str.indexOf("G");              // between space after "Red" and
                                            // the letter G of "Green"
    substr = str.substring(indexS, indexF);
    R = substr.toInt();
    indexS = indexF + 6;                    // parse green color component
    indexF = str.indexOf("B");              // between space after "Green"
                                            // and the letter B of "Blue"
    substr = str.substring(indexS, indexF);
    G = substr.toInt();
    indexS = indexF + 5;                    // parse blue color component
```

```
    substr = str.substring(indexS);  // following space after "Blue"
    B = substr.toInt();
                                     // display color components
    Serial.printf("RGB: %d %d %d \n", R, G, B);
    color = ring.Color(R, G, B);     // convert RGB values to color
    ring.fill(color);                // set the LED color
    ring.show();                     // update LED ring color
  }
}
```

Wi-Fi Communication

The app layout with Wi-Fi communication is similar to the app layout with Bluetooth communication. The *Listpicker*, *Button*, and *Label* components, associated with Bluetooth connection status, are replaced by a *Textbox* component in which the last two numbers of the IP address of the server, which is the ESP32 microcontroller, are entered for Wi-Fi communication. The *Web* component, located in the *Connectivity* palette and displayed below the app layout as a *Non-visible component*, performs the *HTTP GET* request with the ESP32 microcontroller (see Figure 12-38).

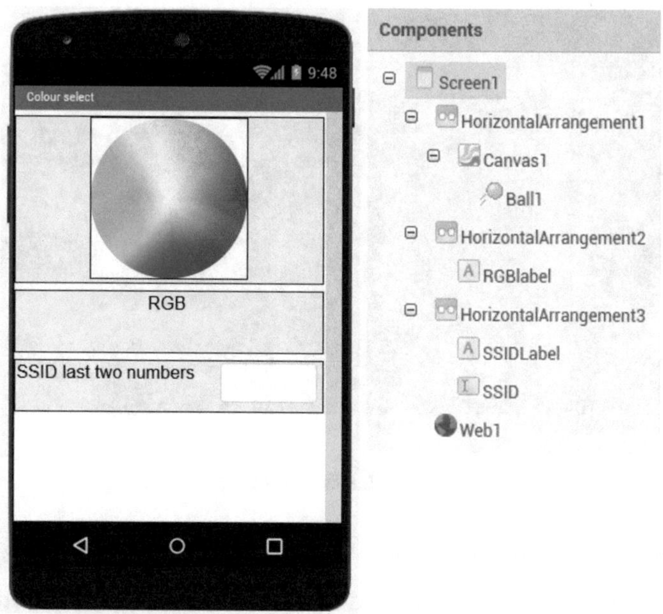

Figure 12-38. *Color selection on a color wheel app with Wi-Fi*

Blocks to move the *Ball* component across the *Canvas* component and obtain the red, green, and blue color components are identical to the blocks in Figures 12-33 and 12-34. When the screen is no longer touched, the *RGBlabel* text is displayed, and the content of the URL, to be transmitted to the server, is generated by the *URL* procedure (see Figure 12-39). The format of the URL content is *R=valR&G=valG&B=valB*, where *valR*, *valG*, and *valB* are the RGB color components obtained from the block in Figure 12-39. In Figure 12-33, the block to call the *URL* procedure is added after the block to call the *labels* procedure.

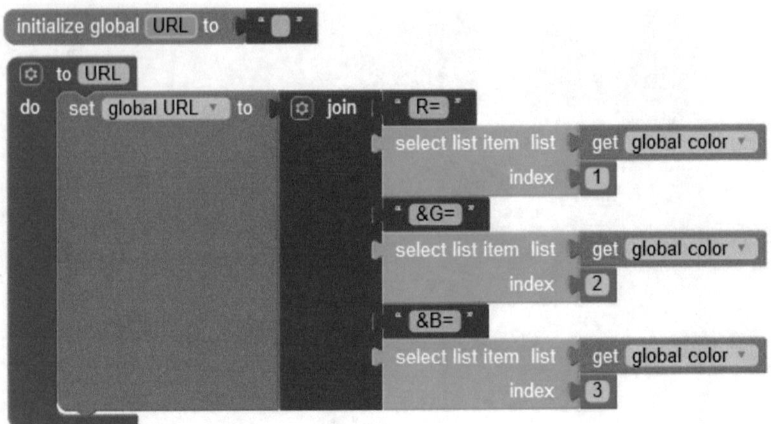

Figure 12-39. *Color components with Wi-Fi*

The *Web* component transmits, to the server, an *HTTP GET* request URL consisting of the server IP address, the */wheel?* label, and the RGB values formatted as *name=value* pairs. For example, given a server IP address of *192.168.1.219*, the URL is formatted as `http://192.168.1.219/wheel?R=valueR&G=valueG&B=valueB` (see Figure 12-40), and the *HTTP GET* request is *GET /wheel?R=valueR&G=valueG&B=valueB HTTP/1.1*.

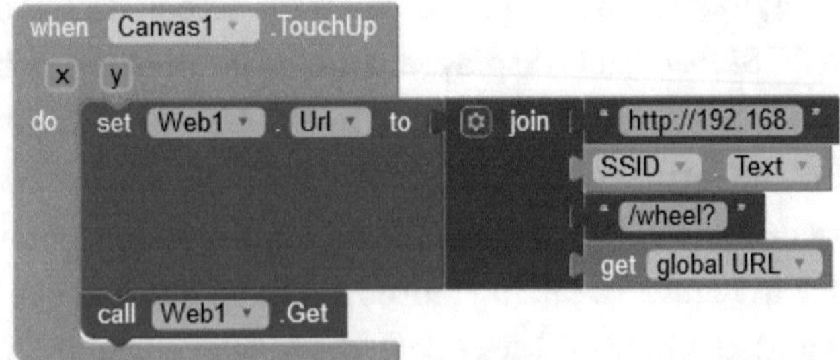

Figure 12-40. *Wi-Fi communication*

The sketch in Listing 12-6 is the Wi-Fi communication equivalent of Listing 12-5 for Bluetooth communication. The message received by the ESP32 microcontroller contains the text "*R=N&G=N&B=N HTTP*", with *N* representing a number between 0 and 255. The message is parsed into the three RGB color components with substrings from the character after "*R=*" to the ampersand before the letter *G*, from the character after "*G=*" to the ampersand before the letter *B*, and from the character after "*B=*" to the letter *H*. The RGB color components are converted to a 32-bit integer to set the RGB LED color and update the WS2812 5050 RGB LED ring display.

Listing 12-6. WS2812 color selection with Wi-Fi

```
#include <WiFi.h>                    // include WiFi library
WiFiClient client;                   // associate client and server with
                                     //   WiFiClient and WiFiServer libraries
WiFiServer server(80);
#include <ssid_password.h>           // file with SSID and password
#include <Adafruit_NeoPixel.h>       // include Neopixel library
int LEDpin = 25;                     // define data pin
int LEDnumber = 12;                  // number of LEDs on ring
int32_t color;                       // color is 32-bit or signed long
                                     // associate ring with Neopixel library
Adafruit_NeoPixel ring(LEDnumber, LEDpin, NEO_GRB + NEO_KHZ800);
String str;
int R,G,B, indexS, indexF;

void setup()
{
  Serial.begin(115200);              // Serial Monitor baud rate
  WiFi.begin(ssid, password);        // initialize and connect Wi-Fi
  while (WiFi.status() != WL_CONNECTED) delay(500);
                                     // display server IP address
  Serial.println(WiFi.localIP());
  server.begin();                    // initiate server
}
```

```
void loop()
{
  client = server.available();
  if (client)                    // initialize client connection
  {                              // no client request, do nothing
    while (!client.available()) {};
                                 // map str to message
    str = client.readStringUntil('\r');
    Serial.println(str);         // display HTTP GET request
    indexS = str.indexOf("R="); // position of "R=" in string
    indexF = str.indexOf("G=");
                                 // red color component
    R = str.substring(indexS, indexF-1);
    indexS = indexF;
    indexF = str.indexOf("B=");
                                 // green color component
    G = str.substring(indexS, indexF-1);
    indexS = indexF;
    indexF = str.indexOf("H");
                                 // blue color component
    B = str.substring(indexS, indexF-1);
                                 // display color components
    Serial.printf("RGB: %d %d %d \n", R, G, B);
    color = ring.Color(R, G, B); // convert RGB values to color
    ring.fill(color);            // set the LED color
    ring.show();                 // update LED ring color
    client.stop();               // close connection
  }
}
```

CHAPTER 13

Remote Control Motors

Servo motors are used in a variety of applications, such as robotics, tracking systems, and positioning devices, with DC (direct current) motors also used in portable power tools and electric vehicles. This chapter describes controlling servo motors and DC motors with the ESP32 microcontroller and also with the combination of an app and the ESP32 microcontroller.

Servo Motor

A servo motor is controlled by the pulse length of a 50Hz square wave, which has a wavelength of 20ms. The Tower Pro SG90 servo motor moves to angle 0° or 180° with a square wave pulse length of 500μs or 2500μs, while a pulse length of 1000μs or 2000μs is required for the Tower Pro MG995 servo motor. For both servo motors, a 50Hz square wave with pulse length of 1500μs, corresponding to a duty cycle of 7.5% = 1.5ms/20ms, moves a servo motor to an angle of 90°.

A servo motor has three connections normally colored red for power, brown or black for GND, and orange or white for signal. A servo motor runs at 5V and uses up to hundreds of milliamps during the few

N. Cameron, *ESP32 Formats and Communication*,
https://doi.org/10.1007/978-1-4842-9376-8_13

milliseconds that the motor is turning, which exceeds the 40mA output of an ESP32 module GPIO pin. A servo motor requires an external power supply with GND of the external power supply connected to the ESP32 module GND. The ESP32 microcontroller controls a servo motor position by either generating the square wave pulse length directly with the *ledc* function or using the *ESP32Servo* library instructions. Controlling a servo motor with both methods is described in this chapter.

ledc Function

The *ledc* function is primarily for *LED C*ontrol by generating a PWM (Pulse-Width Modulation) signal to vary the brightness of an LED. All ESP32 microcontroller GPIO pins, except the input-only pins (GPIO 34, 35, 36, and 39), are PWM pins to generate a square wave with variable duty cycle. The three instructions required to generate a square wave are

```
ledcAttachPin(wavePin, channel)       // define PWM channel
ledcSetup(channel, freq, resolution)  // frequency (Hz) and resolution
ledcWrite(channel, duty)              // scaled duty cycle (0 to 255)
```

with the parameters GPIO pin to output the square wave (*wavePin*), PWM output channel (*channel*) between 0 and 15, square wave frequency (*freq*), PWM resolution (*resolution*), and scaled duty cycle (*duty*). The *ledc* instructions are available in the file *User\AppData\Local\Arduino15\packages\esp32\hardware\esp32\version\cores\esp32\esp32-hal-ledc.cpp*. The ESP32 microcontroller uses 8-, 10-, 12-, or 15-bit resolution for PWM, providing ranges of 0–255, 0–1023, 0–4095, or 0–32767, respectively, for the scaled duty cycle.

A Tower Pro SG90 servo motor moves to an angle between 0° and 180° with a square wave signal of frequency 50Hz and a pulse length between 500μs and 2500μs. The square wave pulse length of *(500 + 2000 × angle/180)*μs and wavelength of $(10^6/frequency)$μs correspond to a duty cycle equal to pulse length/wavelength, which is scaled by the PWM resolution. For example, moving a Tower Pro SG90 servo motor to an angle of 45° requires a 50Hz square wave signal with a pulse length of 1000μs, which corresponds to a duty cycle of 0.05, given the signal wavelength of 20ms. The 8-bit PWM resolution has a maximum value of $255 = 2^8 - 1$, and the scaled duty cycle is $0.05 \times 255 = 12.75$. Instructions to generate a square wave to move a servo motor to a given angle are shown in Listing 13-1. The sketch on the right of Table 13-2 illustrates controlling a servo motor with the *ledc* function.

Listing 13-1. ledc function instructions

```
freq = 50                          // square wave frequency
wavelength = pow(10,6)/freq        // wavelength (μs)
resolution = 8                     // PWM resolution
pulse = 500+2000*angle/180         // pulse length (μs)
                                   // scaled duty cycle
duty = round(pulse*(pow(2,resolution)-1)/wavelength)
ledcWrite(channel, duty)           // generate square wave
```

The available *ledc* channels are 0–15. The ESP32-CAM module accesses *ledc_channel_0* on *ledc_timer_0*, as indicated in Listing 11-3, so other *ledc* channels are utilized if controlling a servo motor with an ESP32-CAM module. Details of the 16 *ledc* channels, as defined in the file *esp32\version\cores\esp32\esp32-hal-ledc.cpp*, are given in Table 13-1. One group of channels operates in a high-speed mode and the other group in a low-speed mode with an updated PWM duty cycle implemented in hardware and software, respectively. Further details are available at `docs.espressif.com/projects/esp-idf/en/latest/esp32/api-reference/peripherals/ledc.html`.

Table 13-1. *ESP32 ledc channels and timers*

Channel	Timer	Group 0 ledc_channel	Group 1 ledc_channel
0	0	0	8
1	0	1	9
2	1	2	10
3	1	3	11
4	2	4	12
5	2	5	13
6	3	6	14
7	3	7	15

ESP32Servo Library

With the *ESP32Servo* library, the servo motor is moved to angle θ° by either the instruction `write(θ)` or `writeMicroseconds(N)`, where *N* is the corresponding square wave pulse length. The square wave frequency of 50Hz is defined with the `setPeriodHertz(freq)` instruction.

The *ESP32Servo* library includes the parameter pair *DEFAULT_uS_LOW* and *DEFAULT_uS_HIGH*, which define the range of pulse lengths required to move a servo motor from angle 0° to 180°, and the parameter pair *MIN_PULSE_WIDTH* and *MAX_PULSE_WIDTH*, which define the minimum and maximum square wave pulse lengths.

A servo motor is initialized with the `attach()` instruction, which has two formats. With the `attach(servoPin)` instruction, the subsequent `write()` instruction maps the angles 0°–180° to the range *DEFAULT_uS_LOW* to *DEFAULT_uS_HIGH* microseconds. With the `attach(servoPin, min, max)` instruction, the angles are mapped to the range *min* to *max* microseconds, provided *min* is not less than *MIN_PULSE_WIDTH* and *max* is not greater than *MAX_PULSE_WIDTH*.

The `write(N)` instruction has dual functionality, as when the parameter *N* is greater than *MIN_PULSE_WIDTH*, the instruction is interpreted as `writeMicroseconds(N)`. If the *ESP32Servo* library parameter pairs are unequal, then the `write()` instruction with the parameter equal to an angle or to the corresponding square wave pulse length does not move the servo motor to the same position. For example, in the library *ESP32Servo.h* file, the *DEFAULT* values are 544–2400, and the *PULSE_WIDTH* values are 500–2500. Use of the `attach(servoPin)` instruction results in the `write(N)` function mapping the parameter *N* to the 544–2400μs range or to the 500–2500μs range, with the parameter *N* equal to an angle or to a square wave pulse length.

The `attach(servoPin, min, max)` instruction ensures that the `write(N)` instruction moves the servo motor to the same position irrespective of the parameter *N* being equal to an angle or to a square wave pulse length. If the pulse length required to move the servo motor to 0° is less than *MIN_PULSE_WIDTH*, then the line `#define MIN_PULSE_WIDTH 500` of the *ESP32Servo.h* file must be updated.

The sketch in Listing 13-2 calibrates a servo motor by entering different microsecond values on the Serial Monitor and measuring the servo motor angle. For example, values of 800μs and 1700μs corresponded to angles of 45° and 135° giving the equation *pulse = 350 + 10 × angle = 350 + (2150 – 350) × angle/180* and a pulse length range of 350–2150μs to move the servo motor between angles of 0° and 180°. The *ESP32Servo.h* file must be updated, as the pulse length required to move the servo motor to an angle of 0° is less than the *MIN_PULSE_WIDTH* value of 500.

Listing 13-2. Servo motor calibration

```
#include <ESP32Servo.h>                // Servo library for ESP32
Servo servo;                           // associate servo with library
int servoPin = 5;                      // servo pin
int pulse;

void setup()
{
  Serial.begin(115200);                // Serial Monitor baud rate
  servo.attach(servoPin);              // initialize servo motor
}

void loop()
{
  if(Serial.available())               // text entered in Serial Monitor
  {
    pulse = Serial.parseInt();         // parse text to integer
    servo.writeMicroseconds(pulse);    // move servo motor
  }
}
```

The sketch on the left of Table 13-2 illustrates controlling a servo motor with the *ESP32Servo* library by moving the servo motor to angles of 45°, 90°, and 135°, given that a 50Hz square wave with pulse length of 350μs or 2150μs moves the servo motor to angle of 0° or 180°, respectively. The corresponding sketch with the *ledc* function is also shown in Table 13-2. Differences between the *ESP32Servo* library and *ledc* function instructions are highlighted in bold.

Table 13-2. *Servo motor control*

ESP32Servo library	ledc function
#include <ESP32Servo.h>	
Servo servo;	**int channel = 0;**
int servoPin = 5;	int servoPin = 5;
int angle, pulse, freq = 50;	int angle, pulse, freq = 50, **duty, resol = 8**;
int low = 350, high = 2150;	int low = 350, high = 2150;
void setup() {	void setup() {
servo.attach(servoPin, low, high);	**ledcAttachPin(servoPin, channel);**
servo.setPeriodHertz(freq);	**ledcSetup(channel, freq, resol);**
}	}
void loop() {	void loop() {
for (int i=1; i<4; i++)	for (int i=1; i<4; i++)
{	{
angle = 45*i;	angle = 45*i;
pulse = low + (high-low)*angle/180.0;	pulse = low + (high-low)*angle/180.0;
// servo.write(angle);	**duty = pulse*freq*(pow(2,resol)-1) * pow(10,-6);**
servo.writeMicroseconds(pulse);	**ledcWrite(channel, duty);**
delay(1000);	delay(1000);
} }	} }

App to Control a Servo Motor

A demonstration app with a slider to control a servo motor is illustrated in Figure 13-1. When the slider is moved, the app transmits the corresponding servo angle to the ESP32 microcontroller. A software-enabled access point, *softAP*, is provided by the ESP32 microcontroller for communication with the app. The *softAP* IP address of *192.168.4.1* is displayed by the ESP32 microcontroller on the Serial Monitor. Remember to connect the Android tablet or mobile phone hosting the app to the *softAP*. The *softAP* IP address is preset, so a server IP address does not have to be defined by the user for communication between the ESP32 microcontroller and the Android tablet or mobile phone hosting the app.

Figure 13-1. *App slider to control a servo motor*

The app layout is shown in Figure 13-2 with the horizontal slider defined by the *Slider* component properties, as described in Chapter 12, "Control Apps." The servo motor angle range of 0°–180° defines the minimum and maximum values of the slider, with the initial slider position set to 90. The *Web* component, located in the *Connectivity* palette and displayed below the app layout as a *Non-visible component*, performs the *HTTP GET* request by the client, which is the app, to the server, which is the ESP32 microcontroller.

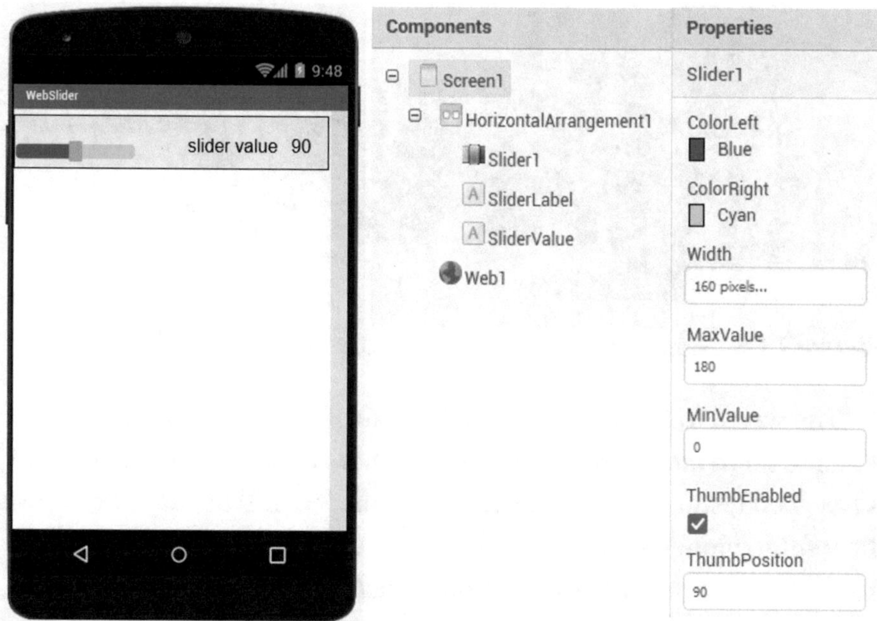

Figure 13-2. *Slider control app layout*

Blocks for the slider and the *HTTP GET* request are shown in Figure 13-3. When the slider position is changed to the value *N*, the app generates the URL `http://192.168.4.1/slider?value=N`, for the *softAP* IP address of *192.168.4.1*. The *Web* component transmits, to the server, the *HTTP GET* request of *GET /slider?value=N HTTP/1.1*. The slider minimum value is on the left of the slider, while a servo motor angle of 0° moves the servo motor to the right. For consistency, the slider position, *thumbPosition,* is transformed to the servo motor angle of 180-*position.*

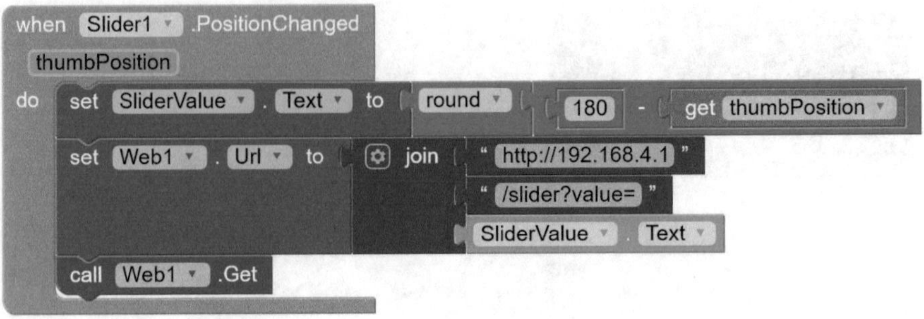

Figure 13-3. *Blocks for an app to control a servo motor*

The sketch to control a servo motor with an app transmitting the required servo motor angle to the ESP32 microcontroller (see Listing 13-3) is based on Listing 12-3 and the sketch on the left of Table 13-2, which uses the *ledc* function. When the server receives the *HTTP GET* request from the client, the transmitted servo motor angle is extracted from the *HTTP GET* request, and the corresponding duty cycle for the 50Hz square wave is determined. The server response to the *HTTP GET* request only confirms the request as no data is transmitted to the client.

Listing 13-3. App to control a servo motor

```
#include <WiFi.h>                // include WiFi library
WiFiClient client;               // associate client and server with
WiFiServer server(80);           // WiFiClient and WiFiServer libraries
char ssidAP[] = "ESP32";         // softAP SSID and password
char passwordAP[] = "12345678";
String str, NNN;
int indexS, indexF;
int servoPin = 5;                // servo motor pin
                                 // ledc channel, frequency and resolution
int channel = 1, freq = 50, resol = 8;
int low = 350, high = 2150;      // pulses to move to 0° and 180°
int angle, pulse, duty;
float scalar;
```

```
void setup()
{
  Serial.begin(115200);                   // Serial Monitor baud rate
  WiFi.softAP(ssidAP, passwordAP);        // connect to softAP
  Serial.println(WiFi.softAPIP());        // display softAP IP address
  server.begin();                         // initiate server
  ledcAttachPin(servoPin, channel);       // initialize ledc channel
  ledcSetup(channel, freq, resol);
  scalar = freq*(pow(2,resol)-1)/pow(10,6);
}

void loop()
{
  client = server.available();
  if (client)                             // initialize client connection
  {
    while (!client.available()) {};       // no client request, do nothing
    str = client.readStringUntil('\r'); // map str to message
    Serial.println(str);
    indexS = str.indexOf("value");        // position of "value" in string
    indexF = str.indexOf("HTTP");         // value=NNN HTTP
    NNN = str.substring(indexS+6, indexF-1);
                                    // HTTP header and response code
    client.println("HTTP/1.1 200 OK");
                                          // \n to generate blank line
    client.println("Content-type:text/html\n");
    client.stop();                        // close connection
    angle = NNN.toInt();                  // servo motor angle
    pulse = low + (high-low)*angle/180; // square wave pulse length
    duty = round(pulse*scalar);           // scaled duty cycle
    ledcWrite(channel, duty);             // generate square wave
  }
}
```

When the app slider is moved, multiple *HTTP GET* requests are transmitted to the server for every slider position between the initial and final slider positions. One solution is to only transmit an *HTTP GET* request when the user is no longer touching the slider, with the *touchup* function. The *SliderTools* extension provides the required functionality, and installation of the *SliderTools* extension is described in Chapter 12, "Controlling apps," section "Horizontal Slider Touchdown and Touchup." The slider is registered with the *SliderTools* component, the *Changed* block displays the current slider position, and the *TouchUp* block transmits the *HTTP GET* request with only the last slider position (see Figure 13-4). The *SliderTools* component is displayed below the app layout as a *Non-visible component.*

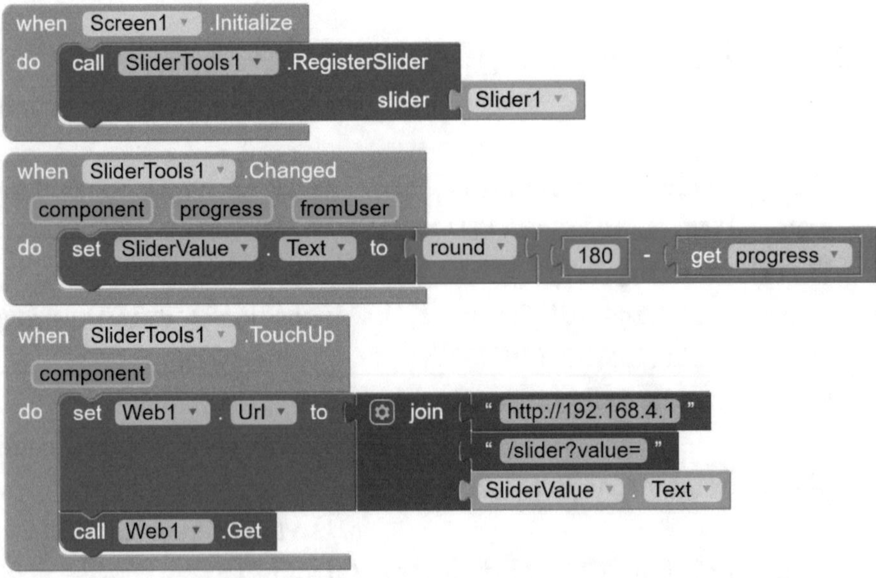

Figure 13-4. *Blocks for an app to control a servo motor with a final slider position*

Alternatively, a button is included in the app, and when the button is clicked, the client *HTTP GET* request is transmitted to the server. Button images are uploaded in the *Media* palette and then mapped to a button in the *Button Properties* palette (see Figure 13-5).

***Figure 13-5.** Slider control app with a button layout*

When the slider is moved, the *SliderValue* label is updated with the slider position. When the button is clicked, the *HTTP GET* request containing the final slider position is transmitted to the server (see Figure 13-6).

The effect of including the *SliderTools* extension or the button is the same, but with the former the app layout does not include an additional button, and with the latter an extension is not required.

```
when Slider1 .PositionChanged
  thumbPosition
do  set SliderValue . Text to  round  180 - get thumbPosition

when Button1 .Click
do  set Web1 . Url to  join  " http://192.168.4.1 "
                              " /slider?value= "
                              SliderValue . Text
    call Web1 .Get
```

***Figure 13-6.** Blocks for a slider control app with a button*

DC Motors

A DC (direct current) brushed motor has an operating voltage of 3–12V, with a recommended voltage of 6–8V. The DC motor contains gears with a gear ratio of 1:48 to turn the axle at a lower speed than the DC motor speed and increase the torque delivered by the motor.

The TB6612FNG and L298N motor driver boards control the direction and speed of a DC motor with an H-bridge and with Pulse-Width Modulation (PWM), respectively. The H-bridge is formed by two pairs of switches, on opposite sides of the motor, and the direction of current, through the motor, changes as each diagonally opposite pair of switches opens. With Pulse-Width Modulation, the pulse length of a square wave is varied, with a longer pulse length equivalent to a higher duty cycle of the square wave, corresponding to a faster motor speed, when a DC motor is controlled by a TB6612FNG or a L298N motor driver board.

The TB6612FNG and L298N motor driver boards, shown to scale in Figure 13-7, both control two DC motors.

Figure 13-7. *TB6612FNG and L298N motor driver boards*

Features of the TB6612FNG and L298N motor driver boards are given in Table 13-3. A TB6612FNG motor driver board H-bridge consists of MOSFETs, rather than BJTs as in a L298N motor driver board, that increases the efficiency and the maximum motor speed (RPM, Revolutions Per Minute) compared with the L298N motor driver board (see Figure 13-8). Efficiencies of 71–94% with a TB6612FNG motor driver board are substantially higher than with a L298N motor driver board, as shown in Table 13-3 and Figure 13-8. Efficiency is defined as power output, the voltage across a DC motor × current, divided by power input. Voltage across a DC motor is higher with a TB6612FNG motor driver board powered at 6V, 9V, or 11.9V than with a L298N motor driver board. The higher efficiency, due to the lower relative-voltage drop (voltage output divided by voltage input) of a TB6612FNG motor driver board compared with a L298N motor driver board, reduces heat loss, and consequently a heat sink is not required. Efficiency values in Figure 13-8 for a L298N motor driver board with a scaled duty cycle of 50 are for 9V and 11.9V inputs, as the DC motor used in this chapter did not turn with a scaled duty cycle of 50 and a 6V input. The *duty* parameter in Table 13-3 corresponds to the scaled duty cycle of an 8-bit-resolution PWM square wave. For example, a motor speed at half of full speed requires a 50% duty cycle. Given PWM with 8-bit resolution, equating to 256 =2^8 PWM levels from 0 to 255, then the scaled duty cycle is 50% × 256 = 128.

Table 13-3. *TB6612FNG and L298N motor driver boards*

Feature	TB6612FNG	L298N
Dimensions	20 × 20 × 3mm	43 × 43 × 27mm
Operating voltage	4.5–13.5V	4.5–46V
5V power supply for ESP32 module	No	Yes
Current output	1.2A	2A
H-bridge switches	MOSFET	BJT
Voltage drop with 6V, 9V, or 11.9V	48, 18, or 6%	80, 45, or 14%
Heat sink	Not required	Required
Efficiency at 50, 150, or 250 duty	71, 80, or 94%	18, 38, or 68%
Maximum RPM at 6V, 9V, or 11.9V	194, 294, or 348 RPM	136, 246, or 315 RPM

On balance, the TB6612FNG motor driver board has the advantage of efficiency and size over the L298N motor driver board, but an additional buck converter is required with the TB6612FNG motor driver board to provide 5V for powering the ESP32 module.

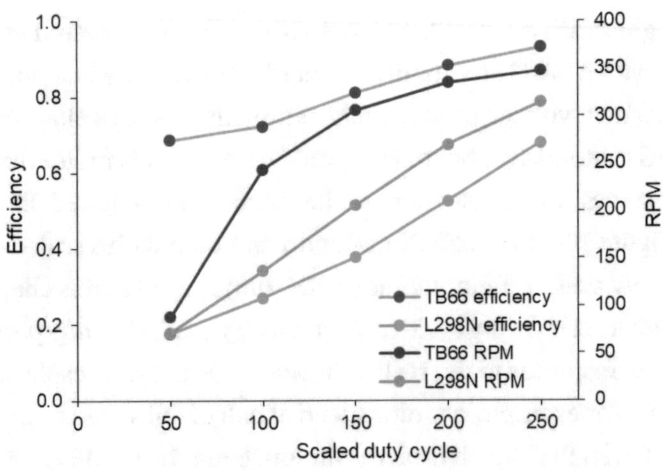

Figure 13-8. *Efficiency of TB6612FNG and L298N motor driver boards*

DC motor speed (RPM) is determined with the built-in Hall effect sensor of the ESP32 microcontroller, which measures the strength of a magnetic field. The `hallRead()` instruction returns the Hall effect value, with positive or negative values indicating the direction of the magnetic field. The DC motor speed is determined by attaching a magnet to a wheel connected to the DC motor, and the rotation time is measured by the Hall effect sensor detecting when the magnet passes the ESP32 module. The sketch in Listing 13-4 measures the Hall effect and calculates the DC motor speed. The Hall effect state is converted from *LOW* to *HIGH* when the Hall effect measurement exceeds a threshold, which depends on the magnet strength and distance between the magnet and the ESP32 microcontroller. When the Hall effect state changes, the DC motor speed is calculated from the time since the last state change, which occurred at the start of the wheel revolution. The ESP32 microcontroller Hall effect sensor measures the magnetic field strength 5100 times a second, and, in the sketch, false-positive state changes are discarded if the interval since the last state change is less than 100ms.

When a DC motor is controlled by a TB6612FNG or a L298N motor driver board, motor speed is dependent on the square wave pulse length on the motor driver board PWM pin, which has 8-bit resolution. The pulse length is equivalent to the scaled duty cycle equal to 256 × pulse length/wavelength, given the 8-bit PWM resolution with 2^8 PWM levels from 0 to 255. In Listing 13-4, the PWM resolution is defined as 8-bit, for consistency with subsequent sketches with a TB6612FNG or a L298N motor driver board. The scaled duty cycle, *duty*, is entered on the Serial Monitor to change the motor speed, which is determined with the Hall effect sensor. The state of an LED, connected to the ESP32 module, is alternated on each revolution to reflect the changes in motor speed in response to changes in the scaled duty cycle. Controlling DC motors with the scaled duty cycle is described for both the TB6612FNG and the L298N motor driver boards.

Listing 13-4. DC motor speed and Hall effect sensor

```
int IN1 = 25, IN2 = 26;                 // DC motor control input pins
int chan = 1, chanNull = 2;             // ledc channel numbers
int duty, freq = 1000, resol = 8;       // PWM frequency, 8-bit PWM
unsigned long revol, last = 0;
int hallThresh = 60;                    // Hall effect threshold
int hall, hallState = LOW, oldState = LOW, RPM;
int LEDpin = 2;                         // ESP32 module LED pin

void setup()
{
  Serial.begin(115200);                 // Serial Monitor baud rate
  ledcAttachPin(IN1, chan);             // allocate ledc channels to GPIO
  ledcAttachPin(IN2, chanNull);
  ledcSetup(chan, freq, resol);         // square wave for each channel
  ledcSetup(chanNull, freq, resol);
  pinMode(LEDpin, OUTPUT);              // define LED pin as OUTPUT
}

void loop()
{
  if(Serial.available())                // scaled duty cycle
  {                                     // entered on Serial Monitor
    duty = Serial.parseInt();           // convert to integer
    ledcWrite(chan, duty);              // generate PWM signal
    ledcWrite(chanNull, 0);             // channel with no signal
  }
```

```
  hall = hallRead();                      // read Hall effect sensor
                                          // low Hall effect value detected
  if(hall < hallThresh) hallState = LOW;
  else hallState = HIGH;                  // Hall effect value > threshold
  if(hallState == HIGH && oldState == LOW)  // change in state
  {
    revol = millis() - last;              // revolution time (ms)
    if(revol < 100) return;               // 100 ms equivalent to 600 RPM
    last = millis();                      // update time of last state change
    RPM = 60000.0/revol;                  // determine motor speed
    Serial.printf("duty %d revol %d RPM %d \n", duty, revol, RPM);
    digitalWrite(LEDpin,                  // alternate
    !digitalRead(LEDpin));                //LED state
  }
  oldState = hallState;                   // update change state
}
```

TB6612FNG Motor Driver Board

On the TB6612FNG motor driver board, each DC motor has two control input pins, a PWM input pin, and two output voltage pins (see Figure 13-9). The TB6612FNG motor driver board standby pin, *STBY*, must be set *HIGH*.

motor voltage VM
ESP32 voltage VCC
GND
motor A output voltage A1
A2
motor B output voltage B2
B1
GND
TB6612FNG
PWMA motor A PWM input
AIN2 motor A control input
AIN1 (HIGH or LOW)
STBY Standby: HIGH
BIN1 motor B control input
BIN2 (HIGH or LOW)
PWMB Motor B PWM input
GND

Figure 13-9. *TB6612FNG motor driver board*

When the motor control input pins *IN1* and *IN2* are *HIGH* and *LOW*, respectively, a DC motor turns clockwise, but anti-clockwise, when the control input pins *IN1* and *IN2* are *LOW* and *HIGH*, respectively. If a DC motor does not turn in the required direction, then the DC motor connections to the output voltage pins should be reversed. When both control input pins are *HIGH*, a DC motor stops immediately, while a DC motor stops gradually when both control input pins are *LOW*. Motor speed is controlled by the PWM pin with 8-bit resolution with a maximum value of $255 = 2^8 - 1$. If the voltage supply to a DC motor is too low, either by setting the motor speed too low or power to the motor is too low, when the motor is battery powered, then the DC motor produces a buzzing sound and stops turning. Example instructions to rotate DC motor A in a clockwise direction at half of full speed are shown on the left side of Table 13-4. The parameters *IN1*, *IN2*, and *PWM* correspond to the *AIN1*, *AIN2*, and *PWMA* pins for DC motor A or to *BIN1*, *BIN2*, and *PWMB* pins for DC motor B.

Table 13-4. *DC motor control with TB6612FNG and L298N motor driver boards*

With input control and PWM pins	With input control pins	Comments
int freq = 1000	int freq = 1000	Square wave frequency
int resol = 8	int resol = 8	8-bit PWM resolution
digitalWrite(IN1, HIGH)		Control input pin 1 HIGH
digitalWrite(IN2, LOW)	digitalWrite(IN2, LOW)	Control input pin 2 LOW
ledcAttachPin(PWM, channel)	ledcAttachPin (IN1, channel)	Attach PWM or IN1 pin to channel
ledcSetup(channel, freq, resol)	ledcSetup (channel, freq, resol)	Define square wave on channel
ledcWrite(channel, 128)	ledcWrite(channel, 128)	Scaled duty cycle for half speed

Alternatively, DC motor speed and direction are controlled by a PWM signal on one of the pairs of input pins, and the PWM pin is set *HIGH* (see Figure 13-10). Controlling a DC motor with only the input pins requires two connections between an ESP32 module and a TB6612FNG motor driver board, rather than three connections. The corresponding instructions to rotate DC motor A with two connections are shown in the middle column of Table 13-4. If both DC motors are required to only turn in one direction, such as clockwise, then only the IN1 control input pin is required to provide the PWM signal, as the IN2 control input pin is connected to the ESP32 module GND pin.

The TB6612FNG motor driver board does not have a 5V output to provide power for the ESP32 microcontroller. One solution is to connect a LM2596 buck converter between the battery power supply and the ESP32 module to reduce the high voltage, required to supply the DC motors, down to 5V to power the ESP32 module. For example, Figure 13-10 illustrates an ESP32-CAM module controlling a servo motor and two DC motors with a TB6612FNG motor driver board, and power is provided by two 18650 lithium ion rechargeable batteries. In Figure 13-10, the servo motor and ESP32 module are powered from the LM2596 buck converter, while the DC motors are powered directly by the batteries. Connections are given in Table 13-5.

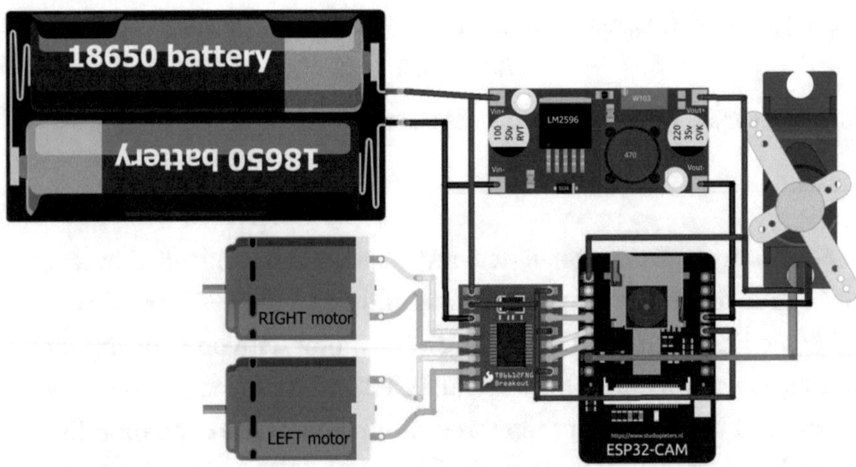

***Figure 13-10.** TB6612FNG motor driver board and ESP32-CAM*

Table 13-5. *TB6612FNG motor driver board and ESP32-CAM*

Component	Connect to	then to
TB6612FNG VM	18650 batteries positive	LM2596 IN positive
TB6612FNG VCC	ESP32-CAM VCC (3.3V)	
TB6612FNG GND	18650 batteries negative	LM2596 IN negative
TB6612FNG A1	Motor A, right DC motor	
TB6612FNG A2	Motor A, right DC motor	
TB6612FNG B2	Motor B, left DC motor	
TB6612FNG B1	Motor B, left DC motor	
TB6612FNG PWMA	TB6612FNG VCC (3.3V)	
TB6612FNG AIN2	ESP32-CAM GPIO 12	
TB6612FNG AIN1	ESP32-CAM GPIO 13	
TB6612FNG STBY	TB6612FNG VCC (3.3V)	
TB6612FNG BIN1	ESP32-CAM GPIO 15	
TB6612FNG BIN2	ESP32-CAM GPIO 14	
TB6612FNG PWMB	TB6612FNG VCC (3.3V)	
TB6612FNG GND	ESP32-CAM GND	LM2596 OUT negative
Servo motor signal (orange)	ESP32-CAM GPIO 2	
Servo motor VCC (red)	ESP32-CAM 5V INPUT	LM2596 5V OUT positive
Servo motor GND (brown)	ESP32-CAM GND	

L298N Motor Driver Board

For each DC motor connected to the L298N motor driver board, there are two control input pins, a PWM pin, and two output voltage pins (see Figure 13-11), which is identical to a TB6612FNG motor driver board.

When the L298N module input voltage is less than 12V, the built-in voltage regulator supplies a 5V output pin for powering an ESP32 module. If the input voltage is greater than 12V, then the *5VEN* (enable) voltage jumper behind power connections must be disconnected, as well as an external 5V supply provided for the ESP32 module.

Figure 13-11. *L298N motor driver board*

DC motor A is controlled by the two input pins, *IN1* and *IN2*; the PWM signal pin, *ENA*; and the two output voltage pins, *OUT1* and *OUT2*. Similarly, DC motor B is controlled by the two input pins, *IN3* and *IN4*; the PWM signal pin, *ENB*; and the two output voltage pins, *OUT3* and *OUT4*. When DC motor A control input pins *IN1* and *IN2* are *HIGH* and *LOW*, respectively, DC motor A turns clockwise, but anti-clockwise, when the control input pins *IN1* and *IN2* are *LOW* and *HIGH*, respectively. Motor speed is controlled by the PWM pin with 8-bit resolution with a maximum value of $255 = 2^8 - 1$. The instructions to rotate DC motor A in a clockwise direction at half of full speed are given on the left side of Table 13-4. The parameter *PWM* corresponds to the *ENA* pin for motor A.

Motor speed and direction are controlled by a PWM signal on one of the pairs of input pins on the L298N motor driver board, which is similar to the TB6612FNG motor driver board, and the PWM pin is connected to 5V with the *ENA* or *ENB* voltage jumper (see Figure 13-12). The corresponding instructions to rotate DC motor A with two connections are shown in the middle column of Table 13-4. Figure 13-12 illustrates an ESP32-CAM module controlling a servo motor and two DC motors with a L298N motor driver board, with power provided by a 9V battery. Connections are given in Table 13-6.

If the voltage supply to a DC motor is too low, either by setting the motor speed too low or the battery power is too low, then the DC motor produces a buzzing sound and stops turning.

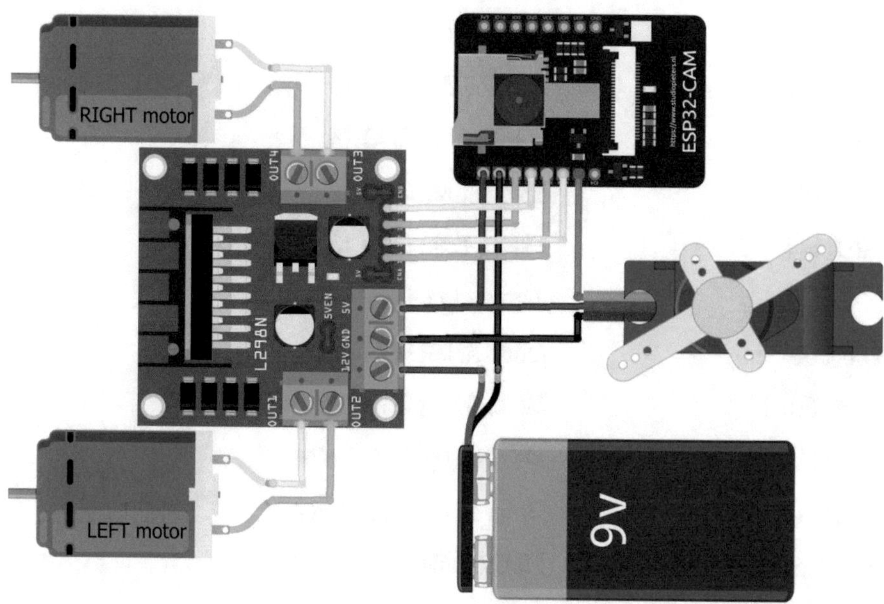

Figure 13-12. *L298N motor driver board and ESP32-CAM*

Table 13-6. *L298N motor driver board and ESP32-CAM*

Component	Connect to	then to
L298N 12V	9V battery positive	
L298N GND	9V battery negative	ESP32-CAM GND
L298N 5V	ESP32-CAM 5V INPUT	
L298N 5VEN	Jumper across pins	
L298N ENA	Jumper to 5V pin	
L298N IN1	ESP32-CAM GPIO 15	
L298N IN2	ESP32-CAM GPIO 14	
L298N IN3	ESP32-CAM GPIO 12	
L298N IN4	ESP32-CAM GPIO 13	
L298N ENB	Jumper to 5V pin	
L298N OUT1	Motor A, left DC motor	
L298N OUT2	Motor A, left DC motor	
L298N OUT3	Motor B, right DC motor	
L298N OUT4	Motor B, right DC motor	
Servo motor signal (orange)	ESP32-CAM GPIO 2	
Servo motor VCC (red)	L298N 5V	
Servo motor GND (brown)	L298N GND	

The TB6612FNG and L298N motor driver boards operate in a similar manner. The advantage of the L298N motor driver board is the board powers an ESP32 module directly, without requiring a buck converter module. The advantage of the TB6612FNG motor driver board is the higher efficiency, higher maximum motor speed, and smaller size.

Motor Driver Control

Both the DC motor rotation direction and speed are able to be controlled by one potentiometer. A linear potentiometer rather than a log potentiometer is required. High, intermediate, or low potentiometer voltages correspond to a fast, clockwise direction, no movement, or a fast, anti-clockwise direction, respectively. The intermediate potentiometer voltages, corresponding to no motor movement, are defined as the average of the minimum and maximum potentiometer voltages plus or minus an arbitrary buffer of 100mV. No motor movement with intermediate potentiometer voltages enables a smooth transition between clockwise and anti-clockwise motor movements, ensures there is sufficient power to turn a DC motor, and prevents a buzzing sound being made by the DC motor.

For the potentiometer used in this chapter, the minimum and maximum potentiometer voltages of 220 and 3100mV result in an intermediate range of 1560–1760mV (see Figure 13-13a), given the buffer value of 100mV. A minimum scaled duty cycle of 50 is required for a DC motor to turn and to prevent the motor producing a buzzing sound. The maximum scaled duty cycle of $255 = 2^8 - 1$ results from the 8-bit resolution of a PWM signal for controlling motor speed.

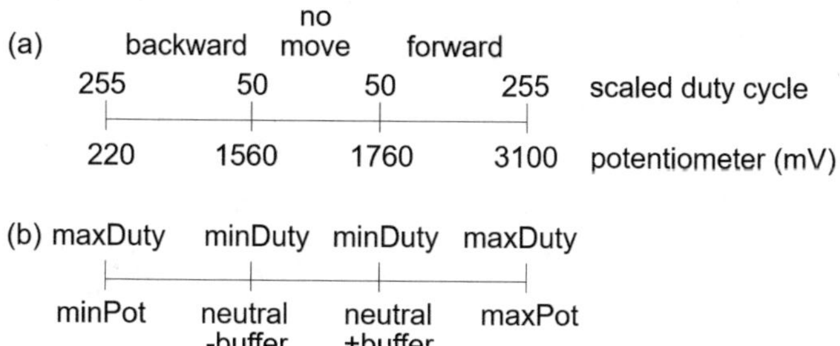

Figure 13-13. *Motor control with potentiometer voltage*

The minimum and maximum potentiometer voltages, *minPot* and *maxPot*; the minimum and maximum scaled duty cycles, *minDuty* and *maxDuty*; and the buffer size, *buffer*, are included in the mapping of potentiometer voltage, *pot*, to motor rotation direction and scaled duty cycle, *duty* (see Figure 13-13b). The scaled duty cycle, *duty*, is $a + b \times pot$, where $b = \frac{maxDuty - minDuty}{(maxPot - minPot)/2 - buffer}$ and $a = maxDuty - b \times maxPot$ or $a = maxDuty + b \times minPot$, when *pot* is greater than *neutral* + *buffer* or less than *neutral* - *buffer*, respectively. The *neutral* value is the average of the minimum and maximum potentiometer voltages.

Listing 13-5 is for an ESP32 DEVKIT DOIT or a TTGO T-Display V1.1 module to control a DC motor with either a TB6612FNG or a L298N motor driver board. A potentiometer is connected to GPIO 33, which supports ADC (analog to digital conversion). PWM signals are generated with the *ledc* function.

Listing 13-5. Motor driver control

```
int IN1 = 25, IN2 = 26;                 // control input pins
int LEDC1 = 1, LEDC2 = 2;               // ledc channels
int pot, potPin = 33;                   // potentiometer pin
           // min and max potentiometer voltages and scaled duty cycle
int minPot = 220, maxPot = 3100;
int minDuty = 50, maxDuty = 255;
int buffer = 100;                       // buffer > noise level
int freq = 1000, resol = 8;             // square wave freq, 8-bit PWM
float neutral, aHigh, aLow, b;          // regression coefficients
int duty, chan, chanNull;
```

```
void setup()
{
  ledcAttachPin(IN1, LEDC1);                  // allocate ledc channels
  ledcAttachPin(IN2, LEDC2);
  ledcSetup(LEDC1, freq, resol);              // PWM frequency and
  ledcSetup(LEDC2, freq, resol);              //resolution
  neutral = (maxPot + minPot)/2.0;            // middle of pot range
  b = (maxDuty - minDuty)/((maxPot - minPot)/2.0 - buffer);
                    // regression coefficients for high and low pot voltages
  aHigh = maxDuty - b * maxPot;
  aLow  = maxDuty + b * minPot;
}

void loop()
{                      // potentiometer voltage constrained between limits
  pot = analogReadMilliVolts(potPin);
  pot = constrain(pot, minPot, maxPot);
  motor();                                    // call motor function
}

void motor()
                       // function to control direction and speed of rotation
{                                   // high or low potentiometer voltage
  if(pot >= neutral + buffer) duty = round(aHigh + b * pot);
  else if(pot <= neutral - buffer)
         duty = round(aLow - b * pot);
  else duty = 0;                    // potentiometer voltage in neutral zone
  chan = 1 + int(pot/neutral);                // channel with PWM signal
```

```
  chanNull = 3 - chan;
  ledcWrite(chan, duty);                  // generate PWM signal
  ledcWrite(chanNull, 0);                 // channel with no signal
}
```

App to Control DC Motors with a Heading Angle

Instead of controlling two DC motors with two potentiometers, the motor directions of rotation and motor speeds are controlled by the heading angle. The circular slider app in Chapter 12, "Control Apps," provides the mechanism for defining the heading angle. For example, in a right turn movement, the left DC motor turns faster than the right DC motor, with the difference in DC motor speeds proportional to the heading angle.

The heading angle, θ, is derived from a point on the perimeter of a circle, with the point coordinates $(cos(\theta), sin(\theta))$ (see Figure 13-14). Note that heading angles of 0°, 90°, 180°, and 270° correspond to a right turn, to forward, to a left turn, and to backward, respectively. The absolute values of the point coordinates are combined with the minimum and maximum scaled duty cycles, *minDuty* and *maxDuty*, to define the forward-backward, $FB = minDuty + (maxDuty - minDuty)\ |sin(\theta)|$, and left-right, $LR = minDuty + (maxDuty - minDuty)\ |cos(\theta)|$, components of the required direction of travel. Note that $|x|$ is the absolute value of x. Scaled duty cycles of the two DC motors are the sum, $FB + LR/scalar$, and the difference, $FB - LR/scalar$, of the *FB* and *LR* components, with the *LR* component weighted by a *scalar* of 2.

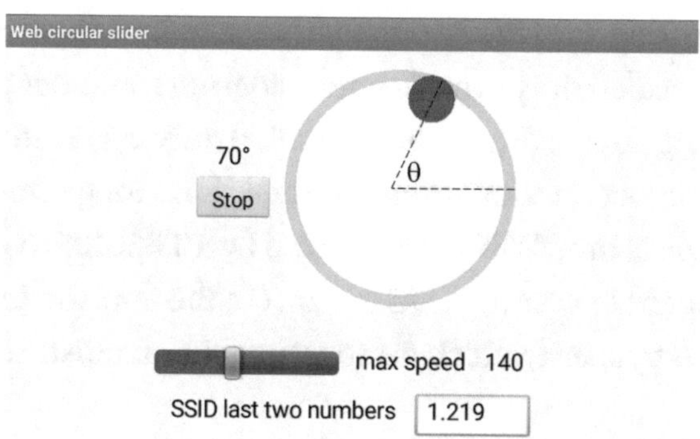

Figure 13-14. *App for motor control with a heading angle*

When the heading angle is between 90° and 270°, *cos(θ)* is less than zero, and the right and left DC motor scaled duty cycles are the sum and difference of the *FB* and *LR/scalar* components, respectively. Otherwise, the right and left motor scaled duty cycles are the difference and sum of the *FB* and *LR/scalar* components, respectively.

For example, movement to a heading angle of 70° with minimum and maximum scaled duty cycles of 50 and 200 corresponds to the forward-backward and left-right components of $FB = 50 + (200 - 50) \times 0.940 = 191$ and $LR = 50 + 150 \times 0.342 = 101$, with sin(70°) and cos(70°) equal to 0.940 and 0.342, respectively. The corresponding scaled duty cycles for the right and left motors are $191 - 101/2 = 140$ and $191 + 101/2 = 242$, with the latter constrained to the maximum motor speed of 200. When the heading angle is between 180° and 360°, *sin(θ)* is less than zero, and both DC motors turn anti-clockwise in the backward direction. For example, a heading angle = 220° corresponds to point coordinates (*cos(θ), sin(θ)*) of (–0.766, –0.643), and as both parameters are less than the buffer, the right and left DC motors turn backward and to the left.

An app to transmit the heading angle and maximum scaled duty cycle to the ESP32 module connected to the DC motors is shown in Figure 13-15. A circular slider app and a horizontal slider app with the *touchup* function are described in Chapter 12, "Control Apps." The red circle is moved around the gray ring, and the corresponding heading angle is displayed. The maximum scaled duty cycle is obtained from the slider position, and both the heading angle and maximum scaled duty cycle are transmitted to the ESP32 microcontroller, when the slider is no longer touched. The scaled duty cycle is the PWM value utilized by a TB6612FNG or a L298N motor driver board to control a DC motor. On the app, the term *scaled duty cycle* is replaced by *speed*, which is the motor characteristic of relevance to the user.

The ESP32 microcontroller and the Android tablet or mobile phone hosting the app are connected to the same WLAN (Wireless Local Area Network) for communication between the ESP32 microcontroller and the app. The ESP32 microcontroller IP address is displayed on the Serial Monitor, and the last two digits of the IP address are entered in the textbox by the user (see Figure 13-14 for an IP address of *192.168.1.219*). The first two digits of the IP address, *192.168*, are incorporated with the last two digits by the app for communication with the ESP32 microcontroller.

The app layout and components consist of a circular slider, as described in Chapter 12, "Control Apps," to indicate the heading angle; a horizontal slider to determine the maximum scaled duty cycle with a *ResetButton* button, labeled *Stop*; and a textbox to enter the last two numbers of the IP address (see Figure 13-15). When the circular or horizontal slider is moved, the slider position is updated on the app. The *Web* component, located in the *Connectivity* palette and displayed below the app layout as a *Non-visible component*, performs the client *HTTP GET* request, when the circular slider is no longer touched.

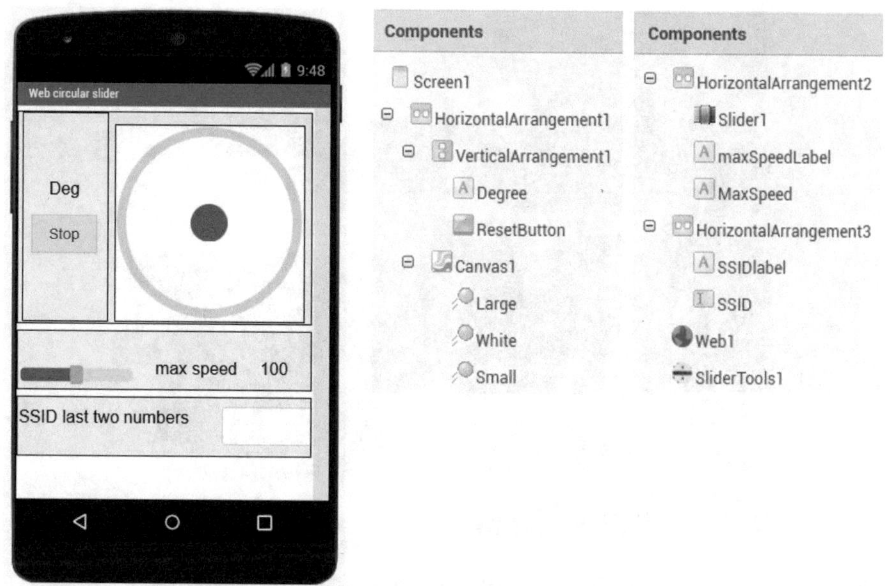

***Figure 13-15.** App layout for motor control with a heading angle*

Blocks for the circular slider are described in Chapter 12, "Controlling Apps." The additional blocks to transmit the circular slider position to the ESP32 microcontroller through the client *HTTP GET* request are shown in Figure 13-16. When the user stops touching the circular slider, which is the *TouchUp* action, the *transmit* procedure is called to transmit an *HTTP GET* request containing the two parameters, *degree* and *max*, representing the heading angle and the maximum scaled duty cycle. The app generates the URL `http://192.168.1.219/slider?heading=degree&maxSpd=max`, for the server IP address of *192.168.1.219*. The *Web* component transmits the *HTTP GET* request of *GET /slider?heading=degree&maxSpd=max HTTP/1.1*

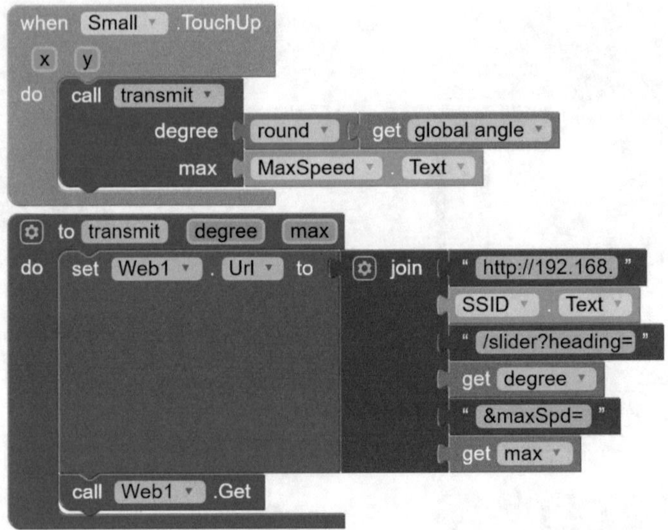

***Figure 13-16.** Blocks to transmit a circular slider position*

When the *ResetButton* button next to the circular slider is clicked, the small *Ball* center is moved to the center of the large *Ball,* and the displayed circular slider degree is reset (see Figure 13-17). The blocks are similar to those of the circular slider in Chapter 12, "Controlling Apps" (see Figure 12-22), with addition of the *transmit* procedure and *degree* set to 999, to indicate to the ESP32 microcontroller to stop both DC motors.

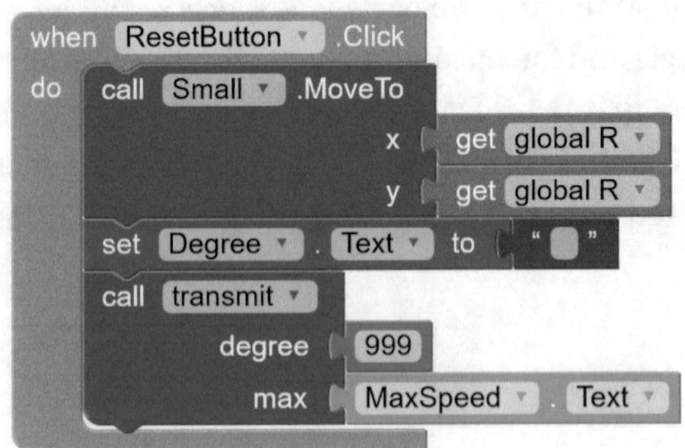

***Figure 13-17.** Blocks to reset a circular slider*

Blocks for the horizontal slider to display the maximum scaled duty cycle when the slider is moved, but to only call the *transmit* procedure when the slider is not touched, are shown in Figure 13-18.

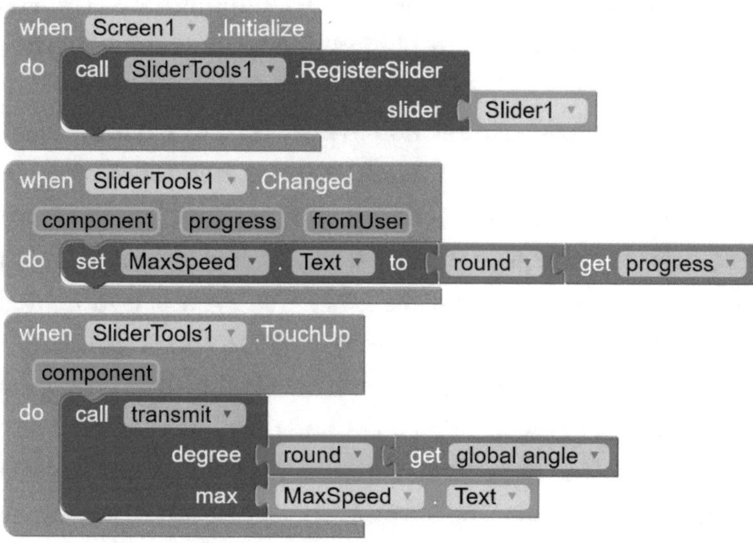

Figure 13-18. *Blocks for a horizontal slider*

The sketch to control the directions of rotation and speeds of two DC motors based on the heading angle transmitted by the app to an ESP32-CAM module connected to a TB6612FNG or a L298N motor driver board is shown in Listing 13-6. The first section of the sketch loads the *WiFi* library and establishes the Wi-Fi client and server for communication between the app and the ESP32 microcontroller, respectively. PWM signals, generated by the *ledc* library, drive the DC motors, and *ledc* channels are defined in the `chans[]` array. The ESP32-CAM module uses channel 0, so the *ledc* channels 1–4 are utilized. The heading angle coordinates, ($cos(\theta)$, $sin(\theta)$), range from –1 to +1, and a buffer value of 0.1 is chosen to ensure a smooth transition between clockwise and anti-clockwise motor movements over the range (–1 to -0.1, +0.1 to +1).

In the *setup* function, the ESP32 microcontroller connects to the WLAN, and the microcontroller IP address is displayed on the Serial Monitor. The last two numbers of the IP address are entered on the app by the user. The GPIO pins connected to the DC motors are mapped to the *ledc* channels, and an 8-bit resolution PWM square wave is defined for each channel.

In the *loop* function, a connection to the client, which is the app, is established, and when a client *HTTP GET* request is received, a string, *str*, is mapped to the received message, but the carriage return character, *\r*, is excluded. The string is split into components using the *indexOf* function. In the example, the *HTTP GET* request is formatted as *GET /slider?heading=deg&maxSpd=max HTTP/1.1* and contains the *name=value* pairs of *heading=deg* and *maxSpd=max*, with *deg* and *max* corresponding to the heading angle and maximum scaled duty cycle, respectively. The *deg* parameter is located between the *"heading"* and *"&max"* substrings, and the *max* parameter is located between the *"maxSpd"* and *"HTTP"* substrings, with the substring starting positions obtained with the *indexOf* function.

The heading angle and maximum scaled duty cycle are converted to scaled duty cycles for the two DC motors with the *convert* function. The *motor* function generates a PWM signal on the two *ledc* channels of each DC motor.

Listing 13-6. Control DC motors with a heading angle

```
#include <WiFi.h>                    // include WiFi library
WiFiClient client;                   // associate client and server
WiFiServer server(80);               // with library
#include <ssid_password.h>           // file with SSID and password
int pins[] = {12, 13, 15, 14};       // DC motor pins
int chans[] = {1, 2, 3, 4};          // ledc channels
```

```
int freq = 1000, resol = 8;              // frequency and resolution
int minDuty = 50, maxDuty;          // min and max scaled duty cycles
float scalar = 2.0, buffer = 0.1;
float sinDeg, cosDeg, FB, LR, Sum, Dif;
int degree;
int motorR, motorL, chanR, chanRnull, chanL, chanLnull;
String str, NNN;
int indexS, indexF;

void setup()
{
  Serial.begin(115200);                    // Serial Monitor baud rate
  WiFi.begin(ssid, password);              // initialize and connect Wi-Fi
  while (WiFi.status() != WL_CONNECTED) delay(500);
  Serial.println(WiFi.localIP());          // display server IP address
  server.begin();                          // initiate server
  for (int i=0; i<4; i++)
  {
    ledcAttachPin(pins[i], chans[i]);      // match pins[] to channels
    ledcSetup(chans[i], freq, resol);      // and define PWM
  }                                        // square wave
}

void loop()
{
  client = server.available();             // initialize client connection
  if(client)
  {
    while (!client.available()) {};      // no client request, do nothing
                                         // map str to HTTP GET request
    str = client.readStringUntil('\r');
```

```
    indexS = str.indexOf("heading");
    indexF = str.indexOf("&max");
    NNN = str.substring(indexS+8, indexF);  // heading=NNN &max
    degree = NNN.toInt();                   // transform received value
    indexS = str.indexOf("maxSpd");
    indexF = str.indexOf("HTTP");           // maxSpd=NNN HTTP
    NNN = str.substring(indexS+7, indexF-1);
    maxDuty = NNN.toInt();
          // HTTP header & response code with \n to generate blank line
    client.println("HTTP/1.1 200 OK");
    client.println("Content-type:text/html\n");
    client.stop();                          // close connection
    if(degree == 999) motor(0,0,0,0);       // stop DC motors
    else convert();                         // call function to convert
  }                                         // degree to DC motor speeds
}
void convert()          // function to convert degree to DC motor speeds
{
    sinDeg = sin(DEG_TO_RAD*degree);        // point co-ordinates from
    cosDeg = cos(DEG_TO_RAD*degree);        // heading angle
    FB = 0;
    LR = 0;
    if(abs(sinDeg) > buffer)          // forward-backward component
       FB = minDuty + (maxDuty - minDuty) * abs(sinDeg);
    if(abs(cosDeg) > buffer)                // left-right component
       LR = minDuty + (maxDuty - minDuty) * abs(cosDeg);
    Sum = FB + LR/scalar;                   // sum and difference of
    Dif = FB - LR/scalar;                   // FB and LR components
    if(Sum > maxDuty) Sum = maxDuty;        // constrain values
    if(Dif < minDuty) Dif = 0;
    motorL = 0;
```

```
    motorR = 0;                       // map motor speed to each motor
    if(cosDeg < 0) {motorR = round(Sum); motorL = round(Dif);}
    else           {motorR = round(Dif); motorL = round(Sum);}
    if(sinDeg < 0) motor(0, motorL, 0,  motorR);  // move backward
    else           motor(motorL, 0,  motorR, 0);  // move forward
}
                              // function to create PWM signal on each channel
void motor(int leftF, int leftB, int rightF, int rightB)
{
    ledcWrite(chans[0], leftF);                  // left-side DC motor
    ledcWrite(chans[1], leftB);
    ledcWrite(chans[2], rightF);                 // right-side DC motor
    ledcWrite(chans[3], rightB);
}
```

Motor Speed Variation

When the sum of the forward-backward, *FB*, and scaled left-right, *LR*, components exceeds the maximum scaled duty cycle, the sum is constrained. The constraint on the sum of *FB* and scaled *LR* components reduces variation in the scaled duty cycle and consequently on DC motor speeds across a range of heading angles. Alternatively, if the sum of the forward-backward and scaled left-right components is proportionally reduced, with the maximum value of the reduced sum equal to the maximum scaled duty cycle, then variation in DC motor speeds is maintained. The maximum value of the sum, sum_{max}, occurs at a heading angle of *arctan(scalar),* and the sum is reduced to $a + b \times sum$, where $b = \frac{\max Duty - minDuty}{sum_{max} - minDuty}$ and $a = minDuty \times (1 - b)$. For example, given a maximum scaled duty cycle of 200, the sum of the forward-backward and scaled left-right components exceeded the maximum scaled duty cycle for heading angles between 40° and 140° (see Figure 13-19a). Constraining the sum to the maximum scaled duty cycle resulted in similar values across a range of heading angles, while the reduced sum maintained the variation. The impact of constraining the sum on the scaled duty cycles is illustrated in Figure 13-19b. For the right DC motor, the scaled duty cycle is the same with the constrained sum or with the reduced sum for heading angles between 0° and 100°. For heading angles between 100° and 180°, reducing, rather than constraining, the sum of components maintained variation in the scaled duty cycle. The impact of reducing the sum of components on the left DC motor is, correspondingly, on the complementary heading angles to the right DC motor.

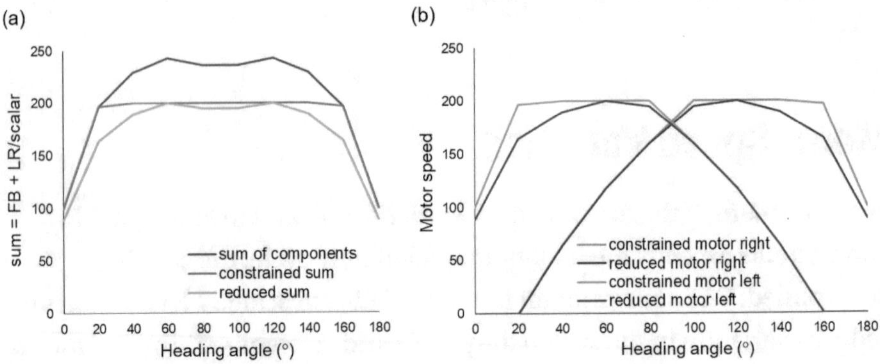

***Figure 13-19.** Constraint on motor speed components*

The *adjust* function in Listing 13-7 determines the regression coefficients, *a* and *b*, to reduce rather than constrain the sum of the forward-backward, *FB*, and scaled left-right, *LR*, components. In the *convert* function of Listing 13-6, the instruction `if(Sum > maxDuty) Sum = maxDuty` is replaced by the instructions `adjust()` and `Sum = a + Sum * b`.

Listing 13-7. Maintain variation in DC motor speed

```
void adjust()
{
  float maxAngle, maxFB, maxLR, maxSum;  // heading angle for
  maxAngle = atan(scalar)*180.0/PI;      // maximum sum value
  maxFB = minDuty + (maxDuty - minDuty) * sin(DEG_TO_RAD*maxAngle);
  maxLR = minDuty + (maxDuty - minDuty) * cos(DEG_TO_RAD*maxAngle);
  maxSum = maxFB + maxLR/scalar;         // maximum sum value
  b = (maxDuty - minDuty)/(maxSum - minDuty);     // slope
  a = minDuty * (1.0 - b);                        // intercept
}
```

CHAPTER 14

Remote Control an ESP32-CAM Robot Car

The ESP32-CAM module streams images to an app, hosted by an Android tablet or mobile phone, with Wi-Fi communication over a WLAN or a software-enabled access point, *softAP*, provided by the ESP32 microcontroller (see Figure 14-1). The robot car is powered by two DC motors with the ESP32-CAM module mounted on a servo motor tilt bracket to provide different observation positions. The app transmits *HTTP GET* requests, to the ESP32-CAM microcontroller, containing the image resolution, direction or heading angle, and motor speed for the robot car and the servo motor inclination angle. The ESP32-CAM module updates the camera image resolution and responds to the *HTTP GET* request by providing the image resolution details. The heading angle is converted to the rotation directions and speeds for the two DC motors to update the direction of travel of the robot car. The response to the *HTTP GET* request also includes direction of travel and motor speed information and the Wi-Fi signal strength for display on the app.

N. Cameron, *ESP32 Formats and Communication*,
https://doi.org/10.1007/978-1-4842-9376-8_14

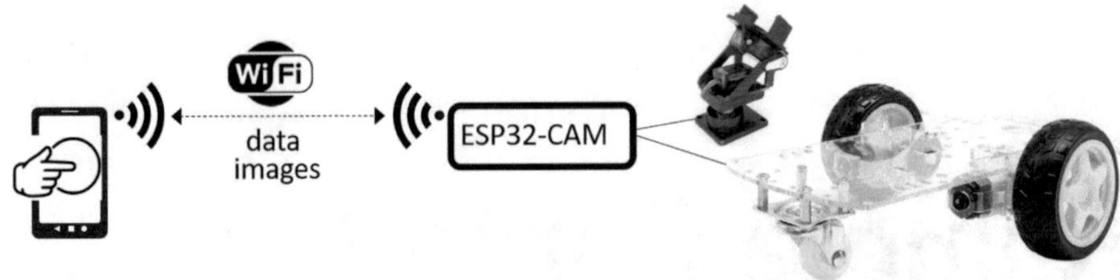

***Figure 14-1.** ESP32-CAM and app to control a robot car and motors*

The two DC motors are powered directly by two 18650 lithium ion rechargeable batteries with a LM2596 buck converter reducing 7.4V from the batteries to 5V to supply power to both the ESP32-CAM module and the servo motor (see Figure 14-2). The TB6612FNG motor driver board has the advantage of efficiency and size over the L298N motor driver board (see Chapter 13, "Remote Control Motors"). For each DC motor, the motor speed and direction are controlled by a PWM signal on one of the pairs of motor control input pins, and the motor PWM pin on the TB6612FNG motor driver board is set *HIGH*. Connections are given in Table 14-1.

Note that on the app, the term *speed* refers to the scaled duty cycle input of the PWM signal to a TB6612FNG motor driver board to control DC motor speed, which is the motor characteristic of relevance to the user.

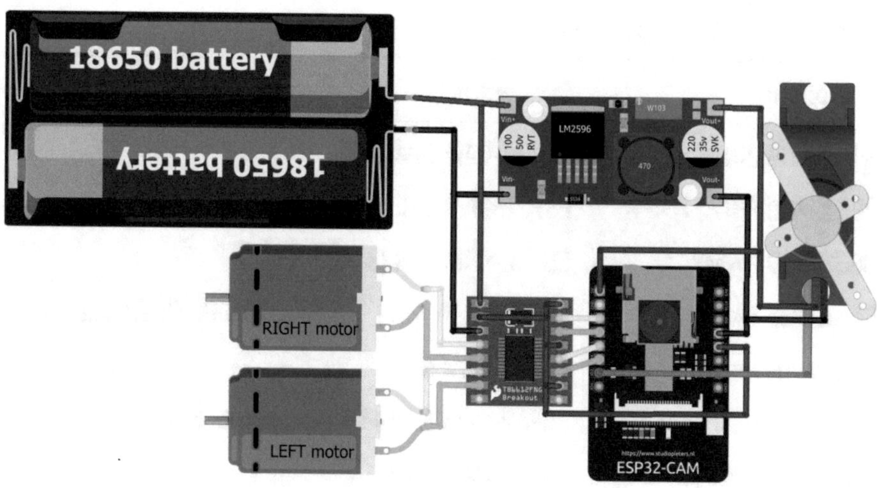

Figure 14-2. *ESP32-CAM robot car*

Table 14-1. *ESP32-CAM robot car connections*

Component	Connect to	then to
TB6612FNG VM	18650 batteries positive	LM2596 IN positive
TB6612FNG VCC	ESP32-CAM VCC (3.3V)	
TB6612FNG GND	18650 batteries negative	LM2596 IN negative
TB6612FNG A1	Right DC motor, motor A	
TB6612FNG A2	Right DC motor, motor A	
TB6612FNG B2	Left DC motor, motor B	
TB6612FNG B1	Left DC motor, motor B	
TB6612FNG PWMA	ESP32-CAM VCC (3.3V)	
TB6612FNG AIN2	ESP32-CAM GPIO 12	
TB6612FNG AIN1	ESP32-CAM GPIO 13	
TB6612FNG STBY	ESP32-CAM VCC (3.3V)	

(*continued*)

Table 14-1. *(continued)*

Component	Connect to	then to
TB6612FNG BIN1	ESP32-CAM GPIO 15	
TB6612FNG BIN2	ESP32-CAM GPIO 14	
TB6612FNG PWMB	ESP32-CAM VCC (3.3V)	
TB6612FNG GND	ESP32-CAM GND	LM2596 OUT negative
Servo motor signal (orange)	ESP32-CAM GPIO 2	
Servo motor VCC (red)	ESP32-CAM 5V INPUT	LM2596 5V OUT positive
Servo motor GND (brown)	ESP32-CAM GND	

App with Direction Buttons

An app to display streamed images from the ESP32-CAM module is shown in Figure 14-3, with buttons to control motor direction, horizontal sliders to control motor speed and image resolution, and a vertical slider to control the servo motor inclination angle. The app image and control functions are displayed in parallel in Figure 14-3.

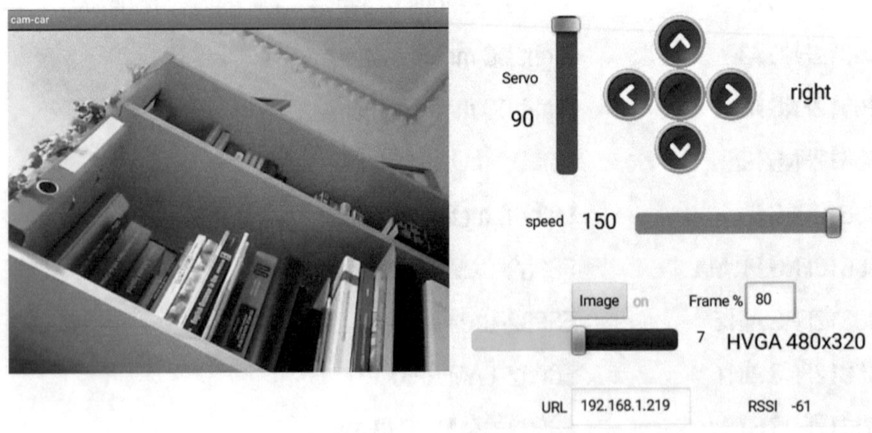

Figure 14-3. *ESP32-CAM robot car app with direction buttons*

Streamed images from the ESP32-CAM module are displayed on the app after the IP address of the ESP32-CAM microcontroller is entered in the *URL* textbox and the *StatusButton*, labeled *Image*, is clicked. The ESP32-CAM image resolution is updated with the lower slider, and the value in the *Frame %* textbox determines the image frame size. When a direction button is clicked, both DC motors turn at the set motor speed either forward or backward, or one motor turns at a slower speed for a left or a right turn. The center button stops the DC motors. The vertical slider displays the servo motor angle, and the tilt bracket, which is attached to the servo motor, is vertical when the servo motor inclination angle is 90°.

The server, which is the ESP32-CAM microcontroller, responds to the *HTTP GET* request from the client, which is the device hosting the app, by transmitting descriptions of the travel direction and image resolution with the Wi-Fi signal strength or RSSI (Received Signal Strength Indicator), which are displayed on the app (see Figure 14-3).

The app layout is shown in Figure 14-4. Note that the vertical slider is not visible in the Designer window of *MIT App Inventor*. The height of the *HorizontalArrangement* containing the *WebViewer* component is reduced from 400 pixels to 60 pixels for inclusion of the app components in Figure 14-4. App components to display ESP32-CAM steamed images are included in Chapter 11, "ESP32-CAM Camera," and Chapter 12, "Control Apps." Chapter 13, "Remote Control Motors," describes the app design to control the servo motor and the DC motors. The app layout in Figure 14-4 is based on the app layout for image streaming and control functions in Figure 12-13, with addition of the vertical and horizontal sliders to control servo motor inclination angle and to set DC motor speed, respectively.

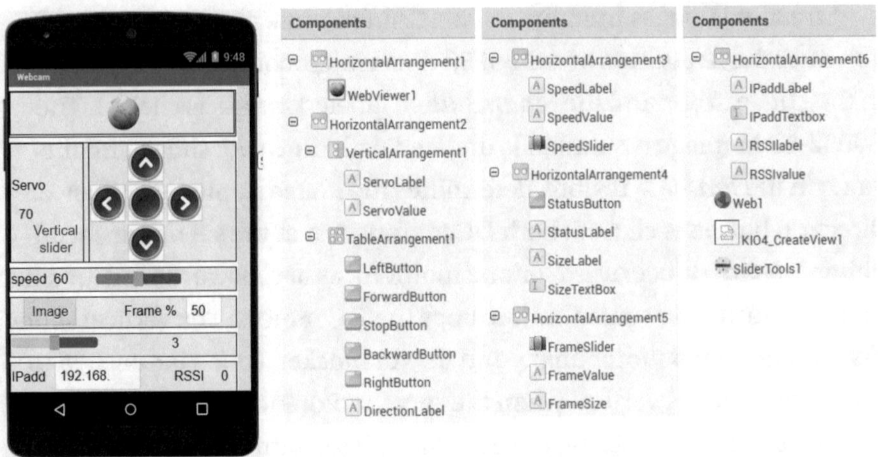

***Figure 14-4.** Layout of the ESP32-CAM robot car app with direction buttons*

The ESP32-CAM microcontroller IP address, which is displayed on the Serial Monitor, is entered in the *IPaddTextbox,* labeled *IPadd,* to enable the app to communicate with the ESP32-CAM microcontroller with Wi-Fi communication. The first two numbers of the IP address, *192.168,* are preloaded in the textbox. The *StatusButton* button, labeled *Image,* is clicked to control the display of streamed images from the ESP32-CAM module, with the text *On* or *Off* displayed beside the button (see Figure 14-3).

Several block combinations to display the image streaming status (see Figure 12-6), to generate the HTML code for streaming images as a URL (see Figure 12-7), and to receive the server response to the client *HTTP GET* request (see Figure 12-16) are based on the blocks in Chapter 12, "Control Apps." Blocks to display the image streaming status are unchanged. In blocks to generate the HTML code, *URLtextBox* is renamed *IPaddTextbox.* Blocks to receive the server response are expanded to include the *RSSIvalue* (see Figure 14-10).

When a direction button is clicked or a slider position is changed, *procedure2* updates the global variable *direct* and sends an *HTTP GET* request to the server to obtain a response, such as changing the DC motor speed or the image resolution. The *HTTP GET* request includes the server IP address, motor direction (*direct*), image resolution (*FrameValue*), DC motor speed (*SpeedValue*), and servo motor angle (*ServoValue*) (see Figure 14-5). In an *HTTP GET* request, parameters are formatted as *name=value* pairs, such as *speed=90*, separated by an ampersand, &, symbol. The *Web* component transmits to the URL *http://server IP address* the *HTTP GET* request of *GET /button?direct=R&frame=7&speed=150&servo=90 HTTP/1.1*, corresponding to the right button being pressed and slider positions of 7 for image resolution, 150 for scaled duty cycle, and 90 for servo motor inclination angle.

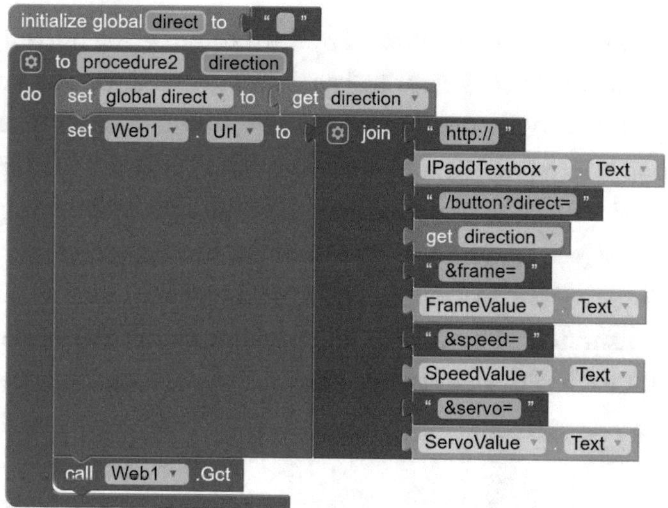

***Figure 14-5.** Blocks for a client HTTP GET request*

Blocks for the direction buttons (see Figure 14-6) call *procedure2* with the parameter corresponding to the direction, such as *R, L, F, B,* and *S* for right, left, forward, backward, and stop. The horizontal *FrameSlider* controls the image resolution value, *FrameValue,* and when the slider position is changed, the *FrameValue* label is updated with the slider position and *procedure2* is called, with the global variable *direct* (see Figure 14-6).

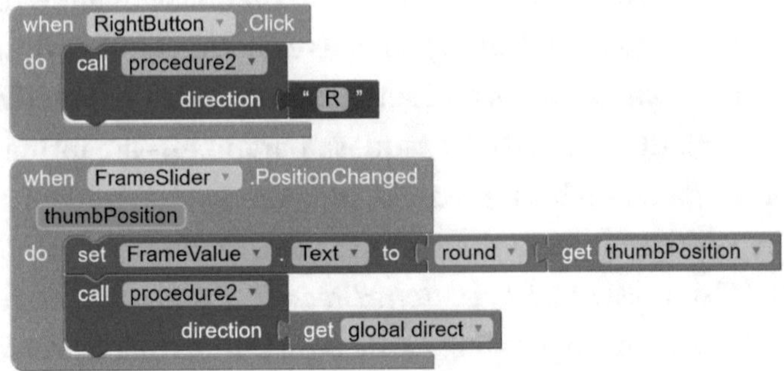

***Figure 14-6.** Blocks for updating motor direction and image resolution*

The DC motor speed is controlled by the position of the horizontal *SpeedSlider* with the *SpeedValue* displayed next to the slider. The extension component *SliderTools* is installed, as described in Chapter 12, "Control Apps," section "Horizontal Slider Touchdown and Touchup." The *SpeedSlider* is registered with the *SliderTools* extension component, when the app screen is loaded (see Figure 14-8). The *Changed* block displays the current slider position, *progress,* but the *TouchUp* block ensures that one *HTTP GET* request is transmitted with the last slider position, rather than several *HTTP GET* requests, each with an intermediate slider position (see Figure 14-7).

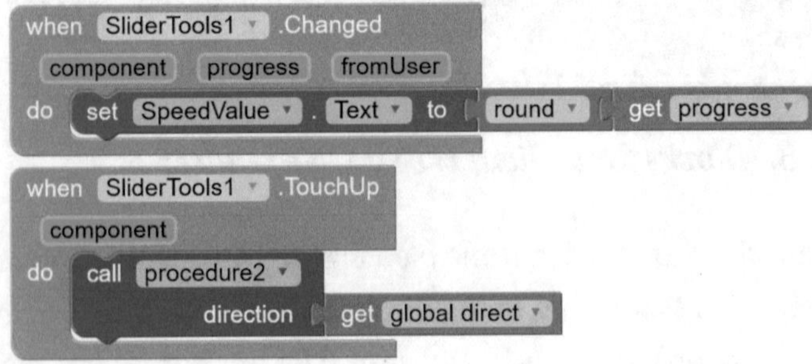

***Figure 14-7.** Blocks for a maximum motor speed slider*

The vertical slider for the servo motor inclination angle requires the *KIO4_CreateView* extension, as described in Chapter 12, "Control Apps." The slider parameters are relative to a horizontal slider, so the width and height parameters refer to the height and width of the vertical slider (see Figure 14-8). A negative value of the *leftMargin* property of the *Slider* block moves the slider to the left of the *VerticalArrangement* containing the slider, with the *AlignHorizontal* property of the *VerticalArrangement* set to *Left*. The *TopMargin* property of the *Slider* block positions the slider vertically in the *VerticalArrangement*. The *minValue* and *maxValue* parameters are the maximum and minimum values of the vertical slider.

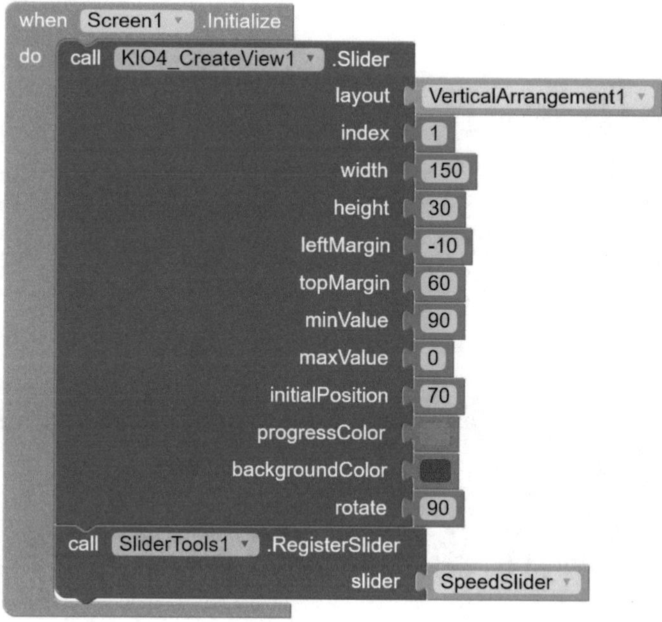

Figure 14-8. *Blocks for a vertical slider (1)*

When the vertical slider is moved, the slider position is displayed with the *PositionChanged* block (see Figure 14-9). When the vertical slider is no longer touched, the vertical slider is effectively redrawn by the *StopTrackingTouch* block with the *Slider* block repeated, but with the initial position updated to the vertical slider position, *thumbPosition*. The two block structures, *KIO4_CreateView.Initialize* and *KIO4_CreateView.StopTrackingTouch*, are identical apart from inclusion of the *RemoveViewAt* block and replacement of the *initialPosition* property by the *get thumbPosition* block.

The updated vertical slider position is included in the *HTTP GET* request generated by *procedure2*, but only when the vertical slider is no longer touched.

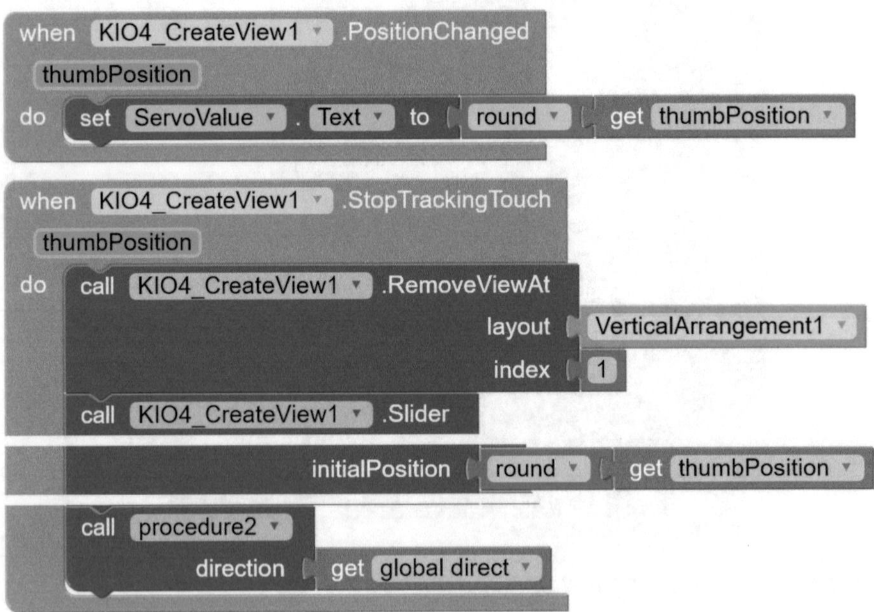

***Figure 14-9.** Blocks for a vertical slider (2)*

The content of the server response to the client *HTTP GET* request is allocated to a list, with comma-separated values, and split into three components, which are allocated to the corresponding textboxes (see Figure 14-10). For example, the server response to the client *HTTP GET* request of *GET /button?direct=R&frame=7&speed=150&servo=90 HTTP/1.1* is *right, HVGA 480x320, -61*, corresponding to the direction, image resolution, and Wi-Fi signal strength (see Figure 14-3), respectively.

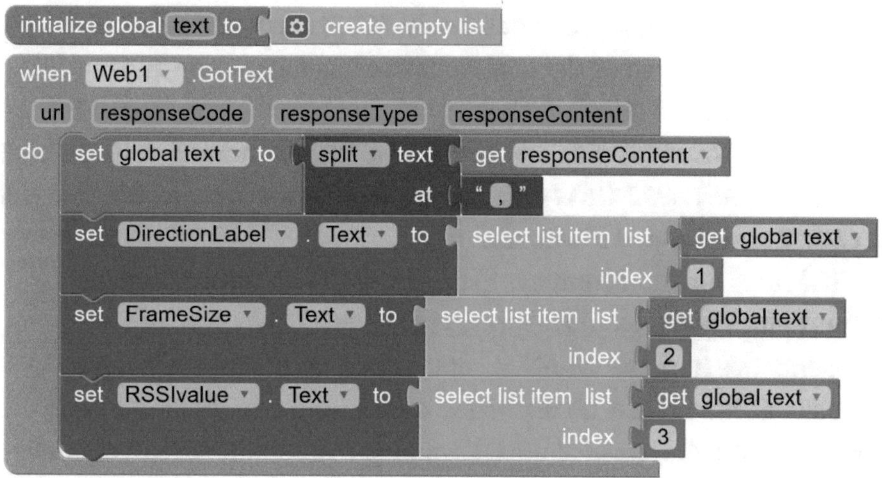

Figure 14-10. *Blocks for a response to an HTTP GET request*

The sketch to control the ESP32-CAM robot car when buttons on the app define the direction of travel is given in Listing 14-1. The sketch is a combination of Listings 12-4 (app with image streaming and control functions), 13-3 (servo motor control), and 13-5 (DC motor control).

The *ledc* function controls the servo motor position and the DC motor speed. The available GPIO for connecting servo motors and DC motors to the ESP32-CAM module are limited to GPIO 12, 13, 14, 15, and 2. GPIO 16 on the ESP32-CAM module is connected to the CS (chip select) pin of PSRAM. GPIO 0 and 16 are each connected to an internal 10kΩ pull-up resistor. GPIO 4 is connected to the module COB LED. GPIO 1 and 3 are TX and RX Serial communication pins, respectively.

The first section of the sketch in Listing 14-1 includes the *Wi-Fi* and *ESP32-CAM* libraries and defines the Wi-Fi client and server for communication between the mobile device hosting the app and the ESP32-CAM microcontroller. The two DC motors are connected to GPIO pins 12, 13, 15, and 14, which are mapped to *ledc* channels 1–4, as channel 0 is used by the ESP32-CAM microcontroller. The servo motor is connected to GPIO 2 and mapped to *ledc* channel 6.

The *setup* function connects to the WLAN, but a software-enabled access point, *softAP*, would be provided by the ESP32-CAM for independence from the WLAN. A servo motor requires a 50Hz square wave signal, but there is no restriction on the frequency of the square wave to control the speed of the DC motors. The square wave frequency for a DC motor is defined as 1000Hz to provide sufficient resolution for a scaled duty cycle with 256 levels. The *ledc* setup instructions, `ledcSetup()`, include different frequencies for the servo motor and for the DC motors.

When a client *HTTP GET* request is received by the server, the request is parsed into the direction, the image resolution category, the DC motor speed, and the servo motor inclination angle, which are updated by the server. For forward and backward directions, the speeds of both DC motors equal the value set by the position of the *SpeedSlider* slider. For a left or right turn, the corresponding DC motor turns at the defined *slowSpeed*.

The server responds to the client *HTTP GET* request with descriptions of the direction of travel, the image resolution, and the Wi-Fi signal strength.

Listing 14-1. Control of an ESP32-CAM robot car with direction buttons

```
#include <WiFi.h>                    // include libraries
WiFiClient client;                   // associate client and server with
WiFiServer server(80);               //  WiFiClient and WiFiServer lib
#include <esp_camera.h>
#include <esp_http_server.h>
#include "stream_handler.h"          // stream handler function
#include <ssid_password.h>           // file with SSID and password
//char ssidAP[] = "ESP32CAM";        // softAP SSID and password
//char passwordAP[] = "pass1234";
int servo, oldServo, pulse, duty; // servo pin and channel
int servoFreq = 50, servoPin = 2, servoChan = 6;
int low = 1500, high = 2500;         // pulses to move to 0° and 90°
int pins[] = {12, 13, 15, 14};       // left and right DC motor pins
int chans[] = {1, 2, 3, 4};          // ledc channels
int freq = 1000, resol = 8;          // frequency and resolution
String str, reply, direct;
String frames[] = {"96x96","QQVGA 160x120","QCIF 176x144",
  "HQVGA 240x176","240x240","QVGA 320x240","CIF 400x296",
  "HVGA 480x320","VGA 640x480","SVGA 800x600","XGA 1024x768",
  "HD 1280x720","SXGA 1280x1024","UXGA 1600x1200"};
int indexS, indexF, frm, oldfrm = 0;
int speed, slowSpeed = 70;           // slow motor speed for turns
```

```
void setup()
{
  Serial.begin(115200);                // Serial Monitor baud rate
//  WiFi.softAP(ssidAP, passwordAP); // option for softAP
//  Serial.println(WiFi.softAPIP());
  WiFi.begin(ssid, password);        // initialize and connect Wi-Fi
  while (WiFi.status() != WL_CONNECTED) delay(500);
  Serial.println(WiFi.localIP());    // display server IP address
  configCamera();                      // functions to configure camera
  startServer();                       // and start server
  server.begin();                      // initiate server
           // match servo pin to channel and define PWM square wave
  ledcAttachPin(servoPin, servoChan);
  ledcSetup(servoChan, servoFreq, resol);
  for (int i=0; i<4; i++)
  {            // match pins[] to channels and define PWM square wave
    ledcAttachPin(pins[i], chans[i]);
    ledcSetup(chans[i], freq, resol);
  }
}

void loop()
{
  client = server.available();
  if (client)                          // initialize client connection
  {
    while (!client.available()) {}; // no client response, no action
    str = client.readStringUntil('\r');        // map str to message
```

```
Serial.println(str);                    // display HTTP GET request
indexS = str.indexOf("frame");          // position of "frame" in string
indexF = str.indexOf("&speed");
frm = (str.substring(indexS+6, indexF)).toInt(); // to integer
if(frm != oldfrm)                       // image resolution changed
{
  oldfrm = frm;
  sensor_t * s = esp_camera_sensor_get();       // update image
  s->set_framesize(s, (framesize_t)frm);        // resolution
}
indexS = str.indexOf("speed"); // identify maximum motor speed
indexF = str.indexOf("&servo");
speed = (str.substring(indexS+6, indexF)).toInt();
indexS = str.indexOf("servo");          // identify servo angle
indexF = str.indexOf("HTTP");
servo = (str.substring(indexS+6, indexF-1)).toInt();
if(servo != oldServo)
{                          // square wave pulse length and duty cycles
  pulse = low + (high-low)*servo/90.0;
  duty = round(pulse*servoFreq*(pow(2,resol)-1)/pow(10,6));
  ledcWrite(servoChan, duty);           // generate square wave
  Serial.printf("image %d speed %d servo %d \n",
                frm, speed, servo);
}
                                        // map direction to motor speed
     if(str.indexOf("R") != -1)
         {direct = "right"; motor(slowSpeed, 0, 0 ,0);}
else if(str.indexOf("L") != -1)
         {direct = "left";  motor(0, 0, slowSpeed, 0);}
else if(str.indexOf("F") != -1)
         {direct = "forward";  motor(speed, 0, speed, 0);}
```

```
    else if(str.indexOf("B") != -1)
             {direct = "backward"; motor(0, speed, 0, speed);}
    else if(str.indexOf("S") != -1)
             {direct = "stop"; motor(0,0,0,0);}
    reply = direct +","+ frames[frm] +","+ String(WiFi.RSSI());
  // HTTP header starts with response code with \n to generate blank line
    client.println("HTTP/1.1 200 OK");
    client.println("Content-type:text/html\n");
    client.println(reply);           // display response client request
    client.stop();                   // close connection
  }
}
                           // function to create PWM signal on each channel
void motor(int leftF, int leftB, int rightF, int rightB)
{
    ledcWrite(chans[0], leftF);       // left-side DC motor
    ledcWrite(chans[1], leftB);
    ledcWrite(chans[2], rightF);      // right-side DC motor
    ledcWrite(chans[3], rightB);
}
```

App with Heading Angle Control

The app to display streamed images from the ESP32-CAM module with DC motor direction defined by the heading angle, rather than a direction button, is shown in Figure 14-11. The format of the app description is the same as for the *app with direction buttons.*

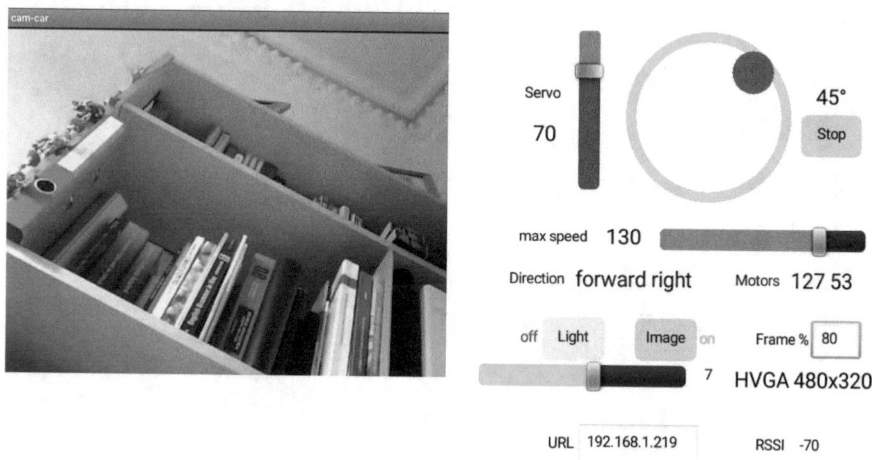

Figure 14-11. *ESP32-CAM robot car app controlled with a heading angle*

The app layout is shown in Figure 14-12. The vertical slider is not visible in the Designer window of *MIT App Inventor*, as with Figure 14-4, but the slider position is indicated in Figure 14-12. The primary difference between the app with direction buttons and the app with the heading angle is the replacement of the direction buttons (*TableArrangement* in Figure 14-4) by the circular slider (*Canvas* and *VerticalArrangement2* and *HorizontalArrangement4* in Figure 14-12) to define the heading angle.

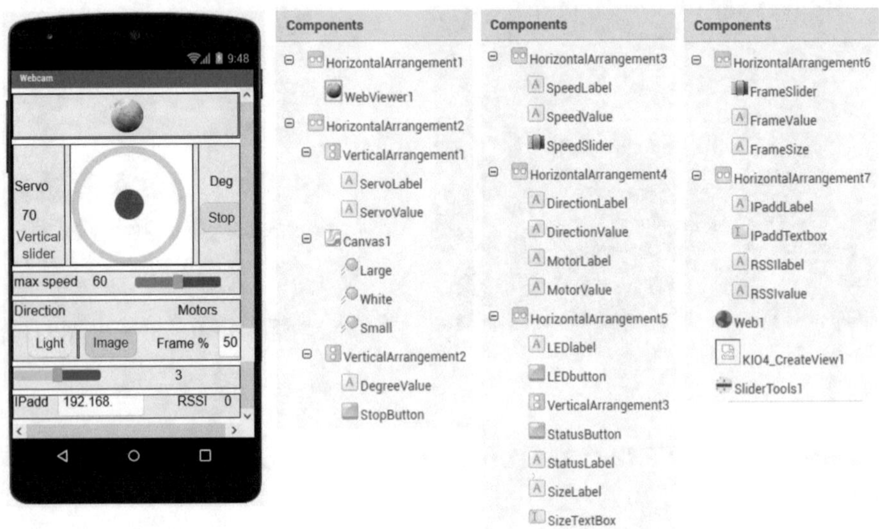

***Figure 14-12.** Layout of an ESP32-CAM robot car app with heading angle control*

Several block combinations are identical between the two apps. Blocks for image streaming control (see Figure 12-6), HTML code to display streamed images (see Figure 12-7), sliders for image resolution and maximum motor speed (see Figures 14-6 and 14-7), the vertical slider (see Figures 14-8 and 14-9), and the server response to the client *HTTP GET* request (see Figure 14-10) are unchanged.

Blocks for moving the *Small* ball around the gray ring of the circular slider to define the heading angle are described in Chapter 12, "Control Apps" (see Figure 12-20). The corresponding blocks are shown in Figure 14-13 with addition of the condition to constrain the heading angle to positive.

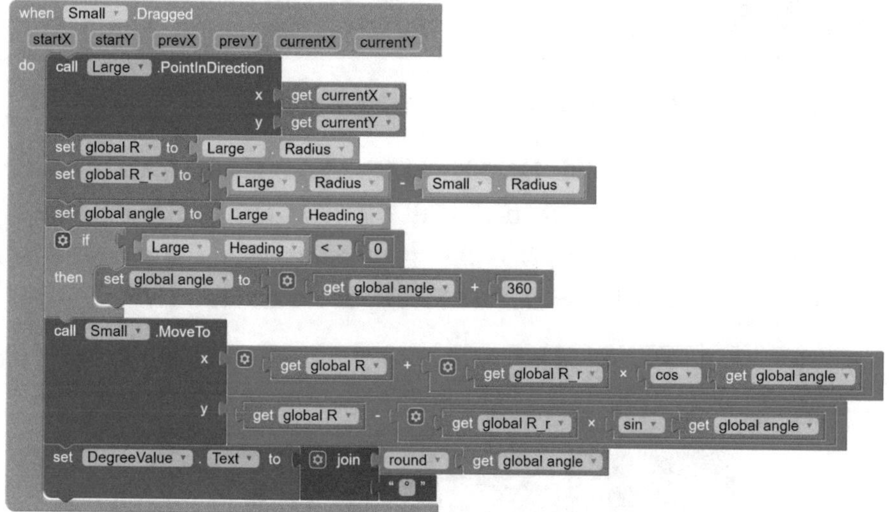

Figure 14-13. *Circular slider for heading angle (1)*

While the *Small* ball is dragged, the heading angle is updated on the app screen, but the client *HTTP GET* request is only sent, by the *transmit* procedure (see Figure 14-16), when the *Small* ball is no longer touched by the user (see Figure 14-14). When the *StopButton* button is clicked, the *Small* ball is returned to the center of the circular slider, the *degreeValue* is reset, and the *transmit* procedure is called with the heading angle set to 999, to indicate to the server to stop the DC motors.

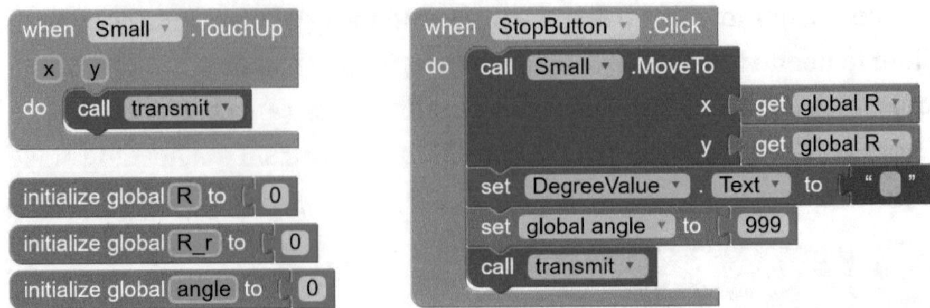

***Figure 14-14.** Circular slider for heading angle (2)*

The ESP32-CAM module includes a COB LED on GPIO 4, and the LED is turned on or off by inclusion of the *LEDbutton* button on the app (see Figure 14-15). The LED state, *N*, is alternated between zero and one as the button is clicked, and the *LEDlabel* text is updated accordingly.

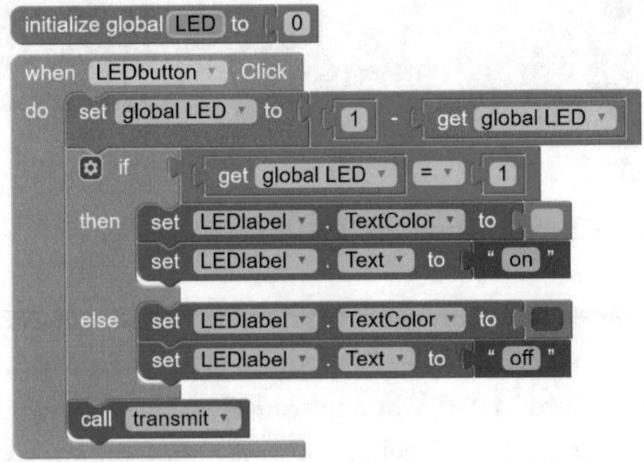

***Figure 14-15.** ESP32-CAM COB LED update*

The *transmit* procedure for generating the client *HTTP GET* request is shown in Figure 14-16. The *transmit* procedure blocks are similar to those of the app with direction buttons (see Figure 14-5), except that direction is replaced with heading angle and the COB LED state is included.

The sketch to control the ESP32-CAM robot car with a heading angle, rather than with direction buttons, is given in Listing 14-2. Only the instructions specific to the heading angle control are annotated to emphasize the instructions differing from Listing 14-1. The first section of the sketch and the *setup* function are identical to Listing 14-1, other than the definition of variables to generate the motor speeds and motor directions from the heading angle.

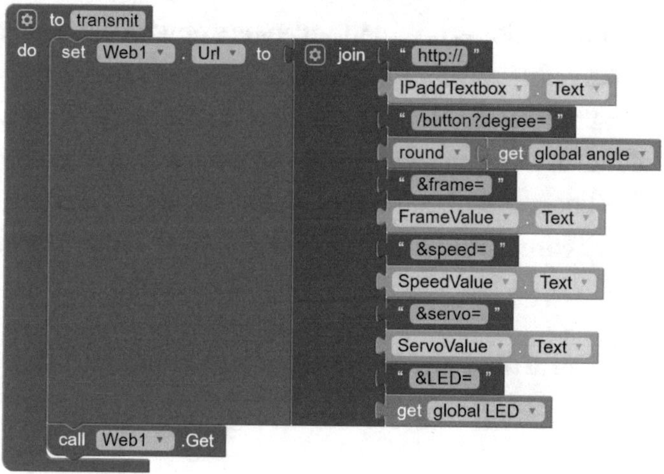

Figure 14-16. *Blocks for an HTTP GET request with a heading angle*

When the heading angle is updated, the *splitStr* function is called to parse the *HTTP GET* request string into the heading angle (*degree*), image resolution category (*frm*), maximum motor speed (*maxSpeed*), servo motor inclination angle (*servo*), and COB LED status (*LEDval*). The string is parsed in the same manner as in Listing 14-1, by searching the string for substrings and defining the required value with the location indices of the bounding substrings. The `str.substring(indexS, indexF)` instruction extracts a substring, from the *str* string, between positions *indexS* and *indexF-1*.

The *convert* function is called to convert the heading angle to the directions and speeds of the two DC motors. The sum and difference of the forward-backward, *FB*, and left-right, *LR*, components, with the latter divided by a scalar, are reduced to the maximum motor speed, *maxSpeed*, and to a minimum of zero, respectively. The *adjust* function determines the regression coefficients, slope and intercept, as described in Chapter 13, “Remote Control Motors.” The angle at which the maximum sum of the forward-backward and weighted left-right components occurs is $\tan^{-1}$(*scalar*), and the slope, *b*, and intercept are obtained as *(maxSpeed – minSpeed)/(maxSum – minSpeed)* and *minSpeed* × *(1.0 – b)*, respectively.

The left and right motor speeds are equal to the reduced sum and difference of the forward-backward and weighted left-right components. The forward or backward direction of DC motor rotation is determined by which DC motor connection has a PWM signal, as the opposite connection has no signal.

Listing 14-2. Control of an ESP32-CAM robot car with a heading angle

```
#include <WiFi.h>
WiFiClient client;
WiFiServer server(80);
#include <esp_camera.h>
#include <esp_http_server.h>
#include "stream_handler.h"
#include <ssid_password.h>
int servo, oldServo, pulse, duty
int servoFreq = 50, servoPin = 2, servoChan = 6;
int low = 1500, high = 2500;
int pins[] = {12, 13, 15, 14};
int chans[] = {1, 2, 3, 4};
int freq = 1000, resol = 8;
```

```
String str, reply;
String frames[] = {"96x96","QQVGA 160x120","QCIF 176x144",
  "HQVGA 240x176","240x240","QVGA 320x240","CIF 400x296",
  "HVGA 480x320","VGA 640x480","SVGA 800x600","XGA 1024x768",
  "HD 1280x720","SXGA 1280x1024","UXGA 1600x1200"};
int indexS, indexF, frm, oldfrm = 0;
int minSpeed = 50, maxSpeed;      // min and max. motor speeds
float a, b, scalar = 2.0, buffer = 0.1;
float sinDeg, cosDeg, FB, LR, Sum, Dif;
int degree;
int motorR, motorL, chanR, chanRnull, chanL, chanLnull;
String directFB, directLR;
int LEDval = 0, LEDpin = 4;       // COB LED on GPIO 4

void setup()
{
  Serial.begin(115200);
  WiFi.begin(ssid, password);
  while (WiFi.status() != WL_CONNECTED) delay(500);
  Serial.println(WiFi.localIP());
  configCamera();
  startServer();
  server.begin();
  ledcAttachPin(servoPin, servoChan);
  ledcSetup(servoChan, servoFreq, resol);
  for (int i=0; i<4; i++)
  {
    ledcAttachPin(pins[i], chans[i]);
    ledcSetup(chans[i], freq, resol);
  }
  pinMode(LEDpin, OUTPUT);      // LED pin as output
}
```

```
void loop()
{
  client = server.available();
  if (client)
  {
    while (!client.available()) {};
    str = client.readStringUntil('\r');
    Serial.println(str);
    splitStr();                     // call function to parse string
    if(frm != oldfrm)
    {
      oldfrm = frm;
      sensor_t * s = esp_camera_sensor_get();
      s->set_framesize(s, (framesize_t)frm);
    }
    if(servo != oldServo)
    {
      oldServo = servo;
      pulse = low + (high-low)*servo/90.0;
      duty = round(pulse*servoFreq*(pow(2,resol)-1)/pow(10,6));
      ledcWrite(servoChan, duty);
    }
    reply = frames[frm] +","+ String(WiFi.RSSI());
    if(degree != 999)               // updated heading angle
    {                               // call function to convert
      convert();                    // heading angle to motor speeds
      reply = reply +","+ directFB +" "+ directLR;
      reply = reply +","+ String(motorL) +" "+ String(motorR);
    }
```

```
    else
    {
      motor(0,0,0,0);                    // stop DC motors
      reply = reply +", , ";             // no directions or speeds in reply
    }
    digitalWrite(LEDpin, LEDval);        // update COB LED state
    Serial.println(reply);
    client.println("HTTP/1.1 200 OK");
    client.println("Content-type:text/html\n");
    client.println(reply);
    client.stop();
  }
}

void splitStr()                          // function to parse HTTP GET request
{                                        // indices of starting and final substrings
  indexS = str.indexOf("degree");
  indexF = str.indexOf("&frame");
  degree = (str.substring(indexS+7, indexF)).toInt();
  indexS = str.indexOf("frame");
  indexF = str.indexOf("&speed");
  frm = (str.substring(indexS+6, indexF)).toInt();
  indexS = str.indexOf("speed");
  indexF = str.indexOf("&servo");
  maxSpeed = (str.substring(indexS+6, indexF)).toInt();
  indexS = str.indexOf("servo");
  indexF = str.indexOf("&LED");
  servo = (str.substring(indexS+6, indexF)).toInt();
  indexS = str.indexOf("LED");
  indexF = str.indexOf("HTTP");
  LEDval = (str.substring(indexS+4, indexF-1)).toInt();
}
```

```
void convert()           // function to convert degree to DC motor speeds
{
    sinDeg = sin(DEG_TO_RAD*degree);    // point co-ordinates from
    cosDeg = cos(DEG_TO_RAD*degree);    // heading angle
    FB = 0;
    LR = 0;
    if(abs(sinDeg) > buffer)        // forward-backward component
       FB = minSpeed + (maxSpeed - minSpeed) * abs(sinDeg);
    if(abs(cosDeg) > buffer)        // left-right component
       LR = minSpeed + (maxSpeed - minSpeed) * abs(cosDeg);
    Sum = FB + LR/scalar;           // sum and difference of
    Dif = FB - LR/scalar;           // FB and LR components
//    if(Sum > maxSpeed) Sum = maxSpeed;
    adjust();                  // function to derive regression coefficients
    Sum = a + Sum * b;                   // reduced Sum
    if(Dif < minSpeed) Dif = 0;          // restrict Dif
    directLR = "";
    directFB = "";
    if(cosDeg > buffer) directLR = "right";       // motor direction
    else if(cosDeg < -buffer) directLR = "left";
    if(sinDeg > buffer) directFB = "forward"; // for display on app
    else if(sinDeg < -buffer) directFB = "backward";
    motorL = 0;
    motorR = 0;                            // map motor speed to each motor
    if(cosDeg < 0) {motorR = round(Sum); motorL = round(Dif);}
    else           {motorR = round(Dif); motorL = round(Sum);}
    if(sinDeg < 0) motor(0, motorL, 0, motorR); // move backward
    else          motor(motorL, 0,  motorR, 0); // move forward
}
```

```
void adjust()              // function to determine regression coefficients
{
  float maxAngle, maxFB, maxLR, maxSum;
  maxAngle = atan(scalar)*180.0/PI;       // angle for maximum value
  maxFB = minSpeed + (maxSpeed - minSpeed) *
                                     sin(DEG_TO_RAD*maxAngle);
  maxLR = minSpeed + (maxSpeed - minSpeed) *
                                     cos(DEG_TO_RAD*maxAngle);
  maxSum = maxFB + maxLR/scalar;  // maximum function value
  b = (maxSpeed - minSpeed)/(maxSum - minSpeed);       // gradient
  a = minSpeed * (1.0 - b);                            // intercept
}

void motor(int leftF, int leftB, int rightF, int rightB)
{
    ledcWrite(chans[0], leftF);
    ledcWrite(chans[1], leftB);
    ledcWrite(chans[2], rightF);
    ledcWrite(chans[3], rightB);
}
```

CHAPTER 15

Libraries

Libraries are used in the majority of the sketches in the book. Many LCD displays and sensors have libraries to manage the input and output of information with the Arduino website `www.arduino.cc/reference/en/libraries/` listing over 5800 libraries. Libraries combine instructions for managing a sensor, for example, with the main sketch only having to call the corresponding library function, rather than include all the instructions for managing the sensor. For example, a temperature reading from a DHT11 sensor library is simply obtained with the instruction `dht.readTemperature()`. Inclusion of a library in a sketch makes the sketch more readable and easier to interpret.

This chapter describes aspects of the *TFT_eSPI* library, which is used extensively throughout the book, and provides details of libraries utilized in the book. The process of creating a library is demonstrated with an example library.

TFT_eSPI Library

The *TFT_eSPI* library by Bodmer is recommended for displaying images on an LCD (Liquid Crystal Display) screen, and the library is available within the Arduino IDE. The library references the *User_Setup_Select.h* file to define the screen drivers and settings for several screen types. In the *TFT_eSPI* library, comment out `#include <User_setup.h>` in the *User_Setup_Select.h* file and un-comment one option according to the device or screen:

N. Cameron, *ESP32 Formats and Communication*,
https://doi.org/10.1007/978-1-4842-9376-8_15

```
                                                   // M5Stack Core2
#include <User_Setups/Setup12_M5Stack_Basic_Core.h>
                                                   // 1.3" 240×240 TFT LCD
#include <User_Setups/Setup24_ST7789.h>
                                                   // TTGO T-Display V1.1
#include <User_Setups/Setup25_TTGO_T_Display.h>
                                                   // ILI9341 LCD screen
#include <User_Setups/Setup42_ILI9341_ESP32.h>
                                                   // not required
#include <User_Setups/Setup45_TTGO_T_Watch.h>
```

If a 240 × 240-pixel ST7789 LCD screen is powered by an ESP32 DEVKIT DOIT module, then the *TFT_eSPI* ➤ *User_Setups* ➤ *Setup24_ST7789* file must be modified. The *Setup24_ST7789.h* file includes GPIO definitions for the ESP8266 and ESP32 microcontrollers, with default values for the ESP8266 *NodeMCU*. For the ESP32 microcontroller, un-comment the *Generic ESP32 setup* and comment out the *NodeMCU* lines. The ESP32 *TFT_DC* pin is mapped to GPIO 2, which is connected to the ESP32 DEVKIT DOIT built-in blue LED. The *TFT_DC* pin is mapped to GPIO 15 by changing the instruction `#define TFT_DC 2` to `#define TFT_DC 15`. The `#define TFT_INVERSION_ON` instruction must be un-commented.

The library for the TTGO T-Watch V2 (see Chapter 4, "TTGO T-Watch V2") references a version of the *TFT_eSPI* library, so editing the *TFT_eSPI* library *User_Setup_Select.h* file is not required.

The TTGO LoRa32 V2.1 1.6 module includes an OLED screen, which requires the *Adafruit_SSD1306* library rather than the *TFT_eSPI* library.

Library Functions

A selection of the *TFT_eSPI* library functions to display information on the TFT screen are used in the book. The `setTextColor(color)` color options are listed in the library *TFT_eSPI.h* file with the corresponding HEX color codes, color names, and 8-bit RGB values. The `setTextColor(foreC, backC)` instruction overwrites existing text with foreground, *foreC*, and background, *backC*, colors, respectively. If the existing text is longer than the current text, then the remaining characters are overwritten by drawing a rectangle filled with the background color over the existing text or filling the screen in the background color before printing the current text.

Rectangles and triangles are drawn with the `fillRect(xStart, yStart, width, height, color)` and `fillTriangle(xPeak, yPeak, xLeft, yLeft, xRight, yRight, color)` instructions. The `fillRoundRect(xStart, yStart, width, height, radius, color)` instruction includes a parameter for the radius of a quarter circle instead of corners on the rectangle. The `fillCircle(xCenter, yCenter, radius, color)` instruction displays a circle. Strings, integers, or real numbers are displayed starting at position *(x, y)* with the `drawString(string, x, y, font)`, `drawNumber(number, x, y, font)`, or `drawFloat(number, DP, x, y, font)` instruction. If the font is not included in the `drawString` instruction, then the font defined by the `setTextFont` instruction is used.

The `setTextSize(S)` instruction has values of 1–7, and the `setTextFont(F)` instruction has values 1, 2, 4, 6, and 7, with font 7 representing 7-segment display characters. Text height is $8 \times S \times F$, except for font 4, which is $26 \times S$, and font 7, which is the same as font 6. The instructions `getCursorX()` and `getCursorY()` return the cursor position. Text fonts 6 and 7 essentially only print numbers.

Screen orientation is defined by the `setRotation(N)` instruction for portrait, with *N* equal to 0 or 2 (180° rotation), or landscape, with *N* equal to 1 or 3. For the TTGO T-Display V1.1 module, font size, *S*, of 1–4 requires $8S \times 16S$ pixels, which enables 8, 4, 2, or 2 rows of 30, 15, 10, and 7 characters per row with landscape orientation and 15, 7, 5, and 3 rows of 16, 8, 5, and 4 characters per row with portrait orientation. Note that for a real number, the `print` and `printf` instructions default to 2DP and 6DP, respectively.

Fonts

In addition to the seven default fonts of the *TFT_eSPI* library, there are several custom fonts in the *TFT_eSPI\Fonts\Custom* folder, such as *Orbitron_Light* with font sizes of 24 or 32 bitmap points. Additional fonts are generated using the `oleddisplay.squix.ch` web page by Daniel Eichhorn. For example, Figure 15-1 illustrates selection of the *Rock Salt* font, size 24, and *Adafruit GFX Font* options with the font illustrated on the web page, with an ILI9341 LCD screen or an OLED 0.96" (128 × 64) screen.

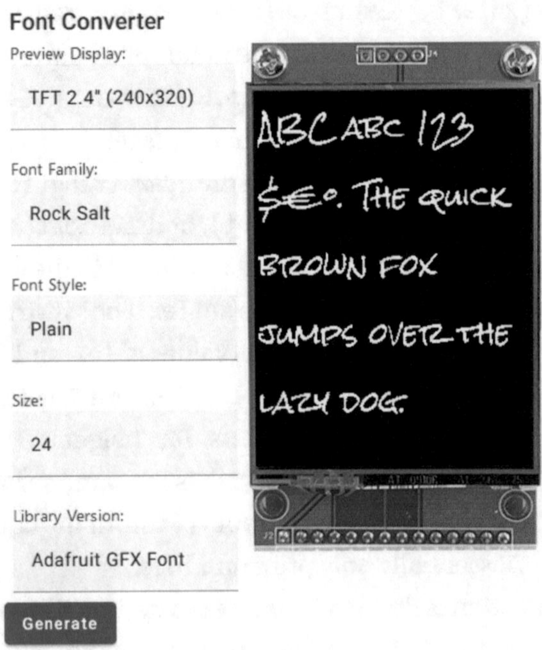

Figure 15-1. *Generate an additional font*

The generated bitmap data (see Listing 15-1) is copied onto a tab, such as *newfont.h*, in the sketch, and the tab is loaded with the `#include "newfont.h"` instruction. The font is defined by the `tft.setFreeFont(&Rock_Salt_Regular_24)` instruction, prior to a `print`, `drawString`, or `drawNumber` instruction. The font name is highlighted in bold in Listing 15-1.

Listing 15-1. Bitmap of an additional font

```
const uint8_t Rock_Salt_Regular_24Bitmaps[] PROGMEM = {
// Bitmap Data:
0x00, // ' '
⋮
{  5400,   4,  25,   8,    1,  -20 }, // '|'
{  5413,  14,  32,  15,   -2,  -22 } // '}'
};
const GFXfont Rock_Salt_Regular_24 PROGMEM = {
(uint8_t  *)Rock_Salt_Regular_24Bitmaps,
(GFXglyph *)Rock_Salt_Regular_24Glyphs,0x20, 0x7E, 58};
```

The sketch in Listing 15-2 displays the text in Figure 15-1 on a 2.4" 320 × 240-pixel ILI9341 SPI TFT LCD screen with the *Rock Salt* font of size 24. The text is displayed as a string with the `print` instruction, which automatically wraps text. After a delay, the parsed text is displayed, without splitting words, by the *splitText* function from Listing 2-7 with the *line* variable changed from 25 to 13 and `M5.Lcd.println` replaced by `tft.println`.

Listing 15-2 with the *Rock Salt* font of size 14 is applicable to a TTGO T-Display V1.1 module, which includes a TFT ST7789 1.14" LCD screen with 135 × 240 pixels.

Listing 15-2 is adapted for an SSD1306 0.96" OLED screen with 128 × 64 pixels by replacing the *TFT_eSPI* library with the *Adafruit_SSD1306* library, defining the font with the `setFont(&Rock_Salt_Regular_8)` instruction, and increasing the *line* variable to 20. Chapter 6, "LoRa and Microsatellites," includes sketches for an OLED screen with the TTGO LoRa32 V2.1 1.6 module.

Listing 15-2. Display an additional font

```
#include <TFT_eSPI.h>            // include TFT_eSPI library
#include "newfont.h"             // tab containing Listing 15-1
TFT_eSPI tft = TFT_eSPI();
String str = "ABC abc 123 $@. The quick brown fox jumps over
  the lazy dog";

void setup()
{
  Serial.begin(115200);
  tft.begin();                   // init() and begin() are equivalent
  tft.setFreeFont(&Rock_Salt_Regular_24);        // additional font
  tft.setRotation(0);
  tft.fillScreen(TFT_BLACK);
  tft.setTextColor(TFT_WHITE);
  tft.setTextSize(1);
  tft.setCursor(0,30);
  tft.print(str);                // display text with wrap around
  delay(5000);
  tft.fillScreen(TFT_BLACK);
  tft.setCursor(0,30);
  splitText(str);                // display parsed text
}

void splitText(String text)      // see Listing 2-7

void loop()                      // nothing in loop function
{}
```

The `drawString(text, x, y, 1)` instruction and the `print` instruction with `setTextSize(1)` result in identical characters. The `drawString` instruction with font 4 and text size 1 is recommended for characters (see Figure 15-2). The drawString instruction with font 6 is, essentially, only for digits, and text size 1 is sufficient. Comparable character sizes are obtained with drawString font 4 and text size 2. The print instruction with text size 2 provides smaller characters than drawString font 4 and text size 1. The drawString instruction with font 2 for text size 2 produces "thin" characters, and text size 3 with the print instruction results in "square-ish" characters.

A subset of text sizes and fonts is highlighted in bold in Listing 15-3 with the corresponding display on a TTGO T-Watch V2 shown in Figure 15-2.

Listing 15-3. Alternative text and font sizes

```
#define LILYGO_WATCH_2020_V2     // define T-watch model
#include <LilyGoWatch.h>         // include library
TTGOClass * ttgo;                // associate objects with libraries
TFT_eSPI * tft;                  // graphics library

void setup()
{
  ttgo = TTGOClass::getWatch();
  ttgo->begin();                       // initialize ttgo object
  ttgo->openBL();                      // turn on backlight
  tft = ttgo->tft;                     // shorthand for object
  ttgo->bl->adjust(64);                // reduce brightness from 255
  tft->fillScreen(TFT_BLACK);          // screen background color
  tft->setTextSize(1);
  tft->setCursor(0,0);
```

```
  tft->println("ABab123");                        // too small
  tft->drawString("ABab123", 0, 10, 2);           // minimum readable
  tft->drawString("ABab123", 0, 30, 4);           // recommend
  tft->drawString("123",     0, 60, 6);           // digits only
  tft->setCursor(0,110);
  tft->setTextSize(2);
  tft->println("ABab123");                        // smaller alternative
  tft->drawString("ABab123", 0, 130, 2);          // thin characters
  tft->drawString("ABab123", 0, 170, 4);          // similar to size 1 font 6
//tft->setTextSize(3);                            // square-ish characters
//tft->setTextSize(4);                            // poor quality characters
}

void loop()                                       // nothing in loop function
{}
```

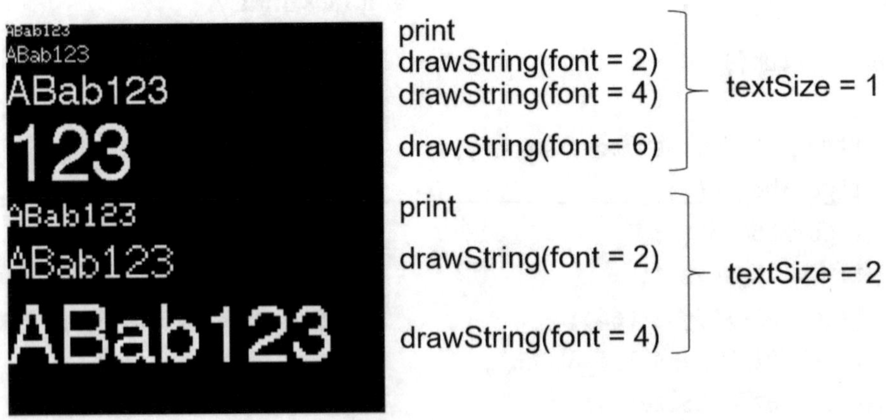

Figure 15-2. Alternative text and font sizes

Libraries to Access Time Data

There are several libraries to source time information, and three libraries are illustrated with an example to continuously display the current time. A Wi-Fi connection is initially required to obtain the time from the Network Time Protocol (NTP), and then the Wi-Fi connection is turned off. Details of NTP pools are available at `www.ntppool.org`.

time Library

The current time is obtained with the *time* library (see Listing 15-4), which is used in Chapter 9, "MQTT" (Listing 9-5), and in Chapter 10, "Managing Images" (see Listing 10-18). Connection to the local NTP pool is obtained with the `configTime(GMT, daylight, pool)` instruction, where *GMT* and *daylight* are the offsets for Greenwich Mean Time (GMT) and for daylight saving, both measured in seconds. The `getLocalTime(&timeData)` instruction generates the *timeData* structure containing time variables, such as *tm_hour* and *tm_min*, for the current hour and minutes, respectively. Details of the time structure are available at `cplusplus.com/reference/ctime/tm/`.

Listing 15-4. time library and current time (1)

```
#include <WiFi.h>                     // include Wi-Fi library
#include <ssid_password.h>            // file with logon details
#include <time.h>                     // include time library
struct tm timeData;                   // structure with time data
int GMT = 0, daylight = 3600;         // GMT, daylight saving (sec)
unsigned long last;
int wd, hh, mm, ss, dd, mn, yy;
String days[] = {"Sun","Mon","Tues","Wed","Thur","Fri","Sat"};
String mon[] = {"Jan","Feb","Mar","Apr","May","Jun",
                "Jul","Aug","Sep","Oct","Nov","Dec"};
```

```
void setup()
{
  Serial.begin(115200);                 // Serial Monitor baud rate
  WiFi.begin(ssid, password);           // initialize and connect to Wi-Fi
  while (WiFi.status() != WL_CONNECTED) delay(500);
  configTime(GMT, daylight, "uk.pool.ntp.org");   // NTP pool
  while (!getLocalTime(&timeData)) delay(500);    // get valid time
  WiFi.disconnect(true);                // disconnect Wi-Fi
  WiFi.mode(WIFI_OFF);
}

void loop()
{
  if(millis() - last > 1000)            // at every second
  {
    last = millis();
    getLocalTime(&timeData);            // obtain current time
    wd = timeData.tm_wday;              // day of week starts at 0
    hh = timeData.tm_hour;
    mm = timeData.tm_min;
    ss = timeData.tm_sec;
    dd = timeData.tm_mday;              // day in month
    mn = timeData.tm_mon;               // month starts at 0
    yy = timeData.tm_year + 1900;
    Serial.printf("%s %02d:%02d:%02d %02d %s %d \n",
                  days[wd], hh, mm, ss, dd, mon[mn], yy);
  }
}
```

The sketch in Listing 15-5 parameterizes the NTP time as the Unix epoch time, which is the number of seconds since January 1, 1970. Given the Unix epoch time, held by the *epoch* variable, the current time is displayed, in the default *Www Mmm dd hh:mm:ss yyyy* format, with the `Serial.print(ctime(&epoch))` instruction. The Unix epoch time is converted to a time structure, *timeData*, with the `localtime_r(&epoch, &timeData)` instruction. The time components of the *timeData* structure are displayed on the Serial Monitor by referencing the terms *%A, %B, %d, %Y, %H, %M,* and *%S* for day of week, month, day, year, hour, minute, and second, respectively. The time components of the *timeData* structure are accessed as shown in Listing 15-5, such as `timeData.tm_sec`. Instructions differing from Listing 15-4 are commented.

Listing 15-5. time library and current time (2)

```
#include <WiFi.h>
#include <ssid_password.h>
#include <time.h>
time_t epoch;                                   // time library variable
struct tm timeData;
int GMT = 0, daylight = 3600;
unsigned long last;

void setup()
{
  Serial.begin(115200);
  WiFi.begin(ssid, password);
  while (WiFi.status() != WL_CONNECTED) delay(500);
  configTime(GMT, daylight, "uk.pool.ntp.org");
                                          // wait for connection to NTP
  while (time(nullptr)< 1000) delay(500);
  epoch = time(nullptr);                  // set the Unix epoch time
```

```
  WiFi.disconnect(true);
  WiFi.mode(WIFI_OFF);
}

void loop()
{
  if(millis() - last > 1000)
  {
    last = millis();
    time(&epoch);                        // current Unix epoch time
    Serial.print(ctime(&epoch));         // time in default format
                                  // convert Unix epoch time to structure
    localtime_r(&epoch, &timeData);
    Serial.print("time ");
    Serial.println(&timeData, "%H:%M:%S");
    Serial.printf("sec %d \n\n", timeData.tm_sec);
  }
}
```

RTC Library

Accessing time components with the system RTC (real-time clock) library, *soc/rtc*, is similar to the approach in Listing 15-4, with the `getLocalTime(&timeData)` instruction replaced by the `RTC_Date timeData = ttgo->rtc->getDateTime()` instruction. The RTC library was used with the TTGO T-Watch V2 module in Chapter 4, "TTGO T-Watch V2" (Listing 4-15). In Listing 15-6, instructions differing from Listing 15-4 are commented.

Listing 15-6. RTC library and current time

```
#include <WiFi.h>
#include <ssid_password.h>
#define LILYGO_WATCH_2020_V2
#include <LilyGoWatch.h>        // TTGO T-Watch library
#include <soc/rtc.h>            // library for real-time clock
TTGOClass * ttgo;
struct tm timeData;
int GMT = 0, daylight = 3600;
unsigned long last = 0;
int hh, mm, ss;

void setup()
{
  Serial.begin(115200);
  ttgo = TTGOClass::getWatch();
  ttgo->begin();                // initialize ttgo object
  WiFi.begin(ssid, password);
  while (WiFi.status() != WL_CONNECTED) delay(500);
  configTime(GMT, daylight, "uk.pool.ntp.org");
  getLocalTime(&timeData);      // get valid time data
  WiFi.disconnect(true);
  WiFi.mode(WIFI_OFF);
}

void loop()
{
  if(millis() - last > 1000)
  {
    last = millis();            // obtain current time
    RTC_Date timeData = ttgo->rtc->getDateTime();
```

```
    hh = timeData.hour;
    mm = timeData.minute;          // access time variables
    ss = timeData.second;
    Serial.printf("%02d:%02d:%02d \n", hh, mm, ss);
  }
}
```

TimeLib and NTPtimeESP Libraries

The *TimeLib* and *NTPtimeESP* libraries provide access to the current time (see Listing 15-7). The *TimeLib* library by Paul Stoffregen is available in the Arduino IDE and is listed as *Time*. The *NTPtimeESP* library by Andreas Spiess is downloaded from `github.com/SensorsIot/NTPtimeESP`. A valid time is obtained from the NTP, and the *timeData* structure is equated to the Unix epoch time, which is the number of seconds since January 1, 1970. The time components are derived from the Unix epoch time.

The Greenwich Mean Time (GMT) and daylight saving effect adjustments are both measured in hours, rather than in seconds as in Listing 15-4. In Listing 15-7, the day of the week and the month number both start at one, while in Listing 15-4, both start from zero, and 1900 must be added to *year*. Instructions that differ from Listing 15-4 are annotated.

Listing 15-7. TimeLib and NTPtimeESP libraries and current time

```
#include <WiFi.h>
#include <ssid_password.h>
#include <TimeLib.h>                // include TimeLib and
#include <NTPtimeESP.h>             // NTPtimeESP libraries
NTPtime NTP("uk.pool.ntp.org");     // define NTP
strDateTime dateTime;               // NTPtimeESP library structure
int GMT = 0, daylight = 1;          // GMT, daylight saving (hr)
unsigned long last;
int wd, hh, mm, ss, dd, mn, yy;
```

```
String days[] = {"Sun","Mon","Tues","Wed","Thur","Fri","Sat"};
String mon[] = {"Jan","Feb","Mar","Apr","May","Jun",
                "Jul","Aug","Sep","Oct","Nov","Dec"};

void setup()
{
  Serial.begin(115200);
  WiFi.begin(ssid, password);
  while (WiFi.status() != WL_CONNECTED) delay(500);
                                        // obtain valid NTP time
  dateTime = NTP.getNTPtime(GMT, daylight);
  while (!dateTime.valid) dateTime = NTP.getNTPtime(0, 1);
  setTime(dateTime.epochTime);          // TimeLib library command
  WiFi.disconnect(true);                // disconnect Wi-Fi
  WiFi.mode(WIFI_OFF);
}

void loop()
{
  if(millis() - last > 1000)
  {
    last = millis();
    wd = weekday();                     // day of week starts at 1
    hh = hour();
    mm = minute();
    ss = second();
    dd = day();
    mn = month();                       // month starts at 1
    yy = year();                        // actual year value
    Serial.printf("%s %02d:%02d:%02d %02d %s %d \n",
     days[wd-1], hh, mm, ss, dd, mon[mn-1], yy);
  }
}
```

System Time Library

The time elapsed between the ESP32 microcontroller entering sleep mode and being reset is obtained from the system *time* library. The sketch in Listing 15-8 illustrates the method, which was used in Chapter 5, "BLE Beacons" (see Listing 5-2). The time when the ESP32 microcontroller entered sleep mode is stored in real-time clock (RTC) memory, as in sleep mode the ESP32 microcontroller CPU and memory are disabled. During sleep mode, information is retained in RTC memory by including `RTC_DATA_ATTR` in the variable definition instruction. The `gettimeofday(&timeData, NULL)` instruction obtains the current system time.

Listing 15-8. Elapsed time between sleep mode and reset

```
#include <sys/time.h>                      // system time library
RTC_DATA_ATTR time_t rebootTime;           // variable in RTC memory
struct timeval timeData;                   // time structure
int interval, sleepSec;
unsigned long uSec = 1000000;

void setup()
{
  Serial.begin(115200);
  gettimeofday(&timeData, NULL);           // time at reboot
                                           // interval (sec) since reboot
  interval = timeData.tv_sec - rebootTime;
  Serial.printf("slept for %d s \n", interval);
  rebootTime = timeData.tv_sec;            // update reboot time
  sleepSec = random (1, 10);
  Serial.printf("sleep for %d s \n", sleepSec);
  esp_deep_sleep(sleepSec * uSec);         // sleep for sleepSec seconds
}

void loop()
{}                                         // nothing in loop function
```

Libraries Used

Several libraries are automatically installed with updates to the *esp32* Boards Manager, with details available at `github.com/espressif/arduino-esp32/tree/master/libraries`. The libraries are located in *User\AppData\Local\Arduino15\packages\esp32\hardware\esp32\version*.

Table 15-1 lists the libraries used in the book with details of the author and source, if the source is not the Arduino IDE, and the library version. Information on updates to Table 15-1 is available on the *GitHub* website for the book: `github.com/Apress/ESP32-Formats-and-Communication`.

Table 15-1. *Details of libraries*

Library	Chapter	Author and source, if not Arduino IDE
Adafruit_DRV2605	4	Adafruit TTGO_TWatch_Library
Adafruit_GFX	6	Adafruit
Adafruit_Neopixel	12	Adafruit
Adafruit_SSD1306	6	Adafruit
ArduinoJson	3	Benoît Blanchon
ArduinoWebSockets	7	Gil Maimon
AsyncTCP	3	Hristo Gochkov
Audio (ESP32-audioI2S)	2	Wolle (schreibfaul1) `github.com/schreibfaul1/ESP32-audioI2S`

(*continued*)

Table 15-1. (*continued*)

Library	Chapter	Author and source, if not Arduino IDE
BLE2902 BLEAddress BLEBeacon BLEClient BLEDevice BLEScan BLEServer BLEUtils	5	Neil Kolban Updated Boards Manager
BluetoothA2DPSink (ESP32-A2DP)	2	Phil Schatzmann `github.com/pschatzmann/ESP32-A2DP`
BluetoothSerial	3	Evandro Luis Copercini Updated Boards Manager
BTLE	5	Florian Echtler
CayenneArduinoMQTTClient (CayenneMQTT)	9	myDevices
CayenneMQTTESP32 (CayenneMQTT)	9	myDevices
CCS811	9	Maarten Pennings `github.com/maarten-pennings/CCS811`
ElegantOTA	1	Ayush Sharma
esp_adc_cal	1	Espressif Updated Boards Manager
esp_camera	11	
esp_http_server	11	

(*continued*)

Table 15-1. (*continued*)

Library	Chapter	Author and source, if not Arduino IDE
ESP_Mail_Client	7	K. Suwatchai (Mobizt)
esp_now	9	
ESP32 BLE Arduino	5	Neil Kolban Updated Boards Manager
ESP32Servo	13	Kevin Harrington and John K. Bennett
ESPAsyncWebServer	8	Hristo Gochkov `github.com/me-no-dev/ESPAsyncWebServer`
ESP-Dash	8	Ayush Sharma
esp-wifi	9	
FastLED	1	Daniel Garcia
FFT	2	Robin Scheibler
HTTPClient	4	Markus Sattler Updated Boards Manager
IRremote		Ken Shirriff
IRremoteESP8266, IRsend	4	David Conran et al.
LittleFS	10	Hristo Gochkov Updated Boards Manager
LoRa	6	Sandeep Mistry (`github.com/sandeepmistry/arduino-LoRa/blob/master/API.md`)
M5Core2	1	M5Stack
M5Unified	1	M5Stack

(*continued*)

Table 15-1. *(continued)*

Library	Chapter	Author and source, if not Arduino IDE
NTPtimeESP	9	Andreas Spiess `github.com/SensorsIot/NTPtimeESP`
painlessMesh	3	Coopdis et al.
RF24	5	J. Coliz
SD	2	Updated Boards Manager
soc/rtc	4	
SPI	5	Hristo Gochkov Updated Boards Manager
SPIFFS	10	Hristo Gochkov, Ivan Grokhotkov Updated Boards Manager
TaskScheduler	3	Anatoli Arkhipenko
TFT_eSPI	1	Bodmer
time	9 and 10	Paul Stoffregen
TJpg_Decoder	11	Bodmer
TTGO_TWatch_Library	1	TTGO `github.com/Xinyuan-LilyGO/TTGO_TWatch_Library`
WebSerial	8	Ayush Sharma
WebServer	7	Ivan Grokhotkov Updated Boards Manager
WebSocketsClient	11	Marcus Sattler
WebSocketsServer (WebSockets)	7	

(continued)

Table 15-1. (*continued*)

Library	Chapter	Author and source, if not Arduino IDE
WiFi WiFiClient WiFiServer	12	Hristo Gochkov Updated Boards Manager
Wire	6	Hristo Gochkov Updated Boards Manager

Several *esp* libraries are located in *User\AppData\Local\Arduino15\packages\esp32\hardware\esp32\version\tools\sdk\esp32\include*, while *esp* functions, such as the *ledc* function, are located in the *version\cores\esp32* folder.

Create a Library

A library contains at least the first three files in the following list:

- *Header file* (*library.h*) – Library variable definitions.
- *Source code* (*library.cpp*) – Library function instructions; cpp may represent Cplus-plus.
- *Keyword file* (*keyword.txt*) – Keywords used in the library.
- *Information file* (*library.txt*) – Details of the library author, version, function, etc.
- *Example files* (*sketch.ino*) – Example sketches illustrating use of the library.

A library file style guide is available at `www.arduino.cc/en/Reference/APIStyleGuide`.

Creating a library is illustrated with the example of a library, called *flashLibrary*, to flash an LED every second and display on the Serial Monitor the time that the LED state is *HIGH*. The initial *HIGH* time is 100ms, which is changed with the user entering the value in the Serial Monitor. The original sketch, without a library, is shown in Listing 15-9.

Listing 15-9. Original sketch

```
const int totalTime = 1000;         // total of LED on and off times
int LEDpin = 4;                     // define GPIO pin
int LEDtime = 100;                  // initial LED on time

void setup()
{
  Serial.begin(115200);             // Serial Monitor baud rate
  pinMode(LEDpin, OUTPUT);          // LED pin as OUTPUT
}

void loop()
{
                                    // new LED on-time
  if(Serial.available()) LEDtime = Serial.parseInt();
  digitalWrite(LEDpin, HIGH);       // turn on LED
                                    // display LED on-time
  Serial.printf("HIGH time %d \n",LEDtime);
  delay(LEDtime);
  digitalWrite(LEDpin, LOW);        // turn off LED
  delay(totalTime-LEDtime);
}
```

The sketch is reformatted to establish a *class* containing functions and variables that are either available to the main sketch, termed *pubic* variables, or are only available to the *class*, termed *private* variables. The instructions in the *loop* function are also reformatted as a *public* function.

The main function, called a *constructor* of the class, has the same name as the library and passes variables from the main sketch to the library. In the example, the GPIO pin and the time that the LED state is *HIGH* are passed from the main sketch to the library by the *flashLibrary* constructor. The *begin* library function initializes Serial communication with the default baud rate set at 115200Bd and defines the GPIO pin as `OUTPUT`. The second library function, *flashLED*, is equal to the contents of the *loop* function in the original sketch. In the example, the time that the LED state is *HIGH* is updated if data is available in the Serial buffer, and then the LED is turned on and off, with the total time equal to the value of the *totalTime* constant.

The two functions, *begin* and *flashLED*, are defined as *public* and are called by the main sketch. The *LEDpin* and *LEDtime* variables, which are local to the library, are defined as *private*.

The expanded sketch, in Listing 15-10, now incorporates the *flashLibrary* instructions. The instruction `flashLibrary flash(4, 100)` associates *flash* with the *flashLibrary* class and passes the GPIO pin number and the time that the LED state is *HIGH*. The *setup* and *loop* functions only contain the `flash.begin()` and `flash.flashLED()` instructions. Note that the class functions of *begin* and *flashLED* are prefixed with *flash*, which is associated with the *flashLibrary* class.

Listing 15-10. Expanded sketch

```
const int totalTime = 1000;
class flashLibrary
{
  public:
    flashLibrary(int pin, int time)  // constructor has same name
    {                                // as library
      LEDpin = pin;                  // LEDpin and LEDtime are
      LEDtime = time;                // local variables to the library
    }
```

```
    void begin(int baud = 115200)
    {             // function called by main sketch with a default baud rate
      Serial.begin(baud);
      pinMode(LEDpin, OUTPUT);
    }
    void flashLED()                          // function called by main sketch
    {
      if(Serial.available()) LEDtime = Serial.parseInt();
      digitalWrite(LEDpin, HIGH);
      Serial.printf("HIGH time %d \n",LEDtime);
      delay(LEDtime);
      digitalWrite(LEDpin, LOW);
      delay(totalTime-LEDtime);
    }
  private:                                   // variables local to library
    int LEDpin;
    int LEDtime;
};                                           // note semi-colon

flashLibrary flash(4, 100);      // associate flash with library
void setup()                     // and pass GPIO pin and LED time
{
  flash.begin();                 // main sketch calls begin function
}
void loop()
{
  flash.flashLED();              // main sketch calls flashLED function
}
```

Source File

The library source and header files are generated from Listing 15-10 with the files edited by a text editor, such as WordPad or Notepad. A folder, with the name of the library, is created to store the library files. Using the preceding example, the files *flashLibrary.h* and *flashLibrary.cpp* are created and stored in the *flashLibrary* folder. The source file contains the library constructor and functions, which are easily extracted from the expanded sketch in Listing 15-10. The double colon preceding a function indicates that the function is part of the *flashLibrary* class. The first instruction of the source code file calls the library header file. For the example, the file *flashLibrary.cpp* is shown in Listing 15-11.

Listing 15-11. Library source code file

```
#include <flashLibrary.h>          // include header file
flashLibrary::flashLibrary(int pin, int time)
{
  LEDpin = pin;
  LEDtime = time;
}

void flashLibrary::begin(int baud)
{                                  // equal to public
  Serial.begin(baud);              // definitions
  pinMode(LEDpin, OUTPUT);
}

void flashLibrary::flashLED()
{
  if(Serial.available()) LEDtime = Serial.parseInt();
  digitalWrite(LEDpin, HIGH);
  Serial.printf("HIGH time %d \n", LEDtime);
```

```
  delay(LEDtime);
  digitalWrite(LEDpin, LOW);
  delay(totalTime-LEDtime);
}
```

Header File

The header file defines the library functions and variables as public or private. Instructions to define the library header file, if it has not been defined, and include the Arduino library of standard types and constants precedes the library instructions. One convention for indicating a private variable is to precede the variable name with an underscore. Note that the close bracket of the class definition is followed by a semicolon. For the example, the file *flashLibrary.h* is shown in Listing 15-12.

Listing 15-12. Library header file

```
#ifndef flashLibrary_h      // note underscore h and not dot h
#define flashLibrary_h
#include <Arduino.h>

class flashLibrary                        // same name as library
{
  public:                                 // functions called by main sketch
    flashLibrary(int pin, int time);
    void begin(int baud = 115200); // default value for baud rate
    void flashLED();
    const int totalTime = 1000;     // value accessed by main sketch

  private:                                // variables local to the library
    int LEDpin;
    int LEDtime;
};                                        // note semi-colon
#endif                                    // note #endif at end of header file
```

The library folder is moved to the Arduino libraries folder, and the Arduino IDE is restarted. The Arduino IDE does not have to be restarted after making changes to either the library header or source code file, but the main sketch does have to be recompiled and loaded. An example sketch using the *flashLibrary* is given in Listing 15-13. Note that the library functions are preceded by *flash,* the term associated with the library, when called by the main sketch.

Listing 15-13. Sketch including the library

```
#include <flashLibrary.h>               // include library
flashLibrary flash(4, 100);             // associate flash with library
                                        // pass GPIO pin and LED time
void setup()
{
  flash.begin();                        // call library function
}

void loop()
{
  flash.flashLED();                     // call library function
  Serial.println(flash.totalTime);      // display library variable
}
```

Figure 15-3 illustrates the original sketch (left side) and the sketch accessing the library (right side). The example demonstrates the easier broad interpretation of the sketch accessing the library with the details available in the library source file. Note that the two sketches essentially require the same storage space, 34.7KB, as the sketch accessing the library has to load both the sketch and the library (see Figure 15-3).

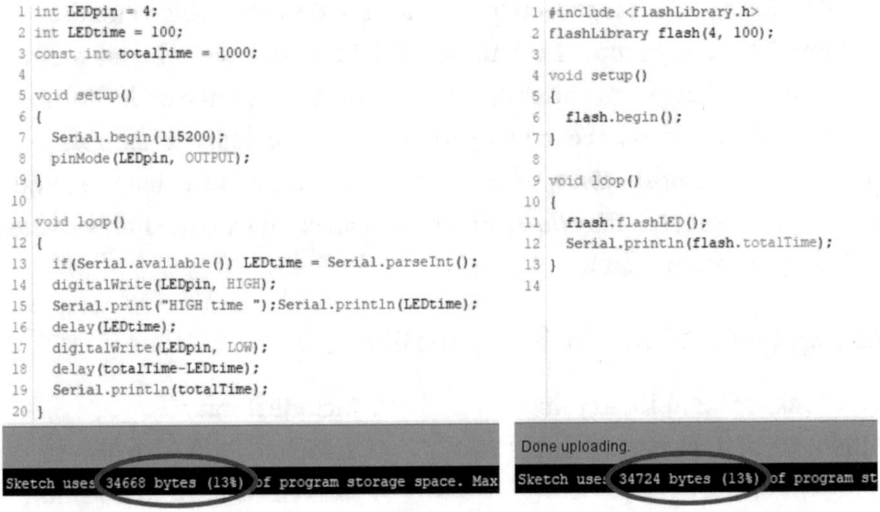

```
int LEDpin = 4;
int LEDtime = 100;
const int totalTime = 1000;

void setup()
{
  Serial.begin(115200);
  pinMode(LEDpin, OUTPUT);
}

void loop()
{
  if(Serial.available()) LEDtime = Serial.parseInt();
  digitalWrite(LEDpin, HIGH);
  Serial.print("HIGH time ");Serial.println(LEDtime);
  delay(LEDtime);
  digitalWrite(LEDpin, LOW);
  delay(totalTime-LEDtime);
  Serial.println(totalTime);
}
```

```
Sketch uses 34668 bytes (13%) of program storage space. Max
```

```
#include <flashLibrary.h>
flashLibrary flash(4, 100);

void setup()
{
  flash.begin();
}

void loop()
{
  flash.flashLED();
  Serial.println(flash.totalTime);
}
```

```
Done uploading.
Sketch uses 34724 bytes (13%) of program st
```

Figure 15-3. *Sketch without and with a library*

Keyword File

The *keyword* file indicates "words" that are highlighted in a sketch, with `KEYWORD1` for classes, `KEYWORD2` for functions, and `LITERAL1` for constants. The format of the keyword file is shown in Listing 15-14, with the hash symbol, #, indicating a comment. When changes are made to the *keyword* file, the Arduino IDE must be restarted for the changes to be implemented. Figure 15-3 (right side) illustrates the color highlighting of the library name (bold orange), library functions (orange), and library constants (blue). The color format of highlighted words in a non-library sketch (see Figure 15-3 (left side)) is defined in the file *C:\Program Files (x86)\Arduino\lib\theme\theme.txt*, with a list of Arduino keywords and categories available at *C:\Program Files (x86)\Arduino\lib\keywords.txt*.

Listing 15-14. Keyword file

```
# Syntax For flashLibrary

# Classes
flashLibrary KEYWORD1      // tab after keyword not spaces
# Methods and Functions
begin        KEYWORD2
flashLED     KEYWORD2

# Constants
totalTime    LITERAL1
```

The penultimate lines of the two sketches in Figure 15-3 display the value of the constant, *totalTime,* on the Serial Monitor. In the sketch accessing the library (see Figure 15-3, right side), the constant, *totalTime,* is preceded by *flash,* which is associated with the *flashLibrary* library. The constant, *totalTime,* is defined in the library header file as *public* to be accessible to the main sketch. The "word" *totalTime* is formatted in blue, as the term represents a constant, whose format is defined in the *flashLibrary* library *keyword* file.

Information File

The library *information* file contains details of the library author and maintainer with contact details, the library version number, a sentence and paragraph describing the library function, details of library website information, and any library dependencies.

A recommended format of a library information file with the *flashLibrary* as an example is

> *name=flashLibrary*
> *version=1.0*
> *author=Neil Cameron*
> *maintainer= Neil Cameron (email address)*
> *sentence=flash a LED with variable LED on time*
> *paragraph= flash a LED with variable LED on time, which the user enters on the Serial Monitor with a maximum value of one second.*
> *category=Display (or Device or Sensors or Communication etc)*
> *url=*`http://github.com/xxx`
> *architectures=AVR (or ESP8266 or ESP32 etc)*
> *depends=none*

Components

Components listed by chapter

Component	Chapters (quantity if more than one)
18650 battery charging shield	9
18650 lithium-ion-battery	9, 13 (2), 14 (2)
4Ω speaker	2 (2)
9V battery	13, 14
Arduino Uno or Nano	5
Button switch	3 (2)
Capacitor	9 (10μF), 12 (100μF)
CCS811 air quality sensor	9
DC motors	13 (2), 14 (2)
ESP32 DEVKIT DOIT	1, 2, 3, 4, 5, 7, 8, 9, 10, 11, 12, 15
ESP32-CAM camera	11, 12, 13, 14
Externally powered speaker	2
FT232RL FTDI USB to TTL Serial converter	11
ILI9341 TFT LCD 2.4" screen 320×240 pixels	11
Infrared sensor VS1838B	4
LED and 220Ω resistor	3, 5 (2), 7 (2), 8, 15 (2)

(continued)

N. Cameron, *ESP32 Formats and Communication*,
https://doi.org/10.1007/978-1-4842-9376-8

Component	Chapters (quantity if more than one)
LM2596 buck convertor	13, 14
M5Stack Core2	1, 2, 7, 10, 11
M5Stack Core2 Battery Base	1
MAX98357 decoder	5 (2)
Micro-SD card	2
nRF24L01 transceiver	5
OLED screen 128×96 pixels	2, 10
PCM5102 decoder	5
Potentiometer 10kΩ	2
Relay KY-019	3
Resistor	9 (10kΩ×2, 22Ω), 12 (470Ω)
SCT013 current transformer	9
SO-239 connector	6
ST7789 TFT LCD 1.3" screen 240×240 pixels	10
TB6612FNG or L298N motor driver board	13, 14
TowerPro SG90 servo motor	13, 14
TTGO T-watch V2	4, 11
TTGO LoRa32 V2.1 1.6	6 (2)
TTGO T-Display V1.1	1, 3 (2), 5, 9 (2)
Wire lengths	6 (18cm×4, 16.4cm)
WS2812 RGB LED ring	12

Index

A

B

N. Cameron, *ESP32 Formats and Communication*, https://doi.org/10.1007/978-1-4842-9376-8

C

D

F

G

H

I

J

K

L

M

N

O

P

Q

R

S

T

U

V

W, X, Y, Z

Printed in the United States
by Baker & Taylor Publisher Services